The Microsoft® EXCHANGE USER'S HANDBOOK

Includes Microsoft Outlook, Exchange 5.0, and Windows Messaging

SUE MOSHER

DUKE PRESS

A Division of
DUKE COMMUNICATIONS INTERNATIONAL
Loveland, Colorado

Library of Congress Cataloging-in-Publication Data

Microsoft Exchange user's handbook / by Sue Mosher. — 1st ed.
   p.   cm.
Includes index.
ISBN 1-882419-52-9
1. Microsoft Exchange. 2. Client/server computing.   I. Title.
Mosher, Sue, 1953-
QA76.9.C55M68 1997
005.7'13769—dc21   96-45905
                              CIP

Copyright © 1997 by DUKE PRESS
DUKE COMMUNICATIONS INTERNATIONAL
Loveland, Colorado

It is the reader's responsibility to ensure procedures and techniques used from this book are accurate and appropriate for the user's installation. No warranty is implied or expressed.

This book was printed and bound in Canada.

ISBN 1-882419-52-9

1 2 3 4 5 IB 9 8 7

To Robert, whose love has led me on the greatest adventure of all.

Acknowledgments

I'm still amazed that this book actually happened over the same months that my family and I moved from Arlington, Virginia, to Moscow, Russia. Perhaps it's a true testament to the robust qualities of Exchange that I could take it on the road and even run Exchange Server on a Pentium laptop computer (I didn't say it ran well, but it did work fine for experimenting).

First and foremost thanks must go to my husband, Robert, and daughter, Annie, for accommodating my need to upload at odd hours, meet deadlines, test lengthy procedures, and carry on e-mail conversations with dozens of Exchange users around the world. You enabled me to give a lot of myself to many, many people. I hope I can give as much and more to you over the coming months.

To Valda Hilley go my admiration for the number of projects she can juggle (including mine) and my appreciation for getting me into the book business. It's hard to believe that we met only once, at Comdex several years ago, and have built not just a working relationship but a friendship via e-mail and many long phone calls. Keep that room in the country waiting for me.

This book wouldn't exist without Microsoft Exchange and the excitement it's generated, so I extend my thanks to the whole Exchange team at Microsoft, but particularly Brian Valentine, Elaine Sharp, Scott Briggs, and Rob Shurtleff for staying on the front lines with the right answers and Kai Ichikawa for his quick responses. I owe more gratitude that I can possibly express to my personal team of Microsoft Exchange gurus — Tom Laciano, who double-checked tricky procedures, fielded my bug reports, and still managed to pass his TCP/IP test; and Alec Dun, who stemmed my panic the week that the Windows Messaging update for Windows 95 was released.

The team at Duke Press has been just great to work with, always friendly and flexible. Janet Robbins, Sharon Hamm, Margaret McDonald, John Morris-Reihl, Dawn Cyr, Rob Carson, Martha Nichols — please take a bow.

There's a long list of people who provided moral support, tips, resources, and inspiration. When you see them online in the newsgroups, say hi! for me: my fellow MVPs and newsgroup habitués Rob Ingham (especially for his help with Microsoft Phone), Hal Hostetler, Graham Smith, Heath Perryman (especially for his assistance with Transend MAPI ConnectorWare for cc:Mail), Uncle Gus Hallgren, Colene Allen, and Joe Ventola; Peter Bowyer at Verity for managing the msexchange discussion list; Don Adams for his Exchange Information Service and Exchange Page; Anthony M. Humphreys for his comments on my Web site and many messages about new doodads; Ben Goetter, widget wizard extraordinaire; Allan N. Robinson at US Connect for the Exchange test server; Mr. WordMail, Scott Marquardt; Marc Seinfeld and Scott English at Microsoft; Dirk Bischoff at Verity; Andy Sumberg and Judy

Cole at Wang; John Young at Nemx; Irving Caplan; Shelly Sofer at Delrina; Fred Krefetz at Transend; Terry Beavers and Wesley Peace for Exchange Server 5.0 connections; Larry Burton for his technical review of the manuscript; and all the other vendors and programmers who've created add-ons for Exchange.

A final wave of appreciation goes out to Lee Perryman at Associated Press Broadcast Services, who loaned his lab, sent lists of Exchange annoyances, and helped out in many transatlantic crunches; and to Wayne Cook at Microsoft PSS for leading the way through the Windows 95 launch and beyond.

Despite the efforts of all these wonderful people to keep me on track, any errors and omissions found herein are all my burden to bear. Fortunately, in this age of the Internet, a book can become a living document with an online counterpart where corrections can (and will) be made.

Sue Mosher

Slipstick Systems, Moscow
http://www.slipstick.com
December 1996

Table of Contents at a glance

Table of Contents

Chapter 1

Quick Start

Let's assume you bought this book, not because you want to learn all the theory of electronic mail, but because you want to send some! We'll spend time in Chapter 2, "What Is Exchange?," discussing the components and functions that make Exchange tick. But for now, let's concentrate on the basics.

The best way for you to get to know Exchange is to start using it. In this chapter, we're going to explore what you need to get Exchange up and running, then get enough of Exchange installed so you can send your first message. If you already have Exchange set up and are eager to send that first message, feel free to skip ahead to the section "Sending Your First Message" later in this chapter (page 7).

You may already be an experienced Exchange user. In that case, you may want to learn more about how Exchange is put together in Chapter 2 or turn directly to the chapters in Part II on setting up specific Exchange services. You may find new tips on the Exchange services you already use in the "Tips and Tricks" sections at the end of the chapters in Parts II and III. Advanced topics such as security, Internet e-mail, workgroup postoffice management, and features of Microsoft Exchange Server are covered in Part IV.

This book is unique in that it covers both the version of Exchange that comes with Windows 95 and Windows NT 4.0 (this version is also sometimes known as Windows Messaging) and the version distributed with Microsoft Exchange Server. This means that, whether you send e-mail via a network at your office or operate solely on a standalone machine, you'll find information here that will make you a more effective Exchange user.

What You Need to Get Started

Exchange is all about making connections — connections to a Microsoft Mail server, to a Microsoft Exchange server, to the Internet, to a single fax machine, or to available online services.

Any Exchange connection consists of three elements:

* Something to do the connecting = software
* Something to connect with = hardware
* Something to connect to = mail servers and e-mail accounts (or fax machines)

Why is each of these essential? Without the proper software, you won't be able to run Exchange at all. If you have inadequate hardware, Exchange will be sluggish at best. And without servers to relay your messages (or fax machines to receive them), your messages will be all dressed up with nowhere to go. We'll look at each of these three elements, starting with the software, because the choice of a particular Exchange version governs what you need in the way of hardware and accounts.

Exchange Software: The Program Itself

Understanding Exchange is complicated by the fact that there are seven versions of Exchange, each with different requirements and opportunities to customize the program.

* Exchange operating system version for Windows 95 — comes with the Windows 95 operating system. An upgrade to this version is called Windows Messaging.
* Windows Messaging operating system version for Windows NT 4.0 — comes with the Windows NT 4.0 Workstation operating system
* Exchange Server client for Windows 95 — distributed with Exchange Server
* Exchange Server client for Windows NT — distributed with Exchange Server
* Exchange Server client for Windows 3.1x (i.e., Windows or Windows for Workgroups 3.1 and 3.11) — distributed with Exchange Server
* Exchange Server client for DOS — distributed with Exchange Server
* Exchange Server client for Macintosh System 7 — distributed with Exchange Server

Microsoft has changed the name of its e-mail program for Windows 95. It's now Windows Messaging, instead of Microsoft Exchange, and that's also the name of the e-mail program included with Windows NT 4.0. The reason for the name change was to distinguish the operating system e-mail program from the full Exchange Server product. However, since both use essentially the same interface and have the same basic features, this book will continue to call them both Exchange.

Special Note

As you can see, the versions break down into two groups — those included with the Windows 95 and Windows NT operating systems and those distributed with Exchange Server. We sometimes use the word *client* instead of *version*, especially for the Exchange Server versions, because they're part of a client/server combination. *Client/server* describes an arrangement in which much of the processing for a program is done on a central server, to which multiple client computers send their information requests and commands.

The Exchange Server clients include advanced features, such as *assistants* to manage incoming messages, *public and private folders* for group discussions, and customizable *views*. Assistants and public folders require a connection to Exchange Server, the "back" side of Microsoft Exchange, which runs on Windows NT Server.

Throughout this book, we'll spend our time on the four Windows 95 and Windows NT versions, because they support more features and plug-ins. If you will be using the full Exchange Server client, but haven't installed it yet, feel free to skip ahead to "Installing and Updating the Exchange Server Client," page 103 in Chapter 5.

Exchange Software: Information Services

Installing the Exchange program by itself is not enough. The program is just a framework for an array of *information services* that plug in to Exchange. Without information services, Exchange is like a car with no gas, no oil, and no driver. It might look cool in your driveway, but it isn't going to get you anywhere. Examples of information services include address books, message storage files and folders, and transport services.

Transport services (also known as *transport providers*) are information services that let you send different types of e-mail to various recipients. All Exchange clients come with at least two transport services. You can add more later, depending on the version of Exchange, but the following are the basics:

All Exchange clients come with at least two transport services; you can add more later.

- For the Exchange Server clients, your basic transport service is the Microsoft Exchange Server service. You can also use Microsoft Mail.

- The Windows 95 operating system comes with Microsoft Mail, for exchanging messages within your organization, and Microsoft Fax.
- The Windows NT operating system comes with Microsoft Mail and Internet Mail, for exchanging messages with people on the Internet.

"Transport Services" in Chapter 2 (page 17) includes a list of some of the other available transport services. Many of these services can be downloaded for free or are available as part of services you already subscribe to or other programs you already own.

Hardware

You need either a network card for a local area network connection, or a modem.

Exchange is not a small program; it requires a substantial commitment of both memory (RAM) and hard-drive space. A system meeting the bare minimum standards for Windows 95 cannot run Exchange. Table 1.1 summarizes the hardware requirements for each version. Add 4 MB to the memory requirements for the Exchange Server Windows clients if you want to design forms on the machine.

Table 1.1 Hardware Requirements for Exchange

Client	Memory (MB)	Free Hard-Drive Space (MB)
Operating System Clients		
Windows 95	8 (8–16 recommended)	5–7
Windows NT 4.0	12 for Intel; 16 for MIPS, Alpha, PowerPC (16–32 recommended)	5
Exchange Server Clients		
Windows 95	8 (12 recommended)	12–22
Windows NT (Intel)	16 (20 recommended)	12–22
Windows NT (MIPS, Alpha, PowerPC)	20 (24 recommended)	15–22

The figures for free hard-drive space do not cover storage of address books and message folders on the local drive. These items can grow to several megabytes in size, so you'll want to have room for them, too.

In addition to sufficient memory and hard-drive storage, you need either a network card for a local area network (LAN) connection, or a modem to connect to various dial-up information services or to Exchange Server from remote locations. More memory is recommended if you plan to use Microsoft Word as your e-mail editor (this Word option is known as WordMail).

Servers and Accounts

The final required components are

- a server that connects you to an information service, and
- an account on that server

These components could be a Microsoft Mail account on a Microsoft Mail server, a mailbox on a Microsoft Exchange server, or an e-mail account on an Internet POP3/SMTP server, among others. You need to know both how to connect to the server (the phone number or network path) and the details of your account — that is, your user ID and password. Microsoft Fax is an exception here, because you connect directly to the recipient's system. All you need is the receiving fax machine's phone number. But we can generalize in this fashion: Before you can send a message, you must have either an e-mail account to send from or a fax number to send to.

Before you can send a message, you must have either an e-mail account to send from or a fax number to send to.

Setting Up Exchange Using the Defaults

The method you use to set up Exchange depends on the version you're using. The Windows 95 and Windows NT 4.0 operating system clients install through the Control Panel, while the Exchange Server clients run a separate Setup.exe program.

Setting Up Exchange Through the Control Panel

If you are running Windows 95 or Windows NT 4.0 and want to use the version of Exchange that comes with the operating system, install it through the Control Panel following these steps:

1. Click Start, then Settings, then Control Panel.

2. Double-click Add/Remove Programs, then switch to the Windows Setup tab, shown in Figure 1.1.

Figure 1.1

For Windows 95, check Microsoft Exchange and, optionally, Microsoft Fax and The Microsoft Network. For Windows NT, you will see a Windows Messaging component.

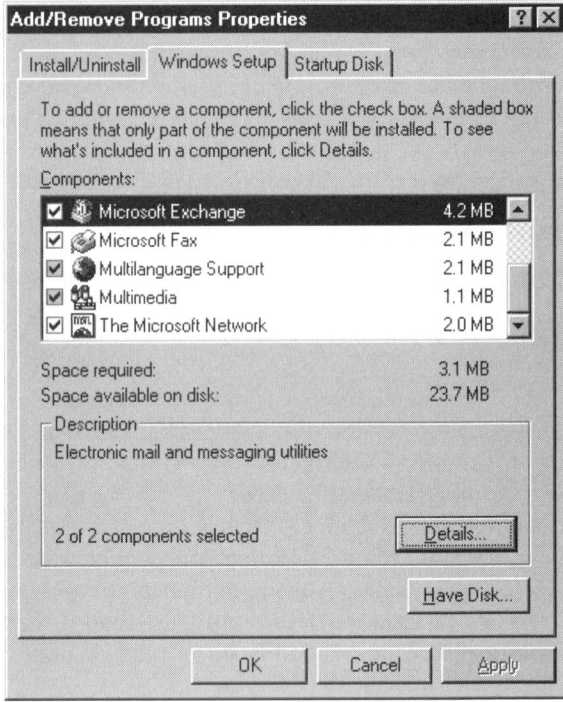

3. If you are using Windows 95, check the box marked Microsoft Exchange. If you are using Windows NT, check the box marked Windows Messaging.
4. If you are a Windows 95 user, you also can check Microsoft Fax if you want to send faxes, and/or The Microsoft Network if you want to send mail through the MSN online service.
5. Click the OK button to install the components you've selected.

After you've installed Exchange, you can run it. The first time you start Exchange, the Exchange Setup Wizard will help you configure your Exchange *profile*, a collection of settings for your mail accounts. See "Configuring Your Profile" on the following page.

Setting Up Exchange Server Clients

If you are going to connect to Exchange Server on a network, your system administrator should give you instructions on how to install Exchange using a Setup.exe program either from the network or from a CD or diskette. You'll find details on this process in Chapter 5, "Setting Up the Microsoft Exchange Server Service."

The setup process will probably create and configure a default Exchange profile for you, without any work on your part. However, if this doesn't happen, then the Exchange Setup Wizard will help you configure your profile the first time you run Exchange, as we'll see in the next section.

Configuring Your Profile

Once you've installed Exchange, the next step is to configure your profile. Start Exchange by double-clicking the Inbox icon on the desktop. You can also click the Start button, then choose Programs, Microsoft Exchange (or Windows Messaging, if you are using Windows NT 4.0).

The Exchange Setup Wizard launches and walks you through a series of questions designed to set up all the information services you'll use in Exchange. For e-mail (the Microsoft Exchange Server service, Microsoft Mail, Internet Mail, Microsoft Network), you'll need details about the name and password for your mail account and the location of the mail server. For Microsoft Fax, you'll just need your fax number (the one you'll be transmitting from).

We'll go into the details of all the settings for the different information services in Part II of this book; but for now, just try to answer as best you can. (One hint: Don't configure the Microsoft Mail service if you're working on a computer that never connects to a network.) You can use the defaults that Exchange suggests as the locations for your Personal Folders and Personal Address Book. You'll learn how to change those locations later in the book.

Sending Your First Message

It's time to send that first message! This is going to take one double-click, a few button clicks, and a little typing. For the purpose of this demonstration, we're going to assume that you have either the Microsoft Exchange Server service, Microsoft Mail, or Microsoft Fax installed. For other services, you'll need to learn how to enter addresses. Let's go through the process step by step:

Start Exchange

1. Double-click the Inbox icon on your desktop to start Exchange.

The four steps necessary to send a message are address, compose, send, and deliver. Delivery is often (but not always) automatic.

Create a new message

2. Click the New Message button on the Exchange toolbar (Figure 1.2), or choose Compose, New Message, or press Ctrl+N to open a New Message window (Figure 1.3).

Figure 1.2

To create a message, click the New Message button.

New Message

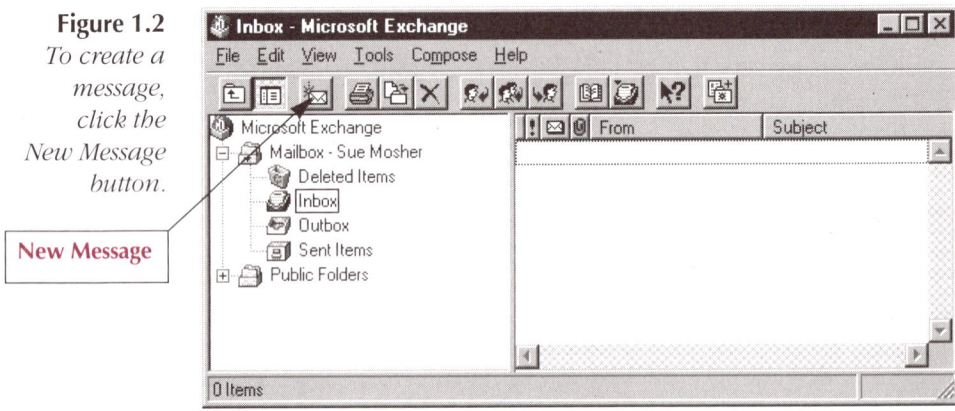

Figure 1.3

To address the message, click the To button.

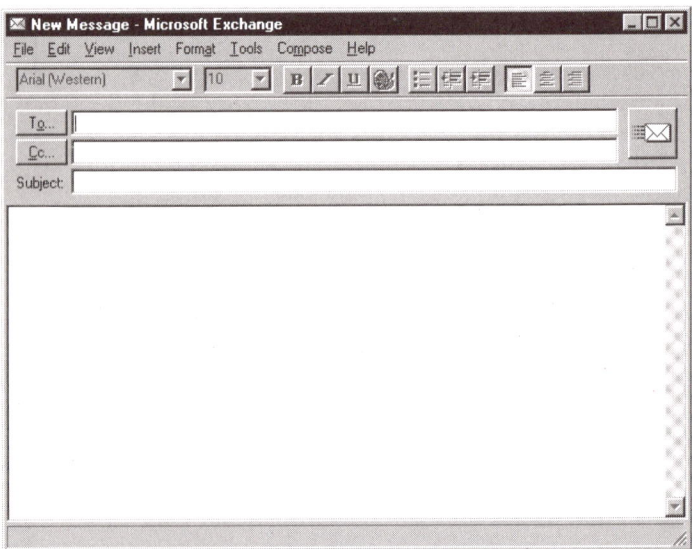

Address the message

3. If you're sending an e-mail message, click the To button to view the Address Book (Figure 1.4). From the Show Names list, pick Postoffice Address List or the Global Address List, depending on which one you see.

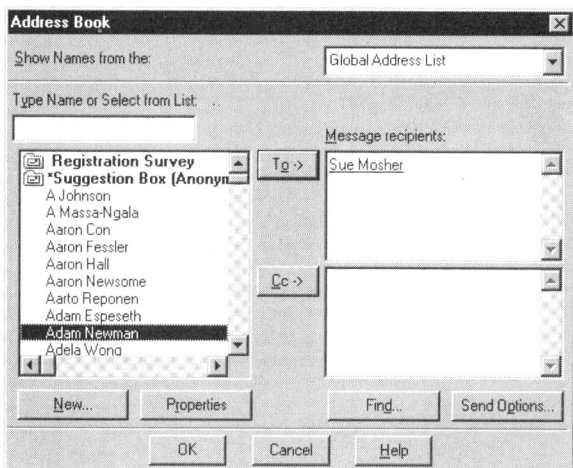

Figure 1.4
Select names from the address list for your organization.

4. Double-click any name on the left side of the Address Book, which will copy that address to the Message Recipients list in the To box. Click OK to return to the New Message window, where you'll see the name you picked in the To box.

Address the message (fax)

5. If you're sending a fax, choose Tools, Fax Addressing Wizard. If instead you're sending a message, proceed to step 7.

6. In the Fax Addressing Wizard (Figure 1.5), enter the name of the person you're sending the fax To, the Country, and the Fax Number. Click Add to List, then click Finish to return to the New Message window.

Give the message a subject

7. Click in the Subject box (or press Tab twice to get there), then type in the subject of this message. "Hello, world!" will do just fine.

Figure 1.5

*For each copy of the fax
you want to send, fill in the
information at the top of
the Fax Addressing Wizard.*

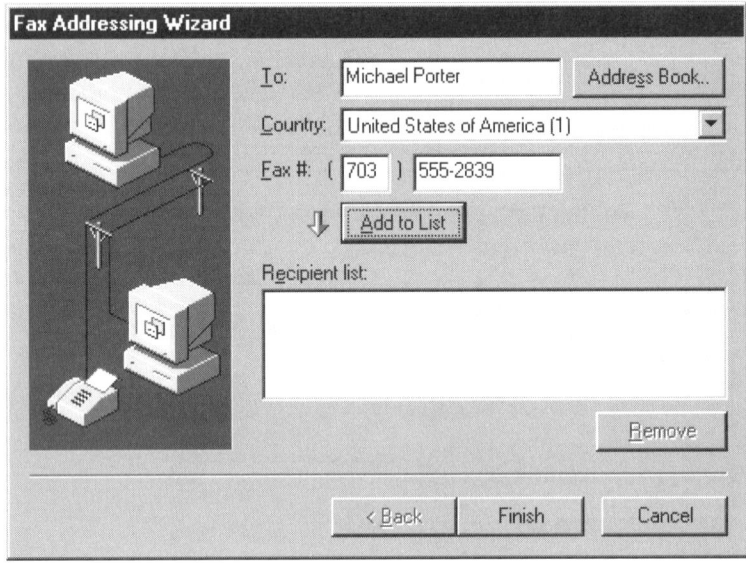

Compose the body of the message

8. Press Tab to move from the Subject box to the large text box, where you write the message. You can type in "Hello, world!" or make the message as elaborate as you want. Figure 1.6 shows how the message will look when it's ready to be sent.

Send the message

9. Click the Send button.

Deliver the message

10. If you sent a fax, you should hear the modem begin to dial the number. If you sent an e-mail message via Microsoft Mail, the mes-sage will be delivered the next time Exchange checks for new messages. Or you can transmit the message to the server imme-diately. To do that, choose Tools, Deliver Now. For Exchange Server e-mail, the message is processed by the server automatically just a few seconds after you send it.

To sum up, the four steps necessary to send a message are address, compose, send, and deliver. As you'll see in Chapter 11, "Sending E-Mail Messages,"

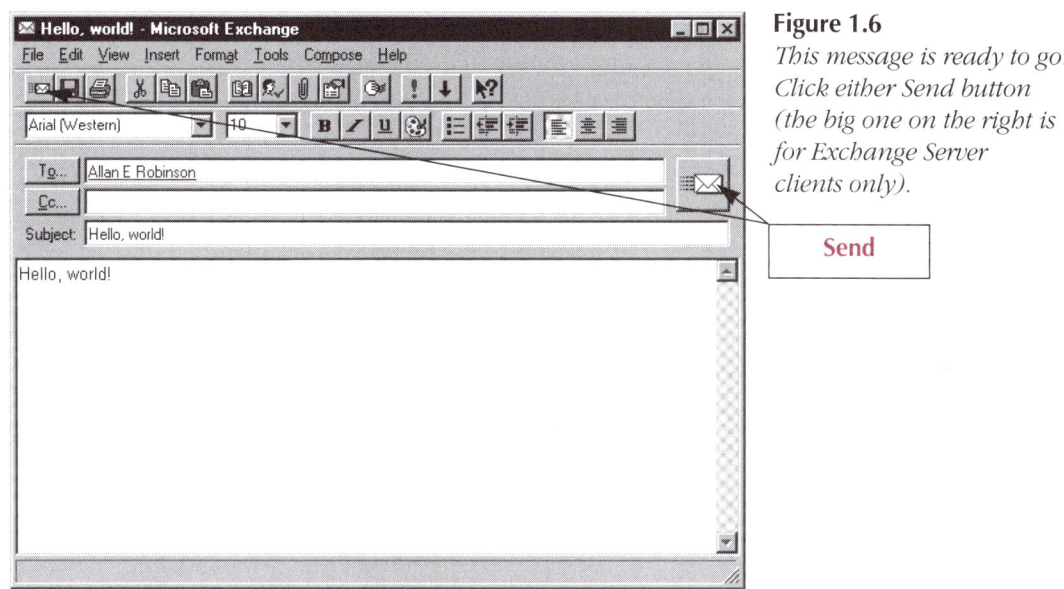

Figure 1.6
This message is ready to go. Click either Send button (the big one on the right is for Exchange Server clients only).

delivery isn't always automatic. Sometimes, you must take an extra step to deliver your messages to their destination.

Summary

You should now have Exchange set up on your system with at least a basic profile. And you've seen how to send a message using the New Message function. If you're using one of the Exchange Server clients on a network, you might want to send a message to your system administrator to let him or her know that you've successfully installed Exchange and are ready to learn more. Most importantly, you should understand that Exchange is not just a single program. It has many components that work together to store your addresses and to format, store, and deliver your messages.

Key Points

- Exchange is all about making connections.
- All Exchange clients come with at least two transport services; you can add more later.
- You need either a network card for a local area network (LAN) connection, or a modem.

- Before you can send a message, you must have either an e-mail account to send from or a fax number to send to.
- The four steps necessary to send a message are address, compose, send, and deliver. Delivery is often (but not always) automatic.

For More Information

In the next chapter, we'll continue our discussion of the components that make up Exchange, introducing you to profiles and explaining the differences between the different Exchange clients. Then, Section II covers the Exchange configuration issues, both individual information services and concepts such as how to set up remote access to your network and the Internet. We'll cover the services that Microsoft provides with Exchange, plus many of those services available from other providers. Section III shows you how to use Exchange to send and receive messages and faxes and to store information. In Section IV, we'll look at the advanced features of the Exchange Server clients, discuss the issues involved with mail on the Internet, and show you how to manage a workgroup postoffice if you want to use the Microsoft Mail service in Exchange. Finally, in Section V, you'll find a summary of features in the latest members of the Exchange family — Microsoft Exchange Server 5.0 and Microsoft Outlook.

Chapter 2

What Is Exchange?

It would be nice if I could tell you that Exchange is just a program for sending e-mail. If that were all it did, this book would be a lot shorter. But Exchange is so much more than a simple messaging program that I think it's important to understand what it can do and what each Exchange component does.

Microsoft Exchange really is an application for managing all types of information, not just messages. This flexibility comes in part from Exchange's ability to accept a wide variety of plug-in additions, which can be added either on the user's computer or as part of Exchange Server. Other enhancements use a special programming interface called MAPI to help other programs communicate directly with Exchange. For example, Exchange can be implemented as a simple e-mail application for sending messages to the Internet or as an enterprise-wide information system with thousands of mailboxes and hundreds of public folders for sharing documents. Third-party add-ons can enhance Exchange with advanced search capabilities, wireless messaging, and other tools. Electronic forms can turn Exchange into an instrument for collaboration with others both within and outside your organization.

To get the most out of Exchange, you'll want to understand the different elements that help Exchange operate in so many different ways. In the next few pages, we'll look at the functions Exchange offers and the components that make those functions operate. You might want to pay particular attention to the section on "Differences Between Exchange Versions," because the two basic versions — the one that comes with the Windows 95 and NT operating systems and the version included with Exchange Server — have different capabilities.

Exchange Functions

Exchange's main functions are sending and receiving messages, storing messages and documents, and helping you work with that information.

The first and most obvious function of Exchange is to send and receive messages. These messages can be e-mail messages or faxes, with or without attachments. With the right Exchange setup, it's possible to send a message to anyone, anywhere, even if the recipient doesn't have electronic mail. (How? You could use a service that prints your e-mail message on paper and delivers the message either to the post office or directly to the recipient.)

Exchange's second function is to store messages and other documents. Messages you receive and send are automatically kept in a *message store*, which can be either on your local drive or on a network server. You can also keep documents in Exchange — spreadsheets, proposals, presentations, any file at all. By organizing messages and documents together into folders related to projects and issues, you can see the "big picture" along with all the details. Put all those messages and documents in a public folder, and everyone will get the picture.

The final function of Exchange is to provide the tools to help you work with all that information. You get an address book for storing information about the people you send messages to. Depending on the version of Exchange, you may have a simple Find tool for searching messages or sophisticated *assistants* and *views* to impose your own rules on how messages should be handled. Some Exchange tools work totally behind the scenes to "glue" groupware together or to help you move project tasks from one person to another. Dozens of companies are creating new tools to enhance Exchange with advanced search capabilities, electronic data interchange, group conferencing, and other mechanisms to improve the way you handle information.

One of the goals of this book is to show you how to use the tools that are packaged with Exchange and to introduce you to other tools available as add-ons. But before we can do that, we need to examine the components that make up Exchange.

Exchange Components

The most visible components of Exchange are the *information services* that define what kinds of messages you can send, where your messages are stored, and how your address book is kept. Other components, such as the Messaging Application Programming Interface (MAPI) and forms, add new functions and enable other programs to tie into Exchange.

Where do you see these components of Exchange? You can find them within your Exchange profile and among the options available for Exchange. You'll also find them added to menus, particularly the Compose menu.

Each user has a *profile,* which keeps details about what information services are set up for that user, where messages are stored, and where personal addresses are stored. An example of a profile for a user named Tom Jones is shown in Figure 2.1. We'll spend all of Chapter 4, "Configuring Profiles," looking at different ways to set up users with Exchange.

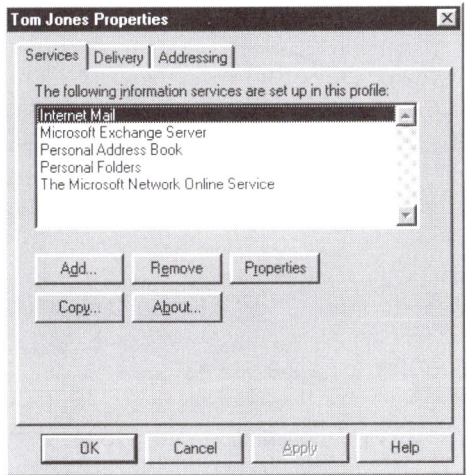

Figure 2.1

A typical profile consists of one or more information services (such as Internet Mail, Microsoft Exchange Server, or The Microsoft Network), plus Personal Address Book and possibly Personal Folders.

Another place to look for Exchange components is in the Options dialog box, shown in Figure 2.2. Some add-ons — usually those that do not install in your profile as Exchange services — place additional tabs here, where you can configure their settings.

A third place to look for enhancements to Exchange is on the program menus. On the Compose menu, you'll find options for sending and posting

Figure 2.2

This Exchange user has added two enhancements — a preview utility and an antivirus program — to Exchange. Both are controlled on the Options dialog box, rather than through profile settings.

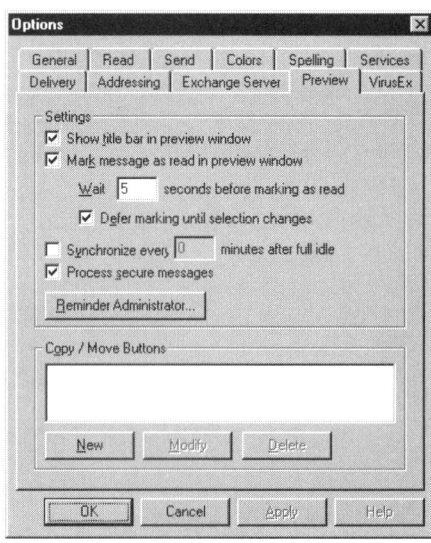

new types of items, such as the New Winfax choice shown in Figure 2.3. You may also find new functions such as the Resend options in Figure 2.3. Also check the File, View, and Tools menus. Some add-ons even put entirely new menus on the menu bar.

Figure 2.3

Additions to Exchange for this user result in several new choices on the Compose menu — New WinFax, plus two Resend options.

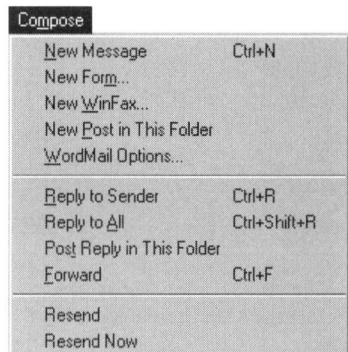

Information Services

As we discussed briefly in the previous chapter, Exchange consists of the program itself and the information services that operate inside it. There are three types of information services: message store services, directory services, and transport services. You need all three types of services to make Exchange work.

Message Store Services

As you'd probably guess, *message store services* provide a place to store messages and ways to manage them. There are both private and public message stores. A private store is for your personal use. The public stores are located on servers and shared with other Exchange users.

In the Windows 95 and Windows NT operating system versions of Exchange, the private message store is called *Personal Folders*. You can have more than one Personal Folders file associated with your profile, and Personal Folders can be stored either on your local system or on a network device.

In the Exchange Server clients, you will have a private information store, called a *mailbox*, which is kept on the server, so you don't have to worry about backups. If you travel, you'll also have offline folders on your computer that will be synchronized with the mailbox on the Microsoft Exchange server. You can have Personal Folders in the Exchange Server client, too. (Archives are a good reason to have Personal Folders in any version of Exchange, as we'll see in Chapter 4, under "Uses for Secondary Personal Folders.")

If you use Exchange on a local area network, you probably also work with public information stores — either public folders on Exchange Server or shared folders with Microsoft Mail. These don't appear in your profile.

Exchange includes three types of information services: message store services, directory services, and transport services.

Directory Services

Directory services is a fancy name for address lists, places to look up names so you don't have to enter the details of each person's address every time you want to send a message. E-mail addresses can get quite complicated when mailboxes are scattered across multiple servers, so this is a useful, time-saving feature.

It is possible to enter almost any type of address by hand without looking it up, but it's not easy; so you're better off using Exchange's directory services.

When you look at the Address Book (see Figure 2.4), you'll see your Personal Address Book and — if you're connecting to Exchange Server or a Microsoft Mail postoffice — one or more lists of addresses for your organization.

Transport Services

The *transport service* or *transport provider* is the part of Exchange that takes your messages, formats them, and transmits them to the recipients. Examples include the Microsoft Exchange Server service, Microsoft Mail, Microsoft Fax, Netscape Internet Mail, AT&T Mail, CompuServe Mail, and Microsoft Network mail.

You can — and probably will — use more than one transport service with Exchange. Exchange is often called the "universal inbox" because of its

Figure 2.4

The Microsoft Exchange Server service, Microsoft Mail, Microsoft Network, and some other information services add their own address lists to those accessible from the Address Book.

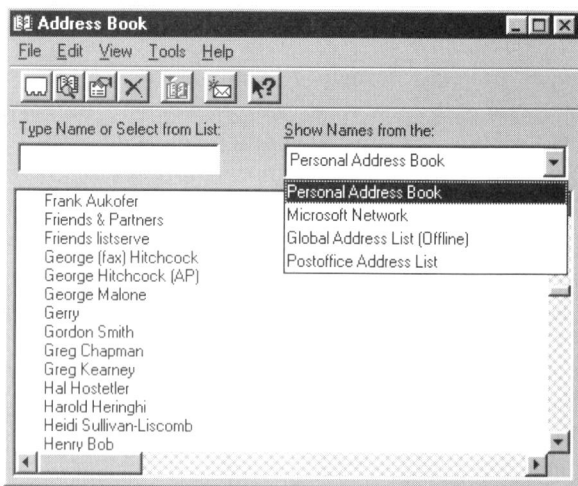

ability to let you access messages from a variety of sources using different transport services. New transport services are being introduced all the time, often coupled with their own directory services to manage compatible addresses or with a special entry type for use in the Personal Address Book.

Closely related to the transport services are *connectors* and *gateways*. These, too, contribute to making Exchange a universal inbox. Connectors and gateways link either Exchange Server or Microsoft Mail Server to other types of messaging, such as the Internet, mainframe mail servers, a fax server, wireless messaging, or a voice-mail server. These links don't add anything to your profile, since they interact directly with the server. But they may add other components to Exchange — a new address book entry type and/or one or more forms (see Figure 2.5) used to create a specific type of message. We'll discuss the role forms play in a little more detail in an upcoming section.

Table 2.1 lists some of the available transport services and connectors. Those that work only with the Exchange Server clients are marked with an asterisk.

Profiles

Tying all these information services together for an individual user is the *profile*. Everybody has a profile, whether or not you've seen it. If Exchange was installed on your system for you, then a profile probably was created for you. If that's not the case, then you'll be prompted to answer various questions the first time you run Exchange, and from the answers, a profile will be built.

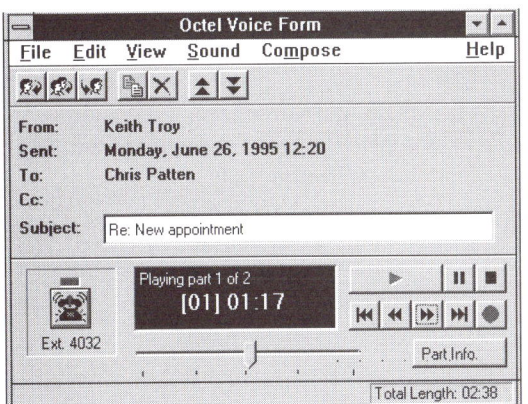

Figure 2.5

This voice-mail service added to Exchange installs a special form for composing and listening to voice mail. Notice that the form combines recording and playback controls (at lower right) with reply and forward buttons (at upper left).

Table 2.1 Exchange Transport Services and Connectors	
Type	**Services**
Workgroup/enterprise mail	Microsoft Exchange Server * Microsoft Mail MAPI ConnectorWare for cc:Mail Lotus Notes
Internet mail	Microsoft Internet Mail Microsoft Internet Mail Connector * Netscape Internet Mail Transport netApps Internet Series Workgroup Internet Gateway
Fax	Microsoft Fax Active Voice ViewMail * Fenestrae Faxination * Octel Unified Messaging * OMTOOL Fax Sr. * Optus FACSys *
Voice mail	Active Voice ViewMail * Applied Voice CallXpress3 Octel Unified Messaging *

* Works only with Exchange Server clients

continued

Table 2.1 Exchange Transport Services and Connectors, continued	
Type	**Services**
Wireless messaging and paging	ARDIS Mobile Office * Integra Wireless Messaging Server * Marcwell MobyMail * Mobileware Personal Omnitrend PageMaster/ex *
Online services	CompuServe Mail The Microsoft Network
Other services	AT&T Mail

* Works only with Exchange Server clients

You can have more than one profile, and more than one user can have a profile on any given computer. In Chapter 4, "Configuring Profiles," we'll look at some reasons for having multiple profiles and explore various sample profiles for different situations.

Other Components

Two other Exchange components deserve special attention: Messaging Application Programming Interface (MAPI) and forms. Without MAPI, there would be no Exchange. Forms expand Exchange from simple messaging to groupware, and from groupware to integrated applications that haven't even been imagined yet.

MAPI

If information services are the basic building blocks of Exchange, MAPI is the mortar that binds these building blocks together.

If information services are the basic building blocks of Exchange, *MAPI* is the mortar that binds these building blocks together. MAPI, the Messaging Application Programming Interface, gives programmers the ability to peer into Exchange's structure of messages, folders, users, and addresses, present that information to other applications, and create add-ons that integrate neatly into the Exchange client itself.

In fact, every time you do File, Send from an application to send a document via e-mail, you put MAPI to work. Many of the enhancements for Exchange included on this book's CD, and many of those available from other sources, use MAPI. If you're a programmer, you can even write your own add-ons for Exchange using tools such as C++ and Visual Basic, plus MAPI.

To show you the wide range of MAPI products, Table 2.2 lists just a sampling of those available, along with some of the other plug-ins for Exchange that you might want to try. The list grows every day. A relatively simple MAPI program such as WinFax may access only folders and the

Table 2.2 MAPI-Integrated and Other Exchange-Compatible Products	
Type	**Product**
Workflow	Action Workflow System *
	Integrated Work WinWork and RIO *
	Keyfile KeyflowT *
	PC DOCS Interchange *
	Reach WorkMAN Route&Track *
Mobile computing	Ericsson Virtual Office
Forms	Shana Informed Electronic Forms
	Delrina FormFlow 2.0
	JetForm
Group discussion	Mesa Conference+
	Trax TeamTalk *
	Verity TEAM 97 *
Fax	Delrina WinFax Pro version 7.0
Antivirus tools	VirusEx
	netApps ThunderBYTE Anti-Virus for
	Microsoft Exchange
Search tools	Fulcrum Find *
	Verity Search 97 for Exchange *
Security tools	Deming Secure Messenger
	PGP Extension for Microsoft Exchange
Voice mail	Mediatrends Quip
	Microsoft Phone
	Bonzi Voice E-mail

Works only with Exchange Server clients.

Personal Address Book. The most sophisticated products use the full power of Exchange Server to build applications that automate the flow of projects and documents or that manage group discussion forums.

Forms

Every time you create or read a message or post a document in Exchange, you're working with a form.

Every time you create or read a message or post a document in Exchange, you're working with a *form*, a template for creating a particular type of message or document. The simplest form is the basic New Message form. You can also have fill-in-the-blank forms and forms that take specific actions based on information you provide, such as routing forms.

Forms are so important to Exchange that the Exchange Server clients come with Exchange Forms Designer software that lets you create your own forms, even if you don't know how to write programming code (see Chapter 20, "Using and Creating Exchange Forms").

Differences Between Exchange Versions

Exchange comes in two flavors: a basic version included with the Windows 95 and Windows NT 4.0 operating systems, and the full program that works with Exchange Server.

Exchange comes in two flavors: a basic version included with the Windows 95 and Windows NT 4.0 operating systems; and the full program that works with Exchange Server, and with clients for DOS, Windows 3.1x, Macintosh, Windows 95, and Windows NT. Where we need to distinguish between the two, this book refers to the *Exchange operating system clients* and the *Exchange Server clients*.

Figure 2.6 helps you recognize the different clients. The Exchange Server client is the version with the fancier icons (and yes, the Outbox reverts to an empty tray when all its messages have been delivered).

Operating System Clients

On Windows NT 4.0 and on some Windows 95 systems, Exchange goes by the name of Windows Messaging, Microsoft's effort to distinguish this version from the full Exchange Server client. We've stuck to the Exchange name in this book to keep things simple.

The operating system clients let you plug in a wonderful array of information services to access many different kinds of messaging services and even perform some groupware functions. But the one service you can't install in an operating system client is the Microsoft Exchange Server service. To use all the features detailed in the next section — or any of the services and applications listed in Tables 2.1 and 2.2 as exclusive to Exchange Server — you must upgrade the Exchange operating system client to the version that comes with Exchange Server. This also will automatically install the Microsoft Exchange Server service in your default profile.

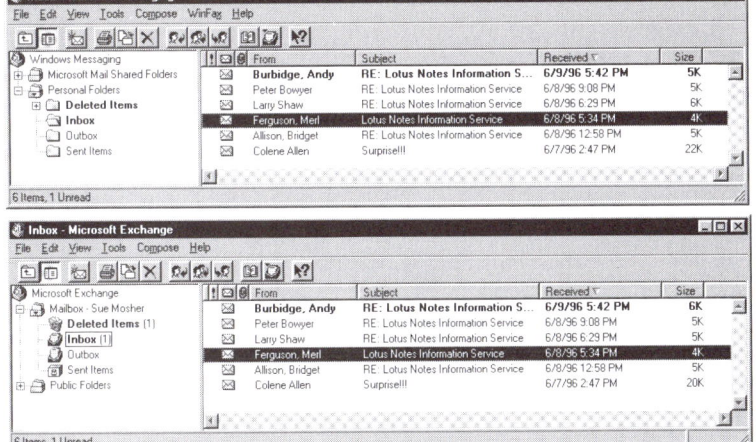

Figure 2.6
The window at the top shows the Exchange program from the Windows 95 operating system, sometimes known as Windows Messaging. The bottom window is the Windows 95 Exchange Server client. Note the presence of Public Folders and the more elaborate icons under the Mailbox folder, which represents a private message store on the Exchange Server.

On the other hand, the Exchange Server client works very nicely on a standalone machine, even one that never connects to Exchange Server. See Appendix B, "Exchange Resources," for information about how to download a trial copy of this version.

One other note: A spelling checker is not included with the operating system clients. To add a spelling checker to the Windows 95 and NT 4.0 clients, you need to add the 32-bit version of Microsoft Word or Works to your system.

Exchange Server Clients

Exchange Server includes clients for DOS, Windows 3.1x, Windows 95, Windows NT, and Macintosh. This book concerns itself with the Windows 95 and NT clients, which are the most fun because they use all the features of Exchange.

The Exchange Server clients are actually three programs in one. In addition to Exchange, they also include Schedule+ and Exchange Forms Designer, both of which are worthy subjects for entire books by themselves.

Schedule+ (Figure 2.7) is a perfect example of MAPI and forms combining with Exchange to create a powerful tool, in this case an application for personal and group scheduling. Schedule+ uses Exchange Server public folders to keep the free/busy times for all users, making it possible to do scheduling across an entire enterprise, not just in one small office. Schedule+ also includes special forms for requesting and confirming meetings.

On Windows NT 4.0 and on some Windows 95 machines, the operating system client goes by the name of Windows Messaging.

Users of the operating system Exchange clients can do group scheduling with the version of Schedule+ included with Office 95 and a Microsoft Mail or workgroup postoffice. Be aware, however, that you won't be able to exchange schedule information with Windows 3.1 or Windows NT 3.51 users working with the older version of Schedule+.

Electronic Forms Designer (EFD) is just what the name says it is — a tool for creating electronic forms that plug right into Exchange. No previous programming experience is required. We'll take a brief tour of EFD in Chapter 20.

One other component shipped with the Exchange Server clients that isn't included with the operating clients is the spelling checker, the same proof-reading engine included with Microsoft Word or Works.

Finally, a question that often arises is whether the Exchange Server client will work on a standalone machine that doesn't have a way to connect to a Microsoft Exchange server. The answer is, yes, it works just great, giving you access to features such as views and AutoSignature.

If you use the Exchange Server client as a replacement for the operating system Exchange client on a standalone machine without a Microsoft Exchange server to connect to, you will not be able to use the Inbox Assistant to handle incoming messages. This feature works only when the Microsoft Exchange Server service is installed in your profile and an Exchange Server connection is available.

Figure 2.7

The version of Schedule+ that comes with Exchange Server allows you to set up a meeting with anyone listed in your organization's address book.

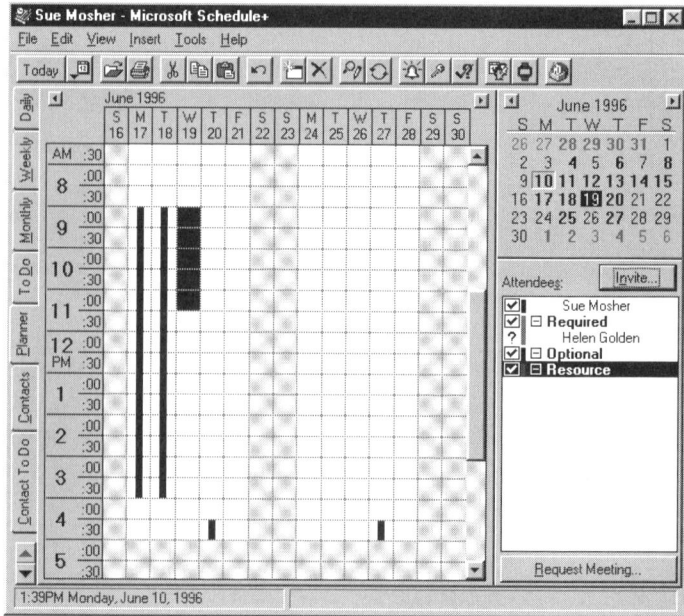

Summary

This is the end of our introductory chapter about Exchange. From here on, it's time to dig into practical matters — configuring and using Exchange. If you've been patient enough to get this far in our one theoretical chapter, good for you! Understanding some of the underlying structure of Exchange really will help you get more out of Exchange. The next time the boss asks whether Exchange can help streamline a particular business process, you'll be able to think about whether a new information service, a MAPI-enabled add-on, or a simple form might do the trick.

New additions to the Exchange family are emerging at a steady pace. For example, Exchange Server 5.0 adds the capability to access your mailbox through an Internet Web browser. Microsoft Office 97 includes a new Exchange client called Outlook that integrates messages, forms, contacts, and scheduling into a single desktop information management system. You'll learn more about both those additions in Chapters 25 and 26.

Key Points

- Exchange's main functions are sending and receiving messages, storing messages and documents, and helping you work with that information.
- Exchange includes three types of information services: message store services, directory services, and transport services.
- If information services are the basic building blocks of Exchange, MAPI is the mortar that binds them together.
- Every time you create or read a message or post a document in Exchange, you're working with a form.
- Exchange comes in two flavors: a basic version included with the Windows 95 and Windows NT 4.0 operating systems, and the full program that works with Exchange Server.
- On Windows NT 4.0 and on some Windows 95 machines, the operating system client goes by the name of Windows Messaging.

For More Information

Throughout the book, I've highlighted a wide variety of the information services and MAPI applications available for Exchange. The most important of these get their own chapters, while others may appear only as screen shots or passing mentions. See Appendix B, "Exchange Resources," for contact information if you want to find out more.

Another class of add-ons to watch for throughout this book is the "widget." In general, widgets are small programs that enhance particular functions — such as adding a signature line or performing optical character recognition on a fax. Many are mentioned in the text and in Appendix B, but new ones are sprouting up all the time. Check the CD that came with this book for the best of the bunch.

Chapter 3

Making Connections

Even if your computer is on a desk by itself, with no network to plug into, working with Exchange is still largely a matter of making connections. You dial a fax machine across town or connect to the Internet to send mail around the globe. Perhaps you travel and need to reach your Microsoft Exchange server to get your mail and check essential public folders. You can connect not only with a dedicated bank of dial-up modems, but also via the Internet.

In this chapter, we'll review some of the essential skills involved in making and maintaining such connections. For the most part, I assume that, if you're working in a network environment, the network is already set up and running fine; or if you're connecting via modem, you have the modem installed and working. We'll concentrate mostly on issues using modem connections, but we'll also highlight the skill of sharing network folders. You'll learn how to

- Tell Windows where you're dialing from
- Instruct Windows how to dial with your credit card
- Adjust your international dialing code if it changes in your country
- Make dial-up connections to the Internet or to a network mail server
- Create a shared folder for network faxing or for a Microsoft Mail postoffice

While Windows 95 and NT dialing locations, calling cards, and dial-up networking (DUN) work more or less the same, there are some differences in the dialog boxes that I'll highlight as we go along.

Configuring Dialing Locations

Windows keeps phone numbers separate from dialing location settings, then puts the two together when you dial.

Have you ever traveled from city to city and reset the settings for a half-dozen communications programs at every stop? You need to change the code to get an outside line in every program and turn off the call-waiting code you had on your office phone. Windows solves that problem with the concept of dialing locations, which are completely separate from phone numbers. Each time you need to call from somewhere different, you configure all the dialing settings in one place, then they automatically apply to every number you dial with any Windows communications program that supports the Telephony Application Programming Interface (TAPI).

In the next few sections, you'll learn how to set up a dialing location, how to switch between different locations, and how to set up calling cards.

Basic Settings

To work with dialing locations, you need to display the Dialing Properties dialog box. This can be done from any dialog box where you see a Dialing Properties button, such as the one in the Microsoft Fax Properties dialog box's Modem tab. You can also get to the Dialing Properties dialog box from the Control Panel. In Windows NT, run the Telephony applet. In Windows 95, you can use the Telephony applet if you have one, or choose Modems, then click the Dialing Properties button. You'll see a dialog box like that in Figure 3.1.

Figure 3.1

Create new dialing locations and switch between locations in the Dialing Properties dialog box. Note that Windows 95 users will not see the Telephony Drivers tab, which is part of the Telephony applet in Windows NT.

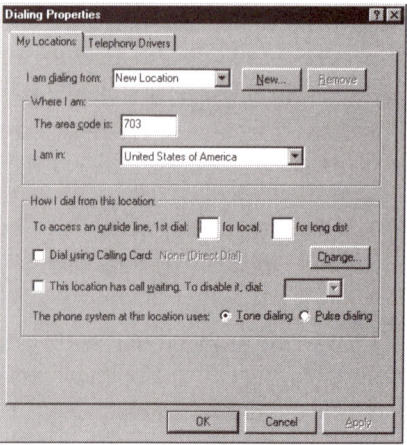

Each *location* is a collection of dialing settings specific to a particular place, such as your office, your home, a hotel room in Poughkeepsie, or a client's office in Bonn. By switching locations, you can change all the dialing settings at once, rather than having to change each one individually.

Let's first complete the setup of your default location. If you work at a desktop computer that never travels, this is all you need. First, in the Dialing Properties dialog box (Figure 3.1), enter your area code in the "The area code is" box and select a country from the "I am in" list if they're not already filled in. You can also change the name of the location, if you like, in the "I am dialing from" box.

Next, consider what changes you may need to make under "How I dial from this location." Some examples are

- If you need to dial a number to obtain an outside line for both local and long distance calls, enter that number in the "for local" box and again in the "for long dist." box.
- If you dial two different numbers for local and long distance access, enter the appropriate numbers in the "for local" and "for long dist." boxes.

Do not enter 1 in the "for long dist." box, even if all your long distance calls must start with a 1, as they generally do in the U.S. and Canada. Windows 95 has a table of codes for each country that indicate what number(s) to dial for long distance and even for international long distance. We'll look at these in more detail later in this chapter, when we discuss calling cards.

Special Note

- If your line has call waiting, check the box labeled "This location has call waiting." Then either pick a code from the "To disable it, dial" list (such as *70) or enter a different code.
- If your phone system uses pulse dialing rather than the default tone dialing, click "Pulse dialing."

The dialing properties are global within Windows; they affect all Windows communications programs that support TAPI, not just dial-up networking (DUN) and Microsoft Fax.

Special Note

You've probably realized by now that we have skipped the "Dial using Calling Card" settings. Calling cards cover virtually any type of dialing situation that doesn't fit the normal area code + number format. This includes telephone credit cards, PBX dialing without a 1 in front of long distance numbers, accounting codes after a number, and new international long distance codes. We're going to explore calling cards later in the chapter.

When you've finished setting up the default location, click OK to close the Dialing Properties dialog box.

Working with Locations

To create a new location,

1. Click the New button in the Dialing Properties dialog box (Figure 3.1).
2. In Windows 95, give the location a name in the Create New Location dialog box, then click OK. In Windows NT, the name New Location is entered for you in the "I am dialing from" box; change this name to something more meaningful.
3. Enter the country, area code, call waiting, and other settings for the new location in the Dialing Properties dialog box.

To switch locations, choose a location from the "I am dialing from" list. To remove a location, select it in the "I am dialing from" list, then click Remove.

Calling Cards

A Windows calling card is more than a telephone credit card; the calling card can solve a number of dialing-code problems.

A *calling card* in the context of Windows dialing is not the same as a telephone credit card. Calling cards are used in a variety of situations to apply extra settings beyond those available in the Dialing Properties dialog box. Examples include the following:

- Calls made through a preferred long distance provider
- Telephone credit card calls
- An accounting code added to the end of the number dialed
- A change in the international access code within a country
- A PBX where you need to omit the 1 before making long distance calls

Each calling card consists of three sets of codes that define the way calls are dialed:

- Within the same area code
- Outside the same area code, but within the same country (long distance calls)
- To another country (international calls)

To use a calling card as part of a dialing location, follow these steps:

1. Open the Dialing Properties dialog box, as described above under "Configuring Dialing Locations."
2. Check the box marked "Dial <u>u</u>sing Calling Card," or click the C<u>h</u>ange button.

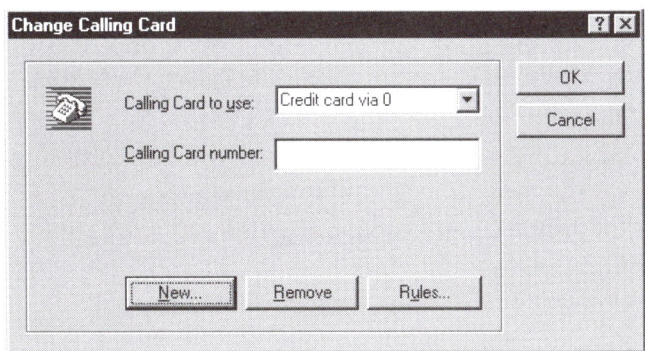

Figure 3.2
This is the Windows NT version of the Change Calling Card dialog box. On the Windows 95 version, the Rules button is instead labeled Advanced, but it does the same thing — it gives you a place to enter dialing codes.

3. In the Change Calling Card dialog box (Figure 3.2), select the "Calling Card to <u>u</u>se."
4. If the calling card incorporates a credit card, the "<u>C</u>alling Card number" box will become active. Enter your number.
5. Click OK to save that calling card as part of the current dialing location.

Next, we'll create some examples of different types of calling cards, starting with dialing long distance. When you create a new calling card, you generally use an existing card as a template.

Dialing a Preferred Long Distance Provider

The calling cards provided with Windows include several used to dial long distance through a specific provider with a special code. For example, in the U.S., you can prefix a long distance call with 10ATT (or 10288) to force the call to go through AT&T.

Here are the long distance calling cards included with Windows and how each dials a long distance number:

AT&T Direct Dial via 10ATT1   10288 + 1 + area code + number
MCI Direct Dial via 102221   10222 + 1 + area code + number
Sprint Direct Dial via 103331   10333 + 1 + area code + number

Like all the calling cards installed with Windows, these can be copied but not directly edited. Instead of changing one of these calling cards, you can create a new card, copy the settings from an existing card, then make any desired changes.

To create and use a new calling card by copying one of the cards included with Windows, follow these steps:

1. In the Dialing Properties dialog box (Figure 3.1), click the Change button. (In Windows 95, you first must check the "Dial using Calling Card" box.)

2. In the Change Calling Card dialog box (Figure 3.2), click the New button.

3. Give your new calling card a name, then click OK to return to the Change Calling Card dialog box, where the new card is now selected.

4. In Windows 95, click the Advanced button. In Windows NT, click the Rules button.

5. In the Dialing Rules dialog box, click the Copy From button.

6. In the Copy Dialing Rules dialog box, choose the card you want to use as a template, specifically one of the three listed above, then click OK. Figure 3.3 shows the result of copying the dialing rules for the AT&T Direct Dial Via 10ATT1 card. You see the three different sets of codes for three kinds of calls. Table 3.1 lists the meanings of the different codes you'll see in the Dialing Rules dialog box.

Figure 3.3
The rules shown here are for a calling card to dial a number directly via AT&T by dialing 10ATT, then the area code and number.

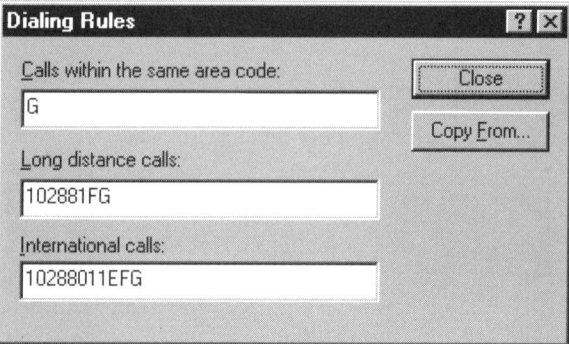

7. Under "Long distance calls" and "International calls," change the 288 (or other code, if you didn't use AT&T as the template) to the dialing code for the long distance provider you prefer.

Table 3.1 Codes Used for Calling Cards	
Code	**Description**
E	Country code
F	Area or city code
G	Local number
H	Calling card number
P	Switch to pulse dial
T	Switch to tone dial
W	Wait for a second dial tone
@	Wait for a ringing tone, followed by five seconds of silence
$	Wait for a credit card prompt ("bong")
?	Display an on-screen prompt to the user to continue dialing
,	Include a two-second pause
!	Hookflash (1/2 second on-hook, 1/2 second off-hook)

8. Click Close when you've finished with the Dialing Rules dialog box, then click OK to close the Change Calling Card dialog box and return to Dialing Properties.

Dialing with a Credit Card

At the beginning of this section on calling cards, we looked at the basic procedure for using a credit card as part of a dialing location. You select the calling card, then enter the "Calling Card number" in the Change Calling Card dialog box. Calling cards to handle credit card dialing in the U.S. and other countries are installed with Windows, including a basic Calling Card via 0 that lets you dial 0, followed by the number, then your credit card.

Sometimes you need to alter the setting for one of these credit card calling cards. In particular, if you're using a calling card with Microsoft Fax, you may need to replace the $ code (used to wait for the credit card "bong") with a series of commas, each representing a two-second pause. Microsoft Fax does not properly handle the $ code unless your modem directly supports it, with the result that your credit card number might be omitted from the call.

To make a copy of a calling card so that it uses a comma for pauses, follow these steps:

1. In the Dialing Properties dialog box (Figure 3.1), click the Change button.

2. In the Change Calling Card dialog box (Figure 3.2), click the New button.

3. Give your new calling card a name, then click OK to return to the Change Calling Card dialog box, where the new card is now selected.

4. In Windows 95, click the Advanced button. In Windows NT, click the Rules button.

5. In the Dialing Rules dialog box, click the Copy From button, choose the card you want to use as a template, then click OK. This example uses the Calling Card Via 0 card.

Figure 3.4

This is a basic calling card for credit card dialing in which you dial 0, then the number, then the credit card number. Notice the H code, which represents your credit card number.

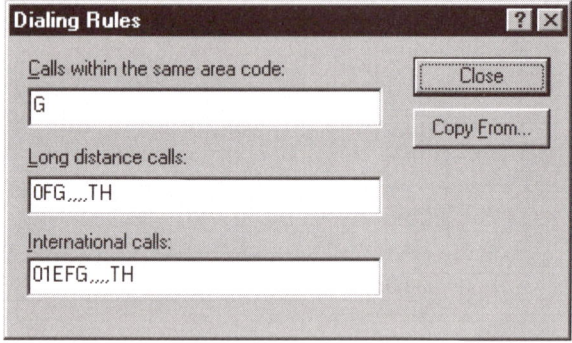

---

6. Back in the Dialing Rules dialog box, replace the $ with four commas. Each comma represents a two-second pause. The result is shown in Figure 3.4.

7. Click the Close button to return to the Change Calling Card dialog box (Figure 3.2).

8. Enter your credit card number in the "Calling Card number" box.

9. Click OK to save that calling card and make it part of the current dialing location.

Changing the International Access Code

Each country has its own code to indicate that a call is being made to a number outside the country. If this access code changes, you'll need to update the dialing properties to accommodate the new code. An easy way to do that is by adding a calling card. Here's how:

1. In the Dialing Properties dialog box (Figure 3.1), click the Change button.
2. In the Change Calling Card dialog box (Figure 3.2), click the New button.
3. Give your new calling card a name, then click OK to return to the Change Calling Card dialog box, where the new card is now selected.
4. In Windows 95, click the Advanced button. In Windows NT, click the Rules button.
5. In the Dialing Rules dialog box, define the rules you want to use, such as

Same area code:	G
Long distance:	0FG
International calls:	0061EFG (where 0061 is the new international access code).

See Table 3.1 for the meaning of the E, F, and G codes, which represent parts of the actual number to be dialed.
6. Click the Close button to return to the Change Calling Card dialog box.
7. Click OK to save that calling card and make it part of the current dialing location.

For Windows 95, Microsoft provides another way to update the international codes via the addition of a [Country Overrides] section to the Telephon.ini file in your Windows folder. The necessary settings can be found in article Q142328 (dated March 1996) in the *Microsoft Knowledge Base*. A utility is also expected from Microsoft to handle this.

Special Note

Dialing Through a PBX

For our final calling card example, we'll create a calling card that lets you dial long distance without first dialing 1, as many PBXs require. Use the Dialing Properties dialog box to enter the 8 or 9 or other code(s) needed to access local and long distance lines. Then create a new calling card to handle the rest of the dialing rules, like this:

1. In the Dialing Properties dialog box (Figure 3.1), click the Change button.
2. In the Change Calling Card dialog box (Figure 3.2), click the New button.

3. Give your new calling card a name, then click OK to return to the Change Calling Card dialog box, where the new card is now selected.

4. In Windows 95, click the Advanced button. In Windows NT, click the Rules button.

5. In the Dialing Rules dialog box, define the rules you want to use, such as

Same area code:	G
Long distance:	FG
International calls:	011EFG

Note the omission of the 1 under "Long distance calls."

6. Click the Close button to return to the Change Calling Card dialog box.

7. Click OK to save that calling card and make it part of the current dialing location.

Dial-Up Networking

Dial-up networking (DUN) connects you to either Exchange Server or a Microsoft Mail server at your office, or to an Internet mail server.

Dial-up networking (DUN) connects you to either Exchange Server or a Microsoft Mail server at your office, or to an Internet mail server. You can even use the Internet to connect with Exchange Server — a real boon if you travel.

There are two phases to setting up DUN:

- Installing DUN itself and any network protocol you need that isn't already on your computer

- Creating DUN connection settings to link you to specific network resources (Under Windows 95, these settings are called *connectoids*; Windows NT calls them *phonebook entries.*)

You may already have DUN installed; you certainly will if you've used any Windows 95 or Windows NT utilities to connect to the Internet. Open My Computer on your desktop. If you see an icon for Dial-Up Networking, then DUN is definitely installed.

Chances are that your system is also already configured for the network protocols you need to connect to various servers. However, just in case it isn't, we'll cover TCP/IP installation, because TCP/IP is the protocol used to connect with the Internet and it is also increasingly used on local area networks. You might use a different protocol, perhaps NetBEUI, to connect to a Windows NT server running Remote Access Server (RAS) for connections to a Microsoft Mail server, or IPX/SPX to connect to a NetWare server. The basic procedure for installing NetBEUI or IPX/SPX would be the same as that for installing TCP/IP, only there aren't as many settings for those two as as there are for TCP/IP.

What You Need to Know for Dial-Up Networking

Before you get started with DUN, it pays to do a little homework. When you create a phonebook entry for Windows NT or a DUN connectoid for Windows 95, you need to know the answers to many questions about the server you want to connect to. Here's a checklist you can use to gather this information all in one place:

Dial-Up Networking Checklist

☐ Log-on name: _____

☐ Password: _____

☐ Domain (if you connect to a Windows NT server): _____

☐ Telephone number: _____

☐ Alternate numbers: _____

☐ Use Telephony (for dialing   ☐ Yes
    locations and calling cards):   ☐ No

☐ Use a log-on script: ☐ No
                                    ☐ Before connection
                                    ☐ After connection

☐ Name of script: _____

☐ Network Protocol: ☐ TCP/IP
    (check all that apply)   ☐ NetBEUI
                                      ☐ IPX/SPX

☐ IP Address   ☐ Server provides
    (TCP/IP only)   ☐ I provide: _____

☐ DNS Server Address :   ☐ Server provides
    (TCP/IP only)   ☐ I provide: _____

☐ WINS Server Address :   ☐ Server provides
    (TCP/IP only)   ☐ I provide: _____

☐ Type of TCP/IP   ☐ PPP
    connection: ☐ SLIP

You use log-on scripts to automate the connection process when the server requires you to enter a user ID and password. The Windows 95 dial-up scripting language works for both Windows 95 and Windows NT, though NT also has its own scripting language. You are not required to log on with a script; but once you have one, logging on is easier. You can either write your own script or check with the network administrator to see if one has already been written.

The IP address is the network address assigned to your computer while the computer is using the DUN connection. The IP address will be different from the address for any network adapter card installed in your computer.

DNS and WINS are techniques for locating servers on the network. You may need either a DNS or WINS server address, but not both, for any given connection. In some cases, the remote server will provide the DNS and WINS server addresses automatically.

Once you've gathered this information, you can start working with DUN connections. In the rest of this chapter, we cover the basic installation procedure for DUN and show you how to create DUN connections to different servers.

Configuring DUN for Windows 95

If you don't see a Dial-Up Networking icon in My Computer, then you need to install DUN; here's how to do it on a Windows 95 system:

1. In the Control Panel, choose Add/Remove Programs, then switch to the Windows Setup tab.

2. Select Communications, then click the Details button.

3. Check the Dial-Up Networking box.

4. Click OK, then OK again to install Dial-Up Networking.

Ask your Internet Service Provider (ISP) whether you'll connect with Point-to-Point Protocol (PPP) or with Serial Line Internet Protocol (SLIP). If it's SLIP, then you'll need to follow these steps to install support for SLIP from your Windows 95 CD. Also use this procedure to install Dial-Up Scripting if your ISP requires a manual log-on through a terminal window.

1. In the Control Panel, choose Add/Remove Programs, then switch to the Windows Setup tab.

2. Click the Have Disk button.

3. Point to the Admin\Apptools\Dscript folder on the Windows 95 CD.

4. Select Rnaplus.inf from the list, then click OK.

5. Click the OK button to copy the manufacturer's files from the Dscript folder.

6. Click the box for SLIP and Scripting for Dial-Up Networking.

7. Click Install to complete the SLIP and Scripting installation.

8. Click OK to close the Add/Remove Programs window.

The SLIP and Scripting support files can also be downloaded from Microsoft support sites and are available as part of the Microsoft Plus! CD and the Internet Jump-Start Kit.

Special Note

Installing a Network Protocol

The next step is to install the TCP/IP protocol (or another protocol if you need it) if TCP/IP is not already active on your system. You need TCP/IP mainly if you're connecting to the Internet, though a growing number of private LANs also use it. In Windows 95, follow these steps:

1. In the Control Panel, choose Network.

2. In the Network dialog box, click the Add button. Then select Protocol and click Add again.

3. Under Manufacturers, select Microsoft. Under Network Protocols, select TCP/IP. Then click OK.

If you need to use IPX/SPX or NetBEUI to access an NT or NetWare server, then choose that protocol instead of TCP/IP.

Special Note

4. Click OK to close the Network dialog box, then restart your computer when you're prompted to do so.

Do not configure any of the TCP/IP settings through Control Panel, Network. The defaults will do fine. We'll make specific changes later for individual DUN connectoids.

Creating a DUN Connectoid

Now you need to create a DUN connectoid to link you to specific network resources. To make a new connectoid, follow these steps:

1. Open My Computer, then choose Dial-Up Networking. You'll see any existing DUN connectoids, including one for The Microsoft Network, if you have joined MSN. You can also start DUN by clicking Start, then choosing Programs, Accessories, Dial-Up Networking.

2. Choose Make New Connection.

3. In the first screen of the Make New Connection wizard, give this connection a name, perhaps the name of the computer you're dialing. Also, select a modem from the list of those installed on your system. Click Next to continue.

4. Enter the Area Code, Telephone Number, and Country Code for the computer you want to call; then click Next to continue and Finish to complete the wizard.

   This process creates a new connectoid with default settings to connect to a Windows 95, Windows NT, or Internet server. Here's where we get into the specific settings for your connection. You'll need to know

   - Your user name
   - Your password
   - Whether or not a terminal window is used for logging on
   - For TCP/IP, whether or not the server assigns an IP address
   - For TCP/IP, whether or not the server assigns name server (DNS and WINS) addresses

   Once you have this information, right-click on the connectoid in the Dial-Up Networking folder and choose Properties. In the Properties dialog box for the connectoid (Figure 3.5), click the Configure button to display the properties for the selected modem, then switch to the Options tab (Figure 3.6) to set the connection options listed in Table 3.2.

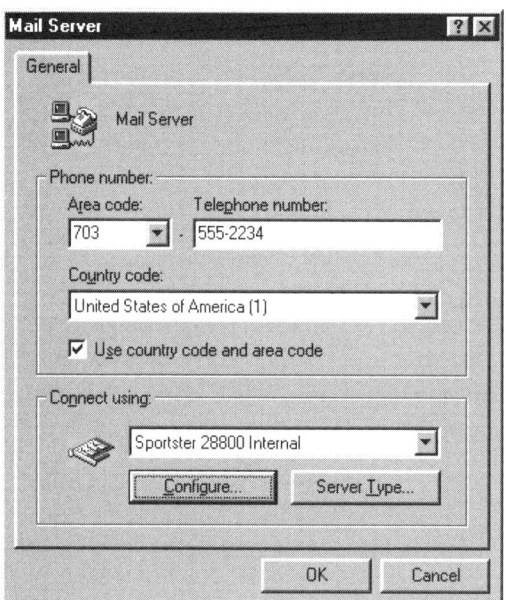

Figure 3.5
You can change the settings entered in the Make New Connection Wizard in the Properties dialog box for the connection.

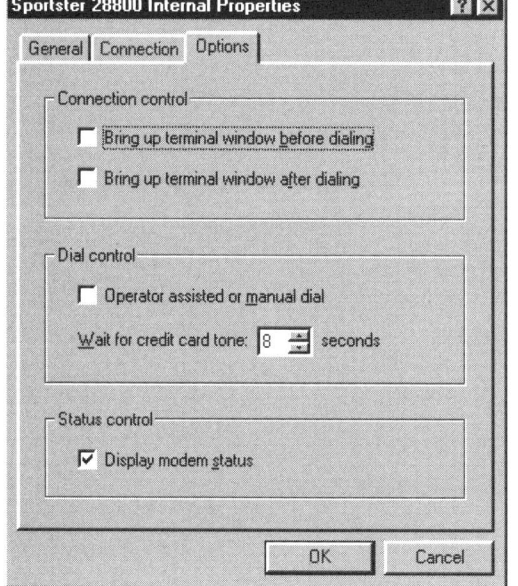

Figure 3.6
Configure the way the modem will connect on the Options tab.

Table 3.2 Connection Options

Option	Description
Bring up terminal window before dialing	Use this if you need to be able to type commands directly to your modem before dialing.
Bring up terminal window after dialing	Use this if you need to enter a user ID and password after dialing.
Operator assisted or manual dial	Use this if you need to go through an operator or if you need to dial manually for some other reason. When you hear the computer answer, click Connect.
Wait for credit card tone	This option indicates the number of seconds to wait for a credit card tone before continuing dialing.
Display modem status	This option displays a status window that shows the state of the connection.

When you've finished with these options, click OK to return to the properties for the connectoid, then click Server Type for additional options, as shown in Figure 3.7. These options are also listed in Table 3.3.

Figure 3.7

Using the Server Types dialog box, you can configure a DUN connectoid to connect with all kinds of servers.

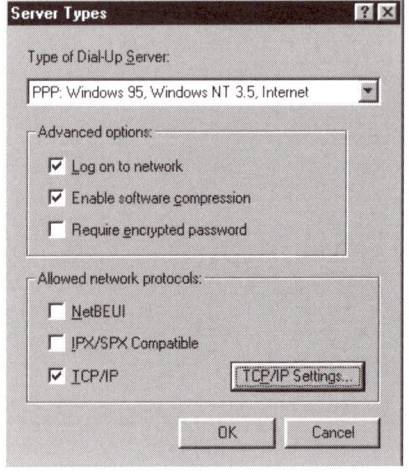

Table 3.3 Server Type Options

Option	Description
Type of Dial-Up Server	The type of machine you're dialing into; the choices are • CSLIP: Unix Connection with IP Header Compression (only if SLIP is installed) • NRN: NetWare Connect • PPP: Windows 95, Windows NT 3.5, Internet (default) • SLIP Internet: Unix Connection (only if SLIP is installed) • Windows for Workgroups and Windows NT 3.1
Log on to network	DUN will try to log on to the network using the user name and password you used to log on to Windows, or a different user name and password specified for this connectoid.
Enable software compression	Speed up the transfer of information by compressing it before it is sent, assuming the computer on each end supports it. (PPP only)
Require encrypted password	Add security by specifying that your computer will send and receive only encrypted passwords. This is useful only if the computer you're connecting to supports password encryption. (PPP only)
Allowed network protocols	For maximum efficiency, select only the protocol(s) that you actually need to connect to the other computer. The choices are • NetBEUI (PPP and RAS) • IPX/SPX Compatible (NRN and PPP only) • TCP/IP (CSLIP, PPP, and SLIP only)

Special Note

PPP connections also can be made to Shiva LanRovers and other third-party remote access products.

If you choose TCP/IP as one of your protocols, click TCP/IP Settings for a final set of connectoid options, listed in Table 3.4.

Table 3.4 TCP/IP Options	
Option	**Description**
Server Assigned IP Address (Default)	Choose this if you get a different IP address every time you log on to the remote computer.
Specify an IP Address	Use a specific IP address for this connection; enter it under IP Address.
Server Assigned Name Server Addresses (Default)	Let the remote computer indicate the addresses of the computers that maintain a database of host computer names and IP addresses.
Specify Name Server Addresses	Use specific computers for the name servers; enter their IP addresses in the areas provided for Primary and Secondary DNS and WINS.
Use IP Header Compression (Default)	Optimize data transfer by adding compression; not all remote computers support this option. (affects PPP only)
Use Default Gateway on Remote Network (Default)	Instruct the connectoid to connect to the DUN server before trying to connect to any gateways listed in the TCP/IP Properties from the Network dialog box in the Control Panel.

Setting the User ID and Password

By default, a DUN connectoid uses the same user name and password that you specified when you logged on to Windows. You'll want to change this in some cases, particularly if you're using the connectoid to log on to an Internet mail server. Follow these steps:

1. Double-click the connectoid in the Dial-Up Networking window.
2. In the Connect To dialog box (Figure 3.8), enter the User name and Password that you want to use to connect to this server.

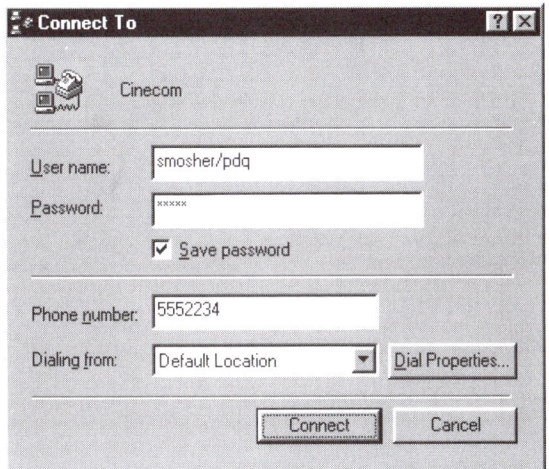

Figure 3.8
When you launch a DUN connectoid, the Connect To dialog box gives you a chance to change the "User name," "Password," "Phone number," or "Dialing from" location.

3. Click the "Save password" box if you want this password to be saved as part of your Windows password list, so you won't be prompted for it again.
4. Click the Connect button to apply the new user name and password to this connectoid and to try to make a connection.

Scripting the Log-On Process

Some ISPs automatically handle the log-on process, based on the user name and password you provided. Others require you to enter that information manually, responding to prompts on the screen. It's possible to automate your log-on process with a script. If you installed support for SLIP, as described earlier under "Configuring DUN for Windows 95," then script support is already available. If not, follow the steps in that section to install it.

You can automate your dial-up log-on process with a script.

Before writing a script, use the connectoid at least once and jot down all the prompts that appear in the terminal window, as well as your responses. To see those prompts, you need to select Bring Up Terminal Window Before Dialing, as described in Table 3.2.

To use Dial-Up Scripting, click Start, then choose Programs, Accessories, Dial-Up Scripting Tool. You will see the dialog box shown in Figure 3.9.

Figure 3.9

The Dial-Up Scripting Tool for Windows 95 associates log-on scripts with your different DUN connectoids.

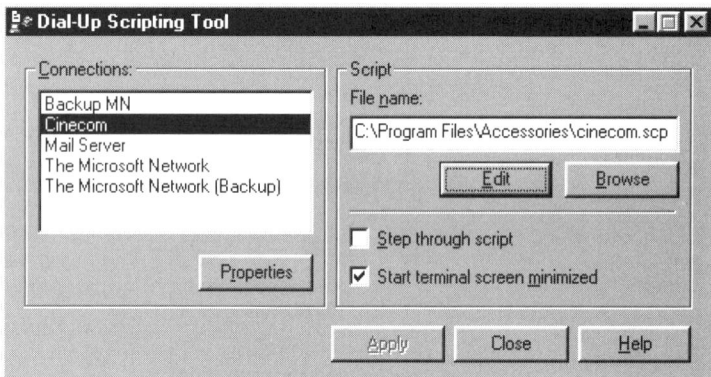

To add a script to a DUN connectoid, follow these steps:

1. Under Connections, select the connectoid you want to work with.

2. In the "File name" box, type a name for the script you want to create. Use .scp as the extension; for example, My Connection.scp.

3. Click Edit to open the blank script in Notepad.

4. Enter a **proc main** command to begin the script and an **endproc** to end it.

5. Between **proc main** and **endproc**, enter commands from those listed in Table 3.5. Alternate a **waitfor** or **delay** command with one or more **transmit** commands, as shown in the sample script on page 48.

6. Close Notepad and save the script.

7. If you want to test your script when the connectoid starts, check "Step through script."

8. In the Dial-Up Scripting Tool dialog box, click the Apply button to link the script with the selected connectoid, then click Close.

Table 3.5 Commands Commonly Used for Dial-Up Scripting

Command	Result
proc *<name>*	Begins the script procedure. All scripts must have a main procedure (**proc main**). The script begins running at the main procedure and stops at the end of the main procedure.
Endproc	Ends the script procedure. When this command is reached in the main procedure, Dial-Up Networking will start PPP or SLIP.
Delay *<n seconds>*	Pauses for *n* seconds before executing the next command. For example, **delay 2** will pause for two seconds.
waitfor "*<string>*"	Waits until the specified characters are sent by the computer you are connecting to before executing the next command. See the table entry for *<string>* for details on special characters. The value you specify for *<string>* is case-sensitive. For example, **waitfor "USERNAME"** waits until "USERNAME" (in all capital letters) is received from the computer you are connecting to.
transmit "*<string>*" transmit $USERID transmit $PASSWORD	Sends the specified characters or your user name or password to the computer you are connecting to. The user name and password variables are automatically set to the user name and password for the Dial-Up Networking connection that you assign the script to. The **transmit $USERID** or **transmit $PASSWORD** command is usually needed, followed by **transmit "^M"** to send a carriage return character.
;	Indicates a comment. All text preceded by a semi-colon is ignored; for example, **;this is a comment**.

continued

Table 3.5 Commands Commonly Used for Dial-Up Scripting, continued	
Command	**Result**
<string>	You can use any character as part of a string, including **^char**. If **char** is a value between @ and _, then the character sequence is translated to a single-byte value between 0 and 31. For example, **^M** is converted to a carriage return. If **char** is a value between a and z, then the character sequence is translated to a single-byte value between 1 and 26. If **char** is any other value, then the character sequence is not treated specially. <cr> Sends or receives a carriage return. <lf> Sends or receives a line feed. \ " Includes a double quote as part of the string. \< Includes a < as part of the string. \ \ Includes a backslash as part of the string. For example, **transmit "Joe^M"** sends Joe, followed by a carriage return, to the remote computer; **waitfor "Joe<cr><lf>"** waits to receive Joe, followed by a carriage return and a line feed, from the remote computer before executing the next command in the script.

Once you've added a script to a connectoid, the script will automatically execute each time you use that connectoid, saving you from having to enter your user ID and password in the terminal window.

Here's an example of a simple script you can use to wait for various prompts and enter the required information:

```
proc main
   ; wait for prompt for user name
   waitfor "User ID:"
   ; send user ID
   transmit $USERID
   transmit "^M"
   ; wait for prompt for password
   waitfor "Password:"
   ; send password
```

> **transmit $PASSWORD**
> **transmit "^M"**
> **endproc**

In addition to the common commands shown in Table 3.5, a number of others are available to address specific log-on issues. For example, to establish a PPP connection using CompuServe, you must change the communications port settings to log on, then restore them to complete the connection. To find out about these commands, click the Help button in the Dial-Up Scripting Tool dialog box. Look in the Program Files\Accessories folder for more examples of scripts, stored as .scp files.

Configuring DUN for Windows NT

Under Windows NT 4.0, DUN is part of Remote Access Service (RAS) and is installed as part of the network setup, following these steps:

1. Click the Start button, then choose Settings, Control Panel.

2. In the Control Panel window, double-click Network, then switch to the Services tab in the Network dialog box.

3. On the Services tab, click the Add button. (If this button is disabled, that means you don't have the right privileges to change your network setup. See your system administrator for assistance.)

4. In the Select Network Service dialog box, select Remote Access Service, then click OK.

5. In the Windows NT Setup dialog box, enter the path to the CD, diskette, or network folder where the NT setup files can be found, then click Continue.

6. After the Remote Access Service files are copied to your system, the Add RAS Device dialog box (Figure 3.10) appears. Under RAS Capable Devices, choose the modem you want to use for DUN. (You can also click the Install Modem button to add a new modem to your system.) Click OK when you have selected the modem.

7. You should now see your modem listed in the Remote Access Setup dialog box (Figure 3.11). Your modem is set by default for dial-out access only. Click the Network button to bring up the Network Configuration dialog box shown in Figure 3.12.

8. In the Network Configuration dialog box (Figure 3.12), check TCP/IP or the other network protocol you need, then click OK.

9. Back in the Remote Access Setup dialog box, click the Continue button.

10. Restart your system when you're prompted to do so.

Figure 3.10
When installing Remote Access Service under Windows NT, choose from the available modems or first install a new modem.

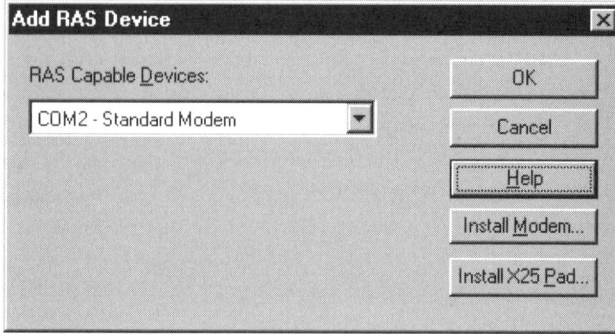

Figure 3.11
Select how each RAS port will be used (for dialing out, receiving calls, or both) with the Configure button. Use the Network button to configure the protocols for each port.

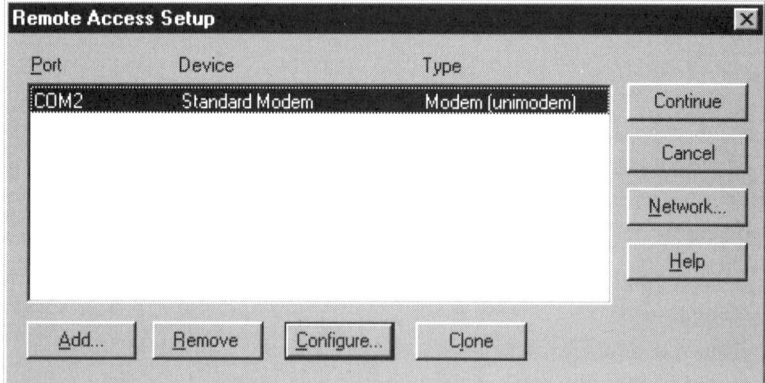

Figure 3.12
Check the protocol(s) you need to access various mail servers. For example, Internet Mail requires TCP/IP protocol.

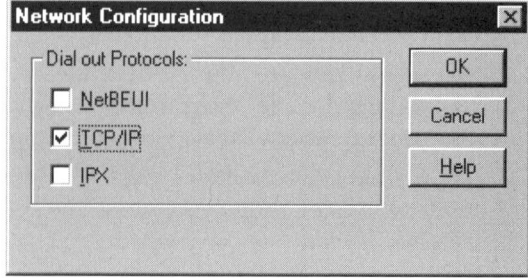

If you want to add dial-in access to your modem, click the Configure button shown in Figure 3.11. This will turn your workstation into a remote access server that other people can dial into. You will then also see additional options for the RAS server in the Network Configuration dialog box. For Exchange, though, you need only the dial-out access.

Special Note

Installing a Network Protocol

The next step is to install the TCP/IP protocol for accessing the Internet (or another protocol if you need it) if TCP/IP is not already active on your system. Follow these steps to install TCP/IP:

1. Click the Start button, then choose Settings, Control Panel.

2. In the Control Panel window, double-click Network, then switch to the Protocols tab in the Network dialog box.

3. On the Protocols tab, click the Add button.

4. In the Select Network Protocol dialog box, select TCP/IP Protocol, then click OK.

5. You'll be asked whether you want to use DHCP to dynamically obtain an address for your network adapter. Click Yes if your computer is connected with a network card to a LAN that has a DHCP server available. Otherwise, click No. (Click No if you use this machine only for DUN, not for connecting on a local network.)

6. In the Windows NT Setup dialog box, enter the path to the CD, diskette, or network folder where the NT setup files can be found, then click Continue.

7. After files are copied to your system, you'll be asked whether you want to configure RAS to support the TCP/IP protocol. Click OK.

8. In the Remote Access Setup dialog box (Figure 3.11), select the modem you use for RAS, then click the Network button.

9. In the Network Configuration dialog box (Figure 3.12), check TCP/IP, then click OK.

10. Back on the Remote Access Setup dialog box, click the Continue button. Then, in the Network dialog box, click Close.

11. If you did not choose DHCP in Step 5, you'll see the Microsoft TCP/IP Properties dialog box, where you will need to enter configuration settings for your network card on four separate tabs, then click OK to save them (get the information you need from your system administrator). For DUN, these settings are handled on each phonebook entry, as you'll see in the

next section; so you won't see this dialog box if you use only DUN and no network card.

12. Restart your computer when you're prompted to do so.

Creating a Phonebook Entry

Now you need to create one or more phonebook entries to link you to specific network resources. To make a new phonebook entry, follow these steps:

1. Open My Computer, then open the Dial-Up Networking folder, or click the Start button, then choose Programs, Accessories, Dial-Up Networking. If you've never previously had a DUN or RAS phonebook on this computer, a dialog box will appear where you need to click OK to add the first entry.

   If you have an existing phonebook, you'll see the Dial-Up Networking dialog box shown in Figure 3.13. Click the New button to create a new phonebook entry.

Figure 3.13

From the Dial-Up Networking dialog box, select the "Phonebook entry...," change your "Dialing from" location, and create additional phonebook entries.

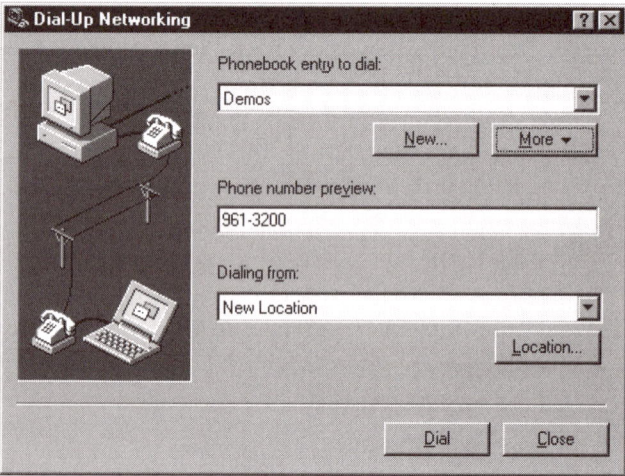

2. On the first screen of the New Phonebook Entry Wizard (Figure 3.14), give the phonebook entry a name, then click the Next button. (If you'd prefer not to use the wizard for this and future entries, check "I know all about phonebook entries and would rather edit the properties directly." See Figure 3.18 for the phonebook entry properties dialog box.)

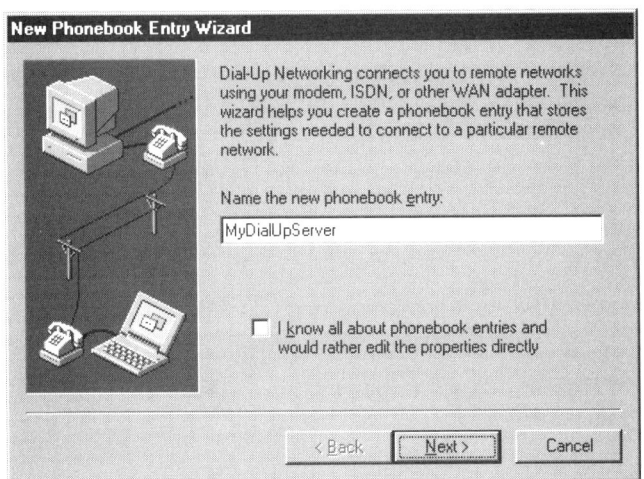

Figure 3.14
Each phonebook entry needs a unique name.

3. On the Server dialog box (Figure 3.15), you have three options to consider. If you plan to use this phonebook entry to reach the Internet, check "I am calling the Internet." If the server you will connect to does not support encrypted passwords, check "Send my plain text password if that's the only way to connect." If you must enter a user name and password to log on to the server or if you need to supply an IP address for your computer or for a DNS or WINS server, check "The non-Windows NT server I am calling expects me to type login information after connecting, or to know TCP/IP addresses before dialing."

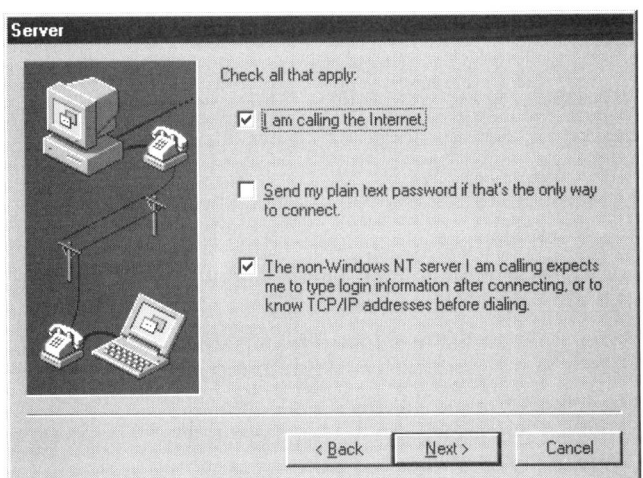

Figure 3.15
Choose from the most common server options, such as connection to the Internet.

When you have made your choices on the Server screen, click the Next button.

4. On the Phone Number dialog box (Figure 3.16), check the "Use Telephony dialing properties" box if you plan to travel with this computer; that way, the phone number you enter will work with different dialing locations, as described earlier in the chapter. Enter the "Country code," "Area code," and "Phone number" in the boxes provided. If you do not check the "Use Telephony dialing properties" box, you will see just a "Phone number" box where you should enter the number.

Figure 3.16

Computers used for travel should use the Telephony dialing properties.

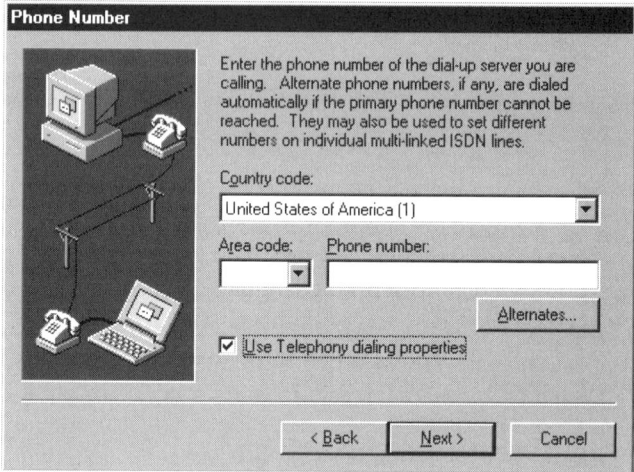

5. If there are alternate numbers for this server, click the Alternates button and enter the additional numbers, which will be tried if Windows can't connect to the first number. When you have finished entering primary and alternate phone numbers, click the Next button on the wizard to continue.

6. On the Serial Line Protocol screen, choose either Point-to-Point Protocol (PPP), the default selection, or Serial Line Internet Protocol (SLIP), whichever the server supports. Click the Next button to continue.

7. If you indicated in Step 3 that you need to log on, you will see the Login Script screen (Figure 3.17). Choose None if you do not need to do a text log-on for this server. Choose "Use a terminal window" if you want to enter the user ID and password manually each time. Choose "Automate with this script" if you want to use a log-on script to automate the process.

If you choose "Automate with this script," you also need to either select a script from the list of those that have been created previously on your computer or click the "Edit script" button to create a new script.

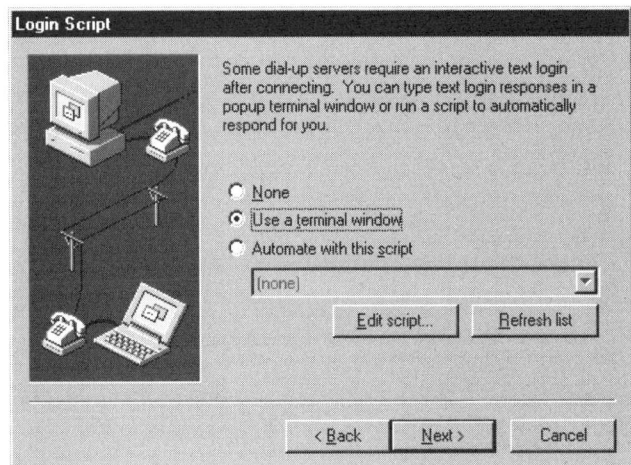

Figure 3.17
If you need to enter a user ID and password to log on, you may choose to use an interactive text log-on process in a terminal window or to automate your log-on process with a script.

Scripts can use either the Windows NT RAS scripting language, which is described in the Winnt\System32\Ras\Switch.Inf document (this document appears when you first click the "Edit script" button) or the Windows 95 dial-up scripting language, which is covered in "Scripting the Log-On Process" earlier in this chapter.

When you have decided how to log on, click the Next button to continue.

8. If you indicated in Step 3 that you know the specific IP addresses before connecting, you'll enter those addresses on the final screens of the wizard. On each screen, enter the address that the remote network's administrator provides. Otherwise, if the server you dial in to provides the address, leave the address as 0.0.0.0. Click the Next button when you're done with each screen.

9. Click the Finish button to save the settings for this phonebook entry, and display the Dial-Up Networking dialog box.

The wizard returns you to the Dial-Up Networking dialog box (Figure 3.13), where you can now click the Dial button to test your new phonebook entry. Enter your user name, password, and, if you are connecting to a Windows NT server, domain name in the dialog boxes provided, then click OK to dial the server.

In the Dial-Up Networking dialog box, you not only can dial the phonebook entry you've just made, but you also can create new entries, edit existing entries, and change the dialing location. To change dialing location, click the Location button.

To create a new phonebook entry, click the <u>N</u>ew button. The New Phonebook Entry Wizard will start; or if you checked "I <u>k</u>now all about phonebook entries and would rather edit the properties directly" in step 2 above, a tabbed Edit Phonebook Entry dialog box (Figure 3.18) appears. You need to enter information on each of the first four tabs and, if you connect via a public X.25 communications network, also on the X.25 tab.

Figure 3.18

All the settings for a Windows NT DUN connection are collected in the Edit Phonebook Entry dialog box.

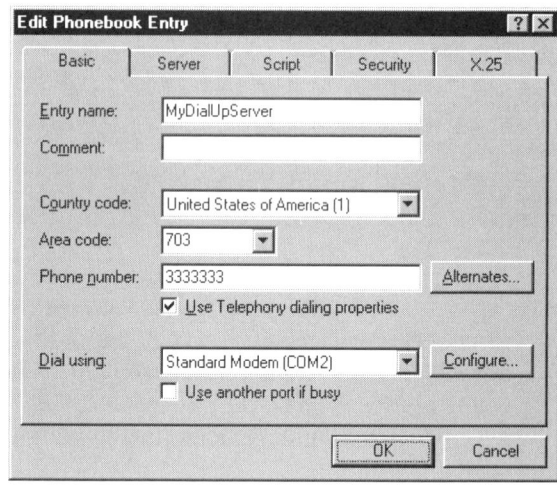

To edit any of the properties of a phonebook entry, follow these steps:

1. Open My Computer, then open Dial-Up Networking, or click the Start button, then choose <u>P</u>rograms, Accessories, Dial-Up Networking.

2. In the Dial-Up Networking dialog box (Figure 3.13), select the "Phonebook ent<u>r</u>y to dial" that you want to edit.

3. Click the <u>M</u>ore button, then choose "<u>E</u>dit ent<u>r</u>y and modem properties" to display the Edit Phonebook Entry dialog box shown in Figure 3.18.

The tabs on the Edit Phonebook Entry dialog box and the options on the More button in the Dial-Up Networking dialog box will lead you to a number of settings and tools to help you manage connections. For example, you can create a phonebook that can be shared with other people or copied from your desktop computer to the one you travel with. We'll look at that technique in the "Tips and Tricks" section at the end of this chapter.

Sharing Network Resources

By sharing either your folders or your printer(s), your system becomes a network server (called a *peer-to-peer server* because it's a peer of the other systems that will be accessing those resources). The server can be a dedicated server — used only for sharing — or a non-dedicated server, on which you run other applications.

> **By sharing either your folders or your printer(s), your system becomes a network server.**

The files needed for sharing are installed on Windows NT by default. You also need to start the Server service. To do so, follow these steps:

1. Click the Start button, then choose Settings, Control Panel. Open the Services applet in the Control Panel.

2. In the Service list in the Services dialog box, select the Server service, then click the Start button. After the Server service starts successfully, you will see Started in the Status column.

3. Click the Close button to quit the Services applet.

Note that in the Startup column you should see the word Automatic. This means that, during future sessions, the Server service will start up automatically.

To enable sharing under Windows 95,

1. Click the Start button, then click Settings and Control Panel.

2. In the Control Panel folder, double-click Network.

3. In the Network dialog box, click File and Print Sharing.

4. In the File and Print Sharing dialog box, check the boxes to give others access to your files and/or to allow others to print to your printer(s), then click OK.

5. Click Yes when you're asked whether you want to restart your computer.

To share a folder, follow these steps:

1. Right-click on the folder in My Computer or Explorer, then choose Sharing.

2. In the Sharing dialog box, choose Shared As and enter a Share Name.

3. If this is a Windows 95 computer and share-level security is in effect, select the Full access type and enter a password if you prefer. If you are set up for user-level security on a Windows 95 computer, you must choose the users or groups you want to grant access to. Click the Add button. In the Add Users dialog box, select users or groups, then click the Full Access button. Click OK to close the Add Users dialog box.

If you are set up for user-level security for Windows NT, the default is to grant access for the maximum number of users (10 on an NT Workstation computer), with full access for everyone, as shown in Figure 3.19. If you want to limit access to certain groups or users, click the Permissions button.

Figure 3.19
Here the WGPO0000 folder is being shared on a Windows NT computer with the name WGPO, with full access to the folder given to all users.

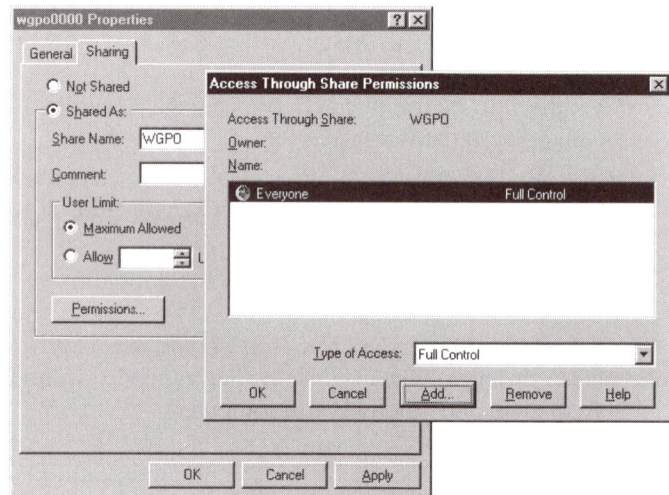

4. Click OK when you've finished setting up the share.

Users at other workstations will now be able to connect to that shared folder by specifying your computer name and the share name (the one you just entered), in this format: *computername**sharename*. For example, if the computer name is MAILMAN and you shared the WGPO0000 folder with the share name WGPO, users will use the path \\MAILMAN\WGPO to connect to the folder.

Tips and Tricks

Windows NT 4.0 offers several useful tools for working with dial-up connections, including the ability to copy phonebook entries to another computer (something Windows 95 can't do!). Also in this section, as either a Windows 95 or Windows NT user, you will learn how to make a connection when you can't dial directly.

Creating a Portable Windows NT Phonebook

What if you use two different computers, one in the office and one for travel? Wouldn't it be nice to be able to copy all the DUN connection settings from one machine to the other? This is relatively easy to do with Windows NT by creating a personal phonebook. Unfortunately, Windows 95 doesn't offer a similar function.

The phonebook entries you create with Windows NT are initially contained in a system phonebook, one that is shared by everyone who uses the computer. You can copy these entries to a personal phonebook, which consists of a .pbk file. Here's how:

1. Open My Computer, then open Dial-Up Networking, or click the Start button, then choose Programs, Accessories, Dial-Up Networking.

2. In the Dial-Up Networking dialog box (Figure 3.13), click the More button, then choose "User preferences." In the User Preferences dialog box, switch to the Phonebook tab.

3. On the Phonebook tab (Figure 3.20), you will see that "The system phonebook" is selected. This means that DUN is using a phonebook that is available to everyone who uses the computer.

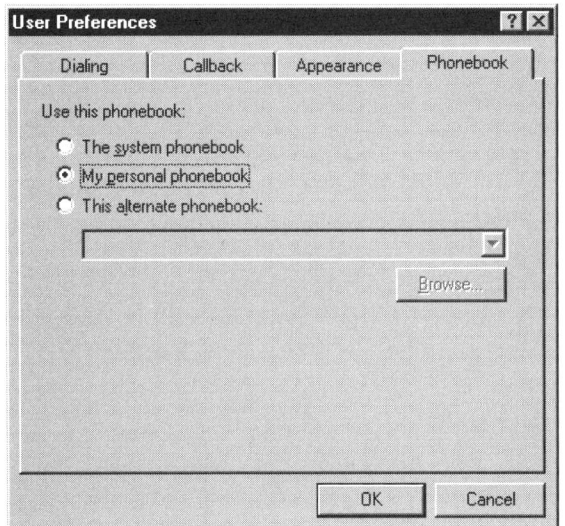

Figure 3.20

The system phonebook is available to all users of your computer, but you can also have a personal phonebook or work with other lists of DUN settings.

4. Select "My personal phonebook," then click the OK button. Phonebook entries from the system phonebook are copied to a new phonebook file. Click OK to return to the Dial-Up Networking dialog box, where you'll now see the entries for the new personal phonebook.

The new phonebook is a .pbk file named for your user name. For example, the Administrator account would have a personal phonebook named Administ.pbk. This file is stored in the Winnt\System32\Ras folder. (The system phonebook is itself a file of this type: Winnt\System32\Ras\Rasphone.pbk.)

To use your personal phonebook on another computer, follow these steps:

1. Copy the .pbk file to the other machine.

2. Follow Steps 1 through 3 above to access the Phonebook tab (Figure 3.20).

3. Select "This alternate phonebook," and either enter the path and file name, or click the Browse button to locate the file.

4. Click OK to switch DUN to use the phonebook you specified.

Making a Manual Connection

You may find yourself at a location where it's impossible to make a phone call without going through an operator. In that case, you need to configure DUN to allow you to dial the number manually. When you hear the computer answer, you'll be able to continue the connection process.

For Windows NT, manual dialing is turned on and off in the Dial-Up Networking dialog box (Figure 3.13). Click the More button, then choose "Operator assisted or manual dialing." This option will appear checked the next time you click More. Use the same procedure to turn off manual dialing.

On Windows 95, manual dialing must be set for each particular DUN connectoid. To set manual dialing, follow these steps:

1. Open My Computer, then open Dial-Up Networking, or click the Start button, then choose Programs, Accessories, Dial-Up Networking.

2. Right-click the DUN connectoid that you want to use manual dialing, then choose Properties.

3. On the General tab, click the Configure button, then switch to the Options tab.

4. Check "Operator assisted or manual dial."

5. Click OK twice to return to the Dial-Up Networking folder.

To use manual dialing once you've enabled it, follow these steps:

1. Start to connect with the desired DUN connectoid or phonebook entry. On Windows 95, a Manual Dial dialog box will appear. On Windows NT, it's an Operator Assisted or Manual Dial dialog box.

2. Place your call.

3. On Windows NT, click the OK button as soon as you've finished dialing, then replace the telephone handset. On Windows 95, wait until you hear the computer at the other end, then click the Connect button and replace the handset.

Summary

Connecting your computer with others is what Exchange is all about. Such connections include dialing up to the Internet, or to your office Microsoft Exchange server or Microsoft Mail server. One of the most ingenious Windows aids to making connections is the concept of dialing locations. Your address book and DUN phone numbers stay the same, while you change access codes and credit card numbers with a single command.

Key Points

- Windows keeps phone numbers separate from dialing location settings, then puts the two together when you dial.

- A Windows calling card is more than a telephone credit card; a Windows calling card can solve a number of dialing-code problems.

- Dial-up networking (DUN) lets you connect with either a Microsoft Exchange server or a Microsoft Mail server at your office, or with an Internet mail server.

- You can automate your dial-up log-on process with a script.

- By sharing either your folders or your printer(s), your system becomes a network server.

For More Information

One of the places where you'll apply your new knowledge of connections is in using Remote Mail, which we discuss in Chapter 13. Microsoft Fax (Chapter 14, "Sending Faxes") also depends a lot on your having the right dialing location so Microsoft Fax can determine what codes to dial.

If you want to go beyond a standard dial-up connection to a high-speed ISDN link, you may want to obtain Microsoft's Get ISDN for Windows, a free program that helps you order ISDN service from your telephone company. See Appendix B, "Exchange Resources," for details about how to download this program from Microsoft's Web site.

Finally, if installing a modem is something that's new to you, both the Windows 95 and Windows NT help files have lots of information to assist you in what is a largely automatic process. Click the Start button, then choose Help. On the Index tab, search for "modems" to get a list of relevant topics.

Chapter 4
Configuring Profiles

Exchange gives you the ability to store multiple configurations on a single machine and lets you choose which configuration to apply for any given session. These configurations are called *profiles*, and in this chapter we'll discuss what makes profiles tick.

In the first part of the chapter, we'll look at the elements of a profile and factors to help you decide where to locate key components such as the Personal Address Book and your main message store. In the second half of the chapter, you'll learn how to create and set up profiles.

What's in a Profile?

A profile stores information about your mail accounts, address book, message store, and the types of messages you can send.

A profile stores information about your mail accounts, address book, message store, and the types of messages you can send. The profile can be very simple, consisting of just the Microsoft Exchange Server transport service and your Personal Address Book, as seen in Figure 4.1; or it can contain many information services and more than one message store.

While you will probably start out with a single Exchange profile, having multiple profiles can be very useful for troubleshooting and for separating Exchange services that don't coexist well. For example, you might want to keep Microsoft Fax in a profile by itself and use it only when you want to send and receive faxes.

Use the Mail and Fax (or Mail, for the Windows Messaging clients) applet in the Control Panel to set up profiles. Table 4.1 lists the services and other Exchange settings that are stored in your profile and configured through Mail and Fax. Other settings, related to the way you operate Exchange, are handled through the Options dialog box in Exchange itself. We'll cover those as we discuss Exchange functions in Parts III and IV of this book.

Figure 4.1

A simple profile for an Exchange Server user consists of just the Microsoft Exchange Server service, which includes the user's mailbox, and a Personal Address Book.

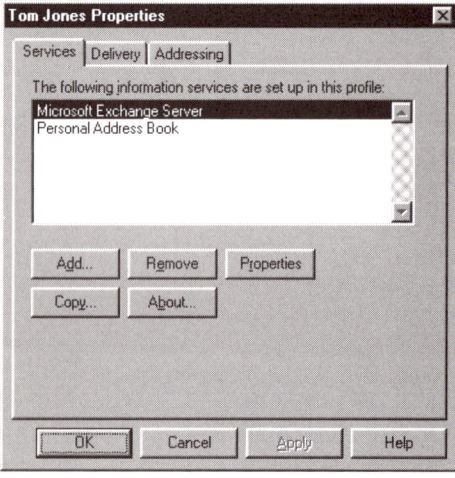

Table 4.1 Elements of a Profile

Element	Description
Services	
Transport Services	Services such as Microsoft Exchange Server, Microsoft Mail, Internet Mail, and CompuServe Mail that deliver your messages.
Message Stores	Separate storage locations such as Personal Folders and Delrina WinFax PRO Logs. Also, settings that determine whether you use an offline message store with Exchange Server.
Address Books	Personal Address Book and other address lists, such as the CompuServe Address Book.
Settings	
Delivery Location	The message store where incoming mail will be delivered.
Delivery Order	The order in which Exchange delivers messages using different transport services.
Preferred Address List	The address list shown first when you open the Address Book.
Personal Address List	The address list where you want to keep personal addresses — almost always the Personal Address Book.
Check Names Order	The order in which Exchange tries to match addresses on outgoing messages with addresses on various address lists.

Understanding User Profiles vs. Exchange Profiles

If you use Windows NT, then you're familiar with the concept of a user profile, since you must log on with a valid user name. When you log on, you are using the default user profile unless your system administrator has created a specific profile for you and your environment.

Your Exchange profile is part of your Windows user profile.

For Windows 95, user profiles are not always required or even visible. Your machine may be configured so that you're never asked to log on. However, if you do log on under a particular user name, this means you have a *user profile* — settings that govern your Windows working environment. (Even if you never log on, you still have a profile: the default profile for the computer.)

A user profile includes the way your desktop looks, the programs on the Start menu, and the Exchange profiles available to you. Exchange profiles are part of the user profile. If you log on as a different user, you see different Exchange profiles.

Profiles for Roving Users

If you don't sit at the same desk every day, you need to take a little extra care to make sure you can use Exchange the same way at each machine you use. The procedures vary, depending on whether you have a network log-on procedure that copies your user profile from a central location every time you log on.

If you see a Windows NT domain log-on option or a Novell NetWare log-on option every time you start Windows, then your network is at least capable of storing your user profile for you. Check with your system administrator to see whether your profile is currently being saved and, if not, to have the settings for your user ID changed so your profile is saved on the server.

If you are using Windows 95 or NT without connecting to a Windows NT or NetWare server, then your Windows user profile cannot be stored centrally. Instead, you must create a new Exchange profile on each machine you use, taking care to set up the profile for your specific user account(s). An important part of that process will be setting the location of your Personal Folders file, which we'll discuss later in this chapter.

When to Use Multiple Profiles

Just as a single user might have profiles on several machines, a single machine might have several profiles on it for different users. But a single user might also have a need for more than one Exchange profile. Table 4.2 lists several reasons for using multiple profiles.

Table 4.2 Reasons for Using Multiple Profiles	
Reason	**Description**
Troubleshooting	An important first step in troubleshooting is to isolate the particular Exchange service that seems to be causing a problem. This is most often done by creating a new profile with only that service, plus a new Personal Address Book and Personal Folders.
Managing a Microsoft Mail Postoffice	If you are responsible for managing the workgroup postoffice, then you may have two different accounts — one account for your personal mail and a separate account for the postoffice manager. Create two profiles, one for each account.
Separate Services That Don't Coexist Well	Some Exchange services, such as Microsoft Fax and Internet Mail, do not always work well together in one profile. Many users like to keep Microsoft Fax in its own separate profile, for use only when fax services are needed.
Different Users on the Same Machine	The best way to handle multiple users on a single machine is to have each one log on to Windows under a separate user ID. Where this is not practical, you would need to create an Exchange profile for each user.
Setting up Resources for Schedule+	Though Schedule+ isn't covered in this book, multiple profiles are commonly used for this application, because each resource — such as a conference room or electronic whiteboard — must use its own profile, at least for initial configuration.
Multiple Internet Service Providers (ISPs)	If you depend on the Microsoft Internet Mail service to get messages through an ISP, you can set up a second profile to access a second ISP but deliver mail to the same mailbox or Personal Folders.

Where Should Messages Be Stored?

The most important decision related to an Exchange profile is where incoming and outgoing messages will be stored. Exchange Server users have more choices than users of the operating system client do.

Operating System Client Message Locations

If you use the operating system version of Exchange, messages always reside in a Personal Folders file, which can be located either on your local hard drive or on a network drive. In Table 4.3, look for your particular situation and find a recommended location for the Personal Folders file.

Table 4.3 Locations for Personal Folders	
If You . . .	**Put Your Personal Folders . . .**
Always work at the same computer and are the only person working on that system	On the local hard drive. No password protection is needed for the Personal Folders file.
Always work at the same computer, which is also used by other people	On the local hard drive. Use password protection.
Work at different computers	On a network drive. Use password protection.
Work sometimes in the office, sometimes at remote locations	On a local or network drive on your desktop system and in My Briefcase on your remote computer. Use password protection if you keep Personal Folders on the network or if more than one person uses your computer.

   In the first two cases, you also may have the option of keeping Personal Folders on a network drive. An advantage of keeping Personal Folders on a network drive is that they will be included in network backups, as long as you have shut down Exchange so the Personal Folders file is no longer open when the backup occurs.

We'll look at My Briefcase and other methods for synchronizing Personal Folders for remote users in Chapter 13, "Working Remotely."

Exchange Server Client Message Locations

For users of the full Exchange Server client, Personal Folders is an extra message store option. Your primary message location should be the mailbox for your account on the Microsoft Exchange server.

Unlike Personal Folders, the server-based mailbox message store is not a separate single file, but a data structure within Exchange Server. Even though it might seem convenient to keep messages in Personal Folders on your local drive, there are several very important reasons for putting them on the Microsoft Exchange server instead:

- Your mailbox is backed up as part of any regular Exchange Server backup procedure. If you put your messages in Personal Folders, then you may be responsible for your own backups.

- Keeping messages in the Exchange Server mailbox is a more efficient use of disk space.

- The Exchange Server administrator may do periodic cleanups for you, to empty out old messages. Otherwise, you'll have to do this chore yourself.

- You can easily access messages in your Exchange Server mailbox from a remote location, without the need to synchronize Personal Folders between desktop and remote locations.

But making the Exchange Server mailbox your primary message location doesn't mean you can't use Personal Folders as well, as you'll see in the next section.

Exchange Server gives you an optional third message storage location, called offline folders. Of particular value to remote users, offline folders include both your Exchange Server mailbox and any public folders you've designated as favorites and set up to keep synchronized with the server. Details about setting up offline folders are included in Chapter 5, "Setting Up the Microsoft Exchange Server." We'll look at favorite folders in Chapter 16, "Working with Messages and Folders."

Uses for Secondary Personal Folders

All versions of Exchange can use Personal Folders and can have more than one Personal Folders file in a profile. Even if you have an Exchange Server

For Exchange Server clients, the primary message store should be the mailbox for your account on the Microsoft Exchange server.

mailbox, you probably will find uses for Personal Folders. Here are some ideas:

- Use a Personal Folders file to archive your incoming and outgoing messages for each month.
- Instead of archiving by date, store all messages related to completed projects in Personal Folders files, one for each project.
- If you subscribe to a mailing list, move all messages from that list into a separate Personal Folders file for later reference. You can even send that file to other users who want to get up to speed on the list topic.
- Test new Exchange forms and folders in Personal Folders first, before moving them to the Exchange Server public folders.

For more information about Personal Folders, turn to the section "Configuring Personal Folders" on page 81.

Address Book Locations

The same rules that govern Personal Folders locations generally apply to the location of your Personal Address Book (PAB), used for the addresses you access most often:

- Put the PAB on a server if you move around.
- Keep the PAB on your local drive (or a network drive if automatic backup is available) if you work at the same desk every day.
- Put the PAB in My Briefcase if you work at both a desktop computer and remotely.

No password protection is available for the Personal Address Book.

Use the Mail and Fax (or Mail) applet in the Control Panel to configure Exchange profiles.

Working with Profiles

Dealing with profiles consists of two activities: manipulating the profiles themselves and working with the services that are the components of each profile.

Throughout the rest of this chapter, we'll be working with the Mail and Fax applet (or Mail for Windows Messaging, the new name for the operating system version of Exchange) in the Control Panel (Figure 4.2). Let's examine the steps involved in creating and configuring a profile, and how to select a profile to use as the default profile.

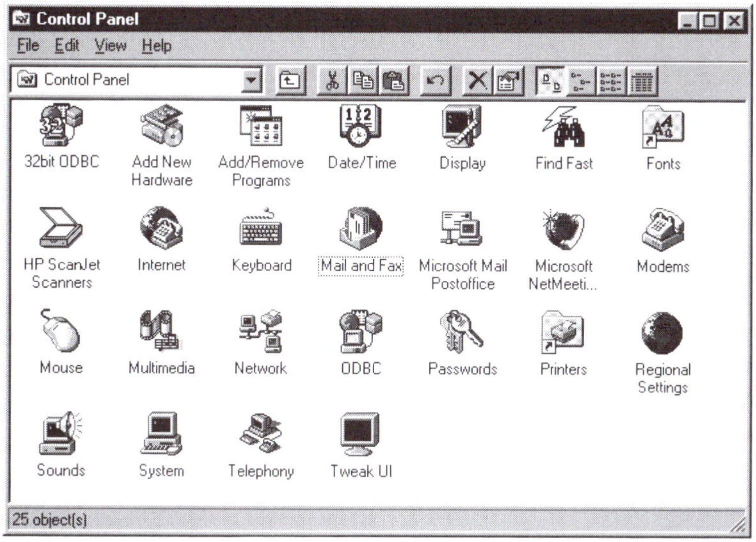

Figure 4.2
Users of Windows NT and Windows Messaging for Windows 95 will see a Control Panel icon for Mail, rather than for Mail and Fax.

Creating a Profile

There are three ways to create a new Exchange profile:

• Add a profile and use the Setup Wizard to configure its services
• Add a profile and manually configure its services
• Copy an existing profile

I recommend that you start by using the Inbox Setup Wizard (also called the Microsoft Exchange Setup Wizard), then learn how to copy an existing profile and copy services from one profile to another.

Using the Setup Wizard

To add a profile using the Setup Wizard, follow these steps:

1. Run the Mail and Fax (or Mail) applet in the Control Panel.
2. Click the Show Profiles button.
3. Choose Add.
4. In the first screen of the Setup Wizard (Figure 4.3), choose "Use the following information services" and check the ones you want to use. Click Next to continue.

Figure 4.3

Either choose the services you want to install and let the Setup Wizard help you, or choose to manually configure the profile by adding each service you want to use.

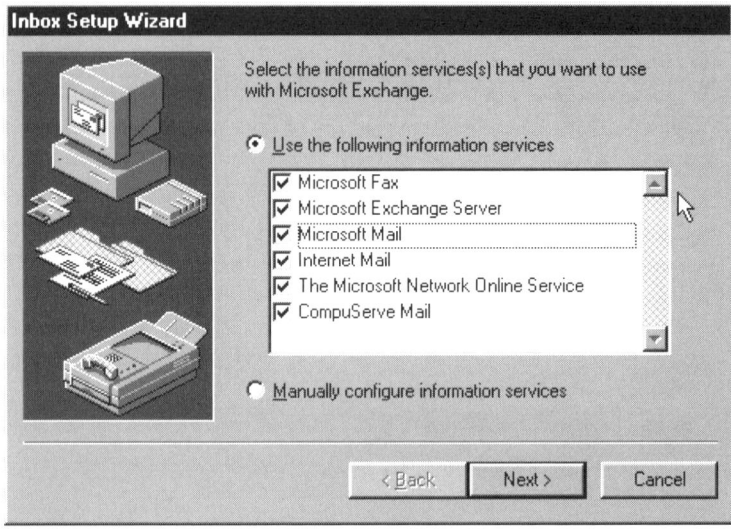

5. Enter a Profile Name. Make the name descriptive, such as MS Fax Only, or use your user name. This profile name appears in a list where you can change profiles either in the Control Panel or before starting Exchange, so you should use a name that makes it easy to remember the purpose of a particular profile.

6. Click the Next button to continue through the wizard, answering questions for each service. We will discuss the details about these settings in subsequent chapters about the individual information services.

7. On the Personal Address Book screen of the Setup Wizard, give the location for the PAB. This may be the path to an existing .pab or a new location. Click Next to continue.

8. If you are not installing the Microsoft Exchange Server service, the Setup Wizard will ask you for the location of the Personal Folders file. This may be the path to an existing .pst file or a new location. (For Exchange Server clients, the Setup Wizard does not add a Personal Folders file; instead, it uses your Exchange Server mailbox as the primary message store.) Click Next to continue.

9. Choose whether you want Exchange added to your Startup group so it loads whenever you start Windows. Click Next to continue, then Finish to complete the profile setup process.

If you were previously using a different profile, you might want to make this new profile your default. See the instructions for setting the default profile on page 76 in "Other Profile Actions" later in this chapter. You should also check the settings on the Delivery and Addressing tabs, as described in the "Delivery Settings" and "Addressing Settings" sections, also later in this chapter.

Manually Configuring Services

To add a profile by manually configuring services, follow these steps:

1. Run the Mail and Fax (or Mail) applet in the Control Panel.
2. Click the Show Profiles button.
3. Choose Add.
4. In the first screen of the Setup Wizard (Figure 4.3), choose "Manually configure information services." Click Next to continue.
5. Enter a descriptive Profile Name, one that makes it easy to remember the makeup of the profile when you see it again in a list of all the profiles on your machine.
6. Add services to the profile, as described in the "Working with Services" section later in this chapter. Subsequent chapters provide details about the settings for each service.
7. Check the settings on the Delivery and Addressing tabs, as described in "Delivery Settings" and "Addressing Settings" later in this chapter.
8. Click OK to save the new profile.

If you were previously using a different profile, you might want to make this new profile your default. See the instructions for setting the default profile on page 77 of "Other Profile Actions" later in this chapter.

Copying an Existing Profile

Once you have configured your first profile, the job of creating a new one becomes just a little bit easier. You can copy the existing profile — with all its settings for information services, messages stores, and the Personal Address Book — then add and remove services to customize the new version. Here's how:

1. Run the Mail and Fax (or Mail) applet in the Control Panel.
2. Click the Show Profiles button.
3. Select the profile to be copied, then choose Copy.
4. Enter a descriptive New Profile Name. Click OK to add this profile to the profiles list.

5. Select the new profile, then click the Properties button.

6. Add, remove, and edit services as described in the "Working with Services" section later in this chapter.

7. Check the settings on the Delivery and Addressing tabs as described in the next two sections.

8. Click OK to save the new profile.

Delivery Settings

The Delivery tab (Figure 4.4) contains two settings that are configured for you automatically.

Figure 4.4

The order of services on the Delivery tab is critical if you have more than one service that can handle Internet mail. Messages with Internet addresses are always delivered by the first Internet-capable service in the delivery order list.

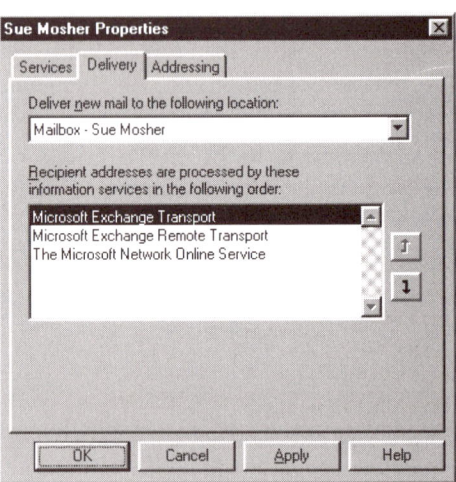

The first setting on the Delivery tab is the delivery location, the location where new (incoming) messages are sent. If you are using the Microsoft Exchange Server service, the default location is your mailbox. Otherwise, the default location is the profile's Personal Folders file. If you have more than one Personal Folders file, you can designate which file will be used for Inbox and Outbox functions.

Special Note

To send and receive messages, you must have at least one message store location in the profile, either an Exchange Server mailbox or a Personal Folders file. If the Microsoft Exchange Server service is part of your profile, then you automatically have a mailbox, and it doesn't appear as a separate service.

The second setting on the Delivery tab is the delivery order, which affects several different aspects of Exchange:

- When you send a message to the Internet, the message is delivered by the first service on this list that is capable of handling Internet addresses. For example, if you have both Exchange Server with a connection to the Internet, and The Microsoft Network, as shown in Figure 4.4, you should put Microsoft Exchange Transport (the transport for the Microsoft Exchange Server service) first, so it will deliver your mail.

- Delivery order is the order in which messages are delivered when you choose Tools, Deliver Now Using, All Services. It often takes some experimentation to get the order right, because some services that dial out don't release the phone line in time for the next service on the list to use it.

- The Microsoft Fax service needs to appear first in the delivery list in profiles where either Microsoft Mail or the Microsoft Exchange Server service is also installed. Otherwise, fax messages will either be returned as undeliverable or left in the Outbox.

To change the delivery order of messages, select a service, then use the up or down arrow button to move the service up or down in the list.

You can also reach the settings on the Services and Delivery tabs from within Exchange (for the current profile only) using Tools, Services (or Tools, Options, then switching to the Delivery tab). However, most changes do not take effect until you exit and log off Exchange, then restart the program. Therefore, I recommend that you get in the habit of making changes to services and delivery options through the Control Panel, which will also give you access to every profile, not just the one currently loaded.

Special Note

Addressing Settings

On the Addressing tab (Figure 4.5), you'll find three settings for the profile. Under "Show this address list first," select the address list you want to see when you open the Address Book. This address usually will be your PAB. Under "Keep personal addresses in," select the address list to use for personal addresses. Again, this address should be your PAB.

If you are using CompuServe mail, the CompuServe Address Book will appear as an option under "Keep personal addresses in." Do not use this option for storing personal addresses, because you can keep only CompuServe addresses here; if you try to add other types of addresses, you will get an error message.

Special Note

Figure 4.5

The Addressing tab governs the way the Address Book operates.

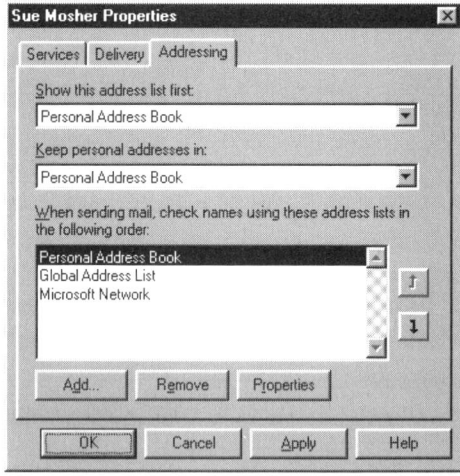

The last setting specifies the order in which the address lists will be checked to try to match an existing address with the recipient name you enter on a message. When you use Tools, Check Names on a message or send the message without first using Check Names, Exchange tries to match the addresses you've entered against the available address lists. You can speed up this process by setting the order so that the list where most of your recipients are stored comes first on the list. This could be the PAB, the Global Address Book, or a Postoffice Address list, depending on your configuration and preference. In general, you'll want to put the PAB first if you send most of your messages to the people listed there.

You can also change any of the above settings for the current profile while you have Exchange loaded. Choose Tools, Options, then switch to the Addressing tab. Any changes will take effect immediately.

Other Profile Actions

Before we move on to the details of how to edit a particular profile, you need to know about a few other basic profile actions. For example, to delete a profile,

1. Run the Mail and Fax (or Mail) applet in the Control Panel.

2. Click the Show Profiles button.

3. Select the profile you want to delete.

4. Click the Remove button.

To use a different profile as your default,

1. Run the Mail and Fax (or Mail) applet in the Control Panel.
2. Click the Show Profiles button.
3. Select the new default profile from the list labeled "When starting Microsoft Exchange … Always use this profile."
4. Click the Close button to save the new default.

The default profile comes into play in two different ways. You can tell Exchange to always use the default profile — without asking you first. Or you can choose to select a profile when Exchange starts, with the default profile shown first.

The setting that controls this profile is accessible only when you have Exchange loaded. Choose <u>T</u>ools, <u>O</u>ptions. On the General tab (Figure 4.6), you'll see two choices under "When starting Microsoft Exchange":

Prompt for a profile to be used
Display a list of all profiles, with the default profile selected (Figure 4.7)

Always use this profile
Make the selected profile the default profile every time Exchange is started

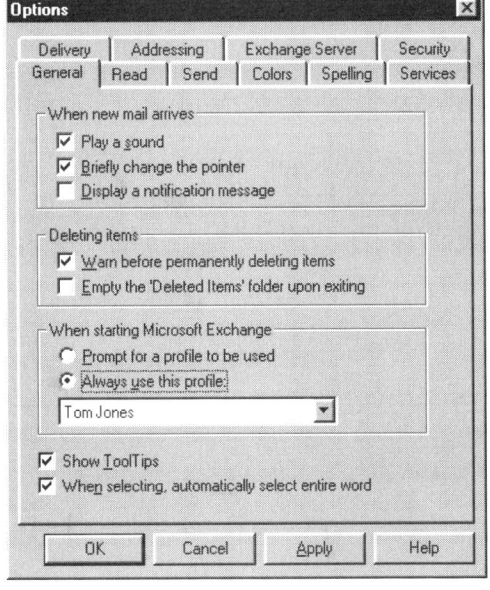

Figure 4.6
The two choices under "When starting Microsoft Exchange" let you choose to always use one profile, or to select a different profile each time you use Exchange (see Figure 4.7).

Figure 4.7

If you choose to be prompted for a profile, you'll see this dialog box every time you start Exchange. Click the New button if you want to create a new profile.

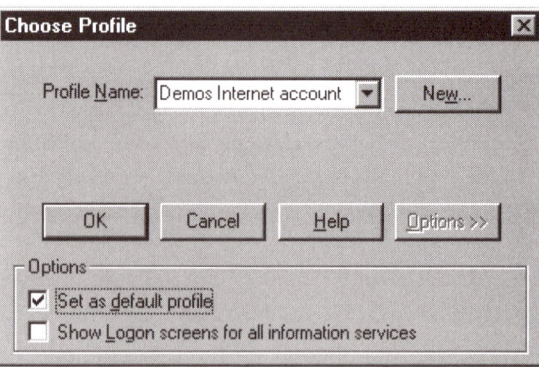

The Options shown in Figure 4.7 appear when you click the Options button. Notice that this gives you yet another place to change the default profile.

Working with Services

Profiles can be dynamic, changing as you expand Exchange with new services and as you change the way you work with existing services. To make these changes, you need to know how to work with the individual services in your profile.

Before you can add services to a profile, those services must be installed on your computer. When you first run Mail and Fax (or Mail) from the Control Panel, on the Services tab you will see the services contained in the current default profile (see Figure 4.1 on page 64 at the beginning of this chapter). Some services are installed through the Control Panel, and others through a separate setup program. We will discuss details for individual services in the next few chapters.

To work with services in a different profile, follow these steps:

1. Run the Mail and Fax (or Mail) applet in the Control Panel.
2. Choose Show Profiles.
3. Select the profile you want to work with.
4. Click the Properties button.

Special Note

You can also make changes to the services in your current profile with Tools, Service, but the changes won't take effect until you exit, then restart, Exchange.

Adding a Service

Once you have selected a profile to modify, there are two ways to add a service — either directly or by copying the settings from another profile. To add a service to a profile directly, follow these steps:

1. Run the Mail and Fax (or Mail) applet in the Control Panel.

2. If the profile you want to work with isn't the default profile, click the Show Profiles button. Select the profile you want to modify, then click the Properties button.

3. On the Services tab (Figure 4.1), click the Add button.

4. In the Add Service to Profile dialog box (Figure 4.8), select the service you want to add, then click OK.

If you try to add a service (other than Personal Folders) that is already in your profile, you get an error message.

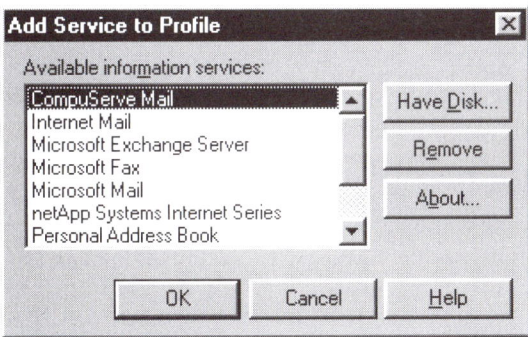

Figure 4.8
When you choose to add a service to a profile, you can pick that service from all the Exchange services installed on your computer, or you can add a new service.

Alternatively, if you have a new service, you may need to use Have Disk to install it. Check the setup instructions for the service.

Do not use the Remove button found in the Add Service to Profile dialog box (Figure 4.8). This does not remove a service from the profile, but instead removes it from your system so that it is no longer available to any profiles.

Caution

Here's how to copy a service from another profile:

1. Run the Mail and Fax (or Mail) applet in the Control Panel.
2. Click the Show Profiles button.
3. Select the profile from which you want to copy a service.
4. Click the Properties button to bring up the properties for that profile.
5. Select the service you want to copy, then click Copy.
6. In the Copy Information Service dialog box, select the profile you want to copy to, then click OK.

If you try to add a service that is already in your profile, you will get an error message. Only Personal Folders can be added to your profile more than once. In particular, this means that you cannot have more than one PAB, nor can you add the Internet Mail service twice to get mail from two different Internet service providers.

Removing or Modifying a Service

To remove a service from a profile,

1. Run the Mail and Fax (or Mail) applet in the Control Panel.
2. If the profile you want to work with isn't the default profile, click the Show Profiles button. Select the profile you want to modify, then click the Properties button.
3. Select the service you want to remove.
4. Click the Remove button.

This process does not remove the profile from your system — only from the profile you're currently working with. Also, removing Personal Folders or the PAB from a profile does not remove the actual .pst or .pab file. The file remains available for use in this and in other profiles.

To modify the settings for a service,

1. Run the Mail and Fax (or Mail) applet in the Control Panel.
2. If the profile you want to work with isn't the default profile, click the Show Profiles button. Select the profile you want to modify, then click the Properties button.
3. Select the service you want to work with.
4. Click the Properties button.

The next few chapters give you details about the settings for the different services. Because any profile can contain Personal Folders information, we'll go ahead and examine the Personal Folders settings here.

Configuring Personal Folders

Once you add Personal Folders to your profile, you can customize the folders in several ways. To view the Personal Folders properties,

1. Run the Mail and Fax (or Mail) applet in the Control Panel.
2. If the profile you want to work with isn't the default profile, click the Show Profiles button. Select the profile you want to modify, then click the Properties button.
3. Select the Personal Folders in your profile.
4. Click the Properties button.

You will see the dialog box shown in Figure 4.9.

If you put Personal Folders on a network drive or on a local hard drive used by several people, use password protection.

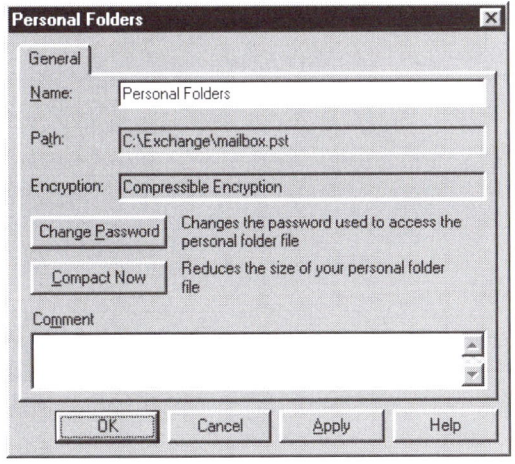

Figure 4.9
It's easy to change the name of Personal Folders to something more descriptive.

Under Name on the General tab, you can change the display name for this Personal Folders file. This name is shown on the left-hand folder pane in the Exchange Viewer, so you may want to use a name that describes the content of the Personal Folders, especially if it's a file used for a special purpose. For example, if this Personal Folders file is an archive of all messages sent and received in June 1996, you might want to call it June 1996 Mail Archive.

If the Personal Folders file resides on a network server or on a computer used by several people, you should protect the file with a password. To add a password, follow these steps:

1. In the Personal Folders properties dialog box (Figure 4.9), click Change Password.

2. In the Change Password dialog box, leave the Old Password blank.

3. Enter the desired password in both the New Password and Verify Password boxes. Note that the password for a Personal Folders file is case-sensitive.

4. If you always log on to Windows under your own user name, check the box labeled "Save this password in your password list." This will put the password in the list kept for your user ID. However, do not check this option if you share the computer with other people and do not use an individual Windows log-on process.

5. Click OK to save the password.

To change your password, follow the same steps, entering the old password in the appropriate box and providing a new one. Again, note that the password for a Personal Folders file is case-sensitive.

Tips and Tricks

If you work with multiple profiles, you'll be interested in the tip here on launching Exchange with a particular profile using a desktop shortcut. Among other tricks, you'll also find out how to move a Personal Folders file to a new location.

Keeping a Library of Services

Earlier in this chapter, you learned how to create profiles and add services by copying from existing profiles. If you find yourself experimenting a lot with Exchange, you may want to create one or more library profiles that contain every service available on your system, with your preferred settings for each. Once you have such a library, creating a new profile will be a simple matter of copying the desired services to the new profile.

Making a Shortcut for Each Profile

Exchange does not provide any mechanism for loading with a particular profile other than through the selection dialog box (Figure 4.7). However, the CD for this book does include a utility, Exchange Profile Selector (EPS), that lets you use shortcuts to launch Exchange with any profile you want. Here's how to use EPS:

1. After you've installed EPS, create a shortcut to the Eps.exe file.
2. Right-click on the shortcut, and choose Properties, then switch to the Shortcut tab.
3. In the Target box, add the name of the profile, in quotation marks, after the Eps.exe command.
4. For example, if you have installed Eps.exe in your C:\Exchange folder and have created a profile called Fax Only, the Target box should read C:\Exchange\Eps.exe "Fax Only".
5. Click OK to save the shortcut.

Another utility to accomplish the same task is included on the CD as part of the Widgets for Microsoft Exchange. It's called MAPI Logon and works from shortcuts just the same as EPS.

Moving a Personal Folders File

You may have noticed in Figure 4.9 that there's no way to change the Path for a Personal Folders file. However, it's relatively easy to move the file; to do so, follow these steps:

1. Use File, Exit and Log Off to shut down Exchange.
2. Move the Personal Folders file to its new location.
3. Restart Exchange.
4. When you're prompted for the location of the Personal Folders file, enter the new path.

After Exchange confirms that the Personal Folders file can be found at a new location, it updates your profile.

Moving from Personal Folders to an Exchange Server Mailbox

If you switch to the Exchange Server client after you've been using Exchange for a while, you may want to migrate your messages from Personal Folders to your new mailbox on the server. This move requires two steps.

First, change the Delivery settings (see the earlier section, "Delivery Settings") so that new (incoming) mail is delivered to your mailbox instead of to

Personal Folders. Second, the next time you run Exchange, drag all the messages from your Personal Folders to the corresponding folders in your mailbox.

What if you change the delivery location for new mail from your Exchange Server mailbox to a Personal Folders file? The results are surprising. All the messages in the mailbox's Inbox are automatically moved to the Inbox in the Personal Folders file. You might have expected those messages to stay put, with only new (incoming) messages going into the Personal Folders file's Inbox. But instead, the entire Inbox is cleared out and its contents moved to the new delivery Inbox.

Summary

Profiles tie together all the components of Exchange and customize them for your personal use. You can have multiple profiles for different purposes. In this chapter, we've shown you how to create and modify profiles and we've identified the factors that determine where you should tell Exchange to store your messages.

Key Points

- A profile stores information about your mail accounts, address book, message store, and the types of messages you can send.
- Your Exchange profile is part of your Windows user profile.
- For Exchange Server clients, the primary message store should be the mailbox for your account on the Microsoft Exchange server.
- Use the Mail and Fax (or Mail) applet in the Control Panel to configure Exchange profiles.
- If you try to add a service (other than Personal Folders) that is already in your profile, you will get an error message.
- If you put Personal Folders on a network drive or on a local hard drive used by several people, use password protection.

For More Information

In the rest of the chapters in this part of the book, we'll look at individual information services and their settings, including all the services available from Microsoft and many of those available for use with both the operating system clients and the Exchange Server clients.

You'll also learn more about the Personal Address Book in Chapter 17, "Using the Address Book."

Chapter 5

Setting Up the Microsoft Exchange Server Service

With the Microsoft Exchange Server service, you can

- Exchange e-mail with other people in your organization who have Exchange Server mailboxes
- Exchange e-mail with people on other mail systems or even send faxes or voice mail (if your Microsoft Exchange server is connected to the Internet or to other messaging systems)
- Post documents in public folders, participate in group discussions, and use workgroup applications designed for Exchange Server
- Manage your incoming messages with the Inbox Assistant and the Out-of-Office Assistant

Note that this chapter concerns itself with the Microsoft Exchange Server service that's installed on client machines, not with the configuration of a Microsoft Exchange server, which would be a book and a half in itself.

Requirements

To use the Microsoft Exchange Server service, you must have

You cannot use the Microsoft Exchange Server service with the operating system version of Exchange; you must install the Exchange Server client.

- A Windows NT domain log-on user name and password
- An Exchange Server mailbox
- A way to connect to the Microsoft Exchange server, either on the LAN or via dial-up networking (DUN)
- The Exchange Server client software installed (See the sidebar "Installing and Updating the Exchange Server Client" on page 103 at the end of this chapter.)

Your system administrator can provide the domain log-on account details, plus information about your Exchange Server location and mailbox. If you'll be connecting remotely, be sure to check with the administrator for the specifics about either dialing into the network or reaching it via the Internet. Note that you cannot use the Microsoft Exchange Server service with the operating system version of Exchange; you must install the Exchange Server client.

Basic Setup

Depending on how Exchange was set up on your system, you may already have the Microsoft Exchange Server service in your default profile. But assuming you don't, we'll walk through the two different methods of adding it: with the Setup Wizard and by manually configuring the service. See Chapter 4, "Configuring Profiles," if you need a refresher on how to add a service to an Exchange profile.

Using the Setup Wizard

The Setup Wizard is available only when you create a new profile through the Mail and Fax (or Mail) applet in the Control Panel. To add a profile using the Setup Wizard, follow these steps:

1. Run the Mail and Fax (or Mail) applet in the Control Panel.
2. Click the Show Profiles button.
3. Choose Add.
4. In the first screen of the Setup Wizard, choose "Use the following information services" and check the ones you want, in this case being sure to include the Microsoft Exchange Server service.

5. Click Next to continue, and give the profile a name on the next screen of the wizard, then click Next again to begin configuring the Exchange Server service and any other services you selected.

Here are the steps in the Setup Wizard that are specific to the Microsoft Exchange Server service:

1. The Setup Wizard asks the name of your Microsoft Exchange server and your Mailbox name (see Figure 5.1). If you don't know your mailbox name, enter your Windows user name or ask your system administrator. You need to double-check the mailbox name anyway, after the wizard completes it work, as described under "Checking Your Mailbox." Click Next to continue.

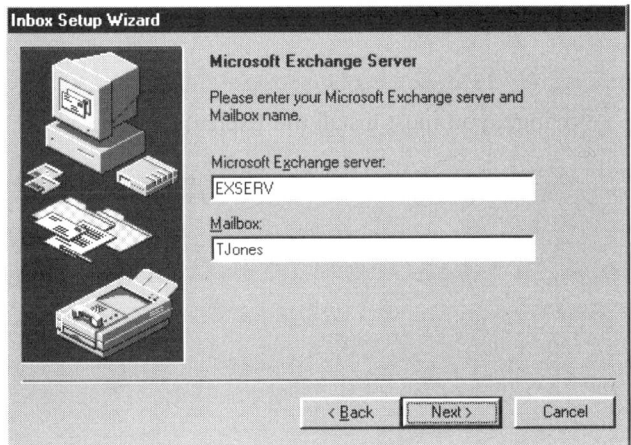

Figure 5.1

To use the Setup Wizard, you must know the names for the Exchange server and your mailbox.

2. Next, the Setup Wizard asks whether you travel with this computer. Answer Yes or No as appropriate.

3. Click Next to continue and finish answering the questions posed by the Setup Wizard about other services.

If you choose to install only the Microsoft Exchange Server service, the Setup Wizard creates a profile with only two services in it: the Microsoft Exchange Server service and the Personal Address Book.

Once you've completed the Setup Wizard, use the Mail and Fax applet in the Control Panel to bring up the properties for the Microsoft Exchange Server service to check some additional settings. If you are working from a computer connected to a network, follow the procedure described in the next section, "Checking Your Mailbox." If you'll be working from outside your office, follow the instructions under "If You're Connecting Remotely."

Checking Your Mailbox

Before you log on to Exchange Server for the first time, it's a good idea to make sure you have entered the right server name and mailbox; otherwise, you'll get an error message about not being able to log on. To check your mailbox, follow these steps:

1. Go to the Control Panel and run the Mail and Fax applet.

2. If the profile you want to work with is not the default profile, click the Show Profiles button. Then select the desired profile and click the Properties button.

3. Select the Microsoft Exchange Server service, then click the Properties button.

4. On the General tab (Figure 5.2), click the Check Name button.

Figure 5.2

Once the server and mailbox have been validated with the Check Name button, they'll appear underlined. Notice how the mailbox now shows the full display name for the user, rather than the mailbox name you saw in Figure 5.1.

5. If the server and mailbox both can be located, the exact display name of the mailbox will be shown, and both the mailbox name and the server name will be underlined. You can then click OK and run Exchange for the first time with the Microsoft Exchange Server service installed.

6. If you get the message

   *The name could not be resolved. Network problems are preventing
   connection to the Microsoft Exchange Server computer.*

   then either the name of the server is not correct or you have a network
   connection problem. Either way, the problem needs to be resolved before
   you can connect to the Microsoft Exchange server.

7. If you get the message

   *The name could not be resolved. The name could not be matched
   to a name in the address list.*

   then the name of the server is OK, but your mailbox can't be found. Check
   the spelling of the mailbox name or try entering your first or last name (or
   maybe just the first few characters). Exchange will search the Microsoft
   Exchange server's user list to try to find your mailbox for you.

   Once the server and mailbox names are both underlined, you're ready to
run Exchange and access your Exchange Server mailbox.

Manually Configuring the Microsoft Exchange Server Service

If you are not creating a completely new profile, there's no wizard to help
you. You must manually configure the Microsoft Exchange Server service as
part of the process of adding it to an existing profile (see "Adding a Service,"
page 79 in Chapter 4). Follow these steps:

1. Run the Mail and Fax (or Mail) applet in the Control Panel.

2. If the profile you want to work with isn't the default profile, click the
   Show Profiles button. Select the profile you want to modify, then click the
   Properties button.

3. On the Services tab, click the Add button.

4. In the Add Service to Profile dialog box, select the Microsoft Exchange
   Server service, then click OK.

5. On the General tab (Figure 5.2), enter the name of your Microsoft
   Exchange server and the Mailbox name.

6. Follow the procedure in steps 4 through 7 under "Checking Your Mailbox" (skip this step if you're working remotely).

7. If your machine sometimes or always dials in to a network to get mail,
   then continue with the next section, "If You're Connecting Remotely."

Otherwise, you have completed all the required settings for the Microsoft Exchange Server service. Click the OK button to save the configuration.

There are a number of other settings for the Microsoft Exchange Server service that you may want to review; the "Options" section details them all.

If You're Connecting Remotely

If you are a remote user of the Microsoft Exchange Server service, you will need to take additional steps to

Before you can use offline folders, you must activate them by connecting to the Microsoft Exchange server and synchronizing the folders.

- Specify how you will connect to the Microsoft Exchange server
- Activate a message file for offline storage

If you still have the Microsoft Exchange Server properties d ialog box (Figure 5.2) open from the previous section, pick up at step 4 below; otherwise, start with step 1.

1. Run the Mail and Fax (or Mail) applet in the Control Panel.

2. If the profile you want to work with isn't the default profile, click the Show Profiles button. Select the profile you want to modify, then click the Properties button.

3. Select the Microsoft Exchange Server service, then click the Properties button.

4. On the General tab (Figure 5.2), the default is "Connect with the network." You can change this to "Work offline and use dial-up networking" if your preference is to compose messages offline.

5. If you chose "Work offline…," select "Choose the connection type when starting." (You need this option to make the initial connection to the Microsoft Exchange server to check the mailbox name and activate offline folders.)

6. Switch to the Advanced tab (Figure 5.3).

7. Clear the box labeled "Use network security during logon." If you connect to Exchange Server over the Internet, check the box "Encrypt Information … When using dial-up networking."

8. Click the Offline Folder File Settings button.

9. In the Offline Folder File Settings dialog box (Figure 5.4), enter the path to the File used to synchronize your mailbox and favorite public folders for offline use. This file should be on your local hard drive; Exchange will create the file if it doesn't already exist.

Figure 5.3
The Advanced tab controls network security, the offline folder file, and additional mailboxes you might need to access.

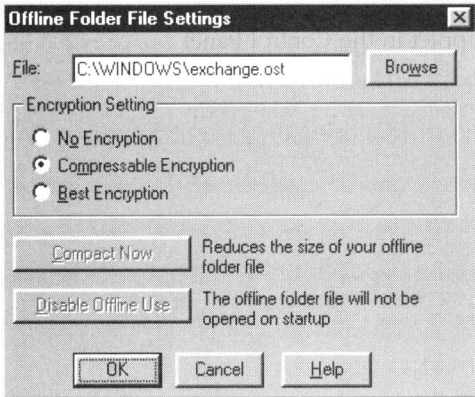

Figure 5.4
The offline folder file should be located on your local hard drive.

10. Choose the Encryption Setting from the following choices:

No Encryption	Does not encrypt the offline folder file.
Compressable Encryption (default)	Encrypts your offline folder file so it can be compressed if your computer uses disk compression.
Best Encryption	Encrypts your file in a format that offers the greatest degree of protection. Some compression is still possible, but much less than with Compressable Encryption.

11. Click OK to close the Offline Folder File Settings dialog box. Answer Yes if you're asked whether you want to create the file.

12. Switch to the Dial-Up Networking tab (Figure 5.5).

Figure 5.5

Set the connection type for remote connections on the Dial-Up Networking tab.

13. If you dial into the network, choose "Dial using the following connection" and pick a DUN connection (see "Dial-Up Networking," page 36 in Chapter 3) from the list. You can also click the New button if you need to add a new connectoid.

14. Enter the "User name," Password, and Domain for the Windows NT user account you use to access the network. The user name is likely to be the same as your Exchange Server mailbox name, but it doesn't have to be. Passwords aren't necessarily the same, either.

15. If you connect to the Microsoft Exchange server from a remote LAN without dialing, then click "Do not dial, use existing connection."

16. Click OK to save the settings (we'll cover the settings on the Remote Mail tab in the next section).

To complete the setup for remote use, you need to connect to the Microsoft Exchange server and validate the mailbox, as described under "Checking Your Mailbox." You'll see a Windows NT domain log-on dialog box when you try to connect to the Microsoft Exchange server. The later section, "Network Security," explains why.

While you are still connected to the server, activate the offline folders file by choosing Tools, Synchronize, All Folders. Once synchronization is complete, you're ready to disconnect from the network and take your folders on the road.

Options

Like all Exchange services, the Microsoft Exchange Server Properties dialog box includes multiple tabs for a variety of options. Table 5.1 lists these settings and their default values. You've already seen some of the settings, because they're included in the basic settings discussed above.

Table 5.1 Settings for Microsoft Exchange Server	
Setting	**Default**
General Settings	
Microsoft Exchange Server	None — entered by user or supplied by custom setup
Mailbox	Name given when the Exchange Server client was installed — needs to be changed to the actual Mailbox name (usually by using the Check Name button)
When starting	Connect with the network
Choose the connection type when starting	For computers that don't travel, disabled. For computers that do travel, enabled.
Advanced Settings	
Open these additional mailboxes	None
Encrypt information … When using the network	Disabled
Encrypt information … When using dial-up networking	Disabled
Use network security during logon	Enabled
	continued

Table 5.1 Settings for Microsoft Exchange Server, continued	
Setting	**Default**
Offline Folder File path (accessed via the Offline Folder File Settings button)	Exchange.ost in the Windows folder
Offline Folder File encryption (accessed via the Offline Folder File Settings button)	Compressable Encryption
Dial-Up Networking Settings Dial/do not dial	"Dial using the following connection," but no connection specified
Remote Mail Settings Process marked items/retrieve items	Process marked items
Disconnect after connection is finished	Enabled
Schedule Next Connection	None scheduled

The next few sections highlight some of the changes you're most likely to want to make to these default settings. Note that the offline folder file and DUN settings are discussed in the earlier "If You're Connecting Remotely" section.

Startup Connection

If you always want to connect to the server immediately, even when you are working remotely, choose "Connect with the network" on the General tab (Figure 5.2). This is also the right choice if you always work at a desktop computer attached to the network. If you often travel with your computer and want to save phone costs by reading and composing messages offline before connecting, then choose "Work offline and use dial-up networking." You can also give yourself the opportunity to choose between connecting immediately and working offline. Check the box marked "Choose the connection type when starting."

Network Security

The setting on the Advanced tab for "Use network security during logon" requires a little explanation, because the name doesn't clearly explain the function. When enabled, this setting uses your log-on account for the Windows NT domain to verify your status as a valid user with access to one or more Exchange mailboxes. If you log on as Paul Dill when Windows starts, you automatically will have access to Paul Dill's mailbox, without going through a separate log-on procedure for Exchange. You never see a log-on option for the Exchange Server mailbox, because it knows which users are allowed access to which mailboxes; no further validation is necessary.

Contrary to how it might appear, clearing the "Use network security..." box does not let you bypass domain security; this setting just makes the Exchange Server connection procedure more flexible. Each time you connect to your Exchange server, you are asked to enter your user name, password, and domain name. This means you can use any NT domain and user name. Here are some situations where this flexibility might be appropriate:

- You need to access Exchange servers at more than one location, and in different domains (for example, you're a consultant who needs access to an Exchange Server mailbox at two different companies)

- You travel with your computer and use DUN to connect with Exchange Server over the Internet

- You need to log on to Exchange Server with more than one user name from the same computer

When you use network security, Exchange uses your log-on account for the Windows NT domain to verify your status as a valid user. This approach gives you automatic access to your mailbox, so you never see a log-on dialog box for Exchange Server.

When "Use network security during logon" is checked, anyone sitting at your computer can access your mailbox just by starting Exchange. If the security of your mail is important, either use a password-protected screen saver or log out of Windows before you leave your desk.

Caution

Additional Mailboxes

Exchange lets you work with other people's mailboxes, assuming you have permission. For example, if you share customer-support responsibilities with three other people, you might all have access to a special mailbox for customer-support messages.

To add a second mailbox to your profile, follow these steps:

1. Run the Mail and Fax (or Mail) applet in the Control Panel.
2. If the profile you want to work with isn't the default profile, click the Show Profiles button. Select the profile you want to modify, then click the Properties button.
3. Select the Microsoft Exchange Server service, then click the Properties button. Switch to the Advanced tab (Figure 5.3).
4. Choose Add, and enter either the mailbox name or the user name in the Add Mailbox dialog box.
5. If the mailbox is found on the server, it is added to the "Open these additional mailboxes" list.
6. If the mailbox can't be found, you'll get an error message; you can try entering the name again (but maybe you ought to check with the system administrator first to make sure you have the correct name).

This is one case where you can make a change to your profile while Exchange is running and have it take effect immediately. From Exchange, to look at another mailbox right away, use Tools, Services from the Exchange menu, then add the mailbox as described in steps 3 through 6 above. You instantly see the additional mailbox in the folder pane on the left side of the Exchange Viewer.

Note that, when you add the mailbox, Exchange does not check to see whether you have sufficient permission to open it. If you add a mailbox that you don't have permission for, you will get a warning only when you actually try to open the folders. You'll learn how to grant permission for other people to work with your mailbox in Chapter 19, "Using Exchange to Collaborate."

Encryption

The encryption settings on the Advanced tab deal with the way information is sent from your computer to the Microsoft Exchange server, rather than with encryption of individual messages, which we'll cover in Chapter 21, "Message Security." You can choose to use encryption when you're connected via the LAN, when you are connected with DUN, or both. Check the appropriate box(es) under "Encrypt information" on the Advanced tab.

Remote Mail

The settings on the Remote Mail tab (Figure 5.6) govern the way the Microsoft Exchange Server service operates when you connect via DUN and use the Remote Mail window. Start Remote Mail by choosing Tools, Remote Mail from the Exchange Viewer. You can change these settings while Exchange is loaded, so they take effect immediately.

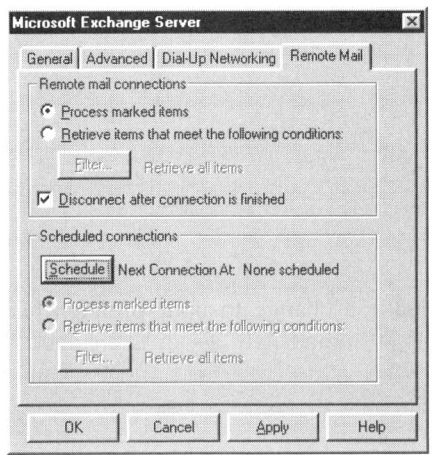

Figure 5.6
You can establish both manual and scheduled remote connections to selectively retrieve either marked or filtered messages.

To change the Remote Mail settings while Exchange is running, follow these steps:

1. From the Exchange menu, choose Tools and then Services.
2. Select the Microsoft Exchange Server service, then click the Properties button.
3. Select the Remote Mail tab on the Microsoft Exchange Server properties dialog box.

During a Remote Mail session, Exchange always sends any items pending in the Outbox folder and updates the list of headers for messages waiting for you. Exchange also processes the headers you have marked (for retrieval and/or deletion) *or* it downloads either all items or selected items that meet criteria you've set. What this means is that you can tell Exchange to download only messages from your boss, your spouse, your kids, and the client who's about to sign a million-dollar deal with your company.

Better yet, because you have the option of separate settings for scheduled and manual Remote Mail sessions, you can download messages from your boss automatically every hour, then manually browse through the remainder of your messages — viewing just the headers and retrieving only those that need your immediate attention.

To set up a scheduled session, follow these steps:

1. On the Remote Mail tab (Figure 5.6), click the Schedule button to display the Schedule Remote Mail Connection dialog box (Figure 5.7), where you can schedule a connection at a specific time each day, at regular intervals, or both.

Figure 5.7
Schedule automatic connections at a particular time of day, at regular intervals, or using both methods.

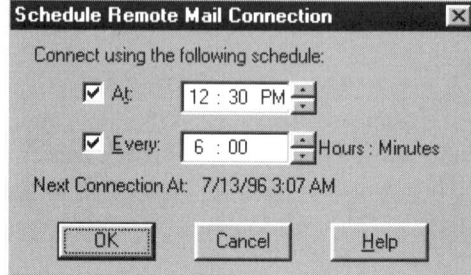

2. To schedule a specific daily connection, check At and enter the time.

3. To schedule a connection at regular intervals, check Every and enter the interval in hours and minutes.

4. Click OK to close the Schedule Remote Mail Connection dialog box.

5. If you want to work just with your message headers in the Remote Mail dialog box, then choose "Process marked items" (the default). If you want to retrieve all your pending messages each session, then choose "Retrieve items that meet the following conditions." If you want to retrieve only certain items, click the Filter button and enter the filter conditions (see "Working with Filters," page 237 in Chapter 10).

The filter for Remote Mail does not let you scan by text in the message body or by folder properties, but otherwise it works like a folder filter. Click OK to close the Filter dialog box.

To configure the actions for manual Remote Mail sessions, follow step 5 above. If you want to stay online after you run a manual Remote Mail session, clear the box labeled "Disconnect after connection is finished." You can then quickly review your headers and retrieve the messages of interest, then disconnect the connection yourself (scheduled connections always disconnect automatically). We'll go into the step-by-step operation of Remote Mail in Chapter 13, "Working Remotely."

Tips and Tricks

The main issues surrounding the Microsoft Exchange Server service are related to performance. We look at two here, both of which may require some assistance from your system administrator. Also, there's some advice for those of you who may have upgraded to the Exchange Server client from an operating system version of Exchange.

Speeding Up Exchange on Windows 95

In some network configurations, Exchange starts very slowly on Windows 95 machines, taking as long as several minutes to load. Fixing this problem is not difficult, but it does require the assistance of your network administrator to re-adjust some network settings that control how the Exchange client communicates with the Exchange Server. The problem described in the next section can also increase the startup time for Exchange.

Stopping Exchange from Dialing the Internet

Under Windows 95, if you have a DUN adapter configured for TCP/IP (see "Dial-Up Networking," page 36 in Chapter 3) and you also connect to your Microsoft Exchange server on a LAN using TCP/IP, your computer may try to dial your Internet service provider whenever you load Exchange.

What's happening is that Exchange is trying to find the Microsoft Exchange server, but it's looking on the Internet first, rather than on your LAN. There is no perfect fix for this problem, but you can try one of several workarounds:

- Add a HOSTS or LMHOSTS entry for the Exchange server. See your network administrator for details.
- Ping the Microsoft Exchange server before launching Exchange. (Ping.exe is a TCP/IP utility included with Windows 95. To run the application, open a DOS window, then enter "PING" followed by the address of the server.) This verifies the location of the Microsoft Exchange server, loading its address into a cache. Exchange will get the location of the server from that cache rather than by trying to dial out. Ask the network administrator what address to use with the Ping.exe application included with Windows.

- Run the Internet applet on the Control Panel. On the Connection tab, clear the box labeled "Connect to the Internet as needed" or "Dial whenever an internet connection is needed." Note that this turns off the feature in Windows 95 that automatically makes a DUN connection to the Internet whenever you try to open an "http://" reference or other Internet link.

Configuring Offline Folders for Online Users

The section "If You're Connecting Remotely" discussed how to set up offline folders for use by remote users who have to dial in to the Microsoft Exchange server or connect via a remote LAN. I recommend that you set up offline folders and occasionally synchronize them even if you spend all your time at the same desktop computer and never work remotely. It's good, cheap insurance against the possibility that one day you might not be able to connect to the Microsoft Exchange server because of network problems or some other cause. If you have offline folders set up, you'll still be able to create new messages and work with older messages from the last time you synchronized.

There is one situation in which you would not want to set up offline folders for a desktop computer: in the event that you have limited hard drive space on the machine.

Removing Old Exchange Files

If you upgrade to the full Exchange Server client after using the operating system version of Exchange or Windows Messaging, you can choose to put Exchange in the old Exchange or Windows Messaging folder or install it in a different folder. If you don't install over the previous version, the old folder is not removed. The default location for this folder depends on the operating system and Exchange version:

Windows 95 (original version)	C:\Program Files\Microsoft Exchange
Windows 95 (Windows Messaging update)	C:\Program Files\Windows Messaging
Windows NT	C:\Program Files\Windows NT\ Windows Messaging

As long as this folder does not contain any .pst or .pab files that might be used by a profile, you can safely delete the folder and all its contents.

One consequence of removing the folder is that any shortcuts to the now deleted Exchng32.exe file will, of course, no longer work. When you use such a shortcut, you'll be prompted to specify the new location for Exchng32.exe, which is in the folder where you installed the Exchange Server client, usually C:\Exchange. If you use the Microsoft Office Shortcut Bar, you will also need to update the path to Exchng32.exe on any buttons that point to Exchange.

Do not use the Add/Remove Programs in the Control Panel to remove the older version of Exchange on Windows 95 systems. Doing so will cause the Microsoft Fax service for Exchange and The Microsoft Network online service to be removed from the computer. The only way to restore these services would be to re-install the operating system version of Exchange. You would then need to re-install the Exchange Server client.

This is a less critical issue on Windows NT computers. If you remove Windows Messaging from NT through the Control Panel, you lose the use of the Internet Mail service for Exchange. If your Exchange server handles Internet messages, then you don't need Internet Mail anyway.

Caution

Summary

Installation of the Microsoft Exchange Server service requires access to the Microsoft Exchange server and a mailbox on the server. Remote users need to follow an additional procedure to activate the offline folders file, which is used to synchronize Exchange folders on the local computer with those on the Microsoft Exchange server itself.

Key Points

- You cannot use the Microsoft Exchange Server service with the operating system version of Exchange; you must install the Exchange Server client.

- Before you can use offline folders, you must activate them by connecting to the Exchange Server and synchronizing the folders.

- When you use network security, Exchange uses your log-on account for the Windows NT domain to verify your status as a valid user. This approach gives you automatic access to your mailbox, and you will never see a log-on dialog box for Exchange Server.

For More Information

Remote users will want to read Chapter 13, "Working Remotely," thoroughly to learn how to use Remote Mail and other techniques for downloading and uploading messages and for maintaining access to favorite public folders.

Features exclusive to Exchange Server are covered throughout Parts III and IV, particularly in the following chapters:

- Chapter 16 , "Working with Messages and Folders," which describes the properties of public folders;
- Chapter 18, "Exchange Assistants," where you'll learn how to make the Inbox Assistant and Out-of-Office Assistant process incoming messages, even when you're not there;
- Chapter 19, "Using Exchange to Collaborate," which covers Public Folders and access to other users' mailboxes;
- Chapter 20, "Using and Creating Exchange Forms," which describes how to go beyond simple messages to forms for collecting, presenting, and managing all types of information;
- Chapter 21, "Message Security," which deals with the mechanics of sending encrypted messages and messages with digital signatures.

Installing and Updating the Exchange Server Client

The Exchange Server client can be installed from CD, from a seven-disk installation set, or from a network drive. It can be installed over the operating system version of Exchange or Windows Messaging. If the Exchange Server client is not already installed on your system, follow these steps:

1. Run Setup.exe from the location indicated by your system administrator.

2. In the initial dialog boxes, accept the end-user license and confirm your name and organization (the name you provide will be used to locate your Exchange Server mailbox, so make sure you enter the name correctly). You will also have an opportunity to specify where you want Exchange installed on your computer.

3. You may see a choice of Typical, Custom, Laptop, or (if you are installing from a shared network installation) Workstation installation. Usually, the Exchange administrator has customized the settings so that either Typical or Laptop (or Workstation if available) installs the components you need. The Laptop installation leaves out the spelling checker and Windows Help files. Choose Laptop if you have limited space on your hard drive and don't need these files.

   If you want to see what components will be installed and possibly change them, choose the Custom installation. You will need to click the Continue button to complete the installation after you select what components to install.

4. If you choose Typical, Laptop, or Workstation, the setup program begins installing files immediately.

5. Restart your computer if you are prompted to do so.

This process will 1) install the Exchange Server client on your computer and 2) add the Microsoft Exchange Server service (and Microsoft Mail if you so choose) to your default profile. If you have not used a previous version of Exchange on this computer, the newly created profile is called Default Exchange Profile. You will still need to double-check the mailbox as described under "Checking Your Mailbox" on page 88.

Be aware that if your system administrator has customized the Exchange setup program, you may see slightly different options (such as

continued

Installing and Updating the Exchange Server Client, continued

only a Typical installation choice) from those listed above. If you installed the Exchange Server client over a previous version of Exchange, you may want to check the section "Removing Old Exchange Files" at the end of this chapter. If you want to add or remove Exchange Server client components (for example, to add the spelling checker if you didn't do so during the initial installation), you need to use the setup program again. Here's how to do it:

1. Go to the Control Panel, and start the Add/Remove Programs applet.

2. On the Install/Uninstall tab, select Microsoft Exchange from the list of programs at the bottom of the dialog box. Then click the Add/Remove button. This starts the Microsoft Exchange Setup program. You may be prompted to insert the Exchange CD or diskette — the same one you used to install the Exchange Server client.

3. On the Microsoft Exchange Setup dialog box (Figure 5.A), click the Add/Remove button.

Figure 5.A

After installing the Exchange Server client, you can use the maintenance program to update, add, or remove components. Choose Reinstall if you just want to refresh all the program files for your current Exchange setup.

4. On the Microsoft Exchange - Maintenance dialog box (Figure 5.B), select Exchange under Options, then click the Change Option button.

continued

Installing and Updating the Exchange Server Client, continued

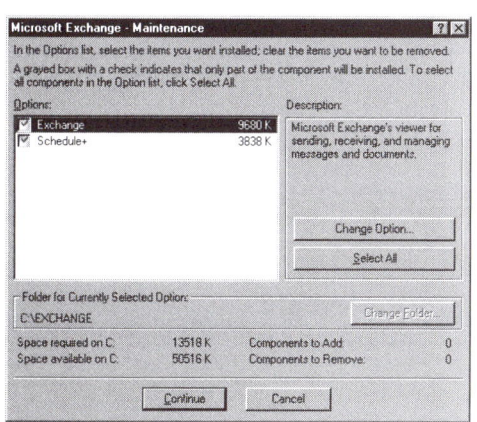

Figure 5.B
Components for both Exchange and Schedule+ can be updated. If the checkboxes are gray, as shown here, it means that these programs are only partially installed. You could add additional components to your system.

5. On the Microsoft Exchange - Exchange dialog box (Figure 5.C), check the box for any component you want to add, or clear the box to remove a component.

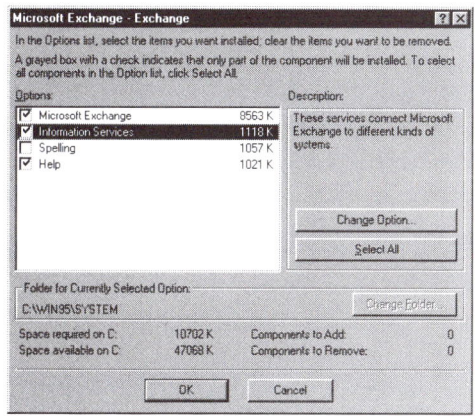

Figure 5.C
You can add or remove information services, the spelling checker, or Windows Help files. Don't clear the box for Microsoft Exchange, because that removes the program itself.

6. To add or remove a particular information service, select Information Services under Options, then click the Change Option button.

continued

Installing and Updating the Exchange Server Client, continued

7. On the Microsoft Exchange - Information Services dialog box (Figure 5.D), check the box for any component you want to add, or clear the box to remove a component. Then click OK to return to the Microsoft Exchange - Exchange dialog box.

Figure 5.D

The Exchange Server client includes four different information services.

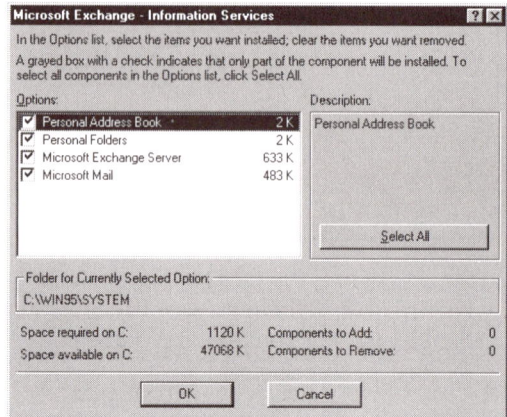

8. When you have finished selecting components, click OK to return to the Microsoft Exchange - Maintenance dialog box, then check the Continue button to complete the update. If you installed the Exchange Server client from diskettes, you probably will be asked to insert one or more disks as part of the process.

Chapter 6
Setting Up Microsoft Mail

As we continue this series of chapters spotlighting the details of different Exchange services, let's look at the Microsoft Mail service, which supports both local and remote connections within the same Exchange profile. (The older Microsoft Mail program that you might be familiar with required a separate Microsoft Mail Remote for roving users.) With the Microsoft Mail service, you can

- Exchange e-mail with other people in your organization who have Microsoft Mail addresses
- Exchange e-mail with people on other mail systems, if your postoffice is connected to a *gateway*, or even send faxes (A *gateway* is a way of connecting a Microsoft Mail Server to other types of mail systems, such as an Internet mail server or Novell NetWare mail.)
- Post information in shared folders for other members of your postoffice to see

In general, Microsoft Mail is a mail service for organizations, not individuals. You do not need the Microsoft Mail service unless you are part of an organization that uses Microsoft Mail for its internal messages.

Requirements

Microsoft Mail is a mail service for organizations, not individuals.

To use the Microsoft Mail service for Exchange, you must have

- A Microsoft Mail postoffice to connect to. You will need to know the network path to the postoffice.
- An account in that postoffice and the password for that account.
- An update to Exchange that adds the capability to access Microsoft Mail shared folders (if you are using the version of Exchange that comes with Windows 95). The update will be either Service Pack 1, the Windows Messaging update, or a later update (see Appendix B, "Exchange Resources," page 639).

Note that last requirement carefully. Both the Windows NT operating system version (Windows Messaging) of the Microsoft Mail service and the version distributed with the Exchange Server clients handle shared folders just fine. But if you want to use these versions with Windows 95, you need an update; the original version on the Windows 95 CD does not give access to shared folders (also see the section "Activating Shared Folders" at the end of the chapter).

The postoffice can be a full postoffice created with Microsoft Mail Server. The postoffice also can be a workgroup postoffice created either by the Mail program that comes with Windows for Workgroups or Windows NT 3.x, or by the Microsoft Mail Postoffice applet in the Windows 95 or Windows NT 4.0 Control Panel. If you've never used Microsoft Mail on your network, you can create your own postoffice and add user accounts. See Chapter 23, "Managing a Workgroup Postoffice," page 513 for details. If you have previously used Microsoft Mail on your computer, you'll have the opportunity to import addresses and messages from your old message file (named Msmail.mmf or something similar).

Basic Setup

Depending on how Exchange was set up on your machine, you may already have Microsoft Mail in your default profile; but assuming you don't, we'll walk through the two different methods of adding it: via the Setup Wizard and by manually adding the service. See Chapter 4, "Configuring Profiles," if you need a refresher on how to add a service to an Exchange profile.

The advantage of using the wizard is that it lets you pick your name from the list of people with accounts in the postoffice; you don't have to know your actual mailbox name. The advantage to manual configuration is that you get the chance to establish all the settings at once. If you tend to veer from the defaults (see Table 6.1), then manual configuration is probably your best bet. Manual configuration will also be the most efficient method if you're setting up Microsoft Mail on a laptop or on any system that isn't currently connected to the network where the postoffice resides. We'll discuss both setup methods after taking a quick look at some preparation you'll need if you're upgrading to Exchange from an older version of Microsoft Mail.

If You've Used Microsoft Mail Before

Before you set up the Microsoft Mail service, make sure that your old messages are available for Exchange to import. These old messages are stored in an .mmf file, either in the postoffice or on your local drive. Locally stored messages are usually in a file called Msmail.mmf in your Windows folder. If the messages are on the server, you will need to use the old Microsoft Mail program to move or copy them so Exchange can import them.

If you have old Microsoft Mail messages, put them where Exchange can find them to import them.

To copy the old messages, follow these steps:

1. Start Microsoft Mail and log on to your account. (You may need to do this from another workstation; Mail will not start on some machines where Exchange already has been installed.)

2. Choose File, Export Folder.

3. Specify a name for your export file, then click OK.

4. In the Export Folders dialog box, choose Select All Folders.

5. Click Copy to copy all the folders and your Personal Address Book to the export file. Click the Close button when you're finished.

6. Choose File, Exit and Sign Out to close Mail.

Alternatively, if you prefer to move the message file from the server to another location,

1. Run Mail and log on to your account. (As noted above, you may need to do this from another workstation, because Mail doesn't always start on a machine where Exchange has been installed.)

2. Choose Mail, Options.

3. From the Options dialog, click the Server button.

4. Choose Local and, in the File box, specify a path to the .mmf file; this path can be either on a local drive or at another server location.

5. Click OK twice to return to the main Mail window.

6. Choose File, Exit and Sign Out to close Mail.

Using the Setup Wizard

Now that you have access to any earlier Microsoft Mail .mmf file, you can add Microsoft Mail to your profile. As noted earlier in this chapter, there are two ways to do this — using the Setup Wizard or manually.

The Setup Wizard is available only when you create a new profile through the Mail and Fax (or Mail) applet in the Control Panel. To add a profile using the Setup Wizard, follow these steps:

1. Run the Mail and Fax (or Mail) applet in the Control Panel.
2. Click the Show Profiles button.
3. Choose Add.
4. In the first screen of the Setup Wizard, choose "Use the following information services" and check the ones you want, in this case being sure to include Microsoft Mail.
5. Click Next to continue, and give the profile a name on the next screen of the wizard, then click Next again to begin configuring Microsoft Mail and any other services you selected.

Here are the steps in the wizard that are specific to Microsoft Mail:

1. The wizard asks the path to your postoffice (Figure 6.1). This path is likely to be \\<servername>\wgpo0000 or something similar if the postoffice is on a workstation or an NT server. You may be able to locate the path by

Figure 6.1

Check with your system administrator to get the path to the Microsoft Mail postoffice before you run the Setup Wizard.

browsing the LAN through Network Neighborhood, but it's probably quicker just to ask the system administrator. Click Next to continue.

2. If you've entered the postoffice path correctly and the wizard can connect to it, the system will display a list of Microsoft Mail users (Figure 6.2). Pick your name, then click Next to continue.

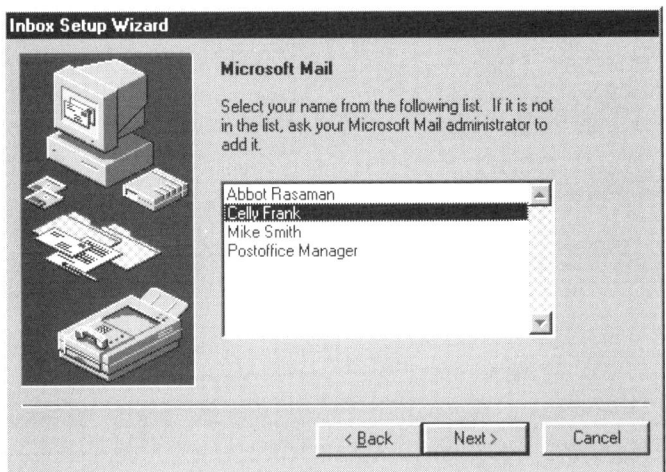

Figure 6.2
Pick your name from the list of Microsoft Mail users.

3. If you see the list of users, but your name isn't there, then you don't have an account in the postoffice and therefore will not be able to set up Microsoft Mail. Click the Cancel button and make sure you get an account before you try to configure Microsoft Mail again. If you don't see a list of users, skip to step 5.

4. Enter your password on the next screen (Figure 6.3), then click Next to continue and skip to step 6.

5. If the wizard can't find the postoffice, it will tell you so (this will almost always be the case if you're configuring Microsoft Mail just for remote use). Click Next to continue. Then in the dialog box shown in Figure 6.4, enter the name of your mail account and its password. The system administrator should be able to give you that information if you don't have it already. Click Next to continue.

6. If you have used Mail on this machine and have moved the .mmf file to local storage (as described in the previous section), the wizard should offer to convert it for you (see Figure 6.5). You can choose "Convert the file now" or "Don't convert the file." (If the wizard does not offer to convert the file, follow the instructions in the section "Importing an .mmf File" on page 115.)

Figure 6.3

You must know the password for your Microsoft Mail account before you can use Microsoft Mail from Exchange. The mail administrator can reset your password for you if necessary.

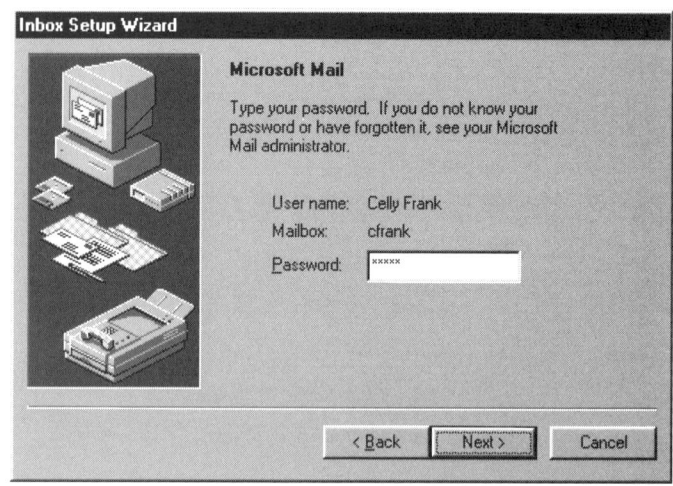

Figure 6.4

If you are working remotely, you'll need to enter the actual Mailbox name rather than pick from a list of users.

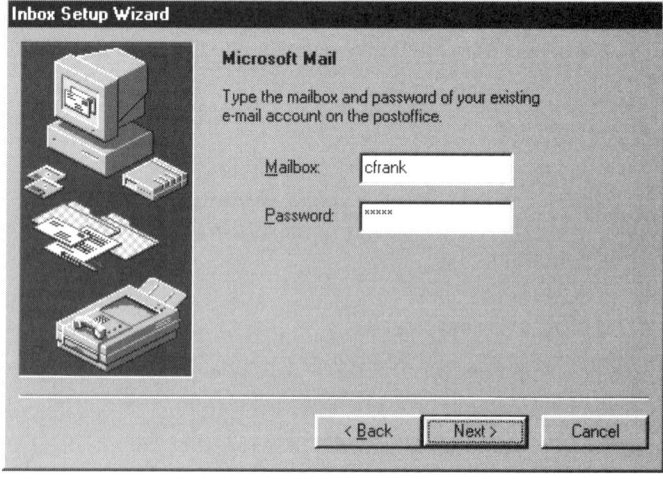

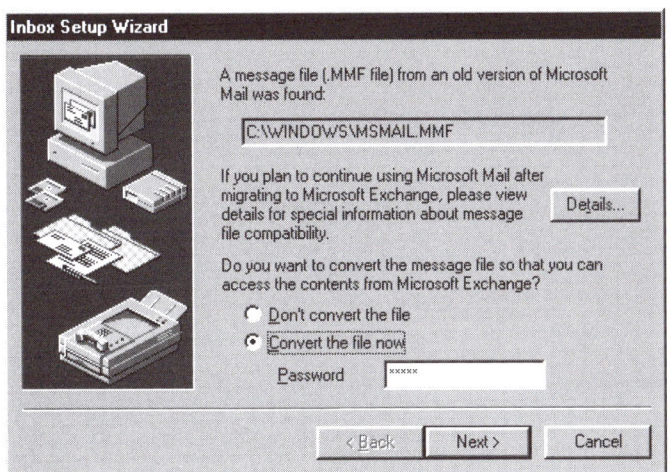

Figure 6.5
Old messages and addresses are not actually converted, but instead are imported. The original .mmf file remains intact.

There is no direct way to export messages from Exchange back to an .mmf file. The best workaround is to create a Microsoft Mail shared folder, then move all the messages from the Exchange folders to that shared folder. You can then quit Exchange, start Microsoft Mail, and move the messages from the shared folder to the Microsoft Mail folders. For addresses, there is no way to export from Exchange back to Microsoft Mail.

Special Note

Manually Configuring Services

If you add Microsoft Mail to an existing profile, you configure the mail services through the Microsoft Mail properties dialog box, which consists of eight tabs of settings. You also use the properties dialog box if you create a new profile, then choose "Manually configure information services" when the Setup Wizard launches.

After adding Microsoft Mail to an existing or new profile, follow these steps on the properties dialog box to configure the minimum required settings. Other settings are discussed in "Options" later in this chapter.

1. On the Connection tab (Figure 6.6), "Enter the path to your postoffice," as described in the previous section.

2. Switch to the Logon tab (Figure 6.7).

3. Enter your mailbox or account name and the password for the account.

Figure 6.6

Before you can use Microsoft Mail, you must enter the network path to your postoffice.

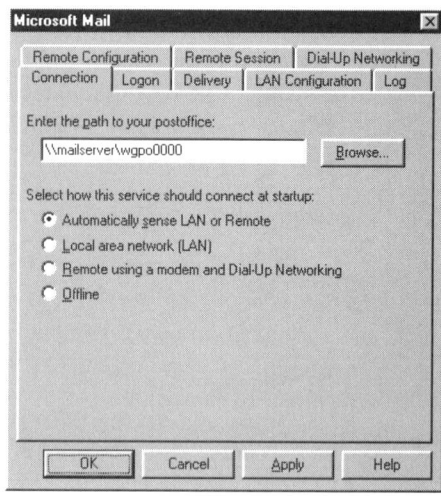

Figure 6.7

When you type in your password, your keystrokes are masked so no one can look over your shoulder and learn your password.

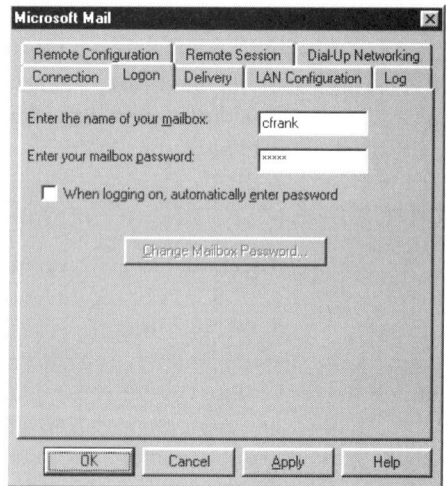

If your machine sometimes or always dials in to the network to get mail, and if you're connecting remotely, then continue with the "If You're Connecting Remotely" section on page 117. Otherwise, you have completed all the required settings for Microsoft Mail. Click the OK button to save the configuration for this service. There are, however, many more settings to review; and we detail all of them in the "Options" section that follows.

Remember that, with Exchange, you can have multiple profiles that define how you connect and to what services. If you carry a laptop computer between home and office, you may want to use two different Exchange profiles to connect to your Microsoft Mail postoffice, one for remote use and another for times when you're in the office.

Special Note

Importing an .mmf File

If you configured Microsoft Mail manually or if an existing .mmf was not imported by the Setup Wizard, you can also import the messages and addresses through Exchange. To do so, follow these steps:

1. On the Exchange menu, choose File, Import to display the Specify File to Import dialog box (Figure 6.8).

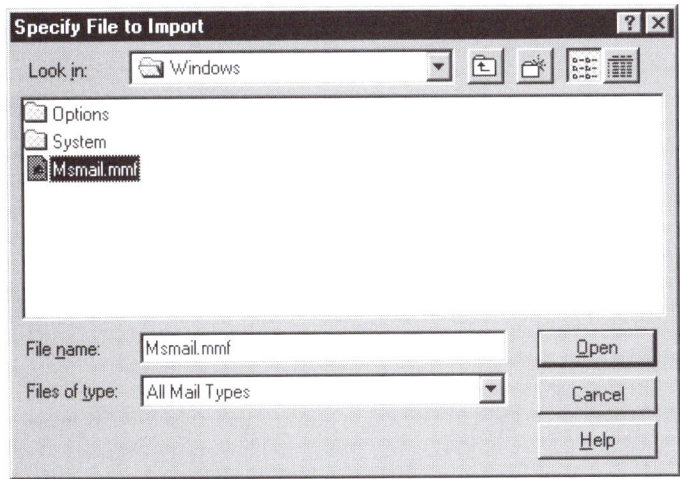

Figure 6.8
An old Microsoft Mail file is most likely to be found in the Windows folder.

2. Switch to the folder where the .mmf file is located, select the file, then click the Open button.

3. In the Import Mail Data dialog box (Figure 6.9), enter the Password for the .mmf file.

4. Select whether to "Import messages," "Import personal address book entries," or both, then click the OK button.

5. If you choose to import messages, a second Import Mail Data dialog box appears, as shown in Figure 6.10.

Figure 6.9

You can choose to import just messages, just address book entries, or both types of data from your old Microsoft Mail file.

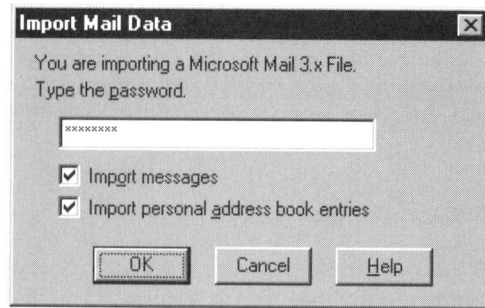

Figure 6.10

Messages can be imported into any set of folders in your current profile or into a new set of Personal Folders.

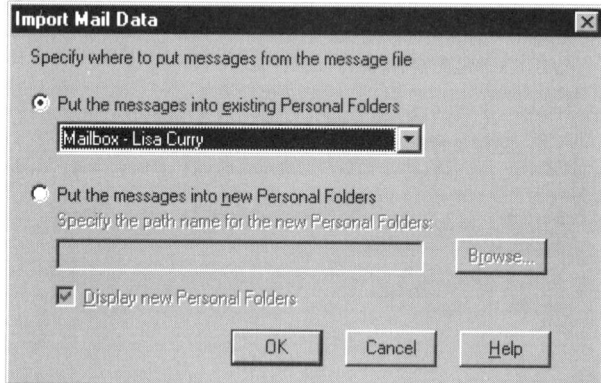

Specify where you put the messages. If you want them to go into either your Exchange Server mailbox or an existing Personal Folders file, choose "Put the messages into existing Personal Folders," and select from the folders available in the current profile. If you want to copy the old messages into a new Personal Folders file, choose "Put the messages into new Personal Folders" and provide a location (path name) either by typing the path name into the box provided or using the Browse button to point to it. If you don't want these new folders to appear in the current profile, then clear the Display New Personal Folders box.

6. When you've chosen the location for the messages, click OK to continue. Exchange will import the data from the .mmf file, then display a log showing how many messages and address book entries where imported. Click OK to close the log and return to Exchange.

If You're Connecting Remotely

To establish your Microsoft Mail connection for remote use, switch to the Dial-Up Networking tab on the Microsoft Mail properties dialog box (Figure 6.11). You must designate the DUN connectoid or phonebook entry that you want to use for Microsoft Mail connections (see Chapter 3, "Making Connections," for details about setting up DUN). Make your selection from the list shown under "Use the following Dial-Up Networking connection."

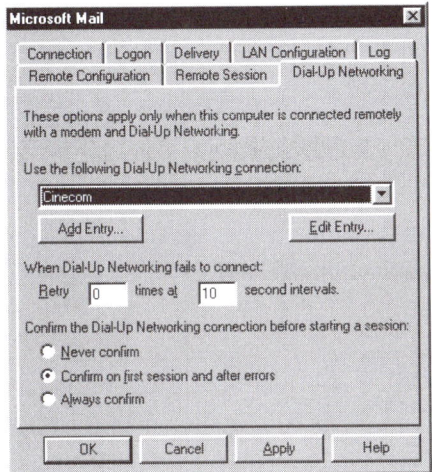

Figure 6.11

When you connect to the Microsoft Mail postoffice from remote locations, Exchange will use the DUN connection or phonebook entry that you specify.

You also have the option to create a new connectoid or phonebook entry. Click the Add Entry button to proceed. When you've selected the DUN connectoid or phonebook entry, click the OK button to save the configuration for this service.

Options

Like all Exchange services, Microsoft Mail includes an extensive properties dialog box with multiple tabs for a variety of options. Table 6.1 lists these settings and their default values; some you've already seen, because they're included in the basic settings discussed above. We'll look at the other settings on the Microsoft Mail properties dialog box in this section. The next few sections highlight some of the changes you're most likely to want to make to these default settings.

Table 6.1 Settings for Microsoft Mail

Setting	Default
Connection settings	
Path to your postoffice	None — entered by user
How the service should connect at startup	Automatically sense LAN or Remote
Log-on settings	
Mailbox name	None — entered by user
Mailbox password	None — entered by user
Automatically enter password	No
Delivery settings	
Enable incoming mail delivery	Yes
Enable outgoing mail delivery	Yes
Enable deliver to address types (Press the Address Types button to see what types are available.)	All
Check for new mail	Every 10 minutes
Immediate notification (requires NetBIOS)	No
Display Global Address List only	No
LAN Configuration settings	
Use Remote Mail	No
Use local copy of the postoffice address list	No
Use external delivery agent	No
Location of the session log	Msfslog.txt in the Windows folder

continued

Table 6.1 Settings for Microsoft Mail, continued

Setting	Default
Remote Configuration settings	
Use Remote Mail	Yes
Use local copy of the postoffice address list	Yes
Use external delivery agent	No
Remote Session settings	
Automatically start Dial-Up Networking	No
Automatically end Dial-Up Networking after retrieving mail headers	No
Automatically end Dial-Up Networking after sending and receiving mail	Yes
Automatically end Dial-Up Networking when you exit Exchange	Yes
Dial-Up Networking settings	
Dial-Up Networking connection	None — entered by user
Retry	0 times at 10-second intervals (Exchange Server clients)
	0 times at 120-second intervals (Windows 95 and Windows NT 4.0 clients)
Confirm Dial-Up Networking	On first session and after errors

Startup Connection

Return to the Connection tab on the Microsoft Mail properties dialog box (Figure 6.6) and look at the setting under "Select how this service should connect at startup." If this machine is always connected to the LAN, choose "Local area network (LAN)." If this machine sometimes travels, then your best choice is "Automatically sense LAN or Remote." If this machine is always on the road, choose "Remote using a modem and Dial-Up Networking."

The Offline setting is of limited usefulness, because you can't send or receive mail when Offline is selected. Use this setting only in a profile where you will not need to connect to the mail server at all. To deliver any mail that you compose while working offline in this fashion, you will need to change the startup connection setting to one of the other choices, quit Exchange, then restart Exchange.

Password

Password settings are on the Logon tab (Figure 6.7). To change the password on your Microsoft Mail account, use the Change Mailbox Password button. (You can also change your password from within Exchange by choosing Tools, Microsoft Mail Tools, Change Mailbox Password.) If you want Exchange to enter your password automatically, check the box labeled "When logging on, automatically enter password." This will save your password in the password cache for your Windows user profile.

Special Note

You may have several passwords associated with Exchange. The password for your Microsoft Mail account is separate from any password you may have set for Personal Folders.

Delivery

You can turn off delivery of incoming and outgoing messages by clearing the appropriate checkboxes on the Delivery tab shown in Figure 6.12. This might be useful, for example, if you want all outgoing messages held for delivery at one time or if you don't want to be distracted by incoming messages while you are working on an urgent project.

If you are connecting to a full Microsoft Mail server, rather than to a workgroup postoffice, you can use the Address Types button to enable or disable delivery to types of mail recipients other than Microsoft Mail. The types listed (Figure 6.13) will depend on the mail gateways connected to your mail server.

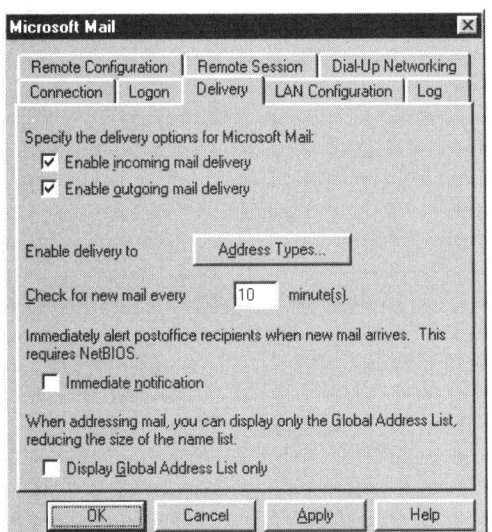

Figure 6.12
The Delivery tab includes a number of settings that determine how Microsoft Mail messages are sent.

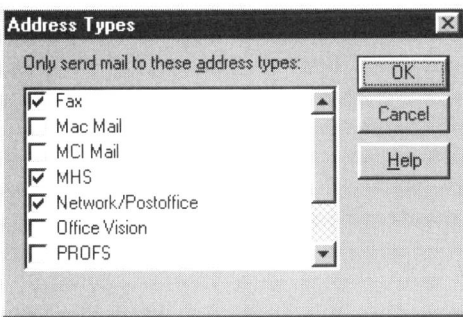

Figure 6.13
If your Microsoft Mail server uses one or more gateways to reach other messaging systems, possibly including fax recipients, you can send messages to these other address types.

For full Microsoft Mail server connections, you may also want to check the "Display Global Address List only" box at the bottom of the Delivery tab. This can speed things up if people in your organization are scattered among a number of different postoffices, each with its own address list.

Set the interval in which you want Exchange to check the postoffice for new mail in the box on the Delivery tab. Exchange will also send messages when it makes that check. This setting only applies if you have not checked the Use Remote Mail box on the LAN Configuration tab.

To be notified immediately when new messages arrive at the postoffice for you, check the Immediate Notification box. You will need to have Net-BIOS enabled in your network settings. The server where the postoffice is located must also support NetBIOS. See your system administrator to find out whether this setting is appropriate.

LAN Configuration

There are only three settings to consider if you operate Exchange directly connected to a LAN. These settings appear on the LAN Configuration tab, shown in Figure 6.14.

Figure 6.14

The settings on the LAN Configuration tab affect mainly slow LANs and situations where you need to leave messages on the server. The default settings are for all options to be disabled.

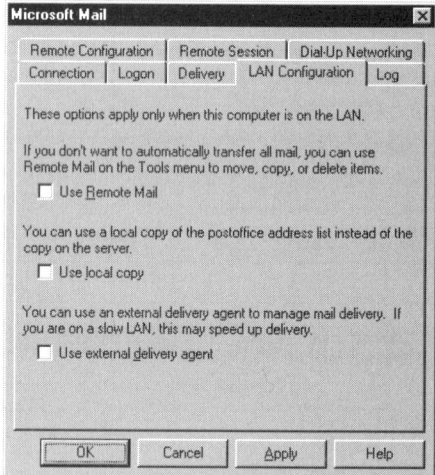

Perhaps the most important of these settings is Use Remote Mail on the Remote Configuration tab. Choose this if you want to delete messages from the server only on command, rather than delete them all automatically once Exchange has retrieved them. For more about this issue, see "Retaining Messages on the Server," page 127, later in this chapter.

If your LAN is slow or the postoffice is large, you may want to check the box labeled "Use local copy" on the LAN Configuration tab. This will keep a copy of the postoffice address list on your local system. To refresh the list, occasionally choose Tools, Microsoft Mail Tools, Download Address Lists.

The third setting, "Use external delivery agent," is relevant only if you're connecting to a full Microsoft Mail Server postoffice (this setting is also mainly for slow networks). See your system administrator to find out whether this setting is appropriate for you.

Log

By default, Exchange keeps a log of your Microsoft Mail sessions, using the location specified on the Log tab (Figure 6.15). To view the log from Exchange, choose Tools, Microsoft Mail Tools, View Session Log.

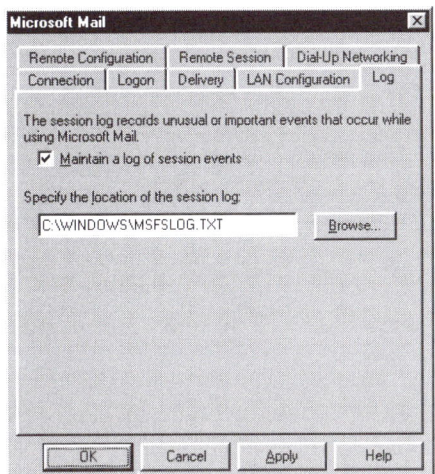

Figure 6.15
Track your Microsoft Mail sessions with a log file.

Remote User Settings

The settings for connecting remotely to the Microsoft Mail postoffice are complex enough to cover three tabs. The Remote Configuration tab includes the same settings as the LAN Configuration tab discussed previously. The Remote Session tab determines when you'll connect and disconnect. Finally, the Dial-Up Networking tab governs how you'll connect.

One thing to consider as you work with these settings is whether you want to use Remote Mail to get your messages by selecting the ones to retrieve from a list of headers. This is an alternative to getting all your messages at once, either on demand or through a scheduled mail download. For a complete discussion of the difference between these methods, see Chapter 13, "Working Remotely."

Remote Configuration

The settings available on the Remote Configuration tab (Figure 6.16) are the same as those for the LAN Configuration tab that we've already looked at in the "LAN Configuration" section, page 122. Those on the LAN Configuration

Figure 6.16

*The Remote Configuration
tab includes the same
settings as the LAN
Configuration tab
(Figure 6.14), but the
defaults for dial-up
networking connections
are different.*

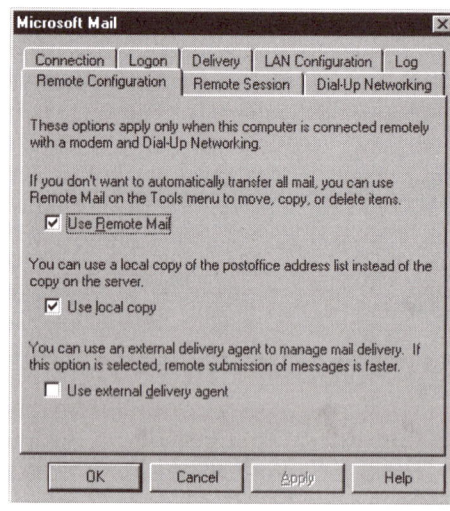

tab affect Exchange sessions when you are directly connected to the postoffice via a LAN. Those on the Remote Configuration tab are in effect when you use DUN to connect to the postoffice.

As you might guess, the settings on the LAN Configuration tab that were appropriate for slow LANs are also appropriate for remote connections, which are also slower than direct LAN connections.

The Use Remote Mail box on the Remote Configuration tab is checked by default. That's the best setting, because it gives you the option of using the Remote Mail feature if you want to retrieve messages selectively. You should also check Use Remote Mail if you want to delete messages from the server only on command (see "Retaining Messages on the Server," page 127).

Because you're likely to be composing messages when you are not connected to the postoffice, leave the box labeled "Use local copy" checked. This will keep a copy of the postoffice address list on your local system. To refresh the list, occasionally choose Tools, Microsoft Mail Tools, Download Address Lists.

The third setting on the Remote Configuration tab, "Use external delivery agent," is relevant only if you're connecting to a full Microsoft Mail Server postoffice. See your system administrator to find out whether this setting is appropriate for you.

Dial-Up Networking

On the Dial-Up Networking tab (Figure 6.11), you must select a "Dial-Up Networking connection" from among those you've already configured and tested

(see "Dial-Up Networking," page 36 in Chapter 3). You can also choose A<u>d</u>d
Entry to create a new connectoid or phonebook entry or <u>E</u>dit Entry to alter the
one that's currently selected.

If the remote connection fails, you can have Exchange retry the connection a certain number of times at a specified interval of seconds. Enter the
number of retries in the <u>R</u>etry box and the interval in the "<u>A</u>t X second intervals" box.

You can choose one of three methods for confirming that you want to
use a particular DUN connection:

Never confirm	Does not confirm the dial-up network-ing connection, always using the DUN connectoid or phonebook entry selected on the Dial-Up Networking tab
Confirm on first session and after errors	Confirms when you first connect and if errors occur (default), so you have a chance to switch DUN connectoids or perhaps change dialing locations
Always confirm	Confirms the DUN connectoid or phonebook entry each time you log on

If you travel, you'll probably want to stick with the default choice —
Confirm on first session and after errors — to get an easy opportunity to
change dialing location to match the city where you're working today. An
alternative is to choose "Always confirm choice." This will give you an easy
way to switch to a different DUN connectoid or phonebook entry each time
you dial the postoffice server.

Remote Session

Switch to the Remote Session tab (Figure 6.17) to specify when Exchange will
connect to the remote postoffice. If you want to connect to the postoffice
whenever you start Exchange, check the box marked "When this service is
started." A connection will be made when you start Exchange. Then you can
use either <u>T</u>ools, <u>R</u>emote Mail or <u>T</u>ools, <u>D</u>eliver Now to send and retrieve mail.

The settings under "Automatically end a Dial-Up Networking session"
affect what happens during a session. The normal configuration is to stay connected after retrieving message headers ("After retrieving mail headers" is
cleared), but to disconnect after sending and receiving with Remote Mail or
Deliver Now ("After sending and receiving mail" is checked). This gives you a
chance to quickly review the headers and mark which messages you want to
retrieve.

**Microsoft Mail
offers many
ways to
schedule
automatic
connections.**

Figure 6.17

Microsoft Mail has many flexible options for setting up automatic remote-connection sessions.

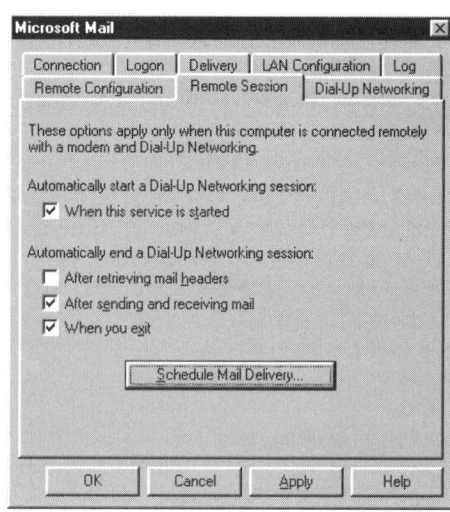

You'll probably also want to break the DUN connection when you exit Exchange, so the box marked "When you e_x_it" is checked by default.

Click the _S_chedule Mail Delivery button to display the Schedule Remote Mail Delivery dialog box (Figure 6.18), where you can set up as many automatic mail sessions as you like. You can also schedule sessions from Exchange by choosing _T_ools, Microsoft _M_ail Tools, Schedule Remote Mail Delivery.

Figure 6.18

In an automatic mail session, Exchange delivers any messages pending in the Outbox for your Microsoft Mail postoffice and retrieves any messages waiting for you.

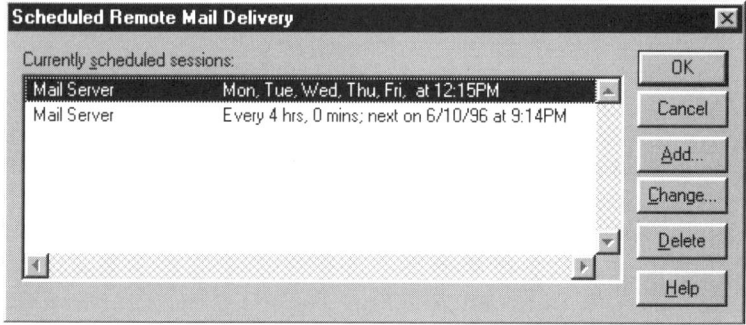

Click the _A_dd button to bring up the Add Scheduled Session dialog box, shown in Figure 6.19. Under _U_se, choose the DUN connectoid or phonebook entry you want to use.

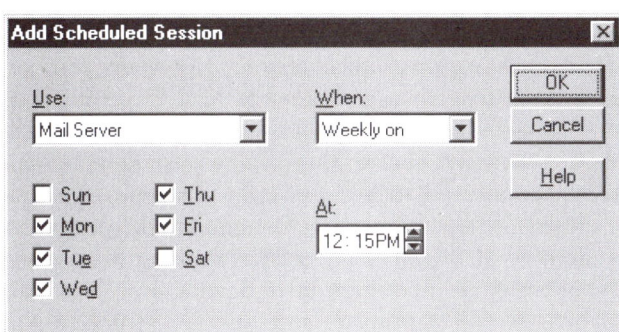

Figure 6.19
Automatic connections can be scheduled at regular intervals of several hours, on a daily or weekly basis, or as on-off events.

You have three choices under When:

Every	At a specified interval, defined in hours and minutes
Weekly on	Each week on a particular day (or days), at a particular time
Once at	On a particular date, at a particular time

For example, to set up Microsoft Mail to connect every weekday during your lunch hour, choose Weekly and check the boxes for Monday through Friday, then set the At time to 12:15 p.m. or whenever you go to lunch. An example appears as the first connection listed in Figure 6.18.

Click OK to save the scheduled session and return to the Scheduled Remote Mail Delivery dialog box, where you can also use Change and Delete to reschedule and remove sessions. When you're done scheduling connections, click OK to return to the Microsoft Mail properties dialog box.

Tips and Tricks

Now that you have the Microsoft Mail service set up the way you like it, let's look at a way to make Exchange act more like the old Microsoft Mail program. We'll also cover some special situations you might encounter.

Retaining Messages on the Server

One of the most frequently asked questions about the Microsoft Mail service in Exchange is whether it's possible to leave messages on the server. Exchange normally downloads all messages into your Exchange message store and deletes them from the postoffice. If you log on from different locations and want to see your messages, or if you are still using Microsoft Mail (without Exchange) from some workstations, this can be a problem.

The key to keeping messages on the server is to always use Remote Mail, even when you're connected to the LAN.

In the standalone Microsoft Mail application, this problem was solved with a feature called *inbox shadowing* that allowed you to leave messages on the server. Exchange does not have any similar feature. However, you can achieve the same result through diligent use of Remote Mail to get all your messages.

The key is to configure Microsoft Mail so that you can use Remote Mail even when you're directly connected to the LAN. Do this with the Use Remote Mail setting described earlier under "LAN Configuration," page 122. Then always use Tools, Remote Mail (see Chapter 13, "Working Remotely") to retrieve headers for your messages and mark to retrieve a copy. You can also mark messages for deletion when you are sure you won't need them any longer.

Another way to make sure that messages stay on the server is to temporarily disable Exchange's ability to retrieve Microsoft Mail messages. Here's how:

1. Choose Tools, Services and bring up the properties for Microsoft Mail.
2. Switch to the Delivery tab.
3. Clear the box for "Enable incoming mail delivery."
4. Click the OK box to save the change, which takes effect immediately without the need to restart Exchange.

Activating Shared Folders

If you have used the Exchange version that comes with Windows 95, you probably noticed that Microsoft Mail shared folders were not available. As noted at the beginning of this chapter (under "Requirements"), you need to install an update to get access to shared folders. But there's a little more to it than that. While new profiles can see shared folders just fine, old ones can't.

To gain access to Microsoft Mail shared folders with an old profile, you must remove the Microsoft Mail service from that profile, then add it back to the profile. That makes the change needed so you can work with shared folders.

Adding Microsoft Mail to an Exchange Server Client

If you look back at the sidebar "Installing and Updating the Exchange Server Client," page 103 in Chapter 5, you'll notice that there is an option for adding the Microsoft Mail service. What if somehow you overlooked that during the installation? How do you go back and add the Microsoft Mail service to a computer where the Exchange Server client is installed? Here's the procedure to follow:

1. Go to the Control Panel, and start the Add/Remove Programs applet.

2. On the Install/Uninstall tab, select Microsoft Exchange from the list of programs at the bottom of the dialog box. Then click the Add/Remove button. This starts the Microsoft Exchange Setup program. You may be prompted to insert the Exchange CD or diskette, the same one that you used to install the Exchange Server client.

3. In the Microsoft Exchange Setup dialog box, click the Add/Remove button.

4. In the Microsoft Exchange - Maintenance dialog box, select Exchange under Options, then click the Change Option button.

5. In the Microsoft Exchange - Exchange dialog box, select Information Services under Options, then click the Change Option button.

6. In the Microsoft Exchange - Information Services dialog box (Figure 6.20), check the box for Microsoft Mail, then click OK twice to return to the Microsoft Exchange - Maintenance dialog box.

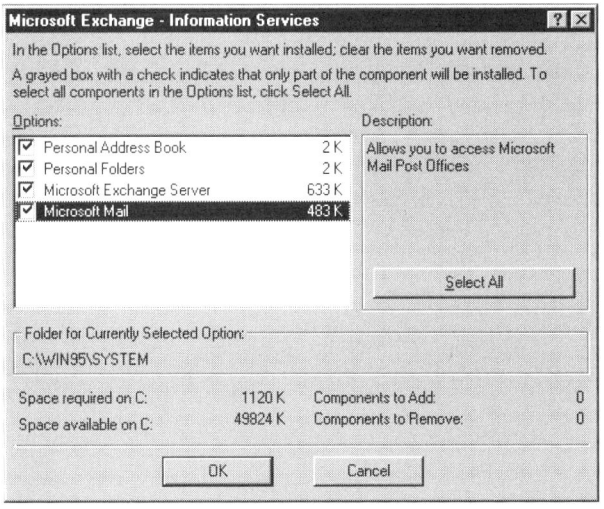

Figure 6.20
For Microsoft Exchange Server clients, use the setup program to add Microsoft Mail if you didn't do so when you installed the client software.

7. In the Microsoft Exchange - Maintenance dialog box, click the Continue button to complete the installation of the Microsoft Mail service. If you installed the Exchange Server client from diskettes, you will be asked to insert one or more disks as part of the process.

After the Microsoft Mail service is installed, you can add it to one or more Exchange profiles. Note that we added Microsoft Mail using the Microsoft Exchange entry on the Install/Uninstall tab of the Add/Remove Programs applet, not by using the Microsoft Exchange or Windows Messaging entry on the Windows Setup tab.

Checking the Delivery Order

If you have both the Microsoft Exchange Server and Microsoft Mail services installed in your Exchange profile, then the delivery order may affect your replies to messages from Microsoft Mail users. This order is part of the profile settings and governs what service delivers a message when more than one service is capable of doing it (see "Delivery Settings," page 74 in Chapter 4). This is an issue only when the Microsoft Exchange Server is set up to transfer messages to and from a full Microsoft Mail server; it does not affect workgroup postoffices (those created with Windows 95, Windows NT, or Windows for Workgroups).

In this case, if the Microsoft Exchange Server service is first, then a Microsoft Mail recipient will see your new Exchange Server mailbox (actually what's known as a "proxy address") as the return address. If the Microsoft Mail service is first, then the Microsoft Mail recipient sees your old Microsoft Mail address as the return address.

To help with the transition from Microsoft Mail to Microsoft Exchange Server, it's best to put the Microsoft Exchange Server service first. Follow these steps:

1. From the Exchange Viewer menu, choose Tools, Options, then switch to the Delivery tab in the Options dialog box.

2. In the delivery order list at the bottom of the Delivery tab, select the Microsoft Mail service.

3. Use the down arrow to move Microsoft Mail so that it appears below Microsoft Exchange Transport and Microsoft Exchange Remote Transport on the delivery list.

4. Click OK to close the Options dialog box.

This change becomes effective after you quit and restart Exchange.

Summary

Microsoft Mail is one of the most powerful services available for Exchange. Microsoft Mail supports both LAN and remote use and includes many flexible settings for tailoring its operation to your needs. One configuration that is not supported by Microsoft is using Exchange to retrieve Microsoft Mail from one workstation but using the original Microsoft Mail application from another machine. For best results, you should go with Exchange across the board. If you need to log on to your Microsoft Mail account from multiple workstations, then make sure your primary message store is either an Exchange Server mailbox or a Personal Folders file located on a network drive, so you can access it from anywhere.

Key Points

- Microsoft Mail is a mail service for organizations, not individuals.
- If you have old Microsoft Mail messages, put them where Exchange can find them to import them.
- Microsoft Mail offers many ways to schedule automatic connections.
- The key to keeping messages on the server is to always use Remote Mail, even when you're connected to the LAN.

For More Information

Once you've configured remote access for Microsoft Mail, you'll want to learn how to use it in Chapter 13, "Working Remotely."

A number of the procedures in this chapter require familiarity with DUN. See Chapter 3, "Making Connections," for details about how to use DUN for remote access.

If you're using Microsoft Mail for the first time and have been given responsibility to manage the postoffice, all the information you need is in Chapter 23, "Managing a Workgroup Postoffice."

Chapter 7

Setting Up Microsoft Fax

With the Microsoft Fax service, you can

- Send messages as faxes
- Receive faxes
- Send documents as faxes by printing them from any Windows program
- Send and receive editable documents and executable programs from other Microsoft Fax (and compatible software) users

The capability to exchange not just faxes, but the actual documents themselves, is called *binary file transfer* (BFT). This feature turns Microsoft Fax into a point-to-point electronic mail system, making it easy for a writer to send an article directly to an editor or for a sales representative to send a proposal, without requiring e-mail accounts for everyone involved.

Requirements

To use Microsoft Fax, you must have

- Windows 95
- A compatible modem attached to a telephone line or access to a computer elsewhere on your network that is running Microsoft Fax with a modem attached

The Microsoft Fax service does not ship with Windows NT 4.0. Instead, Microsoft has developed an add-on called Personal Fax for Windows NT (see Appendix D), which can be downloaded from the Microsoft Web site. For information about alternative fax services, see "WinFax PRO 7.0," page 210 in Chapter 9, and "Using Third-Party Fax Services," page 335 in Chapter 14.

The fax modem can be located either on your local system or on a network fax server that is also running Exchange. There are three common types of fax modems. Microsoft Fax supports two of them — Class 1 and Class 2. Class 1 fax modems can send documents to each other as binary files — that is, as editable documents or executable programs. Class 1 fax modems also can send and receive in facsimile format. Class 2 fax modems can send and receive in facsimile format only.

The third common type of fax modem, CAS, is not supported by Microsoft Fax. However, a firmware revision is available from Pure Data for the Intel SatisFAXtion 400i CAS modem to make it compatible with Class 1 (see Appendix B, "Exchange Resources," for contact information).

Basic Setup

The following sections look at the Microsoft Fax setup from two different points of view, based on whether you installed Microsoft Fax as part of the Windows installation or you are adding it later.

If You Installed Microsoft Fax During Windows 95 Setup

If you chose to install Microsoft Fax when Windows 95 was set up, you were prompted to give the following information:

- What modem to use
- Your name
- Your return fax number
- Your country

Checking Out Your Modem

On a Windows 95 system, you can determine the fax class of your modem through a diagnostic tool built into the Modems applet in the Control Panel. Follow these steps:

1. Click the Start button, point to Settings, and then click Control Panel.
2. In the Control Panel folder, double-click the Modems icon.
3. Switch to the Diagnostics tab.
4. Select your modem, then click the More Info button.
5. In a moment, you'll see the More Info dialog box, shown in Figure 7.A. The fax class information is at the bottom of the Command/Response list, in the listing for the command AT +FCLASS=?. In Figure 7.A, the listed modem supports both Class 1 and Class 2 fax.

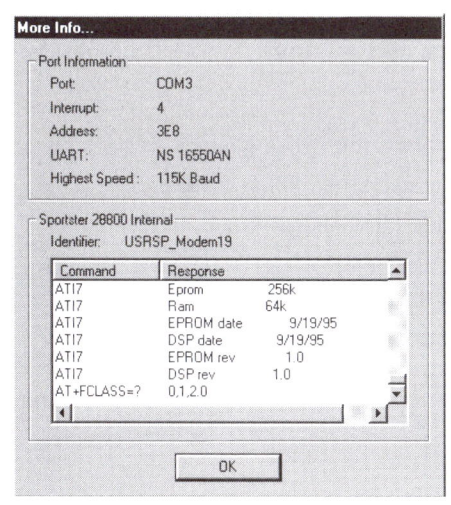

Figure 7.A
Diagnostic information about your modem is available from the Modems applet in the Control Panel.

Exchange then added Microsoft Fax to the default profile with default settings that work for most users. Before using Microsoft Fax for the first time, you should

• Check for the presence of the Microsoft Fax printer driver
• Confirm your name and other user settings
• Update the Dialing Properties, if necessary

Check for the presence of the Microsoft Fax printer driver. If your system had no modem when you did the setup, Microsoft Fax will be missing an essential component — the Microsoft Fax printer driver. Without this printer driver, you cannot send faxes in facsimile format. Therefore, it's a good idea to check for the presence of this driver even if you did have a modem when Microsoft Fax was installed.

To check for the Microsoft Fax printer driver and re-install it if necessary,

1. Click the Start button, point to Settings, and then click Printers.
2. If the Microsoft Fax icon is not present, proceed to Step 3. If you do see the Microsoft Fax icon, proceed to Step 5.
3. Click the Start button, then click Run.
4. In the Open box, type the following file name, then click OK:

      Awadpr32.exe

   Running the Awadpr32.exe program builds the Microsoft Fax printer driver.
5. Close the Printers folder.

Confirm your name and other user settings. To view and, if needed, change these settings,

1. Click the Start button, point to Settings, then click Control Panel.
2. In the Control Panel folder, double-click the Mail and Fax icon.
3. In the Properties dialog box, double-click Microsoft Fax to display its properties.
4. Switch to the User tab, which is shown in Figure 7.1.
5. Once you've made any desired changes to your user information, click OK to save the changes and return to the Properties dialog box. Then click OK again to close the Properties dialog box and return to the Control Panel.

If you already have Exchange running, another way to get to your user settings is to choose Tools, Microsoft Fax Options from the main menu, then switch to the User tab. For more information about the user settings and how they work with cover pages, see "Editing User Information" later in this chapter.

Update the dialing properties, if necessary. If you need to dial 9 or another number to use an outside line, use a telephone credit card, or use call waiting, then you should reconfigure the dialing properties that Windows 95 uses. See "Configuring Dialing Locations," page 28 in Chapter 3. Once you've

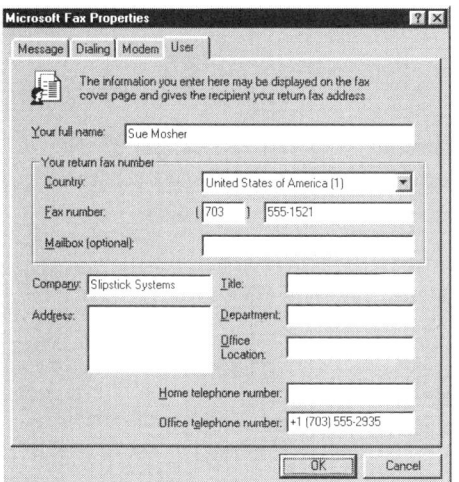

Figure 7.1
*Before sending your
first fax, confirm the
settings for your name
and phone number
on the User tab.*

checked the dialing properties, you're ready to send your first fax, which we will discuss in Chapter 14, "Sending Faxes."

If You're Installing Microsoft Fax for the First Time

On a machine where Microsoft Fax has not been installed, you need to

- Add a fax modem to your system if you don't have one already (unless you are planning to fax through a network fax server).
- Install the Microsoft Fax service.
- Add Microsoft Fax to your Exchange profile.
- Confirm your name and other user settings (see the previous section if you need help doing this).
- Update the dialing properties, as described in the previous section.

Add a fax modem. As we discussed under "Requirements" at the beginning of this chapter, this must be either a Class 1 or a Class 2 modem.

Install Microsoft Fax. To add Microsoft Fax to a Windows 95 system, follow these steps:

1. Click the Start button, point to Settings, then click Control Panel.
2. In the Control Panel folder, double-click Add/Remove Programs.
3. Switch to the Windows Setup tab.
4. Check the box next to Microsoft Fax.

5. Click OK to close Add/Remove Programs and add Microsoft Fax to your system, inserting a CD or disk as prompted.

6. If you are notified that you need to restart Windows, do so.

Special Note

There are two special considerations for using Microsoft Fax with the Exchange Server client or Windows Messaging update. First, you cannot add the Microsoft Fax service to your computer after installing either of these versions. You must first do the installation in this order:

1. Install the Windows 95 operating system client and Microsoft Fax.

2. Make a backup copy of Mapisvc.inf.

3. Install the Exchange Server client or Windows Messaging update.

If you already have the Exchange Server client and want to add MIcrosoft Fax, then remove the Exchange Server client first and follow the above procedure. Do the same if you have the Windows Messaging update and want to add Microsoft Fax.

Second, even if you follow the above installation sequence, you may no longer be able to add Microsoft Fax to a profile because of a damaged Mapisvc.inf. That's the reason for step 2 above. Use the backup copy of Mapisvc.inf to restore missing information as described in "Restoring a Missing Service," page 529 in Chapter 24.

Using the Setup Wizard

Once Microsoft Fax has been installed through the Control Panel, you can add it to one or more Exchange profiles. There are two ways to do this — using the Setup Wizard or manually. The Setup Wizard is available only when you create a new profile through the Mail and Fax (or Mail) applet in the Control Panel.

To add a profile using the Setup Wizard, follow these steps:

1. Run the Mail and Fax (or Mail) applet in the Control Panel.

2. Click the Show Profiles button.

3. Choose Add.

4. In the first screen of the Setup Wizard, choose "Use the following information services" and check the ones you want, in this case being sure to include Microsoft Fax.

5. Click Next to continue, and give the profile a name on the next screen of the wizard; then click Next again to begin configuring Microsoft Fax and any other services you selected.

Here are the steps in the wizard that are specific to Microsoft Fax:

1. The wizard asks you to choose a fax modem. Any modems installed on your system are listed in the "Select a fax modem" box (see Figure 7.2.) If the modem you want to use is already listed, select it, then click the Next button and skip to step 3.

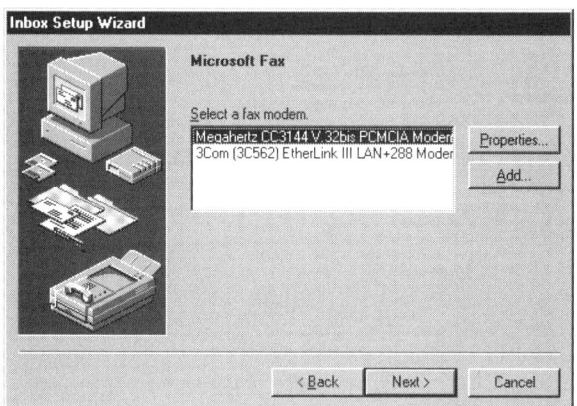

Figure 7.2
The first step in adding Microsoft Fax to a profile is to decide what modem to use.

2. If you need to install a new modem or use a network fax server, click the Add button. The Add a Fax Modem dialog box (Figure 7.3) appears. To install a new modem, select "Fax modem" and click OK, then follow the steps in the Install New Modem wizard. To connect to a network fax modem, select "Network fax server" and click OK. Enter the Path to the network fax server in the Connect to Network Fax Server dialog box, then click OK. When you have finished adding modems, click OK to close the Add a Fax Modem dialog box (for more information about using a network fax modem, see "Connecting to a Network Fax Server" later in this chapter). On the Setup Wizard (Figure 7.2), select the modem you want to use for faxing, then click the Next button.

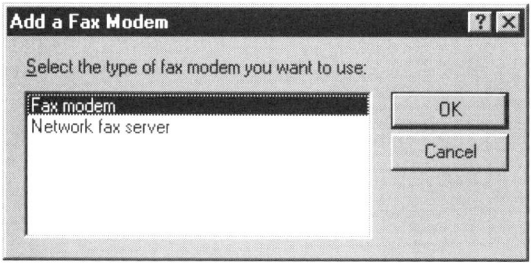

Figure 7.3
You can add either a new fax modem installed on your computer or a fax modem installed on a computer running Microsoft Fax elsewhere on the network.

3. In the second screen of the Setup Wizard (Figure 7.4), indicate whether you want Microsoft Fax to answer all incoming calls. Click the Next button to continue.

Figure 7.4

You can set Microsoft Fax to answer all incoming calls.

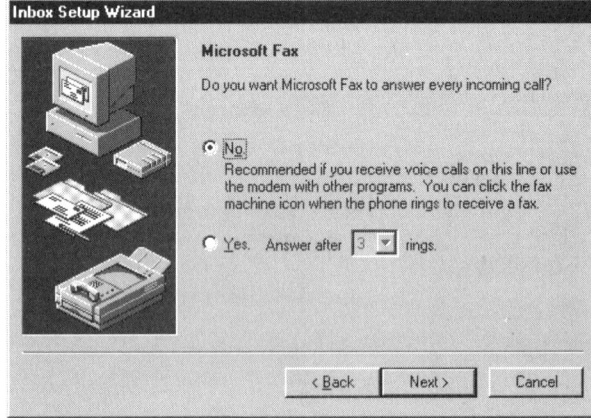

4. Finally, enter "Your full name," "Country," and "Fax number," as shown in Figure 7.5. Click Next to continue and finish answering the questions posed by the Setup Wizard about other services.

Figure 7.5

The last Microsoft Fax information requested by the Setup Wizard is your name and complete fax number, including country code.

Once you've completed the Setup Wizard, use the Mail and Fax (or Mail) applet in the Control Panel to bring up the properties for the Microsoft Fax service to check the settings. In particular, see the instructions earlier in this chapter for how to "Update the dialing properties, if necessary" (page 136) and check the section "Editing User Information" (page 149).

Manually Configuring Microsoft Fax

If you are not creating a completely new profile, there's no wizard to help you. You must manually configure the Microsoft Fax service as part of the process of adding it to an existing profile (see "Adding a Service," page 79 in Chapter 4). To add Microsoft Fax to a profile,

1. Click the Start button, and choose Settings, Control Panel. Then start the Mail and Fax (or Mail) applet.

2. If the profile you want to work with isn't the default profile, click the Show Profiles button. Select the profile you want to modify, then click the Properties button.

3. On the Services tab, click the Add button.

4. In the Add Service to Profile dialog box, select Microsoft Fax, then click OK.

5. Answer Yes when you're asked whether you want to specify your fax details. If you don't have this information handy, you can answer No, in which case you'll be prompted for this information the next time you run Exchange.

6. In the Microsoft Fax Properties dialog box, fill in the information on the User tab (see Figure 7.1 in the previous section). Your name and return fax number (with country) are required. It's also a good idea to add your company name, if appropriate, and your office or home telephone number, so people will know how to reach you if there's a problem with your fax.

7. When you've completed the user information, switch to the Modem tab (Figure 7.6), where you should see the modem(s) installed on your system. If you want to fax with a modem installed on your system, select the modem, then click the Set as Active Fax Modem button. If you want to fax with a network fax modem, see "Connecting to a Network Fax Server" later in this chapter.

8. Click OK to close the Microsoft Fax Properties dialog box to complete the basic installation of the Microsoft Fax service.

There are a number of other settings for the Microsoft Fax service that you may want to review; the "Options" section later in this chapter details them all.

Figure 7.6

A fax modem can be either local or on another machine on the network. You can also share your own fax modem with other Microsoft Fax users.

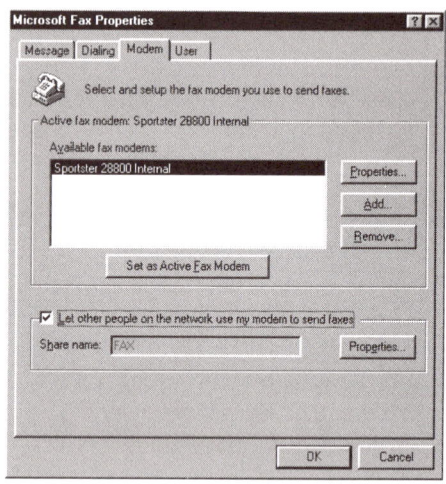

Microsoft Fax on a Network

Microsoft Fax works both on a standalone PC and in a network environment. One modem can send and receive faxes for a group of people. The machine where this modem is located is called the *fax server*.

Setting Up a Fax Server

A network fax server must be running Exchange at all times.

The first step in establishing a fax server is to decide which machine to use. Here are some key issues to consider:

- The fax server must be running Exchange at all times. This arrangement leaves fewer resources for other applications; so if you plan to run other programs on the fax server, you should use a relatively fast machine with 16 MB or more of RAM.

- You normally can't use the same machine both as a fax server that sends and receives faxes and as a dial-up networking (DUN) host for remote users to connect to. If both DUN and Microsoft Fax are active on the same machine, DUN will always take the incoming call and you will not be able to receive incoming faxes. This is not a problem, however, if you use the fax server only for outgoing faxes. See "Sharing a Modem Between Microsoft Fax and Dial-Up Networking" on page 174 for other approaches to this problem.

- If you are receiving faxes on a machine using the version of Exchange that comes with Windows 95, someone at the fax server may need to print out or forward all incoming faxes. (The client that comes with Exchange Server does allow automatic forwarding and printing through the use of the Inbox Assistant, discussed in Chapter 18, "Exchange Assistants," page 411. Another approach to managing incoming faxes is to use the Print Fax utility included on the CD.)

- The network fax server needs to have plenty of hard-drive space to hold incoming and outgoing faxes; this storage requirement can easily be 100K or larger.

A Windows for Workgroups system running Microsoft Mail cannot send faxes through a Windows 95 Microsoft Fax server. The reverse is also true: A Windows 95 PC using Microsoft Fax cannot send a fax through a Windows for Workgroups machine acting as a fax server using the At-Work Fax capability of Mail. While Microsoft promised a patch when Windows 95 was released to resolve this incompatibility, such a patch has not been delivered.

Special Note

To use a system as a Microsoft Fax server, you will need to

- Enable file sharing
- Designate a modem as a shared fax modem
- Share the folder that will be used by Exchange for network faxes

Enable file sharing. If you haven't done it already, change your system settings to allow other users access to files stored on your system. For details, see "Sharing Network Resources," page 57 in Chapter 3.

Designate a modem as a shared fax modem. To do this, follow these steps:

1. In Exchange, choose Tools, Microsoft Fax Tools, Options. (You also can use the Control Panel's Mail and Fax (or Mail) applet to open the properties dialog box for Microsoft Fax.)

2. In the Microsoft Fax Properties dialog box, switch to the Modem tab, shown previously in Figure 7.6.

3. Check the box marked "Let other people on the network use my modem to send faxes." If you have more than one drive on your system, you'll be asked which drive you want to use for the shared fax folder. You cannot put the shared fax folder on a different machine; the folder must be on a local drive.

4. Click OK to close the Microsoft Fax Properties dialog box, which completes the process of sharing the fax modem.

Sharing the fax modem creates a new folder called NetFax on the drive you indicate. This folder is shared with the default share name FAX. If you are using share-level security on Windows 95, the folder is automatically shared with Full access.

If you are working with user-level security on a Windows 95 machine, you will need to grant access to different users and groups explicitly. Return to the Microsoft Fax Properties dialog box, switch to the Modem tab, then click the Properties button next to the "Share name" box. You can then use the Add and Remove buttons to grant access to people who need to send faxes.

Connecting to a Network Fax Server

Once the network fax server is running Exchange with Microsoft Fax installed and its fax modem shared, other workstations can start connecting to the server. You must know the path to the network fax server. This path is a combination of the fax server's computer name (which you can see in Network Neighborhood) and the share name given to the NetFax folder; FAX is the default share name. For example, if the computer name is Faxmanager, the path would be \\Faxmanager\fax. If you don't know the name of the computer, you can browse Network Neighborhood, shown in Figure 7.7 as you see it in Explorer, to find a folder named fax.

Figure 7.7

Locate the fax server in Network Neighborhood, usually as a shared folder named fax.

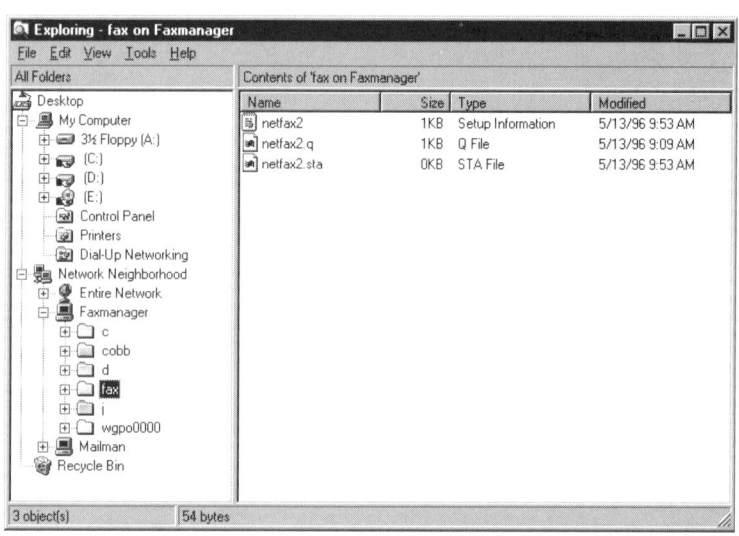

To connect to a network fax server,

1. In Exchange, choose Tools, Microsoft Fax Tools, Options. (You can also use the Control Panel's Mail and Fax (or Mail) applet to open the properties dialog box for Microsoft Fax.)

2. In the Microsoft Fax Properties dialog box, switch to the Modem tab.

3. Click the Add button.

4. In the Add a Fax Modem dialog box, select Network Fax Server, then click OK.

5. In the Connect to Network Fax Server dialog box, enter the path, such as \\Faxmanager\fax, then click the OK button to return to the Microsoft Fax Properties dialog box.

6. If you see more than one modem on the Modem tab, select the modem represented by the network fax path you just entered (rather than a locally installed modem), then click the Set as Active Fax Modem button.

7. Click OK to close the Microsoft Fax Properties dialog box.

If the network fax modem is the first fax modem installed on this machine, you should check for the presence of the Microsoft Fax printer driver, as described in "If You Installed Microsoft Fax During Windows 95 Setup" earlier in this chapter, and install the driver if it is not present.

Options

While the default settings for Microsoft Fax enabled by the Setup Wizard will certainly get you started, you will probably want to review those options to make sure they fit the way you plan to send faxes. Table 7.1 summarizes the settings available in Microsoft Fax. In the next few sections, we'll examine these settings in detail.

Table 7.1 Settings for Microsoft Fax

Setting	Default
Cover Page Settings	
Use a cover page	Yes
Default cover page	Generic (Generic.cpe)
User Information (appears on cover pages)	
Name	As entered in the Setup Wizard
Country	As entered in the Setup Wizard
Fax number	As entered in the Setup Wizard
Mailbox (options)	(blank)
Company	(blank)
Address	(blank)
Title	(blank)
Department	(blank)
Office location	(blank)
Home telephone number	(blank)
Office telephone number	(blank)
Message Settings	
Time to send	As soon as possible
Message format	Editable, if possible
Paper size/orientation	Letter 8.5 x 11 inches, portrait orientation, best available image quality

continued

Table 7.1 Settings for Microsoft Fax, continued

Setting	Default
Show incoming faxes with a fax icon or with an editable subject line and a file attachment	With a fax icon
Dialing Settings	
Dialing properties	Default Location: tone dialing, no pre-fixes to reach an outside line, disable call waiting, and no calling card
Prefixes within your area code that need a + 1 + area code	(blank)
Retries	Retry 3 times, with 2 minutes between retries
Modem Settings	
Answer mode	Auto-answer or don't answer, depending on your choice in the Setup Wizard
Speaker volume	Turn off after a connection is made
Call preferences	Wait for a dial tone before calling, hang up if busy, and wait 60 seconds for an answer
Error handling	Error correction enabled; accept incoming fax pages with a high number of errors
Maximum fax transmission/ reception speed	Depends on the modem; some default to 9,600 rather than 14,400 bps
Force operation as a Class 2 fax machine	Disabled
Compression	Disabled

Cover Pages

The first thing you'll probably want to change after you install Microsoft Fax is the cover page and the information about you that the cover page displays. To access the cover page settings, choose Tools, Microsoft Fax Tools, Options to display the Microsoft Fax Properties dialog box, shown in Figure 7.8. (You can also work with these settings in Control Panel, Mail and Fax, by bringing up the Properties for the Microsoft Fax service.)

Figure 7.8

Select the cover page you want to use from those listed on the Message tab of the Microsoft Fax Properties dialog box.

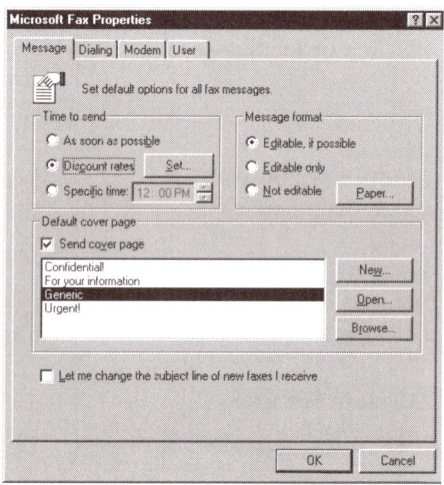

Setting the Default Cover Page

U.S. law requires each fax transmission to be clearly identified.

Microsoft Fax includes the following four cover pages, which you can customize or copy to create new cover pages. They are stored as .cpe files in your Windows folder.

- Confidential!
- For your information
- Generic
- Urgent!

The Generic cover page is set as the default when Microsoft Fax is installed. To change the default cover page, select the cover page you want to use from those listed on the Message tab of the Microsoft Fax Properties dialog box (Figure 7.8). We'll discuss editing and creating cover pages in "Using the Cover Page Editor" a little later in this chapter. If a company cover page has been created for your organization — perhaps with your company logo — and the cover page is stored on a network server, choose Browse to locate it. A shortcut to that cover page will be added to your Windows folder and the name of that cover page will appear in the list on the Message tab.

You probably noticed that you can disable the sending of a cover page as a default setting for faxes. U.S. law requires each fax transmission to be clearly identified with the sender, sender's phone number, and date and time of the transmission (see the sidebar "Fax Legalities"). Therefore, it's recommended that you select a cover page for use with Microsoft Fax as a default. You will still be able to disable the cover page for individual faxes if, for example, the document you're faxing already includes that identifying information.

Editing User Information

When you use the Setup Wizard to install Microsoft Fax, the wizard queries you for only a minimum of information — your name, country, and fax number. However, the cover pages that come with Microsoft Fax include fields for your company name, address, and office and home phone numbers. These fields will be left blank unless you fill them in on the User tab of the Microsoft Fax Properties dialog box (Figure 7.1).

Fax Legalities

The U.S. Telephone Consumer Protection Act of 1991 requires that fax transmissions be identified clearly with the

- Name of the person or organization sending the fax
- Sender's phone number (either fax or voice)
- Date and time the fax was sent

Standalone fax machines and many fax programs meet these requirements with a header at the top of each fax page. Microsoft Fax does not support the fax page header. Therefore, you must either use a cover page with your name and number on it or include that information on the first page of the document you are faxing.

Also note that you are not allowed to fax unsolicited advertisements, except to someone with whom you have an existing business relationship. If a customer or prospect in such a relationship asks you to stop sending faxes, you must honor that request.

If you don't want to show your home telephone number on fax cover pages, you can either leave the Home Telephone Number field blank on the User tab, or remove it from the cover page completely with the Cover Page Editor.

If your organization has Exchange Server or an Exchange add-on capable of routing inbound faxes, then check with your system administrator to find out what you should use in the Mailbox box to identify those faxes intended for you. When you enter a Mailbox, Exchange adds this to your fax number so that recipients see your return fax address as "mailbox@+1 (703) 555-1234" or whatever your fax number is, where *mailbox* is the information you entered in the Mailbox field.

Other Message Defaults

You can change the cover page or override any other message default for a particular fax.

When and how your message is sent is governed by the settings on the Message tab in the Microsoft Fax Properties dialog box (Figure 7.8). Keep in mind that these are default settings. You can change any of them for a particular fax transmission.

For example, you may choose to have most faxes sent when rates are lowest. But for a fax that needs to be transmitted right now, you can change the "Time to send" to "As soon as possible." You can do this by choosing File, Send Options if you're working in a message window or by clicking the Options button if you're using the Compose New Fax wizard.

Time to Send

Three choices are available for the default "Time to send" a fax:

- As soon as possible
- Discount rates
- Specific time

The first two choices, "As soon as possible" and "Discount rates," are the most commonly used. If you choose "Discount rates," then click the Set button to display the Set Discount Rates dialog box, where you need to tell Microsoft Fax when discounted phone rates begin and end. The default is for discount rates to start at 5:00 p.m. and to end at 8:00 a.m.

Message Format

Microsoft Fax offers two ways for you to send information. As mentioned at the beginning of this chapter, in addition to fax images that can be printed out, you also can (under certain conditions) send the actual documents, a technique called *binary file transfer* or BFT (see "Sending a File (BFT)," page 324 in Chapter 14).

The distinction between these two types of transmissions is made on the Message tab (Figure 7.4). A message that you want to send only as a facsimile image is a *non-editable* message. A message that you'd like to send as the document itself is an *editable* message. You have three choices for Message Format:

- Editable, if possible
- Editable only
- Not editable

The default is to send all messages "Editable, if possible." This is the best choice for general use, because it means that recipients will get your messages by the most efficient transmission means available. If the recipient is using Microsoft Fax, WinFax PRO 7.0, or another application capable of BFT, the document you send can be opened on the recipient's system. If the recipient has a paper fax machine or fax software that doesn't support BFT, a facsimile image will be received.

Also shown under Message Format on the Message tab is a Paper button. Use this to set the default paper size and orientation for your transmissions to paper fax machines and non-BFT fax software. See the Message Format dialog box shown in Figure 7.9.

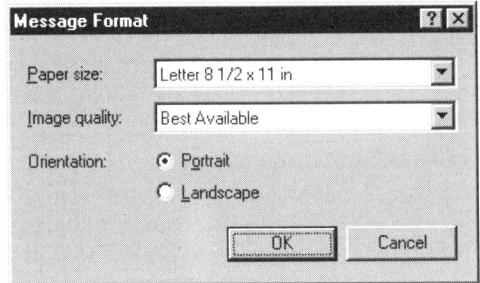

Figure 7.9
Set the paper size, orientation, and image quality for fax format transmissions with the Message Format dialog box.

Choose either Letter or A4 for "Paper size," depending on which your recipients are more likely to use. For "Image quality," keep the default, Best Available. Under Orientation, the default Portrait is suitable unless you are planning to send most of your faxes in Landscape format, with a landscape cover page included.

Let Me Change the Subject Line ...

This setting, whose full title is "Let me change the subject line of new faxes I receive," controls a lot more than you might think; it even governs how faxes appear in the Inbox. Table 7.2 summarizes the results of checking and unchecking this box.

Table 7.2 Controlling How Faxes Appear in the Inbox		
	"Let me change the subject line of new faxes I receive"	
	Checked (=enabled)	Unchecked (=disabled)
Can change the subject line of incoming faxes	Yes	No
Appearance of new faxes in Inbox folder	Envelope icon + paper clip	Fax machine icon
Procedure to view fax	Open message, then double-click fax icon in the body of the message (2 steps)	Open message (1 step)

If you're mostly concerned about finding faxes quickly in your Inbox and viewing them, then disable this setting by clearing the "Let me change the subject line..." box. If, on the other hand, you like to refile incoming faxes in other folders, possibly changing the subject lines, and you don't mind taking an extra step to open a fax, then check the "Let me change the subject line..." box.

Dialing and Modem Properties

Earlier in this chapter, we discussed how to set up the modem that you use for faxing — either a local modem installed on your machine or a network fax modem on another system. One of the first things you may need to do after installing Microsoft Fax is to adjust the way Exchange dials out. In this section, you'll also learn how to avoid conflicts with other communications programs.

Dialing Properties

Do you need to configure such things as a prefix to access an outside line or to disable call waiting? If so, then on the Dialing tab of the Microsoft Fax Properties dialog box, shown in Figure 7.10, click the Dialing Properties button to bring up the My Locations dialog box, which we discuss in detail in "Configuring Dialing Locations," page 28 in Chapter 3. If you are faxing through a network fax server, these settings will have no effect. The dialing properties on the fax server itself are the ones that will be used.

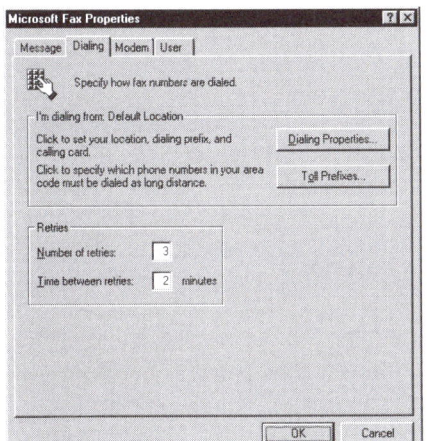

Figure 7.10

From the Dialing tab, configure the way your fax modem dials. The Dialing Properties button lets you add codes for call waiting, credit cards, and access prefixes.

Toll Prefixes

In some cases, you might be in a city where you need to dial a number in your area code as if it were a long-distance number. In the U.S. and Canada, this means that you'd dial 1, then the area code, then the number. Usually, the numbers that need to be dialed this way can be distinguished by their prefix — that is, by the first three digits of the local number.

To specify that numbers with certain prefixes be dialed as long-distance numbers, click the Toll Prefixes button. In the Toll Prefixes dialog box (Figure 7.11), select in the left column those prefixes to be dialed as long-distance numbers and use the Add button to move the prefixes to the right column.

Note that the Toll Prefixes list only lets you specify which local numbers need full 1 + area code dialing. If you have numbers that need to use the area code, but without the initial 1, see "Handling Multiple Local Area Codes," page 342 in Chapter 14.

Figure 7.11

Some local numbers may need to be dialed as long-distance numbers. Select the prefixes for these numbers in the Toll Prefixes dialog box.

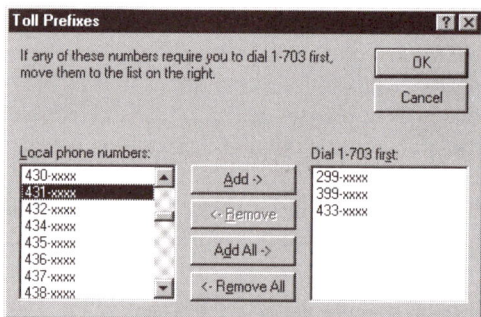

Retries

If Microsoft Fax gets a busy signal or does not find a working fax machine at the number for the recipient, it will retry the number several times. Enter the number of retries you prefer in the "Number of retries" box on the Dialing tab of the Microsoft Fax Properties dialog box. The default is three retries. Set the "Time between retries" to the number of minutes you prefer. The default is two minutes.

Special Note

Other conditions that cause a fax to fail, such as a noisy phone line, will not necessarily result in Microsoft Fax retrying the number. If you use the Hang Up button on the Fax Status dialog box (see "When You Send a Fax," page 324 in Chapter 14) to abort a fax transmission, the number definitely will not be retried. Also, Microsoft Fax does not keep any record of how many retries it makes for a given fax message.

Modem Properties

We first visited the Modem tab on the Microsoft Fax Properties dialog box earlier in this chapter (Figure 7.6) when we installed and connected to a network fax modem. You should already be familiar with the use of the Add button to add a new fax modem and the Set as Active Fax Modem button to tell Exchange which modem to use if you have more than one modem. Let's turn now to the properties you can set for a fax modem on your local system and for a network fax modem.

Properties for Local Fax Modems

On the Modem tab, select a modem (a local modem, not a network fax modem), then click the Properties button. You'll see the Fax Modem Properties dialog box (Figure 7.12). You can also open this dialog box with the fax machine icon that appears in the Windows taskbar when you have Exchange loaded. Right-click on that icon, then on <u>M</u>odem Properties.

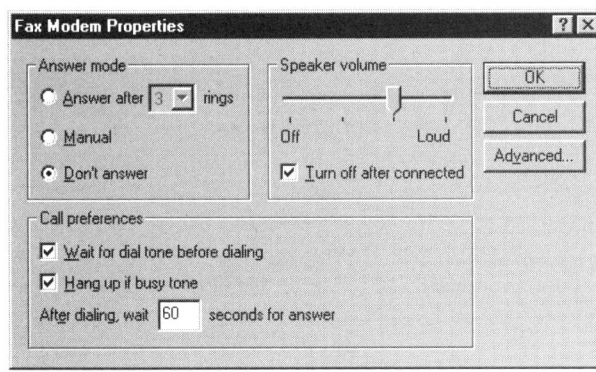

Figure 7.12
The most important properties of your fax modem are in the Fax Modem Properties dialog box.

The most important setting for the fax modem has to do with how it responds to incoming calls, as listed under "Answer mode." Your choices are

Answer after 2–10 rings   Choose this if you want Microsoft Fax to automatically answer all incoming calls to your modem.

Manual   Exchange pops up a dialog box when an incoming call is detected, asking you whether or not you want Microsoft Fax to answer.

Don't answer   With this setting, there is no detection of incoming calls, but you can still use the Answer Now button in the Microsoft Fax Status dialog box to respond to an incoming call. This setting is a good one to choose if your fax phone line also rings somewhere else and you don't want the fax modem to answer automatically.

If you still use communications programs designed for Windows 3.x, you will have problems if Microsoft Fax is set to either automatic or manual answering, because other communications programs will not be able to gain access to your modem. Either exit Exchange or switch to "<u>D</u>on't answer" before using those other applications. Once all your communications programs are 32-bit versions using the Telephony Application Programming Interface (TAPI) built into Windows 95 to facilitate sharing of modems by different programs, this problem will no longer exist.

Note that if you do choose automatic answering, the minimum number of rings is two; this is a limitation of Microsoft Fax. The fax modem takes several seconds to initialize once it detects the incoming call, so it can't answer on the first ring.

Also in the Fax Modem Properties dialog box are other assorted preferences for placing calls and listening to the connection dialog.

For troubleshooting fax connection problems, click the Advanced button. You should try the first four settings in the Advanced dialog box (shown in Figure 7.13) one at a time if you're having problems. You can also adjust the tolerance for rejecting pages with errors. If you choose very low tolerance, Microsoft Fax rejects incoming faxes with even a small number of errors.

Figure 7.13
The Advanced dialog box for modem properties is used mainly for troubleshooting.

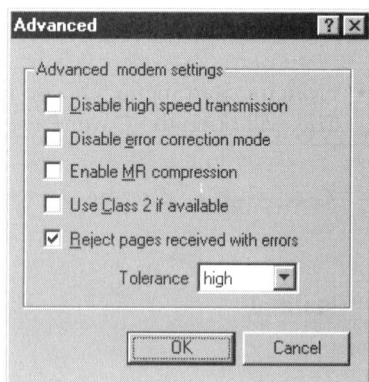

Network Fax Modem Status Checks

You can set only one property for a network fax modem: how often the queue on the fax server will be checked to see how your faxes are doing. To set this property, select a network fax modem on the Modem tab, then click the Properties button to display the Configure Network Fax dialog box, shown in Figure 7.14. Adjust the time to Very often, Often, or Rarely.

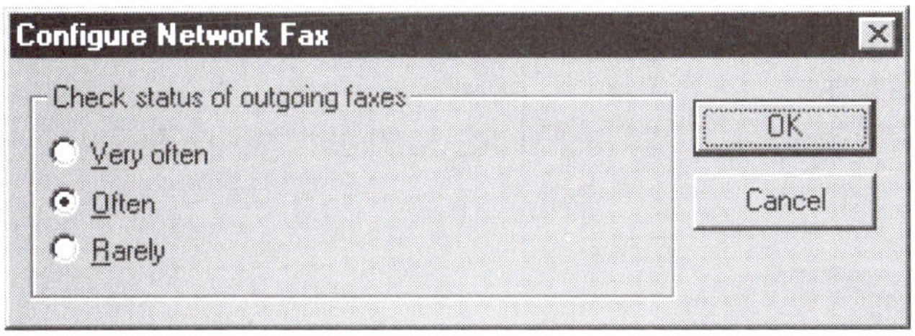

Figure 7.14
You can control how often Exchange checks the status of any faxes you've sent to the network fax server.

Using the Cover Page Editor

If you do much faxing, you'll probably want to create your own fax cover page, perhaps with your company logo. Included with Microsoft Fax is the right tool for the job, the Cover Page Editor, and four sample cover pages to get you started with some ideas. You can make changes to one of those pages or start your own cover page from scratch.

You can launch the Cover Page Editor from the Start menu or from within Exchange:

• From the Start menu, choose Programs, Accessories, Fax, Cover Page Editor. This will open the Cover Page Editor to a new, blank cover page.

• From within Exchange, choose Tools, Microsoft Fax Tools, Options. In the Microsoft Fax Properties dialog box (Figure 7.8), either select a cover page and click Open to edit it in the Cover Page Editor, or click the New button to start a fresh cover page.

I recommend that you start by editing an existing cover page, rather than starting from scratch. You'll save a lot of time this way, because most of the information you need will already be on the page. As an example, let's work with the Generic cover page. You'll learn how to add information about yourself or the people you're sending faxes to, and also how to change a font and insert a graphic.

After you open a cover page, but before you make changes, you may want to save the document under a new file name so you can use the original cover page again. In Figure 7.15, we've opened the Generic cover page, then used File, Save As to make a copy called New Generic, which is the one we're going to edit.

Figure 7.15

Microsoft Fax includes a Cover Page Editor that handles text, graphics, and information from your address book.

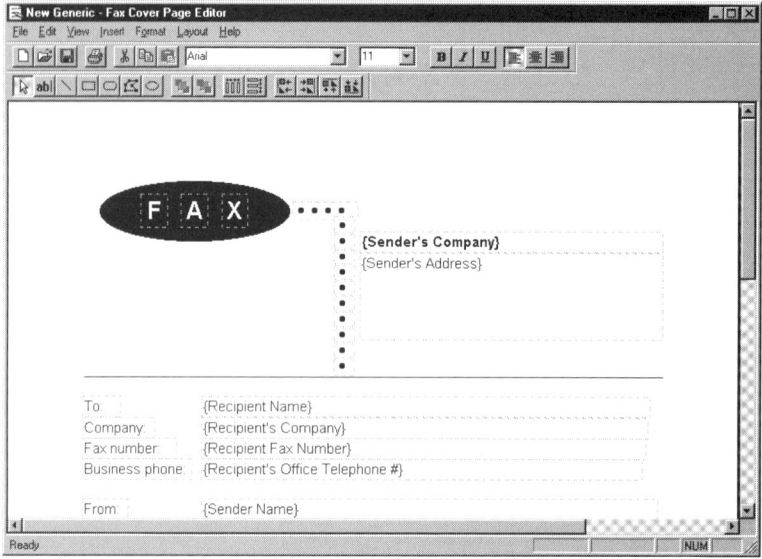

The cover page in Figure 7.15 may look complicated, but it really consists of just three basic elements:

- Text boxes that contain information about the sender, the recipient, or the message itself. These field names are enclosed in curly braces, such as {Sender's Company}.
- Plain text boxes, such as the letters F, A, and X that spell out FAX at the top.
- Graphics, such as the black ellipse at the top or the horizontal line.

All the tools you need are on the style toolbar and the drawing toolbar. You can hide either toolbar by unchecking it on the View menu. Table 7.3 lists the toolbar controls and their functions.

The Cover Page Editor includes an Undo function. You can choose Edit, Undo or press Ctrl+Z to undo a series of actions, one by one.

Table 7.3 Cover Page Editor Toolbar Controls

Control	Name	Description
Style Toolbar		
	New	Close the cover page that is currently open and open a new, blank cover page
	Open	Present an Open dialog box where you can choose a cover page file to work on
	Save	Save the current cover page
	Print	Print the current cover page
	Cut	Remove the selected object(s) and copy to the clipboard
	Copy	Copy the selected object(s) to the clipboard
	Paste	Paste the contents of the clipboard (only if the clipboard contains a graphic or a Cover Page Editor text box)
	Font Name	Set the font used for a text box or boxes
	Font Size	Set the font size used for a text box or boxes
	Bold	Toggle bold for a text box or boxes
	Italic	Toggle italics for a text box or boxes

continued

Table 7.3 Cover Page Editor Toolbar Controls, continued

Control	Name	Description
U	Underline	Toggle underline for a text box or boxes
	Align Left (text)	Justify text to the left of the text box
	Center	Center text in the text box
	Align Right (text)	Justify text to the right of the text box
Drawing Toolbar		
	Select	Select one or more objects
abl	Text	Insert a plain text box
	Line	Draw a line
	Rectangle	Draw a rectangle or square
	Rounded Rectangle	Draw a rectangle or square with rounded corners
	Polygon	Draw an irregular shape
	Ellipse	Draw a circle or ellipse
	Bring to Front	Move the selected object(s) so they appear in front of other objects
	Send to Back	Move the selected object(s) so they appear behind other objects
	Space Across	Adjust the selected items so they have equal horizontal space between them

continued

Table 7.3 Cover Page Editor Toolbar Controls, continued

Control	Name	Description
	Space Down	Adjust the selected items so they have equal vertical space between them
	Align Left (object)	Adjust the selected items so their left edges line up with the left edge of the left-most object
	Align Right (object)	Adjust the selected items so their right edges line up with the right edge of the right-most object
	Align Top	Adjust the select items so their top edges line up with the top edge of the upper-most object
	Align Bottom	Adjust the selected items so their bottom edges line up with the bottom edge of the bottom-most object

Inserting Text and Information Boxes

Text on a cover page can be contained in either text boxes or information boxes. Use an information box when you want to include information about the sender, the recipient, or the fax itself. When you insert an information box, an accompanying text box is also added to provide a label for the information box.

Use a text box where you want to add specific text that is unrelated to any of the information box fields. To add text to the cover page, follow these steps:

1. Click the Text button on the Drawing toolbar. The pointer will turn into a black cross.
2. Click and drag a rectangle at the location where you want the text box.
3. Type in the text.
4. Make any desired changes as described in "Formatting Text" later in this chapter.

To add a field that refers to information about yourself, your recipient, or the message itself, follow these steps:

1. Use the scroll bars on the Fax Cover Page Editor window to position the cover page so the place where you want the field to go is roughly in the center of the screen.
2. Choose Insert, then pick a Recipient, Sender, or Message field from the list of information fields shown in Table 7.4.

Table 7.4 Information Fields	
Field	**Entry**
Recipient fields	Name
	Fax Number
	Company
	Street Address
	City
	State
	ZIP Code
	Country
	Title
	Department
	Office Location
	Home Telephone Number
	Office Telephone Number
	To: List
	CC: List
Sender fields	Name
	Fax Number
	Company Address
	Title
	Department
	Office Location
	Home Telephone Number
	Office Telephone Number
Message fields	Subject
	Time Sent
	Number of Pages
	Number of Attachments

3. The field and a plain text box with the title of the field will be inserted in the middle of the displayed portion of the cover page. Position the pointer over the field and text box so that it shows a four-sided arrow, then click the mouse and drag the new elements to where you want them to be on the cover page.

All the Recipient fields except To: List and CC: List are drawn from information in the address book entry for the recipient (see "PAB Address Details," page 397 in Chapter 17). If you don't plan to fill in those fields in the address book entry, don't put them on your cover page.

The To: List and CC: List fields show the names of all the people to whom a particular fax was sent — including any e-mail recipients. (One of the great features about Exchange is that you can use a single message to send a document to a variety of people, some via fax and others via e-mail.)

Selecting Elements

To change the format of a text box, to alter the properties of a graphic element, or to move or align elements, you will need to select the element(s) first. There are two ways to do this:

- Click the Select tool in the Drawing toolbar, then draw a rectangle around the elements you want to work with. If an element's border is entirely within the rectangle you draw, it will be selected.

- Hold down the Ctrl key while you click on different elements with the mouse. You can also de-select an element with this method.

Formatting Text

The default format for text boxes is 11-point Arial. To change the font, first select an element or elements, then use the Font, Font Size, Bold, Italic, and Underline buttons as needed. Alternatively, you can choose Format, Font and change most font properties with the Font dialog box. Oddly, the Font dialog box offers no choice for underlining; you must do that from the toolbar.

To change the way text is aligned, use the Align Left, Align Center, and Align Right buttons; or choose Format, Align Text. One popular use for this feature is to right-align the text boxes that contain the titles for fields. We've done that in our sample makeover for the New Generic cover page, shown in Figure 7.16.

Figure 7.16

The New Generic cover page now has bold, right-aligned labels for information fields and a full-page border inserted as a graphic object then sent to the back of the other objects. Also, a black rectangle has replaced the black ellipse.

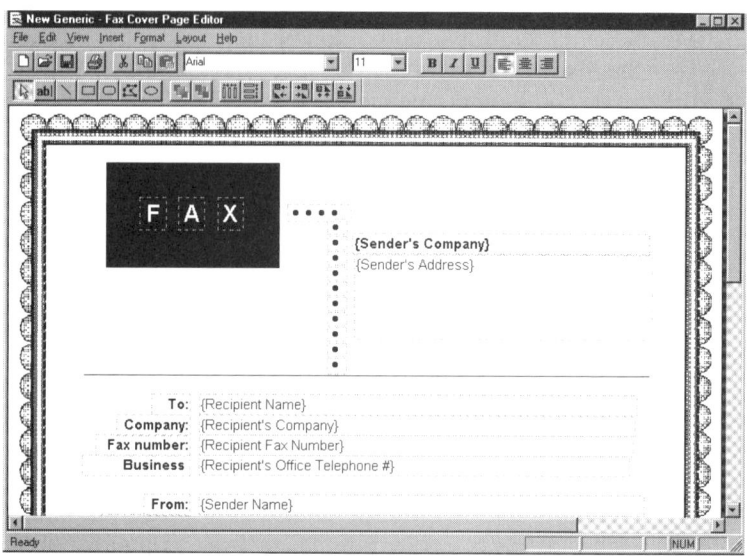

To change the color of the text, choose Format, then Line, Fill and Color, to display the dialog box shown in Figure 7.17. The "Text color" list offers choices of black, white, and three shades of gray. To create the white-on-black effect in the New Generic cover page, set Color under "Fill color" to Black and the "Text color" to White. If you use gray, see "Darkening or Lightening Faxes" in the "Tips and Tricks" section later in this chapter for details about how to control the darkness of outgoing faxes.

Figure 7.17

Add borders around elements, control the thickness of lines, set the fill color for elements, and change the text color.

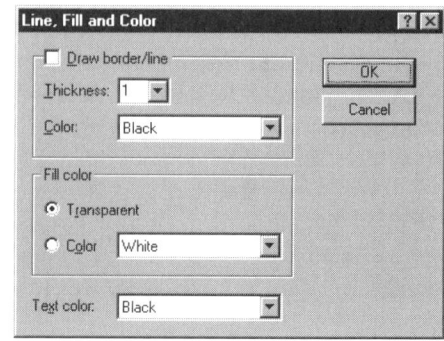

Adding and Formatting Graphic Elements

With the Drawing toolbar, you can add lines, rectangles (with square or rounded corners), ellipses, and freehand shapes (polygons). The black FAX on the Generic cover page is actually a black ellipse behind three text boxes spelling out F-A-X.

To add a line or shape, click the appropriate toolbar button, then click and drag to create the shape. For a perfect square or circle, hold down the Shift key while you drag. To make a vertical or horizontal line or a line at a 45-degree angle, hold down the Shift key while you drag.

You can change the line width and color for any line or shape. Choose Format, then Line, Fill and Color, to display the Line, Fill and Color dialog box shown in Figure 7.17. You get five color choices: black, white, and three shades of gray. If you use gray, see "Darkening or Lightening Faxes" in the "Tips and Tricks" section later in this chapter for details about how to control the darkness of outgoing faxes.

If you want to add a company logo or other graphic to your cover page, the graphic element must be in a format associated with a graphics program on your system. A .pcx or .bmp file will always work, because Microsoft Paint, a Windows 95 accessory, can read those files. To insert a graphic, follow these steps:

1. Choose Insert, Object.
2. In the Insert Object dialog box, choose Create from File.
3. Either enter the name of the graphic file in the File box, or click the Browse button to find it on your system.
4. Check Link if you want your cover page to be updated whenever the graphic file changes.
5. Click OK to paste the graphic into your cover page.
6. Click on the graphic, then drag it to the location where you want it to appear.

Arranging Elements

Once you have all the text boxes and graphics you want on your cover page, you may want to rearrange them. Table 7.5 lists a number of techniques you can use to rearrange one or more objects.

Table 7.5 Techniques for Arranging Cover Page Objects

Action	Technique
To move	Click and drag to the new location.
To resize	Select, then move the pointer over one of the small black square "handles" on the sides and corners until the pointer turns into a double-headed arrow. Then drag that handle until the object is the size you want.
To remove	Select, then press Delete.
To cut	Select, then choose Edit, Cut or press Ctrl+X.
To copy	Select, then choose Edit, Copy or press Ctrl+C.
To paste	Choose Edit, Paste or press Ctrl+V.
To center on the page	Select, then choose Layout, Center on Page, then choose either Width or Height.
To space evenly	Select at least three elements, then click the Space Across or Space Down button (or choose Layout, Space Evenly, and either Across or Down).
To line up elements	Select at least two elements, then click the Align Left, Align Right, Align Top, or Align Bottom button (or choose Layout, Align Objects, where you can pick the same alignment choices as the buttons; in addition, you can align relative to the Horizontal Center or Vertical Center).
To move behind other elements	Select, then click the Send to Back button; or choose Layout, Send to Back; or press Ctrl+B.
To move in front of other elements	Select, then click the Bring to Front button; or choose Layout, Bring to Front; or press Ctrl+F.

Printing and Saving the Cover Page

When you've finished working on a cover page, save it by clicking the Save button or by choosing File, Save. You also can just close the Cover Page Editor. If you've been working on a new cover page, you'll be asked to give it a file-name. You should store cover pages in your Windows folder.

To print a cover page, click the Print button or choose File, Print. This printout will probably look better than the cover page you send with your faxes, because a laser or inkjet printer has a higher resolution than a fax machine. So you may also want to test your cover page by sending it to a plain-paper fax machine or by using the [FAX: me] technique described in "Tips and Tricks" later in this chapter.

You can't export Microsoft Fax cover pages to another program, because they're stored in a special .cpe format. Even if you select all or part of the elements on the page and use Edit, Copy, you won't be able to paste them anywhere except in the Cover Page Editor.

Special Note

Imaging for Windows

Imaging for Windows is an application developed by Wang for Microsoft that replaces the Fax Viewer that ships with Microsoft Fax; Imaging for Windows adds support for annotations, .tif file export, and scanning. Depending on your version of Windows, you may already have Imaging installed. If not, you can obtain it free from the sources listed in Appendix B. (A slightly different version of Imaging is included with Windows NT 4.0. Also, starting in the fall of 1996, new computers with Windows 95 pre-installed have Imaging instead of the Fax Viewer.)

Imaging for Windows replaces the Fax Viewer that ships with Microsoft Fax; Imaging for Windows adds support for annotations, .tif file export, and scanning.

Basic Setup

Once you've obtained the Img_us.exe file (or the file name for your language version), run it in an empty folder to extract the component files. If you have a scanner and are installing Imaging for Windows 95, check the Readme.txt file to see if your scanner supports TWAIN version 1.6, and what version of your scanner software is required to work with Imaging. (TWAIN is a technology used to acquire an image from a scanner and insert it into a document.) Then run the Setup.exe that you'll find in the folder where you extracted the setup files. The only option during setup is to install support for TWAIN 1.6, which you'll want to do if your scanner supports it.

Options

To launch Imaging, you can either double-click on a fax you've received in Exchange or use the Start menu. You'll find Imaging on the Programs, Accessories menu. To specify the size at which faxes and other image documents should be displayed, choose View, Options, General to display the General dialog box, shown in Figure 7.18. Make your choice from the "Open documents zoomed to" list. In the General dialog box, you also can set the toolbar button size and toggle scroll bars on and off.

Figure 7.18

Select how you want faxes to be displayed when Imaging first opens them.

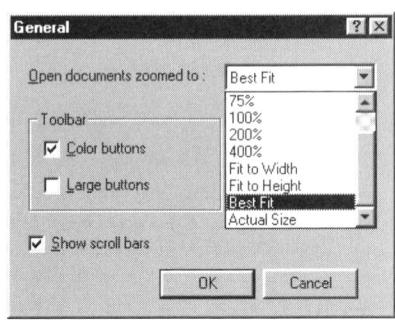

When you start Imaging, it always defaults to a view of one page. You can see a page and thumbnails, or just thumbnails, by using the appropriate buttons or the corresponding choices on the View menu. To change the size of the thumbnails, choose View, Options, Thumbnail and drag the corner of the sample thumbnail (Figure 7.19) to the desired size. The default "Aspect ratio" is Letter, but you have a choice of several other aspect ratios; or you can choose Unconstrained to control both the height and width of the thumbnail directly.

Imaging installs itself as the registered application for a number of different file types, including the following:

AWD	Microsoft Fax format
DCX	Fax format
PCX	PC Paintbrush format
TIF	Tagged Image File format

You can double-click any of these types of files, either in Exchange or in an Explorer folder, or on your desktop, to open that file in Imaging. For more information about Imaging, see "Using Imaging," page 357 in Chapter 15.

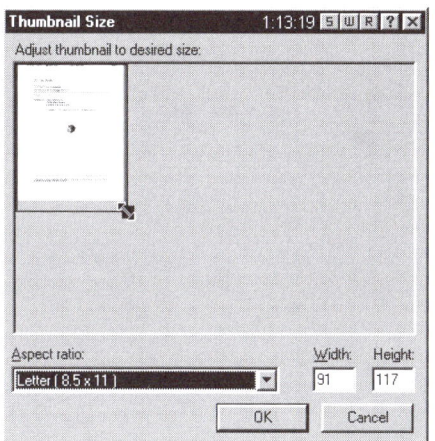

Figure 7.19
Change the size and shape of the thumbnail used to preview fax pages in Imaging.

Imaging for Windows NT does not include support for Microsoft Fax .awd files.

To uninstall Imaging,

1. Open the Control Panel and choose Add/Remove Programs.
2. Switch to the Windows Setup tab and select Accessories.
3. Click the Details button, then clear the Imaging box on the Components list.
4. Click OK twice to close the Accessories and Add/Remove Programs dialog boxes.

Tips and Tricks

Getting cover pages just right can take some effort. We provide several tips to help you with special characters and give you the opportunity to preview cover pages just as the recipients will see them. You'll also learn how to make Microsoft Fax coexist with other Exchange services and communications programs and get more configuration secrets.

Figure 7.20

An alternative to using graphics on your cover page is to use characters from special fonts such as WingDings.

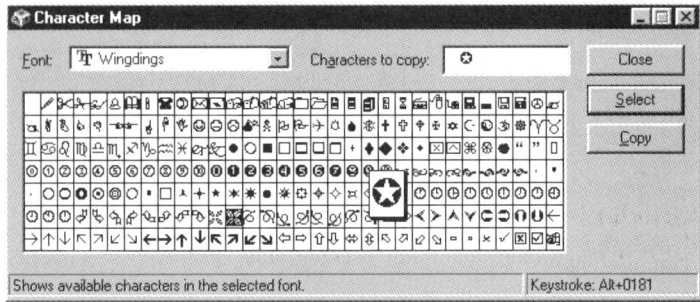

Setting the Archive Property for Cover Pages

If the Archive property of the cover page (.cpe) files is turned off — as it usually is after you run a backup program — you may not be able to use those cover pages with Microsoft Fax. Microsoft has provided a patch that fixes this problem. See Appendix B, "Exchange Resources," for details about where to obtain the Microsoft Fax Cover Page Fix.

Another way to solve this problem is to reset the Archive property after each backup. You can put the following command in your Autoexec.bat file to have it fix the Archive attribute each time you start Windows 95:

```
attrib +a C:\Windows\*.cpe
```

where C:\Windows is your actual Windows 95 folder.

Adding Special Characters to Cover Pages

Text boxes on a cover page can contain more than just words; you can use any of the special characters included in the various fonts you might have installed on your system. For example, the two lines of dots in the New Generic cover page (Figure 7.16) are not graphics. They're actually text boxes formatted with 10-point Marlett, a TrueType font included with Windows 95 and mainly used for dialog boxes and windows. WingDings is another font with special characters you might want to use.

To see what characters are available, click the Start button, then the Programs, Accessories, Character Map (Figure 7.20). Pick a font from the Font list. Once you locate a character you want to use, click it and note the keystroke equivalent, given in the bottom right corner of the Character Map window. You will need to use this keystroke to enter the character in your cover page text box, because copying from other applications, including Character Map, doesn't work with the Cover Page Editor. If the keystroke is, for example,

Alt+0181 (a star inside a circle in WingDings), this means to hold down the Alt key, type 0181, then release the Alt key.

After you've noted the keystroke equivalent, switch back to the Cover Page Editor and enter it in the text box where you want to use the special character. Then, if you haven't done so already, format the text box to use the appropriate font, following the instructions found in "Formatting Text," page 163.

Using [FAX: me] to Get a Rendered Copy of a Fax or Cover Page

Unlike most fax applications, Microsoft Fax does not keep complete copies of the versions of faxes sent to paper fax machines — in other words, the "rendered" or facsimile version. All you will see in Sent Items is the text of any cover page note and icons for any attached files. Or if you sent a document by printing it to the Microsoft Fax printer, you'll see the document pages but not the cover page.

However, there is a trick for seeing exactly what your recipients will get. You can use this procedure to test your cover pages, as well as to preview documents that you want to send. This is also an essential troubleshooting technique to determine whether the Microsoft Fax printer driver is operating properly. With this procedure, you actually send a fax to yourself without using a modem. Here's how:

1. From the Exchange Viewer window, use Compose, New Fax to start the Compose New Fax Wizard (or print to the Microsoft Fax printer to start the wizard if you're working in an application).

2. For Country, choose (None — Dial as Entered), which appears at the top of the list.

3. Under Fax #, the area code box will be disabled. In the box for the local number, enter "me," again without the quotes.

4. Press Enter to add "me" to the recipient list and proceed to the next screen of the wizard.

5. Click the Options button.

6. On the Send Options dialog box, click "Not editable" under Message Format, then click OK.

7. Click the Next button to move to the next screen.

8. Enter a Subject and a Note if you want one.

9. Click the Next button to move to the next screen.

10. Click the Add File button to add any files that you also want to preview in their fax-rendered form.

11. Click the Next button to move to the next screen, then Finish to send the fax to yourself.

After a few moments, a copy of the rendered fax will appear in your Inbox. When you open this document, you'll see exactly what a fax recipient would get, except that the cover page will be addressed to "me."

If you don't need to see the cover page with the note on it, you can use Compose, New Message to display the normal New Message window and enter the address [FAX:me] in the To: box. You also will need to set the message format to "Not editable."

If you find the [FAX:me] technique useful, you might want to add an address for it to your Personal Address Book. To do so, follow these steps:

1. Click the Address Book button or choose Tools, Address Book to display the Address Book window.

2. Choose File, New Entry.

3. In the New Entry dialog box, choose the entry type Other Address, then click OK.

4. For Display Name, enter FaxMe or whatever name you'd like to use for this address.

5. Under E-mail Address, enter "me" (without the quotes).

6. For E-mail Type, enter FAX.

7. If you plan to use this address to test cover pages, you may want to switch to the Business tab and enter sample information in the fields you find there. This will help you get an idea of how these recipient information fields will look on your cover pages.

8. Click OK to save the new address.

Now, whenever you want to get a copy of a fax, include FaxMe (or whatever name you entered in step 4) as one of the recipients. If you're using Compose, New Message, you might want to put it in the Bcc: box to get a blind copy of the fax. (See the section "Allowing Blind Carbon Copies," page 252 in Chapter 11.) As we discussed earlier, in the section "Message Format," be sure to set the message format to "Not editable" using the Send Options dialog, or the copy you receive won't be the same as what your addressees received.

Making Microsoft Fax Cooperate

If your Exchange profile includes both Microsoft Fax and Microsoft Mail or the Microsoft Exchange Server service, you may need to adjust the delivery order for these information services. Otherwise, faxes may get stuck in the Outbox and never be sent, or you will get a message that your fax couldn't be delivered because the e-mail address was wrong.

In Exchange, choose Tools, Delivery. In the list of services at the bottom of the dialog box, use the arrow buttons to move Microsoft Fax so that it comes before Microsoft Mail or the Microsoft Exchange Server service.

Keeping Microsoft Fax Connected to FAX: Port

Once Microsoft Fax is properly installed, you will be able to see Microsoft Fax in your Printers folder (click the Start button, then choose Settings, Printers). Right-click on this printer, then choose Properties to view the same sort of printer properties dialog box that you would find for a laser or inkjet printer. On the Details tab, you'll see that the Microsoft Fax printer is connected to FAX: (Unknown local port). This is correct and should not be changed. If you change the connection to COM1: because your modem is on COM1:, Microsoft Fax will not operate correctly. The modem connection for Microsoft Fax must be made on the properties dialog screen for the Microsoft Fax service in Exchange, not on the properties dialog screen for the Microsoft Fax printer.

Darkening or Lightening Faxes

In the properties dialog box for Microsoft Fax in the Printers folder, you can control the darkness of the faxes you send. Switch to the Graphics tab. Under Grayscale — Halftoning, you have these choices:

• Solid Black or White
• Patterned Grays

Patterned Grays is the default and generally the best choice. You will also see a Darkness slider, allowing you to make your outgoing faxes darker or lighter.

Forcing High-Speed Transmissions

During development of its Fax program, Microsoft found that some fax modems are not reliable at higher speeds — among them various U.S. Robotics models, the Gateway Telepath (which is actually a U.S. Robotics modem), and the Intel 14.4 kbps model. Therefore, Microsoft Fax sets the default for these modems at a maximum speed of 9,600 bps. However, if you think your modem can handle it, you can disable that setting and allow Microsoft Fax to try to connect at a higher speed. For example, to try to connect at 14,400 bps,

1. In Exchange, choose Tools, Microsoft Fax Tools, Options.
2. On the Modem tab, select the modem, then click the Properties button.
3. In the Fax Modem Properties dialog box, click the Advanced button.
4. In the Advanced dialog box, clear the Disable High Speed Transmission check box.
5. Choose OK three times to close this and the other dialog boxes and to save the change.

If you find that transmissions at the higher speed are not reliable, then reverse this procedure to limit the modem to 9,600 bps.

Sharing a Modem Between Microsoft Fax and Dial-Up Networking

While you might expect that these two applications could tell what kind of call is coming in — data or fax — it just doesn't work that way. If your PC is acting as a Dial-Up Networking (DUN) server, using the components from Microsoft Plus! For Windows 95, DUN will always take the call.

If you have two modems, however, you can use one for DUN and one for Fax. It is also possible to use the same modem for outgoing faxes and for incoming DUN calls. If you need to receive just the occasional incoming fax, you can temporarily disable the DUN host so it doesn't answer the phone. Here's how:

1. From My Computer or Explorer, open Dial-Up Networking.
2. Choose Connections, Dial-Up Server.
3. In the Dial-Up Server dialog box, click No Caller Access, then click OK.

A newer generation of modems is coming out that supports discrimination between voice, fax, and data calls. The Windows 95 Unimodem V driver included with these new modems is accompanied by a program called Operator Agent. Together with a voice-mail program, such as Microsoft Phone, Operator Agent allows you to take advantage of this call-discrimination feature and direct fax calls to Microsoft Fax and data calls to DUN Server. For more details, see "Microsoft Phone," page 212 in Chapter 9.

Summary

Windows 95 supports the use of Microsoft Fax for sending both faxes to paper fax machines and editable files to compatible systems. Included with Microsoft Fax is a complete Cover Page Editor to help you customize cover pages with text and graphics. Microsoft Fax has been enhanced with the addition of the Imaging for Windows application, which replaces Fax Viewer. Using the [FAX: me] feature lets you see a copy of your fax exactly as your addressees will see it.

Key Points

- To use Microsoft Fax, you must have a compatible modem attached to a telephone line or access to a computer elsewhere on your network that is running Microsoft Fax with a modem attached.

- A network fax server must be running Exchange at all times.

- U.S. law requires each fax transmission to be clearly identified.

- You can change the cover page or override any other message default for a particular fax.

- Imaging for Windows replaces the Fax Viewer that ships with Microsoft Fax; Imaging adds support for annotations, .tif file export, and scanning.

For More Information

Microsoft Fax operations are discussed in Chapter 14, "Sending Faxes," and Chapter 15, "Receiving Faxes." You will find additional information to help with troubleshooting fax problems in Chapter 24, "Troubleshooting."

Chapter 8

Setting Up Internet Mail

With the Internet Mail service, you can

- Exchange e-mail with anyone who has an Internet mail address, including people who use online services such as CompuServe, America Online (AOL), and Prodigy
- Send and receive file attachments without going through a separate encoding or decoding procedure

In general, Internet Mail is a mail service that connects you with people outside your organization. As usual, there are exceptions. For example, your organization may operate an internal mail server to which you can connect using Internet Mail.

If you are using Exchange Server, you may not need Internet Mail. Check with your system administrator to find out whether the Exchange Server already has a connection to the Internet that allows you to send and receive mail without installing this additional service.

Requirements

To use the Internet Mail service for Exchange, you must have

- An account on a mail server that supports POP3 (Post Office Protocol version 3) for incoming mail and SMTP (Simple Mail Transfer Protocol) for outgoing mail
- A way to connect to the mail server, via either dial-up networking (DUN) with a modem or a direct network connection
- Internet Mail service software

If you will be connecting with DUN, create a DUN connectoid or phonebook entry using the procedures in Chapter 3, "Making Connections," and make sure it works before you install Internet Mail.

How to Get an Account

If you don't already have an Internet mail account, I encourage you to get one, even if you already have a mail account with one of the online services.

If you don't already have an Internet mail account, I encourage you to get one, even if you already have a mail account with one of the online services such as CompuServe or The Microsoft Network.

Those online services (as of November 1996) don't yet offer full support for file attachments, as mail through an Internet service provider (ISP) does, though that's likely to change as they offer more to Internet users. Also, if being able to send e-mail is essential to your business, having more than one e-mail account can be a life-saver (I have three accounts at last count).

You can sign up with an ISP for as little as $20 a month (and sometimes even less). For that price, you usually get dial-up access to the provider (often unlimited), an e-mail account, and sometimes even space for a personal Web site. When shopping for an ISP, make sure the provider supports POP3/SMTP mail with MIME (Multipurpose Internet Mail Extensions) attachments.

Many ISPs provide e-mail software such as Eudora or Pegasus when you sign up, but a growing number are also familiar with Microsoft Exchange. They may even offer setup instructions just for Exchange. The advantage that Exchange offers over these other programs is that you can manage not just Internet e-mail, but also messages from other sources, all in the same Inbox and other folders.

Before you set up Internet Mail, get the following information from the ISP (or your network administrator, if the server is local):

- The name or IP address of the mail servers, both the POP3 and SMTP servers, if they're different (Note that this may be different from the address for the dial-up networking connection to your ISP.)

- The name of your mailbox

- Your mail password

- The e-mail address for your mailbox, in the format *name@domain* (The name part is usually the same as the mailbox name, but not always; so be sure to ask.)

Where to Get the Internet Mail Service

Windows NT 4.0 users will find Internet Mail as one of the Windows Messaging services that can be installed through Control Panel, Add/Remove Programs, Windows Setup.

For Windows 95 users, there are a variety of sources for the Internet Mail service:

- On the Microsoft Plus! CD (This version is older than the others. It's recommended that you get the newer version from one of the other sources.)

- Pre-installed on a new computer configured with Microsoft Internet Explorer or Windows Messaging

- As part of the Microsoft Internet Explorer download, available from the Microsoft Web site

- As part of Windows Messaging, which is available on the Windows 95 Software Updates page at the Microsoft Web site

- As a separate download (just Internet Mail) from the Windows 95 Software Updates page at the Microsoft Web site

For details about how to access the Microsoft Web site, see Appendix B, "Exchange Resources." For any file you download, make sure you follow instructions for installing it before you continue with the setup for Internet Mail.

Windows 95 users of the Exchange Server client need to download Internet Mail from the Windows 95 Software Updates page at the Microsoft Web site. Earlier versions don't work with the Remote Mail function in the Exchange Server client.

Special Note

Basic Setup

We're going to walk through two different methods of adding Internet Mail, with the Setup Wizard and by manually adding the service to your Exchange profile. See Chapter 4, "Configuring Profiles," if you need a refresher on how to add a service to an profile.

Using the Setup Wizard

The Setup Wizard is available only when you create a new profile through the Mail and Fax (or Mail) applet in the Control Panel. To add a profile using the Setup Wizard, follow these steps:

1. Run the Mail and Fax (or Mail) applet in the Control Panel.
2. Click the Show Profiles button.
3. Choose Add.
4. In the first screen of the Setup Wizard, choose "Use the following information services" and check the ones you want, in this case being sure to include the Internet Mail service.
5. Click Next to continue, and give the profile a name on the next screen of the wizard; then click Next again to begin configuring the Internet Mail service and any other services you selected.

Here are the steps in the wizard that are specific to Internet Mail:

1. In the first screen of the wizard (Figure 8.1), choose whether to connect to the Internet via Modem or Network. Click Next to continue.

Figure 8.1
You can reach an Internet Mail server either by dialing into it or connecting to it through your local area network.

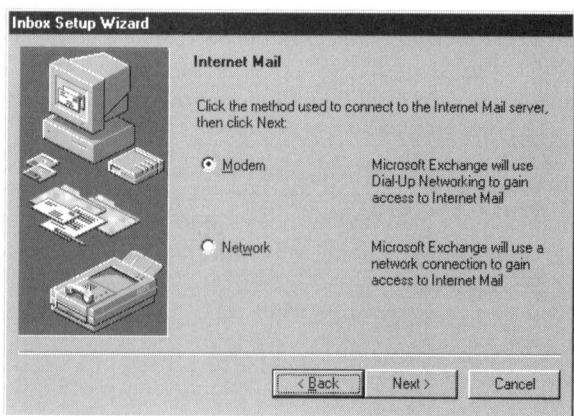

2. If you chose to connect via modem, you see the screen shown in Figure 8.2. Select the DUN connection you want to use with Internet Mail.

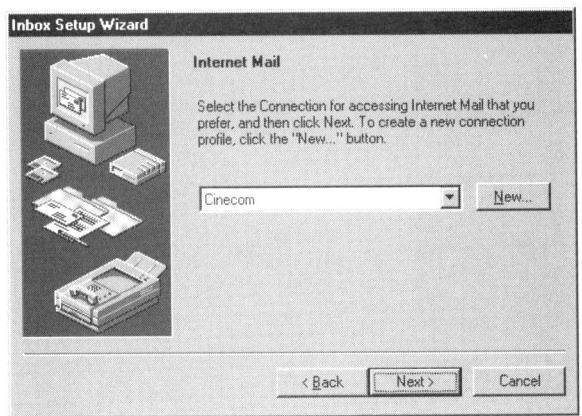

Figure 8.2
Choose a DUN connection to connect to the Internet Mail server.

You can also click the Underline New button if you haven't already set up the connection. Click Next to continue.

3. In the next screen of the wizard (Figure 8.3), enter either the Name or the IP Address for the POP3 mail server, which you obtained from the ISP. Click Next to continue.

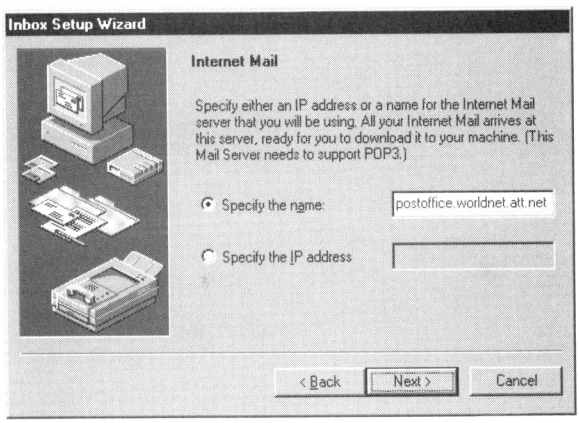

Figure 8.3
Enter either the name or the IP address of the POP3 mail server.

4. Choose Off-line or Automatic connection in the wizard screen shown in Figure 8.4. You can easily change this later. We'll discuss the differences under the "Offline vs. Scheduled Connections" section later in this chapter. Click Next to continue.

Figure 8.4

Internet Mail can either get all your messages automatically or let you use Remote Mail to control which messages to download.

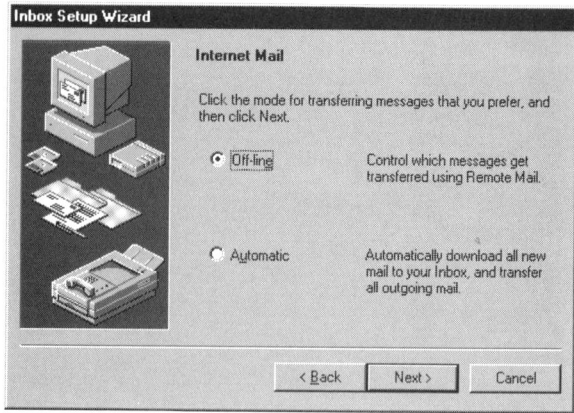

5. Enter your E-mail Address and Full Name, as shown in Figure 8.5. These go on all messages to identify you and to give recipients your return e-mail address. Click Next to continue.

Figure 8.5

The e-mail address entered here becomes the return address for all the Internet messages you send.

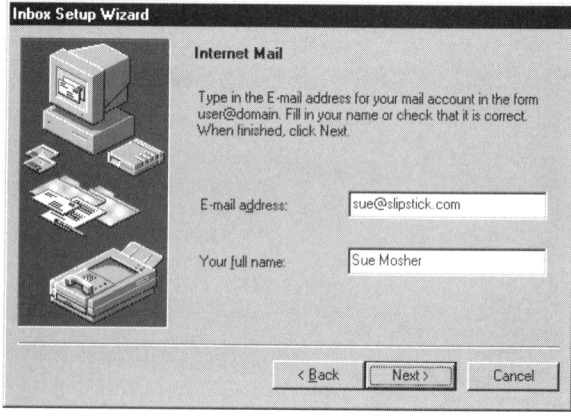

6. Enter the Mailbox Name and Password (see Figure 8.6) that you got from your ISP or system administrator. Note that the Mailbox Name is not the same as your e-mail address. It does not include the domain name (the part after the @ in your e-mail address). And it even may be completely different from the name portion of your e-mail address (the part before the @). Click Next to continue, and finish answering the rest of the questions about other services in this new profile.

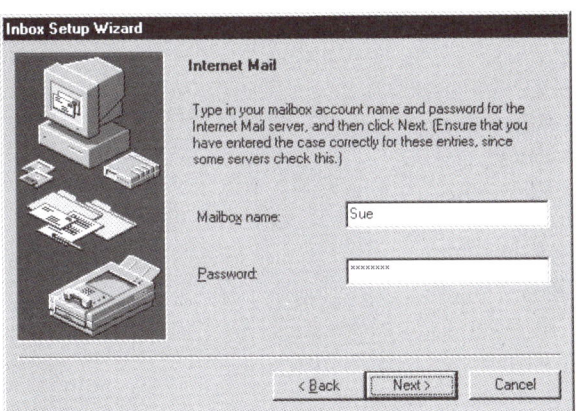

Figure 8.6
Enter the Mailbox Name and Password you received from your ISP or system administrator.

Unfortunately, in many cases, the Setup Wizard does not adequately configure the Internet Mail service. Two more steps are required for most users:

- Adding the SMTP server address
- Adding the user ID and password for the DUN connection

In many cases, the Setup Wizard does not adequately configure the Internet Mail service.

Adding the SMTP Server Address

Quite often, the address for the server handling outgoing mail is different from that for the server where your mail account resides. Your ISP should tell you if this is the case for your mail servers. If so, after running the Setup Wizard, you must add the address for the SMTP server (you will not be able to send any Internet messages until you do so). Follow these steps:

1. Run the Mail and Fax (or Mail) applet in the Control Panel.
2. If the profile you want to work with isn't the default profile, click the Show Profiles button. Select the profile you want to modify, then click the Properties button.
3. On the Services tab, select Internet Mail, then click the Properties button.
4. On the General tab (Figure 8.7), click the Advanced Options button.
5. In the Advanced Options dialog box (Figure 8.8), enter the name or IP address for the SMTP server, then click OK.
6. Keep the Internet Mail Properties dialog box open so you can continue with the next section, beginning with step 4.

Figure 8.7

Enter details about your mail account and return address on the General tab. Use the Advanced Options button to enter the address of your SMTP server if it's different from the POP3 server.

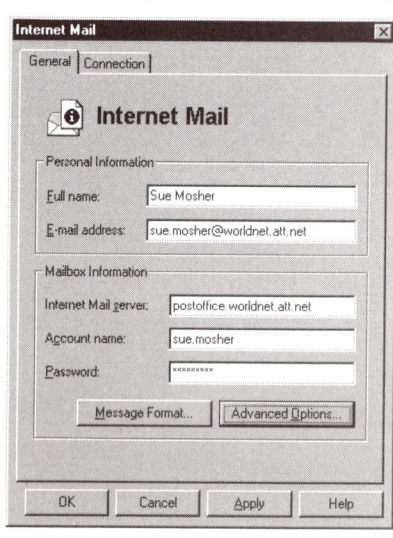

Figure 8.8

Enter the SMTP server name or IP address if it's different from the POP3 server.

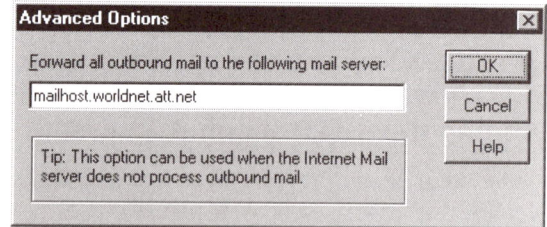

Adding the Log-On Details

If you access the Internet Mail server with a DUN connection, you must enter the user ID and password for that connection, unless you log on with a terminal screen. In other words, if you log on automatically or with a script, Internet Mail needs to know what values to use for the user name and password. Follow these steps to enter those log-on details:

1. Run the Mail and Fax (or Mail) applet in the Control Panel.
2. If the profile you want to work with isn't the default profile, click the Show Profiles button. Select the profile you want to modify, then click the Properties button.
3. On the Services tab, select Internet Mail, then click the Properties button.
4. Switch to the Connection tab (Figure 8.9), then click the Login As button.

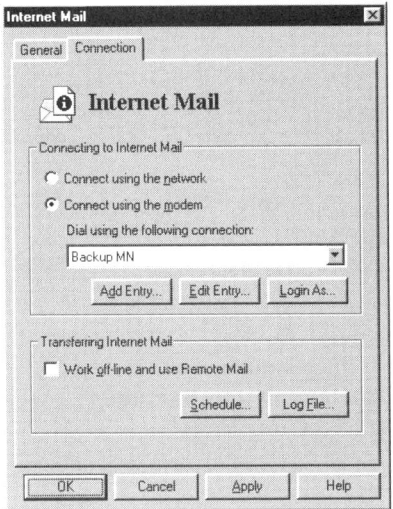

Figure 8.9
On the Connection tab, specify the type of connection and whether you'll use Remote Mail or automatic connections to your mail account. Use the Login As button to enter the user ID and password for a DUN connection.

5. In the Login As dialog box, enter the User Name and Password for the selected DUN connection, then click OK.

6. Click OK to close the Internet Mail Properties dialog box, then click OK again to close the Properties dialog box for the profile.

Manually Configuring Internet Mail

If you are not creating a completely new profile, there's no wizard to help you. You must manually configure the Internet Mail service as part of the process of adding it to an existing profile (see "Adding a Service," page 79 in Chapter 4). To complete the manual configuration, follow these steps:

1. Run the Mail and Fax (or Mail) applet in the Control Panel.

2. If the profile you want to work with isn't the default profile, click the Show Profiles button. Select the profile you want to modify, then click the Properties button.

3. On the Services tab, click the Add button.

4. In the Add Service to Profile dialog box, select the Internet Mail service, then click OK.

5. On the General tab (Figure 8.7), enter your Full Name. Recipients will see this as the From name on messages received from you.

6. Enter your E-mail Address in *name@domain* format. This is the address that will be used when people reply to your messages.

7. Enter the name or IP address of your Internet POP3 Mail Server.

8. Enter your Account Name (mailbox name) on that server and the Password for that account.

9. Click the Advanced Options button. In the Advanced Options dialog box (Figure 8.8), supply the SMTP server name or IP address, then click OK.

10. Switch to the Connection tab, shown in Figure 8.9.

Choose "Connect using the modem" if you always want to use a particular DUN connection to get your Internet Mail. Select the DUN connection you want to use. Click the Login As button, fill in the User Name and Password fields, then click OK to close the Login As dialog box.

Choose "Connect using the network" if any of these situations fit your case: You are using Internet Mail to access an in-house mail server, you have a direct network connection to the Internet, or you want the flexibility of using any DUN connection to get your Internet Mail.

11. Click OK to finish installing Internet Mail.

Options

As with all Exchange services, Internet Mail includes a variety of options. Table 8.1 lists these settings and their default values. Many will be familiar to you from the setup procedures in the previous sections.

Table 8.1 Internet Mail Settings and Default Values	
Setting	**Default**
General settings	
Full name	None — entered by user
E-mail address	None — entered by user
Internet Mail server	None — entered by user
Account name	None — entered by user
Password	None — entered by user
Message format	MIME (other option is UUENCODE)
Character set	ISO 8859-1
	continued

| Table 8.1 Internet Mail Settings and Default Values, continued ||
Setting	Default
SMTP server for outbound mail (click the Advanced Options button for this setting)	The default for Internet Mail is to assume that the SMTP server is the same as the POP3 server, but this is not always the case.
Connection settings Connection method	Network
User name (for DUN connection)	None — must be entered by user
Password (for DUN connection)	None — must be entered by user
Transfer method	Off-line with Remote Mail
Interval for scheduled connections	15 minutes
Log file	No logging
Log file location	Imail.log in the Windows folder

Note that the settings for the SMTP server and DUN user name and password are discussed earlier in the chapter in the sections "Adding the SMTP Server Address" and "Adding the Log-On Details."

Message Format

You can choose between MIME and UUENCODE as the default format for handling the non-text portion of your messages. The default of MIME with the ISO 8859-1 character set is usually the best choice, because it gives you the ability to exchange file attachments with other MIME-compatible recipients, and even to send and receive messages with the rich text formatting that Exchange provides. Because you can change the message format for individual messages, there's really no reason to change this. However, if you do prefer to use UUENCODE as your default or to switch character sets, follow these steps:

1. On the General tab (Figure 8.7), click the <u>M</u>essage Format button.

2. In the Message Format dialog box (Figure 8.10), if you want to use UUENCODE, uncheck the box labeled "Use <u>M</u>IME when sending messages," then click OK.

Figure 8.10
If you clear the MIME box, Exchange will use UUENCODE to format your message attachments.

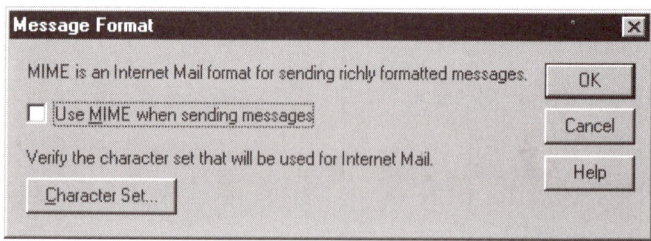

3. If you want to change the character set, click the <u>C</u>haracter Set button and make your selection from the following choices:

> ISO 8859-1 (default)
>
> Norwegian
>
> Swedish
>
> US ASCII

4. Click OK to save the message format and return to the Internet Mail dialog box.

Offline vs. Scheduled Connections

Internet Mail offers a limited range of scheduling options, but these can cause problems for dial-up users.

Internet Mail does not offer as wide a selection of scheduling options as the Microsoft Exchange Server service or Microsoft Mail. In fact, there are only two choices:

Work offline and use Remote Mail	Manual delivery and retrieval with either <u>T</u>ools, <u>R</u>emote Mail or <u>T</u>ools, <u>D</u>eliver Now
Scheduled connections	Automatic delivery and retrieval
	• When Exchange is first loaded
	• At scheduled intervals thereafter

If you connect to the Internet via your LAN, then either choice can work well for you. However, if you connect with a modem, there are potential problems with using scheduled connections:

- If the modem is being used by another program when the time comes to make the scheduled connection, you get an error message.
- When Internet Mail tries to make the connection, it freezes whatever application you're currently working in.

On the other hand, if you choose to work offline, you will be totally in charge of when you gather your Internet Mail, and you'll be able to use either the Remote Mail technique (see Chapter 13, "Working Remotely") or the Deliver Now technique. Even when you're working offline, it's still best, however, to make the connection to your ISP first, then take care of your mail tasks. That way, you can avoid the second problem above and prevent Internet Mail from freezing you out of an application while it connects. Indicate the option you prefer on the Connection tab of the Internet Mail dialog box.

To use scheduled connections, follow these steps:

1. Clear the box on the Connection tab (Figure 8.9) labeled "Work offline and use Remote Mail."
2. Click the Schedule button and enter the number of minutes you want between scheduled connections.

Log File

To keep a record of your Internet Mail connections, follow these steps:

1. On the Connection tab (Figure 8.9), click the Log File button.
2. Choose the level of logging you want. Here are your choices:

No Logging	no log file
Basic	logon and logoff times plus error messages
Troubleshooting	complete protocol interactions with your mail server

3. Give a location for the log file. The default is Imail.log in your Windows folder.
4. Click OK to return to the Internet Mail properties dialog box.

If you choose to keep a troubleshooting log, be sure to turn off logging after you've solved the problem; otherwise, the log file will grow quite large. Review the log by opening it in Notepad or WordPad.

Tips and Tricks

Here are some tips on how to make Internet Mail cooperate if you have more than one e-mail account, and if you also have Microsoft Fax in your profile.

Adding Another Profile or Service for Multiple E-Mail Accounts

What do you do if you have two e-mail accounts? Since you can have only one copy of Internet Mail in your profile, you'll need to consider other options:

- Set up an additional profile using Internet Mail with the other account's settings but pointing to the same Personal Address Book and Personal Folders. Switch between profiles to access the two accounts.
- Add the Netscape Internet Mail Transport to your profile to handle a second account.
- Add the netApps Internet Series to your profile to handle two or more accounts.

Information about the Netscape and netApps services for Exchange is available in Chapter 9, "Setting Up Other Information Services."

Using the Same Return Address for Different Accounts

If you have two e-mail accounts, you may want to use the same return address on both accounts, so you only have to check one server for all your incoming mail. All you need to do is enter the same e-mail address for both accounts, whether in Internet Mail (in the E-Mail Address box on the General tab) or in another Internet mail service in your profile.

Note, however, that some Internet service providers use the return e-mail address as part of processing mail messages. You may want to ask your ISP before changing your return address, or at least send some test messages to make sure this technique works with your ISP.

If you think about it, the ease with which you can use a different return address points out one of the weaknesses in the Internet's handling of mail. There is no requirement that the sender of a message be positively identified, though a thorough look at the Internet header for an incoming message may give you a clue as to whether a sender is legitimate or not.

It's in this context that methods have been developed for adding a digital signature to a message. This signature confirms the sender's identity — at least the e-mail address, not the name — by invoking the authority of a third party who keeps track of such things. We'll look at digital signatures in Chapter 21, "Message Security."

Special Note

Coexisting with Microsoft Fax

If you use scheduled connections, Exchange will try to connect to your mail server when Exchange first loads. If you also have Microsoft Fax in your profile, set to automatic or manual answering, this initial connection will fail, because the fax modem will still be initializing when Internet Mail begins to make its connection.

There are several possible approaches to this problem:

- Ignore it. Leave Internet Mail in the same profile as Microsoft Fax, and click OK when you get a Port in Use message at startup. If you choose this approach, take care not to leave any Internet messages in your Outbox when you exit Exchange. Otherwise, when Exchange starts and the Internet Mail connection fails, you may get an Undeliverable message in your Inbox for each of those messages; any messages returned as undeliverable will need to be resent.

- Put Internet Mail and Microsoft Fax in separate profiles. Because Microsoft Fax makes Exchange load slower, keeping it in a separate profile also should speed up Exchange when you're using just Internet Mail.

- Set Microsoft Fax to Don't Answer. It's easy enough to reset it to answer automatically or manually once Exchange has loaded.

- Set Internet Mail to work offline rather than use scheduled connections.

Summary

Internet Mail is easy to set up — once you have all the necessary information from your ISP or network administrator — and is a powerful tool for communicating with virtually anyone via e-mail. For best results, make sure your mail server supports MIME attachments, so you can easily send and receive files.

Key Points

- In general, Internet Mail is a mail service that connects you with people outside your organization.
- If you don't already have an Internet mail account, I'd encourage you to get one, even if you already have a mail account with one of the online services.
- In many cases, the Setup Wizard does not adequately configure the Internet Mail service.
- Internet Mail offers a limited range of scheduling options, but these can cause problems for dial-up users.

For More Information

If you need help in establishing a DUN connection to your ISP, check out the information in Chapter 3, "Making Connections."

Information about other Internet services for Exchange besides Internet Mail is available in Chapter 9, "Setting Up Other Information Services."

Internet mail is becoming such an essential tool that this book devotes all of Chapter 22 to Internet e-mail issues.

Chapter 9
Setting Up Other Information Services

Whether you use the Microsoft Exchange Server client or the operating system version of Exchange, sometimes known as Windows Messaging, you can expand the capabilities of Exchange with additional information services. New services are being developed at a rapid pace, many available for sampling as downloads from the Internet (see Appendix B, "Exchange Resources"). Some services add new features to Exchange, such as security. Others provide a complete information service with transport and address functions.

The range of available services is greatest for the Exchange Server clients — allowing them to connect to powerful network fax servers or take advantage of direct connections between Exchange Server and other enterprise mail systems. In this chapter, we'll work on a general procedure for installing new services, then we'll look at specific setup issues for some of those services most commonly used.

General Instructions

Always quit Exchange before installing a new service.

Installing a new service in Exchange usually consists of three steps:

1. Install the necessary files and registry entries by running the setup program for the new service.
2. Add the service to your Exchange profile(s).
3. Examine the default settings and make any necessary adjustments. View and change these settings through the Mail and Fax applet (or Mail) in the Control Panel (see "Working with Services," page 78 in Chapter 4).

For services downloaded from the Internet, you may first need to prepare a setup folder to get the setup files ready to install. Before installing any new service, you should quit Exchange if it's open. Choose File, Exit and Log Off to make sure that all Exchange components are shut down.

Preparing a Setup Folder

When you download a service, you usually get a single .exe or .zip file that contains all the components for the service. For some .exe files, starting the program both extracts the component files and runs the setup program automatically. For other .exe files and all .zip files, you need to prepare a folder containing the individual setup files. To do so, follow these steps:

1. Create a new folder on a drive that has a sufficient amount of free space.
2. If you downloaded a .zip file, extract the files to this new folder using your unzip utility (e.g., Pkunzip, WinZip).
3. If you downloaded an .exe file, copy the file to the new folder you created in step 1. Then run the file to extract the setup files into the new folder.

After step 2 or 3, the folder should contain either Setup.exe or Install.exe or something similar. This is the program you'll run in the next phase.

Running the Setup Program

In the setup folder, which could be on your hard drive, a diskette, a CD, or a network driver, run the Setup.exe or Install.exe program. The setup program performs several tasks:

- Copies the necessary files to your Windows folder, Windows system folder, and possibly other folders

- Updates the Mapisvc.inf file and Windows registry with details about the new service
- In some cases, adds the new service to your default Exchange profile

Mapisvc.inf, which is stored in the Windows\System folder for Windows 95 and the Winnt\System32 folder for Windows NT, contains settings used to set up services in Exchange profiles. If you dual-boot Windows 95 and Windows NT — and the service supports both — you must run the setup program two times, once under each operating system.

Some applications, such as Lotus Notes, Netscape, and WinFax PRO 7.0, include Exchange services as a small part of a larger program. In such cases, running the setup program for the main application updates your system to make the Exchange service available. There is no separate setup program just for the Exchange services related to these applications. You will, however, need to add the service to your Exchange profile.

Adding the Service to Profiles

Some setup programs offer to add the service to your default Exchange profile automatically. Go ahead and take advantage of this shortcut feature if it's available. You can always remove the service later if you don't want it in the default profile.

After the setup program completes its work, run the Mail and Fax (or Mail) applet in the Control Panel. If the service has not been added to any profile, add it using the techniques in Chapter 4, "Configuring Profiles." If you plan to use this new service in more than one profile, add the service to a single profile first, then check the settings, as described in the next section. Start Exchange and test the service to make sure it's working correctly. After the service is configured correctly in one profile, return to the Control Panel and copy it to other profiles.

Checking the Configuration

Once the service is part of a profile, select the service in the profile properties dialog box, then choose Properties to check the settings for the service. Review the entries on all the tabs, and be sure to press F1 to bring up the help file for any settings you don't understand.

In the next few sections, we'll look at the settings for some Exchange services you're likely to see.

Enterprise Mail Services

In many cases, connections to other mail services are made directly through either Microsoft Exchange Server or Microsoft Mail. We do not cover this type of connection in this book. However, it's also possible that you will use a separate Exchange service to access mail on other mail servers.

Lotus Notes

Lotus Notes 4.0 includes a limited Exchange service that lets you read Notes messages through a separate Exchange folder when you are connected to the network where the Notes server resides. You also can compose new Notes messages from within Exchange.

Once you install Notes, you must manually add the Lotus Notes service to your Exchange profile. All the necessary settings are picked up from your Notes configuration files. Figure 9.1 shows those settings as they appear in the Properties dialog box for the Lotus Notes service.

Figure 9.1
Settings for the Lotus Notes service are drawn from your Lotus.ini file when you add the service to your Exchange profile.

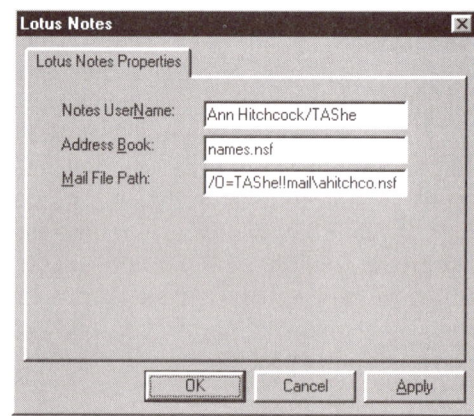

Transend MAPI ConnectorWare for cc:Mail

While Lotus does not provide a cc:Mail client for Exchange, one is available from Transend Corporation (see Appendix B, "Exchange Resources"). MAPI ConnectorWare for cc:Mail supports a full range of features:

- Offline remote operation
- Rich-text formatting of messages to other users of this cc:Mail service for Exchange

- Access to the cc:Mail directory through the Exchange Address Book
- Import of messages from the cc:Mail Inbox, Drafts, Bulletin Boards, and other Folders to the Exchange mailbox or Personal Folders. Two folder groups are created — cc:Mail Bulletin Boards and cc:Mail Folders.

After running the setup program to install MAPI ConnectorWare for cc:Mail, you must add cc:Mail to your Exchange profile. It is listed under the available Exchange services as "cc:Mail 2.0." Figures 9.2 through 9.4 show the configuration options available. You'll need to know your postoffice location, user name, and password.

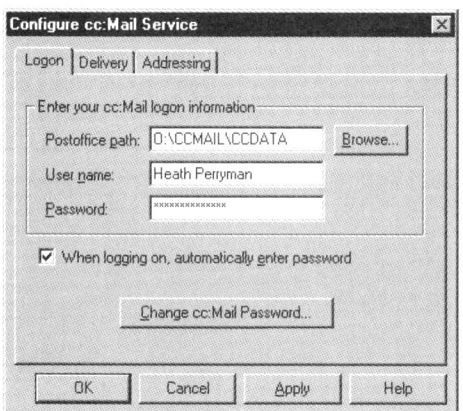

Figure 9.2

Like many Exchange services, MAPI Connector-Ware for cc:Mail needs to know your user name, password, and the location of your mail server.

On the Delivery tab (Figure 9.3), you can choose to retain messages on the cc:Mail server by clearing the "Delete Retrieved Mail" checkbox. You also have the option to send with Microsoft Exchange rich-text format (RTF), but note that this works only when you are sending to other cc:Mail users with Exchange.

If you need to work offline, copy the postoffice address list to your computer using the "Create/Update local copy" button on the Addressing tab (Figure 9.4), and make sure the "Use local copy" box is checked.

You can create new cc:Mail addresses in your Personal Address Book by using the cc:Mail Recipient entry type, which is added by the MAPI Connector-Ware service.

When you create a message offline, save it rather than send it. Then when you reconnect to the LAN, open the message again and, this time, send it. (This is different from other Exchange services, which automatically deliver messages from the Outbox.)

Figure 9.3

Normally you'll want to enable both incoming and outgoing delivery of cc:Mail messages and check frequently for new messages.

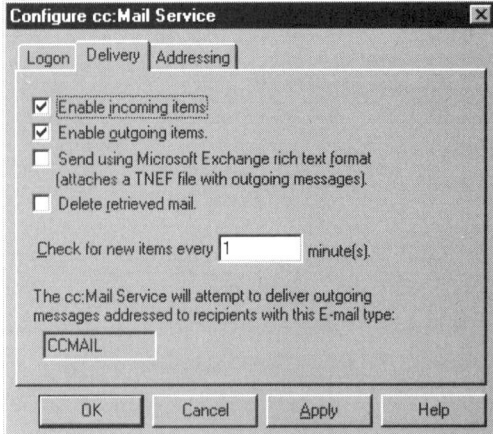

Figure 9.4

The MAPI ConnectorWare service uses both its own address list (either on the postoffice or a local copy) and addresses copied to your Personal Address Book.

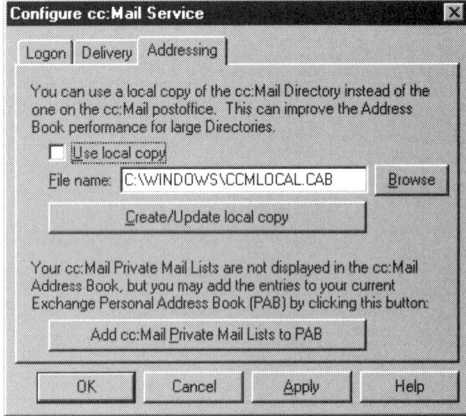

ccXchg

Another cc:Mail service for Exchange is the shareware program ccXchg, which is included on the CD with this book. After you have installed ccXchg, you must add the service to your Exchange profile. The list of available information services shows it as cc:Mail for Exchange. The only information you need to supply is your cc:Mail user name, password, and path to the postoffice (see Figure 9.5).

To send messages to cc:Mail recipients, you can use the cc:Mail address list in the Exchange Address Book or create a new cc:Mail address, either in

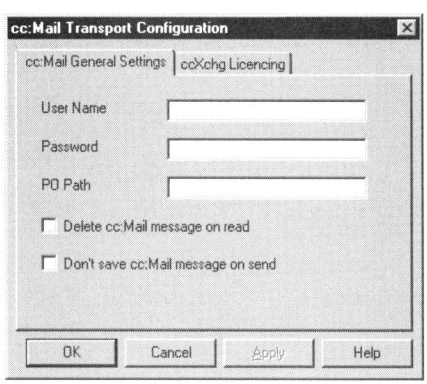

Figure 9.5
Enter details about your cc:Mail account on the cc:Mail General Settings tab. When you register the program, you will receive a license ID to enter on the ccXchg Licencing tab.

your Personal Address Book or just in the message. Follow these steps to create a new cc:Mail address for ccXchg:

1. From the message window, click the To button to display the Address Book dialog box.
2. In the Address Book dialog box, click the New button.
3. In the New Entry dialog box, under Select the Entry Type, choose Other Address, then click the OK button.
4. On the New Other Address Properties dialog box, enter the name of the user in the "Display name" box.
5. In the "E-mail address" box, enter the full address as it would appear in the cc:Mail address book. For someone in the same postoffice as yourself, enter the name as it appears in the cc:Mail address book. For a remote recipient, include the postoffice (e.g., Jeff Banner at SILVER-HQ) (see Figure 9.6).

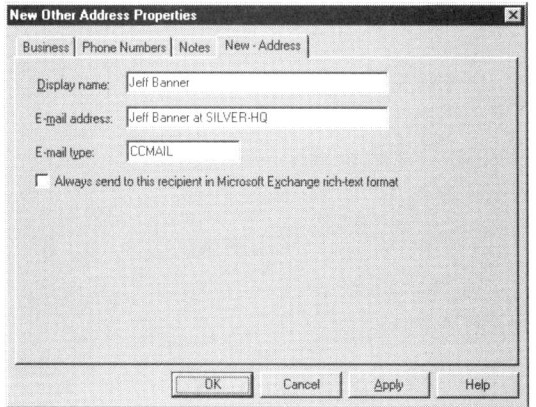

Figure 9.6
Create an Other Address entry, and use CCMAIL for the "E-mail type" when you create a cc:Mail address for ccXchg. Rich-text formatting (RTF) is not supported.

If the cc:Mail postoffice has a gateway to the Internet, you can create Internet addresses as *<name@domain>* at *<InternetGateway>* where *<InternetGateway>* is the name of the postoffice that represents the gateway.

6. In the "E-mail type" box, enter CCMAIL in all caps.

7. Click the OK button to add the address to the message (and to the Personal Address Book if you left that option selected in the New Entry dialog box).

Once you send a message to a cc:Mail user, delivery by ccXchg is automatic; you don't need to use Tools, Deliver Now.

Internet Services

If you use an Internet service but see no Internet address type in the Personal Address Book, use an entry type of Other Address and specify SMTP under "E-mail type."

In this section, we spotlight two individual and two workgroup alternatives to the Internet Mail service provided for Exchange by Microsoft. If you are an Exchange Server user, you can skip this section if you get your Internet mail through the Exchange Server Internet Mail Connector.

One thing all these Internet services have in common is that they do not add an Internet entry type to the Personal Address Book. This doesn't mean you can't add Internet addresses to the PAB; you just need to follow a slightly different procedure. If the only Internet service you have is Netscape, netApps Internet Series, or Workgroup Internet Gateway, then to enter Internet addresses in the PAB, use the Other Address entry type, and specify SMTP under "E-mail type," as shown in Figure 9.7.

The workgroup Internet services — netApps Internet Office and Workgroup Internet Gateway — are interesting alternatives to Exchange Server for small workgroups who want Internet mail but want to keep their configuration simple.

Figure 9.7
If Internet Mail is not a choice for new entries in the Personal Address Book, choose Other Address, then enter SMTP for the "E-mail type."

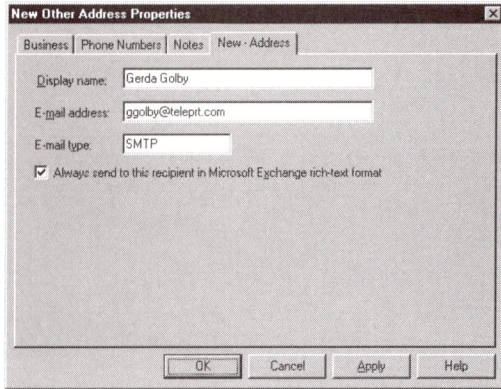

Netscape Internet Transport

Users of Netscape Navigator 2.0 can choose to receive and send mail through Exchange rather than through Netscape's built-in mail features. An Exchange profile can contain both Internet Mail and the Netscape Internet Transport, giving you access to two different mail accounts (see "Delivering Internet Messages," page 502 in Chapter 22).

While the Netscape Internet Transport was included with version 2.0 of Navigator, version 3.0 omits it. Installing version 3.0 over version 2.0 does not remove this service.

Special Note

The Netscape Internet Transport does not include a Remote Mail feature. However, it does have one feature that Microsoft's Internet Mail doesn't: It allows you to retain all messages on the mail server (see Figure 9.8c).

To use the Netscape Internet Transport in Exchange, you must first complete the Netscape Navigator 2.0 setup. Then add the Netscape Internet Transport service to your Exchange profile, completing the information about your Internet mail account shown on the tabs in Figures 9.8a, 9.8b, and 9.8c. You also can create a new profile using the Netscape Internet Transport and let the Setup Wizard walk you through the entry of all the required information.

In both Netscape Navigator 2.0 and the later 3.0 version, there is one other setting related to Exchange. You can control whether Netscape or Exchange is used to compose a mail message when you click on a mailto link on a Web page. (A mailto link is a hotlink to an e-mail address; you click it to send a message.) To view or change this setting, choose Options, Mail and News Preferences. On the Appearance tab, if you want to use Exchange for mailto links, select "Use Exchange Client for mail and news."

Figure 9.8a

The information required for the Netscape Internet Transport is the same as that needed for Internet Mail. Though an NNTP host name for newsgroup postings is also requested, Exchange does not support posting to newsgroups.

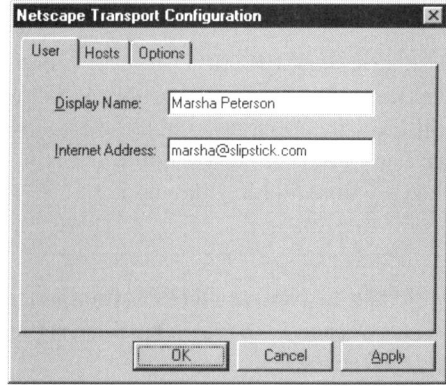

Figure 9.8b

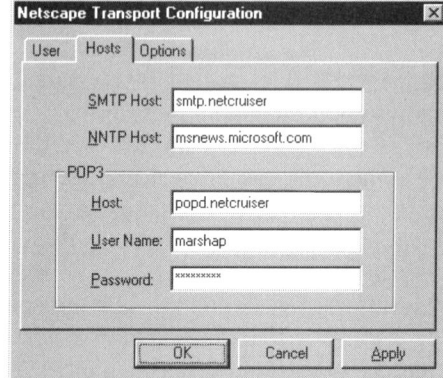

Figure 9.8c

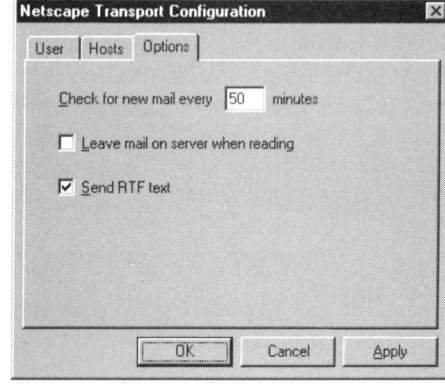

netApps Internet Series

A trial version of the two Internet Series applications from netApps — Internet Personal and Internet Office — is included on the CD. Internet Personal operates as a single-user service with the capability to access more than one Internet mail account. Internet Office functions as a gateway connected to a Microsoft Mail postoffice, either a full Microsoft Mail Server or a workgroup postoffice (see Chapter 23, "Managing a Workgroup Postoffice"). Internet Office allows multiple users to send and receive mail through a single Internet connection. Two components are involved:

- The netApps Systems Internet Series service for Exchange
- Internet Server — a separate program run on the local machine in Personal mode or on a server for Office mode

The Internet Server used in Office mode must be able to connect to the Internet, either with a modem or via a direct network connection. The server does not need to be the same machine as the Microsoft Mail postoffice.

Once you run the setup program, configure the Internet Server. You will also need to add the netApps Systems Internet Series service for Exchange to the profile of each user who wants to send or receive mail via the Internet. Detailed instructions are included on the CD.

Workgroup Internet Gateway

Like the netApps Internet Series, Workgroup Internet Gateway (WIG) lets a group of users send mail through a single (usually dial-up) connection to the Internet. Unlike the netApps Internet Series, WIG establishes a separate database to manage incoming and outgoing Internet messages instead of using the Microsoft Mail postoffice (see Appendix B, "Exchange Resources"). You can use WIG to support multiple Internet mail users in two different ways:

- Through a single Internet mail account that allows multiple "virtual" users
- Through separate Internet mail accounts for each user

You can also combine these two approaches for any given user.

The machine hosting the WIG database is set up as a gateway. Configure the gateway first, following the detailed instructions in the WIG manual. Then add WIG as a service in Exchange on the gateway computer. Finally, add WIG as an Exchange service on the other computers in the workgroup.

Online Services

The Microsoft Network (MSN) and CompuServe make it possible to send and receive mail from your online service's mail account through Exchange. In fact, Exchange is the only way to send and receive MSN messages (at the time this chapter is being written in the fall of 1996). However, that may not be the case for long. Both services are moving toward better integration with the Internet. It's likely that will include standard POP3/SMTP mail servers that can work with any Internet service in Exchange.

The Microsoft Network

MSN is included with Windows 95. The necessary settings for Exchange are added to your system when you install the MSN application (through the Control Panel, Add/Remove Programs, Windows Setup). All you have to do is add MSN to your Exchange profile.

The most important setting for MSN is how you connect to the service. This is not part of the Exchange profile, but is controlled through either The Microsoft Network Sign In dialog box or The Microsoft Network icon on your desktop. Right-click the desktop icon, then choose Connection Settings to display the Connection Settings dialog box (Figure 9.9). You'll also find a Settings button on the Sign In dialog box.

Figure 9.9

You can reach MSN through a direct dial-up number, via a DUN connection to another Internet service provider, or through an MSN access server connected to your local area network.

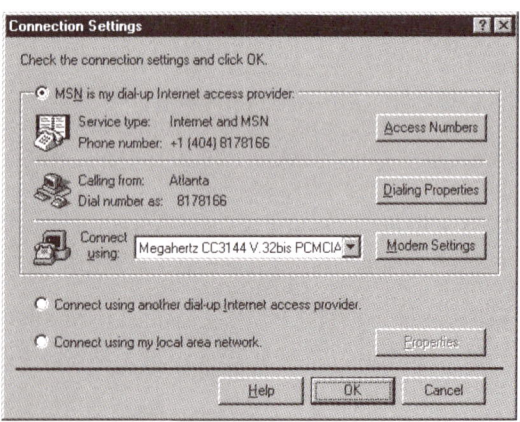

If you have Internet access through a dial-up provider or via your LAN, you can choose to use either of those connections to access MSN. Otherwise, your choice should be "MSN is my dial-up Internet access provider," even if the only local MSN access number is for MSN only, rather than for Internet and MSN. Click the Access Numbers button to select the local access number you want to use.

Table 9.1 lists the Exchange settings for MSN, available in the properties dialog box for the service.

Table 9.1 Microsoft Network Settings

Setting	Description	Default
Download mail when e-mail starts up from MSN	When enabled, MSN messages are automatically downloaded if Exchange is running when you connect to MSN, or if you connect to MSN then start Exchange. If you want to use Remote Mail for MSN, disable this setting. Also disable it if you want to control when you get your MSN messages with Deliver Now.	Enabled
Disconnect after updating headers from Remote Mail	Disconnects the computer from MSN after updating headers in Remote Mail. This setting is effective only for the original Windows 95 operating system version of Exchange, not the Windows Messaging update or Exchange Server client.	Disabled
Disconnect after transferring mail from Remote Mail	Disconnects the computer from MSN after using the Connect function in Remote Mail (or, for the original Windows 95 operating system version, after using the Transfer Mail function).	Enabled
Connect to MSN to check names	Connects to MSN if an address cannot be matched against the Personal Address Book or other local address lists.	Disabled

If mail is waiting for you when you log on to MSN, you'll see a message saying "You have received new mail on The Microsoft Network." Click OK to clear the message, then start Exchange either from the desktop Inbox icon or Programs menu (or you can click E-Mail on the main MSN screen). Once

Exchange starts, the messages will be downloaded automatically if "Download mail when e-mail starts up from MSN" is checked. Otherwise, use either Tools, Deliver Now or Tools, Remote Mail to download your MSN messages.

A few other notes about MSN:

- In an MSN bulletin board, there is an option to reply to the sender of a message via e-mail, even if Exchange is not currently running. However, you may need to start Exchange first to avoid getting an error that the message can't be sent.

- If you are connected to MSN and send a message, it is delivered immediately without any need to use Tools, Deliver Now or Tools, Remote Mail.

- To search the MSN member list, open the Address Book and choose Microsoft Network from the Show Names list. After you connect to MSN, choose Tools, Find.

- To change the properties for your own name on the MSN address list, search the MSN member list as described above. When you find your name, double-click it to open the properties dialog box, where you can enter information about your personal and professional interests.

- If people who aren't MSN users want to send you messages, give them your address as *<MemberID>*@msn.com, where *<MemberID>* is your actual MSN member ID.

- If you get the error message "The MAPI spooler has unexpectedly exited" when you start Exchange, the Remote Mail headers file for MSN may need to be rebuilt. Look in the Windows folder for a file name MOS*<username>*.rhc, where *<username>* is your Windows user name. In other words, if you log on as LisaC, look for MOSLisaC.rhc. Delete this file to resolve the problem. The Remote Mail headers file will be rebuilt automatically.

CompuServe Mail

Version 1.1 of the CompuServe Mail service is available for download on CompuServe (GO CSMAIL). An earlier version can be found on the Windows 95 CD, but that version supports only direct dial-up connections. The later version also supports connections via the Internet through DUN, plus direct connections.

The Remote Mail function of CompuServe Mail is incompatible with all versions of Exchange except the original Windows 95 operating system version. Messages in the Outbox are delivered, but no headers are retrieved for incoming messages.

To install the CompuServe Mail service, run Setup.exe found in the folder for the setup files. The setup program installs the necessary files and offers to add CompuServe Mail to your default profile. You should definitely review the settings for CompuServe Mail, particularly the connection settings, and add scheduled connection times if you wish.

People who want to send mail to your CompuServe account via the Internet need to use an address in this format: *99999.999@compuserve.com*, where *99999,999* represents the user's CompuServe ID. Notice that the comma in the CompuServe ID turns into a period in the Internet address.

Connection Settings

On the Connection tab of the CompuServe Mail Settings dialog box (Figure 9.10), choose how to connect to the CompuServe mail server. Table 9.2 lists the three available choices.

Table 9.2 CompuServe Mail Connection Types	
Connection	**Description**
Windows Modem Settings	By dialing into the phone number listed under Phone Number, using the modem specified under Preferred TAPI Line
Winsock Connection	Using either a dial-up or direct connection to the Internet
Direct Connection	Via a direct serial port connection

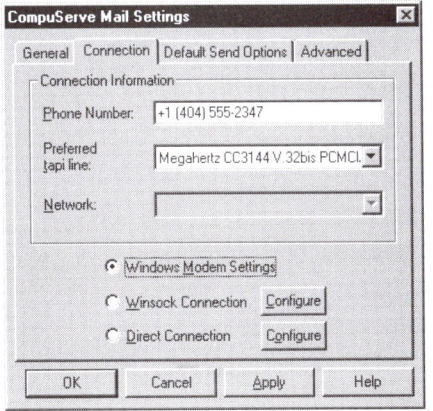

Figure 9.10
CompuServe offers direct dial-up, DUN, and direct connection options.

For a direct dial-up connection (Windows Modem Settings), enter the phone number in international format, with the country and area code as shown in Figure 9.10, if you want to use the Windows dialing properties (call waiting, location, and so on) set up on your computer.

If you choose Winsock Connection, click the Configure button to display the WinSock Settings dialog box shown in Figure 9.11. If you chose during setup to install the CompuServe Dialer, then you can use it to make the connection, rather than Windows DUN. However, if you are already using a Windows dial-up networking connection for Internet access, it's recommended that you clear the Use CompuServe Dialer box. This also has the advantage of letting you check several mail servers (Internet Mail server, Exchange Server, CompuServe, Microsoft Network) via the Internet during one connection. If you choose Direct Connection, click the Configure button to set the communications port and baud rate for the connection.

Figure 9.11

The Internet settings on the WinSock Settings dialog box usually don't need any changes by the user.

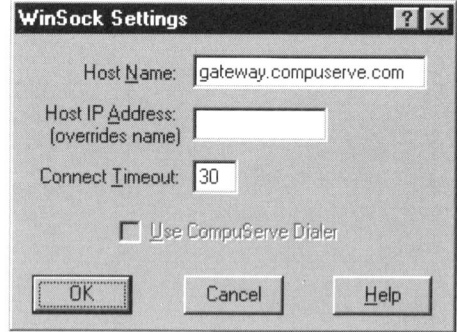

To schedule connections to receive and send CompuServe messages, switch to the Advanced tab (Figure 9.12), and click the Schedule Connect Times button. In the Connection Times dialog box (Figure 9.13), you can choose to receive and send mail

• When Exchange starts
• At a specific time interval
• At a particular time each day

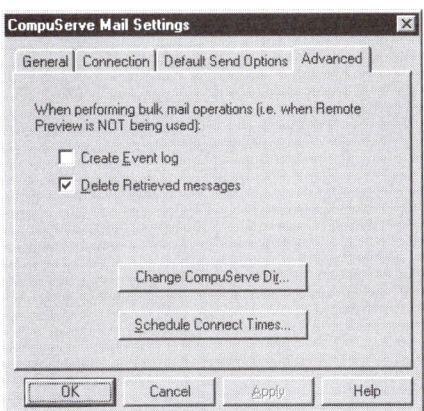

Figure 9.12
Use the Advanced tab for additional settings and to get to the connection scheduling dialog box.

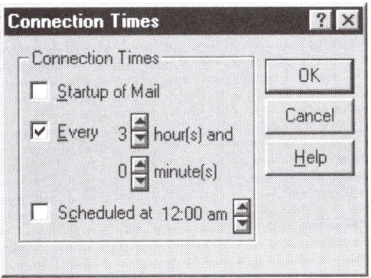

Figure 9.13
CompuServe offers three different ways to schedule mail connections.

Other Settings

Briefly, here are the other settings available for CompuServe Mail. On the General tab (Figure 9.14), set the Name, CompuServe Id, and Password for your CompuServe account.

On the Default Send Options tab (Figure 9.15) are settings for using RTF and setting release and expiration times. You should leave these clear on the CompuServe Mail Settings dialog box. Instead, set these send options for individual messages. Use RTF only when sending to other CompuServe members who are using Exchange. On the Advanced tab (Figure 9.11), clear the "Create Event log" box. You will still receive messages in your Inbox about problems with CompuServe Mail but will not be bothered by routine messages. "Delete Retrieved messages" is checked by default, and that's the preferred setting (otherwise, you'll keep downloading the same messages over and over).

If you use WinCIM or other CompuServe software, Exchange can make use of your CompuServe address book, as long as you indicate the location of your CompuServe folder on the Advanced tab (Figure 9.12). Click the Change

Figure 9.14

Basic information about your CompuServe account is entered on the General tab.

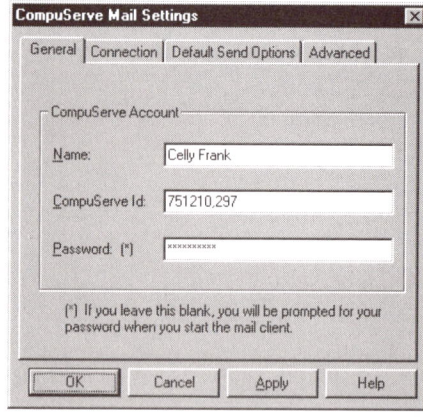

Figure 9.15

Use rich-text format (RTF) only for messages sent to other CompuServe members who rely on Exchange.

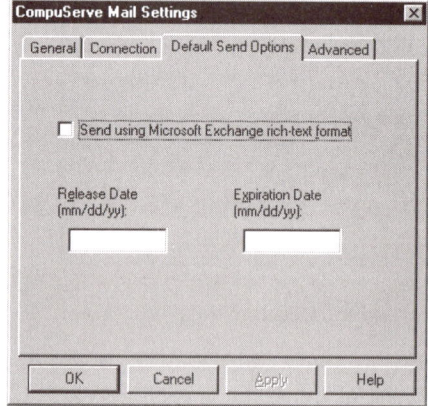

CompuServe <u>Dir</u> button to browse your system for that folder, which will usually be Cserve (use the parent CompuServe folder, not the WinCIM or other subfolder).

WinFax PRO 7.0

WinFax PRO 7.0 adds a New WinFax option to the Compose menu in Exchange and allows you to view incoming and outgoing faxes through the Exchange Viewer. Winfax, however, does not install as a complete service in Exchange. Instead, it uses MAPI (see "Exchange Components," page 15 in Chapter 2) to communicate between the WinFax application and Exchange.

WinFax's integration with Exchange is two-way. You can use Exchange folders and the Exchange Personal Address Book from within WinFax, and you can use the Exchange Viewer to view WinFax's folders for sent and received faxes.

A number of settings related to Exchange are established during WinFax setup. Watch for these options:

- When you choose the type of installation, you'll probably want to pick Typical. If you prefer the Custom installation, take care to select the Exchange option.

- You'll be asked whether you want to use your Exchange folders from within WinFax PRO 7.0 (Figure 9.16). If so, you need to specify how WinFax should deal with Exchange profiles — always use the same profile or prompt on startup.

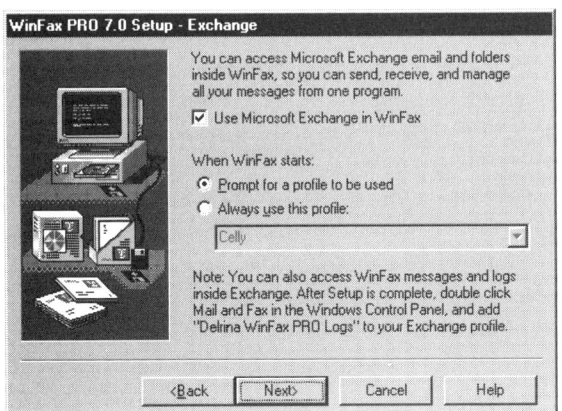

Figure 9.16

If you choose to use Exchange folders from within WinFax PRO 7.0, you must either indicate which Exchange profile to use or choose to select a profile each time.

- When you see the option for uninstalling Microsoft Fax, you may want to choose No (the default is Yes). Doing so will let you wait until you have WinFax working before you delete Microsoft Fax.

After WinFax PRO 7.0 setup is complete, you have one more job to do. If you want to be able to see WinFax faxes, both received and sent, from within the Exchange Viewer, use the Mail and Fax (or Mail) applet in the Control Panel to add the WinFax Logs service to your profile(s). Figure 9.17 shows the options for this service.

Figure 9.17

The properties for the WinFax PRO 7.0 Logs service let you choose how to have incoming faxes delivered and whether to preview outgoing faxes.

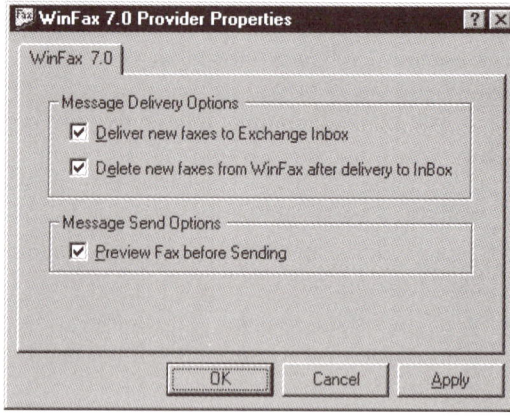

Microsoft Phone

Microsoft Phone turns your computer into a telephone answering machine, delivering voice-mail messages to Exchange, using MAPI in much the same way as WinFax PRO 7.0 does. All the settings for Microsoft Phone's interaction with Exchange are controlled by Microsoft Phone, rather than by your Exchange profile.

Microsoft Phone is available only with certain modems that support the full range of features of Unimodem V, Microsoft's latest universal modem driver for Windows 95. However, the list of Unimodem V modems is growing; this is a feature you should consider in the next modem you buy.

Here's a partial list of computers, modems, and manufacturers that support Unimodem V:

- Compaq Presario models 520, 720, 820, and 920
- Creative Labs Phone Blaster
- Logicode 14.4 data/fax/voice PCMCIA
- Diamond Multimedia TeleCommander 2500
- some Cirrus Logic modems
- some Aztech Systems modems
- some Rockwell design PCMCIA modems

Unimodem V includes a program called Operator Agent that discriminates between voice, data, and fax calls. This means you can automatically route incoming calls to the right program (assuming it is running), all within the same PC. No more fax tones on your answering machine!

To set up Microsoft Phone to add voice mail to Exchange, you must first install the Unimodem V software, then install Microsoft Phone. If you want your modem to handle both voice and fax calls, or voice and data, or all three, then you must also configure Operator Agent.

Configuring Operator Agent

When you install Unimodem V from the disk provided by the modem manufacturer, Operator Agent is installed automatically; to configure it, follow these steps:

1. Click the Start button, then choose Programs, Accessories, Operator. The Microsoft Operator Wizard starts. Click Next three times to move past the dialog boxes that explain how the program works.

2. On the dialog box shown in Figure 9.18, select either the male or female greeting included with Operator Agent. Alternatively, you may record a greeting (assuming your computer has a microphone attached), or select a greeting recorded earlier. This greeting is played to a caller only if the type of call cannot be automatically detected. Click Next to continue.

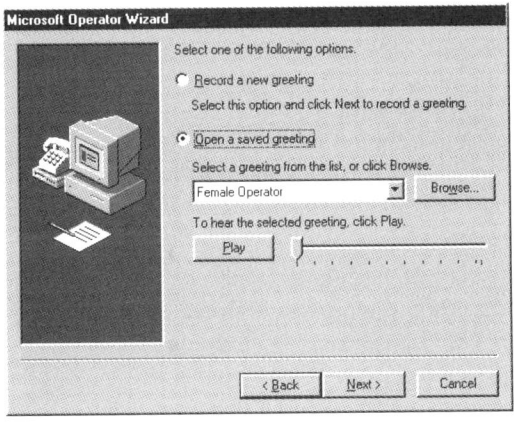

Figure 9.18
Operator Agent includes prerecorded female and male greetings, or you can use one of your own.

3. On the next dialog box of the wizard (Figure 9.19), specify the order in which Operator Agent should try to connect the call to a program if neither automatic detection nor the greeting succeeds in determining the nature of the call. Click Next to continue, then Finish to complete the configuration and start Operator Agent.

Figure 9.19

If the greeting is turned off or the caller doesn't respond, Operator Agent attempts to connect the call to a program in the order you specify in this dialog box.

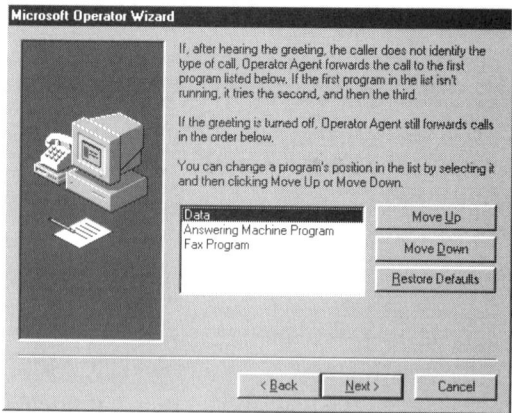

A few additional notes on Operator Agent:

- When Operator Agent is running, it places an icon on the Windows taskbar.

- According to Microsoft, you can't have just data and fax programs running for incoming calls to connect to; you must also be running a voice messaging program, such as Microsoft Phone.

- The default order is voice, fax, data. If you record your own greeting, you should tell the caller to press 1 to leave a voice message, 2 to transmit a fax, or 3 to connect to a data line. However, if you change the call routing order so that, for example, it looks like the order in Figure 9.19, you must also record a new greeting. To match the call routing order in Figure 9.19, you would instruct the caller to press 1 to connect to a data line, 2 to leave a voice-mail message, and 3 to send a fax.

- You can change the call routing order at any time. Double-click the Operator Agent icon on the taskbar to display the Microsoft Operator Agent dialog box, then click the Properties button. Click the Call Routing Priorities button in the Microsoft Operator Agent Properties dialog box.

- If you plan to use Operator Agent for call discrimination to allow Microsoft Fax to coexist with dial-up networking, leave the greeting turned on. Some people find that data, voice, fax is a good response order, though that means that a voice caller who doesn't respond to the greeting will get modem tones as DUN Server tries to take the call. Another approach is to put voice first; in that case, callers who want to make a DUN connection will need to respond properly to the greeting. You may need to experiment to find out what works best for your callers.

Configuring Microsoft Phone

Microsoft Phone (Figure 9.20) is installed with its own setup program. You can find this program on a separate Microsoft disk or CD in the modem package.

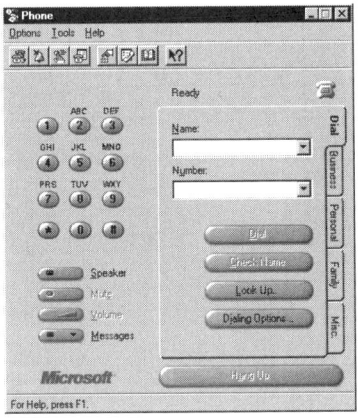

Figure 9.20
Microsoft Phone helps you manage both incoming and outgoing calls.

To start Phone, click the Start button, then choose Programs, Microsoft Phone, Microsoft Phone. You see the Microsoft Phone Startup Wizard, which walks you through the steps needed to set up an answering machine. I recommend that you read "Introducing Microsoft Phone" first and fill out the worksheet before you run the wizard, especially if you want to set up a complex answering system with many options for callers or multiple mailboxes where they can leave messages.

Once you complete the Phone setup with the Startup Wizard, Phone will be configured to place messages directly in your Exchange Inbox using the default Exchange profile. If you want Phone to use a different profile, follow these steps:

1. Choose Options, Phone Properties, then switch to the Messages tab (Figure 9.21).
2. Under "Message storage," select the "Profile name" you want Microsoft Phone to use.
3. If the Inbox for that profile is in a password-protected Personal Folders file, enter the password under "Personal folders password."
4. Click OK to save the changes.

Figure 9.21

Specify the Exchange profile that Microsoft Phone should use for storing messages.

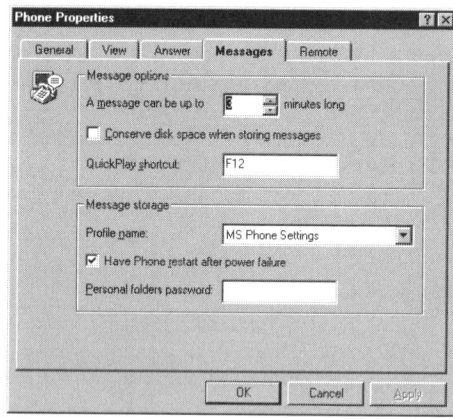

When Microsoft Phone is active, incoming voice-mail messages are stored in Exchange. In the Exchange Viewer, these messages are marked with the talking telephone icon shown in Figure 9.22.

Figure 9.22

Incoming voice messages have their own icon in Microsoft Exchange.

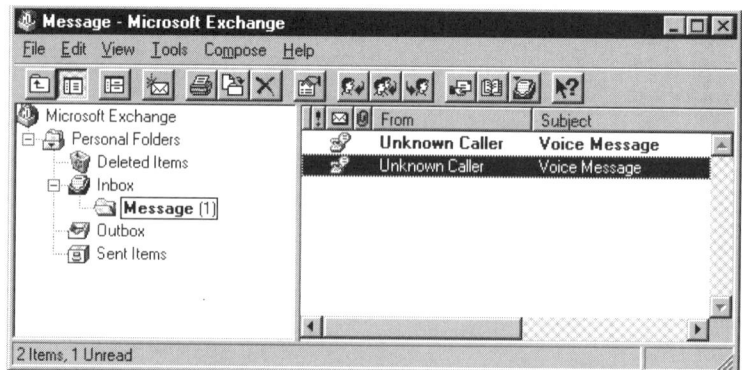

To listen to a voice-mail message, double-click it in the Exchange Viewer. Sound Recorder starts, as shown in Figure 9.23. Click the play button to listen to it.

Microsoft Phone also includes its own QuickPlay viewer to access your voice mail, as an alternative to Exchange. To use QuickPlay, switch to Microsoft Phone (if it's not the active program), then press F12. All your messages will play back in order, as they would on a traditional answering machine.

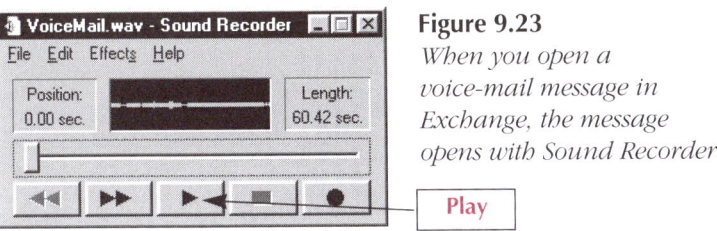

Figure 9.23
When you open a voice-mail message in Exchange, the message opens with Sound Recorder.

Summary

Exchange is designed to accommodate many different kinds of services, both those that connect to different sorts of mail servers and those that add new features such as security or connections to other messaging applications. One good habit is to check the settings for each new service you install, even if a setup wizard seems to have handled everything for you.

In this chapter, we've looked at the settings for a number of Exchange services for connecting to enterprise mail servers, online services, and the Internet. We also reviewed the settings for WinFax PRO 7.0 and Microsoft Phone, which interact with Exchange in a slightly different way from the services that install directly in Exchange. Microsoft Phone is bundled with certain modems; the package also includes Operator Agents, which can discriminate between incoming fax, data, and voice calls.

Key Points

- Always quit Exchange before installing a new service.

- If you use an Internet service but see no Internet address type in the Personal Address Book, use an entry type of Other Address and specify SMTP under E-mail Type.

For More Information

We've spent some time in this chapter discussing the specifics of several Internet mail services. If that's one of your areas of interest, you'll want to review the issues covered in Chapter 22, "Working with Internet E-Mail."

It's not possible to review all the features of the different services available for Exchange, though we try to highlight potential problems and pleasures throughout the rest of the book, as we discuss basic and advanced Exchange functions. The Help file for each service can tell you more. You'll find these Help files on the Help menu in the Exchange Viewer window.

Chapter 10

Using the Exchange Viewer

When you launch Exchange, it opens to the Exchange Viewer, where messages are organized into folders and subfolders. In fact, the Viewer looks a lot like the Windows Explorer in Windows 95 and Windows NT. In this chapter, we'll help you learn how to move around in the Exchange Viewer, how to organize your messages and folders, and, if you're using an Exchange Server client, how to use views and filters to really customize Exchange.

Finding Your Way Around

The Exchange Viewer, shown in Figure 10.1, consists of two panes, one on the left for folders and one on the right to display messages. If you don't see both panes when you start Exchange, choose View, Folders or click the Show/Hide Folder List button (shown depressed in Figure 10.1).

Figure 10.1

The Exchange Viewer gives you a hierarchical view of your personal folders and any public folders in the left pane. Messages and documents are listed in the right pane.

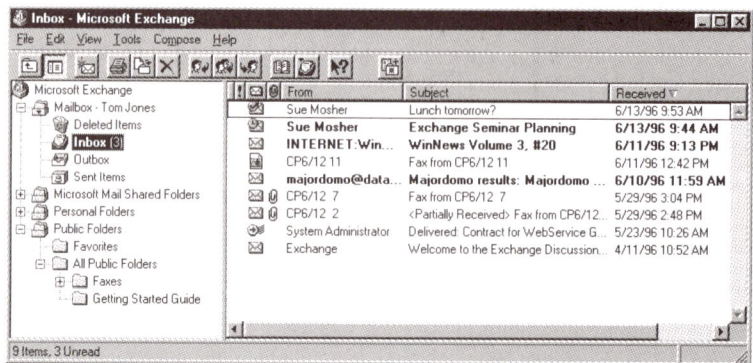

You can turn the toolbar at the top of the Viewer on and off with View, Toolbar. You'll see how to customize the toolbar later in this chapter. At the bottom of the Viewer, a status bar gives the total number of items in the current folder and the number unread. Toggle this status bar on and off by choosing View, Status Bar.

Folders

The list of folders you see on the left of the Viewer will depend on the client you're using and the services installed in your profile.

Depending on the client you're using (operating system or Exchange Server) and the services installed in your profile, you may see a different list of folders on the left of the Viewer. Table 10.1 lists the type of folder sets you're likely to encounter.

The Exchange Server mailbox folder contains four permanent folders. So does the first set of Personal Folders added to an operating system Exchange client profile:

Deleted Items	Items that have been deleted from other folders
Inbox	Incoming messages
Outbox	Outgoing messages that have not yet been delivered
Sent Items	Outgoing messages that have been delivered

Table 10.1 Types of Folder Sets	
Type	**Description**
Mailbox	For Exchange Server clients, a message store on the Exchange Server where your messages are kept. If you are working offline, Exchange reads the copy of your mailbox kept in the offline folders file.
Microsoft Mail Shared Folders	For users of the Microsoft Mail service, a set of folders stored in the postoffice for group access.
Personal Folders	A message store kept as a separate file, either on your system or on a server (for access from multiple workstations). If you are using the Windows 95 or Windows NT operating system client, this may be the only folder set you see.
Public Folders	For Exchange Server clients, a set of folders stored on the server for access by various users, depending on the permissions granted for each folder.

Special Note

You can give other users access to your Exchange Server mailbox folders. For example, you might have an assistant to help manage your mail. See the section "Sharing Mailboxes," page 440 in Chapter 19.

As we discussed in Chapter 4, "Configuring Profiles," a profile can contain more than one set of Personal Folders. When you add a new set of Personal Folders to an existing profile, the only folder created is the Deleted Items folder.

In the Exchange Server clients, the permanent folders have distinctive icons, which you can see in Figure 10.1. In the Windows 95 and NT operating system clients, permanent folders use the same folder icon as other folders. Table 10.2 lists the icons used in the folder pane. We'll look at how to create additional folders and customize them a little later in this chapter.

Table 10.2 Icons in the Folder Pane

Icon	Description
	Primary message store, where new messages are delivered
	Set of folders
	Individual folder
	Open folder
	Folder containing subfolders. To view the subfolders, click on the + icon, press the right arrow key, or press the + key on the number pad.
	Folder open to display its subfolders. To collapse the view, click on the – icon, press the left arrow key, or press the – key on the number pad.
	Subfolder under the Favorites folder (Exchange Server client only; see the "Favorites Folder" sidebar)
	Open subfolder under the Favorites folder (Exchange Server client only)
	Private folder in an Exchange Server client mailbox with synchronization enabled

Messages

Unread messages are shown in bold, and read messages are shown in normal font.

The message pane, on the right side of the Viewer, contains both messages and other documents stored in Exchange. The icons help you identify what kind of item you're looking at. Table 10.3 on page 224 summarizes those icons you are most likely to see.

Previous users of Microsoft Mail may be surprised that there is no open envelope to distinguish read messages from unread. Instead, unread messages are shown in bold, and read messages are shown in normal font. Folders containing unread messages are shown in bold. On the Exchange Server clients, you'll also see the number of unread messages in blue next to the folder name.

Favorites Folder

The Favorites folder is a special folder listed under Public Folders on Exchange Server clients (see Figure 10.1). This folder helps you work more efficiently in two ways:

- By providing a fast way to get to the public folders you use the most
- By keeping selected folders synchronized with the server so you can work with them even when you're not connected to the server

If your organization has a large library of public folders, add to the Favorites folder only that handful that you browse on a regular basis. To add a public folder to Favorites, select the public folder, then choose File, Add to Favorites or click the Add to Favorites button.

To set a Favorites folder so that you can work with it offline, follow these steps:

1. Select the folder.
2. Choose File, Properties, then switch to the Synchronization tab. You can also right-click on the folder, then choose Properties to get to the option tabs.
3. Choose to work with the folder When Offline or Online.
4. Click OK.

We'll talk more about synchronization in Chapter 13, "Working Remotely."

To remove a folder from Favorites, select the folder, then choose File, Remove from Favorites.

Though I often talk about messages in this chapter, all the actions — such as open, delete, move, and copy — can be applied to any type of item.

Special Note

Applications such as Microsoft Schedule+ and Microsoft Project add their own icons for different types of messages. Other applications that build on Exchange's messaging structure also can do this. For familiar document types, such as Excel spreadsheets and Word reports, you'll see the same icons for those documents as you would in Windows Explorer.

Table 10.3 Icons in the Message Pane

Icon	Description
✉	Standard message
✉ 📎	Standard message with attachment
✉	Message with a digital signature
💼	Message sealed with advanced security encryption
⊘	"Not delivered" receipt
⊕	Delivery receipt
❗✉	High-priority message
⬇✉	Low-priority message

Getting Help

You can find detailed information about Exchange procedures on the Help menu. There's a general help file and usually a separate help file for each service you have installed. You can also press F1 to bring up the main help file.

If you want to know what a toolbar button does, leave the mouse pointer over it for a moment and a label will pop up with the name of the button. For a more detailed description of a button or other control, click the Help button, then click the button you want to know more about. The Windows Help topic about that button appears, assuming help is available for that particular button.

Customizing the Toolbar

The most frequently used Exchange functions are on the default toolbar, but you also can customize this toolbar. The available buttons are listed in Table 10.4.

Table 10.4 Toolbar Buttons

Button	Name	Description	On Default Toolbar	Exchange Server Clients Only
	Up One Level	Display the folder one level up	X	
	View Folders	Display the folder pane	X	
	File – Open	Open the selected message(s)		
	File – Save As	Save the selected message(s) as a file		
	File – Move	Move the selected message(s) or folder to a new folder	X	
	File – Copy	Copy the selected message(s) or folder to another folder		
	File – New Folder	Create a new folder		
	File – Delete	Delete the selected message(s) or folder	X	
	File – Rename	Rename the current message or folder		
	File – Properties	Display the properties of the current message or folder		
	File – Print	Print the current message(s)		

continued

Table 10.4 Toolbar Buttons, *continued*

Button	Name	Description	On Default Toolbar	Exchange Server Clients Only
	Edit – Select All	Select all messages in the current folder		
	Edit – Mark as Read	Mark the selected message(s) as read		
	Edit – Mark as Unread	Mark the selected message(s) as unread (i.e., in bold)		
	Tools – Find	Display the Find dialog box		
	Compose – New Message	Compose a new message	X	
	Compose – New Post in This Folder	Compose a new item to be posted		X
	Compose – Reply to Sender	Reply to the sender of the selected message	X	
	Compose – Reply to All	Reply to the sender and all CCs for the selected message	X	
	Compose – Post Reply in This Folder	Post a reply to the selected item		X
	Compose – Forward	Forward the selected item	X	
	Goes to Inbox	Switch to the Inbox folder	X	

continued

Table 10.4 Toolbar Buttons, continued

Button	Name	Description	On Default Toolbar	Exchange Server Clients Only
	Goes to Outbox	Switch to the Outbox folder		
	Tools – Deliver Now	Deliver messages from the Outbox to all services in the profile		
	Tools – Address Book	Display the Address Book dialog box	X	
	Help	Turn the pointer into a Help pointer that you can click on any button or control to find out more about it	X	
	Add to Favorites	Add the selected folder to your Favorites folder	X	X
	Remove from Favorites	Remove the selected folder from your Favorites folder		X
	Folder Design Cue Cards	Display cue cards to help you design new folders		X

To add a button to the toolbar, follow these steps:

1. Choose Tools, Customize Toolbar to open the dialog box shown in Figure 10.2.

2. Select a button from the "Available buttons" list in the Customize Toolbar dialog box.

3. In the "Toolbar buttons" list, select the button where you want the new button to be inserted (it will be added before the button you select). You

can also drag the button directly from the "Available buttons" list to the "Toolbar buttons" list.

4. Click the Add button.

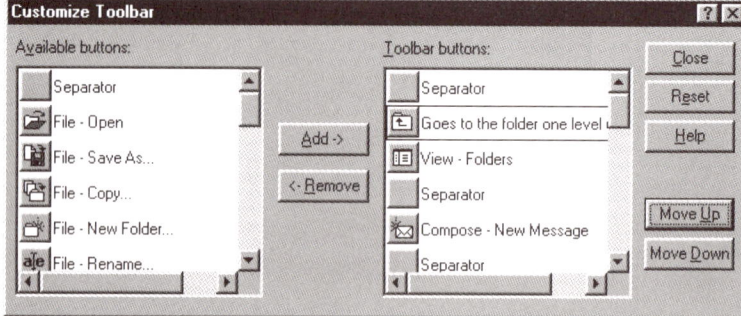

Figure 10.2

Add, remove, and rearrange buttons on the toolbar to fit the way you want to work.

To remove a button from the toolbar, select it in the "Toolbar buttons" list, then click the Remove button. Use the Move Up and Move Down buttons to reposition a button in the "Toolbar buttons" list, or drag the button to the desired position. You also can add a Separator button between any two buttons to put space between them on the toolbar.

Special Note

You can't add a button to deliver mail via a particular service. The Tools – Deliver Now button delivers to all services in sequence. That order happens to be the reverse of the order in which services are listed on the Delivery tab of the Options dialog box, which you can access by choosing Tools, Options (see "Delivery Settings," page 74 in Chapter 4).

If you want to revert to the way the toolbar looked when you first installed Exchange, click the Reset button. Click the Close button when you've finished customizing the toolbar. The changes take effect immediately.

You also can change the spacing and order of the toolbar buttons right from the Exchange Viewer. Hold down the Shift key while you click a button, then drag it to a new location.

Add-ons such as WordMail add their own buttons to the toolbar library; whether to include those buttons on the visible toolbar is up to you.

Working with Messages

To read an item shown in the message pane on the right side of the Exchange Viewer, double-click it or select it, then press Enter. If the message is not a standard message, it will open in the form or application appropriate for the item. A *form* is a special format for creating and/or viewing a specific type of information. The Compose New Message form is itself an example.

To move an item to a different folder, click on the item with the pointer and drag it to the new folder in the folder pane on the left. To copy an item to another folder, hold down the Ctrl key while you click and drag the item to the destination folder.

If you right-click on a message, you'll get a context menu with the most frequently used functions. Figure 10.3 shows the message context menu. "Post Reply in This Folder" appears only on Exchange Server clients.

To read an item in the message pane, double-click it or select it, then press Enter.

Figure 10.3
Right-click on any message or document to get access to the most common functions.

In case you want to give the mouse a rest while reading and responding to messages, Table 10.5 lists the keystrokes used to move around the message and folder pane in the Exchange Viewer.

Table 10.5 Message and Folder Pane Keystrokes

Action	Keystroke	Message Pane	Folder Pane
Read the selected message	Enter	X	
View properties	Alt+Enter	X	X
Print	Ctrl+P	X	
Save as a file	F12	X	
Delete	Del or Ctrl+D	X	X
Move to previous message or folder	Up arrow	X	X
Move to next message or folder	Down arrow	X	X
Move to top of message or folder list	Home	X	X
Move to end of message or folder list	End	X	X
Expand a group of messages or folders	Right arrow or + key on the number pad	X	X
Collapse a group of messages or folders	Left arrow or – key on the number pad	X	X
Switch between folder and message pages	Tab	X	X

Working with Folders

Just a single click on a folder opens it; there's no need to double-click. You can move a folder by dragging it to the destination folder. If you just want to copy a folder, hold down the Ctrl key while you click and drag. In the Exchange Server clients, you also have the option to copy the design of a folder — its rules, forms, views, and permissions. We'll cover that option in Chapter 19, "Using Exchange to Collaborate."

If you right-click on a folder, the context menu of the most frequently used functions pops up, as shown in Figure 10.4.

Figure 10.4
Right-click on a folder and you'll get a context menu of the most common actions.

If you prefer to navigate with the keyboard, then you'll want to learn the keystrokes in Table 10.5.

Creating New Folders

You can create new folders either as top-level folders or as subfolders for existing folders. To create a new top-level folder, follow these steps:

1. Select the folder set where you want to create the new folder.
2. Choose File, New Folder.
3. Give the folder a name, then click the OK button.

To create a new subfolder, follow the same procedure, only start by selecting the folder where you want to create the subfolder.

After you create a new folder, you might want to look at its properties. Select the folder, then choose File, Properties, or click on the folder with the right mouse button, then choose Properties. On all the Exchange clients, you'll see a General tab (Figure 10.5) defining two properties for the folder: its name and Description. You might want to change the name of Deleted Items to Wastebasket.

For a Microsoft Mail Shared Folder, in addition to the General tab, there will be a Permissions tab (Figure 10.6), where you can specify whether or not other users can read, write, or delete items in a folder you created.

The folder properties on an Exchange Server client are more complex. You'll see additional tabs for Views, Administration, Forms, and Permissions. For

You can create new folders either as top-level folders or as subfolders for existing folders.

Figure 10.5

In the operating system clients, you can only change the name of a folder and give the folder an optional description.

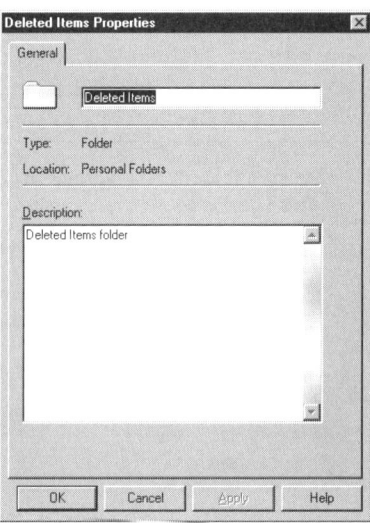

Figure 10.6

By default, new shared folders created in a Microsoft Mail postoffice give users read and write permissions, but not delete privileges.

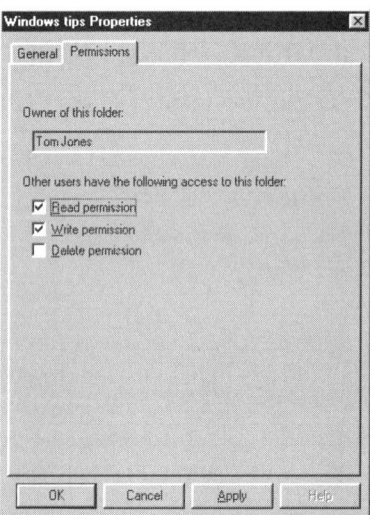

your mailbox folders and Favorites folders, a Synchronization tab determines how the offline folders version is kept up-to-date. We cover these Exchange Server client functions in depth in Chapter 19, "Using Exchange to Collaborate," and Chapter 13, "Working Remotely"; but we'll start looking at Views at the end of this chapter.

Customizing Folders

Once you start creating new folders and moving messages from the Inbox to them, you'll begin thinking about ways to organize those items more effectively. In all the Exchange clients, you can

- Add, remove, and reorder columns
- Change the sort order

  In the Exchange Server clients, you also can

- Filter folders according to particular rules
- Group messages into a tree hierarchy
- Combine grouping, sorting, filtering, and column assignments into saved views

Rearranging Columns

When you create a new folder, Exchange includes these columns by default:

Importance

Item Type

Attachment

From

Subject

Received

Size

If you're collecting all the messages for a project, you might also like to see the To field. That way, you can sort the messages you have sent by the recipient's name. It's easy to add To or any other column to an Exchange folder; to do so, follow these steps:

1. Choose View, Columns to display the Columns dialog box (Figure 10.7).
2. Select the column you want to add from the "Available columns" list on the left.
3. Click Add to add the column to the "Show the following columns" list on the right.

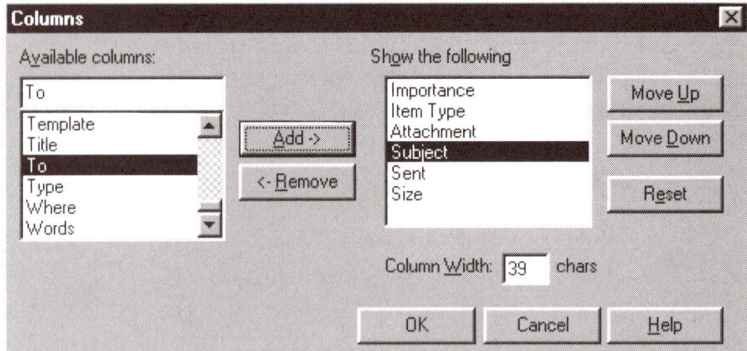

4. Use the Move <u>U</u>p or Move <u>D</u>own buttons to adjust the column's position, if necessary.

5. Click OK to close the Columns dialog box.

Note the <u>R</u>emove button in Figure 10.7. This button is the opposite of the <u>A</u>dd button. Use the Remove button to remove a column from a folder's display. The Columns dialog box also includes a <u>R</u>eset button to restore the columns to the way they were before you began making changes.

Although the Columns dialog box includes a <u>W</u>idth for each column, the width is measured in pixels, which doesn't tell you very much. The best way to adjust column widths is in the Exchange Viewer itself. Click on the border between two columns and drag the line right or left until the column is the width you want.

Sorting Items

To sort items in a folder, click on the column heading.

The quickest way to sort the items in a folder is to click on the heading for the column you want to sort by. Click once to sort in ascending order, click twice for descending order. As you can see in Figure 10.8, the Exchange Viewer indicates the sort column with an arrowhead on the column heading.

Figure 10.8

The down arrowhead on the Received column means this folder is sorted according to the time the messages are received, with the most recent at the top.

! ✉ 📎	From	Subject	Received ▽

Another way to sort is to choose <u>V</u>iew, <u>S</u>ort and choose the "<u>S</u>ort items by" column and order in the Sort dialog box shown in Figure 10.9.

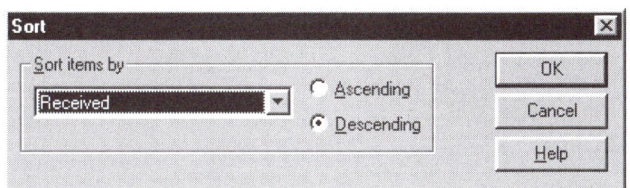

Figure 10.9

The Sort dialog box offers another method for changing the sort order of a folder.

Advanced Customizing with the Exchange Server Client

In the Windows 95 and Windows NT operating system clients, rearranging columns and changing the sort order are the only techniques available to customize a folder. One of the chief advantages of the Exchange Server clients is their ability to alter the appearance of a folder in three additional ways:

- Grouping messages so they appear in a collapsible hierarchy
- Filtering messages to show the partial contents of a folder
- Combining column choices, grouping, sorting, and filtering into saved views — both personal views that can apply to any folder and folder-specific views

These methods work with an Exchange Server mailbox or Public Folders, or with Personal Folders, but not with Microsoft Mail shared folders.

Special Note

Grouping Messages

The Exchange Server client's Group By function combines two techniques for arranging messages: grouping them hierarchically and sorting. Let's look at the Getting Started Guide folder, shown in Figure 10.10, as an example. This is an online Exchange Server user reference manual that your system administrator has probably placed in a public folder.

To see how grouping is set up for the Getting Started Guide, select the guide in the Public Folders folder, then choose <u>V</u>iew, <u>G</u>roup By to display the dialog box in Figure 10.11.

Figure 10.10

Look for the Getting Started Guide in the Public Folders folder on Exchange Server.

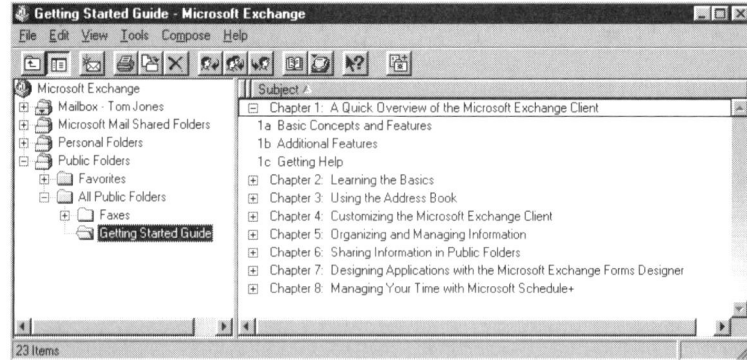

Figure 10.11

You can group items by up to four different fields.

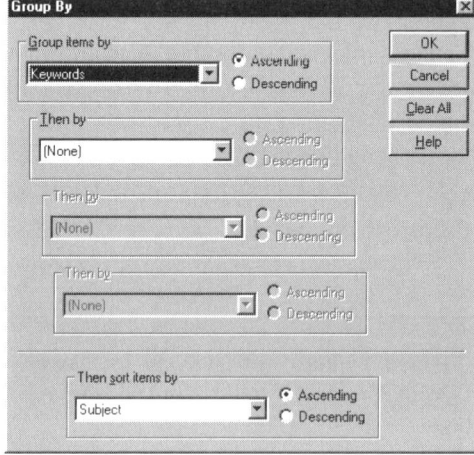

Under "Group items by," you can see that the Getting Started Guide is grouped by the Keywords field, which is available when you post an item in a folder. In this case, the chapter title was entered in the Keywords field when each section was posted. At the bottom of Figure 10.11, under "Then sort items by," the Subject field is used to sort items in ascending order. This puts the sections in alphabetical order under each chapter.

The Getting Started Guide is a relatively simple example of grouping. Because you can group by up to four different fields, grouping can get quite complex, especially when you add fields from custom forms. The fields available for grouping are those you have selected as columns for the selected folder.

Working with Filters

It seems that the more you use e-mail, the faster your Inbox fills up. The capability to filter the items in any folder is provided by one of several tools, such as Inbox Assistant, that the Exchange Server clients offer to help deal with the onslaught. When you use a filter, you tell Exchange to show you only those messages that meet certain criteria. For example, you might create a filter to display only messages

- Sent to your team in the last month by your boss
- From a mailing list you've subscribed to
- With the name of any of your top five customers in the text

As you might have guessed, you can "filter out" and "filter in." By that I mean you can create filters that *include* only certain messages or filters that *exclude* all messages that meet your criteria.

Let's create a simple filter to screen out all the messages from an electronic mailing list you've joined. Imagine that this list is filling your Inbox with 20 to 30 messages a day and you'd like to be able to go through those at your leisure, giving immediate attention to the "real" mail coming in.

Follow these steps to create a filter that shows all the messages in a folder *except* those from a mailing list

1. Switch to the folder you want to use to test your filter.
2. Choose View, Filter to display the Filter dialog box shown in Figure 10.12.

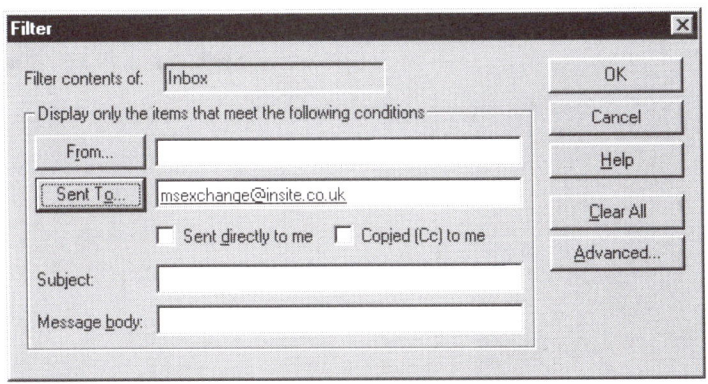

Figure 10.12
Construct a simple filter from the sender's name, the recipient's name, the subject, or text from the message itself.

3. Enter the criteria you want to use. For a mailing list with lots of contributors, this is the hardest part of the job. See the sidebar "Filtering Mailing Lists" for ideas.

4. Click Advanced to see more criteria in the Advanced dialog box shown in Figure 10.13.

Figure 10.13

Advanced filter rules can include date and size criteria, and criteria based on forms and document properties.

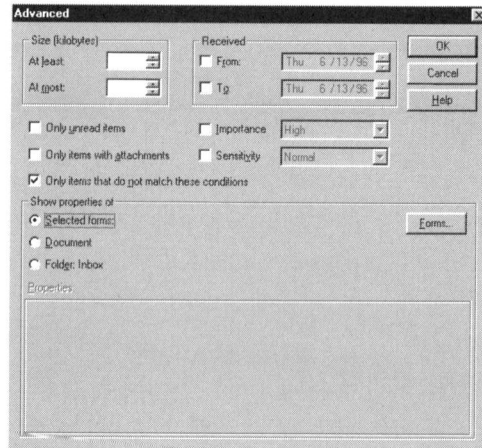

5. Check the box labeled "Only items that do <u>n</u>ot match these conditions." Doing this will cause the filter to hide all messages that match the criteria in the Filter dialog box.

6. Click OK twice to apply the filter to the current folder.

When you apply a filter, a funnel icon appears in the right corner of the status bar at the bottom of the Exchange Viewer. However, you'll see no change in the message counts shown in the status bar and in the unread total in parentheses next to the folder title. Those counts represent totals for the entire folder, not just the items currently filtered.

Now that you've seen how a filter is set up, let's look at the bottom half of the Advanced dialog box (Figure 10.13). Here's what you get from the selections under "Show properties of":

Selected forms	List of forms to choose from so you can filter based on their properties, including any custom fields
Document	List of document summary properties, such as author, number of slides, application name, or title
Folder	Properties associated with the custom forms for a folder

You can set criteria for any of these properties using the boxes and drop-down lists provided on the Advanced form.

Filtering Mailing Lists

There are two basic approaches to isolating messages from a mailing list with a filter. One is to use the address for the mailing list; the other, to locate some unique text in each message.

You can first try typing the e-mail address for the list — the address you'd use to contribute an item — in the Sent To box. This might work some of the time, but if another subscriber uses an alias to send to the list, then that subscriber's messages won't be filtered, because they'll appear in the Sent To column with a different name.

What's happening here is that typing a name in the Sent To box causes Exchange to filter by the display name. What you really want is to filter by the underlying e-mail address.

To filter by the e-mail address itself,

1. First create an entry for the mailing list in your Personal Address Book.

2. Then in the Filter dialog box (Figure 10.12), click the Sent To button to display the Address Book.

3. Select the entry for the mailing list, then click the Sent To button, then click OK to close the Address Book and return to the Filter dialog box.

The address you selected should now appear in the Sent To box, but it will be underlined, indicating that the e-mail address — and not just the display name — will be used in the filter.

The second method for filtering mailing list messages is to look for some common element among the messages. Usually there will be a signature block at the bottom telling you how to contribute to the list and how to end your subscription to the list. Find a unique phrase in that block and enter the phrase in the "Message body" box.

One more tip about filters: Before you set up an Inbox Assistant that acts on messages based on certain criteria, always create a filter with those criteria and test it against several days' worth of messages. For example, it's very bad form to have your Inbox Assistant send a response back every time it gets a message from the electronic mailing list. You'll want to make sure your Inbox Assistant filter ignores any such messages. We'll dig into Inbox Assistants in Chapter 18.

Working with Folder Views

If you construct a filter that works well in one folder, perhaps the filter could help you organize messages in another folder. Exchange offers a way to save that filter as a view so it can be reused.

A *view* is a saved collection of settings — filter, column choices, grouping, or sorting — or any combination of those methods. Earlier in this chapter, we talked about creating a folder and we said that a new folder always contains the same columns. With views, the columns are not a problem: You simply apply your favorite view(s) to the new folder, without going through the tedious task of setting columns, groups, sort, and filter. You can have personal views that work anywhere, plus folder views focusing on a particular folder. Four personal views are already built for you, ready to be applied to any folder. You'll find them on the View, Personal Views menu:

Normal	Columns: Importance, Item Type, Attachment, From, Subject, Received, Size
Group By From	Grouped by From, sorted by Received; same columns, arranged in a different order
Group By Subject	Grouped by Subject, sorted by Received; same columns, arranged in a different order
Group By Conversation Topic	Grouped by Conversation Topic, sorted by Conversation Thread; same columns, arranged in a different order

Group By Conversation Topic is most useful in discussion folders using forms that allow you to follow the history of a topic and the thread subjects developed within it.

These default personal views have two other features in common: They don't use filters, and they can't be changed by the user.

The easiest way to create your own view is to apply the desired filter, grouping, sorting, or columns to a folder, so you can see the results. Then follow these steps:

1. After selecting the folder with the layout you want to save, choose Views, Define Views.

2. In the Define Views dialog box (Figure 10.14), click the New button.

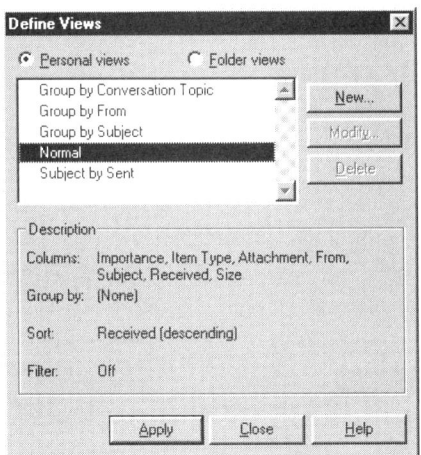

Figure 10.14

Personal views can be applied to any folder, whereas folder views are created for or copied to a specific folder.

3. In the New View dialog box, enter the "View name." Choose a name that describes how items are grouped, sorted, and/or filtered, such as Subject by Sent.

4. The current settings for the folder are already reflected in the Description of the view. Make any changes you need with the Columns, Group by, Sort, and Filter buttons (see Figure 10.15).

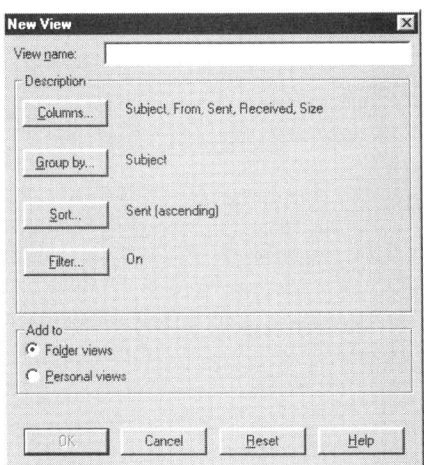

Figure 10.15

A view is a combination of Columns, Group by, Sort, and Filter settings.

Under "Add to," choose "Folder views" to create a view specific to this folder or "Personal views" to create a universal view.

1. Click OK to save the view and return to the Define Views dialog box.

2. If you want to apply this new view to the current folder, choose Apply. Otherwise, choose Close to return to the Exchange Viewer.

You can also use Define Views to delete and modify any views you create. The views you create appear on the View menu under "Personal views" or "Folder views." As you can see in Figure 10.16, new personal views appear at the bottom of the Personal Views menu, beneath a separator line. The two views on the Folder Views menu were created from the mailing list filter we worked on earlier in the chapter.

Figure 10.16

The Personal Views menu shows one user-created view, Subject by Sent, and the Folder Views menu includes two new folder views. The first filters out all messages from a mailing list about Exchange, and the second shows only those mailing list messages.

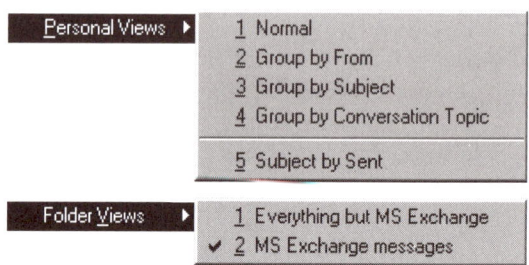

Tips and Tricks

Because Exchange Viewer is such a handy feature, there are many interesting things you can do with it. Here are some tips and tricks that tell you how.

Opening a New Window in Exchange

If one Exchange Viewer is nice, would two be twice as nice? Possibly, where you're dragging many items from one folder to another or want to see two different views of the same folder. Or maybe you want to leave your Inbox right where you stopped reading messages. To keep your place, open a new window to use for browsing other folders. To open a second Exchange Viewer window, choose View, New Window.

Creating Shortcuts to Favorite Folders

You probably won't be surprised to learn that, with the Exchange Server client, you can create shortcuts to your favorite folders, just as you can create a shortcut to almost anything in Windows 95 and Windows NT 4.0. To create a shortcut, select the folder, then choose File, Create Shortcut. You can save the shortcut to the Desktop or to any other Explorer folder. The shortcut will get an .xnk extension; when you launch it, the folder opens in a new Exchange window. You can even drag these shortcuts back into Exchange to create your own library of quick links to favorite folders.

Changing the Color for Groups and Unread Messages

By default, the Exchange Server client shows the number of unread messages in a folder in blue. Blue is also used for the names of groups when you create folder views that group by a particular field. If you'd rather see red (or some other color), follow these steps:

1. Choose Tools, Options and switch to the Colors tab.
2. Under Viewer, change the "Unread number" color, if desired.
3. Also change the "Group labels" color, if you like.
4. Click OK to save the change, which takes effect immediately.

Adding a Preview Pane

If you receive a lot of mail, you probably spend a great deal of time opening and closing messages, just to find out they weren't something you really needed to know about. One of the most useful Exchange enhancements is the addition of a preview pane (Figure 10.17). This pane shares the right side of the Exchange Viewer with the message pane and allows you to see the text of a message without opening it. This is really a big time saver!

Two preview add-ons are available. On this book's CD, you'll find Deming Preview, a freeware preview pane that makes references to Internet resources come alive as hotlinks. Deming Preview installs as a self-executing file (see Appendix A, "CD Contents"). Deming Preview adds a Preview option to the View menu and a Show/Hide Message Preview button to the toolbar. In Figure 10.17, we've scrolled far enough through the text of the highlighted item for you to see a couple of Internet hotlinks. In Deming Preview, these hotlinks are underlined and highlighted in blue. Assuming you're already online or have Windows set up to connect automatically to the Internet, click on one to go to that Web site or to perform other Internet tasks.

The Microsoft Exchange Resource Kit (see Appendix B, "Exchange Resources") also includes a Preview Pane Extension that allows you to set reminders for messages so you can be sure to follow up. To install the

Figure 10.17

A preview pane speeds the job of processing your mail by letting you read a message without opening a separate window.

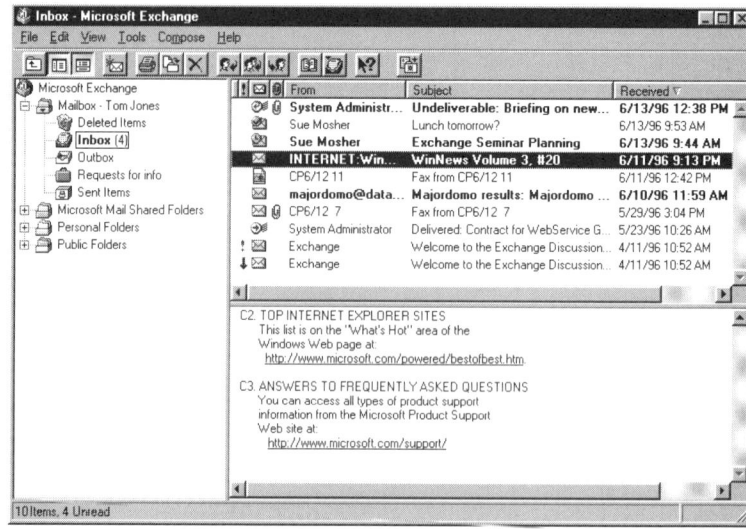

extension, run Setup.exe from the directory where the setup files have been installed. The Preview Pane Extension will add a <u>P</u>review choice to the <u>V</u>iew menu and make various buttons available in <u>T</u>ools, <u>C</u>ustomize Toolbar. Note, though, that it won't display messages larger than about 11K.

Starting Exchange Minimized or Maximized

The easiest way to start Exchange is with the desktop Inbox icon. But if you want Exchange to load minimized or maximized, you need to create a short-cut. To do this, you must know the location of the Exchng32.exe file on your system. Here are the default locations:

Windows 95 operating system client
C:\Program Files\Microsoft Exchange

Windows 95 operating system client with Windows Messaging update
C:\Program Files\Windows Messaging

Windows NT operating system client
C:\Program Files\Windows NT\Windows Messaging

Exchange Server clients
C:\Exchange

If you can't locate Exchng32.exe in any of these folders, click the Start button, then choose <u>F</u>ind, <u>F</u>iles or Folders.

The following procedure tells you how to create a shortcut on the desktop, but you can use the same technique to create a shortcut on the Start menu or in another folder. To start Exchange,

1. Right-click on the Windows 95 desktop and choose New, Shortcut.
2. For the command line, enter

   "C:\ Exchange\Exchng32.exe"

   including the quotes, using the proper path to your own copy of Exchng32.exe.
3. Choose Next to continue.
4. Give the shortcut a name (e.g., My Inbox, Exchange), then click Finish.
5. Right-click the newly created shortcut and choose Properties.
6. On the Shortcut tab, under Run, choose either Minimized or Maximized.
7. Click OK to finish the job.

Adding Command Line Settings to Exchange

You can use the same shortcut technique described in the previous section to take advantage of the command line settings for Exchange. After creating the shortcut, open its properties. Under Target, after the command, add one of the following switches (if the command is in quotation marks, put the switch after the quotation mark):

/n	Compose and send a new message
/s	Open the Find window
/a	Open the Address Book
/I	Open the Exchange Viewer and display the Inbox
/f filename.msg	Open an .msg file as a message
/j	Open the Exchange Viewer with the folder list displayed
filename	Open a new message and insert the specified file as an attachment

Summary

The Exchange Viewer is more than just an Inbox; it's a place for storing information or making it available to others. With the many tools to customize Viewer folders, especially with the Exchange Server clients, you can view messages very efficiently. And though users of the operating system versions of

Exchange don't have filters, they do have a comparable Find command, which we'll cover under "Finding Messages" in Chapter 16.

Key Points

- The list of folders you see on the left of the Viewer will depend on the client you're using (operating system or Exchange Server) and the services installed in your profile.

- Unread messages are shown in bold, and read messages are shown in normal font.

- Applications can add their own icons for different types of messages.

- To read an item in the message pane, double-click or select the item, then press Enter.

- You can create new folders either as top-level folders or as subfolders for existing folders.

- To sort items in a folder, click on the column heading.

For More Information

Chapter 13, "Working Remotely," shows you how to synchronize your mailbox and Favorites public folders if you're using an Exchange Server client.

Chapter 16, "Working with Messages and Folders," has more details about finding messages and managing folders.

In Chapter 19, "Using Exchange to Collaborate," we'll look at some of the situations in which you might want to give someone else access to your Exchange Server mailbox folders. We'll also dip briefly into the special properties of mailbox and public folders with the Exchange Server clients and offer more examples of different kinds of public folders.

Chapter 11

Sending E-Mail Messages

In this chapter and in Chapter 12, "Receiving and Responding to Messages," we finally reach the heart of Microsoft Exchange — sending and receiving messages. Sending a message requires four separate steps:

- Addressing the message
- Composing the message and attaching files
- Sending the message (which places it in the Outbox)
- Delivering the message to the mail server that will forward it to the recipient

Each of these steps is essential and a section of this chapter is devoted to each step. We'll also discuss WordMail as an alternative e-mail editor and look at the techniques for sending mail from within Windows applications.

Using the New Message Window

Let's begin with a look at the New Message window, where you create messages. To start a new message, click the New Message button, or choose Compose, New Message. The New Message window appears (shown in Figure 11.1).

Figure 11.1

A new message starts with a blank form where you enter the address, subject, and text. The large Send button on the right only appears on Exchange Server clients.

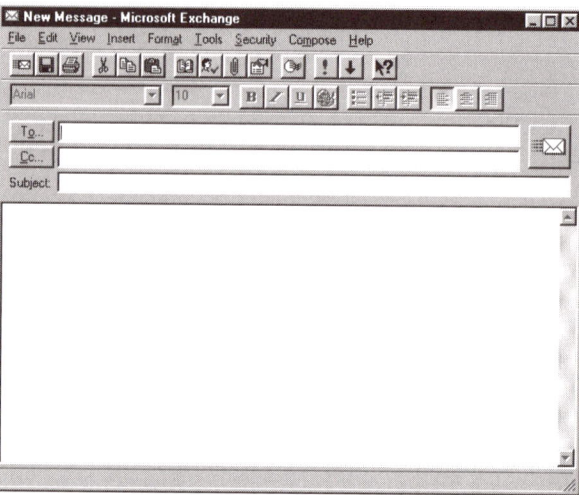

Working with the Toolbars

As with the Exchange Viewer, you can customize the main toolbar (the one on top) in the New Message window. Table 11.1 lists the available toolbar buttons, indicating which appear on the default toolbar and which are available only for Exchange Server clients.

Table 11.1 Message Window Toolbar Buttons

Button	Name	Description	Default	Exchange Server Clients Only
	File – Send	Save the message to the Outbox, ready for delivery	X	
	File – Save	Save the message to the Inbox as a draft	X	
	File – Move	Move the message to another folder		
	File – Copy	Copy the message to another folder		
	File – Delete	Delete the message		
	File – Properties	View and edit the properties for the message	X	
	File – Print	Print the message	X	
	File – Properties – Read Receipt	Get a message from the recipient when your message has been read	X	
	File – Properties – Importance: High	Mark the message as highly important	X	
	File – Properties – Importance: Low	Mark the message as less important	X	
	Edit – Undo	Undo the last changes made to the message		

continued

Table 11.1 Message Window Toolbar Buttons, continued

Button	Name	Description	Default	Exchange Server Clients Only
✂	Edit – Cut	Delete the selection and copy it to the Windows clipboard	X	
📋	Edit – Copy	Copy the selection to the Windows clipboard	X	
📋	Edit – Paste	Copy the contents of the clipboard into the message	X	
⊡	Edit – Select All	Select the entire text of the message		
🔍	Edit – Find	Search for text		
🔍	Edit – Replace	Search for text and replace		
⬆	View – Previous	Open the previous message listed in the Viewer		
⬇	View – Next	Open the next message listed in the Viewer		
📎	Insert – File	Attach a file to the message	X	
🖫	Insert – AutoSig-nature	Insert a selected AutoSig-nature into the message		X
✉	Insert – Message	Insert a message, form, or file stored in an Exchange folder into the message		

continued

Table 11.1 Message Window Toolbar Buttons, continued

Button	Name	Description	Default	Exchange Server Clients Only
	Insert – Object	Insert an imbedded object, such as a Microsoft Word document, into the message		
	Tools – Address Book	Display the Address Book, where you can select recipients and add new entries	X	
	Tools – Check Names	Match the names in the To, Cc, and Bcc boxes with the actual addresses in the Address Book	X	
	Tools – Spelling	Check the spelling of a selected word or an entire message		
	Compose – New Message	Start a new message in another window		
	Help	Get help about any element in the New Message window	X	
	Security – Seal Message with Encryption	Use Exchange Server security to encrypt the message	X	X
	Security – Digitally Sign Message	Use Exchange Server security to add a digital signature	X	X

Choose Tools, Customize Toolbar to change the buttons shown (see the section "Customizing the Toolbar" on page 224 in Chapter 10). Various Exchange add-ons may make additional buttons available to the main toolbar. We'll look at the formatting toolbar in the "Composing Messages" section later in this chapter.

You can toggle both the main toolbar and the formatting toolbar on and off in the New Message window. Use View, Toolbar and View, Formatting Toolbar, respectively. The large Send button on the right side of the New Message window in Figure 11.1 appears only on the Exchange Server clients.

Allowing Blind Carbon Copies

When you compose your first message, only the To and Cc boxes are available. However, blind carbon copies — copies where the recipient name is not shown to other addressees — also can be sent by entering addresses in the Bcc box.

To enable the Bcc box, choose the View, Bcc box in the New Message window. The Bcc box appears below the Cc box and will be on every message until you turn it off from the View menu. On an Exchange Server client, you also can use the View menu to show the From box. However, this is meaningful only in situations where you are sending on behalf of another person, as we'll see in Chapter 19, "Using Exchange to Collaborate."

Addressing Messages

There are three ways to enter an address for a message:

- Pick an entry from the Address Book
- Enter a name and let Exchange match it with an Address Book entry (a procedure known as Check Names)
- Enter the recipient's full address

Using Addresses from the Address Book

To pick recipients from the Address Book, click the Address Book button or choose Tools, Address Book (you also can click the To, Cc, or Bcc button). In the Address Book dialog box (Figure 11.2), select a name in the left pane, then click the To, Cc, or Bcc button to add the name to the message. To pick several recipients at once, hold down the Ctrl key as you click each name in the left pane, then click the appropriate button to add the name to the message.

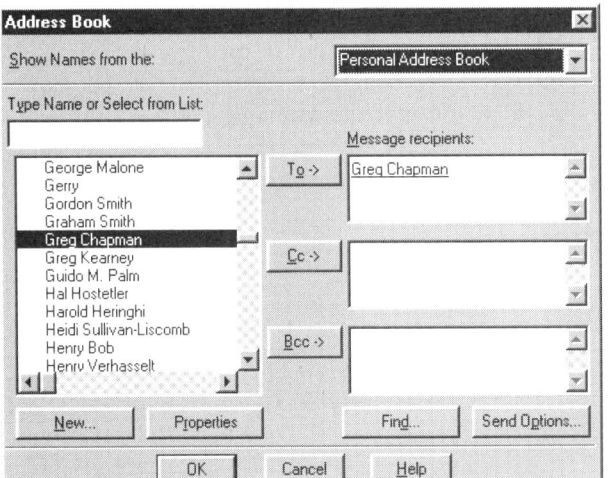

Figure 11.2

From the Address Book, you can choose any name from your Personal Address Book or add addresses from other address lists.

The address list that you see when you open the Address Book is governed by your profile (see the section "Addressing Settings" on page 75 in Chapter 4). You can easily switch between your Personal Address Book (PAB) and any other address lists (such as the Global Address List from Exchange Server). Just pick a different list from the Show Names ... option at the top of the dialog box. To see details about an address, select the address then click the Properties button.

If the name you want isn't already in the Address Book, you can create a new address entry by clicking the New button (see "Managing Your Personal Address Book" in Chapter 17 for details about how to enter new addresses). You also have the option to use that address just for this message, without adding the address to the Personal Address Book.

Some information services may allow certain message options to be set for each recipient (most don't). For those that do support individualized options, you can select a recipient, then click the Send Options button. Note that these options are different from the per-message send options, which we'll cover later in the chapter.

If you have a large address list and want to search for an individual, click the Find button shown in Figure 11.2. For most address lists, including the PAB, you can search for names only. But for Microsoft Exchange Server address lists, including the Global Address List, you can search for both names and other details, such as company, department, office, or city.

Using the Check Names Function

You can type in part of a person's name as the message recipient and have Exchange look up the exact address and enter it for you.

You don't have to use the Address Book for names of message recipients. In fact, you can enter just a person's name or part of a name in the To, Cc, or Bcc box then have Exchange look through the available address entries for you and select the appropriate full address for your message. If you're sending to more than one person, separate addresses (or partial addresses) with a semicolon.

To check the names from those available, click the Check Names button or choose Tools, Check Names. If Exchange finds one matching address, it automatically uses that address (names that have been *resolved* in this way are underlined). If Exchange finds more than one name, you'll be given a chance to choose from the names, as you can see in Figure 11.3. If Exchange finds no names that match, you'll be asked if you want to create a new address.

Figure 11.3

By using the Check Names function, you can enter addresses faster. In this example, the user typed in Henry, then let Check Names find the two Henrys in the Address Book.

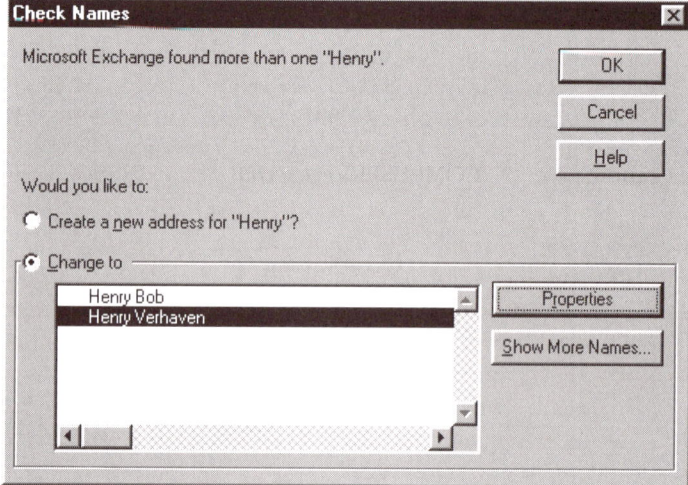

You can even skip the Check Names step. If you don't run Check Names to resolve the addresses after you enter them, Exchange resolves them for you automatically when you send the message. For more on how Check Names works, see "How Exchange Looks Up an Address" on page 393 in Chapter 17.

Entering Other Addresses

The first two addressing techniques we've covered deal with names in the Address Book — either people in your Personal Address Book or those listed in your Microsoft Exchange Server or postoffice list. But you're not limited to sending only to people in the Address Book. You can enter one-time addresses, used for this message only. Each information service (both internal and external) has its own format. The formats you're most likely to encounter are listed in Table 11.2. The brackets are required for those services for which they are listed.

Table 11.2 One-Time Address Formats		
To send to an addressee via	**Use this format**	**Example**
Microsoft Mail	[MS:*network*/*postoffice*/*mailbox*]	[MS:OKNY/PONYMAIL/FRANKC]
Internet (in general)	*address@domain* or [SMTP:*address@domain*]	frankc@okny.com or [SMTP:frankc@okny.com]
Internet (via MSN)	[MSNINET:*address@domain*]	[MSNINET:frankc @okny.com]
CompuServe	[COMPUSERVE:*UserID*]	[COMPUSERVE: 100243,784]
MSN	[MSN:*MemberID*]	[MSN:CellyFrank]
Microsoft Fax (using Dialing Properties)	[FAX:*name*@+1 (*xxx*) *xxx-xxxx*]	[FAX:Celly Frank@+1 (302) 555-4321]
Microsoft Fax (explicit number)	[FAX:*name*@ *xxx xxx-xxxx*]	[FAX:Celly Frank@ (302) 555-4321]

Remember that you must have an appropriate information service to use any of the address types in brackets. For example, if you send a message using a one-time COMPUSERVE address, but you don't have the CompuServe Mail service installed in your current profile, the message will fail.

Notice the two types of Microsoft Fax addresses. As you'll see in Chapter 14, "Sending Faxes," you can use the second type of address, using an explicit number with any dialing prefixes or suffixes, to bypass the dialing properties currently set on your computer.

Composing Messages

The two elements of your message other than the address are the subject and the body of the message. Enter the subject in the Subject box shown in Figure 11.1, then press Tab to move to the large area at the bottom of the window where you write your message. As you move, the title of the window changes from New Message to the subject of your message.

Formatting Your Message

Assuming you have both toolbars turned on, the lower toolbar in the New Message window contains formatting tools, listed in Table 11.3. If you've ever used WordPad, the word processor applet that comes with Windows 95 and Windows NT 4.0, then you already know how to format messages in Exchange, because the editor is the same one.

Table 11.3 Formatting Toolbar Buttons

Button	Name	Description
B	Bold	Make the selected text bold
I	Italic	Make the selected text italic
U	Underline	Underline the selected text
(color)	Color	Change the color of the selected text
(bullets)	Bullets	Start paragraph with a bullet
(decrease indent)	Decrease Indent	Move paragraph to the left
(increase indent)	Increase Indent	Move paragraph to the right
(align left)	Align Left	Left justify paragraph
(center)	Center	Center paragraph
(align right)	Align Right	Right justify paragraph

Figure 11.4 shows a message using the different rich-text formatting (RTF) elements available to you from the formatting toolbar and the Format menu:

- Fonts in different sizes
- Color
- Bold, underline, italics, and strikeout
- Indenting
- Bullets
- Left, center, or right justification

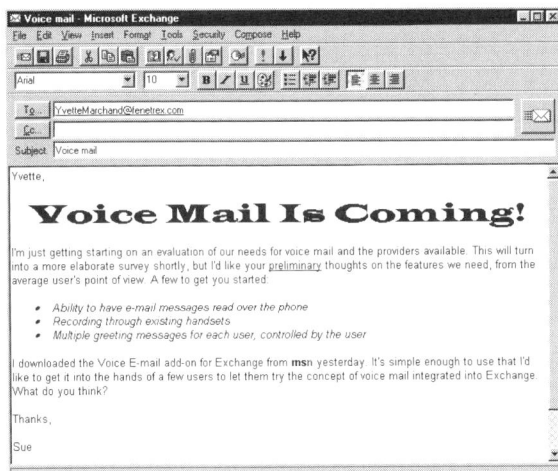

Figure 11.4
Use rich-text formatting (RTF) sparingly, or your message will become cluttered or jarring.

The default font for text in new messages is 10-point Arial. To change the default, choose Tools, Options, then switch to the Send tab and click the Font button to display the Font dialog box. Select the font and characteristics you want to use as the default, then click OK.

Don't go crazy with formatting. Not all recipients can handle RTF (see "When to Use Rich-Text Format," page 507 in Chapter 22), so all some will see is a plain-text equivalent. Even for other Exchange recipients, too much formatting can either clutter the message or make displaying the message take longer. If a message cries out for complex formatting, consider sending it as an attached file rather than as a mail message.

The Spelling Checker

The spelling checker is included with the full Exchange Server client. This tool is also available to the operating system clients if the 32-bit version of either Microsoft Word or Works is installed.

To change the way the spelling checker works, choose Tools, Options, then switch to the Spelling tab shown in Figure 11.5. Notice that you can have the spelling checker ignore text that you're replying to or forwarding. As discussed in the section "Quoting Incoming Messages" on page 292 in Chapter 12, it's best to leave incoming text the way it is, warts and all.

Figure 11.5

The Spelling tab appears for all Exchange clients. However, the spelling checker actually works only with the Exchange Server clients, or if you have Microsoft Word or Works installed.

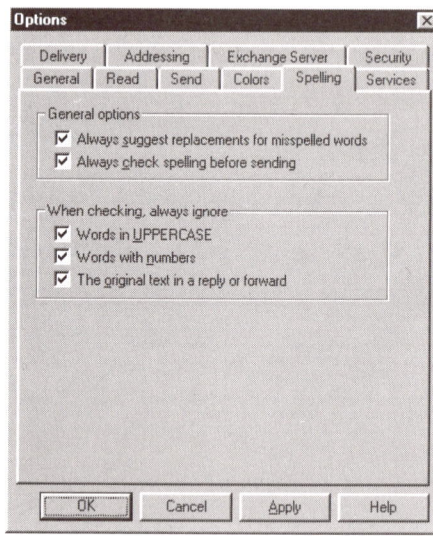

You can check the spelling in a message at any time by choosing Tools, Spelling. Exchange will also check the spelling when you send a message if you have enabled that option.

Special Note

There are two ways to enable the spelling checker, depending on the client you have. If you use the Exchange Server client, then the spelling checker is an installation option. To add it later, follow the instructions in "Installing and Updating the Exchange Server Client," page 103 in Chapter 5. For the operating system clients, you must install the 32-bit version of Microsoft Office, Microsoft Word, Microsoft Excel, or Microsoft Works and specify the spelling checker as part of the configuration options. Exchange uses the spelling checker tool provided with these other programs.

Inserting Files, Messages, and Objects

You can attach files anywhere in an Exchange message. You also can insert an object (such as an Excel spreadsheet) or even other Exchange messages. To attach a file to a message, drag the file from a folder or the desktop into the message; or follow these steps:

You can attach files anywhere in an Exchange message.

1. Position the cursor in the message text where you want the icon for the file to appear.
2. Choose Insert, File, or click the Insert File button. The dialog box shown in Figure 11.6 will appear.

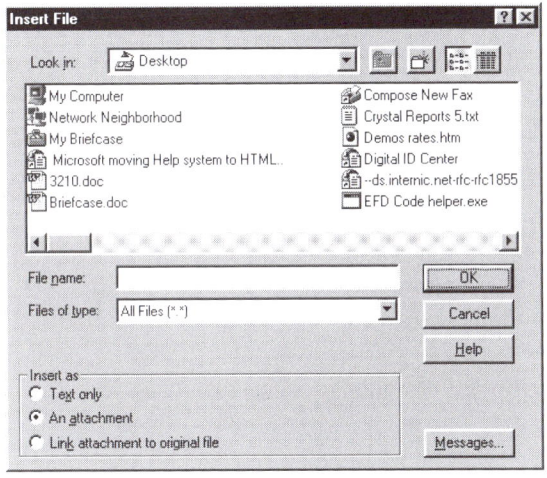

Figure 11.6
Browse your system to locate the file you want to include with your message.

3. Select the file.
4. Select how you want to attach the file; here are the choices:

Text Only	The file is converted to text, which is pasted into the message.
An Attachment	The file itself is attached.
Link Attachment to Original File	A shortcut to the file, which must be on a network drive, is attached.

5. Click the OK button to insert the file. If you want to attach more than one file to a message, you can drag multiple files from a folder or the desktop into the message. However, using Insert, File from the New Message window menu, you can select just one file at a time to attach.

Special Note

It's best to put a file either at the end or in the middle of your message, because sometimes recipients cannot see the icons for files inserted at the beginning when there is no preceding text. Recipients can, however, still extract an attachment that might be hiding at the beginning of a message with File, Save As.

To insert a message in another message, follow the same procedure, only choose Insert, Message instead of Insert, File. You'll be able to browse all the folders in the Exchange Viewer to find the message you want to insert, and you can select multiple messages to insert. This approach is a great way to bring something in a public folder to a colleague's attention, especially if you choose "Link attachment to original file" to send the message as a shortcut.

When you attach an object, you are attaching a chunk of data that works inside a message just as it would inside its normal application. For example, a message about a meeting to review proposals for product logos could include the logos, not as attached files, but as the graphics themselves, which would jump out of the message with greater impact.

There are several ways to insert an object into a message you're working on:

- Choose Insert, Object at the point in the message where you want the object to appear. In the Insert Object dialog box, specify the type of object and choose either to use an existing file or to create a new object.

- Select and drag data from an application into your message (this doesn't work with all applications).

- Select and copy data from the application. Then switch back to your message and choose Edit, Paste Special. You may be able to choose what type of object. For example, a bitmapped graphic can be pasted in an editable bitmap format or in a static Windows Metafile format.

Not all e-mail systems can handle embedded objects, so you may get an undeliverable notice back from some recipients.

Understanding E-Mail Style

E-mail isn't like paper communications. E-mail messages can be printed out, but they're most likely to be read on the computer screen. The limited display area and other technical factors contribute to a consensus about how e-mail exchanges can be conducted most effectively for all parties.

For example, because not all e-mail systems display the sender's address when a message is sent, many people add a line or two to their messages giving their e-mail addresses. We'll look at various methods for handling these *signatures* shortly. Similarly, the need to track the content of a conversation has led to conventions for how (and how much) to quote earlier messages, as you'll see in the next chapter.

As you develop your own e-mail style, you should consider two other major influences:

- Your organization's e-mail policy
- Common sense

Corporate policy may discourage the use of the company-provided e-mail account for personal messages. If no policy has been disseminated, ask around and spread the word that a solid policy on e-mail is good for everyone.

Common sense also gives you a lot to go on. If you're blessed with a direct connection to the Internet, don't assume that your recipients also enjoy such a benefit. They may have 14.4 Kbps (or even slower!) modems. Keep your messages simple and direct. Stick to one specific subject, and put that topic in the Subject field of your message. If you have another topic to discuss with the same person, put it in a separate message. As noted earlier, keep formatting to the minimum needed to get your point across.

Also take some time to analyze incoming messages for their effectiveness: Which are compelling? Which seem disorganized? The goal is to build your own understanding of what makes a good e-mail message.

Online Etiquette

Beyond common sense and company policy, a number of information sources exist that discuss good practices in cyberspace. One source that sums the etiquette up in 10 simple concepts is a book called *Netiquette* by Virginia Shea.[1] Here are her 10 rules:

1. Remember the human.
2. Adhere to the same standards of behavior online that you follow in real life.
3. Know where you are in cyberspace.
4. Respect other people's time and bandwidth.
5. Make yourself look good online.
6. Share expert knowledge.

---

[1] "The Core Rules of Netiquette" are quoted with the publisher's permission from *Netiquette* by Virginia Shea, ISBN 0-9637025-1-3, published by Albion Books, San Francisco. (415) 752-7666; info@albion.com, http://www.albion.com/welcome/albion.

7. Help keep flame wars under control. [In other words, don't start or contribute to discussions that viciously attack other people.]

8. Respect other people's privacy.

9. Don't abuse your power.

10. Be forgiving of other people's mistakes.

For a more elaborate discussion of appropriate online behavior, RFC 1855, *Netiquette Guidelines* (one of the many Request for Comments documents that are part of the standards for the Internet) offers a set of pragmatic directions for e-mail conduct. See Appendix B, "Exchange Resources."

Adding Signatures

As noted above, because you can't count on every mail system to display your return address, it's a good idea to include the address in the body of the message. Typically, this is done with a line or two at the end.

Some people create rather elaborate signatures with a technical tip, quote of the day, and details about their business or perhaps their Web site address. It's best to keep the signature to a couple of lines and, if you feel the need to embellish, keep the content interesting and relevant to the people you're sending the message to. It's a common (but by no means universal) practice to include signatures only in the first message of an online conversation, not in replies and forwards.

Some kind of signature management is a standard feature of most mail applications, especially those for Internet use. If you are using the full Exchange Server client, signatures are built into Exchange. For the operating system clients, you need an add-on program. Here are four different methods for managing signatures:

• (Exchange Server client only) Choose Tools, AutoSignature. In the AutoSignature dialog box, click New. Enter the signature and give it a name (see Figure 11.7). Character and paragraph formatting are supported for signatures, assuming that you're sending with RTF. Note that signatures created with the Exchange Server AutoSignature feature are specific to the computer you're working on, not to your Windows or Exchange profile. If other users share the computer, you all work from the same signature file, Autotext.sig, which is stored in the Windows folder.

• Use an add-on such as Internet Idioms, which is included on the CD for this book, or Exchange Buddy. Both of these let you create and insert a signature, either automatically or on demand.

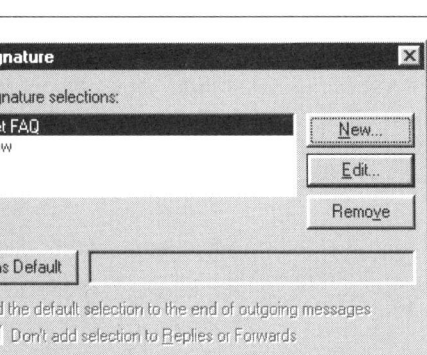

Figure 11.7
*Users of the Exchange
Server client can create
a library of signatures
for all occasions.*

- If you are using WordMail as your Exchange e-mail editor, create an Auto-Text entry named Signature. This text will be appended automatically to new messages (see the section "Using WordMail" later in this chapter).

- Another WordMail technique is to use a more elaborate macro, such as the one from Scott Marquardt's collection on the CD, to manage multiple signatures.

When you put a return Internet address in the signature, preface the address with mailto, as shown in Figure 11.8. This will turn the mailto:*name@domain* address into a hotspot for users of the Exchange Server client and the Deming Preview preview pane (see the section "Adding a Preview Pane" on page 243 in Chapter 10). Recipients will be able to click on the mailto link and immediately open a new message window addressed to you.

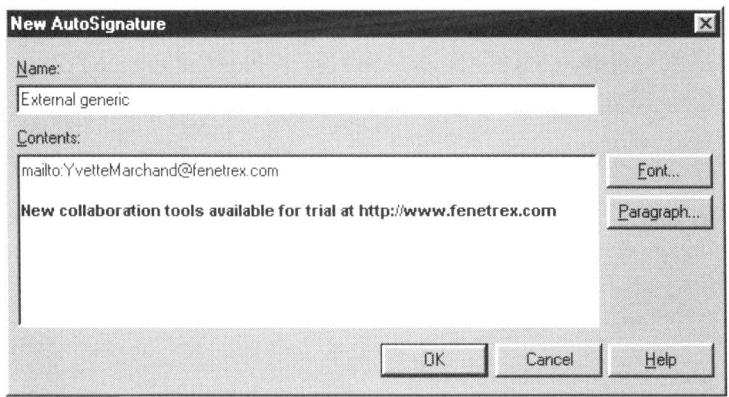

Figure 11.8
*Use mailto: in front of your
return Internet address to
benefit Exchange recipients
who see Internet links in
incoming messages as live
hotspots.*

Adding Internet Links

Mailto addresses aren't the only Internet links you'll find useful to put in your Exchange messages. Use http links (such as http://www.slipstick.com/exchange) to direct recipients to Web sites of interest. Or use ftp links (such as ftp://ftp.microsoft.com/softlib/index.txt) to point directly to a file that can be downloaded.

As noted in the previous section, users of the Exchange Server clients or the Deming Preview add-on will be able to click on these links to access those Internet resources (see "Activating Internet Links," page 288 in Chapter 12).

Saving Drafts

Sometimes you want to create a message, then save it for later revision or perhaps as a template for a report that you need to send every month. Exchange does offer a way to save such drafts. Instead of using File, Send or the Send button to move the message to the Outbox, choose File, Save or just close the message and respond Yes when you're asked whether you want to save changes. This places the message in your Inbox.

When you're ready to send the message, do one of the following:

If you want to keep a copy of the message in your Inbox for later use (as in the case of a monthly report format)	Select the item in the Inbox and choose Compose, Forward or click the Forward button
If you don't want to keep a copy of the message in your Inbox	Open the item, then choose File, Send

You also can move drafts to other folders and forward or send the drafts from there. See the section "Saving Drafts to Other Folders" at the end of this chapter.

Sending Messages

When you've composed and addressed a message, choose File, Send or click the Send button to send the message. This places the message in the Outbox for delivery. Delivery is a separate step, discussed in the upcoming section, "Delivering Messages."

Setting the Send Options and Properties

As part of your profile, Exchange maintains a set of send options and message properties. You can override these options for individual messages. To view and change the default send options, choose Tools, Options and switch to the Send tab, shown in Figure 11.9.

You already encountered the Font button in the earlier section "Formatting Your Message." Table 11.4 lists the other available send options.

For an individual message, you can override the receipts, sensitivity, importance, or Sent Items default. Choose File, Properties, and make your changes on the General tab, shown in Figure 11.10.

For an individual message, you can override the receipts, sensitivity, importance, or other default properties.

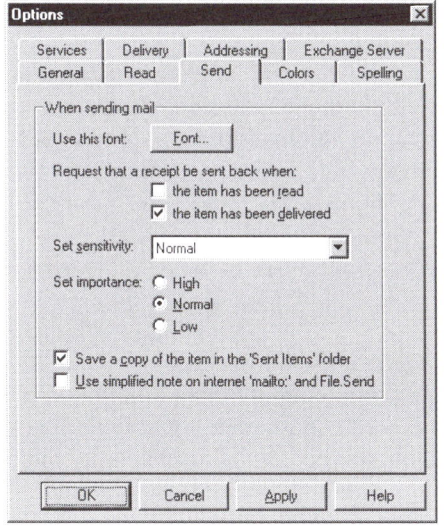

Figure 11.9
For individual messages, you can override the default options that you set on the Send tab.

Other tabs also may be present. If the message is bound for the Internet via the Internet Mail service, you also can change the message format on the Internet tab. We'll look at those settings in Chapter 22, "Working with Internet E-Mail." If the message is to an Exchange Server recipient, you should see a Security tab, where you can encrypt or add a digital signature to the message (see Chapter 21, "Message Security"). Other services installed in your profile may add other property tabs.

Table 11.4 Send Options	
Option	**Description**
Request a receipt when the item has been read	Provides notification when the message has been opened by the recipient.
Request a receipt when the item has been delivered	Provides notification when the message has been delivered to the recipient (assuming the recipient's mail server supports such notifications).
Set sensitivity	Assigns a sensitivity rating, which appears in the Sensitivity column if that column is displayed. Choices are Normal, Personal, Private, and Confidential.
Set importance	Assigns an importance rating, which appears in the Exchange Viewer as a red exclamation point (High) or blue down arrow (Low). Choices are High, Normal, and Low.
Save a copy in the Sent Items folder	Keep a copy of all outgoing messages in Sent Items.
Use simplified note	Enable a different, faster Compose New Message window for sending from an Internet browser or from within other applications (not available on the original Exchange client for Windows 95).

Special Note

When you assign a sensitivity of Private to a message, recipients are not supposed to be able to modify the original message when they reply to it or forward it. However, if the recipient uses WordMail as the e-mail editor, the message can be modified. Therefore, you can't count on the Private sensitivity to protect a message.

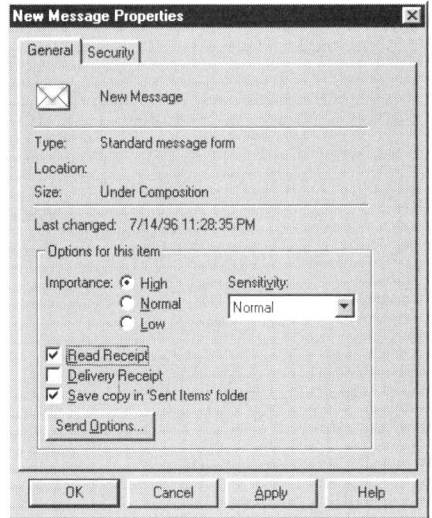

Figure 11.10

The New Message Properties dialog box allows you to ask for a read receipt if you don't normally get one, or to change other defaults.

Service-Specific Send Options

Some information services allow additional properties for each message. You can access these properties through the Send Options button on the New Message Properties dialog box (Figure 11.10). Just as with the New Message Properties dialog box, the tabs visible in the Send Options dialog box (Figure 11.11) depend on the services you have installed. Not all services add send options.

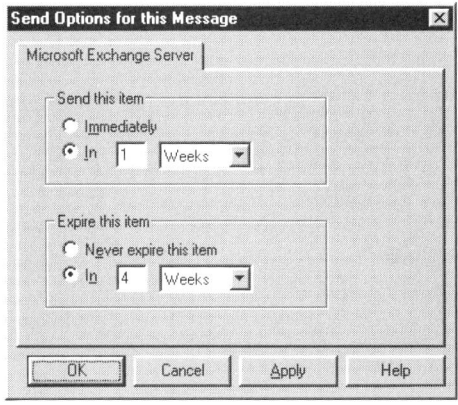

Figure 11.11

Defer delivery and set an expiration date for messages sent via Microsoft Exchange Server.

For Exchange Server messages, you can delay sending a message by a specified number of minutes, hours, days, or weeks, as shown in Figure 11.11. You also can cause a message to be removed after a period of time if it has not been read.

The CompuServe Mail service also allows you to set a release date and expiration date for a message. And you'll see numerous send options for Microsoft Fax when we discuss it in Chapter 14, "Sending Faxes."

Delivering Messages

Sending a message and delivering it are separate steps in Exchange.

Sending a message and delivering it are separate steps in Exchange. Delivery often takes place automatically. Sometimes, depending on the information service and its settings, you need to perform one more task after sending the message to make sure that it's transmitted to the recipients.

If you are connecting to a Microsoft Exchange server on a LAN, messages are delivered immediately. For Microsoft Mail, deliveries take place at a specified interval. For any service where you must make a dial-up networking (DUN) connection, delivery does not occur until the next connection, either manual or scheduled. This is true even if you are connected directly to the Internet. Internet mail is still delivered to the mail server only at the next scheduled connect time or when you use Deliver Now or Remote Mail to deliver mail manually. The chapters in Part II of this book cover delivery options for various information services. Many services allow you to schedule connections either at regular intervals or at a particular time of day.

Two manual techniques exist for delivering messages. We give detailed coverage of Remote Mail in Chapter 13, "Working Remotely." The other manual delivery method is called Deliver Now.

Using Deliver Now

If you have only one information service in your Exchange Profile, choosing Tools, Deliver Now will cause Exchange to connect to that service, send all mail in your Outbox, and download any messages waiting for you. If you have more than one service, the menu changes to Deliver Now Using and brings up a submenu that includes All Services and a list of the information services installed in your profile. You can deliver to all services at once or to each one individually. The order in which delivery occurs for All Services is set with Tools, Options on the Delivery tab. (See the section "Delivery Settings" on page 74 in Chapter 4.)

Note that Deliver Now not only sends all Outbox messages but also retrieves any mail waiting for you on the server. If you want to send but not receive messages, use Remote Mail instead.

When Messages Fail

Sometimes messages don't get through. We discuss related common problems in Chapter 24, "Troubleshooting." If the message fails because Exchange could not deliver it for some reason, you will see an Undeliverable notice in your Inbox from the System Administrator (a mythical person who watches over these things). Open that message to see the reason for the failure. Figure 11.12 shows an example of such a message.

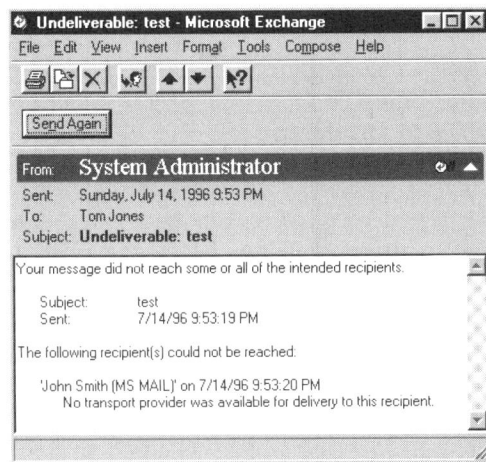

Figure 11.12
Before using the Send Again button to resend an undeliverable message, try to correct the problem listed in the notice.

Click the Send Again button to resend an undeliverable message. If the message was delivered successfully to some recipients, but not to others, the To, Cc, and Bcc boxes will contain only the addresses that failed. You can change any address, but no other part of the message. Click the Send button to put the message back in the Outbox for another delivery attempt.

Resending a Message

You cannot resend a message by dragging it from Sent Items to the Outbox. Here are three alternative methods of resending a message that do work:

* Open the sent message, copy the text to the clipboard, then paste it into a new message. Do the same with the recipient addresses and the subject.

* Use Compose, Reply To All to open the message with the recipient addresses and subject in place. You need to remove the RE before the subject, take your own address out of the To box, and clean up the text to remove the sent message's header and reduce any indenting.

- Use Compose, Forward to open the message. You need to remove the FW before the subject, add recipient addresses, and clean up the text to remove the sent message's header.

Special Note

You also can use the Resend Extension for Microsoft Exchange, included on the accompanying CD, to resend an item directly from the Sent Items folder.

Sending from Applications

Many Windows applications allow you to send the current document as an attachment to an e-mail message.

Many Windows applications allow you to send the current document as an attachment to an e-mail message. Check the File menu for a Send command to see if your application is mail-enabled in this fashion.

When you choose File, Send from within an application, a new message window appears with the current document already inserted. You just fill in the addresses, subject, and any accompanying text, then send the message.

You may see a slightly different window when you use File, Send. This *simplified note* (available in all Exchange clients, except the original Windows 95 operating system version) loads faster than the normal window, because it can't be resized, has only one toolbar, and doesn't support the spelling checker. If you don't want to use the simplified note, you can turn it off by choosing Tools, Options and switching to the Send tab (Figure 11.9). Clear the box labeled Use Simplified Note on Internet 'mailto:' and File.Send.

Using WordMail

You can use Microsoft Word as your e-mail editor instead of the standard editor.

If you have Microsoft Word 7.0, you can use Word as your e-mail editor instead of the standard editor. WordMail will be sluggish on machines with minimal RAM, but you can easily remove it through the Word or Office setup procedure if you don't like the performance.

The clear advantage of WordMail is the way it handles messages for non-RTF recipients. For example, WordMail translates bullets into asterisks; whereas if you use the normal Exchange editor, the bullets are just stripped out when you send messages to non-RTF points. You also gain access to Word's AutoText and AutoCorrect functions, macros, thesaurus, and multiple spelling dictionaries.

Activating WordMail

To enable WordMail on your system, you must have installed Microsoft Word 7.0 with the WordMail option selected. Here's how to activate WordMail if you installed Exchange first, then Word:

1. Choose Compose, WordMail Options.
2. In the WordMail Options dialog box (Figure 11.13), click the checkbox labeled Enable Word as Email Editor.

    If you installed Word first, then Exchange, follow these steps:

1. Load your Microsoft Office or Word CD or Setup disk #1.

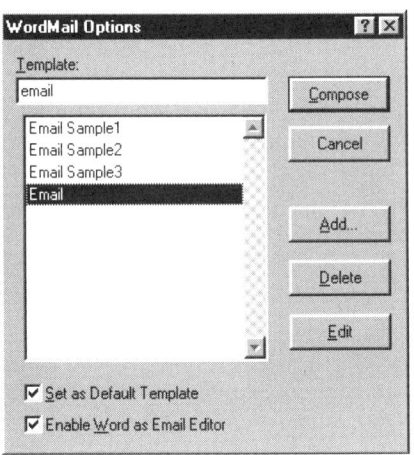

Figure 11.13
WordMail comes with four templates, but you can add more. You use the default template for all replies and forwarded messages.

2. Click the Start button, then choose Run and type in this command:

    d:\setup /Y

    where *d:* is the actual drive letter for the disk or CD. This will reregister Word and set up WordMail.
3. Follow the steps described in the first procedure to enable WordMail within Exchange.

Also use this second procedure if you updated your version of Exchange to Windows Messaging or the full Exchange Server client after you installed Word.

Using Templates

In Figure 11.13, you see four templates installed, with one designated as the default. These are added by the Word setup. Each template includes special styles for the message headers and macros to handle message functions such as Send and Check Names.

When WordMail is activated, Exchange uses the default template each time you open, reply to, or forward a message or start a new message by choosing Compose, New Message from the Exchange Viewer menu. If you want, you can use any other WordMail template to begin a new message. Here's how:

1. From the Exchange Viewer menu, choose Compose, WordMail Options.
2. In the WordMail Options dialog box (Figure 11.13), select the template you wish to use.
3. Click the Compose button.

When editing with WordMail, you get almost all Word functions at your fingertips — AutoText, AutoCorrect, styles, tables, and so on. WordMail intelligently converts any special formatting to a plain-text equivalent and delivers that to recipients who need it, while it delivers the fully formatted message to recipients that can handle RTF.

Editing and Adding Templates

If you want to enhance WordMail with macros or custom toolbars, you must make those changes in a WordMail template (rather than while composing or reading a message with WordMail). To edit an existing WordMail template, follow these steps:

1. From the Exchange Viewer menu, choose Compose, WordMail Options.
2. In the WordMail Options dialog box (Figure 11.13), select the template you wish to edit.
3. Click the Edit button to open the template in Word, where you can modify it.

If you are editing styles, toolbars, or macros, make sure that you specify that changes be saved in the current template, not in Normal.dot.

A collection of WordMail macros is included on the CD accompanying this book. These macros let you activate Internet links in Exchange messages, add signatures, quote incoming messages, and perform many other useful functions. See Appendix A, "CD Contents," for details about how to add these macros to existing WordMail templates.

Special Note

WordMail uses a special toolbar in addition to the Word formatting toolbar. The WordMail toolbar contains buttons for mail functions such as sending messages and checking names, plus Word functions commonly used in creating messages. You cannot, however, edit this toolbar. If you want to add new buttons for WordMail, work with the formatting toolbar (or any other standard Word toolbar) instead, or add your own custom toolbars.

To create a new template, use an existing template as a guide, so the necessary styles and macros are included. Here's how:

1. Choose Compose, WordMail Options.
2. On the WordMail Options dialog box (Figure 11.13), select the template you want to use as a starting point.
3. Click the Edit button.
4. Choose File, Save As to save the template under a new name.
5. Make any changes you want to the template, then save and close it.
6. Back on the WordMail Options dialog box, click the Add button.
7. Select the new template from the Add dialog box, and click the Add button to add the template to the list of templates available to WordMail.

To delete a template from WordMail, select the template, then click the Delete button. This does not remove the .dot file itself; it only makes the file unavailable to WordMail.

Displaying the Bcc Box

As is the case on the normal New Message window, WordMail does not display the Bcc box unless you specifically ask for it. To show the Bcc box in WordMail, follow these steps:

1. Choose File, Properties.
2. In the Properties dialog box, check Show Bcc.
3. Click OK to close the Properties dialog box.

Tips and Tricks

As you can imagine, because sending messages is basic to Exchange, there are some interesting tricks you'll want to try. In this section, you'll learn how to specify a default folder for attachments, save drafts to any folder you like, and make sure your Internet messages are delivered.

Setting the Default Folder for Attachments

If you often create files specifically to attach to Exchange messages, you may want to dedicate a folder for those attachments. To do this, you must start Exchange from a shortcut, rather than with the Inbox icon on the desktop. The following procedure tells how to create a shortcut that uses a particular folder for attachments. You can leave this shortcut on the desktop or drag it to a folder.

1. Click the Start button, then choose Find.

2. Search for Exchng32.exe on your C: drive.

3. When you locate the file, right-click on the file name, then choose Create Shortcut. Answer Yes when you're asked whether you want to put the shortcut on the desktop.

4. On the desktop, right-click the new shortcut, and choose Properties. Switch to the Shortcut tab.

5. Under Start In, enter the path to the folder you want to use as the default for attachments.

6. Click OK to save the changes to the shortcut.

Sending to Yourself to See Plain Text

If you're going to be sending many messages to Internet addresses, you ought to see what a typical message looks like without RTF. Create a sample message using indents, fonts, bullets, and so on, then enter your own Internet address (e.g., *myname@mydomain*) in the To box. When you send and deliver this message, it will come back to you as plain text.

If you are considering using WordMail, use the same procedure with a message you create in WordMail, and you'll see a difference: WordMail converts some rich-text features, such as bullets, into plain-text equivalents.

Sending to a Hidden Exchange Server Address

Not all addresses may be visible in the Exchange Server Global Address List. Some may be hidden by the Exchange administrator for one reason or another. Perhaps the president of the company has a public e-mail address, but also a private address used only by department heads.

If you need to send to a Microsoft Exchange Server user who is not listed in the Address Book, you use the person's X.400 address. X.400 is a standard for messaging systems. Exchange Server supports it, and so do many other mail systems.

Everyone with an Exchange Server account has an address in the X.400 format. This format is a little too tricky to try to enter through the To box. It's better to click the Address Book button, then click the New button on the Address Book dialog box (Figure 11.2) and create a new X.400-type entry, as shown in Figure 11.14. You will need to get the values to fill into the different fields from the Exchange administrator or the person whose hidden address you're planning to use. Exchange Server distribution lists and public folders also have X.400 addresses.

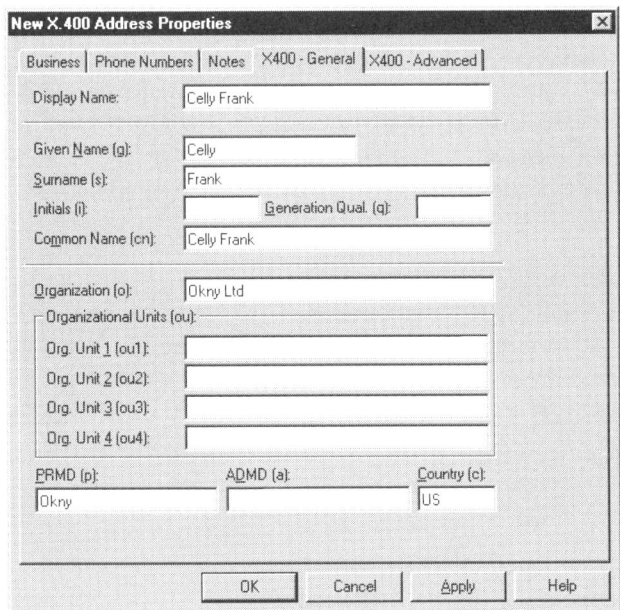

Figure 11.14
Use the X.400 template to add Exchange Server users to your Personal Address Book if they don't appear in the Global Address List.

Saving Drafts to Other Folders

In the earlier section "Saving Drafts," you learned how to use File, Save instead of File, Send to retain a message in your Inbox. It's also possible to save the file to a different folder by following these steps:

1. From the message window, choose File, Move.

2. In the Move dialog box, select the folder where you want to put the message.

3. Click the OK button to close the message and save it in the selected folder.

You can now send the saved message at any time either by forwarding it, if you want to save a copy in the folder, or by opening it and sending it.

Delivering Everything via the Internet

If you have several services in your Exchange profile that can all use Internet connections, you may be able to use a DUN connection to the Internet to deliver all mail (and retrieve all pending messages) with a single phone call.

The trick is to use the same DUN connectoid or phonebook entry for each service. Sometimes you also need to adjust the order of services. You make this adjustment through Tools, Options, on the Delivery tab. I have found that using CompuServe Mail, Internet Mail, and The Microsoft Network, in that order, works quite well (you will need to click the Connect button on The Microsoft Network dialog box). I also like to make the connection to my Internet provider first, then click the Deliver Now button.

Summary

Once you know how to create and send messages, you're well on your way to putting Exchange to work. You have a number of options regarding how messages look, what you include in them, and even what tools you use to create them. As essential as e-mail messages have become in our everyday lives, it's also important to understand e-mail etiquette and what makes a good e-mail message.

Key Points

• You can type in part of a person's name for a recipient address and have Exchange look up the exact address and enter it for you.

• Too much formatting can clutter a message or make the message take longer to display.

• You can attach files anywhere in an Exchange message.

• For an individual message, you can override the receipts, sensitivity, importance, or other default properties.

• Sending a message and delivering it are separate steps in Exchange.

- Many Windows applications allow you to send the current document as an attachment to an e-mail message.
- You can use Microsoft Word as your e-mail editor instead of using the standard editor.

For More Information

For more about how Check Names helps you address messages, see the section "How Exchange Looks Up an Address" on page 393 in Chapter 17.

Sending mail on the Internet requires some understanding of the different possible message formats. We'll look at this topic in Chapter 22, "Working with Internet E-Mail."

Although you can send faxes using the Compose New Message technique, the Compose New Fax Wizard can also walk you through the job. See Chapter 14, "Sending Faxes."

Exchange Server users have access to built-in encryption and digital signature features. These features are available as add-ons to users of the operating system Exchange clients. For more details, see Chapter 21, "Message Security."

Chapter 12

Receiving and Responding to E-Mail Messages

In the previous chapter, we explored Microsoft Exchange's techniques for sending messages. Now let's look at your Inbox and see what you need to do to retrieve your messages and how you can respond to them.

Retrieving Your Messages

Retrieving messages can take place automatically or manually.

Just as with sending messages, retrieving messages can take place automatically or manually. The methods available depend on the information services in your profile and the type of connection you have to the mail server. There are two automatic and two manual procedures, which we will discuss in the next few sections. For details about the retrieval options available for different services, see the related chapters in Part II.

Automatic Retrieval — Unscheduled and Scheduled

If you connect to Microsoft Exchange Server on a LAN, then you do not have to take any action to get your mail. The Exchange Server "pushes" new message headers — containing the subject, sender, and other message properties — to your computer. The message itself remains on the server until you open it. Only at that moment is the text of the message sent to your computer for you to view.

Scheduled retrieval is most commonly used for any service where you connect remotely but want to receive all incoming messages. Scheduling choices for an individual service may include

- When Exchange starts
- At specified intervals, such as every hour
- At a particular time of day (e.g., at 12:30 p.m. while you're at lunch)

Not all services support all these scheduling options.

With Exchange Server, you can use automatic, scheduled retrieval to download only some messages — for example, those that meet certain criteria you set (see the section "Building a Retrieval Filter" in Chapter 13 for details).

Manual Retrieval — Deliver Now or Remote Mail

There are two ways to retrieve your messages manually. From within Exchange, use Tools, Deliver Now (or Deliver Now Using if you have more than one service in your profile) to retrieve all pending messages manually, at the same time sending anything from your Outbox.

The other manual method is Tools, Remote Mail. Remote Mail gives you more control over what messages you download and whether a copy is left on the server (see Chapter 13, "Working Remotely," for more details).

Getting Mail on The Microsoft Network

If you log on to The Microsoft Network (MSN) online service and mail is pending for you, you will receive a notification message from MSN. However, your mail is not automatically displayed. You must start Exchange if it is not already running, then use Deliver Now or Deliver Now Using to retrieve the pending messages.

You must start Exchange to find out whether you have new messages.

New Message Notification Options

How do you know when you have new mail? First of all, Exchange must be running; you won't receive any notice of new messages until you start Exchange (unless you are using one of the mail notifier utilities discussed at the end of this chapter in "Using a Mail Retriever or Notifier").

If you use the Exchange Server client and start Exchange while you are connected to the network, you'll receive notice within a few seconds of any new messages. You can also check the Inbox folder. If a message is shown in bold, then that message hasn't been read. The number of unread messages is shown in parentheses in blue type next to the folder name.

Exchange lets you decide how to be notified of new mail. Choose Tools, Options to display the dialog box shown in Figure 12.1. Under "When new mail arrives" on the General tab, you have these choices:

- Play a sound
- Briefly change the pointer if it is inside a Microsoft Exchange window
- Display a notification message

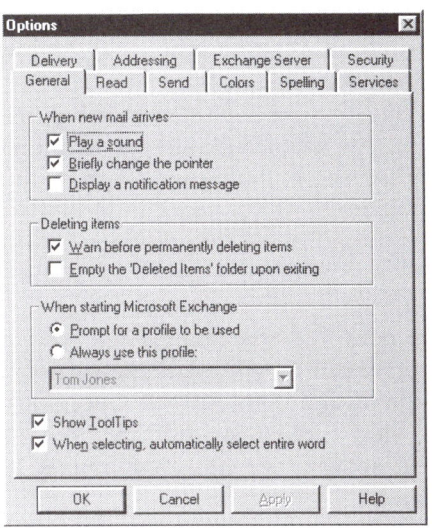

Figure 12.1
Exchange gives you three different ways to be notified of new messages.

If you choose "Play a sound," you can change the New Mail Notification sound in the Sounds applet in the Control Panel (see "Changing the New Mail Notification Sound" at the end of this chapter). If you choose to have Exchange display a notification message, you have the opportunity to read the latest mail immediately.

A fourth indicator that a new message has arrived, one not covered on the General tab, is an envelope icon that appears in the system tray on the Windows taskbar when you have new mail (see Figure 12.2). Also not included on the General tab is a new mail notification option specifically for Microsoft Mail. We discuss this option in Chapter 6, "Setting Up Microsoft Mail."

Figure 12.2
When new messages are pending in the Inbox folder, the envelope icon appears in the system tray on the taskbar.

Remember that these built-in methods work only when Exchange is loaded. Separate utilities are available to get mail, particularly Internet messages, without loading the full Exchange program. The CD for this book includes several of these utilities, which are introduced in the "Tips and Tricks" section at the end of this chapter.

Reading New Messages

New messages appear in your Inbox folder in bold. Messages you have read are in the normal font.

As we mentioned, new messages appear in your Inbox folder in bold. Messages you have read are in the normal font. To read a message, double-click it (or select it, then press Enter). The message opens in a message window (Figure 12.3) similar to that used to compose new messages, but with the formatting toolbar turned off. If you are using WordMail, the message appears in a WordMail window instead, using the default WordMail template (see "Using WordMail" on page 270 in Chapter 11). To open several messages at once, select the messages in the Exchange Viewer by holding down the Ctrl key, then press Enter, or choose File, Open.

The message window's toolbar includes the same buttons that you saw from the Exchange Viewer window for working with incoming messages. There are also two new buttons: the large up and down arrows. Once you've opened a message from the Exchange Viewer, use these buttons to browse through other messages in the same message window without returning to the

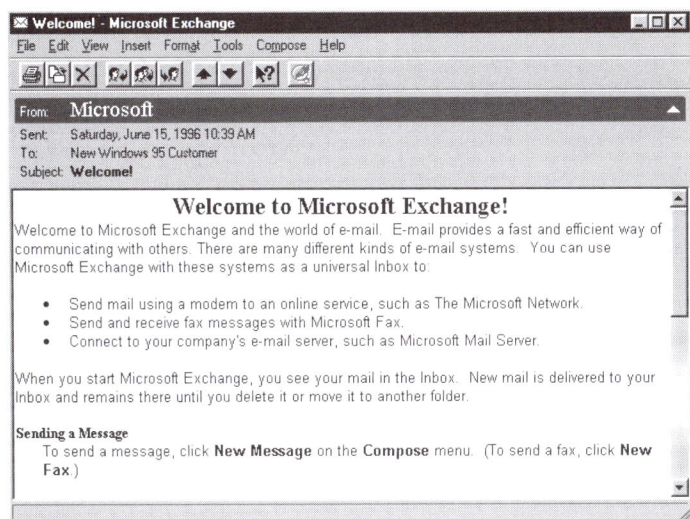

Figure 12.3
In this received message, you can use the up and down arrows on the toolbar to browse the rest of the Inbox without returning to the Exchange Viewer. The contrasting background for the From field is characteristic of the Exchange Server client. The arrow on the right turns the Sent and To fields on and off.

Viewer. In the Exchange Server client, an arrow button at the right side of the message window switches the To and Sent fields on and off. You also can use View, Full Header in the Message window for this task.

   If you add a preview pane to Exchange (described in the "Tips and Tricks" section in Chapter 10), you don't need to open messages. You can read the text in the preview pane. You will, however, need to open the message to use any attached file or view any embedded object.

Message Actions

You can do a number of things with the messages in your Inbox (and other folders):

- Print them
- Delete them
- Copy or move them to another folder
- Save them
- Reply to or forward them
- View the Internet headers
- Work with file attachments
- Link to Internet resources

We will discuss message replies and forwards in an upcoming section. For now, let's look at some of the other actions.

Printing Messages

You can print a single message or a group of selected messages. To select more than one message, hold down the Ctrl key while you click each message. To quickly print the messages, click the Print button. To change the options for printing, choose File, Print. In the Print dialog box shown in Figure 12.4, you can choose the printer destination and number of copies and set two options specific to Exchange:

Start each item on a new page   When disabled (the default), no page breaks are inserted between items. This is an especially good setting if you print all messages related to a topic. When enabled, every item starts on a fresh page.

Print attachments   When enabled, prints attachments using the application associated with the file type (see the sidebar "File Type Associations" on page 325 in Chapter 14).

Figure 12.4

In the Print dialog box, you can change the way multiple messages are printed and enable the printing of attachments.

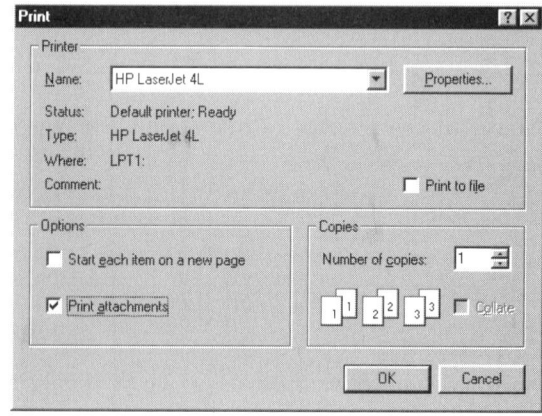

After you've made any changes in the Print dialog box, click the OK button to print the selected message(s).

There are several other printing issues to be aware of:

- The options you set in the Print dialog box, including the destination printer, will be used for all subsequent printing jobs started by the Print button until you change those options again in the Print dialog box.

- Attachments always print to the Windows default printer, even if that is not the printer specified in the Print dialog box (Figure 12.4).

- To print a linked message included as an attachment, open the message first (by double-clicking on it), then print it.

- You cannot drag a message from the Exchange Viewer to a printer. Drag-and-drop printing is not supported for messages.

Deleting Messages

To delete a message from the Exchange Viewer, select the message, then press the Delete key or click the Delete button on the Viewer toolbar. To delete a message while you have it open, click the Delete button or choose File, Delete. What happens next depends on another setting in the Options dialog box (opened with Tools, Options), this time on the Read tab shown in Figure 12.5. Here are your options under "After moving or deleting an open item":

- Open the item above it

- Open the item below it

- Return to Microsoft Exchange

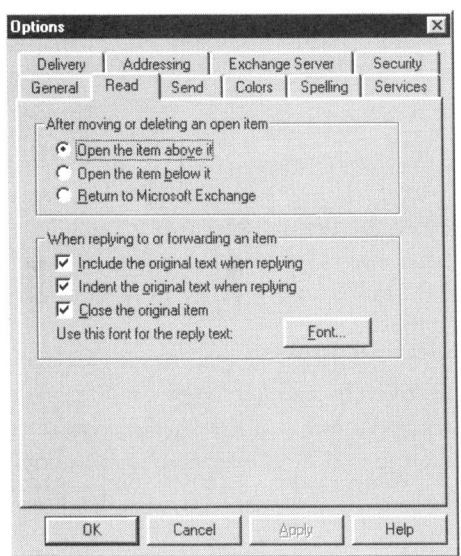

Figure 12.5
Set options for reading, replying to, and forwarding messages on the Read tab.

The first two choices are useful if you like to open a new message, dispose of it, then see the next message immediately. Choose "Return to Microsoft Exchange" if you prefer to go back to the Exchange Viewer window each time you delete or move an open message.

Before you leave the Options dialog box, switch back to the General tab, shown in Figure 12.1. Under "Deleting items," there are two important settings:

- Warn before permanently deleting items
- Empty the 'Deleted Items' folder upon exiting

If the "Empty the 'Deleted Items'..." option is checked, then each time you exit Exchange the Deleted Items folder is purged. This occurs, however, only if you exit Exchange before shutting down Windows. If Exchange is open when you shut down Windows, then deleted items will stay in the Deleted Items folder.

Some mail systems (including Microsoft Exchange Server and Microsoft Mail) support the sending of a "not read" receipt if you delete a message without reading it and the sender has requested a read receipt.

Copying and Moving Messages

To move or copy a message to another folder, choose File, Move or File, Copy. From the Exchange Viewer window, you can also move messages by dragging them to the destination folder. To copy them, hold down the Ctrl key while you drag. When you are moving an open message, the setting described in the previous section determines whether you return to the Viewer window or see another message in the message window.

Saving Messages

You can save messages outside of Exchange in three different formats — as a message format (.msg) file that includes all the header information, as a text-only (.txt) file, or as a rich-text (.rtf) file that preserves all the formatting. A single message can be saved in any of the three formats, either from the open message or from the Exchange Viewer window.

If you select multiple messages in the Exchange Viewer, those messages can be saved only as a .txt file. They are saved in a single .txt file, in the order that you selected them from the Exchange Viewer window. When you save messages to an existing .txt file, you have the option to overwrite the file or to append to it.

To save the selected message(s), follow these steps:

1. Choose File, Save As.

2. In the Save As dialog box shown in Figure 12.6, use the "Save in" list to browse your drive for the folder where you want to save the file.

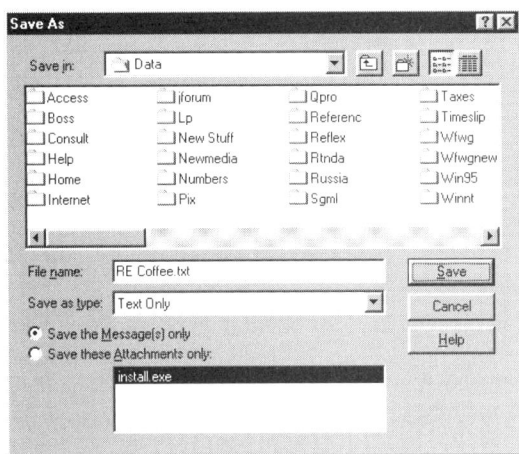

Figure 12.6

You can save a message to your local drive either as a text file, as a message file (including any attachments), or just as an attachment.

3. Select "Save the Message(s) only."

4. Choose the "Save as type," either Text Only, Rich Text Format, or Message Format.

5. Click the Save button.

Viewing the Internet Headers

Messages received from the Internet carry header information to indicate where a message originated and how it was routed to you. To see the header for a message, choose File, Properties and switch to the Internet tab (Figure 12.7) or, for Internet messages received through a Microsoft Exchange server, to the Headers tab.

With the mouse, you can select the header, then press Ctrl+C to copy the header to the clipboard so you can paste it into another application (e.g., Notepad) to better view the header information. We don't have the space in this book to go into the details of reading Internet headers, but many good references are available.

Figure 12.7

The header for an Internet message can help you determine exactly where the message came from and how it was structured.

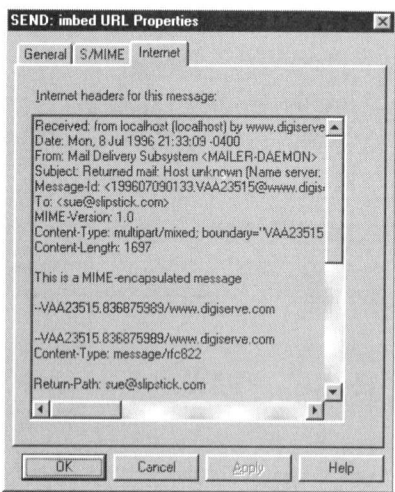

Opening File Attachments

If a message includes an attached file, as indicated by the paper clip icon in the Exchange Viewer, open the message, then double-click the file icon to open the attached file using the application associated with the file type (see the sidebar "File Type Associations" on page 325 in Chapter 14).

To save an attachment as a separate file to your hard drive, follow these steps:

1. Choose File, Save As.
2. In the Save As dialog box shown in Figure 12.6, use the "Save in" list to browse your drive for the folder where you want to save the file.
3. Select "Save these Attachments only."
4. Select the attachment(s) you want to save.
5. Click the Save button.

You can perform this operation either from the open message or from the Exchange Viewer window. In other words, the message doesn't have to be open; you can select it in the Exchange Viewer, then choose File, Save As to save the attachment.

Activating Internet Links

In messages received by the Microsoft Exchange Server clients, links to Internet resources appear in underlined blue text, just as they would in the default colors for a typical Internet browser (see Figure 12.8 for an example of the underlined text). If you move the pointer over this text, it changes to an arrow. Click on an underlined http link to start your Internet browser and go to the World Wide Web site. If the link is a mailto link rather than an http link, a New Message window opens with the address of the recipient filled in.

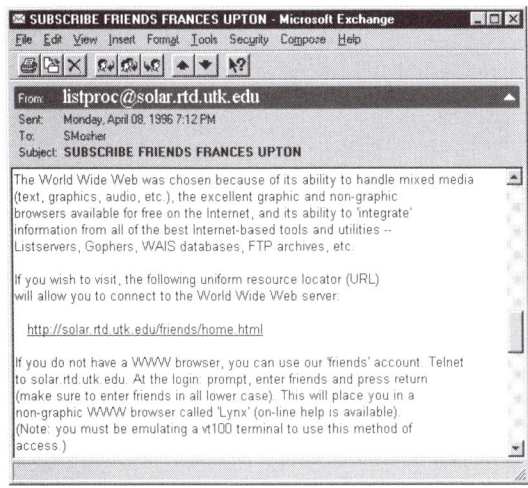

Figure 12.8
Click the underlined (blue) text in the Exchange Server client to activate the Internet link.

To get this same feature with the operating system versions of Exchange, install Deming Preview, an add-on for Exchange included on the accompanying CD. See "Adding a Preview Pane," page 243 in Chapter 10.

Replying to and Forwarding Messages

One of the advantages of e-mail is the ease with which you can reply to or forward a message. The techniques are quite simple. But if you want to be an effective e-mail user, you need to consider the content of your replies and cover notes — in particular, how much text of the incoming message to quote in your own message and how to make that text stand out.

Replying to Messages

To reply either to an open message or to the message selected in the Exchange Viewer, click the Reply to Sender or Reply to All button, or choose Compose, Reply to Sender or Compose, Reply to All. The message opens in a new message window (Figure 12.9) with the addresses already in the To and Cc boxes (Bcc recipients do not receive replies). In some cases, Reply to All

Figure 12.9

When you reply to a message, Exchange automatically fills in the addresses and quotes the incoming message, indenting the message text and including header information.

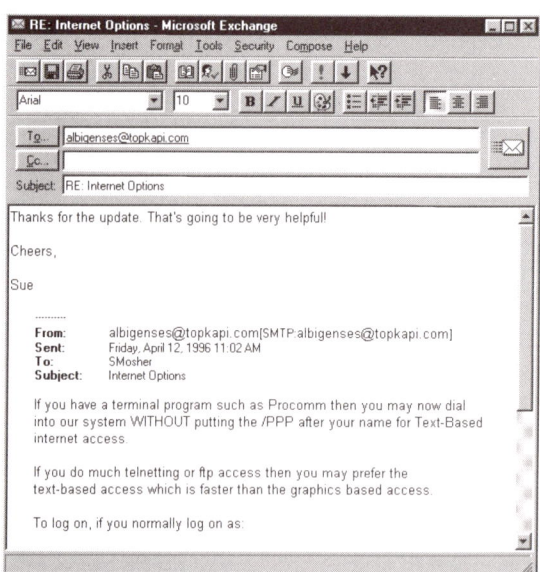

may include your own address in the To box; if this happens, just delete your address.

If there was an attachment in the original message, the reply will include a reference to the file, but not the file itself. Exchange assumes that the person you are replying to already has a copy.

Forwarding Messages

To forward a selected message, choose Compose, Forward. A new message window opens, containing the text of the incoming message, plus any attached files. Enter the addresses of people you want to forward to, just as you would for a new message. Type in a cover note if you want.

You also can select multiple messages in the Exchange Viewer and forward them. Instead of appearing as text, the way a single forwarded message does, these messages will appear as attachments in your new message, using the message file (.msg) format, as shown in Figure 12.10.

Special Note

Only other users of Exchange will be able to read the attached messages if you forward multiple messages using the technique depicted in Figure 12.10. If you need to forward several messages to someone using a different mail program, use Insert, Message instead. Select multiple messages in the Insert Message dialog box, then choose to insert as "Text only" (see "Inserting Files, Messages, and Objects," page 259 in Chapter 11).

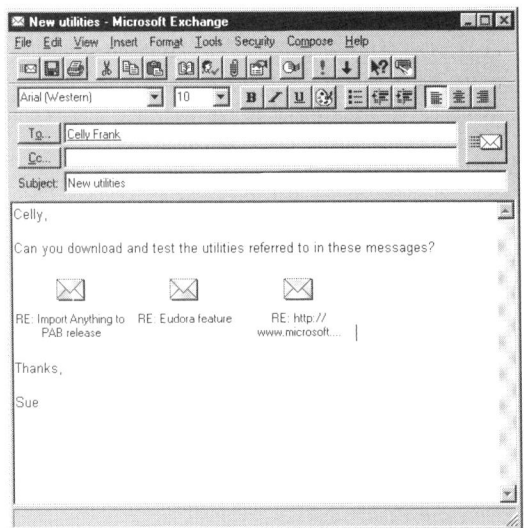

Figure 12.10
When multiple messages are forwarded, they look like file attachments.

Dealing with Custom Messages

Not all incoming messages open in the familiar message window. A Schedule+ meeting request, such as that shown in Figure 12.11, is a good example of a custom message type.

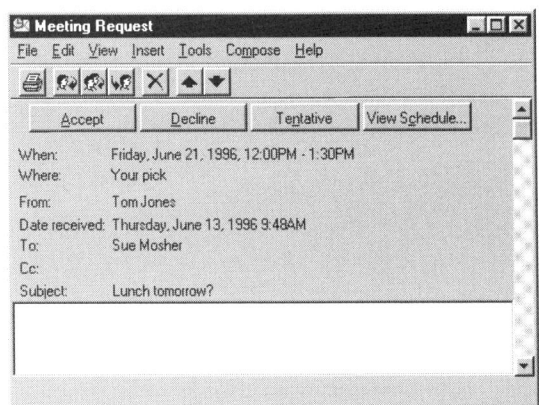

Figure 12.11
Use the Accept, Decline, or Tentative button, rather than the Reply button, to respond to a Schedule+ meeting request.

When you see special buttons on a message such as this, it's safe to assume the buttons are there for a reason. Use the appropriate action button instead of the normal Reply or Reply to All option.

Quoting Incoming Messages

When quoting incoming messages in your replies, use just enough of the original text to get the meaning across.

As soon as your e-mail volume exceeds a couple dozen messages a day, you may find that it's increasingly difficult to recall the earlier portions of a message exchange. This is especially true with mailing lists (which we'll discuss more in Chapter 22, "Working with Internet E-Mail"), where several days may separate the original message and subsequent replies.

The standard method for dealing with this is to quote as much of the original message as necessary to make your meaning clear. Two approaches are recommended, depending on whether or not you're responding point by point:

- If you are responding individually to a series of questions or points in the original message, quote each original question, then add your response.
- If you are responding to the whole incoming message, put that response at the top of the message. Below, include enough of the original message to get the point across.

In either case, remove extraneous material from the original message and rearrange it as needed, but don't edit the remaining text of the message.

On the Internet, it's customary to set off quoted text with a character, usually >, at the beginning of each line. Another way to show that text is included from another message is to put >> at the beginning of the quoted text and << at the end.

Exchange doesn't use either of these methods, though you can employ them with WordMail macros or with add-ons such as Internet Idioms, which is on the CD, and Exchange Buddy, which is listed in Appendix B, "Exchange Resources." However, Exchange does have its own method for setting off quotes. On the Read tab (accessed through Tools, Options — see Figure 12.5), you see two choices under "When replying or forwarding an item":

- Include the original text when replying
- Indent the original text when replying

By default, Exchange uses blue, 10-point Arial text for your reply. To change this, click the Font button. The indenting and blue text will be seen only by recipients capable of handling RTF messages. If you're sending to people who aren't using Exchange, you also may want to use the more traditional quoting method described above.

Tips and Tricks

Many of the utilities developed to enhance Exchange focus on receiving messages. In this section, we spotlight several tools to help you protect against viruses, automatically download your mail, and get alerts when important messages arrive.

Protecting Against Viruses

Eventually, someone is likely to send you a well-meant message about the Good Times virus, which supposedly will wreck your computer if you open an e-mail message with the subject "Good Times." This message, which has been going around for months if not years, is a hoax. You cannot infect your computer with a virus just by opening an e-mail message. However, the threat of viruses being spread through e-mail is real, in the form of attached files. Because it's easy to open attachments by double-clicking them, your system's virus defenses, which depend on files being written separately to the hard drive, are often bypassed.

One of the most recent virus-fighting developments is the advent of Exchange add-ons, such as ThunderBYTE and VirusEx, which inspect file attachments before you open them and warn you of any virus problems. Beta versions of these add-ons are included on the CD.

Changing the Paper Size in WordMail

If you use WordMail to read messages and prefer an A4 paper size for printing, you need to edit the WordMail default template. Otherwise, messages will be formatted for an 8.5-by-11-inch page. To edit the default templates, follow these steps:

1. From the Exchange Viewer menu, choose Compose, WordMail Options.
2. In the WordMail Options dialog box, select the template for which the Set as Default Template box is checked.
3. Click the Edit button to open the template in Word.
4. Choose File, Page Setup, then switch to the Paper Size tab.
5. Select the Paper Size you want to use, then click OK.
6. Choose File, Save to save the changes to the template.

Changing the Color for Sender

In messages opened in the Exchange Server client, the sender of the message is displayed in a distinctive contrasting bar, with white letters on a teal background. To change this color combination, choose Tools, Options and switch to the Colors tab. Select the colors you prefer from the lists for Readbar and Readbar Text. In this dialog box, you can also change the color scheme for unread messages in the Exchange Viewer, as described in the "Tips and Tricks" section in Chapter 10.

Changing the New Mail Notification Sound

By default, Exchange uses a ding sound (Ding.wav) when new mail arrives. If you'd like something snazzier, follow these steps:

1. Click the Start button, then Settings, Control Panel. Next start the Sounds applet.

2. Under Events, select New Mail Notification, listed under Windows sounds.

3. Under Name, choose the sound you want to use for the New Mail Notification event. You also can click the Browse button to locate more sound files on your computer.

4. When you've selected a sound, you can listen to it before finalizing your choice. When you are satisfied, press the OK button to save the new sound.

Using a Mail Retriever or Notifier

The accompanying CD includes several tools to help automate the retrieval of messages with Exchange, especially if you use services other than the Microsoft Exchange Server service:

GetMail	Retrieves mail unattended for all services in a specified Exchange profile, using a specific dial-up networking connection
MailAlert	Provides custom alerts for incoming messages, based on the sender or subject (similar to Inbox Assistant, but for users of the operating system versions of Exchange/Windows Messaging)
	Also automatically retrieves mail via the Internet Mail service at the specified interval (if Internet Mail is configured for scheduled connections)

| **MailFlag** | Alerts the user to new mail in the specified Exchange profile, with the option to set reminders for individual messages |
| **MAPI Download** | Retrieves mail unattended for all services in an Exchange profile |

GetMail and MAPI Download are particularly useful when launched by a scheduler program, such as the System Agent program included with Microsoft Plus!, which starts programs according to a schedule you set. You might also combine GetMail or MAPI Download with MailFlag or MailAlert to receive new mail and get notification of those new messages — without ever starting the full Exchange program. You will find details about how to install and use these programs in Appendix A, "CD Contents."

Summary

It may take some experimentation before you determine the message retrieval methods that work best for you and the services installed in your Exchange profile. But you'll soon become adept at processing new mail using the many techniques that Exchange offers for retaining mail and sharing it with others.

Key Points

- Retrieving messages can take place automatically or manually.

- You must start Exchange to find out whether you have new messages unless you use a mail-notification add-on.

- New messages appear in your Inbox in bold. Messages that you have read are in the normal font.

- When quoting incoming messages in your replies, use just enough of the original text to get the meaning across.

For More Information

The mechanics of scheduling sessions for various services are described in the appropriate chapters in Part II. Delivery of outgoing messages and retrieval of pending mail usually take place together.

Organizing folders to keep track of messages and get rid of the outdated ones is an important task. We'll look at several techniques in Chapter 16, "Working with Messages and Folders."

Exchange Server users have two terrific helpers to keep their Inbox in shape: Inbox Assistant and Out-of-Office Assistant. Both use rules that you define to handle your incoming mail. These tools can route certain messages to your assistant while saving others for your personal review in a separate folder. Chapter 18, "Exchange Assistants," is devoted to these exciting features.

Chapter 13

Working Remotely

One of the chief features of Microsoft Exchange is its capability to gather messages and other information from many sources, no matter where you might be. Staying in touch, whether you're at home, in the office, or on another continent, becomes a matter of pushing a few buttons to connect with your mailbox.

This chapter is not just for travelers, though. If you use Internet Mail, The Microsoft Network, or other similar services, you'll learn how to use the Remote Mail function to browse your messages and download only the most important ones. For those of you who are road warriors, we'll also equip you with tools to keep your Exchange folders and addresses in sync between locations.

Remote Working Environments

Exchange offers three ways to work remotely — online, offline, and synchronized.

Exchange offers three different ways to work remotely:

- Online — connected for an extended period of time directly to your network, but from a remote location — over a dial-up link or perhaps via the Internet
- Offline — connected to the mail server only when you want to download and upload mail
- Synchronized (only available to Exchange Server clients) — offline, but with mirror copies of both your personal folders and favorite public folders

Online Remote Connections

To send and receive messages with an online remote connection, use Tools, Deliver Now from the Exchange Viewer window.

Using Exchange via online remote is just like being in the office, only the slower connection requires more patience. Because you are connected just as any other node on the network is, you have access to everything on the mail server, including public or shared folders if you are using the Microsoft Exchange Server service or Microsoft Mail.

To send and receive messages with an online remote connection, choose Tools, Deliver Now from the Exchange Viewer menu. While no special techniques are involved to send and receive mail, you should check the "Synchronizing Folders" and "Synchronizing Addresses" sections later in this chapter for ideas about how to keep your remote computer in sync with the one in the office. You will want to keep at least the most important messages on both systems. Otherwise, you may end up at a meeting 2,000 miles away, while the agenda and research for the meeting sit back in the Inbox on your desktop computer.

Offline Remote Connections

The offline approach is the most common way to connect remotely with Exchange. Offline is the way you interact with Internet mail servers and online services such as CompuServe and The Microsoft Network. Microsoft Mail also provides offline capabilities for remote users.

Typically, when you work offline, you compose messages while you are disconnected from the network. Then you connect, send those messages, and get (new) incoming mail using Tools, Deliver Now, as described in Chapter 11, "Sending E-Mail Messages." You also can download selected messages with Tools, Remote Mail, as you'll see shortly.

It sounds paradoxical, but you can be connected directly to the network and be working offline. For example, if you use Microsoft Mail and need to keep copies of all messages on the server, you must work offline and use Remote Mail, even from your office computer. See the section "Retaining Messages on the Server" on page 128 in Chapter 6.

Special Note

Synchronized Remote Links

Synchronized remote use is available only to Exchange Server clients. Exchange Server provides a mechanism for keeping an exact copy of both your mailbox and any designated public folders on your remote computer. You can merge changes with the originals on the Microsoft Exchange server when you connect to it.

Using Remote Mail

The idea behind Remote Mail is that, by knowing the who, what, and when of waiting messages, you can decide which messages to download and which to ignore. The who, what, and when of a message is contained in the message *header*, a line in the Remote Mail window that shows you the following information:

- Who sent you the message
- What the message is about (the subject) and whether the message includes an attachment
- When the message was sent

You also will see the size of the message and, depending on the service, the estimated time required to download it.

When you use Remote Mail, you do several tasks in a specific sequence:

1. Download message headers.
2. Select which waiting messages to download and which to delete.
3. Download and delete the selected messages.

Depending on which Exchange client you have, some of these steps may be combined.

Any messages waiting in your Outbox are sent either when you first download the headers, when the messages you marked are processed, or during both operations — again, depending on the client.

The idea behind Remote Mail is that, by knowing the who, what, and when of waiting messages, you can decide which messages to download and which to ignore.

There are two versions of Remote Mail: a multistep version in the Windows 95 operating system client and a one-step version in other Exchange clients.

If you use the original Windows 95 operating system client, you have a multistep version of Remote Mail. A one-step version of Remote Mail is included with the Exchange Server clients, the Windows NT 4.0 operating system, and the Windows Messaging update to the Windows 95 operating system client.

You can see the difference between the two versions of Remote Mail in the toolbar and on the menus. Table 13.1 lists the Remote Mail toolbar buttons. The last two columns indicate which buttons are available in the two versions and what the buttons do.

As you can see, the one-step version of Remote Mail does not include the Update Headers and Transfer Mail functions; instead, it combines them with the Connect function.

Table 13.1 Remote Mail Toolbar Buttons

Button	Name	Multistep	One-Step
	Connect (multistep)	Connect to the mail server	n/a
	Disconnect	Disconnect from the mail server	Disconnect from the mail server
	Update Headers (multistep)	Connect to the mail server Download information about waiting messages	n/a
	Transfer Mail (multistep)	Connect to the mail server Upload Outbox messages Perform actions on marked headers	
	-or-		
	Connect (one-step)		Connect to the mail server Download message headers Upload Outbox messages Perform actions on any marked headers

continued

Table 13.1 Remote Mail Toolbar Buttons, continued

Button	Name	Multistep	One-Step
	Mark to Retrieve	Download the message and delete it from the mail server	
	Mark to Retrieve a Copy	Download the message and keep the original on the mail server	
	Mark to Delete	Delete the message from the mail server	
	Unmark All	Clear all marks	
	Help	Get help about any element of the Remote Mail window	

Preparing for Remote Mail

Before you use Remote Mail, you must set up the individual services in your profile to work with it. See the respective chapters in Part II of this book for details about the settings appropriate for each service.

The CompuServe Mail service (version 1.1 and earlier) is incompatible with the one-step version of Remote Mail. If you use any client other than the original Windows 95 Exchange client, then you must use Tools, Deliver All to get your CompuServe messages.

Special Note

For Internet Mail, you must specifically enable Remote Mail. At the same time, this disables scheduled automatic connections for Internet Mail.

In Chapter 3, "Making Connections," you'll find instructions for building the dial-up networking (DUN) connections that you will likely need for Remote Mail.

Downloading Headers

To make a Remote Mail connection and download headers, follow these steps:

1. Choose Tools, Remote Mail. If more than one service can use Remote Mail, choose which service you want to connect with.

2. In the Remote Mail window (Figure 13.1), click the Connect button (one-step) or the Update Headers button (multistep).

Figure 13.1

This is the one-step Remote Mail window. Users of the Windows 95 operating system client have additional buttons, listed in Table 13.1. Notice the connect icon in the lower right corner, showing whether you're currently connected to the mail server.

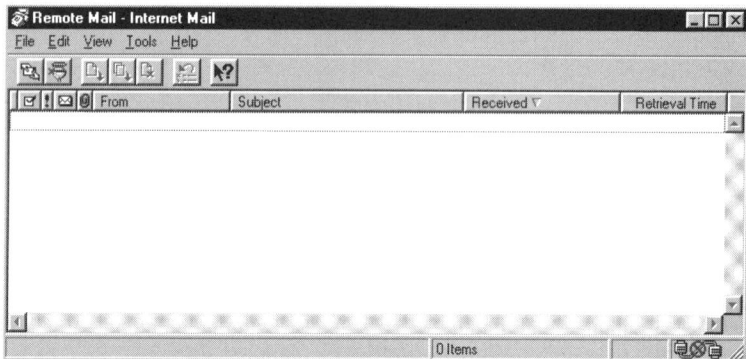

3. If you're connecting to Microsoft Mail, you'll see the dialog box shown in Figure 13.2. Select the actions you want to perform during this connection, then click OK.

Figure 13.2

Each time you start a Remote Mail session for Microsoft Mail, you can select which actions will take place during that session.

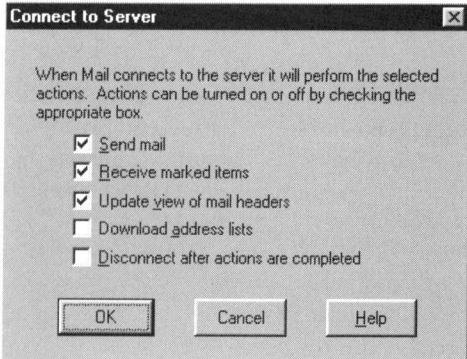

4. Click the Connect button on the Connect To or Sign In dialog box, if one appears as part of your DUN connection.

Exchange connects to the mail server, then downloads headers for waiting messages, displaying the headers in the Remote Mail window. On the one-step Remote Mail, any messages in your Outbox are also sent (unless you are using Microsoft Mail and have cleared the Send Mail box as part of steo 3).

Depending on the particular service and its settings, Exchange may disconnect after updating message headers to give you time to review the headers without running up the telephone bill. The symbol at the lower right of the Remote Mail window (Figure 13.1) indicates whether you are currently connected.

   Connected

   Disconnected

Marking Messages

The next step is to mark the messages you want to retrieve and those you want to delete, using the Mark to Retrieve, Mark to Retrieve a Copy, and Mark to Delete buttons. Figure 13.3 shows headers marked for retrieval and deletion.

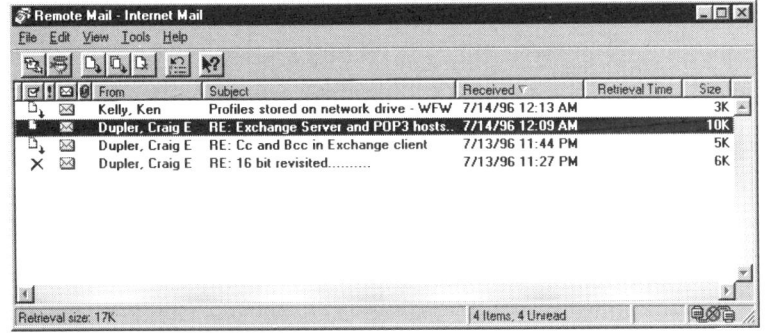

Figure 13.3

After you update headers, mark the items you want to retrieve and delete. Not all services show the Retrieval Time, but the Size column gives you an idea of which messages will take a long time to download.

The information from the headers can help you decide which messages to download. For some services, you'll see an estimated retrieval time, along with the size of the message. Other clues include the Priority, Sender, and Subject, of course; but also pay attention to the presence of any file attachments. As in the Exchange Viewer, you can click on the column heading to sort messages or choose View, Filter to screen out certain messages.

To mark messages, select one or more headers in the Remote Mail window, then click one of the Mark buttons. You also can choose Edit and select any of the Mark choices from that menu. If you don't want to mark headers right away, that's okay. You can close the Remote Mail window and come back to it later. Message headers are kept between Remote Mail sessions, even if you exit Exchange.

Retrieving Messages and Sending Mail

To manipulate the marked messages and send mail from your Outbox,

1. Choose Tools, Remote Mail if the Remote Mail window isn't already open. If more than one service can use Remote Mail, choose which service you want to connect with.

2. In the Remote Mail window (Figure 13.1), click the Connect button (one-step) or the Transfer Mail button (multistep).

3. If you're connecting to Microsoft Mail, you see the dialog box shown in Figure 13.2. Select the actions you want to perform during this connection, then click OK.

4. Click the Connect button on the Connect To or Sign In dialog box, if one appears.

If you're using the one-step version of Remote Mail, any new headers also will be retrieved during this operation.

Holding Items in the Outbox Without Sending Them

With the one-step version of Remote Mail, it's important to realize that your Outbox will be sent each time you click the Connect button or choose Tools, Connect. If you want to defer delivery of an Outbox message, open the message, then close it without sending it. The message will be shown in the Outbox without italics, which means it will not be delivered. When you are ready to send the message, open it again, then choose File, Send.

With one exception, there is no way to disable the entire Outbox; you must defer each individual message. The exception is Microsoft Mail, which allows you to disable delivery of messages to the postoffice. See the section "Delivery," page 120 in Chapter 6.

Synchronizing Folders

If you are a remote user who works on one computer in the office and a different machine at another location, your biggest problem is having access to all mail folders no matter where you're working. Exchange Server clients don't really have a problem with this, as we'll see in a moment, because synchronization is built in. But if you use the operating system Exchange client, you will need to take extra steps to move messages and folders from one computer to another.

Synchronizing Personal Folders

On the Windows 95 and Windows NT operating system clients, folders can be synchronized in two ways:

- Via My Briefcase
- By directly copying Personal Folders files

Exchange Server users also can use one of these techniques to move Personal Folders files back and forth, but the built-in synchronization is a better method of keeping up with the messages in their Exchange Server mailboxes.

Using My Briefcase

If you can connect your remote computer to your office (either via a network card or by DUN), My Briefcase is the easiest way to maintain messages at two locations. If you haven't installed My Briefcase and want to, see the sidebar "Setting Up My Briefcase" on page 308. (If floppy disks are the only means you have to transfer files between the two systems, then it may not be practical to use My Briefcase because of the potential size of Personal Folders files.)

Let's assume you have both an office desktop computer and a notebook that travels with you. To keep your messages updated at both locations, you need to put the Personal Folders file in My Briefcase on the notebook, then set up Exchange on the notebook to use that file. Follow these steps:

Make your Personal Folders file available on the network

1. If you haven't done so already, create a network share on your office computer to the folder that contains your Personal Folders file, usually C:\Exchange or C:\Windows. See the section "Sharing Network Resources" on page 57 in Chapter 3. (Personal Folders is a .pst file. To check its location, choose

For users of the operating system clients, My Briefcase is the easiest way to maintain messages and addresses at two locations.

Tools, Services, then bring up the properties for Personal Folders.)

Copy your Personal Folders file to My Briefcase

2. Connect the notebook to the office network either with a network adapter via DUN, or with a direct cable connection.
3. On the notebook, open the folder (located on the office computer) where your Personal Folders file is located.
4. Drag the .pst (Personal Folders) file to My Briefcase on the Windows desktop on the notebook computer.

Add My Briefcase Personal Folders to your Exchange profile

5. Click Start, choose Settings, Control Panel, then double-click the Mail and Fax (or Mail) icon.
6. Click Add, then select Personal Folders and click OK.
7. In the Create/Open Personal Folders File dialog box (Figure 13.4), use the "Look in" hierarchy to select Desktop. Then double-click My Briefcase to view the files it contains.

Figure 13.4

Use the Personal Folders File from My Briefcase in the profile on your remote computer.

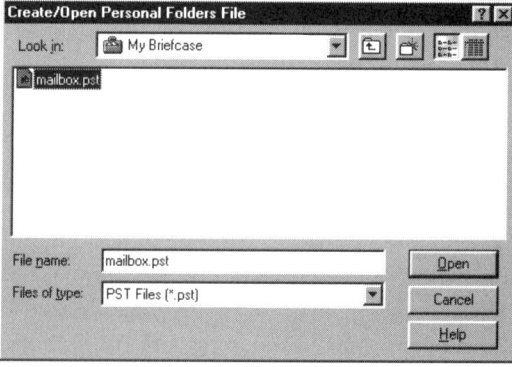

8. Select the .pst file you copied to My Briefcase in step 4, then click Open.

Deliver new mail to My Briefcase Personal Folders

9. If you already had a Personal Folders file in this profile, you may want to remove that file after copying any old messages from it to the new Personal Folders file you just added to the profile.

If you want to keep a previous Personal Folders file in the profile, then you should rename the previous file to distinguish it from My Briefcase Personal Folders. You can do this in the profile properties dialog box by bringing up the properties for Personal Folders.

When you return to the profile properties dialog box, switch to the Delivery tab. Under "Deliver new mail to the following location," select the Personal Folders you just added from My Briefcase.

When you return to the office, you'll connect the notebook to the network again to synchronize My Briefcase with your office computer. Here's how:

1. After connecting the notebook to the network, open My Briefcase from the notebook computer's Windows desktop.

2. Choose Briefcase, Update All.

3. Windows displays the action that needs to be taken to synchronize files, as shown in Figure 13.5.

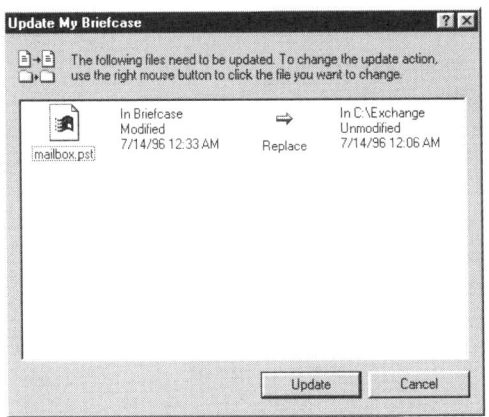

Figure 13.5
When you update My Briefcase, the Personal Folders file on the remote computer replaces the older file on the desktop computer.

4. Click the Update button to copy the Public Folders from the notebook to your office computer.

After the update, start Exchange on the office machine to see all the messages that were sent and received on the notebook.

Setting Up My Briefcase

If you don't see a briefcase icon on your desktop, then My Briefcase is probably not installed on your system. Here's how to add it:

1. Click Start, choose <u>S</u>ettings, <u>C</u>ontrol Panel.
2. Double-click the Add/Remove Programs icon, then switch to Windows Setup in the Add/Remove Programs Properties dialog box.
3. Select Accessories, then click the <u>D</u>etails button.
4. Under <u>C</u>omponents, check Briefcase.
5. Click OK twice to finish adding My Briefcase to your desktop.

My Briefcase is placed on the desktop by default, but you can put a briefcase in any folder on your system. Select the folder, then choose <u>F</u>ile, Ne<u>w</u>, Briefcase.

Before you to take the notebook on the road the next time, just follow steps 1 through 4 again. This time, Windows will copy the file in the other direction, from the office computer to the notebook.

Copying Personal Folders

The other method for synchronizing Personal Folders is simply to copy the .pst file from one computer to another, overwriting the previous version. To make this as easy as possible, use the same file name and folder on both machines. If you are using diskettes and if the .pst file is large, you will need to use a utility such as PKZip to compress the file, possibly onto multiple diskettes, then decompress the file onto the target computer.

Synchronizing Mailbox and Public Folders

The synchronization techniques described for Personal Folders involve copying an entire .pst file, either with My Briefcase or directly. The Exchange Server clients provide a quicker mechanism that updates message by message. This mechanism is called offline folders.

Offline folders include the following:

- Inbox, Outbox, and Sent Items folders from your Exchange Server mailbox
- Any other folders from your mailbox that have been marked for synchronization

- Any public folders from Favorites that have been marked for synchronization

Before you can use offline folders, you must activate them while you're connected with the Microsoft Exchange server (see the section "If You're Connecting Remotely" on page 90 in Chapter 5).

Marking Folders to Be Synchronized

The Inbox, Outbox, and Sent Items folders are always included in offline folders. To use other folders offline, you must set them up to be synchronized. These folders can be either folders from your mailbox or public folders that you've added to the Favorites folder under Public Folders.

To mark a folder for synchronization, follow these steps:

1. Using the Exchange Viewer, select the folder either in your mailbox or under the Favorites folder under Public Folders.

2. Choose File, Properties, then click the Synchronization tab.

3. In the folder's Properties dialog box (Figure 13.6), choose "When offline or online." This marks the folder as one to be synchronized.

4. Click OK to close the folder's Properties dialog box.

Exchange Server's offline folders provide a quicker synchronization mechanism that updates message by message.

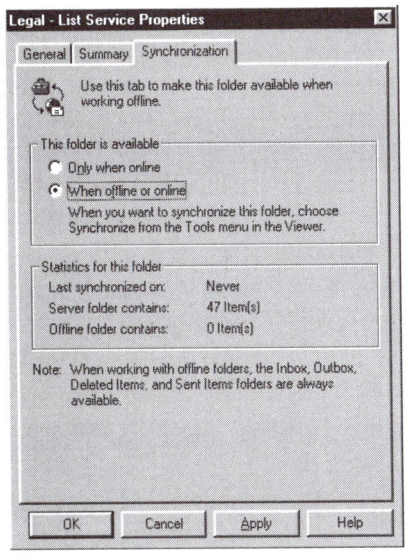

Figure 13.6
Set up offline use and view statistics about the server and local versions of a folder on the Synchronization tab of the folder's Properties dialog box.

Folders marked for synchronization appear in the Exchange Viewer with briefcase rather than folder icons. New folders in your mailbox are set up for synchronization by default. To turn off synchronization, follow the same procedure, but choose "Only when online" in step 3.

Special Note

You can add a public folder to Favorites only when you are connected to the Microsoft Exchange server, not when you are working offline. You might want to make a point of using a full connection from time to time, so you can find out about any new public folders.

Synchronizing Automatically or On Demand

When you connect to the Exchange server (if you've chosen Connect rather than Work Offline for the way you access the Exchange server), folders in your mailbox — including any you've created — are synchronized automatically. Favorite public folders are synchronized only on demand. In Work Offline mode, synchronization for all folders is done only on demand.

To synchronize a single folder, choose Tools, Synchronize, This Folder. To synchronize all folders, choose Tools, Synchronize, All Folders. To see what occurred when you synchronized, look in the Deleted Items folder for a synchronization log listing the actions performed.

Synchronizing Addresses

When you are working remotely, having all your addresses available is just as important as being able to see all your messages. You use different methods for personal and organization address lists. For the Personal Address Book, use the same techniques as for Personal Folders, either with My Briefcase or a simple file copy. For addresses for the organization, Exchange Server clients can download a copy of an offline address list. To do so, follow these steps:

1. Choose Tools, Synchronize, Download Offline Address Book.

2. Choose how much detail you want to download. Your choices are shown in Figure 13.7.

Figure 13.7

The complete Exchange Server address book requires more time to download, but it contains more information and allows you to send encrypted messages.

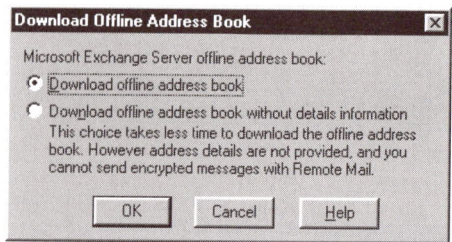

3. Click OK to download the address book.

If you use Microsoft Mail and want a local copy of the organization's address list, choose Tools, Microsoft Mail Tools, Download Address Lists.

Tips and Tricks

Many of the tips and tricks from the two preceding chapters on sending and receiving messages also apply to remote users. However, road warriors need some special techniques of their own. Here you'll learn how to use the Exchange Server client to download messages selectively, how to switch dialing locations from the taskbar, and how various Exchange add-ons can give you new ways to communicate from outside your office.

Building a Retrieval Filter

The Exchange Server clients offer an advanced Remote Mail feature: the ability to retrieve all messages from a particular sender, on a particular subject, or as defined by various other criteria. These filtered messages are downloaded automatically when you connect, without any need to mark the headers. To use this feature, follow these steps:

1. Choose Tools, Services, then select Exchange Server and click Properties.
2. Switch to the Remote Mail tab.
3. Click "Retrieve items that meet the following conditions."
4. Click the Filter button.
5. In the Filter dialog box, set criteria for the messages you want to download. The choices are similar to those available in the Exchange Viewer (see the section "Working with Filters" on page 237 in Chapter 10). However, you cannot filter by words found in the text of the message.
6. When you've finished entering conditions, click OK to close the Filter dialog box, then OK twice more to save the settings.

The next time you use Remote Mail, any items caught by the filter will be downloaded automatically. You'll still see headers for all other messages.

Switching Locations with a Power Toy

For the truly nomadic Windows 95 user, Microsoft has created the TapiTNA Power Toy (Power Toys are add-ons provided without support or warranty by Microsoft). TapiTNA rests as an icon in the system tray on the taskbar.

When you need to switch dialing locations (see the section "Working with Locations" on page 30 in Chapter 3), just click the icon rather than burrow through the Control Panel or Exchange to find the Dialing Locations dialog box. Details about where to get TapiTNA are in Appendix B, "Exchange Resources."

Staying Connected to Internet Mail

Internet Mail automatically disconnects after each Remote Mail connection session (most other services let the user control this action). Sometimes it seems a little silly to have to dial in again after you've marked message headers in the Remote Mail window. Wouldn't it be nice to keep your Internet connection open long enough so you could mark the headers, then download the messages, without having to reconnect?

Maintaining the connection is actually fairly easy to do: Just load your browser before you make the Remote Mail connection. The browser will keep your Internet connection open while you work with the message headers. Just don't forget to disconnect the modem when you're all done with Remote Mail!

Sending Point-to-Point Messages

So far, we've talked about remote messaging only as a way to communicate with mail servers at remote locations; but that's not the only way to work remotely. There are also methods for sending mail directly to another person without going through a mail server. One way is to use Microsoft Fax. If you and the other person both use Microsoft Fax (or WinFax) and Class 1 fax modems, then when you send a fax, it's delivered as an e-mail message. For details about binary file transfer, as this technique is called, see Chapter 14, "Sending Faxes."

Another approach is to use an Exchange service specifically designed for point-to-point communications. MobileWare Personal is such a product for Windows 95 users (see Appendix B, "Exchange Resources"). One advantage that MobileWare Personal has over Microsoft Fax is that with MobileWare Personal more than one message can be delivered in a single phone call.

Sending Wireless Messages

If you work remotely, then you've probably carried a pager at some point — or you frequently need to get in touch with someone who does. Paging gateways, available for Microsoft Mail and Microsoft Exchange Server, let you send an alert to a pager just as easily as you send an e-mail message. You can even set up Inbox Assistant and Out-of-Office Assistant rules to send pages — to yourself or to someone else — in response to particular types of messages.

Pagers are just one example of wireless communications. Various other add-ons for Exchange Server support special Exchange service providers that optimize your messages for wireless transmission to devices such as personal digital assistants with wireless modems.

Summary

In this chapter, we've examined the needs of the remote user with two different goals in mind: showing you how to use the Remote Mail service, and demonstrating how to use Exchange on more than one computer but keep the same messages and addresses available.

Key Points

- Exchange offers three different ways to work remotely — online, offline, and synchronized (for Exchange Server clients only).

- To send and receive messages with an online remote connection, use Tools, Deliver Now from the Exchange Viewer window.

- The idea behind Remote Mail is that, by knowing the who, what, and when of waiting messages, you can decide which messages to download and which to ignore. This information is contained in message headers you can preview.

- There are two versions of Remote Mail — a multistep version in the Windows 95 operating system client, and a one-step version in other Exchange clients.

- For users of the operating system clients, My Briefcase is the easiest way to maintain messages and addresses at two locations.

- The Exchange Server's offline folders provide a quicker synchronization mechanism that updates message by message.

For More Information

Remote Mail is one of two ways to manually send and receive mail. The second method, Deliver Now, is covered in Chapter 11, "Sending E-Mail Messages."

Each information service offers different Remote Mail settings. You might want to review the options for the services installed in your Exchange profile by checking the appropriate chapters in Part II. Also in Part II, you'll find Chapter 3, "Making Connections," to help you get started with dial-up networking.

If you want to use Microsoft Exchange Server security on both your remote computer and the office machine, follow the instructions in the section "Using Exchange Server Security in Multiple Locations" in Chapter 21.

Chapter 14
Sending Faxes

In many respects, sending a fax is just like sending a message. You follow the same basic steps: address, compose, send, and deliver. And if you're faxing a document, Exchange treats the document like an attachment.

There's also another way to fax with Exchange that's not like sending a message; instead, it resembles printing. You can send a fax from virtually any Windows program by printing to a special fax printer driver.

A brief word on terminology before we get into the nitty-gritty details: When I refer to sending a *fax*, I mean sending a message or document without any concern about whether the receiving system is a paper fax machine or another computer. But when I talk about sending a *file*, that narrows the scope of our discussion to sending a file to another computer using binary file transfer (BFT).

The bulk of this chapter deals with Microsoft Fax, which is widely used because it is included with Windows 95. Microsoft Fax does not ship with Windows NT 4.0, but NT does have its own fax service from Microsoft, called Personal Fax, which we discuss in Appendix D, "Personal Fax for Windows NT."

Using Microsoft Fax

Sending a fax is just like sending a message.

In this section, we'll cover several different ways to send a fax with Microsoft Fax and review the process that occurs when you send a fax.

Sending a Fax

Microsoft Fax offers four ways to send a fax (see Figure 14.1):

- From within Exchange
- From within any Windows application
- From any folder within Explorer or My Computer
- From the Start menu, by choosing Programs, Accessories, Fax, Compose, New Fax.

Figure 14.1

Four different ways to send a fax, clockwise from upper left: from Exchange using Compose, New Fax; from a Windows application, using File, Print; after right-clicking on any file in Explorer or My Computer; and from the Start menu.

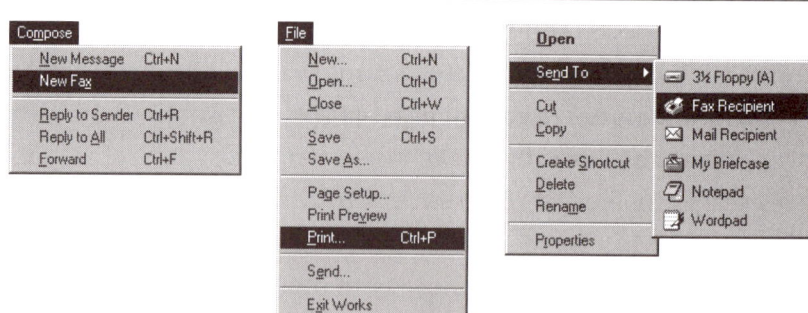

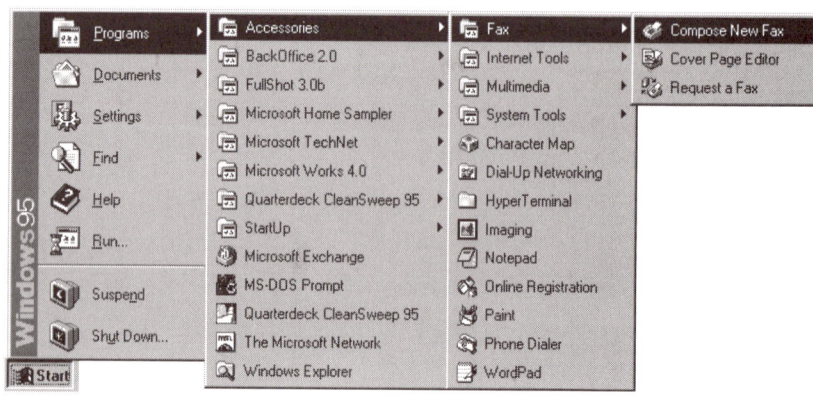

Table 14.1 divides these different methods into two categories: fax wizard methods and e-mail message methods. The fax wizard methods use the Compose New Fax Wizard. The e-mail message methods use Exchange's normal message form. You can use some techniques only when Exchange already has been loaded; these are marked in the table. Other methods are available at any time, whether or not Exchange is active on your system. If Exchange hasn't been loaded, you may be prompted to specify a profile and to log on. Once the fax has been sent, Exchange will unload itself.

Table 14.1 Methods for Sending a Fax	
Methods	**Available Only When Exchange Is Loaded**
Fax wizard In Exchange: Compose, New Fax	X
From Start menu: Programs, Accessories, Fax, Compose New Fax	
From Explorer or My Computer: Right-click on a file, then Send To, Fax Recipient	
From any Windows program: File, Print to Microsoft Fax printer	
E-mail message In Exchange: Compose, New Message	X
From Explorer or My Computer: Right-click on a file, then choose Send To, Mail Recipient	
From some Windows programs: File, Send	

Each set of methods has its advantages. For example, with the fax wizard methods, you can have a note begin on the cover page. With the e-mail message methods, any note will begin on the second page, not on the cover page. Another important distinction is that you can get a delivery receipt only when you use one of the e-mail message methods.

In Table 14.2, you'll find a summary of these methods' different capabilities. You can use this table to help you decide how to send a fax.

Table 14.2 Differences Between Fax Wizard and E-Mail Message Methods		
Option	Fax Wizard	E-Mail Message
Allow note to begin on cover page	X	
Attach multiple documents	If you use Compose, New Fax within Exchange or from the Start menu	X
Allow delivery receipt		X
Send to e-mail as well as fax recipients	X	X
Allow rich-text formatting of cover page note		X
Allow CCs and BCCs		X

As you can see, the main advantage of using the fax wizard methods is that they allow you to put a note right on the cover page, rather than sending the cover page as a separate page.

Using Fax Wizard Methods

When you send a fax via any of the fax wizard methods, the Compose New Fax Wizard launches to walk you through the process. Let's follow along, step by step:

1. The first screen of the Compose New Fax Wizard allows you to confirm or change your dialing location; for example, if you're traveling and need to use a different code to get an outside line from your hotel room. You might not see this screen if you're not using a portable computer. For more about dialing properties, see "Configuring Dialing Locations," page 28 in Chapter 3. Click Next to continue.

2. In the second screen (Figure 14.2), address the fax. You can do this in one of three different ways:

- You can click the Address Book button and pick recipients from your address book.
- You can enter part of a name from your address book, then click the Add to List button and let Exchange find the full address. If Exchange finds more than one match, you'll be asked to select the one you want to use.
- You can enter the full name in the To box, pick the recipient's Country, enter the area code and local number in the Fax # boxes, then click Add to List.

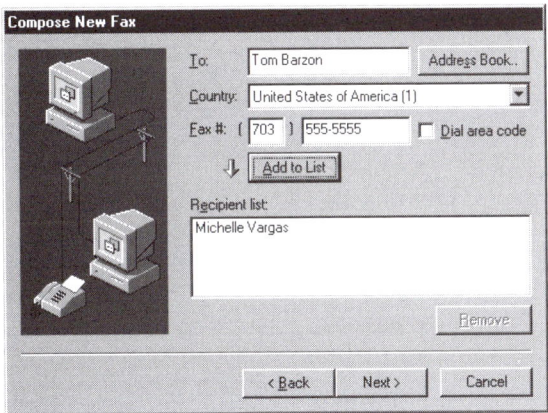

Figure 14.2
Fax recipients can include those entered in your address book and others entered directly in the Compose New Fax screen.

To send a fax to someone from your address book, the recipient must be entered with a fax address. This can be confusing, because the Personal Address Book also allows you to enter a fax number for any recipient on the Phone Numbers tab. However, Exchange does not use this fax number for sending faxes. This means that if you need to reach someone both via e-mail and via fax, you must create two separate entries in your address book, one with the e-mail address, the other with the fax address.

Special Note

3. When you've finished adding to the recipient list, click the Next button to continue.

4. On the third screen of the Compose New Fax Wizard, choose your cover page, or choose No to send none. Remember, though, that at least in the

U.S., you must include information about a fax transmission on the first page. If you decide not to use a cover page, make sure your first fax page includes your name, phone number, and the date and time you sent the fax.

5. If you need to set the time the fax will be sent or change the message format, click the Options button to display the Send Options dialog box (Figure 14.3).

Figure 14.3

Use the Send Options dialog box to override the default options for sending messages.

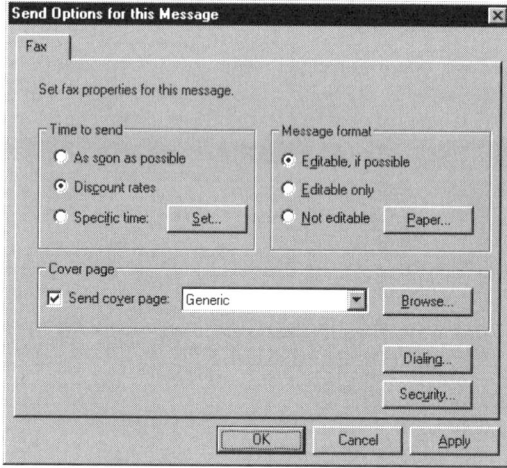

6. In the Send Options dialog box, for "Time to send," you can choose any of the following:

- "As soon as possible"
- During "Discount rates" (you can change the times for this option by changing the options for Microsoft Fax properties, as discussed under "Other Message Defaults," page 150 in Chapter 7)
- At a "Specific time" (you can change the specified time for this option using the Set button)

7. Under "Message format," the best choice is usually "Editable, if possible." However, if you're sending certain types of files (see "Sending a File" later in this chapter), you'll need to switch to "Editable only." If you want everyone to get a fax image rather than an editable document, choose "Not editable." For example, you would choose "Not editable" if you

wanted the recipient to be unable to make changes to the document or if you wanted to send a copy to yourself using the [FAX:me] feature described in "Sending a Fax to Yourself" later in this chapter.

8. You also can change the Paper properties (orientation, fax quality, page size), Dialing properties, and Security (see "Sending Secure Messages via Microsoft Fax," page 488 in Chapter 21) with the appropriate buttons in this dialog box.

9. When you're finished with the Send Options dialog box, click OK to close it and return to the Compose New Fax Wizard. Then click the Next button to continue.

10. In the next screen of the wizard, give your fax a Subject and compose any Note that you want to accompany your fax. If you have a {Note} field on your cover page (as do all the cover pages installed with Microsoft Fax), you will probably want to check the box labeled Start Note on Cover Page. Then click Next to continue.

11. If you used Compose, New Fax either from Exchange or from the Start menu, the next wizard screen lets you attach files. For each file you want to add, click the Add File button and browse your system to select the file, then click the Open button in the Open a File to Attach dialog box. When you've finished adding files, click Next to continue.

You cannot attach additional files if you are printing to the Microsoft Fax printer or if you used Send To, Fax Recipient from a folder. You simply won't see this screen of the wizard.

Special Note

12. On the last screen of the wizard, click Finish to begin the process of preparing your fax in different formats and sending it.

Printing to the Microsoft Fax Printer

You can send a fax from any Windows program by printing to the Microsoft Fax printer. This is another fax wizard method. For some programs, such as Microsoft Works 3.0, this is the only method you can use. The major limitation of this method is that you can send only one document at a time; but if you *are* sending just one document, this is likely to be the fastest fax method.

To print to the Microsoft Fax printer,

1. Choose File, Print from any Windows program.

2. In the Print dialog box, select the Microsoft Fax printer, then click OK.

You can send a fax from any Windows program by printing to the Microsoft Fax printer.

3. The Compose New Fax Wizard will run; just follow the steps described in the previous section.

When you send a fax in this way, you can include an e-mail address, not just a fax recipient. Anyone receiving this message via e-mail will get an attachment with the printed document in Microsoft Fax (AWD) format. (S)he will need to have either Fax Viewer or Imaging for Windows installed to be able to view the attachment.

Special Note

You may see Rendering Subsystem on PUB: listed among your available printers. This is actually part of the Microsoft Fax printer driver, but you should never print directly to the Rendering Subsystem. Always choose the Microsoft Fax printer instead.

If you have a scanner, check to see whether the manufacturer offers a "copier" utility that lets you scan directly to a printer. If so, then you can scan documents directly to the Microsoft Fax printer driver to fax them. We'll look at two other ways to make the scanner part of your faxing arsenal in the sections "Creating a Fax with a Scanner" and "Building a Multipage Fax" later in this chapter.

Using E-Mail Message Methods

Sending a fax using one of the e-mail message methods is almost exactly like composing a regular e-mail message. You can use all the techniques described in Chapter 11, including File, Properties to request a delivery receipt.

If you're not sending to someone in your address book, you might want to use the Fax Addressing Wizard to help you build fax addresses for your recipients. It works just like the addressing screen of the Compose New Fax Wizard. To use the Fax Addressing Wizard, in a Compose New Message window, choose Tools, Fax Addressing Wizard.

To change the fax message format or to send your fax at a time other than the default, from the Compose New Message window, use File, Send Options to display the Send Options dialog box (Figure 14.3) and make changes as described earlier in steps 6 through 8 under "Using Fax Wizard Methods."

There are two limitations with faxes created as e-mail messages:

- Microsoft Fax does not support messages that contain inserted objects. In other words, you can't paste a graphic, chart, or spreadsheet into a fax as you can with an e-mail message.

- You can't include a note on the cover page. Any text you enter in the New Message window will appear on a second page after the cover page, though it will incorporate any rich-text formatting you may have used.

Creating a Fax with a Scanner

If you have a scanner, you can use it to build faxes from paper documents. Microsoft and Wang have made a free tool available, Imaging for Windows, which replaces the Fax Viewer that comes with Microsoft Fax (see "Imaging for Windows," page 167 in Chapter 7).

    To fax one or more documents using your scanner and Imaging,

1. Click the Start button and choose Programs, Accessories, then Imaging.
2. Choose File, New, Scan. The Scan New dialog box (Figure 14.4) will appear.

If you have a scanner, you can use it to build faxes from paper documents.

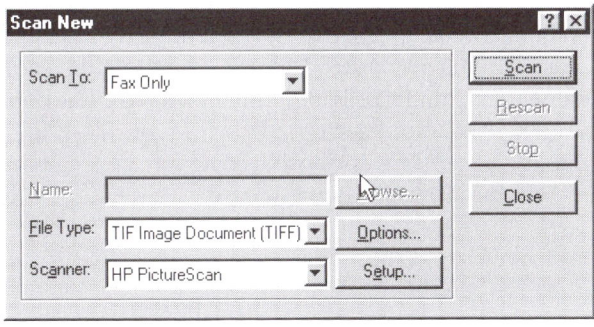

Figure 14.4
With Imaging for Windows, you can scan a document directly to Microsoft Fax.

3. Under Scan To, pick Fax Only.
4. (Optional) Click the Setup button to launch the software for your scanner, scan a preview image, and make any needed adjustments to the scanner settings. Then close the scanner software to return to Imaging.
5. In the Scan New dialog box, choose the File Type you want to use — either Tagged Image File Format (TIFF) or Fax Viewer Document (AWD). TIFF is generally the best choice for documents with graphics.
6. Click Scan to scan the document.
7. If you need to send additional pages, put the next document in the scanner and repeat step 6 (also repeat step 4 as needed; for example, if you switch from a mostly text document to one with graphics or photos). The scanned pages are not displayed in Imaging, but you see the page counter

at the bottom-right corner of the Imaging window increment each time you add a page.

9. When you've scanned all the documents for this fax, click the Fax button to launch the Compose New Fax Wizard. Enter the details for this transmission as usual.

For another method of using your scanner and Imaging, see "Building a Multipage Fax" later in this chapter.

Sending a File (BFT)

As noted at the beginning of this chapter, sending a file means using binary file transfer (BFT) to transmit the actual document, not just a rendered fax image. This approach is possible when both the sender and the recipient are using a Class 1 fax modem and either Microsoft Fax or a compatible fax program.

Normally, you don't have to do anything to use BFT to send a file. The transmission will happen automatically as long as you have the default fax message format set to "Editable if possible." (See "Message Format," page 150 in Chapter 7.) There is a case in which you need to take a couple of extra steps — when you are sending a file that can't be printed. This includes programs and shortcuts (.exe, .com, .bat, and .lnk files), archives (.zip files), and any other binary file that doesn't have an associated program with a Print action (see the sidebar "File Type Associations"). In this case, you must use the Send Options dialog box to set the message format to "Editable only." Otherwise, you will get a System Administrator message in your Inbox telling you that a fax format version of the file could not be created.

When You Send a Fax

When you send a fax, Exchange goes through several steps to assemble your message and attachments in one or two different formats, then it dials each recipient and transmits the fax:

- A version of the message and attachments is prepared in fax format, unless you have set the message format to "Editable only." To prepare the fax format version, Exchange prints the message to the Microsoft Fax printer driver via WordPad (or via Word if you're using WordMail as your e-mail editor) and prints any attachments to the same printer driver using their associated application(s).
- A version of the message and attachments is prepared in e-mail format, unless you've sent to these recipients before and they can all handle only fax format.
- If you've chosen to use a cover page, one is created for each recipient.

File Type Associations

What makes it possible for Microsoft Fax and other fax services to send attached documents as fax images is that Windows keeps a record of what application should be used to print different types of documents. If you watch the fax transmission process closely, you'll see each document opened in its associated application and printed. If Microsoft Fax can't tell what application to use for the printing process, you're likely to get a message that the fax was not deliverable.

Document types are defined by the extension used in the filename. Typically, txt is used for plain text documents (e.g., Readme.txt), doc for Microsoft Word documents, and so on. The command used to print the document is set up when the application is installed.

One way to test whether a document can be sent as an attachment to a fax is to drag the document to a regular printer in your Printers folder. If it prints OK, then it should fax OK. If it doesn't print, then you may want to investigate the file type for that document. To view the file types your system recognizes, go to Explorer or My Computer and choose View, then Options, and switch to the File Types tab in the Options dialog box (Figure 14.A).

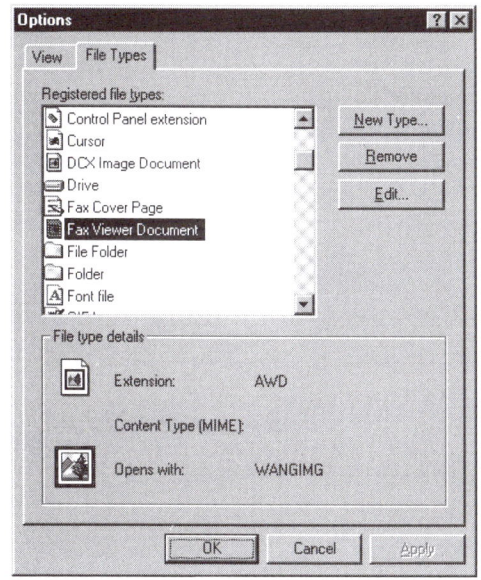

Figure 14.A
You can access file type information from Explorer or from My Computer.

continued

File Type Associations, continued

Each type of registered document is listed here, along with the extension(s) that type of document may use. In Figure 14.A, you can see that the AWD extension is used for Fax Viewer Documents.

To see what application will be used to print a document, select that file type, then click the Edit button. In the Actions list in the Edit File Type dialog box, double-click on Print to display the "Editing action for type" dialog box.

For the Fax Viewer Document type shown in Figure 14.B, the application is Imaging for Windows (C:\Windows\WangImg.Exe). This application, like many Windows programs, allows a command line switch of /p to print a document. The "%1" stands for the filename for the document. The quotation marks are needed to handle long filenames.

Figure 14.B

Editing the Print action lets you see the command used to print a document type.

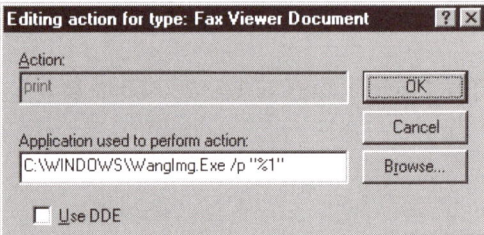

This is a relatively simple example of a Print action. Some Print actions, such as those for Microsoft Word, use dynamic data exchange (DDE) and cannot be entered easily by the user. It's best to let the application setup program do the job of building the file types and actions. The important thing to remember is this: If you don't see a Print action in the Actions list, then you must send this type of document either by opening it and printing it to the Microsoft Fax printer driver, or by sending it as part of a fax with the message format set to "Editable only."

- Each number on the recipient list is dialed in turn. If the number is busy or doesn't answer, Exchange will try again, up to the number of retries you've specified (see "Dialing and Modem Properties" in Chapter 7, page 152).

- After the fax has been transmitted to all recipients (or has failed for some but succeeded for the rest), the message is moved from the Outbox to the Sent Items folder.

- If Exchange could not deliver the fax to one or more recipients, a message from System Administrator appears in your Inbox giving you the reason for the failure(s) and the opportunity to resend the fax to only those recipients who didn't receive it the first time.

If your active fax modem is on a network fax server, but you're not connected to the network or the server is down when you create a message, then that fax will stay in your Outbox. Once you can reconnect to the server, you need to exit Exchange and restart it to queue your fax on the server (see the next section for how to view the fax queue).

You can make the Fax Status dialog box pop up automatically whenever it's processing a fax. In the Fax Status dialog box, choose Options, Display When Active. If you want to monitor the progress of your fax, double-click on the fax machine icon in the system tray at the right side of the Windows taskbar to bring up the Microsoft Fax Status dialog box, shown in Figure 14.5. This dialog box also has a Hang Up button you can use to abort a fax transmission.

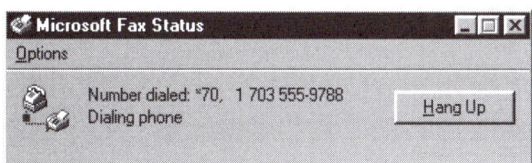

Figure 14.5
To monitor the progress of your faxes with the Fax Status dialog box, double-click the fax machine icon in the system tray on the Windows taskbar.

Viewing the Fax Queue

To see the faxes that are waiting to be sent, choose Tools, Microsoft Fax Tools, Show Outgoing Faxes in the Exchange client window. You also can double-click on the outgoing fax icon (Figure 14.6) in the system tray on the Windows taskbar. The Outgoing Faxes dialog box (Figure 14.7) looks a lot like a printer queue.

In the Outgoing Faxes dialog box, the Sender column distinguishes faxes sent by different users. Notice, though, that this column lists the computer name of the workstation from which each fax was sent, not the user who sent it. To cancel a fax from the Outgoing Faxes dialog box, select the fax you want to cancel, then choose File, Cancel Fax. You can also cancel a fax by deleting it from the Outbox.

Figure 14.6

The fax machine icon appears in the system tray on the taskbar when you load Exchange with a profile that includes Microsoft Fax. The outgoing fax icon appears when a fax is in the queue. Move the pointer over the icon to get a quick pop-up count of the number of faxes in the queue.

Figure 14.7

The Outgoing Faxes dialog box shows the entire network fax server queue, but shows the subjects for only your faxes. The telephone icon marks the fax currently being transmitted.

Sender	Subject	Size	Recipients	Time to Send
FAXMANAGER	...	251 bytes	1	Soon as possible
MAILMAN	Latest logo idea	499011 bytes	1	Discount rates

2 fax(es) in queue

Changing a Fax After It Is Sent

What if you schedule a fax to be delivered during the discount-rate period, but find out that it needs to go right away? Or maybe you realize that you entered the wrong fax number for one of the recipients.

If the fax is a basic cover page with no attachments, you can simply open it in the Outbox, make your changes, then send it again. If there are attachments, however, you need to use a different method. First, cancel the fax from the outgoing fax queue, as described in the previous section. Next, switch to your Inbox, where you'll see an Undeliverable message from the System Administrator. Follow the instructions in the next section to open that message and resend the fax after you make your changes.

Special Note

You may be tempted to try to use Tools, Deliver Now to send a fax immediately. As obvious as that option might seem, it doesn't work. In fact, Deliver Now has no effect at all on faxes.

Resending a Failed Fax

If a fax is not successfully transmitted to all users, Exchange places an Undeliverable message in your Inbox with a reason for each failed transmission (Figure 14.8 shows an example).

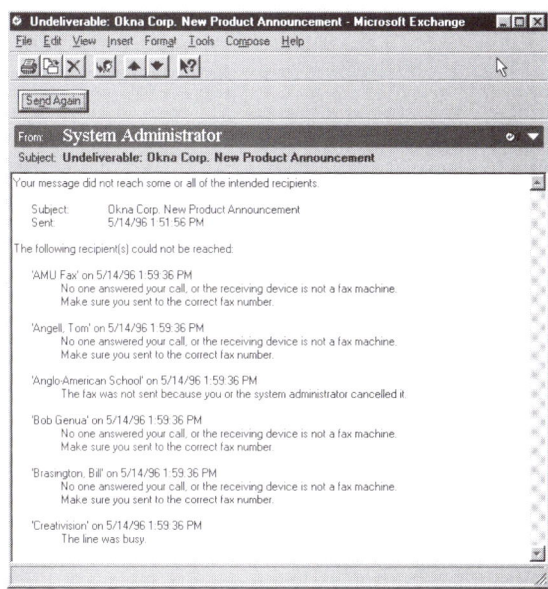

Figure 14.8
If a fax fails, look in the Inbox for a note from the System Administrator telling you why.

To resend a failed fax,

1. Open the Undeliverable message.
2. Click the Send Again button. A copy of the fax will open, but with only those addresses that didn't receive the fax the first time you sent it.
3. Make any needed changes in the fax addresses. (When you resend a fax, you are allowed to change only the addresses, not the subject or the body of the message.)
4. Click the Send button to resend the fax. You also can choose File, Send or press Ctrl+Enter.

Keeping Track of Sent Faxes

Unlike many fax programs, Microsoft Fax does not maintain a log of fax transmissions. It also does not keep a copy of every rendered fax image — only those created by printing to the Microsoft Fax printer driver; and even those do not include the rendered cover page.

When you open a sent fax from the Sent Items folder, it will look like an ordinary e-mail message, with any attachments embedded in the message. If this is a fax generated by printing to the Microsoft Fax printer driver, the attachment will be an .awd file in Microsoft's Fax Viewer format.

At least Microsoft Fax lets you know when things go wrong with your fax. As described in the previous section, if a fax can't be successfully transmitted, you will get a message in your Inbox from the System Administrator advising you of the problem.

There is a way to get notification of successful faxes, but the method has a tradeoff. If you create your fax by using Compose, New Message rather than by using Compose, New Fax (or printing to the Microsoft Fax printer), you can choose File, Properties, then check Delivery Receipt under Options for This Item. When the fax has been sent, a message from the System Administrator will arrive in your Inbox to notify you that the fax was delivered. The tradeoff, of course, is that you can't include a note on the cover page of a fax that you create with Compose, New Message. Still, for many people, getting a delivery receipt is more important.

Creating a Fax for Later Use

If you have standard documents that you often fax to people, you may want to create the faxes ahead of time and store them in Exchange, ready to use. We'll look at two different methods: sending a fax to yourself (without a modem!), and building a multipage fax from existing documents or new scanned pages. You can send a fax to yourself only with the Microsoft Fax service in Exchange. But the second method allows you to create a fax document that can be transmitted with any fax transport provider in Exchange.

Sending a Fax to Yourself

Here's how to fax a document to your own Inbox:

1. Click the New Message button in the Exchange client window, or choose Compose, New Message. Because we aren't using a cover page, we don't need to use the Compose New Fax Wizard.

2. In the To box, enter [FAX me], taking care to include the brackets.

3. Choose File, Send Options.

4. On the Send Options dialog box, set the message format to "Not editable," then click OK to return to the message.

5. Attach the file you want to store as a fax image (see "Inserting Files, Messages, and Objects," Chapter 11, page 259).

6. Click the Send button or choose File, Send.

In a moment, a rendered copy of the document will appear in your Inbox. You can then move the document to another folder.

For more about this [FAX: me] technique, see "Using [FAX:me] to Get a Rendered Copy of a Fax or Cover Page," Chapter 7, page 171.

Special Note

Building a Multipage Fax with Imaging

With Imaging, you can combine scanned images of paper documents with faxes you've received in your Inbox or sent to yourself with [FAX: me], then save the result as an image file (either Microsoft Fax's .awd format or a more generic .tif format) that can be stored in Exchange or on your hard drive. For information about how to obtain and set up Imaging, see "Imaging for Windows," page 167 in Chapter 7.

For another method of building a fax, check out the Scan and Fax Wizard on the CD accompanying this book.

Special Note

Plan your fax before you start. Here are a couple key points to consider:

- Make sure any existing faxes or other image documents you want to include are stored on your system as files, rather than as Exchange documents. To copy a file from Exchange to your system, select the file in the Exchange viewer, then choose File, Save As and specify the location.

- You can't reorder pages in Imaging (though you can insert pages anywhere in the fax). Therefore, you'll want to plan the order in which you want the pages to appear.

To create a new multipage fax that starts with a scanned document,

1. Click the Start button and choose Programs, Accessories, then Imaging.
2. Choose File, New, Scan.
3. In the Scan New dialog box (shown in Figure 14.9), under Scan To, choose Display and File.

Figure 14.9
If you scan documents to a file in Imaging, you can create a fax that can be stored for later transmission.

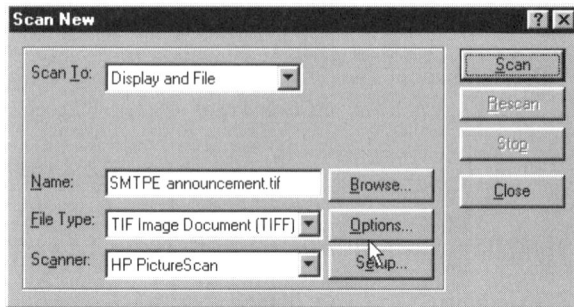

4. Give your fax a Name (with a full path), or use the Browse button to select the folder and specify the name.
5. Select TIF Image Document (TIFF) under File Type. (The .tif format will let you convert any color images to grayscale before faxing them. The Fax Viewer (.awd) format puts everything in black and white, with no grays.)
6. (Optional) Click the Setup button to check your scanner's settings and preview the scan using your scanner's software. Close the scanner software to return to Imaging.
7. In the Scan New dialog box, click the Scan button.
8. If you want to place another scanned page immediately after the first one, put the next document in your scanner, then click Scan again.
9. Repeat step 8 until you have scanned all the pages that you want to appear in this first sequence. Then click the Close button to return to the main Imaging window, where you can continue to add pages either from new scans or from existing image documents or faxes.

Here are two more ways to start a new fax document in Imaging:

• In Imaging, choose File, New, Blank Document. You'll get a blank page, which you'll probably want to delete before you save the fax.

- Modify a fax you've received in Exchange. Start by double-clicking on that fax to open it in Imaging.

Once you have placed an initial sequence of pages in Imaging, choose View, Page and Thumbnails to display a thumbnail list of your pages next to the current page (see Figure 14.10 for an example). This view will make it much easier to navigate as you prepare the rest of the fax, adding and removing pages with the techniques described next.

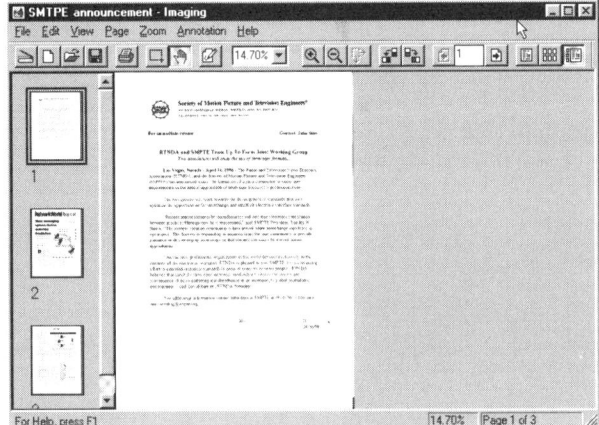

Figure 14.10
Faxes built with Imaging can include pages from existing faxes, from newly scanned documents, or from other image files.

To add a scanned page or pages before the current page,

1. Choose Page, Insert, Scan Page.
2. Scan one or more pages following steps 6 and 7 above.
3. Click the Close button when you're done scanning.

To add a scanned page or pages after the current page,

1. Choose Page, Append, Scan Page.
2. Scan one or more pages following steps 6 and 7 above.
3. Click the Close button when you're done scanning.

If a scanned page doesn't look right, follow these steps to replace it with a new version:

1. Choose Page, Rescan.

2. In the Scan Page dialog box, click the Setup button to re-adjust your scanner settings. Then return to the Scan New dialog box.

3. Click the Scan button to replace the old image with a new version.

4. Repeat steps 2 and 3 as needed to get just the image you want.

5. When you're satisfied with the new image, click the Close button to close the Scan Page dialog box.

To add a page or pages from a fax or other image document before the current page,

1. Choose Page, Insert, Existing Page.

2. In the Insert dialog box, select the file you want to use, then click Open.

3. If the file contains more than one page, indicate the page range in the second Insert dialog box, then click OK.

To add a page or pages from a fax or other image document after the current page,

1. Choose Page, Append, Existing Page.

2. In the Append dialog box, select the file you want to use, then click Open.

3. If the file contains more than one page, indicate the page range in the second Append dialog box, then click OK.

If you add a page from a color document, it will fax better if you convert it to grayscale first (this option is available only if you're saving the document as a .tif file). To convert a page,

1. Click on the page in the thumbnail list to select and display it.

2. Choose Page, Convert.

3. On the Color tab of the Convert dialog box, choose 16 or 256 Shades of Gray.

4. Click OK to close the Convert dialog box.

To delete the current page, choose Edit, Delete Page.

When you're done building this fax, save it on your hard drive if you want to fax it as an attachment, or put it in an Exchange folder so you can easily forward it whenever you need to.

To save the fax document to your hard drive (or a network drive),

- If you started by opening a fax from Exchange, choose File, Save Copy As and provide a filename.
- If you started with a new file, choose File, Save.

To save the fax document to an Exchange folder,

- If you started by opening a fax from Exchange, then choose File, Exit.
- If you started with a new file, choose File, Save. Then, to put that file in an Exchange folder, drag it from an Explorer or My Computer folder into the Exchange Viewer.

For more information about Imaging, including how to add annotations to your faxes, see the next chapter, "Receiving Faxes."

Sending Stored Faxes

When you want to send one of the faxes you've stored in an Exchange folder, select the fax, then forward it by clicking the Forward button; by choosing Compose, Forward; or by pressing Ctrl+F. The original document will remain in its folder. To make these stored faxes available to other Exchange users, copy them to either a Microsoft Mail shared folder or a Microsoft Exchange public folder (see Chapter 16, "Working with Messages and Folders").

Using Third-Party Fax Services

Microsoft Fax isn't the only fax service that integrates with Exchange. We'll look at WinFax PRO 7.0, which has so many features that it's by far the most popular Windows fax solution. We'll also look at some of the fax services that require Microsoft Exchange Server.

Using WinFax PRO 7.0

Unlike Microsoft Fax, WinFax PRO 7.0 is not an Exchange service; it's a separate program. When you use WinFax with Exchange, a built-in Exchange component called MAPI (Mail Application Programming Interface) helps the two programs communicate.

WinFax's integration with Exchange is a two-way street. Exchange's capability to send faxes comes from WinFax, and Exchange accesses WinFax features through several new menu choices. From within WinFax, you can access your Exchange folders. You can send e-mail as well as faxes, mixing and matching recipients from your Exchange address books (not just from the Personal Address Book, but from any enterprise-wide address books as well) and from the separate fax address book that WinFax maintains. You can also view and print your Exchange Personal Address Book, picking which fields you want to include.

It's essential to set up WinFax correctly if you want to use it with Exchange. See Chapter 9, "Setting up Other Information Services," for details.

Sending a Fax with WinFax PRO 7.0

To use WinFax PRO 7.0 from within Exchange, choose Compose, New Win-Fax. You'll see the Delrina WinFax PRO Send dialog box (Figure 14.11), where you can enter recipients and type in a cover page note. To attach files, either from WinFax's Attachments library or from elsewhere on your system, click the Attach button.

Figure 14.11
Rather than a wizard, WinFax presents you with a Send dialog box where you can enter cover text and select recipients.

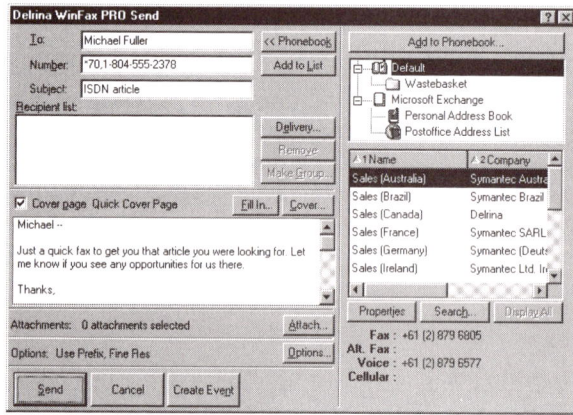

Notice that you have access to the Exchange address books so you can include e-mail addresses as well as fax recipients. However, if you include a Microsoft Fax recipient from your Personal Address Book, the message will be rendered and sent to that person via Microsoft Fax, not via WinFax.

Click the Send button when you're ready to send the fax. Once the fax has been sent, it will appear in the Delrina WinFax Fax Logs Outbox (see Figure 14.12); and if there were any recipients from your Exchange address books, the fax also will appear in the Exchange Outbox. Similarly, once the fax has been sent, it will be listed in the Sent Items folder in Exchange and in the Send Log folder under the Delrina WinFax Fax Logs. Faxes created with WinFax appear with an icon that resembles a torn piece of paper with the word Fax on it.

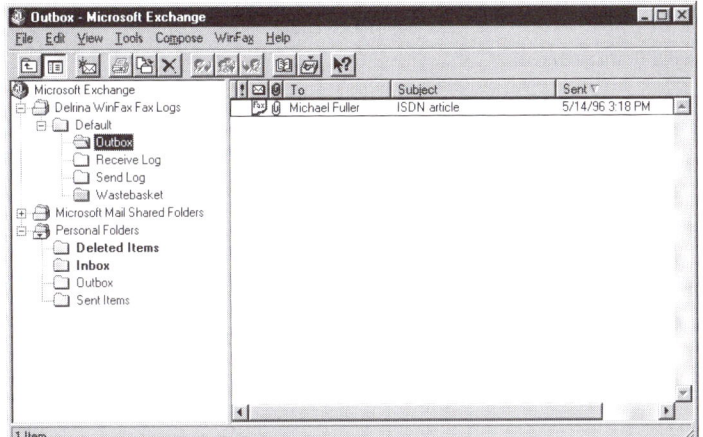

Figure 14.12
Messages received and sent with WinFax PRO 7.0 are stored in a separate set of folders, which you can access from Exchange.

WinFax PRO 7.0 Menu Options in Exchange

In addition to the Compose, New WinFax function, the WinFax PRO 7.0 installation adds an entirely new WinFax menu to Exchange to switch you quickly to the various WinFax functions listed in Table 14.3.

Table 14.3 WinFax PRO 7.0 Menu Choices in Exchange	
Option	**Function**
View/OCR Message	Opens a fax received or created with WinFax
Phonebooks	Displays the Phonebooks window in WinFax
Cover Pages	Displays the Cover Pages window in WinFax
Attachments	Displays the Attachments window in WinFax
Dialing Properties	Displays the Dialing Properties dialog box for WinFax, which is separate from the Windows 95 dialing locations

Binary File Transfer with WinFax PRO 7.0

Like Microsoft Fax, WinFax PRO 7.0 supports sending editable files with BFT. However, whereas Microsoft Fax automatically detects whether a fax recipient supports BFT, with WinFax you must specify the BFT option for each WinFax recipient.

To specify BFT for a recipient of a message you're composing,

1. In the Delrina WinFax PRO Send dialog box, select a recipient from the Recipient List.
2. Click the Delivery button to display the Delivery Properties dialog box.
3. From the Send By list, choose BFT.

Special Note

In the Send By list, you'll also see a choice for Compressed BFT. This option works only when you're sending to another WinFax recipient.

4. Click OK to close the Delivery Properties dialog box, then send your message as usual.

To specify that BFT should be always be used with a recipient, you can work either in the Delrina WinFax PRO Send dialog box or in the Phonebooks window:

1. Double-click the recipient name to bring up the Recipient Properties dialog box.
2. For the primary fax, select a Type of BFT.
3. Switch to the Programs tab.
4. Check the Recipient's Programs list for applications that you know the other user *doesn't* have. Remove any such applications from the list with the Remove button. Otherwise, you might send the recipient a document that can't be opened because (s)he doesn't have the right application.
5. Click OK to close the Properties dialog box.

If a WinFax recipient turns out to be incapable of handling BFT, WinFax will automatically update the send type for that recipient to send fax images in the future.

Using Fax Connectors in Exchange Server

Microsoft Fax is not the only fax solution for Exchange. Several companies also offer fax connectors or gateways that plug into the Exchange Server environment. Whether a particular product is a connector or gateway depends on the way it's integrated with Exchange. I'm going to call them all connectors, to keep it simple. In many cases, these fax connectors support features not found in Microsoft Fax, such as

- Faxing messages containing embedded objects
- Routing of incoming faxes to individual users, to Exchange folders, or to printers
- Confirmation of transmission successes and failures
- Detailed reporting on fax usage and costs
- Least-cost routing for organizations with several fax servers in different cities, to transmit faxes from the fax server closest to the recipient

Appendix B, "Exchange Resources," includes a list of companies offering fax connectors for Exchange Server. Not all fax connectors let you print to a fax printer driver, but you can count on being able to create faxes as e-mail messages. In many cases, you'll be able to attach in a variety of formats and depend on the fax server to convert them to fax images.

Tips and Tricks

Most of the tips and tricks in this chapter refer to Microsoft Fax. However, even if you're using a different fax transport in Exchange, I'd suggest you take a look at the "What Is TAPI?" sidebar for information about this new communications interface, which applies to most 32-bit Windows communications programs. Also highlighted in this section are notes about problems you might encounter when you send faxes from specific Windows applications.

Previewing a Document Before Faxing

Sometimes, because of the resolution difference between a fax and a printed document, fax pages won't break in the same places as on the printed document, or graphics may be shifted. Many applications have a Print Preview function built in, either on the File menu or in the Print dialog box. You can use this to see how your fax will look before you send it — just make sure the default printer is set to Microsoft Fax. You can also preview a document with the technique described in the earlier section "Sending a Fax to Yourself."

Sending a Group of Faxes at a Specific Time

The easiest way to schedule a group of faxes for a particular time is to change the default scheduling parameters for Microsoft Fax, send the faxes, then reset the default. To change the default scheduling parameters,

1. Choose Tools, Microsoft Fax Tools, Options to view the Microsoft Fax Properties dialog box.
2. Under "Time to send," click "Specific time."
3. In the "Specific time" box, specify the time you want your faxes to be transmitted.

After you've sent the faxes, use step 1 to return to the Microsoft Fax Properties dialog box and reset the Time to Send to its previous value (probably "As soon as possible" or "Discount rates").

Two Ways to Speed Up Transmissions

To speed up your fax transmissions, use the Options button on the Compose New Fax wizard or File, Send Options in the New Message window to change the message format to "Editable only" when you're sending to someone who is also using Exchange with Microsoft Fax or another application capable of BFT. When you use "Editable only," only the e-mail format of the message is created. Rendering to the fax format is skipped.

Another way to speed up faxes is to use a lower image quality. To change the image quality for a particular message,

1. Open the Send Options dialog box by clicking the Options button on the Compose New Fax Wizard or choosing File, Send Options in the New Message window, then click the Paper button.
2. Change the Image Quality to Draft.
3. Click OK to close the Message Format dialog box and OK again to close the Send Options dialog box.

If you want to reduce the image quality for all faxes, follow these steps:

1. Choose Tools, Microsoft Fax Tools, Options to view the Microsoft Fax Properties dialog box.
2. Click the Paper button.
3. In the Message Format dialog box, select Draft (200 x 100 dpi) as the new Image Quality.

4. Click OK to close the Message Format dialog box, then OK to save the
   changes to the Microsoft Fax properties.

Saving Copies of Faxes

To see how a fax will look on a paper fax machine, send it to the special
[FAX:me] address described previously in "Sending a Fax to Yourself." Include
this address among the recipients for a fax if you want to receive a copy of
the rendered fax as the other recipients will see it. Remember that you must
set the message format to "Not editable" for [FAX:me] to deliver a rendered
image to your Inbox.

Also, if you send a fax by printing to the Microsoft Fax printer driver, the
message stored in the Sent Items folder will include a rendered copy of the
document, along with the text of any note you included on the cover page.

Using Footers to Avoid Short Pages

If you send a fax to a fax machine that uses thermal paper, the machine will
cut off the page after the bottom of the text on the page. This is by design, to
avoid wasting paper, but it can be very annoying to get these short pages.

To force all your faxes to use a full page, make sure you have a footer
of some kind at the bottom of your cover page — perhaps a company motto
or other tag line, or maybe a border graphic. Also include a footer on any
documents you fax. The date, page number, and name of the document are
good choices for information to include, because the document might get separated from the cover page.

Setting the Font for Cover Page Notes

The font used for fax cover page notes depends on the way you compose the
note. If you use the Compose New Fax Wizard and choose to include the note
on the cover page, then the note will use whatever font you selected for the
{Note} text box in the Cover Page Editor. (See "Using the Cover Page Editor,"
page 156 in Chapter 7.) If you use the Compose New Fax Wizard and decide
not to include the note on the cover page, the note will appear on a separate
page in 10-point Arial. There is no way to change this.

If you want to use rich-text formatting (such as bullets, indents, and a
mixture of bold, underlined, italic, and normal text with different fonts), create
your message as a regular e-mail message, using Compose New Message. The
note will appear on a separate page, but it will appear as you composed it.

Controlling the Order of Attachments

If you send more than one attachment using Compose, New Fax from the Exchange menu, those attachments will be attached to your fax in alphabetical order according to the full path name of the file (e.g., C:\My Documents\ myfile.doc). To control the order in which attachments appear in your fax, use Compose, New Message instead and insert the files in the order you want them to appear.

Handling Multiple Local Area Codes

You may work in a city where you need to dial some numbers with the area code, but without the 1 customarily used for long distance calls in North America. The dialing function in Windows 95 is not designed to handle this situation, but you can trick the function into doing what you need.

For example, if you live in Atlanta and have an area code 404 number, and you need to send a fax to someone in local area code 770, enter the area code for that person as 404, but put the whole 770-*xxx-xxxx* number in the box for the local number (see Figure 14.13). Microsoft Fax will think you're making a local call — because of the 404 area code — but will dial the entire 10-digit number. This works both in the Compose New Fax Wizard and in the Personal Address Book.

Figure 14.13

Sometimes you need to trick Microsoft Fax. In this example, you are located in area code 404 and need to send a fax to someone locally but in area code 770; therefore, the number must be dialed with the 770 area code but without the customary 1 for long distance. The trick is to put 404 — your own area code — in the area code box.

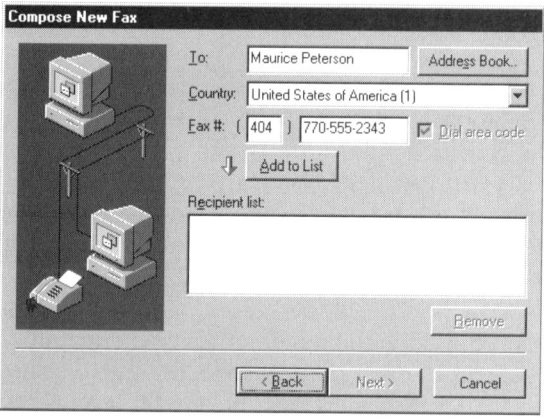

Another way to get around this problem is to enter the fax name and number in the To box as [*FAX:name@xxx-xxx-xxxx*], where name is the recipient's name and *xxx-xxx-xxxx* is the phone number. One drawback to this method is that you won't get any company or other information about the recipient on the cover page.

What Is TAPI?

TAPI stands for Telephony Application Programming Interface. TAPI is a new way of handling communications applications that allows them to cooperate better. For example, one program might be waiting for incoming calls, but other programs can still use the modem. This approach wasn't possible in earlier versions of Windows, where the modem was completely tied up by the program waiting for the call. From a practical standpoint, TAPI means you can have Microsoft Fax set up to answer calls automatically, but you can still dial out to download mail from your Internet mailbox.

There are a couple important things to know about TAPI. One is that older, 16-bit Windows communications programs are not TAPI-compliant. If Microsoft Fax is waiting to receive a fax, one of those older programs will not be able to dial out. You will first need to set the fax modem to Don't Answer. The flip side is also true: If a 16-bit Windows communications program is waiting for a call, your TAPI programs won't be able to dial out.

Some computer manufacturers install fax or other communications software on the system and set it up to answer automatically. If you have problems getting Microsoft Fax to work correctly, check for programs being loaded from either the Run= or Load= line in Win.ini or from the StartUp group in your Start, Programs menu.

The other important fact about TAPI is that the format of a telephone number determines how it is dialed. The properties of your Dialing Location — the numbers to access an outside line, calling card settings, and so on — are only applied if you use the international format (sometimes known as the canonical format), which looks like this:

```
+aa (bb) ccc-cccc    or    +a (bbb) ccc-cccc
```

where *a* or *aa* represents the country code, *bb* or *bbb* the area code, and *ccc-cccc* the local number. The number of digits in each section can vary, depending on where you are in the world.

continued

What Is TAPI?, continued

Most of the time, fax numbers are entered in this format for you. That's why there are three fields in the Compose New Fax Wizard for the three different parts of the number. A Microsoft Fax entry in your Personal Address Book also contains separate boxes for the three components. There are, however, three situations in which the number for a fax recipient might turn out not to be in the international or TAPI format:

- If you upgraded from Windows for Workgroups and imported fax addresses from your Mail message file, you should check those Personal Address Book entries and put them in the TAPI format.
- If you reply to an incoming fax message, the address automatically entered in the To box might not be in the TAPI format. To check it, right-click on it and choose Properties.
- You can enter a fax address directly into the To box using the format [FAX:*name@number*], making sure to include the brackets. If the number is in TAPI format, the Dialing Location properties will be followed. If you enter the address without the plus sign before the country code and the parentheses around the area code, Microsoft Fax will dial the number exactly as you enter it, without a dialing prefix, calling card codes, and the like.

Faxing Works 3.0 Documents

You cannot fax Works 3.0 documents as attachments if you are sending to a paper fax machine. Instead, you must use File, Print and print to the Microsoft Fax printer driver. If you know you are reaching a fax machine that can handle BFT, you can send Works files as attachments as long as you set the message format to "Editable only." This limitation goes away when you upgrade to Works for Windows 95.

Faxing Microsoft Publisher Documents

Publisher requires you to interact with a click while it is rendering a fax that you want to send as an attachment. After you send the fax, Publisher opens the publication document and then displays the Print dialog box. It may look like no printer is selected, and you might be tempted to display the Printer list and pick Microsoft Fax, but don't! You can alter the print range to print only certain pages, but otherwise make no changes to the Print dialog box — just click OK.

If you don't respond to this Print dialog box, eventually you will get a message in your Inbox from the System Administrator advising you that Microsoft Fax was unable to render the fax in the allotted time.

Faxing Office Binder Documents

Don't even think about faxing from the Microsoft Office Binder. At best, you'll get one or two documents to fax as a single transmission, but rarely will you be able to fax the entire contents of the binder. At worst, you'll get six or eight different faxes — one for each document.

Faxing from DOS Programs

You cannot send a fax with Exchange directly from a DOS program, because Microsoft Fax must use a Windows printer driver to convert the file into a fax format. However, if the documents from the DOS application use a file format that's registered on your system, such as .txt for text files, then you can fax such documents as attachments. You also can use BFT to send the documents as editable files to compatible recipients.

Faxing with E-Mail

If you don't have a fax modem at all, either on your local system or on a network fax server, that doesn't mean you can't send faxes. A number of services are available to receive your text as an e-mail message, then send it as a fax to as many people as you like. For example, CompuServe offers such an option as part of its service. Just create the appropriate address type in your Personal Address Book. A resource for several other services is listed in Appendix B, "Exchange Resources."

Sending a fax via e-mail to multiple recipients can be a good cost-containing move if, for example, you are traveling in Europe but you need to get a fax to several people in the U.S. You can send the fax through one of these services and have the call made from a location closer to the receiving fax machines.

Avoiding the General Error Message

When sending a fax with a fax wizard method, you may receive a General Error! message. This is a problem with both the Windows Messaging update for Exchange for Windows 95 (see Appendix C) and the Exchange Server client. There are two workarounds:

- Leave the Subject field blank.

- If you are using Windows Messaging, uninstall it, then re-install the original Windows 95 operating system client or the Exchange Server client.

Summary

We've covered many different methods for using Microsoft Fax in this chapter, along with basic techniques for using WinFax PRO 7.0 and the fax connectors that plug into Exchange Server.

You also should now have a good grasp of how a scanner can be a useful tool for building faxes, both for immediate transmission and as part of a library of information that you might want to send over and over (such as product literature).

Key Points

- Sending a fax is just like sending a message.
- You can send a fax from any Windows program by printing to the Microsoft Fax printer.
- If you have a scanner, you can use it to build faxes from paper documents.
- The format of a telephone number determines how the number is dialed.

For More Information

If you need more details about using rich text in a message or attaching files, skip back to Chapter 11, "Sending E-Mail Messages."

Microsoft Fax supports secure transmissions using binary file transfer. You'll find details about that in Chapter 21, "Message Security."

For help with general fax transmission problems, see Chapter 24, "Troubleshooting."

Chapter 15
Receiving Faxes

In the previous chapter, you learned how to send faxes with Microsoft Fax and other products that plug into Exchange, such as WinFax and various fax connectors. Now it's time for the other side of the fax picture — how to receive faxes with Exchange, using mainly Microsoft Fax but other services as well. We'll also look at what you can do with the faxes once they're in your Inbox, and how to view and print them — even how to turn them into text.

Receiving with Microsoft Fax

You must load Exchange before you can receive a fax with Microsoft Fax.

To receive a fax with the Microsoft Fax service, Exchange must be running. This bears repeating, because it's the most common source of confusion about receiving faxes: You must load Exchange before you can receive a fax with Microsoft Fax.

Here's the source of all the confusion about the above point: If Exchange is not already running when you send a fax, perhaps by printing to the Microsoft Fax printer driver, Exchange loads just enough of itself to transmit the fax. For a while, you'll see the fax machine icon in the system tray on the Windows taskbar. *Even though the icon is on the taskbar, the fax receiving component is not active.* Eventually, the icon will disappear, as the rest of Exchange unloads after the fax transmission. When Exchange is fully loaded with a profile that includes Microsoft Fax, the taskbar will show both the fax icon and a button for Exchange, as shown in Figure 15.1.

Figure 15.1

Exchange can receive faxes only when it's loaded with a profile that includes Microsoft Fax. You'll see both the fax icon and the button for Exchange on the taskbar.

Now that we're perfectly clear on the issue of the disappearing fax icon and the need to run Exchange to receive a fax, we can move on to discuss whether you want reception to be automatic.

Understanding Automatic vs. Manual Reception

You can have Microsoft Fax automatically answer every incoming call to your modem or, instead, you can manually choose which calls to answer. The quickest way to change this setting is to right-click on the fax icon on the Windows taskbar (see Figure 15.1), then choose Modem Properties to display the Fax Modem Properties dialog box shown in Figure 15.2. Another way to get to these properties is from within Exchange; choose Tools, Microsoft Fax Tools, Options, then switch to the Modem tab, select the modem, and click the Properties button. We discussed these fax modem settings in detail under "Modem Properties," page 154 in Chapter 7.

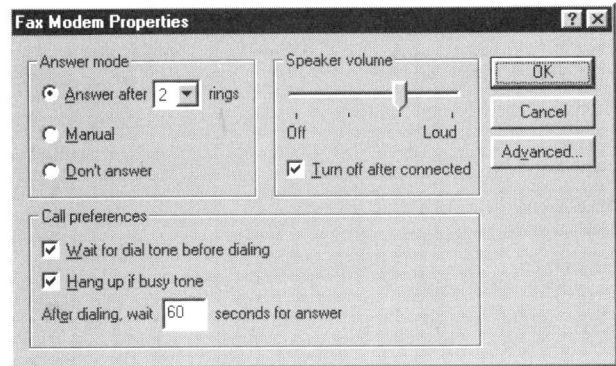

Figure 15.2

Use the Fax Modem Properties dialog box to change how Microsoft Fax responds to incoming faxes.

If the Answer mode is set to "Answer after *X* rings" (minimum 2), then any incoming call to your modem will be picked up by Microsoft Fax without further intervention. With Manual as the Answer Mode, any time a call comes in, a dialog box (Figure 15.3) will pop up asking if you want Microsoft Fax to answer the call. Click Yes to answer or No to ignore the call.

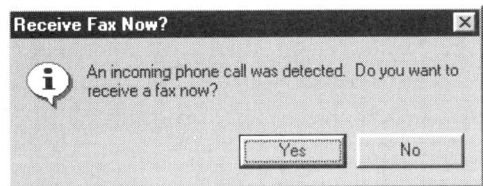

Figure 15.3

With the Answer Mode for Microsoft Fax set to Manual, you're notified any time a call comes in to your PC.

You can still receive faxes if you have the Answer mode set to "Don't answer." Of course, you'll need some way to know that a call is coming in; perhaps the modem shares a line with a regular handset that rings. When you hear the ring, right-click the fax modem icon on the taskbar, then choose Answer Now.

It's quite common to switch back and forth between "Answer after *X* rings" (or Manual, depending on your preference) and "Don't answer." Older Windows communications programs can't dial out except when "Don't answer" is set (see the sidebar "What Is TAPI?" on page 343 in the previous chapter).

As a fax is coming in, you can watch its progress in the Microsoft Fax Status dialog box (Figure 15.4), just as you might monitor an outgoing fax transmission.

Figure 15.4

The progress of incoming faxes is displayed in the Microsoft Fax Status dialog box. For binary file transfer (BFT) transmissions, the page count will always stay at 1.

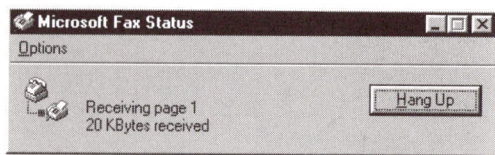

A moment or two after the sending fax machine has hung up, the fax will appear in your Inbox. If you have Exchange set up to notify you of new messages, you'll hear the new-mail-alert sound or see the pop-up message.

Requesting a Fax

Microsoft Fax also can be configured to retrieve a fax from an automated fax retrieval service (often called a fax-back service). There are two ways to do this, depending on the capabilities of the retrieval service: with a wizard and manually.

You can use the wizard only if you are dialing into a service with just one document available or with a library of documents that can be identified by title. Many fax-back services require you to dial in from a fax machine, then enter a series of numbers to select one or more faxes to receive. Microsoft Fax supports this type of retrieval, too, as you'll see in a few minutes.

Using the Request a Fax Wizard

To launch the Request a Fax Wizard, follow these steps:

1. Click the Start button, then choose Programs, Accessories, Fax, Request a Fax. The dialog box shown in Figure 15.5 appears.

2. In most cases, you'll choose "Retrieve whatever is available." (Frankly, I have yet to encounter a fax-back service where you could retrieve documents by name with Microsoft Fax; if you find one, let me know.) Then click Next to continue.

3. Enter the phone number for the fax retrieval service in the next dialog box, then click Next to continue.

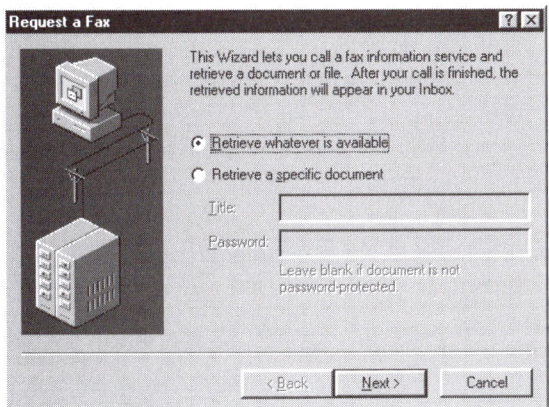

Figure 15.5
In virtually all cases, you'll choose to retrieve whatever fax is available from the fax-back service.

4. In the next dialog box, select when you want to retrieve the fax. Here are your choices:

   - As soon as possible
   - When phone rates are discounted
   - A specific time

5. Click Next to continue, then Finish to complete the entry of the fax retrieval request.

   If you choose to retrieve the fax as soon as possible, the call will be made right away, without any need to launch Exchange (if it isn't already running). However, if you choose to retrieve the fax during the discount rate period or at a specific time, you must make sure that Exchange is loaded at the time specified for the fax request. Otherwise, the call to retrieve the fax is not made. The fax request does remain in the Outbox, however, and Exchange tries to fulfill the request the next time you run Exchange.

Retrieving a Fax Manually

Fax-back services often let you call on your regular phone, select one or more documents, then specify a fax number to have the documents sent to. This process is sometimes known as *two-call* retrieval. There's also a *one-call* technique, in which you dial in from the fax machine and get the documents as part of the same call. Microsoft Fax supports this, as long as you have a regular handset on the same line as your fax modem. Here's how to use the one-call approach:

1. Make sure Exchange is running.

2. Dial the fax service with your regular phone.

3. Follow the instructions you hear, entering whatever codes are needed to select one or more documents.

4. When the fax service tells you to push the start or connect button on the fax machine, right-click the fax icon on the taskbar and choose <u>A</u>nswer Now.

5. When you hear the fax handshake tones from both modems (yours and the fax service's), hang up the regular phone handset.

You can monitor the fax reception progress just as you would with a normal fax.

Receiving with WinFax PRO 7.0

As with Microsoft Fax, WinFax PRO 7.0 can receive faxes either automatically or manually. In either case, WinFax must be loaded first.

To turn automatic receiving on and off, choose <u>R</u>eceive, <u>A</u>utomatic Receive. When WinFax is not receiving automatically, you can still answer an incoming fax (assuming you can hear the phone ring). Choose <u>R</u>eceive, <u>M</u>anual Receive Now. Or right-click the WinFax program button on the taskbar and choose <u>M</u>anual Receive Now.

Incoming faxes can be routed either to your Inbox folder or to the Receive Log subfolder under the Delrina WinFax Fax Logs folder (or to both locations), depending on the settings for WinFax. To change the location for incoming WinFax faxes, follow these steps:

1. Choose <u>T</u>ools, <u>S</u>ervices (or Control Panel, Mail and Fax).

2. Select Delrina WinFax PRO Logs, then click the P<u>r</u>operties button to display the WinFax 7.0 Provider Properties dialog box (Figure 15.6).

3. If you want new faxes to appear in your Exchange Inbox, check the box labeled "Deliver new faxes to Exchange Inbox."

4. If you want new faxes to also appear in the WinFax Receive Log folder, clear the box labeled "Delete new faxes from WinFax after delivery to Inbox."

5. Click OK twice to save the changes made to the WinFax receive locations.

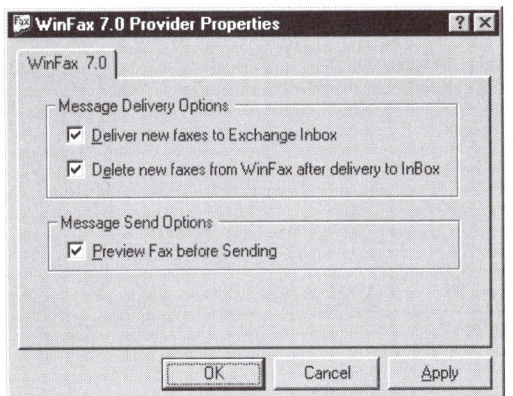

Figure 15.6
The properties for the WinFax PRO Logs service let you choose how to have incoming faxes delivered.

Receiving from a Fax Server

If faxes are being sent not to a fax modem on your PC, but to a fax server elsewhere on the network, the process of receiving faxes is more or less out of your hands. If the fax server is using Exchange and Microsoft Fax, then someone must forward your faxes to you. The faxes will appear in your Inbox as normal e-mail messages with the paper clip icon that shows there's an attachment — in this case, the incoming fax.

If you're using a fax server as a gateway or connector to Microsoft Exchange, most likely some kind of automatic inbound routing will be in place. Some fax connectors allow automatic printing of faxes, as well as automatic routing to your Exchange Inbox. There are many possible methods. If you're curious, your system administrator will be able to tell you what technique is being used on your server.

Working with Incoming Microsoft Fax Faxes

In this section, we're going to concentrate on what you can do with faxes received via the Microsoft Fax service. Other services, including WinFax PRO 7.0 and fax connectors, have their own viewers with similar functions, sometimes including optical character recognition (OCR).

A fax can appear in your Inbox in two different ways, depending on how you have Microsoft Fax set up. The fax can either use the icon for your fax viewer and open with a quick double-click, or it can look like a message with an attachment, using the envelope and paper clip icons. Figure 15.7 shows the difference.

Figure 15.7

You can open the top fax, shown with the Imaging icon, directly with one double-click. The other faxes, with the envelope and paper clip icons, require two steps — opening the message, then opening the .awd file attachment within the message.

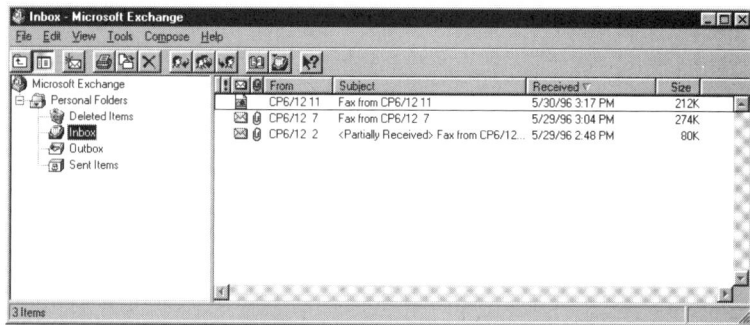

To see new faxes with the viewer icon and be able to open them directly from the Exchange Viewer, choose Tools, Microsoft Fax Tools, Options and clear the box that's labeled "Let me change the subject line of new faxes I receive." To see new faxes as messages with attachments, use the same dialog box, but this time check the Subject Line box. To open these faxes, first open the message, then double-click the .awd file icon you'll find inside.

A file received by your fax modem as a binary file transfer (BFT) will look just like a normal e-mail message, regardless of the setting for the "... change the subject Line" box. See "Sending a File (BFT)," page 324 in Chapter 14, for more about how BFT works.

Forwarding a fax is just like forwarding a message. You can send a fax to either fax or e-mail recipients. To forward a fax to someone else, select the fax, then click the Forward button or choose Compose, Forward. You also can send an incoming fax to someone else by opening it in your Fax Viewer and printing it to the Microsoft Fax printer driver.

Once you receive a fax, you'll want to view it and probably print, save, or copy it — or maybe all the above. You also may be interested in converting the content of a fax into an editable document using optical character recognition (OCR). We'll cover those functions in the next few sections, as we look at the capabilities of the two fax viewers available for Microsoft Fax: the Fax Viewer that ships with Windows 95, and Imaging for Windows 95, developed by Wang for Microsoft. Beginning in the fall of 1996, Imaging replaced Fax Viewer on new PCs shipped with Windows 95 pre-installed. A slightly different version of Imaging that supports .tif files, but not the Microsoft Fax .awd format, is included with Windows NT. You can download Imaging for Windows 95 from Wang (see Appendix B, "Exchange Resources").

Using Fax Viewer

Fax Viewer is part of the default installation of the Microsoft Fax service under Windows 95. When you open a fax in Fax Viewer, the fax is zoomed in to 25 percent of its size so it fills the width of the Fax Viewer window. The first order of business is to get a better view of the image. You may first want to maximize the Fax Viewer window to have more room in which to view the fax, then choose View, Thumbnails or click the Thumbnails button to display thumbnail images to browse the pages of a multipage fax. Finally, choose Zoom, Fit Width to get a good view of the fax (Figure 15.8).

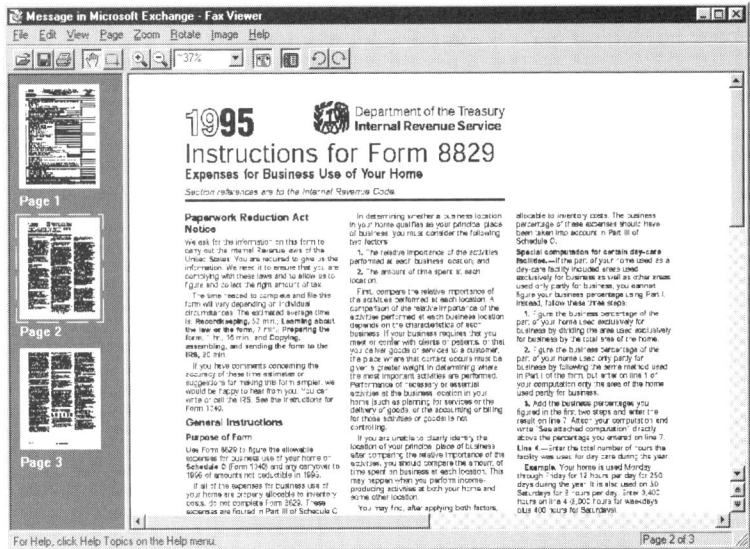

Figure 15.8
Use thumbnails and several zoom settings in Fax Viewer to get the best view of a fax.

Table 15.1 summarizes the buttons available in the Fax Viewer. The Next Page and Previous Page buttons are found on the bottom of the scroll bar on the right side of the Fax Viewer, and the others are on the toolbar along the top.

Table 15.1 Buttons in Fax Viewer

Button	Name	Description
	Drag	Move the image within the Fax Viewer window
	Select	Mark a portion of the image for copying to the Windows clipboard
	Zoom In	Zoom in to magnify the fax image
	Zoom Out	Zoom out to view more of the fax in the Fax Viewer window
	Fit Width	Resize the fax image so it fills the width of the Fax Viewer window
	Show Thumbnails	Show thumbnails of all the fax pages next to the image of the current page
	Rotate Left	Rotate the fax 90 degrees counterclockwise
	Rotate Right	Rotate the fax 90 degrees clockwise
	Previous Page	Display previous page
	Next Page	Display next page

In addition to Fit Width, which is probably the most popular zoom setting, two other zoom levels are available on the Zoom menu:

Fit Height   Resize the fax image so it fills the height of the Fax Viewer window

Fit Both   Resize the fax image to display the entire fax

Once you've opened a fax in Fax Viewer, you can print it, save it, or copy it. Table 15.2 lists these actions and the steps necessary to use them.

Table 15.2 Fax Viewer Actions

Action	Procedure
Save as an .awd fax file	Choose File, Save As
Print	Choose File, Print
Copy an entire page to the clipboard	Choose Edit, Select to activate the selection pointer; then choose Edit, Copy Page
Copy an area to the clipboard	Choose Edit, Select to activate the selection pointer; drag a rectangle around the area you want to copy; then choose Edit, Copy

After you copy all or part of a fax page to the clipboard, you can paste it into another application, for example Word, for annotations.

If you have problems viewing or printing faxes with Fax Viewer, then try Imaging for Windows instead.

Using Imaging

Imaging for Windows includes the same features as Fax Viewer, but adds support for saving faxes as .tif (Tagged Image File Format) files and annotating faxes. Many users also report better quality printouts of faxes from Imaging. As you can see in Table 15.3, the toolbar buttons are quite similar to those for Fax Viewer.

Table 15.3 Buttons in Imaging

Button	Name	Description
	Select	Mark a portion of the image for zooming or for copying to the Windows clipboard
	Drag	Move the image within the Imaging window
	Annotation Toolbox	Toggle the Annotation Toolbox

continued

Table 15.3 Buttons in Imaging, continued

Button	Name	Description
	Zoom In	Zoom in to magnify the fax image
	Zoom Out	Zoom out to view more of the fax in the Imaging window
	Zoom to Selection	Enlarge the selected area so it fills the Imaging window
	Rotate Left	Rotate the fax 90 degrees counter-clockwise
	Rotate Right	Rotate the fax 90 degrees clockwise
	Previous Page	Display previous page
	Next Page	Display next page
	One Page View	Show the fax one page at a time, with no thumbnails
	Thumbnail View	Show thumbnails of all the fax pages
	Page & Thumbnail View	Show thumbnails of all the fax pages next to the image of the current page

Imaging improves the appearance of most faxes by displaying them in grayscale (see Figure 15.9) rather than in stark black and white. You can turn this setting on and off with View, Scale to Gray.

Imaging Zoom Settings

Imaging's Zoom menu includes a wider range of settings than Fax Viewer's:

Fit to Height   Resize the fax image so it fills the height of the Imaging window

Fit to Width   Resize the fax image so it fills the width of the Imaging window

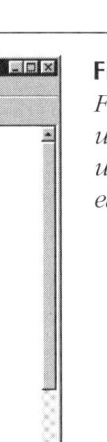

Figure 15.9
Faxes viewed with Imaging use grayscale by default, usually making them easier to read.

Best Fit	Resize the fax image to display the entire fax
Actual Size	Approximates the size of the fax when it will be printed, though usually runs large
25%, 50%, 75%, 100%, 200%, 400%	Resize the image to the specified zoom percentage
Custom	Resize the image to a custom zoom percentage

There's also a very useful Zoom to Selection setting. Here's how to use this setting to zero in on a particular part of a fax:

1. If the current pointer is the "drag" hand, click the Select button to activate the selection crosshairs pointer.

2. Drag a rectangle on the area you want to view more closely.

3. Choose Zoom, Zoom to Selection.

Unlike Fax Viewer, Imaging allows you to set a preferred zoom setting, and it saves the setting between sessions. To set the default zoom setting,

1. Choose View, Options, General.

2. Under "Open documents zoomed to" (Figure 15.10), choose the way you'd like to have faxes appear when you first open them.

3. Click the OK button.

Figure 15.10
With Imaging, you can choose how you want faxes to be displayed when you open them.

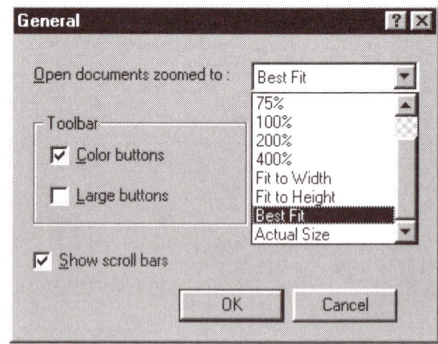

Imaging Annotations

Imaging for Windows provides a rich collection of annotation tools.

Often, you may receive a fax that you want to pass along to someone else, marked to emphasize the important points. Or perhaps a form was faxed to you that needs to be filled out and returned. For these tasks, Imaging provides a rich collection of annotation tools.

To display the toolbox, shown in Figure 15.11, choose Annotation, Show Annotation Toolbox.

To add an annotation, select any tool (other than the selection pointer), then click and drag the pointer to create an annotation of the desired size and shape.

Figure 15.11
Imaging includes both text and graphics annotation tools, including a Rubber Stamp tool you can customize.

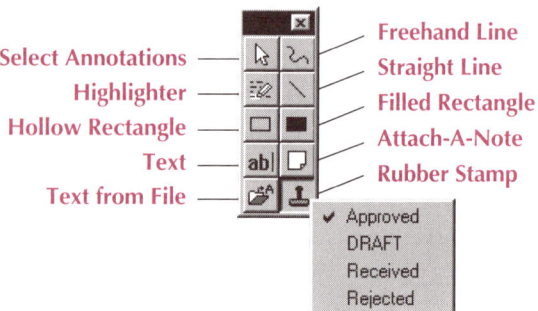

For the text tools — Attach-A-Note, Text, and Text from File — a pop-up dialog box appears to let you enter text or select a file whose text will be added to the fax. To edit the text of an existing annotation, activate the Select Annotations pointer, then right-click on the annotation and choose Edit.

To change font, color, transparency, line thickness, or other properties of an annotation, activate the Select Annotations pointer, then right-click on the annotation and choose Properties.

You can add your own boilerplate text and images, such as a signature, to the Rubber Stamp tools. Choose Annotations, Rubber Stamps to display the dialog box shown in Figure 15.12.

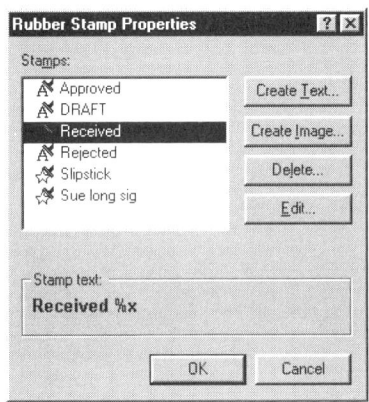

Figure 15.12
Rubber stamps can consist of either text (A+stamp icon) or a graphic (star+stamp icon).

To create a new stamp with boilerplate text, follow these steps:

1. In the Rubber Stamp Properties dialog box shown in Figure 15.12, choose Create Text.

2. In the Create Text Rubber Stamp dialog box (Figure 15.13), enter the Stamp Name as you want it to appear on the list of available stamps.

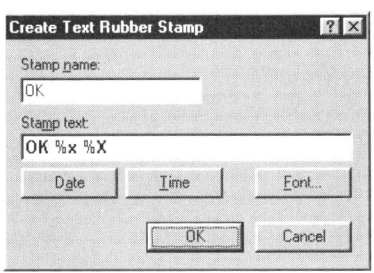

Figure 15.13
You can place any text (up to 231 characters) on a stamp. You also can add the date and/or time.

3. Enter the Stamp Text.

4. If you want to include the current date on your stamp, click the Date button to insert "%x," which will be filled in with the date when you use the stamp.

5. If you want the current time on your stamp, click the Time button to insert "%X."

6. Use the Font button to set the font and color for the stamp.

7. Click OK to finish creating the stamp.

Imaging also can use virtually any graphic image as a stamp. For example, you might scan or fax a copy of your own signature, then save that image to a file and make a stamp out of it. To create a new stamp from an existing image file, do this:

1. In the Rubber Stamp Properties dialog box shown in Figure 15.12, choose Create Image.

2. In the Create Image Rubber Stamp dialog box (Figure 15.14), enter the "Stamp name" as you want it to appear on the list of available stamps.

Figure 15.14
Create a picture stamp from almost any graphic file.

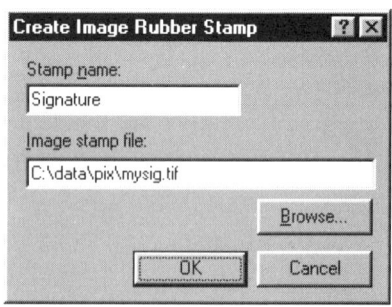

3. Either enter the graphic's file name under "Image stamp file" or click the Browse button to find it on your system.

4. Click OK to finish creating the stamp.

Text and image stamps that you create are listed on the stamp list that pops up when you select the rubber stamp annotation tool, as seen in Figure 15.11.

If you use File, Save to save an incoming fax after adding annotations, the annotations are made a permanent part of that fax. If you want the option to remove the annotations later, then use File, Save As to save the fax to your system as a separate .tif file. That will preserve the original of the incoming fax in your Inbox without annotations. Additionally, annotations in a .tif file can be edited and even removed at a later time.

Converting Faxes to Text

Being able to annotate a fax before forwarding it to a colleague is extremely useful. But sometimes you want to extract the actual text from a fax. The technique used to accomplish this is called *optical character recognition* or *OCR*.

Several add-ons make it easy to perform OCR on faxes received with Microsoft Fax. WinFax PRO 7.0 has its own built-in OCR engine. OCR support is also available in fax connectors that plug into Exchange Server, either directly or through export of a fax image to a file format that a standalone OCR program can read.

If your fax viewer is Imaging for Windows, then you can save faxes in the .tif format, which all standalone OCR programs can use as their data source.

The ability to run OCR on a fax directly from within Exchange is provided by at least two applications, CFax Pro and OmniPage Pro, which we'll look at briefly in the following sections (see Appendix B, "Exchange Resources," for contact information).

Several add-ons make it easy to perform OCR on faxes received with Microsoft Fax.

CFax Pro

CFax Pro is a fax viewer and image processing program. In addition to OCR, CFax Pro includes functions to clean up fax images. When you install CFax Pro, a CFax Pro button is added to the Exchange toolbar (see Figure 15.15) and a CFax Pro item is added to the Tools menu.

Figure 15.15
The button on the far left is inserted when you install CFax Pro to add OCR capability to Microsoft Fax.

To open a fax in CFax Pro, select the fax, then click the CFax Pro button or choose Tools, CFax Pro. To OCR a fax you've opened in CFax Pro, follow these steps:

1. Go to the page you want to OCR, using the choices on the Page menu.

2. Choose Utility, OCR.

3. Click the Go button to begin the OCR process.

After OCR is complete, CFax Pro displays the OCR Editor (Figure 15.16). Words that are not in the CFax Pro dictionary or that contain unrecognizable characters are highlighted in yellow. Double-click on any area to pop up an enlarged image from the fax itself, to help you verify the text. Correct the text as needed, then choose File, Save and Exit. You can choose to store the fax as plain text or in a word-processing or spreadsheet format.

Figure 15.16

As with other OCR programs, CFax highlights questionable words and lets you zoom in on the text. Compare this with OmniPage Pro's Verify Text function, depicted in Figure 15.18.

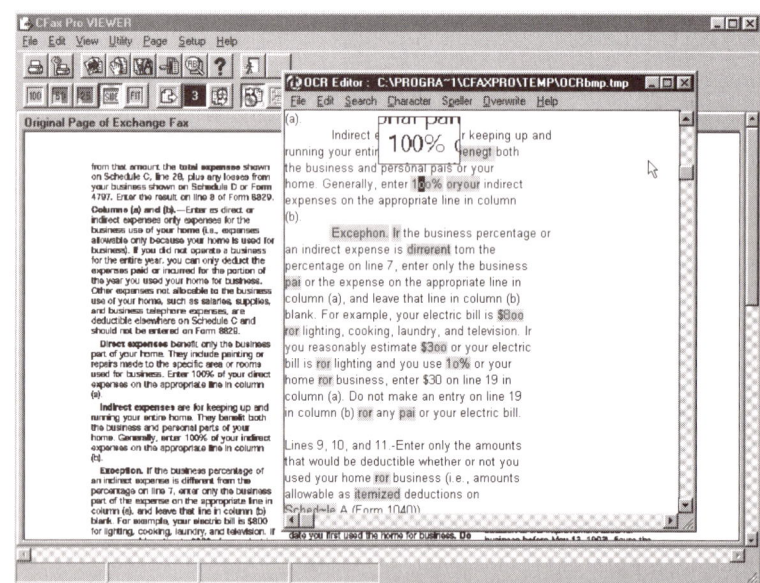

OmniPage Pro

OmniPage Pro is an all-purpose OCR program capable of working directly from scanned images, images saved as files, or faxes received in Exchange with the Microsoft Fax service. OmniPage Pro only works with faxes that appear in your Inbox with the icon for your fax viewer (Fax Viewer or Imaging). It will not work with a fax that appears as a normal message envelope icon with a paper clip.

Follow these steps to check the setting for how faxes are saved in the Inbox and change the setting if necessary:

1. Choose Tools, Microsoft Fax Tools, Options.

2. Make sure that the box labeled "Let me change the subject line of new faxes I receive" is not checked.

3. Click OK to close the Microsoft Fax Properties dialog box.

OmniPage Pro lets you toggle between doing OCR and using your fax viewer to view a fax. To switch back and forth, choose Tools, View Fax with OmniPage Pro. This menu option should appear checked when you want to OCR faxes, unchecked when you just want to view them.

Once you've checked View Fax with OmniPage Pro, double-click on any fax in your Inbox to open it in OmniPage Pro. Thumbnails of the pages will appear on the left, as shown in Figure 15.17.

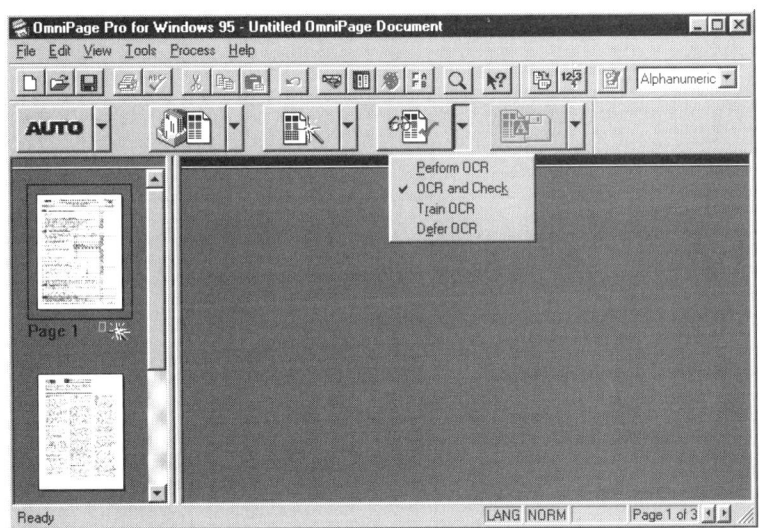

Figure 15.17
Select the page to OCR from the thumbnails on the left side. Select the type of OCR operation with the arrow button next to the OCR button.

To set the type of OCR, click the down arrow to the right of the OCR button to display the menu shown in Figure 15.17. These are your choices:

Perform OCR	Perform OCR on the fax, but do not check for errors
OCR and Check	Perform OCR on the fax, then prompt to correct errors in the text
Train OCR	Teach OmniPage how to recognize special characters
Defer OCR	Schedule OCR for the fax for a later time

The default is OCR and Check. Once you've selected the type of OCR action you want to perform, you don't need to set the type again until you want to change it.

To apply OCR to a fax page, select the page from the thumbnails, then click the OCR button. OmniPage will automatically detect the areas where text occurs (there is also a manual zone setting, if you prefer) and convert the fax to text. If the OCR button is set to Perform OCR, then the converted text will appear in the right-hand pane. The following colors are used to indicate potential problem areas that you'll want to examine more closely:

Blue   Words replaced by the Language Analyst, an optional Omni-Page Pro process that tries to correct unknown words based on context and usage

Green   Questionable characters or words

Red   Characters that OmniPage Pro could not recognize at all

To zoom in on a problem area, right-click it, then choose Verify Text to pop up a detailed view of that part of the page, as shown in Figure 15.18.

Figure 15.18

OmniPage Pro zooms in on questionable text in context. Compare this with the similar CFax Pro function, shown in Figure 15.16.

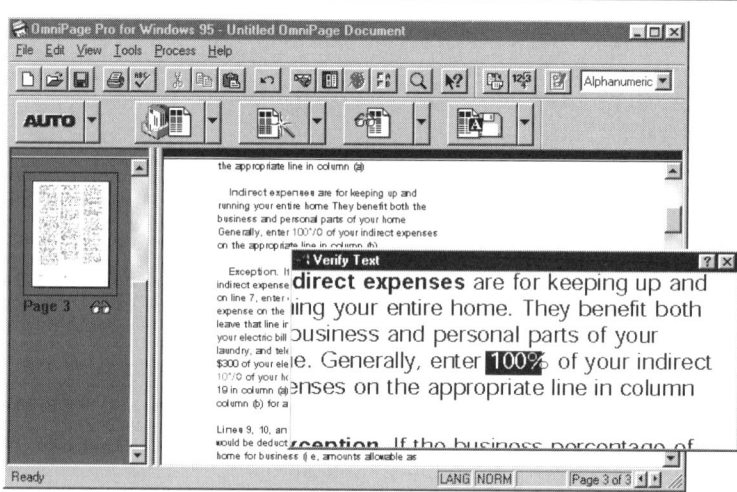

If the OCR button is set to OCR and Check, this verification will take place automatically, giving you a chance to review all changes made by the Language Analyst and check all other questionable or unrecognizable characters. Once you've verified the OCR, choose File, Save As to store the fax either as text or in a word-processing format.

Tips and Tricks

One of the features that people have requested most for Microsoft Fax is to have the capability to print incoming faxes automatically, forward them, or make them available to everyone on the network in some other way. You'll find several alternative procedures here using add-ons, or using the Inbox Assistant function with Microsoft Exchange Server.

Automating Incoming Fax Processing

Microsoft Exchange doesn't include a built-in method for automatically printing incoming faxes, but that doesn't mean it can't be done. On the CD accompanying this book, you'll find Print Fax, a utility for printing received faxes or forwarding them to someone else.

Another solution is an enhanced version of Imaging, called Imaging for Windows Professional Edition, available directly from Wang (see Appendix B, "Exchange Resources"). This program allows you to set rules to process incoming faxes. For any given fax, you can print it, forward it, or apply OCR to turn it into text and graphics.

To set up fax processing in Imaging Pro, you'd use the Flow Wizard to create what's called a *flow*, essentially a flow chart of what actions should be taken on a fax, similar to the Inbox Assistant on the Exchange Server clients. For example, you could configure a flow to apply OCR to each fax, then forward all received faxes containing the word MIS to the director of MIS.

Letting Everyone See Faxes in a Public Folder

One of the drawbacks to using Microsoft Fax is that, unlike the fax connector products, it has no built-in method for forwarding faxes to individual recipients. If you are using Exchange Server, however, you can set up the system running Microsoft Fax to automatically post incoming faxes to a public folder for everyone to review. Here's how:

1. Create an Exchange profile on the network fax server that contains the following services:

   Microsoft Exchange Server

   Microsoft Fax

   Personal Address Book

2. Set the Microsoft Fax modem to "Answer after 2 rings."

With Exchange Server, you can set up a Microsoft Fax server to automatically post incoming faxes to a public folder for everyone to review.

3. Create a public folder called Received Faxes (see "Working with Public Folders," page 427 in Chapter 19). The default permission should be Reviewer, because you don't want everyone deleting each other's faxes.

4. On the fax server, create an Inbox Assistant rule: When the Subject equals "Fax from," move the fax to the Received Faxes folder (see "Inbox Assistant," page 412 in Chapter 18).

5. Leave Exchange running on the fax server at all times.

The Inbox Assistant rule in Step 4 takes advantage of the fact that the subject line for incoming faxes is always "Fax from" plus the CSID that identifies an individual fax machine. Once in a while, you might see an incoming fax from "Unknown Fax Machine," where no CSID has been specified. To handle these situations, you could create another Inbox Assistant rule, perhaps sending the faxes to a different public folder, where they can be reviewed and forwarded. You'd want to adjust the permissions for this folder to give at least one person the permission to edit and delete items in this folder. Note that these rules won't handle incoming binary file transfer (BFT) faxes, because their subject lines won't include the word Fax.

Summary

Received faxes can be viewed, routed, saved, and converted to text, but you may need a combination of several Exchange add-ons to get exactly the fax setup you want. Once Exchange Server enters the picture, you have the option to automatically route faxes to a public folder and to add fax connectors with automatic inbound routing.

Key Points

- You must load Exchange before you can receive a fax with Microsoft Fax.

- Imaging for Windows provides a rich collection of annotation tools.

- Several add-ons make it easy to perform OCR on faxes received with Microsoft Fax.

- With the Microsoft Exchange Server service, a Microsoft Fax server can be set up to post incoming faxes automatically to a public folder for everyone to review.

For More Information

The settings for Microsoft Fax are covered in Chapter 7, "Setting up Microsoft Fax," and those for WinFax PRO 7.0 are in Chapter 9, "Setting Up Other Information Services."

If you have the Microsoft Exchange Server service, this might be a good time to look ahead to the sections "Inbox Assistant" (Chapter 18) and "Working with Public Folders" (Chapter 19) for details about how to use these features. You can put these features together to set up a group repository for incoming faxes.

Modem problems that result in poor fax reception are relatively difficult to diagnose. However, Chapter 24, "Troubleshooting," offers some general procedures to try.

Chapter 16

Working with Messages and Folders

In Chapter 10, "Using the Exchange Viewer," you got acquainted with the Microsoft Exchange hierarchy of folders and subfolders that contain messages and other items. This chapter adds other message and folder procedures to explore as you use Exchange more extensively. These procedures include

- Finding items
- Creating and using archives
- Keeping folders to a manageable size

Finding Messages

You don't have to use e-mail long before the messages start piling up. Either you don't get around to reading them all, or you set some aside for later actions. Eventually, you want to find a message you received (or sent) a few days ago, but you might not remember exactly when. There's more than one way to locate such an item: by browsing the messages, using the Find tool, or using an advanced search tool.

Browsing Messages

If you know the recipient of the item you're trying to find, the subject, or the date it was sent or received — *and you know what folder it's in* — you may be able to find it fastest simply by looking through the messages in that folder. Quickly re-sort the items (by clicking on a column heading) to make it easy to zero in on the one you need.

For example, if you're looking for a message you sent to Kevin Lynch on August 5, click on the Sent Items folder (see Figure 16.1). Normally, this folder is sorted by the date items were sent, with the most recent at the top. Click on the To column heading. This will re-sort the items by recipient, in alphabetical order. For each recipient, the items will be sorted in the order they were sent. If there are not too many items in the folder (say, 100 or fewer), a few more mouse clicks will quickly scroll the list to Kevin Lynch's name and find the August 5 message.

Figure 16.1

This Sent Items folder has been re-sorted to list messages by the recipient. The arrow on the To column indicates that it's in alphabetical order.

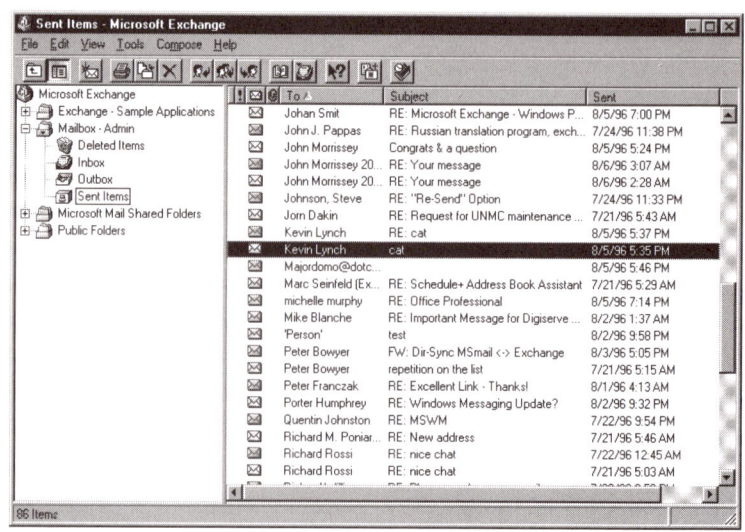

Exchange also supports "prefix searching," in which you enter just the first few characters of the item you're looking for. Here's how to use prefix searching:

1. In the Exchange Viewer, click on the column heading for the column you want to search in to sort the column in ascending order (prefix searching doesn't work with columns sorted in descending order).

2. Type the first few characters of the item you want to find. For example, if you have sorted by the To column, as in Figure 16.1, type the first few letters of the recipient's name. After you stop typing, Exchange will select the first item that matches the characters you typed.

Using the Find Tool

Browsing messages, as described above, is practical only if

Find can search only one public folder (or Microsoft Mail shared folder) at a time.

- You know what folder is likely to contain the item, and
- The folder contains a small number of items

Once folders grow to contain hundreds of messages and other items, browsing is less efficient than the Find tool included with Exchange. To use the Find tool, click Tools, Find to display the Find window shown in Figure 16.2. You'll need to specify where you want to search and what you want to search for.

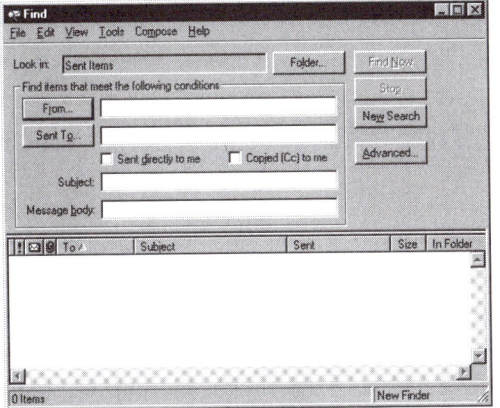

Figure 16.2
The Find tool searches folders for items meeting specific criteria.

By default, the Find tool starts its search in the current folder. If the current folder is in your Exchange Server mailbox or in a Personal Folders file, the find tool also searches all subfolders. To change the starting folder for the search or to turn off subfolder searching, click the Folder button. In the Find Items in Folder dialog box (Figure 16.3), select the folder where you want to begin searching. This is also the dialog box where you can enable or disable subfolder searching.

Figure 16.3

A Find search can begin with a top-level folder or a subfolder.

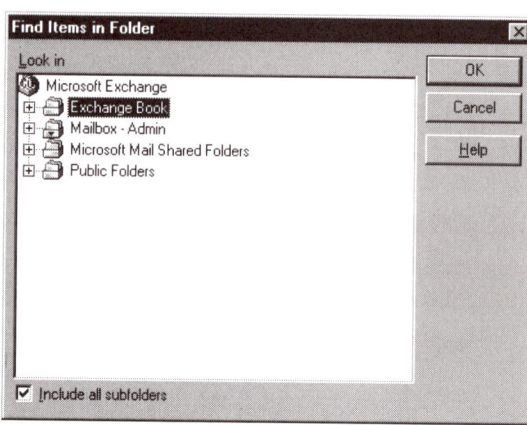

Note that Find can search only one public folder (or Microsoft Mail shared folder) at a time. You must select the specific folder or subfolder where you want to search.

In addition to specifying a start folder, you must enter what you want to search for. You can use each of the boxes shown in Figure 16.2 under "Find items that meet the following conditions" to build your search criteria. When you enter conditions in more than one box, they are combined. For example, you might enter "Celly Frank" under Sent To and add "Performance Review" under Subject. This builds a search for all messages sent to Celly Frank *and* dealing with the subject of Performance Review.

You also can make more than one entry in the boxes. Separate the entries with semicolons, just as you would multiple addresses in an outgoing message. If Sent To contains "Celly Frank; Marsha Patterson," the search will include messages sent either to Celly Frank *or* to Marsha Patterson.

If you don't remember the subject, try searching the body of the message by entering text in the Message Body box.

Setting From and Sent To Criteria

You can set the conditions in the From and Sent To boxes to search either for a name or for the actual e-mail address for that person. If you type in a name (or part of a name) in either the From or Sent To box, the Find tool locates matches for only the display or "friendly" name of the sender or

If you enter a recipient name in the Find window, only the display names are searched. If you instead choose or create an address in the Address Book, Find searches for the underlying e-mail address.

recipient — the name you see in the From or To columns, not the underlying e-mail address.

To search the e-mail addresses themselves, click the From or Sent To button, and choose one or more names from the Address Book dialog box. If the address you want to search for isn't available on an address list, click the New button, and enter the address either as a new Personal Address Book recipient or "In this message only" (in other words, just for this Find session). You can choose to search for the address in the From field of each message or in the Sent To field. Figure 16.4 shows how you build a list of addresses to search from the Address Book.

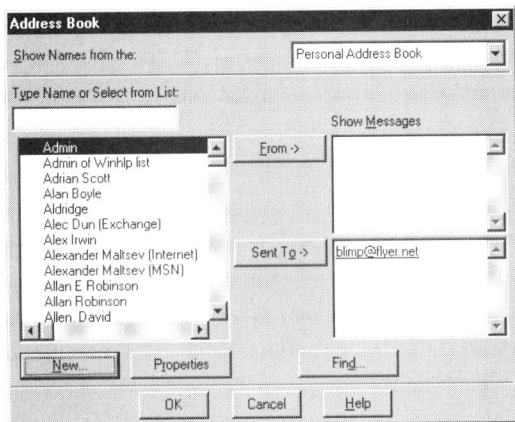

Figure 16.4

To use the underlying e-mail address for a search, you must either choose an address from the Address Book or use the New button to create a new address entry.

Names chosen through the Address Book dialog box appear underlined in the From or Sent To box, which means they've been resolved. For these resolved addresses, Find searches the e-mail addresses rather than the display names.

An example may help illustrate the difference. Let's say you subscribe to a discussion mailing list (see "Mailing Lists," page 505 in Chapter 22) on blimps and zeppelins. The address for posting messages to the list is blimp@flyer.net. If you enter blimp@flyer.net under Sent To in the Find dialog box, you will probably find most of the messages on the list, because most people just send their postings directly to that address. But what if one person has an address book entry for the list, using a display name of just Blimp? You won't find any of his messages, because the name Blimp doesn't match blimp@flyer.net. To find his messages, as well as the others, create a Personal Address Book entry for blimp@flyer.net, then use the Sent To button in the Find dialog box to enter that address for your search. You should see blimp@flyer.net underlined in the Find dialog box, as shown in Figure 16.5.

Figure 16.5

Because the name in the Sent To box is underlined, Find will search for matches for the actual e-mail address, regardless of the display name.

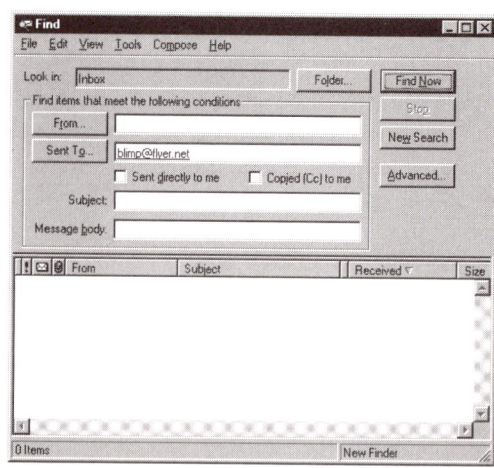

Now the search will find all messages with the e-mail address of blimp@flyer.net, whether the display name is blimp@flyer.net or Blimp or anything else.

To recap, when a name in the Find window is underlined, you're searching for its actual e-mail address (which is not displayed anywhere in the Find window). When a name isn't underlined, Find looks for messages that match the display name, not the e-mail address.

The two checkboxes, "Sent directly to me" and "Copied (Cc) to me," produce inconsistent results if you have more than one service installed in your Exchange profile. Find locates only those items sent directly to you via the first service listed in the delivery order (you can view and change the delivery order by choosing Tools, Options, then switching to the Delivery tab). Therefore, you are better off using a resolved name. Enter your own address (or addresses) in the Personal Address Book. Then use this address in the Sent To box.

Using Advanced Find Conditions

For more Find options, click the Advanced button to use the dialog box shown in Figure 16.6.

From here, you can search by a number of additional criteria:

- The size of the item
- The date the item was received (which is the same as the date sent for messages in the Sent Items folder)

- The importance and/or sensitivity of the item
- Whether the item has been read
- Whether the message included an attachment
- For Exchange Server clients, various properties of forms, documents, and folders

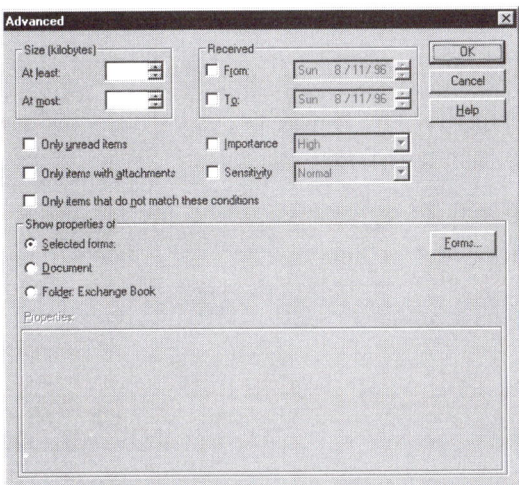

Figure 16.6

Set additional search criteria in the Advanced dialog box of the Find tool. Only Exchange Server clients see the area at the bottom for searching via the properties of forms, documents, and folders.

Also note the checkbox for "Only items that do not match these conditions." The conditions to which this refers are the total criteria from both the basic Find window and the Advanced dialog box (not just the conditions in the Advanced dialog box).

Using Persistent Finders

When you use the Find tool and leave it open, it automatically continues to search for new items that appear in the folder(s) you specified. This type of search is called a *persistent Finder*. If a persistent Finder is active — in other words, the Find dialog box is open — when you quit Exchange, the Find tool will become active again automatically the next time you start Exchange. There is one exception: A persistent Finder on a public folder does not run when you restart Exchange.

Using Other Search Tools

The Find tool has a couple of major limitations:

- It cannot search more than one Exchange Server public folder (or Microsoft Mail Shared Folder). Instead, it searches only one public folder at a time, without searching any subfolders.

- It doesn't search inside attached documents.

Two third-party tools for Exchange Server are available to extend Exchange's search capabilities and overcome these limitations — Fulcrum FIND! and Verity's Search 97. Fulcrum FIND! uses indexes set up by the Microsoft Exchange Server administrator to speed searches of public folders. This tool also includes a flexible viewer, so you don't have to open each document in its native application just to read it.

You can use Search 97 from Verity as both an enterprise search tool — with indexes on public folders — and a personal tool for searching your own mailbox or Personal Folders, as well as Internet or intranet documents.

Managing the Size of Your Folders

Periodically purge your mailbox and/or Personal Folders by deleting unneeded messages and removing duplicate attachments.

Keeping your personal Exchange folders to a reasonable size is an important maintenance task, whether the folders are in a Microsoft Exchange Server mailbox or in a Personal Folders file (or both!). Check with your Exchange Server administrator to see whether your mailbox has a storage limit, designed to help manage the space on the Exchange server. If your mailbox exceeds that limit, you won't be able to send any new messages. While tools are available to Microsoft Exchange Server administrators to help clean user mailboxes, in many cases it will be up to you to make sure that your mailbox is purged of old messages.

If you store items in Personal Folders (as you must if you use the Windows 95 or NT operating system client), trimming the size of the Personal Folders file will help Exchange start faster and make it easier for you to work with messages and folders. (By the way, you can keep up to 16,000 items in a single folder in a Personal Folders file!)

Folder Management Techniques

The main task involved in cleaning up a folder is removing any unnecessary material. We'll look at two techniques for doing this:

- Deleting messages
- Removing attachments

For a Personal Folders file, you'll also want to compact the file to recover the space freed by the cleanup process. If you use Exchange Server, you also can compact your offline folders.

Deleting Messages

Any message you delete is placed in the Deleted Items folder for the message store, either an Exchange Server mailbox or a Personal Folders file. If you have more than one set of folders, each set will have its own Deleted Items folder.

By default, Exchange empties the Deleted Items folder for the primary message store — the one where new messages are delivered — when you quit Exchange. You can change this setting to keep all deleted messages indefinitely. Choose Tools, Options, then clear the box labeled "Empty the 'Deleted Items' folder upon exiting" (see Figure 16.7).

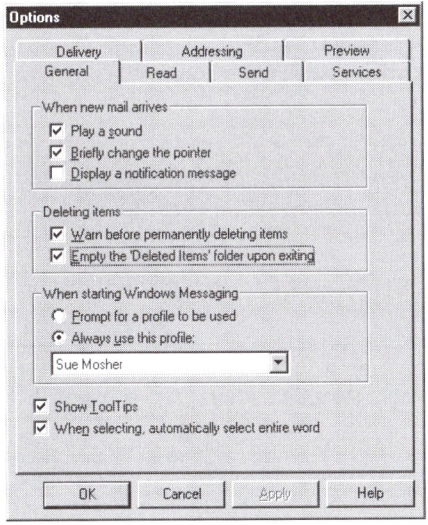

Figure 16.7
Exchange is normally set to permanently remove all items in the Deleted Items folder when you quit Exchange.

If you shut down your computer without first quitting Exchange, the Deleted Items folder is not emptied, regardless of this setting. Also, even if Exchange is set up to empty the Deleted Items folder, it purges only the folder for the primary message store. You must manually purge any other Deleted Items folders on your system by deleting all the items in them. Instead of deleting messages, you may want to move them to a separate Personal Folders file maintained as an archive (see "Archiving Messages" later in this chapter).

Removing Attachments

When you send a message that includes a file from your system, you usually end up with two copies of the file — the original on your system and the copy in the e-mail message (assuming you did not send the attachment as a link rather than as a file).

Because you already have the file on your system, you probably don't need to keep it in your Exchange folder, too. You can open the sent message and remove the attachment. While you have the message open, it's a good idea to type in the name and location of the attachment, to help you remember just what you sent. To locate sent messages with attachments so you can clean them up in this way, use either the Find tool or (on Exchange Server clients) a filter. Check the "Only items with attachments" box on the Advanced Find dialog box shown in Figure 16.6.

Compacting Personal Folders

When you clean up folders in a Personal Folders file, you'll probably want to see immediate results in the form of a smaller .pst file. To compact a Personal Folder file, follow these steps:

1. Choose Tools, Services.

2. In the Services dialog box, select Personal Folders, then click the Properties button.

3. In the Personal Folders dialog box, click the Compact Now button (see Figure 16.8).

Figure 16.8

You can compact a Personal Folders file at any time to recover space freed by deleting or editing messages.

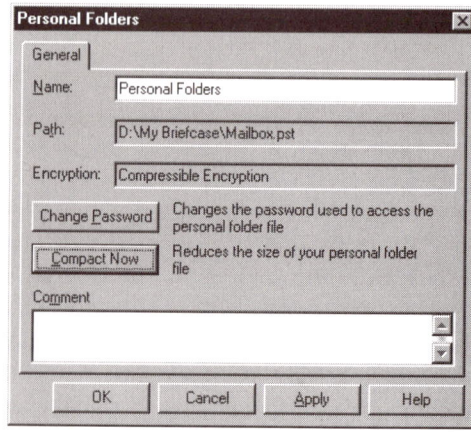

4. When compaction is complete, click OK twice to return to the Exchange Viewer.

A Personal Folders file also will be compacted automatically once the amount of recoverable space exceeds four percent of the total file. If you use a screen saver, you may need to disable it to provide enough idle processor time for the compaction routine to kick in.

Compacting Your Mailbox

Actually, you don't need to compact your Exchange Server mailbox; the server does that for you. But if you are a remote user with offline folders, then you probably do need to compact those folders from time to time. Here's how:

1. Choose Tools, Services. Select Microsoft Exchange Server, then click the Properties button.

2. In the Microsoft Exchange Server properties dialog box, switch to the Advanced tab, then click the Offline Folder File Settings.

3. In the Offline Folder File Settings dialog box (Figure 16.9), click the Compact Now button.

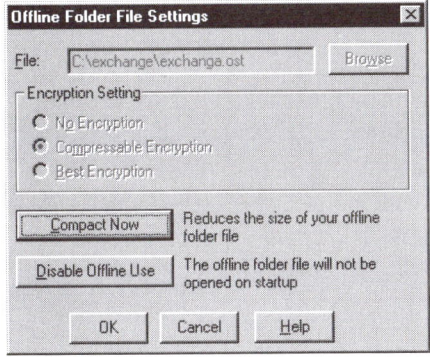

Figure 16.9
The ability to compact the offline folder file is part of the settings for the Microsoft Exchange Server service in your Exchange profile.

Storage Limits on Exchange Server

To control the amount of disk space used on the Microsoft Exchange server, the Exchange administrator can limit the size of your mailbox. If you're a good Exchange housekeeper, this may never affect you. However, if your mailbox does get too large, you'll receive a warning message. You may even see a message such as the one shown in Figure 16.10 alerting you that you will not be able to send any additional messages until you clean out your mailbox.

Figure 16.10
Exchange warns you if the size of your mailbox on the Exchange server grows larger than the limit set by the system administrator.

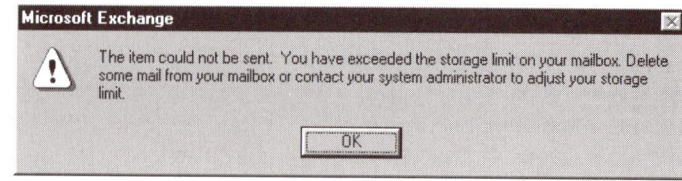

You may want to check with the administrator to find out whether there are any plans to use a cleanup utility to sweep out the old messages automatically.

Archiving Messages

You can store archived messages in a Personal Folders file that can be added to the Exchange Viewer at any time.

Given the need to occasionally purge your mailbox and/or Personal Folders, what should you do with old messages? It's easy to archive them in additional Personal Folders files, which you can create at any time.

To create a new archive file, follow these steps:

1. Choose Tools, Services.

2. Click the Add button.

3. In the Add Service to Profile dialog box, select Personal Folders, then click OK.

4. In the Create/Open Personal Folders File dialog box, select the folder on your system where you want to keep the archive file, then enter the File Name. Use a name that indicates the contents. For example, if you archive by date, use a name such as Jan1997.pst for messages sent and received in January 1997. Click the Open button.

5. In the Create Microsoft Personal Folders dialog box (Figure 16.11), enter a descriptive Name to make it easy to tell the archives from other Personal Folders files in the Exchange Viewer.

6. If more than one person uses your computer, it's a good idea to add a password to the archive file by entering the password in the Password and Verify Password boxes.

7. Click OK twice to return to the Exchange Viewer, where the new set of Personal Folders has been added. Personal Folders will contain only one subfolder, Deleted Items; you may want to create additional folders.

Use the Find tool or a filter to isolate messages by project or by a date range. Then drag those messages from your main message store to the new archive folders. You also can select the messages then choose File, Move.

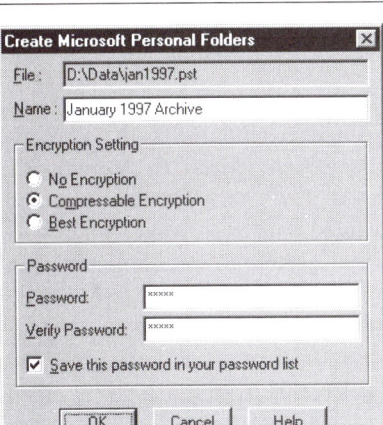

Figure 16.11

Archives are simply sets of Personal Folders, usually with descriptive names to distinguish them from other Personal Folders.

Once you've moved items to the archive folders, you can remove the archive file from the current Exchange profile. Here's how:

1. Choose Tools, Services.

2. Select the Personal Folders file that you created above.

3. Click the Remove button.

Removing a Personal Folders file from the profile does not remove it from your system. The file can be restored to the current Exchange profile at any time (see "Adding a Service," page 79 in Chapter 4), allowing you to search and review all your archived messages.

Posting Documents to Folders

Exchange folders can contain more than just messages. You can put documents created in other applications in your Exchange mailbox, Personal Folders, or Exchange Server public folders. There are two ways to put a document in a folder:

- For Windows 95 or Windows NT 4.0 versions of Exchange, you can drag a document from Windows Explorer or My Computer to an Exchange folder.

- For Exchange Server clients, you can use the Post to Exchange Folder command found on the File menu in Microsoft Office applications.

To use the Post to Exchange Folder command, Office version 7.0a or later is required (see Appendix B, "Exchange Resources"). You should install the Exchange Server client first, then Office. If you installed Office first, then you need to run the Office setup program again after you install the Exchange Server client; this will add the Post to Exchange Folder command.

Changing the Document Subject

When you post a document to an Exchange folder, either by dragging the document to the folder or by using the Post to Exchange Folder command, the subject shown in the Subject column is the file name for the document. To change the subject, you must save the document under a new file name, then post the new document to the folder. You can then delete the old version. There's no way to simply change the subject from within Exchange.

Using Microsoft Office Document Properties

Any Microsoft Office document property can be added to the Exchange Viewer.

Even though you can't easily change the subject of a document, many other properties are available for Microsoft Office documents, including a title field. To view these properties, open a document in its Office application, then choose File, Properties. Properties such as title and author can be changed. Others, such as statistics about the document, are recorded automatically by the application.

To view these Office document properties in an Exchange folder, choose View, Columns, and add the desired properties to the display for the current folder (see "Rearranging Columns" on page 233 in Chapter 10). If you are using the Exchange Server version, you also can add document property columns to a view (see "Working with Folder Views" on page 240 in Chapter 10.) Even custom document properties can be added to an Exchange folder. Here's how:

1. Choose View, Columns.

2. In the Columns dialog box (Figure 16.12), type the name of the custom property in the "Available columns" box (custom document properties are not shown on the available properties list).

Figure 16.12

Because custom properties created in Microsoft Office applications are not shown on the "Available columns" list, you must type in the name of the property you want to display.

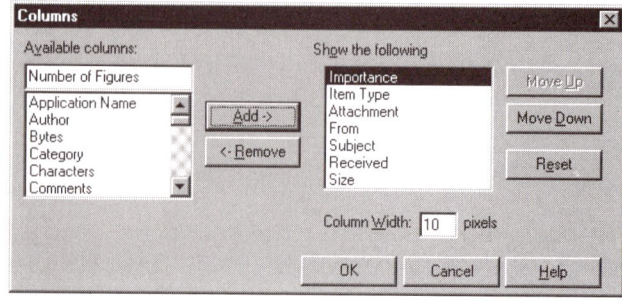

3. Click the Add button to add the property to the "Show the following" list. The Custom Property dialog box, shown in Figure 16.13, appears.

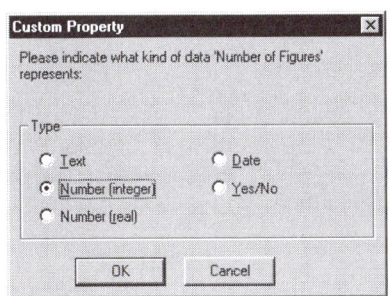

Figure 16.13

When you add a custom document property to the Exchange columns list, you must also specify the type of data.

4. In the Custom Property dialog box, select the Type for the property (this must correspond to the type set when you created the property). Click OK.

5. Use the Move Up or Move Down button, if necessary, to change the placement of the property in the list of columns.

Tips and Tricks

Here are tips on how to check the size of your Exchange folders and use the priority setting to help you keep track of important incoming messages.

Checking Folder Sizes

If you want to clean house, you might want to know which Exchange folder is taking up the most space, and there's nothing built into Exchange to tell you. However, the Preview Pane utility that ships with the Microsoft Exchange Resource Kit (see Appendix B, "Exchange Resources"; this utility is also on the Exchange Technical Resource CD and the TechNet CD) adds a Folder Size item to the File menu. Select a top-level message store (such as your Exchange mailbox or Personal Folders), then choose File, Folder Size to display a list of folders and sizes such as that shown in Figure 16.14.

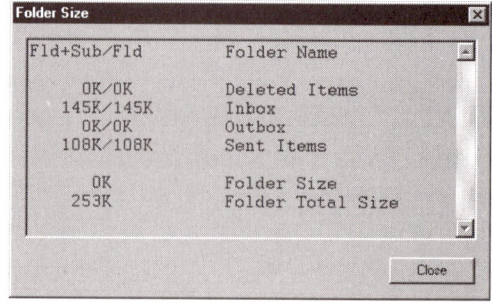

Figure 16.14

Track the size of Exchange folders with the Preview Pane utility included in the Microsoft Exchange Resource Kit.

Changing the Priority on Incoming Messages

Remember that certain properties can be set even for received messages. For example, give a high importance value to messages requiring immediate attention by choosing File, Properties, then selecting High. If you're consistent in the way you use High, Normal, and Low importance, you can then use the Find tool or a sort or filter to quickly locate those items that are higher in priority.

Summary

In this chapter, you've learned how to find messages by browsing, using the Find tool, and employing Exchange Server add-ons. You should also understand the importance of regular housekeeping in your Exchange messages and folders and know several effective techniques for keeping your folders in order. You also now know how to post documents to folders and display even Microsoft Office custom document properties in the Exchange Viewer. When it comes to creating public folders, you know how to copy settings from another folder, set various properties, and make a folder available to all users with the right permissions.

Key Points

- Find can search only one public folder (or Microsoft Mail shared folder) at a time.

- If you enter a recipient name in the Find window, only the display names are searched. If you instead choose or create an address in the Address Book, Find searches for the underlying e-mail address.

- Periodically purge your mailbox and/or Personal Folders by deleting unneeded messages and removing duplicate attachments.

- Archived messages can be stored in a Personal Folders file that can be added to the Exchange Viewer at any time.
- Any Microsoft Office document property can be added to the Exchange Viewer.

For More Information

If you need a refresher on customizing folders, return to Chapter 10, "Using the Exchange Viewer."

Chapter 19, "Using Exchange to Collaborate," shows you how to add custom forms to public folders.

Chapter 17

Using the Address Book

The Address Book is a collection of address lists, both personal lists and those belonging to your organization. Personal lists, such as the Personal Address Book (PAB) and the CompuServe Address Book, are completely under your control; you can add, remove, and edit the addresses in them. Lists tied to your organization's mail system — whether Microsoft Exchange Server, Microsoft Mail, or some other system — are managed by a system administrator.

Working with the Address Book

The Address Book is a collection of address lists, both personal lists and those belonging to your organization.

To open the Address Book (Figure 17.1), click the Address Book button or choose Tools, Address Book. The initial address list shown is controlled by your profile settings (see "Addressing Settings," page 75 in Chapter 4), but you also can change this list from within Exchange.

To change which address list is shown first in the Address Book, follow these steps:

1. Choose Tools, Options in the Exchange Viewer window and switch to the Addressing tab, shown in Figure 17.2.

2. Pick the list you want to display first from "Show this address list first."

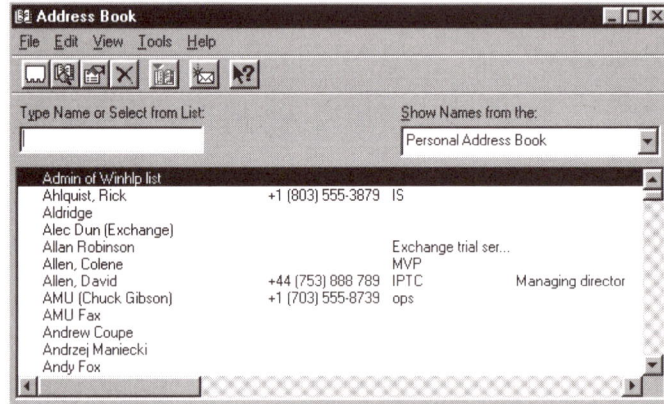

Figure 17.1

The Personal Address Book may be only one of several address lists available in the Address Book, depending on the services you have installed.

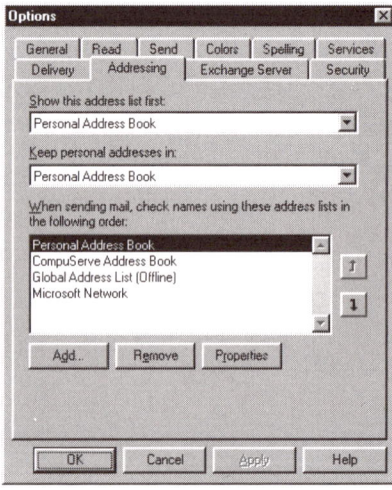

Figure 17.2

On the Addressing tab, you can choose which list to display first when you open the Address Book.

3. Click OK to save the change.

Table 17.1 lists the toolbar buttons found in the Address Book.

Table 17.1 Address Book Toolbar Buttons		
Button	**Name**	**Description**
	New Entry	Add a new address to the current list (available for PAB, other personal lists only)
	Find	Search the current address list
	Properties	Display details for the address
	Delete	Remove the selected address(es) (available for PAB, other personal lists only)
	Add to Personal Address Book	Add the selected name(s) from an organization list to the PAB
	New Message	Compose a new message addressed to the selected name(s)
	Help	Get help on any element of the Address Book window

Notice the scroll bar at the bottom of the Address Book window shown in Figure 17.1. Slide this bar to the right to browse details about the names in the address book. You cannot change the column order or width for this display. Therefore, you'll probably want to concentrate on just the first few visible columns. For the Personal Address Book, these columns are

- Display name
- Primary phone number; this is the number selected on the Business tab (see the section "PAB Address Details" later in this chapter)
- Office
- Title

A little further to the right is a column that shows the type of address — EX for Exchange Server, MS for Microsoft Mail, SMTP for Internet, MSN for The Microsoft Network, and so on.

The first few columns shown for the Microsoft Exchange Server Global Address List are the same as for the PAB, except that the Business phone number is given instead of a user-configurable primary phone number.

Understanding the Address Lists

Most of the address lists you encounter are either personal or organizational. You also may have access to special lists, such as all subscribers to The Microsoft Network. Most of this chapter deals with the PAB, because this list is the main one under your control.

Personal Address Book

A profile can contain only one Personal Address Book (PAB).

The PAB is installed by default in every Exchange profile. You can have only one PAB in a profile (see the "Tips and Tricks" section for a way to switch PABs without restarting Exchange).

The PAB is where you keep addresses for people who are not part of your organization. You also can copy addresses from other address lists into your PAB to keep them handy. For example, if you work for a company with 5,000 employees but regularly send messages to only a dozen other people, those 12 names should be in your PAB; and the PAB should be the place Exchange looks first to resolve addresses (see the section "How Exchange Looks Up an Address" later in this chapter).

Another advantage to keeping commonly used addresses in the PAB is that you can add your own notes, plus details such as telephone numbers. If phone numbers are entered and you have a modem, you can use the Phone Dialer to dial the numbers for you (see the sidebar "Using the Phone Dialer" on page 402). Other applications, such as Microsoft Word, also can use the information contained in the PAB.

Organization Address Lists

Organization or enterprise address lists come in several flavors. A *global address list* (GAL) includes everyone in the organization (or at least everyone the mail administrator wants to include). In addition, you may see *postoffice address lists* (for Microsoft Mail) and *Recipients lists* (for Exchange Server) that represent subsets of the GAL for a particular location. Finally, there may be *gateway lists* that show you addresses on another mail system that is linked to Microsoft Mail or Exchange Server.

Other Address Lists

Different information services may add address-list functions to your profile. CompuServe and The Microsoft Network (MSN) are two examples. The CompuServe Address Book is a personal address list shared with WinCIM or other CompuServe software. However, this address book can contain only CompuServe addresses.

The Microsoft Network provides a searchable address list of all MSN members. When you sign up with MSN, an entry is made in this list with your name and member ID. You also can add your own personal and professional information; here's how:

1. Connect to The Microsoft Network.
2. In Exchange, choose Tools, Address Book or click the Address Book button.
3. In the Address Book dialog box, under Show Names, choose Microsoft Network.
4. Choose Tools, Find.
5. In the Find dialog box, enter your Member ID or Name, then click OK.
6. When the search is completed, you will see your own address. Double-click it to bring up its properties.
7. In the General, Personal, and Professional tabs, enter information you want other MSN members to be able to see, then click OK to save it.

For details about how to search the MSN list, see the section "Finding and Viewing Addresses" later in this chapter.

How Exchange Looks Up an Address

As discussed in Chapter 11, "Sending E-Mail Messages," you don't have to know someone's exact e-mail address as long as (s)he is listed in either your PAB or one of the other lists in the Address Book.

Address name resolution occurs when you click the Check Names button or when you send a message in which the addresses have not already been checked. A critical factor for resolving address names is the order in which address lists are searched. You can save yourself some time and trouble by setting the order in which Exchange searches the address lists.

Setting the Address List Search Order

To set the order for searching the address lists, choose Tools, Options in the Exchange Viewer window, and switch to the Addressing tab, shown in

Different information services may add address-list functions to your profile.

Figure 17.2. The lists that will be checked are at the bottom, under "When ending mail, check names... ." The Personal Address Book is always included in this sequence by default. If the Exchange Server service is installed, you will also see a Global Address List (marked Offline, if you're working offline rather than being connected to the network).

Use the up and down arrows to change the order in which lists are searched. Use the Add and Remove buttons in the Add Address List dialog box shown in Figure 17.3 to add and delete address lists from the search order. You also can make these changes by accessing your profile through the Mail and Fax (or Mail) applet on the Control Panel.

Figure 17.3

Your profile determines which address lists can be searched when you check names. For example, the Global Address List (Offline) belongs to the Microsoft Exchange Server service. A Microsoft Mail user could add the Postoffice Address List.

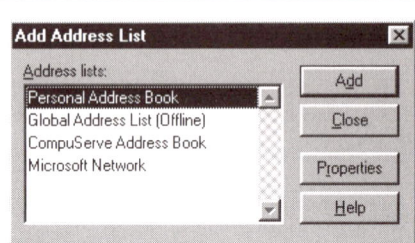

Special Note

The CompuServe Mail service does not automatically add the CompuServe Address Book to the search list. If you want to use the CompuServe Address Book for Check Names, you need to add the service yourself.

Checking Names

When you click the Check Names button in a New Message window, Exchange looks for a match against any part of the display name — the names you see in the first column of the address lists. For example, if you enter John in the To box, then click the Check Names button, possible matches could include Tom Johnson, John Smith, and Melanie Angstrom-Johns. This check is made only against the first part of the name, though, which means Joan Ajohn-ton would not be a match.

If a single match is found on the first address list in the search order, that name is used without the need for any further action on your part. A name that has been resolved is underlined in the T<u>o</u>, <u>C</u>c, or <u>B</u>cc box. If more than one match is found, a dialog box pops up in which you can choose the address to use in your message.

If matches are found in the first address list in the search order, Exchange does not look further. Exchange goes on to the second list only if no match is found in the first list. If no match is found in the second list, Exchange checks the third list, and so on.

For addresses in the Personal Address Book, the e-mail addresses themselves are not searched during the address resolution process. This means you cannot enter ThatCompany.com and see all addresses in your PAB for people with e-mail at the ThatCompany.com domain.

Exchange Server Techniques

For the Exchange Server Global Address List, the search goes beyond the display name. The search also includes a look at the last name, alias, office, and the actual e-mail address for an individual. As you can imagine, this could mean that you get a lot more names than you might want. A check for Smith would turn up Phil Smith as well as Sam Mithers, whose alias happens to be SMithers.

Fortunately, Exchange offers a way to restrict address name resolution to exact matches. Instead of entering Smith in the T<u>o</u> box, use =Smith. The equal sign forces the search to confine itself to perfect matches. You'll get Milo Smith, Judy Haynes-Smith, but not Andrew Smithson or Sam Mithers. It's important to note that use of the equal sign only works in conjunction with the Exchange Server's Global Address List.

Finding and Viewing Addresses

The address resolution procedure described in the previous section is specifically related to sending messages. But there are also times when you want to search the Address Book directly. For this option, select the list you want to search (just one list at a time), then choose <u>T</u>ools, <u>F</u>ind. For many lists, you get a simple dialog box with a box labeled <u>F</u>ind Names Containing. Enter the name you want to search for, then click OK. The selected address list will be filtered to show only those matching names.

To find out more about any address, right-click the address, then choose P<u>r</u>operties. Or you can select the address, then choose <u>F</u>ile, P<u>r</u>operties. The information available varies among address lists, but you will always see at least the display name and actual e-mail address. In the PAB, you see a lot more on the Business, Phone Number, and Notes tabs, which we'll discuss in "PAB Address Details" later in this chapter.

Exchange Server and The Microsoft Network addresses may display additional information. Let's take a look at that information now.

Exchange Server Addresses

You can't change your own Microsoft Exchange Server address details; the system administrator must make the changes.

When you search for addresses in the Exchange Server GAL, you will see a much more detailed dialog box (shown in Figure 17.4) where you can search by many other criteria, including the Department and City.

This form (and the underlying address list) might also be customized for your organization. For example, an international company might want to make information on employees' language skills available, so you can find those rare colleagues who speak Estonian.

When you view the properties of an Exchange Server address for an individual (Figure 17.5), a great deal of information is available on five tabs:

General	Name, address, and affiliation information
Organization	Where the individual is in the hierarchy, including his/her manager and any people who report directly to this individual (see Figure 17.6)
Phone/Notes	Up to eight different phone numbers, plus notes
Member Of	Distribution lists on which the address has been included
E-mail Addresses	All e-mail addresses that can be used to reach this recipient

Figure 17.4

You can search Exchange Server addresses for more than just a name. In this example, we're looking for everyone who works in Nashville.

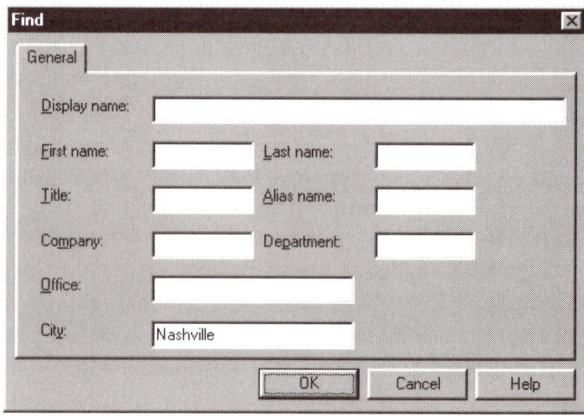

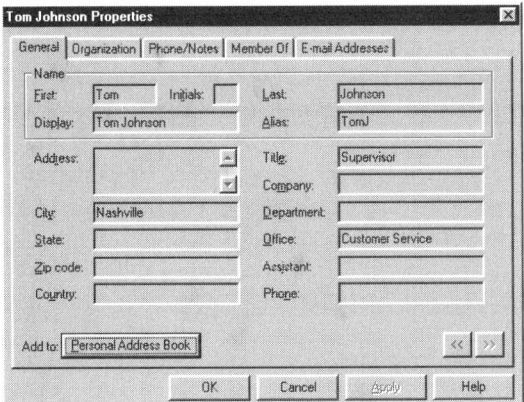

Figure 17.5

The amount of detail available in a Microsoft Exchange Server address record depends on organization policy and the effort of the system administrator to get all desired information collected and entered.

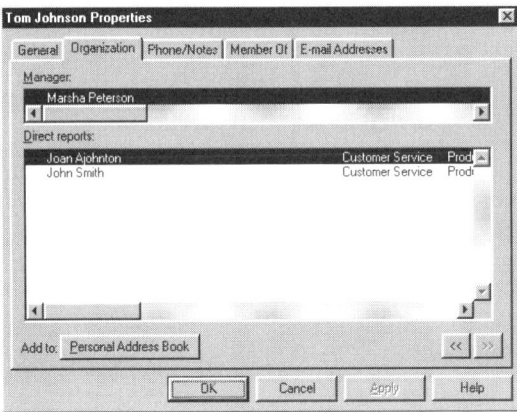

Figure 17.6

A special feature of Microsoft Exchange Server is its ability to maintain an organizational chart as part of individual address records. Here you see where Tom Johnson fits in the hierarchy. Marsha Peterson is Tom's boss, while Joan Ajohnton and John Smith make up his staff.

The Exchange Server administrator manages this information. If details of your own address need to be changed, then you need to have the administrator make the changes; you can't change your own address details.

Aside from individual addresses, you're likely to encounter two other types of Exchange Server addresses:

- Distribution lists
- Public folders

A *distribution list* is a group of recipients who share a single address; this arrangement allows you to send to all of the group by entering just that one address. As with individual addresses, distribution lists include Member Of and E-mail Addresses tabs. The General tab for a distribution list shows the owner and members of the list (see Figure 17.7). To change a list you own, click the <u>M</u>odify Members button.

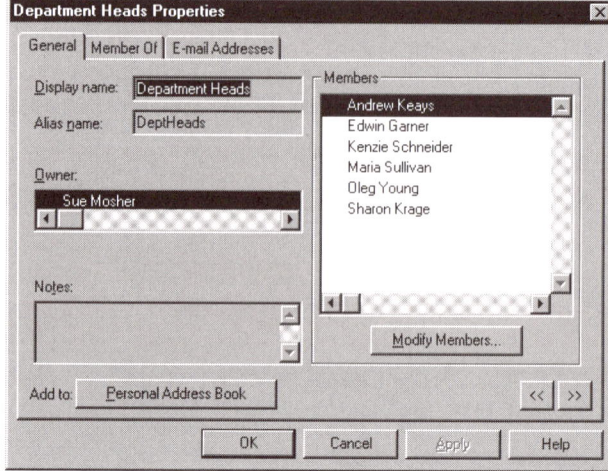

Figure 17.7
This Exchange Server distribution list shows all the members. However, in some cases, the membership of the list may be hidden.

A public folder is marked in the Global Address List with a folder icon. The public folder also has Member Of and E-mail Addresses tabs. The General tab displays the contacts for the folder. If you often post messages to a particular public folder, you might want to add that folder to your PAB. If you don't see the folder in the Global Address List, follow these steps:

1. Right-click the public folder in the Exchange Viewer, then choose <u>P</u>roperties. Switch to the Administrator tab.

2. Click the Personal Address <u>B</u>ook button.

3. Click OK to close the Properties dialog box.

The Microsoft Network Addresses

The Microsoft Network also offers the capability to search member properties, such as those you entered for yourself, as described earlier in this chapter. You must connect to The Microsoft Network to search its address list.

Managing the Personal Address Book

Most of the activity in the Address Book involves the PAB. In this section, you'll learn how to add addresses, create personal mailing lists, and (if you have Microsoft Word) print a copy of the PAB.

Adding PAB Addresses

There are three ways to add an address to the PAB:

1. Copy the address from a message
2. Copy the address from another address list
3. Enter the address by hand

Under the earlier section "Exchange Server Addresses," you'll also find a technique for adding the address for a public folder to the PAB.

To copy an address from a message, open the message so you can see the To and Cc fields. Right-click on the address you want to copy, then choose Add to Personal Address Book. To copy one or more addresses from another address list, follow these steps:

1. Open the Address Book (click the Address Book button, or choose Tools, Address Book).
2. In the Show Names list, choose the address list you want to copy from.
3. Select the address(es) you want to copy.
4. Click the Add to Personal Address Book button, or choose File, Add to Personal Address Book.

One caveat with copying addresses to the PAB from a company address list: If the user's e-mail address changes, you won't know that until a message comes back undeliverable. The PAB is truly personal; you and you alone are responsible for keeping it updated.

To add an address to the PAB by hand, follow these steps:

1. Open the Address Book (click the Address Book button, or choose Tools, Address Book).
2. In the Show Names list, choose Personal Address Book.
3. Click the New Entry button, or choose File, New Entry.
4. In the New Entry dialog box (Figure 17.8), choose the type of address, then click OK.
5. In the New Address Properties dialog box (Figure 17.9), enter the Display Name and the E-mail Address or other address details, which will vary with the type of entry chosen.

You must have a separate Personal Address Book entry for each type of address; for example, Internet Mail and Microsoft Fax.

Figure 17.8

When you add an entry to the Personal Address Book, choose an entry type appropriate for the address.

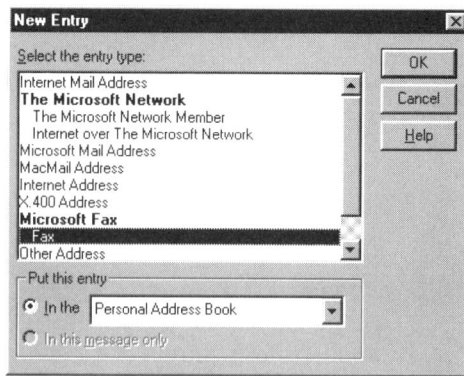

Figure 17.9

For each new PAB entry, enter a Display name and E-mail address. The exact format of this dialog box varies with different entry types.

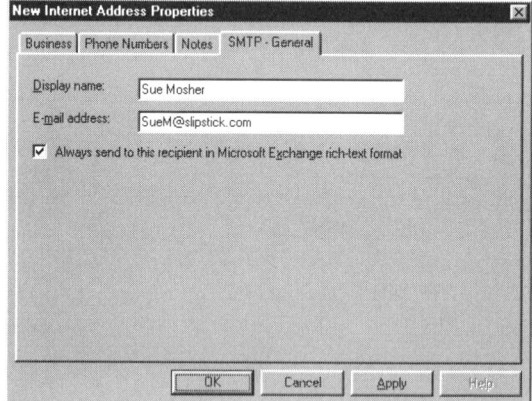

6. For some entries, you will have the option to send messages in Microsoft Exchange rich-text format (RTF). Check this option only if you know the recipient is using Exchange.

7. Add any other information on the Business, Phone Numbers, and Notes tabs (see the next section, "PAB Address Details"), then click OK to save the new address.

The choice of an entry type is critical to entering addresses by hand. You must have a separate entry for each type of address. This means that if you send a message to someone both via Internet Mail and via Microsoft Fax, you need two entries, one with an address type of Internet Mail, the other with an address type of Microsoft Fax.

To make it easy to find the right address type, consider adding (fax) or (SMTP) or (mail) as part of the name. Yes, this will appear in your outgoing messages, but it does make it easier for you to distinguish between different types of addresses for a single individual.

PAB Address Details

Entries in the Personal Address Book can include more than e-mail or fax information. As Figure 17.10 shows, the PAB entry includes four tabs:

Business	Name, address, and affiliation information
Phone Numbers	Eight different phone numbers for business, home, mobile, and so on
Notes	Freeform notes about an entry
Address (labeled with the entry type, such as Fax or SMTP)	E-mail address and type

On the Business tab (Figure 17.10), the "Phone number" list in the second column in the Address Book is used to designate a primary number.

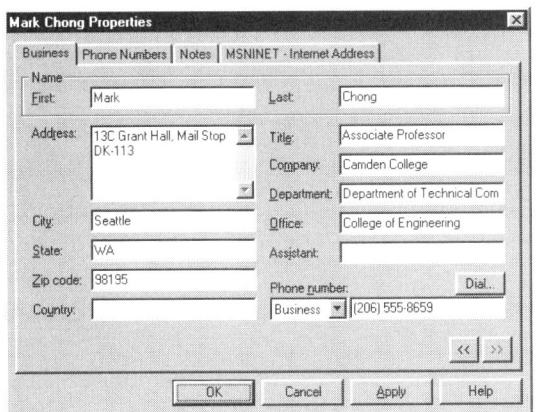

Figure 17.10
The Business tab displays the name, mailing address, affiliation, and primary phone number for a recipient.

On the Phone Numbers tab, enter the numbers in international format if you plan to use the Phone Dialer (see sidebar) and want to use the dialing properties for your location (see the section "Configuring Dialing Locations" on page 28 in Chapter 3). To use the international format, instead of entering 404-555-1234, use +1 (404) 555-1234. The number after the plus sign is the country code. The number in parentheses is the area code.

Using the Phone Dialer

If your computer and telephone use the same phone line, the Phone Dialer can dial numbers in the PAB for you. To install the Phone Dialer, follow these steps:

1. Click the Start button, then choose Control Panel and run the Add/Remove Programs applet. Switch to the Windows Setup tab.
2. Select Communications, then click the Details button.
3. Check the box for Phone Dialer, then click OK twice. Insert your Windows disk if directed to do so.

To use the Phone Dialer, your modem and telephone must be connected to the same phone line. Here's how to use the Phone Dialer:

1. On the Business tab, select the "Phone number" to dial, then click the Dial button. Or on the Phone Numbers tab, click the Dial button next to the number you want to dial.
2. Lift the telephone handset, and click Talk on the Call Status dialog box.
3. In the Active Call dialog box (which popped up before the Call Status was displayed), the name from the PAB entry is already filled in as the "Name to place in call log." Change this name if you like. When you are done with the call, press Enter or click Hang Up to record the call in the Phone Dialer call log.

To view the call log, switch to the Phone Dialer application, which starts when you place a call with the Dial button, and select Tools, Show Log.

The Fax number on the Phone Numbers tab is for reference only; it cannot be used for sending faxes with Microsoft Fax. Instead, you need to create a separate entry of the Microsoft Fax type.

For Exchange Server addresses added to the PAB, you'll see the normal PAB tabs, plus the specific Exchange Server tabs shown in Figure 17.11. The information normally found on the Business tab appears on the EX-General tab as well.

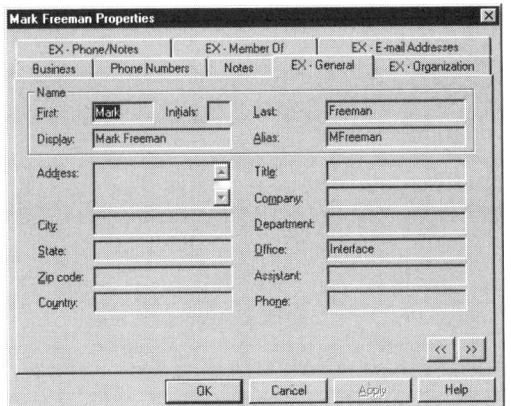

Figure 17.11

The EX tabs on this Exchange Server recipient added to the Personal Address Book list all the Exchange Server address properties.

Personal Distribution Lists

Not only can you place individual addresses in the PAB, but you also can create personal distribution lists that allow you to click one entry to send to a group of people. The addresses on the distribution list can come from entries on any of the address lists in the Address Book. You can mix address types on a distribution list, even including Microsoft Fax recipients. You also can keep addresses exclusively in the distribution list, without entering them in the PAB first.

To create a personal distribution list, follow these steps:

1. Open the Address Book. (Click the Address Book button, or choose Tools, Address Book.)

2. Click the New Entry button, or choose File, New Entry.

3. In the New Entry dialog box (Figure 17.8), choose Personal Distribution List (it's the bottom choice).

4. In the New Personal Distribution List Properties dialog box, give the list a Name.

5. Click the Add/Remove Members button to display the Edit Members dialog box (Figure 17.12).

6. To add members from the PAB or any other address list, with "Show Names from the," select the list that contains the new members.

7. Click OK twice to save the new list.

To add a name to the list without putting the name in the PAB first, follow these steps while you're in the Edit Members dialog box:

Figure 17.12

To add to a personal distribution list, select addresses on the left side, then click Members. You also can use the New button to create a new address.

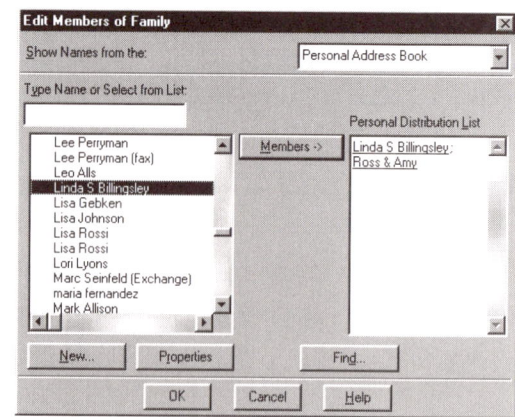

1. Click the New button.

2. In the New Entry dialog box (Figure 17.8), click "Just in This personal distribution list."

3. Select the entry type, then click OK.

4. Fill in the address details on the Properties dialog box.

5. Click the Members button to add the address only to the list.

Remember that, as with any PAB entry, you are completely responsible for the accuracy of a distribution list. If a PAB address changes, it is automatically changed in any personal distribution list; but the same is not true for addresses copied from other address lists, such as the Global Address List. Therefore, it's up to you to keep your personal distribution lists updated. It's also good cyberspace citizenship to respond promptly whenever someone asks to be removed from a distribution list.

To delete an entry from a personal distribution list, follow these steps while you're in the Edit Members dialog box:

1. Select a name (just one name at a time) from the Personal Distribution List box on the right.

2. Press the Delete or Backspace key to remove the name from the list.

Importing and Exporting with the PAB

There is no direct import to or export from the PAB, but workarounds are available.

As convenient as the PAB may be with its many information fields, there is no direct way to import addresses from other programs, such as personal information managers (PIMs). Even Microsoft Schedule+ uses a different address list on its Contacts tabs.

You also cannot have a shared PAB — in other words, a list of customer addresses that everyone on the network can access. It is possible to include such a list in the Exchange Server GAL, but in other configurations you're out of luck. But don't lose hope; there are a few workarounds.

For the shared PAB issue, you can place key addresses in a separate PAB, one you don't normally use with your default profile. Then either mail that PAB to other users or tell them where to find it on the LAN. They can import that PAB into their own PABs by using File, Import in the Exchange Viewer window.

You also can use the Exchange Viewer's File, Import to add addresses from your old Microsoft Mail .mmf file. If you've migrated to Exchange Server, however, those addresses may no longer be valid. If you imported addresses from an .mmf file that were created with the fax option under Windows for Workgroups, you should examine those addresses, too, and make sure the numbers are entered in the proper international format.

It is possible to import to the PAB from other address sources, though it's not easy. Microsoft Word 7.0 includes an AddAddress macro function you can use to transfer address information into the PAB. Examples of such macros are included on the CD for this book.

If you have Word 7.0, export is pretty easy. You can use the mail-merge function, as described in the next section, to create a comma-delimited file that almost any database or PIM program (including Schedule+) should be able to use.

Another way to move addresses from the PAB to Schedule+ is with the Schedule+ Address Book Assistant, another utility included on the book's CD.

Printing PAB Addresses

Printing a copy of your PAB is surprisingly easy if you have Microsoft Word. You do the printing with a mail merge; we don't have space here for a detailed explanation of the process, but you can follow this outline:

1. In Word, choose Tools, Mail Merge.

2. In the Mail Merge Helper dialog box, choose Create, Catalog (assuming you don't already have a mail-merge main document prepared).

3. Choose either to use the Active Window or to create a New Main Document.

4. Choose Get Data, Use Address Book, select the Personal Address Book, then click OK. (Notice that you also can use the Schedule+ Contacts List as an address book in Word.)

Printing a copy of your PAB is surprisingly easy if you have Microsoft Word. Several other programs can also print the PAB.

5. Edit the main document created in step 2 to add the mail-merge fields from the PAB that you want to see in your printout.

6. Choose <u>T</u>ools, Mail Me<u>r</u>ge to return to the Mail Merge Helper. Then choose <u>Q</u>uery Options to filter and sort the PAB. For example, you can print just Microsoft Fax addresses by filtering for Email_Address_Type equal to FAX.

7. On the Mail Merge Help, start the merge by clicking the <u>M</u>erge button.

8. On the Merge window, select where you want to merge, how many records to use in the merge, and the blank line parameters. Click the <u>M</u>erge button to complete the merge and create the address list.

The format of the main document is up to you. Display the addresses in two or three columns if you like. You also can use this technique to create a comma-separated list that can be imported into the Schedule+ Contacts List. Once you've successfully created a main document, save it for future PAB printings.

Several other programs, including Sidekick 95, WinFax PRO 7.0, and Crystal Reports, also have the ability to display and print the PAB. Crystal Reports for Exchange is available for download as part of the Exchange Resource Kit (see Appendix B, "Exchange Resources").

Caution

Microsoft Word 7.0 also can open the PAB directly as a table. This approach is dangerous, however, because if you overwrite the PAB by saving it from Word, you can never use it in Exchange again. It's far better to use the mail-merge technique to get at the PAB data. Or if you feel you must open the PAB directly, save it immediately under a new file name before AutoSave kicks in.

Tips and Tricks

To finish up this chapter, let's learn how to switch between Personal Address Books, how to create nicknames to help you enter addresses quickly, and how to use a different kind of personal address list that comes with WordPerfect.

Switching PABs Without Restarting Exchange

Even though only one PAB is allowed in your Exchange profile, you can switch PABs on the fly, without closing Exchange and restarting it. Here's one way to do it:

1. Choose Tools, Services.
2. On the Services dialog box, select Personal Address Book, then click the Properties button.
3. Under Path, enter the path and file name for a different address book.
4. Click OK twice to make this address book your active PAB.

You also can change address books in the Address Book itself:

1. Choose Tools, Address Book.
2. In the Address Book (Figure 17.1), select Personal Address Book as the current address book from the "Show Names from the" list.
3. Right-click on Personal Address Book in the "Show Names from the" box, and choose Properties.
4. In the Personal Address Book Properties dialog box, enter the path to a different address book, then click OK.

Creating Nicknames with Distribution Lists

It doesn't take long for the Personal Address Book to get quite full, so full that it becomes inconvenient to enter just Rob in the To box and let Check Names do the work of looking up Rob for you. When your list expands to 8 or 10 Robs to choose from, it's time to take another approach.

One solution to the long list of similar names is to change the display name for an entry to use a nickname, such as RobC; but then that nickname would appear on the message. Instead, create a personal distribution list with just one address. Use the nickname as the name for the distribution list. Then put just the entry for that one person in the distribution list. Now you'll be able enter RobC in the To box and still send a message to Rob Cassandite with a dignified display name.

Adding Corel Address Books

An Exchange-compatible address book is included with Corel Office Professional 7 and WordPerfect 7 for Windows 95. The feature that will appeal most to many Exchange users is the capability to have multiple address "books" — and be able to switch between them in Exchange.

The Corel Address Book is installed automatically as part of the Corel Office Professional 7 or WordPerfect setup. To run it as a standalone application (Figure 17.13), click Start, then choose Corel Office 7, Accessories, Corel Address Book 7. If you don't see this option on the Start menu, run the Corel Office Professional or WordPerfect setup program again, choose Custom installation, select the Corel Address Book from the list of Required Shared Components, then complete the setup.

To create a new address book, maybe one to keep personal numbers separate from business contacts, start the Corel Address Book application. In the window shown in Figure 17.13, choose Boo<u>k</u>, New, then give the new address book a name in the Create New Address Book dialog box.

Figure 17.13
The Corel Address Book allows you to keep different types of contacts on separate lists.

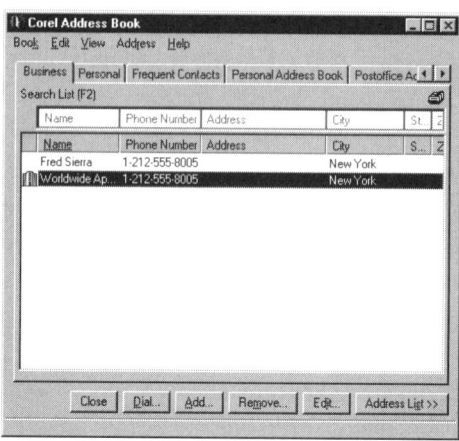

To make the Corel Address Book available to Exchange, add the Corel Address Book service to your Exchange profile (see "Adding a Service," page 79 in Chapter 4). This service is added to your computer as part of the Corel setup. You'll be asked to confirm the location of the address book database.

Once you've added the Corel Address Book to your Exchange profile, you'll find new address lists in the Exchange Address Book the next time you start Exchange. As you can see in Figure 17.14, there's a list for each of the address book tabs in the Corel Address Book — in this instance, Business, Frequent Contacts, and Personal.

The trick to making the addresses from the Corel Address Book work with Exchange is entering the correct e-mail address. To enter an address in the Corel Address Book application, click the <u>A</u>dd button shown in Figure 17.13. In the Properties for New Entry dialog box (Figure 17.15), notice the "<u>E</u>-mail address" and "E-mail t<u>y</u>pe" boxes. The type box corresponds to the entry types from the Exchange Personal Address Book, while the address box contains the address in the proper format for that type. Refer to Table 11.2 on page 253 for the different address types and their syntax.

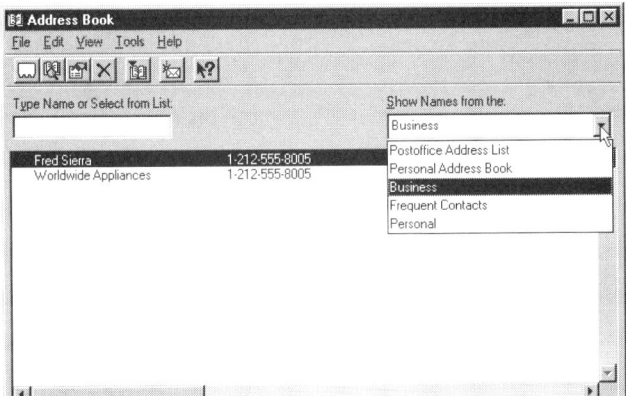

Figure 17.14
Each address book tab in the Corel Address Book appears as a separate address list in the Exchange Address Book.

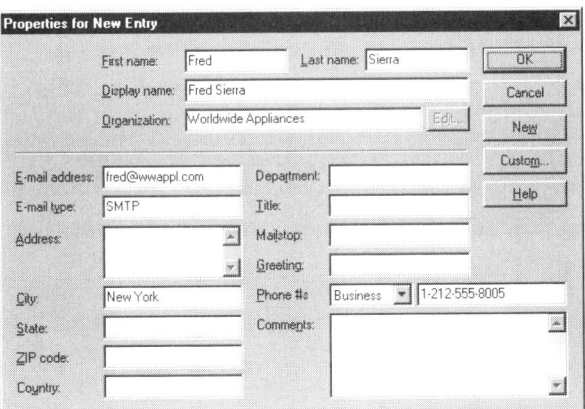

Figure 17.15
You must manually enter the correct "E-mail type" if you want Corel addresses to work with Exchange.

In this example, we're adding an Internet address. The type is SMTP, and the address follows the *name@domain* format. We'll be able to pick this recipient from the Business address book in Exchange and send messages to him or her, because the address is in the correct format.

The Corel Address Book has many other features, including integration with the Corel Office Professional 7 suite and the ability to add new addresses from within Exchange. It's definitely worth checking out, especially if Word-Perfect is your favorite word processing program.

Summary

Several different types of address lists are available in the Address Book. The addresses you use most belong in your PAB, which you control and maintain. When you need to send a message to a group of people, you can create a distribution list mixing addresses from the PAB, from other address lists, and addresses entered just for the list. Exchange Server users will find that their Global Address List contains not just people, but also public folders.

Key Points

- The Address Book is a collection of address lists, both personal lists and those belonging to your organization.
- A profile can contain only one Personal Address Book (PAB).
- Different information services may add address-list functions to your profile.
- You can't change your own Microsoft Exchange Server address details; those changes must be made by the system administrator.
- You must have a separate PAB entry for each type of address; for example, for Internet Mail and Microsoft Fax.
- There is no direct import to or export from the PAB, but workarounds are available.
- Printing a copy of your PAB is surprisingly easy if you have Microsoft Word 7.0. Several other programs can also print the PAB.

For More Information

Chapter 11, "Sending E-Mail Messages," contains more details about the many ways you can enter an address in a new message, both with and without the Address Book.

If you plan to use Microsoft Fax, see Chapter 14, "Sending Faxes," for information about entering fax addresses.

Several Personal Address Book utilities are included on the CD (see Appendix A, "CD Contents") or are available from other sources (see Appendix B, "Exchange Resources").

If you need to send messages while you are away from your office, see Chapter 13, "Working Remotely," to find out how to keep a copy of the Global Address List or Postoffice List on your remote computer.

The newest member of the Exchange client family, Microsoft Outlook, offers many address enhancements through the Contacts folder. You'll find more about these new features in Chapter 26, "Introducing Microsoft Outlook."

Chapter 18

Exchange Assistants

One of the most powerful and versatile features of Microsoft Exchange Server consists of a series of *assistants* that automatically process incoming messages based on rules and actions that you designate. The beauty of these assistants is that they can work when you don't! The Exchange server itself handles most rules, even when you are not currently logged on to Exchange.

It's important to note that the assistants are available only if you are using Microsoft Exchange Server, because the rules are stored on and processed by the server.

Introducing the Assistants

An assistant consists of a series of rules that define what happens to new items that appear in the folder.

Three different assistants are available with Exchange Server:

- Inbox Assistant — for managing new messages delivered to your Inbox
- Out of Office Assistant — for temporary responses and other actions related to messages received when you're not checking incoming mail
- Folder Assistant — for responding to items added to a public folder

An assistant for a folder consists of a series of rules that define what happens to new items. The first two, Inbox Assistant and Out of Office Assistant, work on the messages in the Inbox of your Exchange Server mailbox. You can invoke Folder Assistant for any public folder for which you have responsibility.

We'll look at a few examples of what these assistants can accomplish, then we'll explore how to build the rules that make them work.

Inbox Assistant

The Inbox Assistant can work not only on messages received via Exchange Server, but also on mail received through other services.

To use the Inbox Assistant, choose Tools, Inbox Assistant. The dialog box shown in Figure 18.1 appears. A check in the Status column means the rule is active. A red X means that an error occurred — such as an attempt to move a message to a non-existent folder — and that the rule won't be applied until the problem is fixed. If there is no mark in the Status column, the rule is disabled.

To get an idea of what the Inbox Assistant can do, think for a moment about the kinds of mail you normally receive. There are messages from your subordinates, from members of teams or working groups to which you belong, and from your immediate supervisor. Other messages may come from clients or other regular contacts outside your organization — some of them perhaps strictly personal.

Figure 18.1

Inbox Assistant rules consist of conditions and actions that are applied when the rules are met.

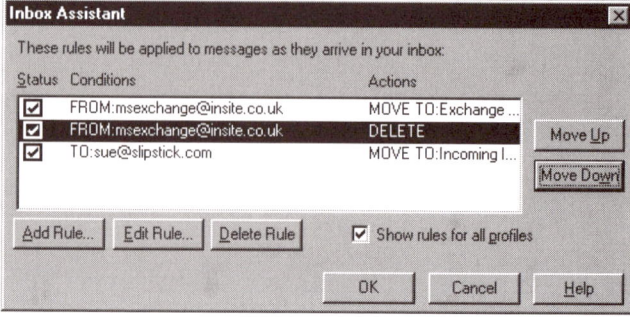

Sorting mail by the sender is one way to use the Inbox Assistant. You can devise rules to move messages into special folders in your mailbox created to hold mail from each of these people or groups with whom you regularly correspond.

Another way to use the Inbox Assistant is to scan either the subject or the message text (or both) for references to key words or phrases related to projects and issues important to you. Again, you might want to group such messages into special folders, but you also might want to send copies to other people working on the same project.

Yet another way for the Inbox Assistant to help you is to filter out "noise" in your mailbox. This can include any Not Read messages (read receipts from people who deleted mail without reading it) or other routine messages that you normally ignore. The Inbox Assistant can take care of deleting these for you.

The Inbox Assistant can work not only on messages received via Exchange Server, but also on mail received through other services installed in your profile. Two conditions apply, however:

- The profile must be set up for delivery to the Exchange Server mailbox, rather than to a set of Personal Folders (see the section "Delivery Settings," page 74 in Chapter 4).

- Inbox Assistant rules act on non-Exchange Server messages only when Exchange is running.

For an example of an Inbox Assistant rule of this type, see "Letting Everyone See Faxes in a Public Folder" in the "Tips and Tricks" section of Chapter 15.

Out of Office Assistant

To use the Out of Office Assistant, choose Tools, Out of Office Assistant. You will see the dialog box shown in Figure 18.2. The Out of Office Assistant works very much like the Inbox Assistant, with a couple of variations:

- The AutoReply function sends a standard response, such as "I'm out of the office until Tuesday," to everyone who sends you a message. Each person receives the response only once, the first time (s)he sends you a message while Out of Office Assistant is turned on.

- For rules, you should use only those actions that can be implemented by the Microsoft Exchange server. As we'll see, certain actions are specific to your profile or even to a particular machine and can run only when

Figure 18.2

The Out of Office Assistant works much the same as the Inbox Assistant, but the Out of Office Assistant also adds an automatic reply to each person who sends you a message.

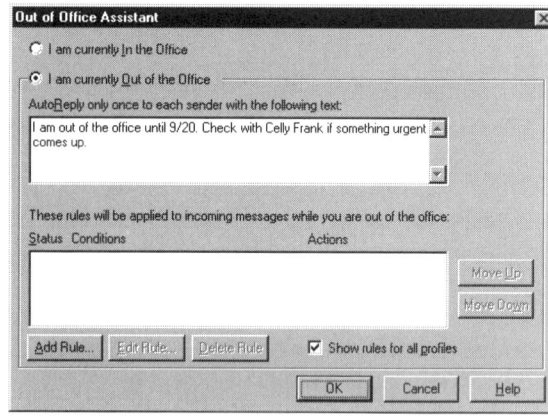

Exchange is running. You should not use those actions with the Out of Office Assistant.

To turn on the Out of Office Assistant, in the Out of Office Assistant dialog box, click "I am currently Out of the Office." Enter the text you want for the AutoReply in the box. If you leave the AutoReply box blank, people who send you messages while you're out will get a blank message back from you. If you don't want to send a reply (especially a blank one!) automatically, use Inbox Assistant rather than Out of Office Assistant to handle your incoming messages.

To turn off the Out of Office Assistant, click "I am currently In the Office." You'll also be prompted to do this when you connect to the Microsoft Exchange server if the Out of Office Assistant is currently turned on.

When the Out of Office Assistant is on, the Microsoft Exchange server tracks the addresses of everyone who sends you a message, so that each person gets only one copy of your AutoReply message. When you turn off the Out of Office Assistant, that list of people who got the Out of Office messages is cleared.

The most obvious use of the Out of Office Assistant is to alert your contacts that you won't be able to respond to their messages for a while. At the same time, you may want to forward particular messages to your assistant or a colleague. Others may need to be filed away in certain folders, just as you might do with Inbox Assistant. Another use is to selectively forward your mail to another account, perhaps an Internet mail account that you can access easily from any location you might travel to.

The AutoSignature default signature is not applied to Out of Office messages. If you want to include a signature, be sure to add it to the AutoReply text.

Folder Assistant

The Folder Assistant works only on public folders. This assistant functions much like the Out of Office Assistant, in that every action involved in executing a rule must take place on the server. These actions are available:

- Return to Sender
- Delete
- Reply With
- Forward

To use the Folder Assistant, follow these steps:

1. Select the public folder you want to work with (you must have Folder Owner permission).
2. Choose File, Properties, then switch to the Administration tab.
3. On the Administration tab, click the Folder Assistant button to display the Folder Assistant dialog box, shown in Figure 18.3.

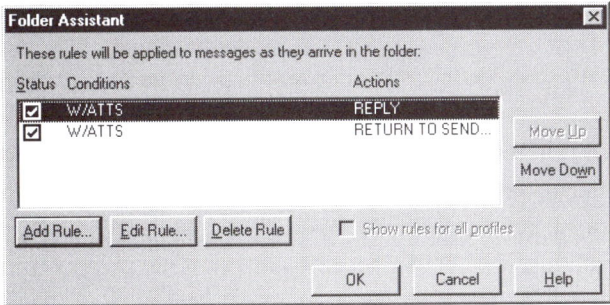

Figure 18.3
The rules for this folder reject any postings with attachments, returning them to the poster and also sending a message about the posting policy for the folder.

Building Rules

There are two parts to every assistant rule:

- a filter that determines what type of messages fall under the rule
- one or more actions performed on those messages

Each assistant dialog box (see Figure 18.1) shows the filters listed in the Conditions column, plus an Actions column. You can have more than one condition and more than one action in each rule, separated by semicolons.

There are two parts to every assistant rule: a filter and one or more actions.

To temporarily disable a rule, clear its box in the Status column. Re-enable the rule by checking its box once again. To add a new rule to an assistant, click the <u>A</u>dd Rule button on the appropriate assistant dialog box to display the Edit Rule dialog box shown in Figure 18.4. Enter the filter conditions in the top portion of the dialog box, then choose one or more actions from the bottom half of the box.

Figure 18.4

You enter the conditions for a rule at the top of the Edit Rule dialog box, and select the actions to be taken at the bottom of the box.

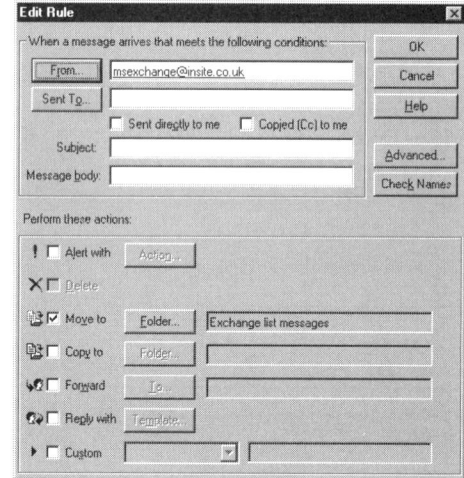

Testing Filter Conditions

We covered filters in Chapter 10, "Using the Exchange Viewer." When you are building rules, it's important to thoroughly test the filter conditions to make sure that a rule works with just a particular set of messages. This is especially true when you are sending automatic replies and forwards; you don't want people to receive unwanted messages from you. Also, if you subscribe to any mailing lists (see Chapter 22, "Working with Internet E-Mail"), take care to ensure that automatic replies are not sent back to the list.

Finally, you need understand how the resolution of From and Sent To names works. As we discussed in the section "Setting From and Sent To Criteria" on page 374 in Chapter 16, you need to use a resolved name from the Address Book if you want to use an e-mail address in a condition. To make that easy to do, the Edit Rule dialog box does include a Chec<u>k</u> Names button.

Note that a message you receive because the sender addressed it to you in the <u>B</u>cc box will not cause a rule to fire, even if you specify your own address in the Sent To box.

Understanding Server Actions

The assistants are one area where the client/server nature of Exchange Server is evident. Assistants are most powerful when rules are implemented to run when you are not connected to the server. However, it's critical that you understand which rules run on the server alone and which require some interaction with your Exchange profile or other settings on your computer. Where this additional interaction is needed, the rule does not run until you are logged on to Exchange.

Table 18.1 lists the actions available for Inbox Assistant (IA), Out of Office Assistant (OOA), and Folder Assistant (FA), along with details about whether the particular action can run when you are not connected to the Exchange server.

Some actions run on the server alone. Others require use of your profile and won't run until you log on to Exchange.

Table 18.1 Actions Available for Assistants

Action	Description	IA & OOA	FA	Runs When Not Connected to Server
Alert with	Play a sound or display a custom message	X		
Delete	Remove the item from the Inbox	X	X	X
Move to	Move the item to a different folder	X		Only if you are moving to another folder in your mailbox
Copy to	Copy the item to a folder	X		Only if you are copying to another folder in your mailbox
Forward	Send the item to another address	X	X	X

continued

		IA &		Runs When Not
Action	**Description**	**OOA**	**FA**	**Connected to Server**
Reply with	Reply to the sender using a custom message, which can also include additional recipients and attachments	X	X	X
Custom	Perform a custom action	X		
Return to Sender	Send the item back to the user who originally posted it		X	

Table 18.1 Actions Available for Assistants, continued

Custom actions are not included with Exchange Server. They are additional actions, such as printing a message, delivered in the form of .dll files that must be installed on your computer. Check with your Exchange Server administrator to see if any custom actions have been developed for your organization.

Note in particular the limitations on the Move and Copy actions. Move and Copy can run on the server only when the target folder is a private folder in your Exchange Server mailbox.

An alternative to Move — when your aim is to move an incoming message to a public folder — is to use Forward instead. To make this work, you need to be able to select the address for the public folder from the Global Address List or your Personal Address Book.

Considering Rule Order

You can combine more than one action into a single rule.

The order in which the rules run matters a great deal. To change the order of rules in an assistant dialog box (see Figure 18.1), select a rule, then click the Move Up or Move Down button to reposition the rule. Each item is matched against the list of rules in the order they are listed. If the item meets the conditions, the associated action occurs. Then the item is compared to the conditions for the next rule. This process continues until either all the rules have been applied or a rule with a Delete action causes the item to be moved to the Deleted Items folder.

Note in particular that a Move action doesn't stop the chain of rules. You can have more than one Move action apply to a particular item, putting it into two different folders. You might, for example, want to move items to two different public folders, one with a short purge interval and the other set up for long-term storage.

In most cases, you can combine more than one different action into a single rule (an exception is the Return to Sender action for public folders). However, you may find it easier to manage the order in which rules run by putting one action in each rule, using the same conditions each time.

Tips and Tricks

One of the best ways to learn about assistants is to look at some specific applications. Below you'll find several useful examples. Instructions are also included for making a backup copy of your Inbox Assistant and Out of Office Assistant rules.

Filtering Posts to Distribution Lists

Imagine you are a section chief and frequently receive messages sent to a distribution list of section chiefs. You also have occasion to post to that distribution list yourself. You might want to use a rule to keep the messages that you send to the list out of your Inbox (since you already have a copy in Sent Items). To do this, create a rule with the Delete action using the following for its conditions:

From	Your name
Sent To	The names of any distribution lists you are on (separated by semicolons)

Click the From and Sent To buttons to pick your name and the distribution lists from the Global Address Book. Or you can enter the names then click the Check Names button to resolve them against the Exchange Server address lists.

Using the Delete Rule and an Alert to Handle "Real" Mail

Let's say you have set up some clever Inbox Assistant rules to move messages from various mailing lists to special folders, thus organizing most of the several dozen messages you get each day. One thing you notice is that, even though those messages have been moved out of the Inbox folder to their own folders, you still see the envelope icon in the system tray indicating that you have new mail. The envelope only tells you that new, unread messages are available. It doesn't tell you whether they're in the Inbox or one of these other folders that you're moving messages to.

In this case, let's assume that you really want to know whether the Inbox itself contains any new messages — in other words, whether any messages have arrived that did not get processed by one of those Move rules you created.

You can handle this with an alert, either a popup message or a sound or both. There are two tricks to making this work. First, you need to add a Delete rule after the Move rule, but use the same selection criteria as the Move rule. The purpose of the Delete rule (even though the item has already been moved) is to stop processing of messages meeting the specified selection criteria.

Any additional messages — those that aren't processed by the Delete rule — fall through to a rule set to produce an alert for all messages. Figure 18.5 shows how this would actually look in the Inbox Assistant.

Figure 18.5
To keep a particular type of message from being processed by rules farther down on the list, add a Delete rule.

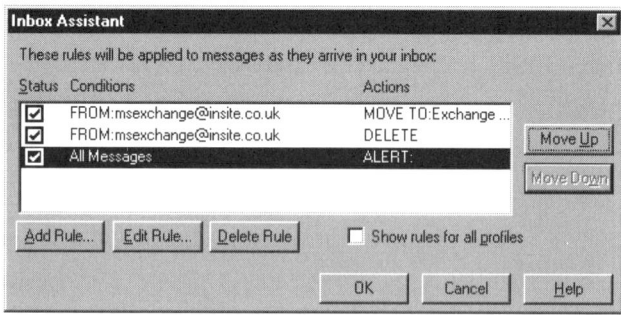

Forwarding Messages to an Internet Mailbox

If you travel, you may find it easier to get your mail from an Internet service provider (ISP) than to connect to your Microsoft Exchange server. You can set up Inbox Assistant to forward messages to your Internet mailbox, assuming your Microsoft Exchange server is capable of delivering Internet mail. You may want to do this selectively, however, to avoid racking up excessive connect time or long-distance charges to collect your mail.

To forward your messages, decide which mail to file for your return to the office and which to forward. For each type of message you want to file, set up two rules: one to move the message to a different folder in your mailbox, then a second rule to delete the item from your Inbox. Make sure the rules are listed in that order — Move, then Delete.

Then put a final rule at the bottom of the list that forwards the remaining mail to your Internet mailing address. This last rule will run only on those messages that have not been filed to other folders then deleted by the preceding rules.

Making a Copy of Inbox and Out of Office Assistant Rules

As you learned earlier in the section on "Understanding Server Actions," some rules depend on a particular Exchange profile being loaded. Wouldn't it be nice if you could copy rules from one profile to another? Even to a copy of Exchange running on a different computer? What about making a backup copy of your rules, just in case something ever happens to your mailbox on the Exchange server?

It's actually quite easy to make a backup copy of your rules and to copy those rules to another profile, through the use of a Personal Folders file. To copy your rules, follow these steps:

1. In the Exchange Viewer, choose Tools, Services.

2. In the Services dialog box, click the Add button, then select Personal Folders from the Add Service to Profile dialog, and click OK.

3. In the Create/Open Personal Folders File dialog box, point to the location where you want to create a new Personal Folders file. In the "File name" box, enter the name "Rules," then click the Open button.

4. In the Create Microsoft Personal Folders dialog box, enter "Rules Backup" in the Name box, then click OK. Click OK to close the Services dialog box.

5. Back at the Exchange Viewer, select the new Rules set of folders, then choose File, New Folder, and enter the name of your current profile in the "Folder Name" box. (If you use only one profile, use the name "My Rules.") Then click OK to create the new folder.

6. Select the new folder under Rules, then choose Tools, Application Design, Copy Folder Design.

7. In the Copy Design From dialog box, select the Inbox folder in your mailbox.

8. Check the Rules box, and clear the Description and Forms & Views boxes.

9. Click OK, then choose Yes when you're asked whether you want to continue.

10. Choose Tools, Services, select the Rules file, then click the Remove button to remove the Rules folders from your profile.

The rules from your Inbox are now saved as part of the folder in the Rules.pst file you just created.

If you use more than one profile, you can log on to Exchange with a different profile, add the Rules.pst Personal Folders file, then repeat steps 5–10 to make a copy of the Inbox rules for that second profile. Note that you won't be able to see the rules while they're in the Rules.pst file, nor will they fire on incoming messages.

To copy the rules from the backup Rules.pst file, you reverse the process. Here's how:

1. In the Exchange Viewer, choose Tools, Services.

2. In the Services dialog box, click the Add button, then select Personal Folders from the Add Service to Profile dialog box, and click OK.

3. In the Create/Open Personal Folders File dialog box, point to the Rules.pst file where you stored the backup copy of your rules, then click the Open button to add the Rule folders to your profile.

4. Select the Inbox folder in your mailbox, then choose Tools, Application Design, Copy Folder Design.

5. In the Copy Design From dialog box, select the Rules folder where you stored the rules for the current profile. (Hopefully, you named it the same as the profile, as suggested above.)

6. Check the Rules box, and clear the Description and Forms & Views boxes.

7. Click OK, then choose Yes when you're asked whether you want to continue.

8. Choose Tools, Services, select the Rules file, then click the Remove button to remove the Rules folders from your profile.

9. Choose Tools, Inbox Assistant to view the copied rules and check the ones you want to use. Repeat with Tools, Out of Office Assistant.

Since you can copy the Rules.pst file to another computer, this provides a convenient way to copy rules from your desktop to your laptop computer or to demonstrate useful rules to another Exchange user.

Summary

Automatic processing of incoming messages is one of the big advantages of Microsoft Exchange Server. Inbox Assistant, Out of Office Assistant, and Folder Assistant can move, copy, reply to, and perform other actions on messages received in your mailbox or a public folder. For each rule, you can specify one or more actions. Rules resemble filters, and you should test the rules thoroughly to make sure the conditions are exactly right.

Key Points

- The Exchange assistants are available only if you use Microsoft Exchange Server.

- An assistant consists of a series of rules that define what happens to new items that appear in the folder.

- The Inbox Assistant can work not only on messages received via Exchange Server, but also on mail received through other services.

- There are two parts to every assistant rule: a filter and one or more actions.

- Some actions run on the server alone; others require use of your profile and won't run until you log on to Exchange.

- You can combine more than one action into a single rule.

For More Information

Other features exclusive to Microsoft Exchange Server are covered in Chapter 20, "Collaborating with Exchange."

For additional details about working with public folders, see Chapter 10, "Using the Exchange Viewer," and Chapter 17, "Working with Messages and Folders."

The latest version of Exchange Server makes it easier to work with rules from multiple profiles and to designate which rule fires last for a particular type of message. See Chapter 25, "Introducing Microsoft Exchange Server 5.0," for details.

Chapter 19
Using Exchange to Collaborate

E-mail is just one example of the many ways Exchange can help individuals and groups collaborate in their work. Groupware is the word generally used to describe such applications. This term usually denotes programs that go beyond messaging to add a structure to the basic processes of an organization. Some examples of groupware might include

- A program to route college applications to different departments (academic, financial, and so on) to verify details of the admissions process
- An application to track progress on a project and automatically request project updates at specific intervals
- A help desk system for tracking user or customer problems with detailed trouble tickets
- A system for responding to information requests from potential customers

All these applications can be built with Exchange, in some cases with just the tools included with the Microsoft Exchange Server service itself, starting with Public Folders, where information can be shared with either a small group or the entire enterprise.

In this chapter, you'll learn how to use and design public folders and how to share mailboxes and send mail on behalf of other users. Our discussion of groupware will continue in the next chapter as we extend public folders through the use of custom forms.

By the way, this chapter and the next one are for Exchange Server users only, because it's only with the full Microsoft Exchange Server service that you can share mailboxes, send e-mail on behalf of other users, design and manage forms for an organization, and take advantage of the many groupware add-ons emerging for Exchange Server.

Using Public Folders

Public folders are the foundation for the concept of Microsoft Exchange Server as a groupware application, or at least a base on which to build groupware. By placing information in a shared location and enhancing it with automatic assistants and powerful forms, Exchange becomes more than just a place to get your mail.

Types of Folders

Exchange Server public folders can be used for reference, news, discussions, and tracking applications.

Public folders come in many flavors, but we can classify them into several basic types:

- Reference — personnel policies, product literature, and other information that doesn't change frequently
- News — news feeds, messages from mailing lists, newsgroup messages, and other information that changes rapidly
- Discussion — topics and responses to those topics (and responses to the responses)
- Tracking — customer contact items and other workflow applications

Public folders can be organized by department, by geographic region, by product line, or in any number of other different ways. Take some time to familiarize yourself with the public folder structure in your organization (Figure 19.1 shows a fairly complex structure). Look for an area where you can create your own public folders to share information with your colleagues.

A variety of sample folder applications is distributed with Exchange Server to demonstrate different types of folders and to provide forms and folder properties that you can adapt to your own needs. One of these is the Getting Started Guide, which we examined briefly in Chapter 10 (see the "Grouping Messages" section on page 235). The sample applications are distributed as a

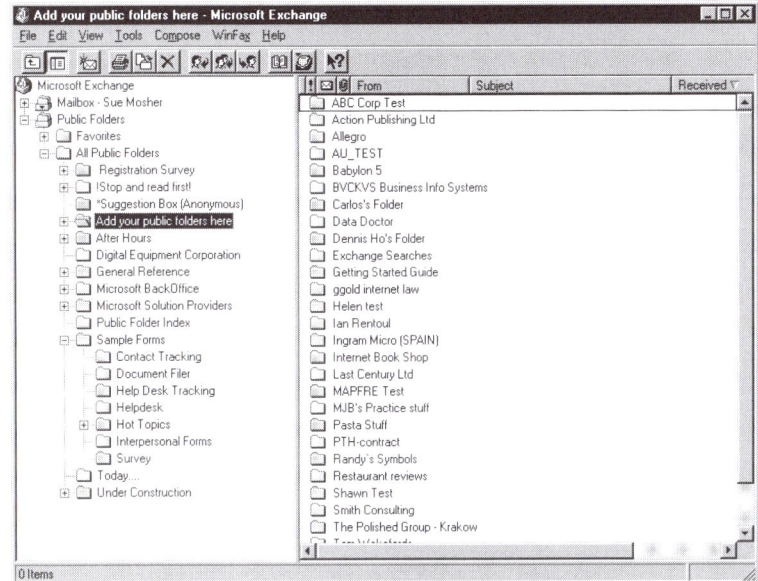

Figure 19.1
The public folders at this Exchange Server trial server (see Appendix B, "Exchange Resources") include many different types of folders, plus an area where users can experiment with their own folders.

single Personal Folders file. Ask your system administrator to point you to this file if the sample folders are not already available in Public Folders.

Working with Public Folders

The main Public Folders folder in the Exchange Viewer has two subfolders, Favorites and All Public Folders. Favorites, where you keep shortcuts to frequently used public folders, will be empty when you first start using Exchange. We'll look at the Favorites folder a little later in this chapter. For now, take a look at the folders under All Public Folders.

When you encounter a public folder for the first time, take a moment to explore. Look at the View, Folder Views menu and experiment with the different available views to develop an understanding of how the information in the folder is organized. Then take a look at the Compose menu. Here you'll find commands for posting items with the standard post form and any custom forms used in the folder, as we'll see in the next sections.

Posting and Replying to Items

Many public folders let you use the standard Exchange post form to add items. Choose Compose, New Post in This Folder to display the New Post form, shown in Figure 19.2.

Figure 19.2

The New Post form, which is used to add items to folders, supports rich-text formatting (RTF), just as the New Message form does.

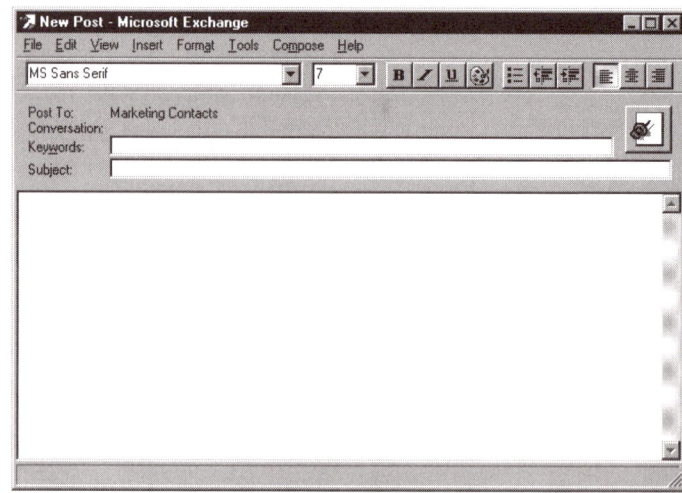

Notice how this form differs from the New Message form:

- There's no <u>T</u>o or <u>C</u>c field.
- A Key<u>w</u>ords field is available.
- Instead of a large Send button, there's a large Post button on the right side of the window.

You can use rich-text formatting (RTF), attached files, and embedded objects in posted items with this form, just as in messages. The Key<u>w</u>ords field is useful mainly in folders that use keywords consistently as a way to organize the information. When you've completed an item for posting, either click the large Post button or choose <u>F</u>ile, <u>P</u>ost.

Posting with Custom Forms

Look on the Compose menu for different ways to post items and responses in a particular folder.

Many folders are designed to use custom forms to enter information in a more structured format that lends itself to more powerful views and Folder Assistant rules. Look on the Co<u>m</u>pose menu for choices available in any particular folder. Sometimes these choices depend on the item currently selected (or opened) in the Exchange Viewer.

For example, the Marketing Contacts folder in Figure 19.3 is based on the Contact Tracking sample application. First, you enter a company profile using the Co<u>m</u>pose, New Company Profile command and a special form. Then, when you select a company, a choice for New Contact Profile appears on the Compose menu.

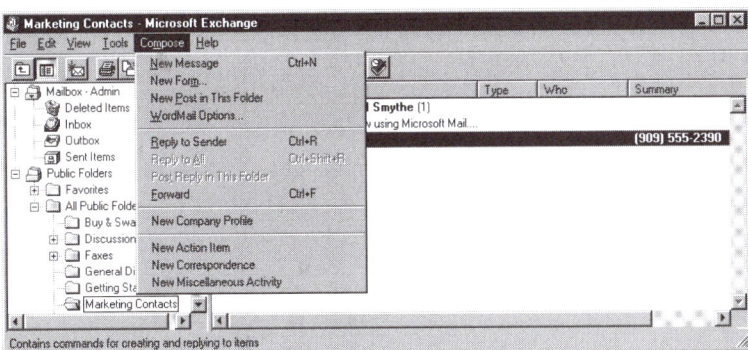

Figure 19.3
Custom forms for a folder are listed at the bottom of the Compose menu.

Finally, when you select a contact, three additional forms become available on the Compose menu — New Action Item, New Correspondence, and New Miscellaneous Activity. If you open the contact record, you also will see these three options on the Compose menu there. Each of these forms uses information from the Company Profile and Contact Profile forms. Figure 19.4 shows the New Correspondence form with the company and contact names filled in automatically.

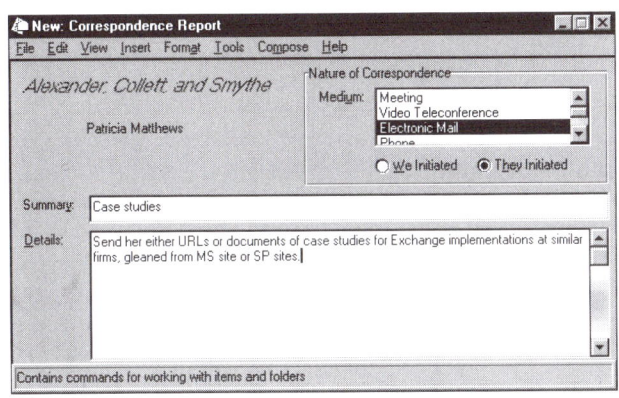

Figure 19.4
A custom folder form can include lists for you to pick from, text boxes to fill in, and a variety of other ways to enter structured information.

If you don't see a Post button on a custom form, choose File, Post to post it.

Using the Favorites Folder

After you've spent some time exploring a public folder, you may decide you'll want to return to it in the future. That makes it a good candidate for inclusion in your Favorites folder, which is a collection of shortcuts to various public folders. Adding a public folder to Favorites has several advantages:

- Navigating to the folder is fast, because Favorites doesn't allow subfolders. Therefore, there's no hierarchy of folders to traverse.

- Exchange keeps track of read and unread messages in Favorites folders, displaying them in bold if there are new items you haven't read. Exchange doesn't do this kind of tracking for the public folders under All Public Folders.

- You can synchronize the folders in Favorites with your offline folders, making it possible for you to access them even when you are not connected to Exchange Server.

If you need more information about setting up offline folders and synchronizing, see "If You're Connecting Remotely," page 90 in Chapter 5, and "Synchronizing Mailbox and Public Folders," page 308 in Chapter 13.

To add a public folder to Favorites, select the public folder, then choose File, Add to Favorites or click the Add to Favorites button. Note that when you add a public folder to Favorites, the subfolders are not added. In fact, Favorites allows only one level of folders. If you want to add a public folder and all its subfolders to Favorites, follow the above procedure to add each folder and subfolder individually.

To remove a folder from Favorites, select the folder, then choose File, Remove from Favorites.

Designing a Public Folder

Be sure to test all folder design elements before you release a public folder for general access.

Public folders generally include many design elements:

- Views
- Forms
- Folder Assistant rules
- Permissions
- Other public folder settings

You should test each of these elements before you release the public folder for general use.

Creating a public folder application can be a complex process. Extra help is available online in the form of cue cards (Figure 19.5) that guide you through each step of the process. To use the cue cards, choose Tools, Application Design, Folder Design Cue Cards.

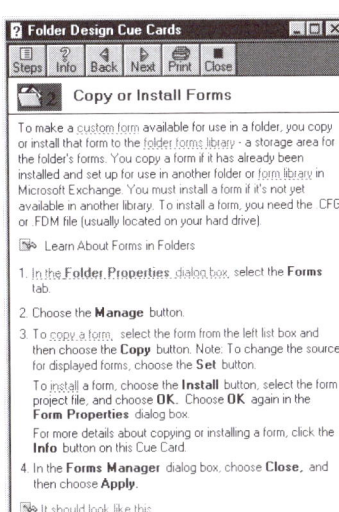

Figure 19.5
You can find details in a series of cue cards about the steps involved in creating a public folder.

In the next section, you'll see how some of the folder techniques you already know, such as views, are combined with other elements to create a public folder application. In the next chapter, "Using and Creating Exchange Forms," we'll look at the process of creating forms that can be used in public folders.

Creating a Folder

In Chapter 10, "Using the Exchange Viewer," you learned how to create a folder using the File, New Folder command. You also can create a new public folder by copying an existing folder using the File, Copy command.

When you copy a folder (see the upcoming section "Copying the Design from Another Folder"), any items, views, and forms the folder contains are copied; but other design elements, such as the initial view and permissions, need to be set separately.

Before you create your first public folder, check with the system administrator to find out where you have permission to create new folders. On some Exchange installations, you may not be allowed to create a new top-level folder (one immediately below the All Public Folders folder in the Exchange Viewer hierarchy); or you may be restricted to creating new subfolders only under certain public folders.

A new public folder automatically inherits two of the design elements from its parent folder:

- The name listed for the sender when items are copied or moved to the folder (see the "Copy/Move Behavior" section later in this chapter)
- Permissions (see the "Permissions" section later in this chapter)

When you create a public folder, by default the folder is available to everyone with the appropriate permissions. To restrict access to the folder while you're working on it, follow these steps:

1. Select the folder in the Exchange Viewer, then choose File, Properties.
2. In the Properties dialog box, switch to the Administration tab (Figure 19.6).

Figure 19.6

While you're designing a public folder, restrict access only to users with Owner permission for the folder.

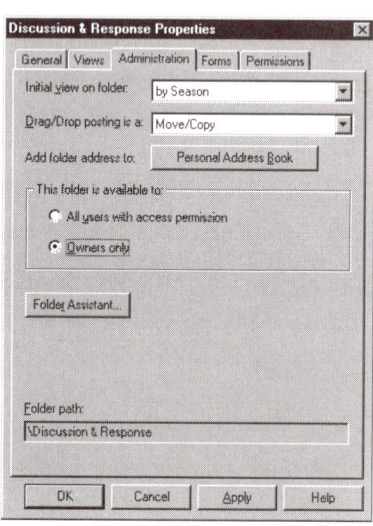

3. Under "This folder is available to," click "Owners only."
4. Click OK to close the Properties dialog box and return to the Exchange Viewer.
5. When you're ready to publish the folder, return to the Properties dialog box and click "All users with access permission."

Special Note

The "This folder is available to" setting doesn't affect subfolders. Users can still work with items in any subfolders, even while you restrict access to the parent folder.

Copying the Design from Another Folder

As noted above, copying a folder with the File, Copy command does not copy the entire design. But there is a way to copy the complete folder design — permissions, rules, description, forms, and views — in a single operation. Follow these steps:

1. Select the public folder you are designing (the folder you want to copy design elements *to*).

2. Choose Tools, Application Design, Copy Folder Design.

3. In the Copy Design From dialog box (Figure 19.7), select the folder whose design you want to copy.

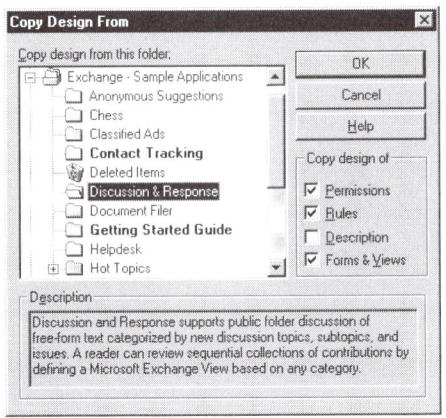

Figure 19.7

In this operation, we are copying the design of the Discussion & Response sample application folder to a new public folder.

4. Check the design elements (Permissions, Rules, Description, Forms & Views) you want to use in the new folder.

5. Click OK to complete the operation. You'll be warned that, in the event of any conflict between properties, the design of the folder that you're copying *from* will be used, replacing the corresponding properties of the folder you're copying *to*.

Once you have copied properties to the new public folder, you may want to check and update them, as described in the next section.

Setting Public Folder Properties

Public folders have the same properties as other Exchange folders, plus some new ones. Properties specific to public folders include

- The view that users see when they first open the folder
- Whether items copied or moved to the folder show the name of the original sender or the name of the person who moved the item
- Permissions for users to work with folder items and create new subfolders
- Folder Assistant rules (see Chapter 18, "Exchange Assistants")

All these properties are found in the Properties dialog box for the folder. To view the Properties dialog box, select the folder, then choose File, Properties (you also can choose Tools, Application Design, Folder Designer).

Name and Description

On the General tab of the folder Properties dialog box (Figure 19.8), you can change the name of the folder and enter a Description. While you might not add a description to a folder created in your mailbox or Personal Folders file, a public folder definitely needs one. The description should explain briefly the purpose for the folder and how the folder should be used.

Figure 19.8

The Description for a public folder should include a statement of purpose and brief instructions.

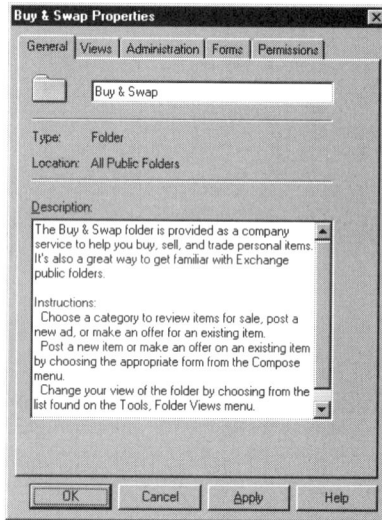

Views

Views for a public folder are created exactly as views for any folder are — on the Views tab of the Properties dialog box, which is shown in Figure 19.9 (see the section "Working with Folder Views" on page 240 in Chapter 10).

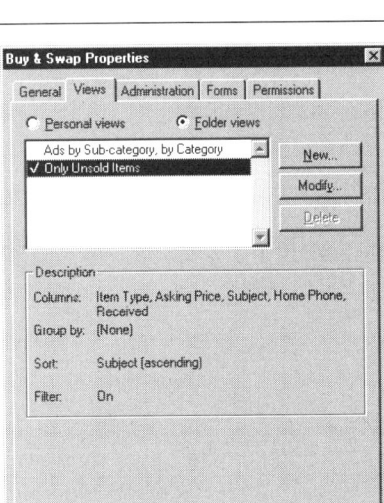

Figure 19.9

Include views that help users browse the contents of the folder in several different ways.

If the folder includes custom forms, you'll probably want to use some of the fields from those forms in one or more views. For example, Figure 19.10 shows a filter being constructed for the "Only unsold items" view, to show only those ads in the Buy & Swap folder that have No for the value of the Sold field.

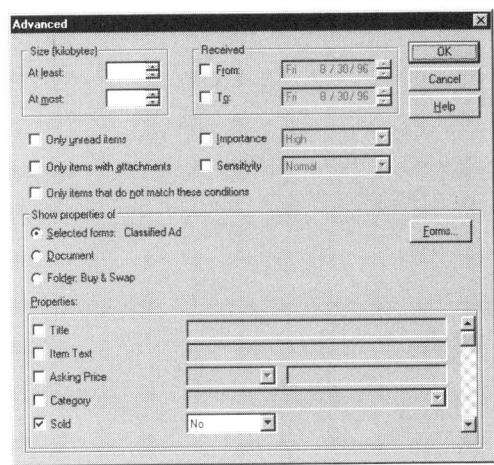

Figure 19.10

A field from a form associated with a folder, here the Sold field, provides yet another way to filter the folder items.

You can control the way users first see the items in the folder by setting the initial view. Switch to the Administration tab (Figure 19.11), and select the view from the "Initial view on folder" list.

Figure 19.11

From the Administration tab, you can set the initial view, change the behavior of moved or copied items, work with the Folder Assistant, and release a folder to all users with access permission.

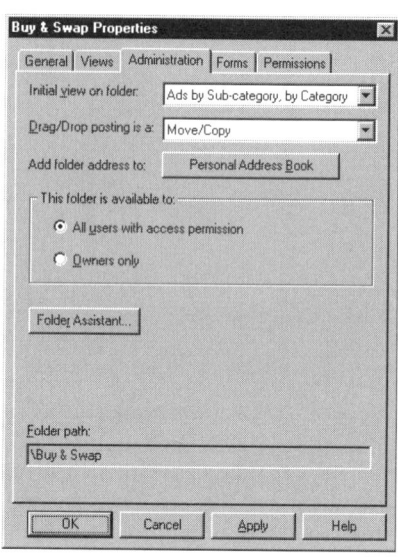

Copy/Move Behavior

Exchange lets you choose whether items copied or moved to the folder show the name of the original sender or the name of the person who moved the item. This choice is made on the Administration tab (Figure 19.11), with the Drag/Drop posting list (note that this affects any moved or copied items, not just those dragged to a folder). If you want copied or moved items to show the original sender, set Drag/Drop posting to Move/Copy. If, instead, you want copied or moved items to show the person who moved the item, set Drag/Drop posting to Forward.

Folder Assistant Rules

You set Folder Assistant rules from the Administration tab. Click the Folder Assistant button. See the section "Building Rules" on page 415 in Chapter 18 for details about constructing Folder Assistant criteria and actions.

Forms

Switching to the Forms tab (Figure 19.12) on the folder Properties dialog box displays the list of forms associated with the folder.

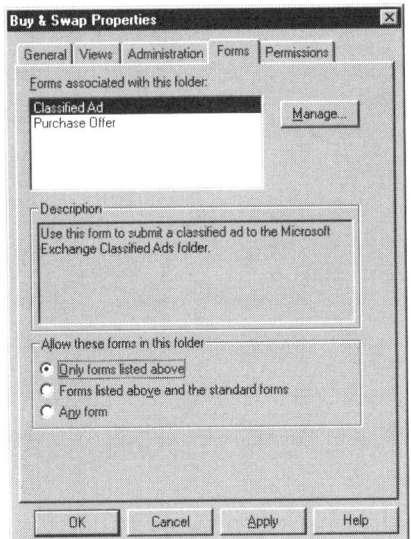

Figure 19.12

A folder may have one or more associated forms.

If you want users to be able to post items to the folder using other forms, then change the setting under "Allow these forms in this folder." For example, it may be desirable to have users add the folder address to their Personal Address Books, then send messages to the folder using the standard message form. In that case, you need to choose "Forms listed above and the standard forms" (which include both the standard message form and the standard folder post form).

Permissions

Access to the contents of the folder is controlled through the Permissions tab, shown in Figure 19.13. The most common permissions are grouped into roles, with Owner having the most control over a folder and None the least (in fact, no access at all).

The creator of a folder is given the Owner role, by default, and also is marked as the "Folder owner" and "Folder contact." The "Folder owner" permission grants authority to view and modify permissions for other users and to delete the folder. In a top-level folder, the default role for other users is Author. Other folders inherit the permissions settings from their parent folders. Table 19.1 lists the different roles and the permissions for each.

Two other roles are possible — None and Custom. Specify the None role when you want to prohibit all access to the folder. Typically, you might use None for the Default user if you want to assign permissions only to specific

Figure 19.13

Define permissions by individual user or by membership on a distribution list. Here, the Department Head distribution list has been given Editor permission, to allow the department heads to delete and edit posted ads.

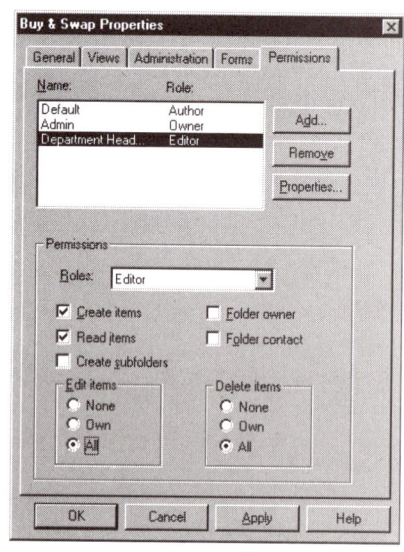

Role	Create Items	Read Items	Create Subfolders	Edit Items	Delete Items
Owner	X	X	X	All	All
Publishing Editor	X	X	X	All	All
Editor	X	X		All	All
Publishing Author	X	X	X	Own	Own
Author	X	X		Own	Own
Reviewer		X		None	None
Contributor	X			None	None

Table 19.1 Permissions for Folder Roles

users. The Custom role is automatically assigned when you select properties inany combination other than those shown in Table 19.1. For example, you might want to assign a group of supervisors the right to delete items, but not to edit them, so you can have a crew to clean up the folder from time to time.

To add a new Name to the list of users with permissions for the folder, follow these steps:

1. Click the Add button.
2. In the left column of the Add Users dialog box (Figure 19.14), select the individual(s) or distribution list(s) for which you want to assign permissions.

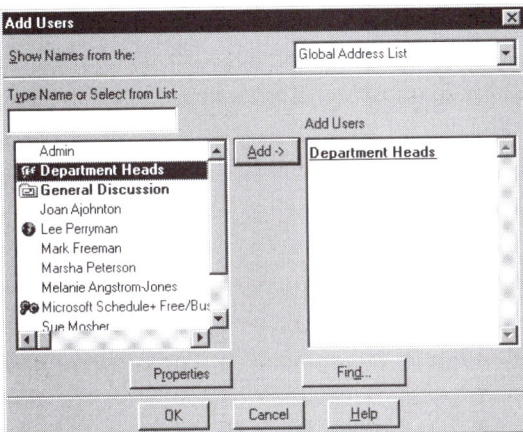

Figure 19.14
Other Exchange Server users in the Global Address List can be given permission to work with your folders, by either choosing the individual users or including a distribution list, as shown here.

3. Click the Add button to copy those names to the Add Users column on the right.
4. Click the OK button to return to the folder Properties dialog box.
5. Assign permissions for the new name(s).

To assign permissions to a group of entries in the Name list, select those names, then assign permissions. Remember that, to give access to anyone other than folder owners, you must switch to the Administration tab (Figure 19.11) and select "All users with access permission."

Special Note

A newly created subfolder inherits the permissions of its parent folder. But if you go back and change the permissions on the parent folder, that change does not trickle down to existing subfolders. Instead, you need to change existing subfolder permissions individually if you want them to have the same permissions as the parent folder.

Notifying Users About the New Folder

Once you've opened access to the new folder, you'll want to spread the word about it. Users who always work connected to the server can just browse the Public Folders area for new folders. Those who work offline, however, and periodically synchronize folders, won't see new folders. They see only those that are listed in their Favorites folder for synchronization.

Different strategies are needed, therefore, to make sure that remote users find out about new folders. These strategies are useful for non-remote users, too. Here are two suggestions:

- Create a New Folder (or Folder Index) public folder and encourage remote users to include that folder among their Favorites. Then post an item in this folder each time a new folder is created. Include a shortcut to the folder.
- Send an e-mail message with a shortcut to the folder to anyone you think might be interested in the information.

A shortcut makes it easy for users to find the new folder, particularly if you have a complex or large Public Folder hierarchy. To create a message or folder post containing a folder shortcut, follow these steps:

1. Select the folder to which you want to create a shortcut.
2. Choose File, Create Shortcut to create a new shortcut to that folder on your Windows 95 or Windows NT 4.0 desktop.
3. Create a new message, or switch to the desired folder and create a new posting.
4. Drag the shortcut from the desktop into the message.
5. Send the message or post the item.

Remote users still need to connect to the Exchange server, then use the folder shortcut to open the folder and use the File, Add to Favorites command to put the new folder in their Favorites list. They also can set the folder for synchronization (see the section "Synchronizing Mailbox and Public Folders" on page 308 in Chapter 13).

Sharing Mailboxes

If you have used Microsoft Schedule+ in a group context, then you're already familiar with the idea of sharing schedules by granting access to other users.

That access can be full access or just the right to respond to meeting requests on your behalf.

Exchange works in a similar way. Other users can be granted access to your mailbox — either full access or permission to send messages using your e-mail address. Here are some examples where this might be useful:

- An executive assistant might be granted full access to his or her supervisor's mailbox so (s)he can read and respond to any of the supervisor's messages.

- Members of a customer support group might both share a Support mailbox *to* which help desk forms are sent, and handle responses *from* that mailbox, rather than from their individual mailboxes.

- A sales group might share a Sales mailbox to which information requests are routed from the company's Web site. Sales representatives then might send responses from their individual mailboxes to establish a personal relationship with potential customers.

Granting Access

Setting up a shared mailbox, such as that for the customer service or sales group described above, is a task that must be handled by the Exchange Server administrator. This is done by giving each user's Windows NT account permission to log on to the shared mailbox. But you do have the power to give other users the capability to work with one or more folders in your mailbox or to send messages on behalf of your mailbox.

Granting Access to Mailbox Folders

To grant access to a mailbox folder, use the same procedure described in the "Permissions" section earlier in this chapter, where you learned how to set permissions for public folders. There are a few special rules for handling access to your mailbox:

- Anyone you want to have access to a mailbox folder must also be granted at least the Reviewer role for your mailbox itself. The Reviewer role provides the "Read items" permission. Without it, a user can't even see the folders in your mailbox, much less open them. Instead, the user sees this error message:

```
The set of folders could not be opened. You do not
have sufficient permission to perform this operation
on this object. See the folder contact or your system
administrator.
```

- Once you give a user "Read items" permission for your mailbox, that user will be able to see the contents of any new folders you create. This is because new subfolders inherit the parent folder's permissions. If you want to hide the contents of the new folder, you must edit its properties to revoke the "Read items" permission.

- If you want someone to be able to delete items in one of your mailbox folders, that user needs both "Delete items" permission on that folder and "Create items" permission on the Deleted Items folder in your mailbox. Without that permission, the user will see this message when they try to delete an item:

```
An item could not be deleted. You do not have permission
to create a message in this folder.
```

Granting Permission to Send on Your Behalf

To grant permission to send on behalf of your mailbox, follow these steps:

1. Choose Tools, Options, then switch to the Exchange Server tab (Figure 19.15).

Figure 19.15

One of the options for your Exchange Server mailbox is to give other users the capability to send messages on your behalf.

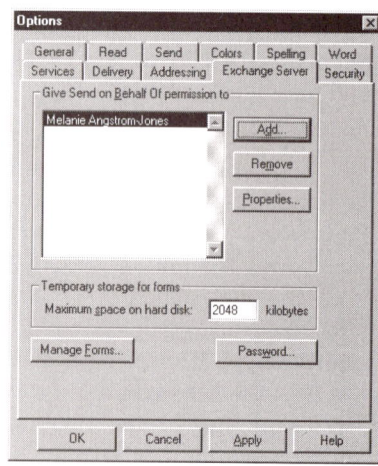

2. Click the Add button.

3. In the Add Users dialog box (Figure 19.16), select names from the left column, then click the Add button to move them to the Add Users column on the right.

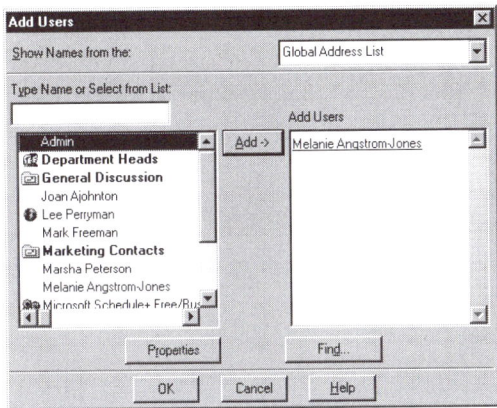

Figure 19.16
From the Global Address List, select those users you want to have the capability to send messages on your behalf.

4. When you've finished adding users, click OK twice to complete the process and return to the Exchange Viewer.

Understanding Send As vs. Send on Behalf Of

There are actually two different permissions that allow you to send from another mailbox. The procedure in the previous section grants Send on Behalf Of permission (the Exchange Server administrator also can grant this permission for a user). The other related permission, which can be granted only by the Exchange Server administrator, is called Send As.

The major difference between these permissions is that the Send As permission hides the name of the actual sender. When Joan Ajohnton uses her Send As permission to send a message as Melanie Angstrom-Jones, recipients see only Melanie Angstrom-Jones on the From field. There is no indication that Joan Ajohnton actually sent the message. On the other hand, if Joan Ajohnton has only Send on Behalf Of permission, recipients will see both her name and Marsha Peterson's name on the incoming message, as shown in Figure 19.17.

For public folders, only Send As permission is available. There is no option for Send on Behalf Of. As with mailboxes, Send As permission for a public folder can be granted only by the Exchange Server administrator.

Special Note

Figure 19.17

A message sent on behalf of another user shows both the actual sender's name and the name of the person for whom it was sent. Notice how the From column in the Exchange Viewer shows a message from Melanie Angstrom-Jones, but the message, when opened, is actually sent on behalf of Melanie by Joan Ajohnton.

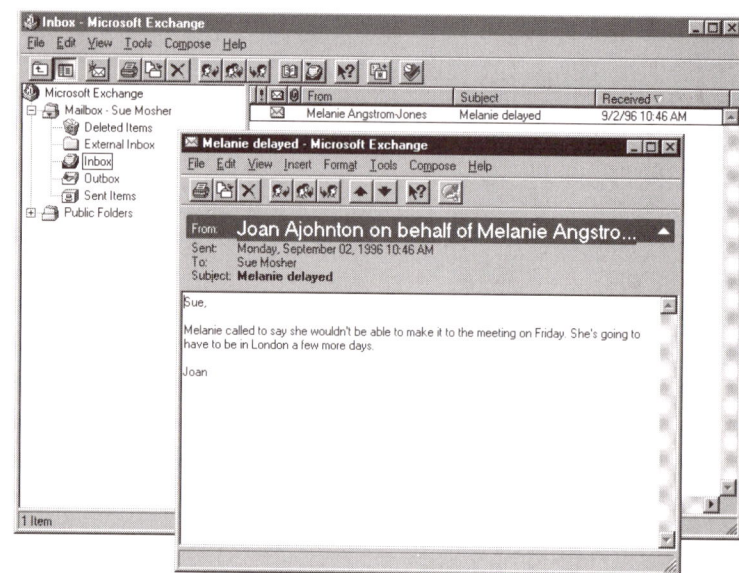

Sending for Another User

Send on Behalf Of shows the names of both the actual sender and the person on whose behalf the message was sent. Send As hides the name of the actual sender.

Regardless of whether you have Send As or Send on Behalf Of permission for another user, the procedure for sending a message for that user is the same. After you start the new message, follow these steps:

1. In the New Message window, choose View, From Box.

2. Enter the name of the person you're sending for in the From box, as shown in Figure 19.18 (or click the From button to select the name from the Global Address List).

3. Complete and send the message as usual. If you don't have permission to send for this person, you'll get a message to that effect.

Opening Additional Mailboxes

Sending for another user is one of two ways that Exchange lets you collaborate on e-mail messages. The other is to open another mailbox, so you can see the Inbox and other folders. Generally, when you are granted the permission to open another mailbox, you also get Send As permission for that mailbox (but you may want to check with the Exchange Server administrator to confirm that, because Send As permission does not *have* to be given).

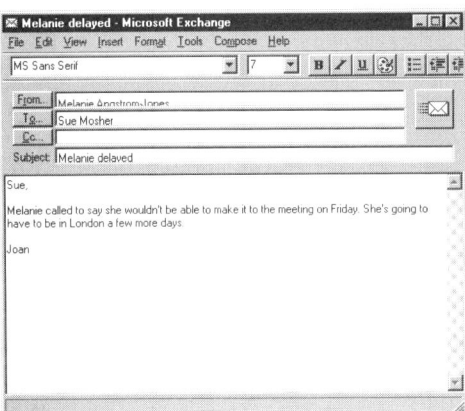

Figure 19.18
Use the View menu to display the From box to send a message for another user.

To add another mailbox to the current Exchange profile, follow these steps:

1. Choose Tools, Services.
2. Select Microsoft Exchange Server, then click the Properties button. Switch to the Advanced tab (Figure 19.19).

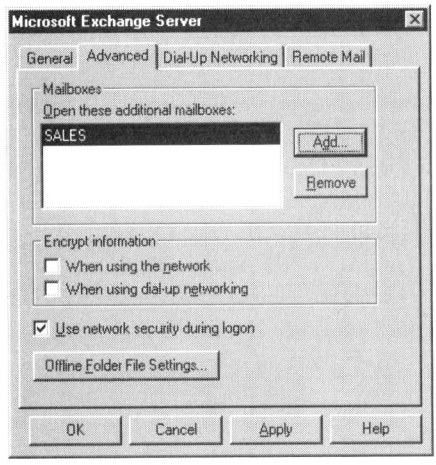

Figure 19.19
The capability to open additional mailboxes is one of the properties for the Microsoft Exchange Server service in your Exchange profile.

3. Click the Add button.
4. In the Add Mailbox dialog box, enter the name of the mailbox you want to open, then click OK. Exchange will try to match the mailbox name

against the Global Address List and, if successful, will add the name to the "Open these additional mailboxes" list.

5. When you've finished adding mailboxes, click OK twice to return to the Exchange Viewer.

When you add a mailbox to your profile, you get immediate access to the mailbox in the Exchange Viewer, as shown in Figure 19.20. It is not necessary to exit and restart Exchange.

Figure 19.20

With more than one mailbox open, incoming messages are sent to and from the main mailbox for the profile. That's the mailbox marked with an arrow, in this case the mailbox for Sue Mosher.

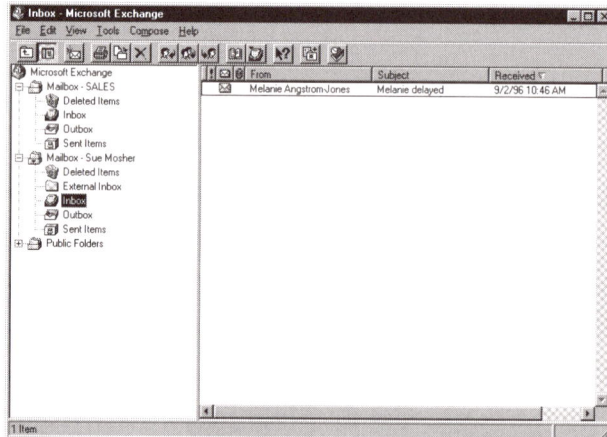

With two Inbox folders and two Outbox folders, how do you tell which one handles incoming messages for the profile? The mailbox marked with an arrow is the primary information store for the profile. Any messages addressed to you will still appear in this mailbox's Inbox, and any messages from you — even those sent for the other mailbox — will be sent from the Outbox for your mailbox. The Inbox for the other mailbox will show messages sent directly to the user for that mailbox; for example, to SALES for the mailbox shown in Figure 19.20. If you want to send a message for the SALES mailbox, you must display the From box and enter SALES there, as described in the earlier section "Sending for Another User."

Tips and Tricks

Here are a few techniques for working with Exchange Server Public Folders.

Designing and Testing a Folder in a .pst File

A public folder can be complex, with many elements that need testing before you make the folder available to users. One design approach is to create the folder outside the Public Folders hierarchy, test the views and forms, install the folder to Public Folders, then finish with the permissions, Folder Assistant rules, and other settings particular to public folders. With this method, you create the folder within a Personal Folders (.pst) file first. Here is an outline of the steps to follow:

1. Create a new Personal Folders file and add it to your Exchange profile (see Chapter 4, "Configuring Profiles"). You might want to call the file Applications or Folders Under Construction to distinguish it from other Personal Folders files.

2. Create a new folder in the Personal Folders file.

3. Either copy the design from an existing folder (see the previous section, "Copying the Design from Another Folder") or design the folder from scratch. Include filters, sorts, views, and forms.

4. Design your new forms and other items.

5. Create a new folder or subfolder under Public Folders.

6. Copy the design for this new folder from the one you designed in step 3.

7. Complete the design with Folder Assistant rules, permissions, and other Public Folder settings.

8. Release the folder for use by everyone with the appropriate permissions.

Of course, you also can create and design the folder under Public Folders, without first using a .pst file. There are, however, two advantages to doing the initial design in the .pst file:

- You can work on the new folder offline, when you're not connected to the Exchange server.

- You can e-mail the .pst file (or a link to it) to other Exchange users if you want them to review or comment on your folder design as it progresses.

Similarly, you could design and test the folder from within your Exchange Server mailbox. I prefer using Personal Folders, though, because that method lets you put away the project simply by removing the Personal Folders file from the current Exchange profile.

Notifying Users of New Public Folder Postings

Unlike folders in your mailbox or Personal Folders, the names of public folders under All Public Folders don't turn bold when they contain messages you haven't yet read. So how are you supposed to keep track of new postings? Or more importantly, how are users expected to learn about new postings?

Two different techniques are available, each suited to a different type of folder. For a folder that changes frequently, encourage users to add the folder to their Favorites folder. Read and unread items are tracked for folders in Favorites, causing those folders to turn bold when they contain unread items. Users can see at a glance whether there's something new they haven't read.

This technique also works, of course, for folders that don't change so often, such as a folder holding product literature. But for those, you might also consider a different method — using a Folder Assistant rule to notify users that a new item has been posted. To use this approach, follow these steps:

1. Create (or have the Exchange Server administrator create) a distribution list of people you want to be notified.

2. Have the Exchange Server administrator give your NT account Send On Behalf Of permission for the public folder.

3. Select the folder under All Public Folders.

4. Choose File, Properties, then switch to the Administration tab and click the Folder Assistant button.

5. In the Folder Assistant dialog box, click the Add Rule button.

6. In the Edit Rule dialog box, check Reply With, then click the Template button.

7. In the Reply Template window, enter the name of the distribution list (created in step 1) in the To box.

8. Under Subject, use "New Posting in," adding the name of the folder.

9. If you like, paste a shortcut to the folder into the body of the message.

10. Choose File, Save & Close to save the reply and return to the Edit Rule dialog.

11. In the Edit Rule dialog box, click OK, then respond Yes when you're asked whether you want the rule to fire for all incoming message.

12. Click OK twice to close the Folder Assistant and Properties dialog boxes and return to the Exchange Viewer.

Be extremely careful when you use this method, because it could flood the Inbox folders of users if traffic in the public folder picks up. Also note that the person who posts the new item also gets a copy of the notification sent as a result of this Folder Assistant rule.

Caution

Setting Age Limits for Public Folders

Actually, you can't set age limits for public folders yourself, but the Exchange Server administrator can. Setting an age limit causes all older messages to be automatically deleted from a public folder. While you wouldn't want a folder such as the Getting Started Guide or one containing human resources policy bulletins to have an age limit, you probably would want a limit on a folder subscribed to a newsgroup, news feed, or mailing list.

Summary

You've learned a lot about public folders in this chapter. You now know how to copy settings from another folder, set various properties, and make a folder available to all users with the right permissions.

In addition, we've explored a couple of ways to collaborate on mail messages, by sharing all or part of your mailbox and by allowing other users to send messages on your behalf.

Key Points

- Exchange Server Public Folders can be used for reference, news, discussions, and tracking applications.
- Look on the Compose menu for different ways to post items and responses in a particular folder.
- Be sure to test all folder design elements before releasing a public folder for general access.
- The Send on Behalf Of permission lets the recipient see the names of both the actual sender and the person on whose behalf the message was sent. Send As permission hides the name of the actual sender.

For More Information

If you need a refresher on customizing folders, return to Chapter 10, "Using the Exchange Viewer."

Remote users will want to learn more about synchronizing public folders in Chapter 13, "Working Remotely."

Chapter 16, "Working with Messages and Folders," contains valuable information about posting documents to folders and finding items in folders.

Chapter 20, "Using and Creating Exchange Forms," includes an introduction to the Exchange Forms Designer and shows you how to add custom forms to public folders.

Chapter 20
Using and Creating Exchange Forms

Continuing our discussion of groupware from the previous chapter, let's turn to forms. As noted back in Chapter 2, "What Is Exchange?", you use forms all the time, whether you realize it or not. The window where you compose a new message is a form, for example.

Forms can do more, though. They can gather information, display the same information different ways, and become interactive components of your Exchange strategy, making it easy for users to send information such as vacation requests or to post information in public folders.

In this chapter, you'll learn more about using forms and see how a simple form is constructed. Our tool will be the Microsoft Exchange Forms Designer, a program for creating electronic forms that is included with Microsoft Exchange Server.

Understanding Post vs. Send Forms

A **send** form can communicate with other users or public folders. A **post** form is used to put information directly into a folder.

There are two basic types of forms:

- *Post* — used to post information directly to a folder, usually a public folder
- *Send* — used to send information from one user to another or to a public folder as a message

Each of these forms comes in two varieties: forms used for new information and forms that respond to that information. For example, a send form to make new time-off requests might have a corresponding response form to approve or disapprove such requests. You access both types of forms through the Compose menu.

Using Post Forms

To use any post forms associated with the folder currently selected in the Exchange Viewer, look at the bottom of the Compose menu for New plus the name of the form. Figure 20.1 shows the Compose menu for a Buy & Swap folder that contains an option for New Classified Ad. Choosing this option brings up a form for posting a new ad in the folder.

Figure 20.1

Forms associated with a particular folder are found at the bottom of the Compose menu.

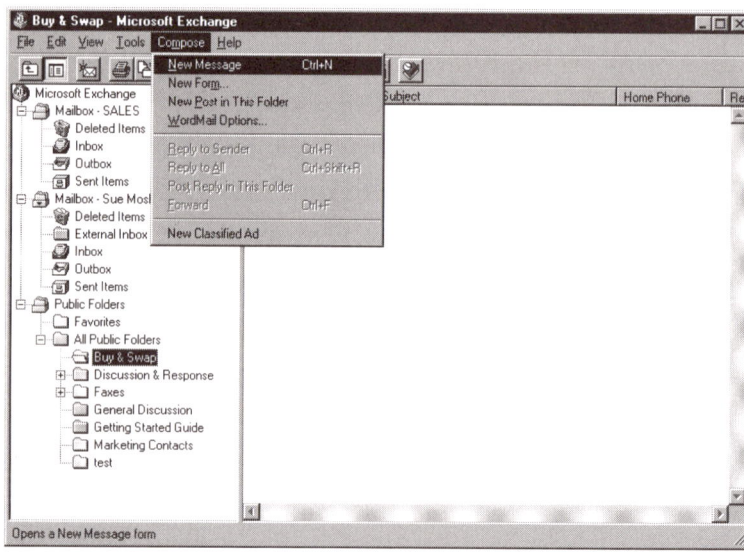

The first time you use the form, you'll see a brief message, Installing the Form on Your Machine, as the form is copied from the Microsoft Exchange server to your local system. This works the same for both the send and post forms.

When you have a folder form open, look for additional post forms on the Compose menu. These will be response forms related to the form you have open. Figure 20.2 shows an open Company Profile form with the Compose menu containing an option to create a New Contact Profile.

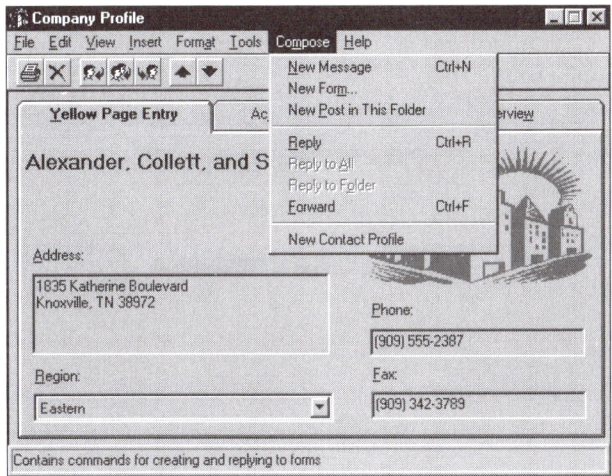

Figure 20.2
Forms that respond to other folder forms are also located on the Compose menu.

The Company Profile and Contact Profile forms are part of a Company Tracking folder included as a sample application with Microsoft Exchange Server. Ask your system administrator where to find this application.

Special Note

Some post forms will have a Post button. For others, you can post the form by choosing File, Post.

Using Send Forms

The purpose of a send form is to handle routine tasks more efficiently. For example, instead of writing a note to your supervisor requesting a week off, you might use a Schedule Time Away form to block out the desired week on a calendar. With a few mouse clicks, you're done, without the need to compose a detailed message.

Send forms are stored either in the Organization Forms library on the Exchange server or in your Personal Forms library (see the section "Managing Forms" later in this chapter). Send forms might include forms to request time off, to obtain a matching contribution for a charitable donation, or even to play chess with another Exchange user!

To use a send form, follow these steps:

1. Choose Compose, New Form.

2. In the New Form dialog box shown in Figure 20.3, use the drop-down list at the top to switch between Organization Forms (those installed on the Exchange server for everyone to use) and Personal Forms (installed directly on your computer).

Figure 20.3

Descriptions and icons for send forms help you decide which one to use.

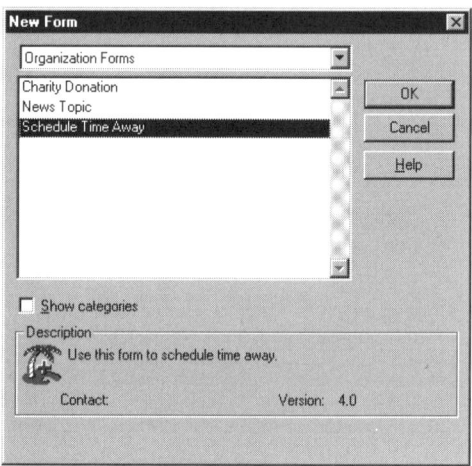

3. In the bottom list, browse the available forms by selecting each one and reading the Description at the bottom of the dialog box.

4. When you have selected the form you want to use, click OK. As with post forms, if the form has not been loaded on your computer, there will be a brief delay as it's copied to your machine.

5. Fill in the information requested in the form (as shown in Figure 20.4), including a To address, then use the Send button or choose File, Send to send the form.

If you want to partially fill in the form, then complete it later, don't send it. Instead, choose File, Save, then close the form. The form is saved in your Inbox, where you can open it later, finish filling in the information, then send it.

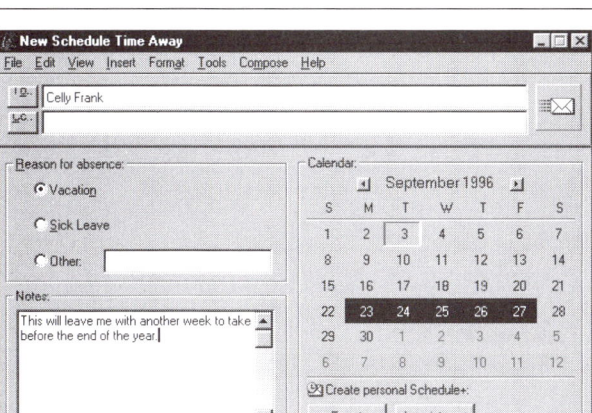

Figure 20.4
Use the Send button on this form to transmit the information once you've filled out the form.

Some send forms may open with the T<u>o</u> address already filled in. An example might be a form for posting information from news articles you've read to a Hot Topics public folder. Instead of going to the folder and using the post form there, you might find that the system administrator has provided a send form with the e-mail address for the public folder filled in. Check with your Exchange Server administrator to see what public folders use send forms as well as post forms.

Getting Started with the Microsoft Exchange Forms Designer

Now that you've seen how forms work, maybe you'd like to create one of your own. The tool you use to create forms is the Microsoft Exchange Forms Designer, which is a separate program. If Forms Designer isn't already installed on your system, get it from your system administrator, then run Setup.exe to install it. Choose the T<u>y</u>pical installation if you want to see sample applications created with EFD, L<u>a</u>ptop if you don't have room for the samples.

You do not need to be connected to the Microsoft Exchange server to design forms. You will, however, need to be connected when you are ready to install a form in the Organization Forms library (see the section "Installing a Form" later in this chapter).

Microsoft Exchange Forms Designer is a separate program included with Microsoft Exchange Server.

Creating a Form

To start the Microsoft Exchange Forms Designer, from the Exchange Viewer, choose T<u>o</u>ols, Applicatio<u>n</u> Design, <u>F</u>orms Designer. The dialog box shown in Figure 20.5 appears.

Figure 20.5

You can select a template either directly or by using the Form Template Wizard; or you can Open an Existing Form Project (.efp) file.

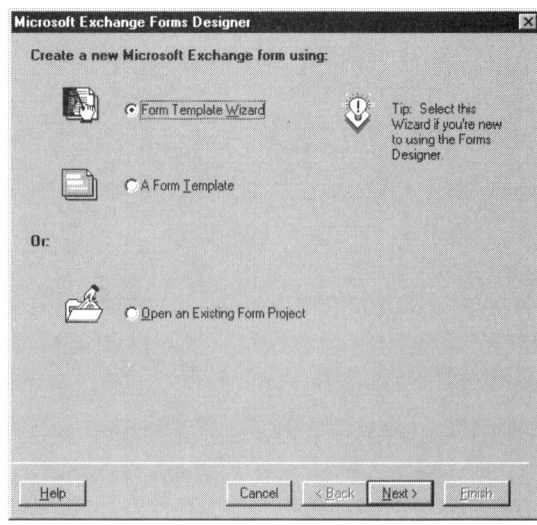

If you use the Form Template Wizard, you'll be asked to make the following choices:

• Whether to create a send form or a post form

• Whether the form will handle new information or a response

• Whether the form should have one or two windows. A two-window form uses one window for entering information and a second window for reading it.

• What you want to name the form and what description to use

This is actually such a simple wizard that I'd recommend you skip it and choose the template directly. The list of available templates is shown in Table 20.1. The file names include hints about the characteristics of each template. For example, if you want to create a send form for gathering information with a single window, look for the file name:

Snd	=	send form
n	=	new information
1wnd	=	single window

or Sndn1wnd.efp.

Table 20.1 Templates Included with Microsoft Exchange Forms Designer			
File Name	Post or Send	New Information or Response	Number of Windows
Pstn1wnd.efp	Post	New	1
Pstn2wnd.efp	Post	New	2
Pstr1wnd.efp	Post	Response	1
Pstr2wnd.efp	Post	Response	2
Sndn1wnd.efp	Send	New	1
Sndn2wnd.efp	Send	New	2
Sndr1wnd.efp	Send	Response	1
Sndr2wnd.efp	Send	Response	2

Figure 20.6 shows a basic one-window template for posting new information, and Figure 20.7 represents a basic send-form template.

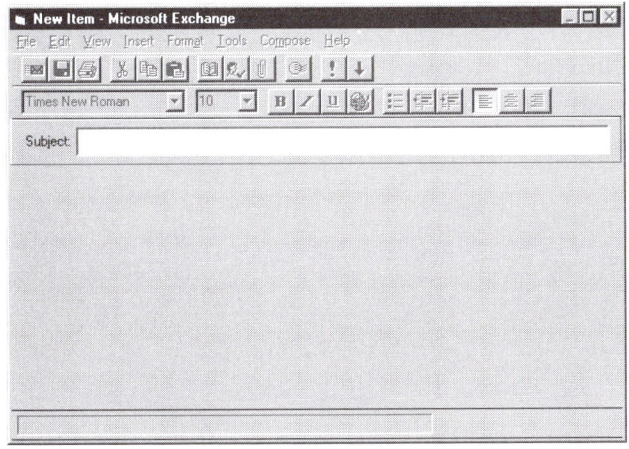

Figure 20.6

A new post form starts with just a Subject field. It's up to you to add other fields.

Figure 20.7

A new send form includes only fields for addressing the message and specifying a subject.

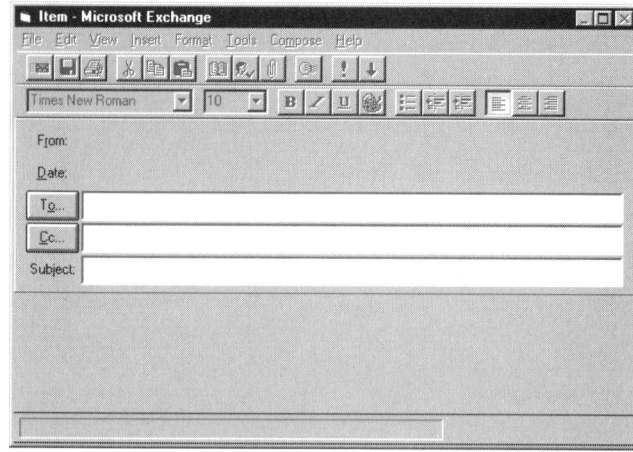

Once you've opened a basic template either directly or with the Form Template Wizard, to finish the form, you need to

- Add fields
- Set form, window, and field properties
- Install the form

You'll be working in the Forms Designer environment (shown in Figure 20.8), which includes three elements in separate, unconnected windows that appear over your desktop:

- The menus and toolbar at the top
- The toolbox at the left, which you use to add fields
- The form you're currently working on

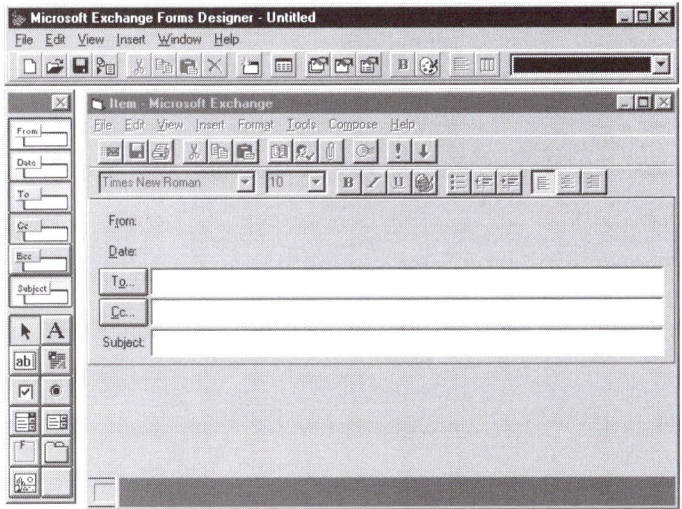

Figure 20.8
Build forms using the Forms Designer menus, toolbar, and toolbox.

Using the Toolbar

Table 20.2 lists the toolbar buttons and explains what each one does.

Table 20.2 Microsoft Exchange Forms Designer Toolbar Buttons		
Button	**Name**	**Description**
	New	Starts a new form project with a template
	Open	Opens an existing form project (.efp) file
	Save	Saves the current project as an .efp file
	Install	Compiles and installs the current project in a folder or forms library
	Cut	Removes the selected item or text from the form and copies it to the clipboard
	Copy	Copies the selected item or text to the clipboard

continued

Table 20.2 Exchange Forms Designer Toolbar Buttons, continued

Button	Name	Description
	Paste	Pastes the contents of the clipboard
	Delete	Removes the selected item or text from the form
	New Window	Adds a new form window to the project
	Insert Field	Adds a field from an existing window either in this project or in a different form project
	Form Properties	Sets the properties for the form
	Window Properties	Sets the properties for the current window
	Field Properties	Sets the properties for the selected field
	Bold	Formats the field as bold
	Field Appearance	Sets the colors and other appearance properties for the field
	Align Left	When two or more fields are selected, aligns them to the leftmost field
	Vertical Spacing	When three or more fields are selected, aligns those in the middle so they're equally spaced between the top and bottom fields

It's a good idea to use the Save button (or choose File, Save) right away to save the project. You will need to specify a folder and file name. Note that the Exchange Forms Designer is a 16-bit application. Therefore, you will not see the long file names or the Desktop that you're accustomed to under Windows 95 and Windows NT 4.0.

As you create your form, continue to save it occasionally. Not only does this protect your work from any possible computer crash, but it also makes it easy to undo a group of changes. If you don't like them, just close the form without saving it, then reopen the saved copy.

Using the Toolbox

You use the toolbox to add fields to the form. Fields provide a way to enter information easily and display that information in an Exchange Viewer column, as well as in the form. The toolbox is divided into two sections. The From, Date, To, Cc, Bcc, and Subject buttons at the top of the toolbox turn these message header fields on or off, always keeping them in the same order at the top of the window as you'd see them on a standard Exchange message. At the bottom of the window are buttons to select and add types of fields to the form. These buttons are described in Table 20.3.

Table 20.3 Toolbox Buttons

Button	Name	Description
�toolbar	Pointer	Selects fields by clicking on them. To select more than one field, hold down the Shift or Ctrl key while clicking.
A	Label Field	Adds a caption, instruction, or other text
ab	Entry Field	Adds a field for entry of unformatted text, usually a single line
🗐	RichEntry Field	Adds a field for entry of rich formatted text, such as a message or note
☑	CheckBox Field	Adds a check box for entry of Yes/No type information
◉	OptionButton Field	Adds a button that can be selected as part of a group. The first time you add an option button, a frame is also added to the form
		continued

Table 20.3 Toolbox Buttons, continued		
Button	**Name**	**Description**
	ComboBox Field	Adds a field where users can select from a list or enter their own value
	ListBox Field	Adds a field where users can select from a list
	Frame Field	Adds a rectangle
	Tab Field	Adds tabs to the form. Each tab can display a separate collection of fields
	PictureBox Field	Adds a picture to the form

The button at the bottom right of the toolbox is inactive.

Selecting Fields

To select a field added to the form so you can change its appearance or other properties, select the Pointer tool from the toolbox; then click either the field or its caption. For the header fields (From, Date, and so on), you can select only one field at a time. For other fields added to the form, hold down the Shift or Ctrl key as you click each field to select a group of fields.

An alternative way to switch to a particular field is to select it from the fields in the drop-down list on the right side of the toolbar.

Some fields may not be visible, because their background color matches the color of the form. Usually, though, the field is placed to the right of its caption. Clicking to the right of the caption is likely to select the field, even if you don't see it.

Example: Equipment Request Form

To demonstrate how to build a form, we're going to create a simple send form for requesting equipment. This is something you might find handy if your organization has a car, scanner, slide projector, or other equipment that everyone shares, but not so much stuff that you need to work out a complex scheduling system. The finished project file is included on the CD for the book in the Equiprpt folder.

The first step in building a form is to open a template. We've chosen the Sndn1wnd.efp template, which is a one-window send form for gathering new information. The blank template is shown in Figure 20.9.

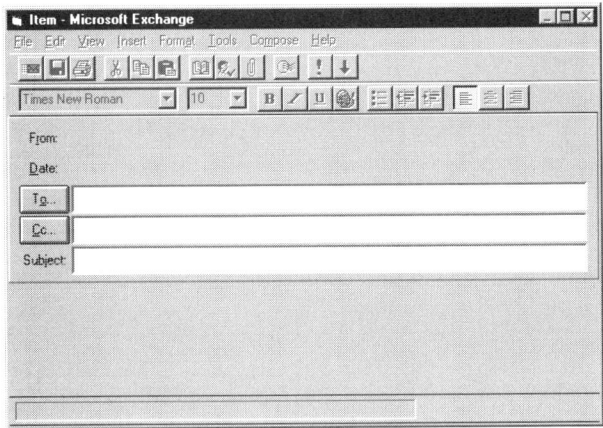

Figure 20.9
A blank send form contains only header fields, some of which you may want to hide in your project.

Setting Header Fields

The first task is to decide which of the message header fields to keep and which to remove. In this case, we want to see the From field, so the person approving equipment requests will know who's asking.

The Date field can be hidden on the form, so that it is available in the Exchange Viewer but doesn't take up space on the form itself. To hide the date, follow these steps:

1. Select the Date field.

2. Choose View, Field Properties or click the Field Properties button.

3. In the Field Properties dialog box (Figure 20.10), check the Hidden box.

4. Click the close button (the one in the upper-right corner with an X) to close the Field Properties box.

The Date field remains on the form as you're designing it, but will disappear when the form is compiled.

Because we want to be able to address the form to whoever is handling equipment requests, leave the To field in place. But we can do without the Cc field. To remove it, click the Cc button in the toolbox. This and the other similar buttons at the top of the toolbox toggle fields on and off. When you click

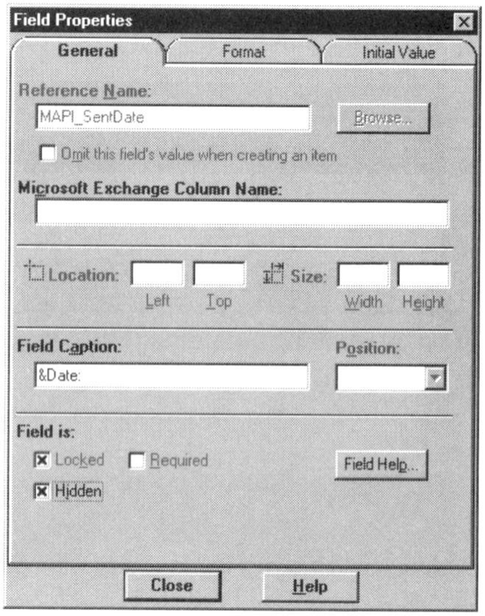

Figure 20.10

For a header field, such as the Date (specifically the sent date), most of the properties are determined by Exchange and cannot be set by the designer.

the Cc button, you should see the Cc field disappear from your form. If you want it back, just click the Cc button again.

To make this form as easy as possible to use, we don't want the user to have to fill in a subject every time. Instead, we'll make the subject always read "Equipment Request," then hide the field, as we did with the Date, so it doesn't take up room on the form.

To specify the subject and hide the Subject field, follow these steps:

1. Select the Subject field.

2. Choose View, Field Properties or click the Field Properties button.

3. In the Field Properties dialog box, click the Hidden box on the General tab.

4. Switch to the Initial Value tab (Figure 20.11) and enter the Subject "Equipment Request."

5. Click the close button (the one in the upper-right corner with an X) to close the Field Properties dialog box.

So far, the changes we've made haven't made that much difference in the form as it's seen in Figure 20.12. The initial values we've set aren't shown on the form as you see it in EFD, but they will appear when the form is compiled and installed. See the section "Setting Initial Values" later in this chapter for more on this subject.

Figure 20.11
The Subject field for a form can be preset by the designer.

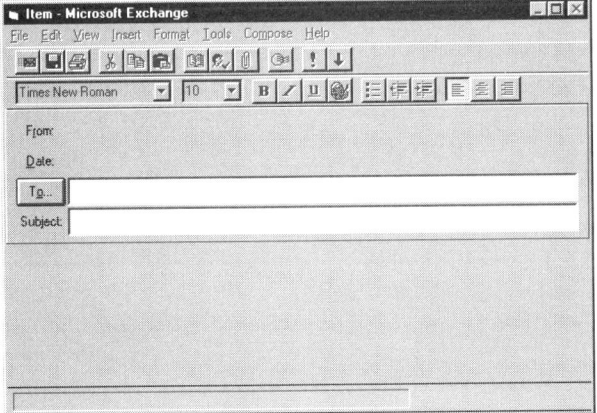

Figure 20.12
After removing the Cc field, we're ready to start adding new fields.

Adding Fields

To complete the Equipment Request Form, we need additional fields for more information on the equipment being requested, the date it's needed, the date it will be returned, and any notes about the request.

Before adding a field, think about the easiest way for users to enter the information you want. Here are some ideas to get you started:

- If the information is text that the user must type in, should it be simple text (Entry field) or richly formatted text (RichEntry field)? Another possibility is a combo box, handy if users often pick from a list; but there's an outside chance they'll need to type in a different value.

- If the information is a Yes or No answer, use a CheckBox field.

- For situations where you want the user to pick from a list (and it's a short list of two or three items), consider a group of OptionButton fields in a Frame. For a longer list, use a combo box or a list box.

Once you've decided on the type of field, select the corresponding tool in the toolbox, then click on the form where you want the field to appear. Let's add a ComboBox field where we can list the equipment that's available. As you can see in Figure 20.13, the Forms Designer makes it easy for you to

Figure 20.13

When you add a field, you get the immediate opportunity to fill in the caption for the field.

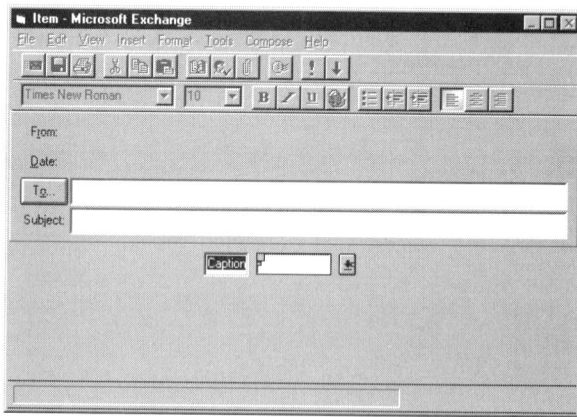

type in a caption for the field immediately, but you can skip that and edit the caption later if you prefer.

After you type in the caption, press Enter. The caption will move to the right or left of the field (depending on the type of field — see the section "Arranging Fields" later in this chapter).

There are a number of changes you can make to the way a field appears and acts by selecting the field, then choosing View, Field Appearance or View, Field Properties from the menu. (You also can double-click on a field to view its properties.) In the next two sections, we'll look at some of the properties you're most likely to work with. For information about others, you can always click the Help button in the Field Properties dialog box or press F1 to bring up the Windows help file for EFD.

Changing a Field's Format

To change the color and general appearance of a field, select the field, then click the Field Appearance button on the toolbar or select View, Field Appearance to display the appearance toolbar shown in Figure 20.14.

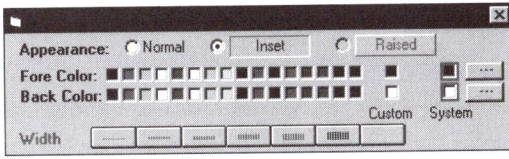

Figure 20.14

With the Appearance toolbar, you can change the colors for a field; give it a three-dimensional effect; and for some fields, change the width of the border.

When you finish making changes with the Appearance toolbar, put it away by clicking the close button — the small square box with the X through the center, located in the upper-right corner of the window frame.

You can make other format changes on the Format tab of the Field Properties dialog box (choose View, Field Properties, then switch to the Format tab). Figure 20.15 shows the Format tab for the Equipment Required combo box added in the previous section and shown in Figure 20.13. Notice in Figure 20.15 how you can switch between the properties for the Field and those for its Caption.

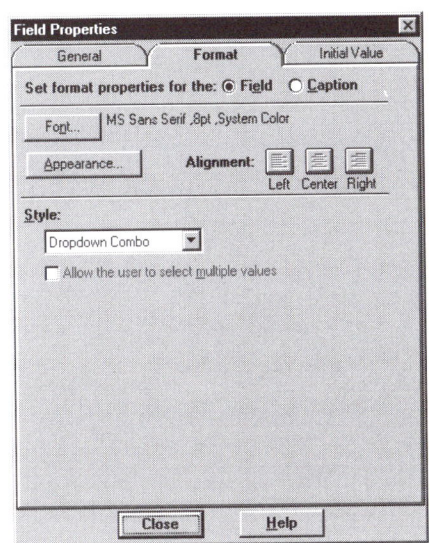

Figure 20.15

The font and other settings are part of the Format properties for a field.

To change the font, click the Fo̲nt button and make changes in the standard Font dialog box that appears. Clicking the A̲ppearance button displays the appearance toolbar, described above. For some fields, you can set the Alignment to Left, Center, or Right. You also can change the S̲tyle for some fields. For example, ComboBox and ListBox fields can be set as Standard List, Dropdown List, or Dropdown Combo, with the option to "Allow the user to select m̲ultiple values."

Setting Initial Values

As we saw earlier with the Subject field, sometimes you'll want to set the initial value of a field for a user. You do this on the Initial Value tab in the Field Properties dialog box. The function of the Initial Value tab varies depending on the type of field. For example, as we'll see in a moment, for combo and list box fields, you need to enter the values for the list. Table 20.4 lists the different kinds of information you can set as the initial value for each type of field.

Table 20.4 Initial Value Settings

Type of Field	Available Initial Value Settings	Default
From	Not available (always uses the sender or poster)	
Date	Not available (always uses the date sent or posted)	
Recipient (To, Cc, Bcc)	Any addresses from any of the available Address Lists	Blank
Subject	Text	Blank
Label	Text	"Label"
Entry	Text	Blank
RichEntry	Text	Blank
CheckBox	Checked or unchecked	Unchecked
OptionButton	Selected or unselected	Unselected

continued

Type of Field	Available Initial Value Settings	Default
Table 20.4 Initial Value Settings, continued		
ComboBox	List of values to be entered by the designer	Blank
ListBox	List of values to be entered by the designer	Blank
Frame	Not available	
Tab	Not available	
PictureBox	Picture file (.bmp, .wmf, .ico, or .dib file) selected by designer	Blank

Most of the time, of course, you'll leave the initial value for entry or rich entry fields blank, so the user can fill them in. Note that initial values are not shown on the form in the Forms Designer. They can be seen only in the compiled and installed form.

If you want the user to be able to see but not change the initial value for a field, switch to the General tab in the Field Properties dialog box, then check Locked.

Since we just added a combo box for Equipment Needed, let's switch to the Initial Value tab, shown in Figure 20.16, and add a list of the equipment that can be checked out. All we need to do is type in a list of the items under "Specify values in the list."

You can rearrange the list by clicking the Sort button to sort the items in alphabetical order, or you can use the up and down arrow buttons to change the order manually. If you want a particular item to be selected when the user opens the form, select that item, then click "Set selection to initial value."

Figure 20.16
For ListBox and ComboBox fields, you must specify the items for the list.

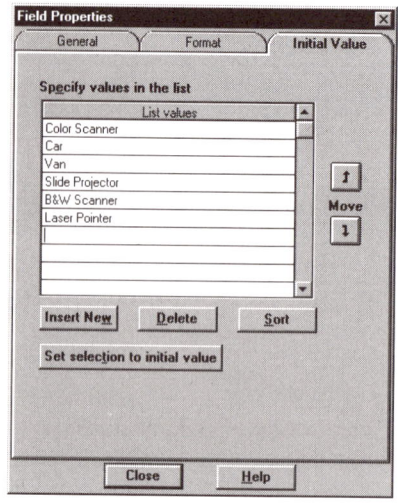

Arranging Fields

The Forms Designer does not include a positioning grid, so it's sometimes difficult to precisely move, size, and align items. The best approach is to place fields roughly where you want them to go, then reposition them. Sometimes you'll want to make position and size changes on the form itself. You may also want to try to make those changes on the General tab of the Field Properties dialog box. In Table 20.5, you'll find details about doing it both ways.

Table 20.5 Techniques for Arranging Fields

Action	Technique
To move (Method 1)	Click and drag to the new location. Caption and field can be dragged separately by the small square in the upper-left corner.
To move (Method 2)	Select, then choose View, Field Properties, and reset the Location on the General tab (Figure 20.17).
To resize (Method 1)	Select, then move the pointer over one of the small black square "handles" on the sides or corners until the pointer turns into a double-headed arrow. Then drag that handle until the object is the size you want.

continued

Table 20.5 Techniques for Arranging Fields, continued

Action	Technique
To resize (Method 2)	Select, then choose View, Field Properties, and reset the Size on the General tab (Figure 20.17).
To remove	Select, then press Delete.
To cut	Select, then choose Edit, Cut or press Ctrl+X.
To copy	Select, then choose Edit, Copy or press Ctrl+C.
To paste	Choose Edit, Paste or press Ctrl+V.
To line up fields along the leftmost edge	Select two or more fields, then click the Align Left button; or choose Edit, Align, Left from the menu bar.
To make fields equidistant vertically	Select three or more fields, then click the Vertical Spacing button; or choose Edit, Align, Vertical Spacing from the menu bar.
To move the caption to a different side of the field	Select, then choose View, Field Properties, and reset the Position on the General tab (Figure 20.17).

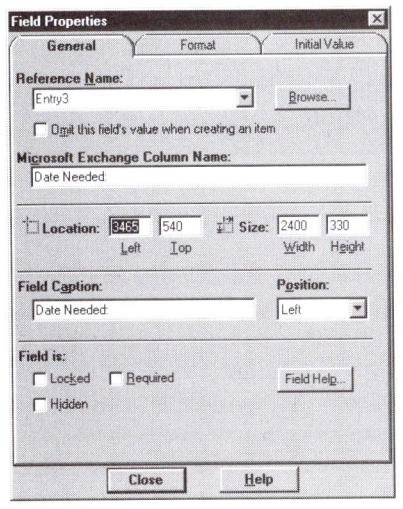

Figure 20.17

You can change the Location and Size of a field on the General tab, along with the position of the caption. You also can hide a field (check Hidden), make it read-only (check Locked), or require entry before the form can be sent or posted (check Required).

Position and size are measured in *twips*, rather than inches or pixels. A twip is a device-independent unit. Forms with size and location measured in twips look the same on all displays. A logical inch contains 1440 twips, while a logical centimeter equals 567 twips.

To complete the layout of the Equipment Request form, we've added three more fields, all text boxes, shown in Figure 20.18. Here's how we positioned and sized them:

First, we selected all four fields, then used the Align Left button to make them line up and the Vertical Spacing button to space them evenly on the form.

The Equipment Needed combo box was resized by dragging the handle on the right side to make it the desired size. We adjusted the size of the Date Needed box the same way, then displayed its Field Properties dialog box to check the exact size, which was 2400 twips wide and 330 high. The next step was to display the Field Properties dialog box for the Will Return text box and use those same values (2400 twips and 330 twips) for its Width and Height.

Like the combo box, the Notes field was resized by dragging a corner handle.

Figure 20.18

The entry fields are complete on the Equipment Request form.

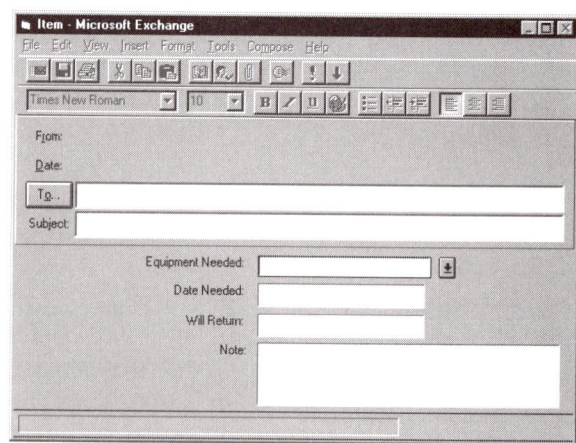

Naming Fields

The Forms Designer gives each field a generic name, such as Entry3 for the third Entry field added to the form. But applying a more descriptive name will make it easier to arrange fields in a convenient order for users to tab through, which is the next step in our design process.

To set the name for a field, bring up the Field Properties dialog box (Figure 20.17). On the General tab, enter the new name under Reference Name.

Setting Window Properties

Form windows have a number of properties of their own, many of which you don't need to worry about when you're just starting out. To work with window properties, choose View, Window Properties or press the Window Properties button. On the General tab of the Window Properties dialog box, shown in Figure 20.19, you'll want to change the Window Caption to something that describes your form.

Let's also look at the tab order and some of the appearance properties. You also may want to experiment with the Menu tab, but you really don't need to make changes there for your first form projects.

Setting the Tab Order

Still on the General tab (Figure 20.19), look at the Field Tab Order section. Fields automatically placed in the tab order are in the right column, under Fields in Tab Order. The other fields are on the left, under Available Fields. Use the left and right arrow buttons to move fields in and out of the tab order, then use the up and down arrow keys to sort the tab order until it reflects the way you want users to move around the form.

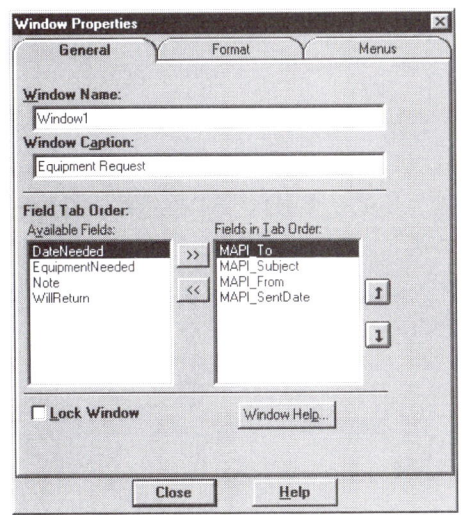

Figure 20.19
We've changed the Window Caption to "Equipment Request," which will appear in the title bar when users open the form. In the Available Fields list, notice that the fields have all been renamed to match their on-screen captions.

Because we want users to be able to move through fields from top to bottom, we'll use the following tab order for the Equipment Request form:

MAPI_To

MAPI_Subject

EquipmentNeeded

DateNeeded

WillReturn

Notes

We'll take MAPI_From and MAPI_SentDate out of the tab order, since the user doesn't see those fields. They're filled in automatically.

Setting Window Appearance Properties

Switch to the Format tab in the Window Properties dialog box to work with the appearance options shown in Figure 20.20.

Here are some of the properties you can set in this dialog box:

- Whether the user can maximize or minimize the form
- What toolbars are visible when the user opens the form
- The icon used for the window in the Exchange Viewer
- The background color for the form
- Whether or not the window can be resized

Figure 20.20

Change the form's overall appearance on the Format tab of the Window Properties dialog box.

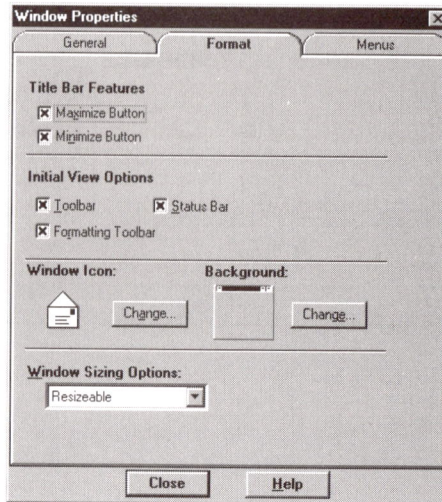

In this case, we're going to turn off the formatting toolbar, because the Equipment Request project uses only Entry fields, no RichEntry fields.

If you have more than one window in a form, each window can have its own icon. We'll set the form icons in the next section.

Setting Form Properties

Our form is nearly done. We just need to set some final properties — the form's description and its icon. Choose View, Form Properties or click the Form Properties button to display the Form Properties dialog box shown in Figure 20.21.

You should set the Form Display Name and Description, which will be shown in the forms and folder libraries. This also is where you set the icons for your form. The large icon is used when you minimize a form or switch to it with Alt-Tab. The small icon is used in the Exchange Viewer.

A number of icons are included with the Forms Designer. To change the icons for the form, follow these steps:

1. On the General tab of the Forms Properties dialog box (Figure 20.21), click the Change button next to the large icon image.

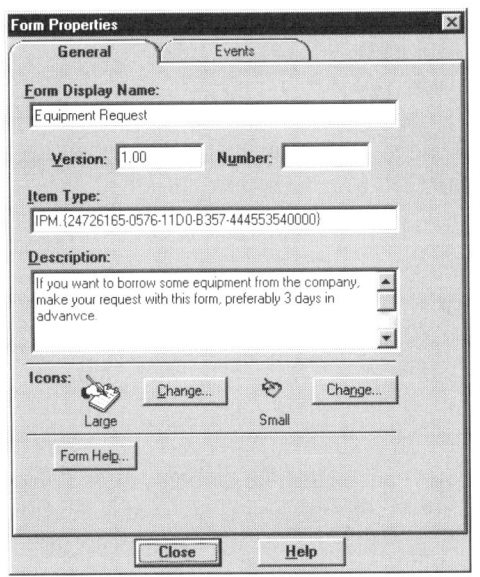

Figure 20.21
Set the Form Display Name, Description, and Icons in the Form Properties dialog box.

2. In the Select Icon dialog box (Figure 20.22), switch to the Icons folder under the folder where EFD is installed.

Figure 20.22

Icons come in two sizes, large and small.

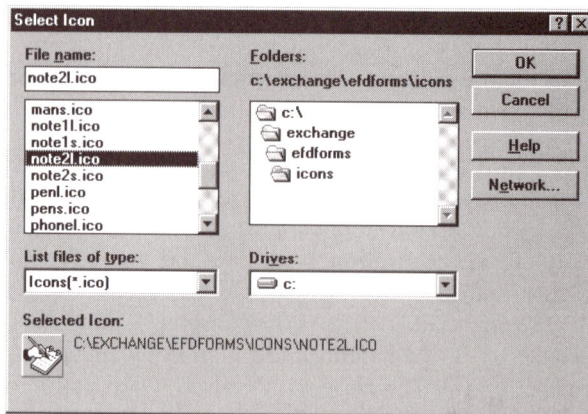

3. Browse the available icons listed in the box on the left. As you select each one, a preview of the icon appears at the bottom. Note that the icons have "l" for large and "s" for small at the end of the file names.

4. When you've selected the large icon you want to use, click OK to return to the Form Properties dialog box.

5. Click the Change button next to the small icon image.

6. Repeat steps 3 and 4 to select a small icon.

7. Click the Close button to save the new properties settings.

If you want to create your own icons, make them in pairs. The large icon should be 32 x 32 pixels; the small one, 16 x 16 pixels.

Saving the Form Project

It's time to save the project (actually, you should have been saving it all along). Choose File, Save As, or click the Save button, The final step is to compile and install the form, which is what the next section is all about.

Installing a Form

Forms can be installed in the Personal Forms library, the Organization Forms library, or a folder.

If you have just created a new form, you must install it from Exchange Forms Designer. For forms that have previously been compiled (as described later under "Installing from the Forms Manager"), use the Forms Manager to install the form.

In either case, you must decide on a destination for the form — the Personal Forms library, the Organization Forms library, or a folder. If you need access to the Organization Forms library or to a particular public folder, see your Exchange Server administrator.

Special Note

Installation of an updated form can affect the display of the information already sent or posted with the older version. A detailed discussion of the implications and possible solutions is beyond the scope of this book, but you can find that information in the MS Application Designer's Guide help file. This help file, **Appdesgd.hlp,** can be found in the folder where EFD is installed. It should also be on the Start, Programs menu on the Microsoft Exchange menu (or other menu you chose during EFD setup).

To install a form after working on it in Exchange Forms Designer, follow these steps:

1. Choose File, Install, or click the Install button.

2. You'll be asked to save the project as an .efp file if you haven't already.

3. The installation process generates code from your project, then Visual Basic for Microsoft Exchange starts and compiles the form. This process can take a few minutes, so feel free to grab a soda or a cup of coffee.

4. After the form is compiled, the Set library To dialog box (Figure 20.23) appears. For a form that will be used only in a particular folder, click Folder Forms library, then select the folder. For a send form or for a post form intended for use in a variety of folders, click Forms library, and choose either Personal Forms or Organization Forms. (A form like the Equipment Request Form would typically be placed in the Organization Forms library.)

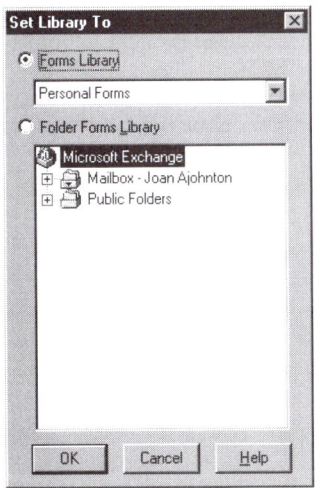

Figure 20.23

As part of the installation process, you must choose the folder or forms library where the new form will be installed.

5. Click OK to close the Set library To dialog box. The Form Properties dialog box appears next (Figure 20.24).

Figure 20.24

Update the form properties as needed as part of the installation.

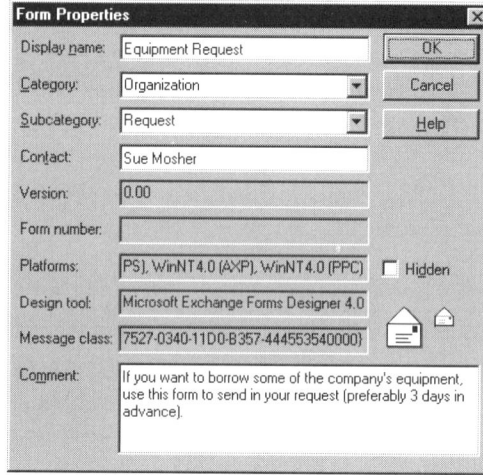

6. In the Form Properties dialog box, update the Display Name and Comment if necessary. It's also a good idea to specify a Contact, in case people have questions about the form. The Category and Subcategory are optional but can be helpful if your organization uses a lot of forms.

7. When you've finished updating the Form Properties dialog box, click OK, and the installation process will finish.

Caution

It's possible (but beyond the scope of this book) to modify forms with Visual Basic to add command buttons and additional code for more powerful functions. Forms that have been extended with such "hand coding" should not be opened in Exchange Forms Designer and installed from there. Instead, use the Forms Manager to install the compiled form using its .cfg file.

Once the Equipment Request form is installed in the Organization Forms library, anyone can use it by choosing Compose, New Form from the Exchange Viewer menu, then selecting the Equipment Request form from the Organization Forms library. As described earlier in this chapter under "Using Send Forms," this will install the form on your computer, then display it, as you can see in Figure 20.25.

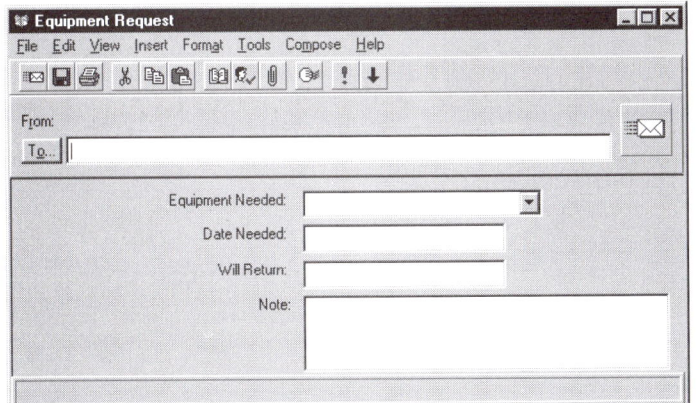

Figure 20.25
Here's what our Equipment Request form looks like now that it's compiled and installed. The Send button was added automatically. The From field will be filled in when a user actually sends a request with this form.

Managing Forms

The Exchange Server client includes a Forms Manager tool for installing forms, saving forms as .fdm files, and copying forms between libraries and folders. Another important aspect of managing forms is setting the maximum amount of space used for forms storage on your computer.

Allocating Space for Forms

You can control the amount of space set aside for forms on your machine. Exchange maintains a local cache of the most frequently used forms, up to the amount of space you specify. Forms saved in this cache load faster. Forms from the Organization Forms library that aren't in the cache must first be copied to your computer. To set the size of the forms cache,

1. Choose Tools, Options, then switch to the Exchange Server tab (Figure 20.26).
2. In the "Maximum space on hard disk" box, enter the size in kilobytes that you want to set aside for storage of forms.
3. Click OK to save the new cache size, which will go into effect only after you exit and restart Exchange.

When you fill up the forms cache, the oldest unused form is removed the next time you need to make room for a new form. The forms cache is located in the Forms folder under the Windows folder.

Figure 20.26

Limit the size of the EFD forms cache by increasing or reducing the number for "Maximum space on hard disk."

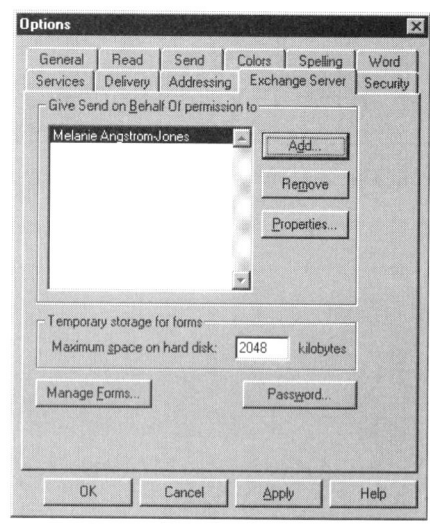

Saving Forms

A form that is saved as an .fdm file can be installed through the Forms Manager. This means you can save the form and e-mail it to a colleague, who can in turn install the form on his or her machine. This can be useful if you have a send form that you don't want to place in the Organization Forms library. To save an installed form as an .fdm file, follow these steps:

1. Choose Tools, Options, then switch to the Exchange Server tab (Figure 20.26) and click the Manage Forms button.

2. Click the Set button on the right side of the Forms Manager dialog box (see Figure 20.27).

3. In the Set library To dialog box (see Figure 20.23 on page 475), choose the library or folder where the form is located, then click OK.

4. Back in the Forms Manager dialog box select the form, then click the Save As button.

5. In the Save As dialog box, enter a file name and, if needed, change the location for the form, then click OK to finish saving it.

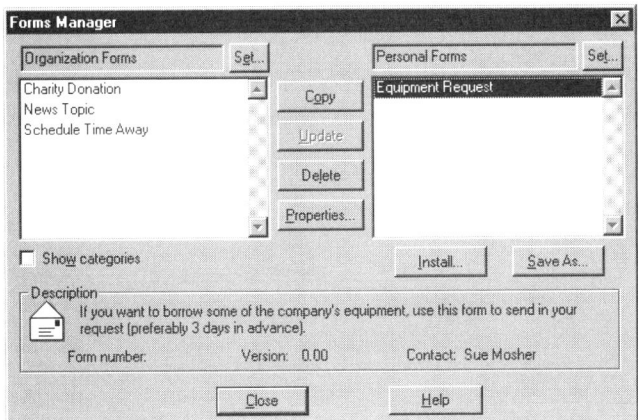

Figure 20.27
From the Forms Manager, you can install new forms, save forms, and copy forms from one library or folder to another.

Installing from the Forms Manager

Forms that have been saved as .fdm files, as described in the previous section, can be installed from the Forms Manager. You also can use the.cfg file from a compiled form for this installation process. The .cfg file for a form is found in a .vb subfolder with the same name as your project. For example, we saved the Equipment Request project as Equip.efp. When the project was compiled, an Equip.vb subfolder was created, and in that subfolder is an Equip.cfg file.

To install a form with the Forms Manager, follow these steps:

1. In the Exchange Viewer, choose Tools, Options, then switch to the Exchange Server tab and click the Manage Forms button.

2. The next step is to set the target library for the form you want to install. Click the Set button on the right side of the Forms Manager dialog box (Figure 20.27) to display the Set library To dialog box.

3. In the Set library To dialog box (see Figure 20.23 on page 477), choose the library or folder where you want to install the form, then click the OK button.

4. Back in the Forms Manager dialog box, click the Install button.

5. In the Open dialog box (Figure 20.28), locate the .cfg or .fdm file for the form you want to install, then click OK to complete the installation process.

As you saw earlier under "Installing from the Forms Designer," once a form has been installed, it can be accessed through the Compose menu on the Exchange Viewer.

Figure 20.28

Choose a .cfg file for a compiled form or an .fdm file for a saved form to install the form through the Forms Manager.

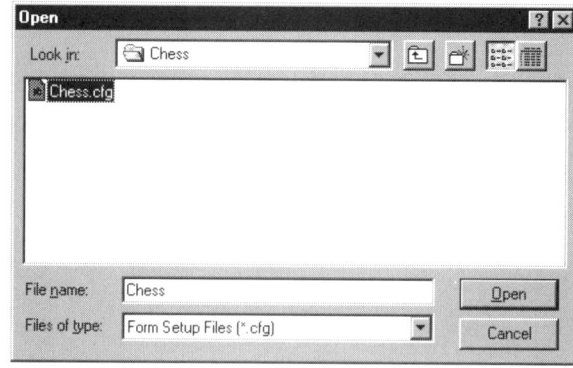

Copying Forms

Another technique for making a form available is to copy an existing form from one library or folder to another. You can copy a form from the Personal or Organization Forms library to a folder or from a folder to one of the two libraries. To copy a form from a library or folder, follow these steps:

1. Display the source and destination, one in each of the two columns in the Forms Manager dialog box (see Figure 20.27 on page 481). Use the two Set buttons and the Set library To dialog box (see Figure 20.23 on page 477) to pick the library or folder. You may find it convenient to always put the source library or folder on the left side and the destination in the right column.

2. Select the form you want to copy, then click the Copy button.

Managing Forms for Remote Users

What about remote users? What forms are available when you work offline and aren't connected to the Exchange Server? If you use offline folders (see the section "Synchronizing Mailbox and Public Folders," page 308 in Chapter 13), any form associated with a message in any of your mailbox folders is copied to the offline folders when you synchronize. You can check this by looking at the synchronization log placed in Deleted items. An example is shown in Figure 20.29.

The same process occurs with any forms associated with folders in your Favorites folder that have been marked for synchronization. If there are other forms that you might want to use while you're offline, you should copy them to your Personal Forms library using the Forms Manager, as described in the previous section, "Copying Forms."

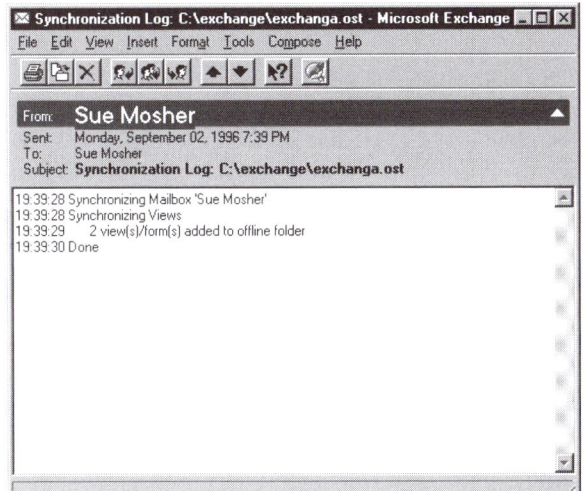

Figure 20.29
New forms and views used in your mailbox are copied to your offline folders during synchronization.

Tips and Tricks

The Equipment Request project just barely scratches the surface of what you can do with the Forms Designer, but I hope it's enough to get you interested in experimenting with forms for your own use, and especially to share with others. In this section, you'll find a technique for keeping column names under control and more ideas on how to extend forms.

Limiting the Number of New Column Names

If you work extensively with the Exchange Forms Designer, you may see the Available Columns list, which is used to customize a folder's display, fill up with all sorts of names.

Each time you create a new field on a form, Exchange Forms Designer uses the caption for that field to also add a column name, by default. If you don't intend a particular field to be used for sorting, grouping, or filtering, then specify that the Microsoft Exchange Column Name is blank, using these steps:

1. In the Exchange Forms Designer, select the field for which you don't want a column name.

2. Choose View, Field Properties.

3. Delete the text entered for Microsoft Exchange Column Name.

4. Click the Close button.

Extending the Reach of Forms

There are many different ways to extend the reach of forms. For example, you might re-create the Equipment Request project as a post form, rather than as a send form, and organize it into a public folder, showing in a custom folder view the date that each piece of equipment is due back in the office. Or you might create a response form where the equipment manager can check whether the request is approved or disapproved.

Forms also can be extended with Microsoft Visual Basic. The Chess form included with the Microsoft Exchange Server sample applications is a good example. This form actually lets you play chess by e-mail with other users and shows you the position of the board after each move.

You can find extensive details about using the Microsoft Exchange Forms Designer in the three help files that accompany the application. You'll find them on the Programs menu, under Microsoft Exchange (Figure 20.30) or whatever menu you chose when you installed EFD.

Figure 20.30

In addition to MS Forms Designer Help for the Forms Designer itself, Microsoft provides an MS Application Designer's Guide help file and OLE MSG Help file for more ambitious form designers.

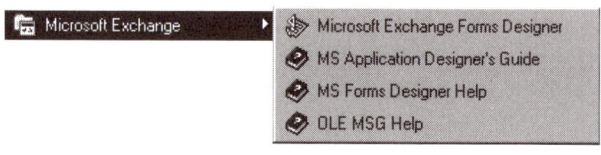

Summary

In this chapter, we've introduced the tools and techniques to build forms to organize information. The process of building a form is rather complex. Naturally, the design process should begin with thoughts about what you want the form to do and how it should look to make it easy to use. Once you've created a form, you can move it between folders and form libraries. You also can save it as an .fdm file to distribute it to other users.

Key Points

- A "send" form can communicate with other users or public folders. A "post" form is used to put information directly into a folder.
- Microsoft Exchange Forms Designer is a separate program included with Microsoft Exchange Server.
- Forms can be installed in the Personal Forms library, the Organization Forms Library, or a folder.
- The Forms Manager in Exchange is used to install forms, save them as files that can be sent to other users, copy forms between libraries and folders, and limit the space allocated for forms on your computer.

For More Information

Forms are only one way to customize public folders. Many more techniques are discussed in Chapter 19, "Using Exchange to Collaborate."

The fields used in a form also appear in Exchange Viewer as new columns. If you need a refresher on how to rearrange columns, see Chapter 10, "Using the Exchange Viewer."

Chapter 21
Message Security

In this chapter, we'll look at one of the more advanced features of Microsoft Exchange — the capability to send secure messages. Two kinds of security are involved:

- Privacy — hiding the contents of a message from everyone except the intended recipient
- Authentication — adding a digital "signature" to positively identify the sender and prove that the message has not been changed since it was sent

Both kinds of security use a system of *keys* to lock and unlock these features. The sender encrypts or signs a message using a *private key* available only to that user. Recipients decrypt the message or verify the signature with a *public key* that the user has distributed. Public keys should be sent to recipients by a secure method (which may rule out e-mail). In some cases, public keys may be stored on public key servers.

Key-based security is built into Microsoft Fax and Microsoft Exchange Server, but this form of security works only with those services. To protect messages sent via the Internet, you need to use an add-on product such as Secure Messenger or PGP Extension for Microsoft Exchange (PGP stands for Pretty Good Privacy, the best known freeware security add-on).

Sending Secure Messages via Microsoft Fax

You can send secure messages directly to another person using Microsoft Fax and Binary File Transfer.

You can send secure messages directly to another person using Microsoft Fax, as long as you and the recipient meet the requirements for using Binary File Transfer. See the section "Sending a File (BFT)," page 324 in Chapter 14. The encrypted or signed message is transmitted as a file rather than as a rendered fax image.

Setting Up Microsoft Fax Security

To set up security for Microsoft Fax, follow these steps:

1. Choose Tools, Microsoft Fax Tools, Advanced Security.
2. In the Advanced Fax Security dialog box (Figure 21.1), choose New Key Set.

Figure 21.1
Security options for Microsoft Fax are maintained through the Advanced Fax Security dialog box.

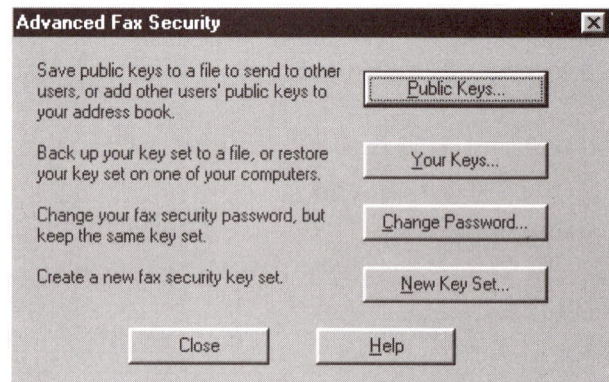

3. In the Fax Security - New Key Set dialog box, enter and confirm a Password. If you are confident that no other person will ever use your computer under your Windows log-on name, you can check the box marked Save the Password in Your Password List.
4. Click OK to continue. Microsoft Fax automatically creates a set of public and private keys.

You now need to send your public key to the people to whom you plan to send secure faxes. Here's how:

1. Back at the Advanced Fax Security dialog box (Figure 21.1), choose Public Keys.

2. In the Fax Security - Managing Public Keys dialog box, click the Save button.

3. In the first Fax Security - Save Public Keys dialog box, select your name from the list on the left, then click the To button to move it to the Save These Keys list on the right. Click the OK button.

4. In the second Fax Security - Save Public Keys dialog box, indicate the location and file name where you want to store the public key file, which uses an .awp extension. Click the Save button to save the file.

You now can send this file to people with whom you will be exchanging secure faxes; those people should send you their public key files, too. Add the public key files to your Personal Address Book (PAB) by following these steps:

1. In the Advanced Fax Security dialog box (Figure 21.1), choose Public Keys.

2. In the Fax Security - Managing Public Keys dialog box, click the Add button.

3. In the Fax Security - Adding Public Keys dialog box, enter the name and location of the public key file you received from another Microsoft Fax user.

4. In the Fax Security - Add Public Keys dialog box (Figure 21.2), select the name(s) to add, then click OK.

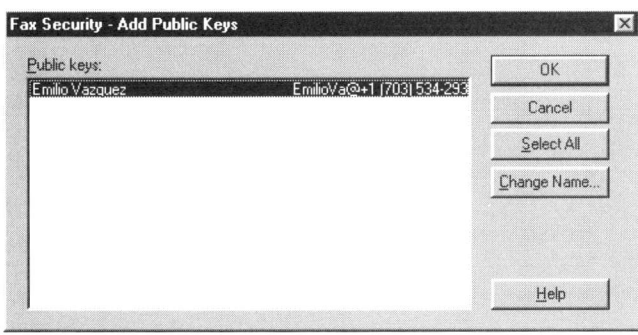

Figure 21.2
A public key file may contain one or many keys. Select those you want to add to your Personal Address Book.

If a name listed in the Add Public Keys dialog box (Figure 21.2) is different from the corresponding entry in your PAB, click the Change Name button to bring up the PAB in the Fax Security - Change Name dialog box so you can match the PAB entry with the key. When you've finished setting up Microsoft Fax security and adding keys, close the Fax Security - Managing Public Keys dialog box and the Advanced Fax Security dialog box.

Sending a Secure Fax

To send a secure fax, follow these steps:

1. Start a new fax by clicking the New Message button or choosing Tools, Compose New Message (*don't* use Compose New Fax).

2. Address the fax and compose the message. You can include file attachments.

3. Choose File, Send Options.

4. On the Fax tab of the Send Options dialog box for the message, set the Message Format to "Editable only." Then click the Security button.

5. In the Message Security Options dialog box (Figure 21.3), choose the security method you want to use. Optionally, choose to "Digitally sign all attachments." Click OK twice to return to the message.

Figure 21.3

Set the security options for an individual fax. Password protection is a simple, alternate method that does not require the exchange of keys.

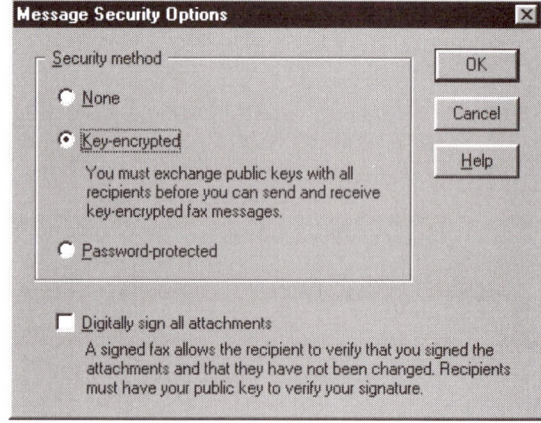

6. Send the message.

Special Note

Figure 21.3 also shows an option for sending a file with password protection rather than key encryption. This is a less secure but easier method, because no exchange of key files is involved. All you need to do is give the recipient the password.

Reading a Secure Fax

If you receive a fax that has been encrypted, <Encrypted> will be included in the subject line. To read the message, follow these steps:

1. Double-click the message to open it.

2. If you did not save the key-set password to your password list, you will see a Fax Security - Key Set Password dialog box. Enter Password for the key set, then click OK.

3. If the sender matches an entry in your PAB, the message is automatically decrypted and a copy placed in the Inbox. Otherwise, you will need to select one of the addresses for which you already hold a public key.

To check whether an incoming fax message has been digitally signed, open the message, then choose Tools, Microsoft Fax Tools, Verify Digital Signature. If the message was signed and the attachments were not tampered with, you see a list of the signed attachments marked Valid. Otherwise, you get a message that the item was not digitally signed.

Working with Microsoft Exchange Server Security

Microsoft Exchange Server security is easier to work with than Microsoft Fax security, because you don't need to maintain a list of public keys. Keys for the entire organization are maintained by a key management server. All you have to do is enable your own mailbox for security, with the help of the Exchange Server administrator.

Setting Up Exchange Server Security

To enable Exchange Server security, the Exchange Server administrator creates an *advanced security token*, a string of letters and numbers that you must then enter to generate your security credentials. To complete this process, follow these steps:

1. Choose Tools, Options, then switch to the Security tab, and click the Set Up Advanced Security button.

2. In the Setup Advanced Security dialog box (Figure 21.4), enter the Token you received from the Exchange Server administrator. Also enter a Password, then confirm it. This password must be at least six characters long.

Microsoft Exchange Server security uses a key management server to store keys for the entire organization.

Figure 21.4

Before enabling Microsoft Exchange Server security, you must get a token from the Exchange Server administrator.

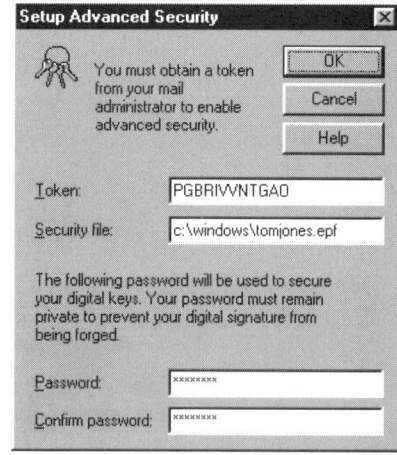

3. A default Security File location is created for you, but you can change that location. The best location is on a network server where files are backed up on a regular basis.

4. Click OK to send a request to enable security to the key management server.

5. A confirmation message will appear indicating that your request was successfully sent to the server, and you will be notified shortly.

6. In a few minutes, you should receive a Reply from Security Authority message. Open this message, then enter the security password you gave in step 2. You will see a message that your mailbox is now enabled for security.

7. (Optional) You may choose Tools, Options again and return to the Security tab (Figure 21.5) to set up default security options for all messages. You have these choices:

   • Encrypt message contents and attachments
   • Add digital signature to message

8. Click OK to close the Options dialog box when you're finished working with security options.

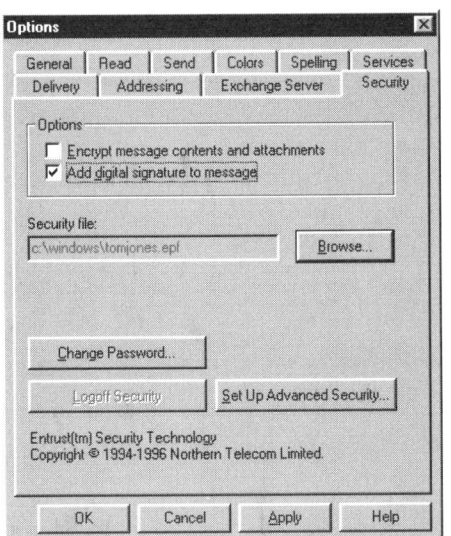

Figure 21.5
You can set up Exchange to use digital signatures on all messages by default.

Using Exchange Server Security

Whenever you use Exchange Server security, you are prompted to enter the security password in the Microsoft Exchange Security Logon dialog box, shown in Figure 21.6. If you forget this password, you must check with the Exchange Server administrator to get a new token to re-enable security.

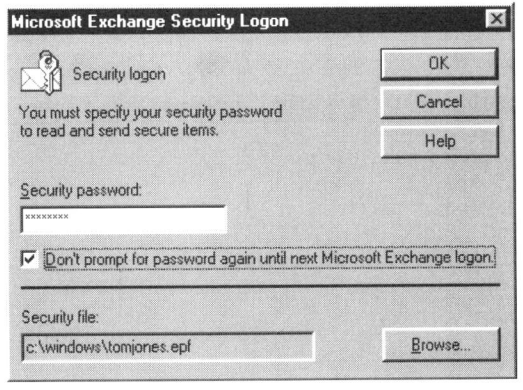

Figure 21.6
You must log on to Microsoft Exchange Server security before you can encrypt or sign messages, or read incoming encrypted messages.

Sending a Secure Message

To send an encrypted or signed message, you must use Exchange Server addresses from the Global Address List, not from your PAB. On the New Message window, choose File, Properties, then switch to the Security tab and check either "Encrypt message contents and attachments," or "Add digital signature to message," or both. You also can add buttons to the message window toolbar to add either option to a message. To do so, choose Tools, Customize Toolbar.

Receiving Secure Messages

When you receive an encrypted message, it appears in the Inbox with a different icon: an envelope with a lock. A message that is digitally signed uses an envelope with a pen for its icon.

Open the message, entering your password in the Microsoft Exchange Security Logon dialog box (Figure 21.6) if that box appears. If the message was digitally signed, the toolbar will include a new button, shown in Figure 21.7, depicting a pen and a magnifying glass (if you don't see this button, you can choose Tools, Customize Toolbar and add it). Click this button to view the Verify Digital Signature dialog box (Figure 21.8).

Figure 21.7
On digitally signed messages, Exchange shows this button on the toolbar. Click the button to verify the message's signature.

Figure 21.8
The Verify Digital Signature dialog box alerts you to any possible compromise in the signature's integrity.

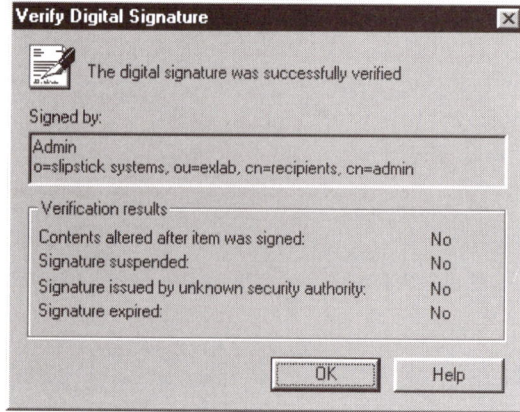

Using Exchange Server Security in Multiple Locations

If you work on more than one machine, copy your security file to a network server where the file will be backed up regularly and securely protected. Follow these steps:

1. Copy the file listed on the Security tab in the Options dialog box (Figure 21.5) to a network server.

2. On that system, choose Tools, Options, then switch to the Security tab.

3. Click the Browse button. In the Locate Security Profile dialog box, select the security file you copied in step 1, then click the Open button.

4. Click OK to close the Options dialog box and enable security for your mailbox on this machine.

If you are working remotely, be sure to download the full Global Address List (see the section "Synchronizing Addresses," page 310 in Chapter 13). You can't send encrypted messages with the smaller version of the Global Address List that does not include security details.

Using Other Security Methods

Microsoft Fax security works only when you dial another person directly. Microsoft Exchange Server security works only within your organization. But what about messages sent via the Internet? Can they be secured?

Yes, they can, through Exchange add-ons. Two add-ons are available so far — PGP Extension for Exchange and Secure Messenger. Both are included on the CD for this book. With these add-ons, you have the option to register your key with a public key server, to make it easier for people to decode and authenticate your messages with confidence that the key is valid.

Messages sent via the Internet can be secured with Exchange add-ons such as PGP Extension for Exchange, and Secure Messenger.

PGP Extension for Exchange

PGP Extension uses Pretty Good Privacy, an encryption application available for download at http://web.mit.edu/network/pgp as freeware for non-commercial use by U.S. citizens in the United States or Canadian citizens in Canada. You also can find links at this site for commercial and export versions.

To install PGP Extension, follow the detailed instructions included with the software on the CD. This extension will add Sign, Encrypt, and Sign and Encrypt choices to the Tools menu. You also can customize the message window toolbar to add the accompanying buttons. The version of PGP Extension on the CD supports only messages without file attachments. A future version (presumably available on the Web site listed above) will support messages with attachments.

Secure Messenger

S/MIME is a new specification for secure electronic mail that Secure Messenger, as well as several other e-mail programs, use.

Secure Messenger is the first Exchange add-on to use S/MIME, a new specification for secure electronic mail. S/MIME stands for Secure/Multipurpose Internet Mail Extensions. This specification is designed to add security to e-mail messages in MIME format (see Chapter 22, "Working with Internet Mail"). There are several other S/MIME-enabled e-mail programs (such as ConnectSoft E-Mail Connection 3.0 and OpenSoft ExpressMail), so recipients don't necessarily have to be using Exchange to decode your messages.

After you install Secure Messenger and add it to your Exchange profile, a new Security menu is added to Exchange. Choose Security, Security Settings to generate keys, set a passphrase, and set the default encryption and signature options for messages.

To set Secure Messenger options for an individual message, choose Tools, Properties, then switch to the S/MIME tab. The first time you send to another S/MIME-enabled address, check the two boxes — Digitally Sign Messages and Attachments, and Send Certificate(s) with Messages. Doing this will allow the recipient to associate your public key (contained in the security certificate) with your e-mail address in his or her PAB.

You'll need to make a similar association for any S/MIME certificates you receive from other users. A signed message, usually sent with a certificate, is represented in the Exchange Viewer as an envelope with a pen. Follow these steps to associate the certificate with an address in your Personal Address Book:

1. Open the S/MIME signed message in your Inbox. This registers the certificate on your system.

2. Click the Address Book button, or choose Tools, Address Book.

3. In your PAB, select the address to associate with the certificate.

4. Click the Address Security Properties button (which Secure Messenger adds to the Address Book), or choose Security, Address Security Properties.

5. In the Address Security Properties dialog box (Figure 21.9), click the Attach New button, select a certificate from the Select a Certificate list, then click OK.

6. Click OK to close the Address Security Properties dialog box.

Once an address has an S/MIME certificate associated with it, you can send that address not only signed messages, but encrypted messages as well.

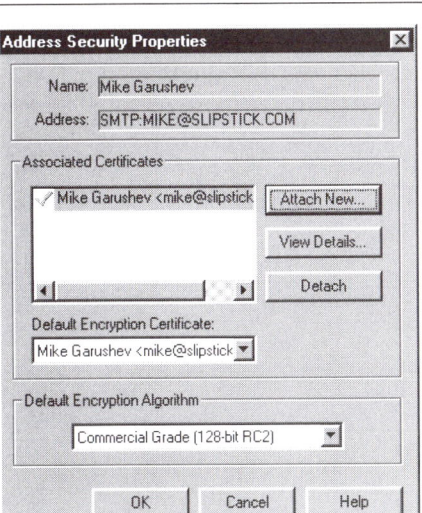

Figure 21.9
Secure Messenger keeps information on public keys in the Personal Address Book as certificates attached to individual addresses.

Summary

We've looked at several implementations of the primary form of message security — the use of private and public keys to encrypt messages and add digital signatures. This area is getting a lot of attention these days as governments rethink their policies on encryption standards — both the use of these standards within their borders and the export of encryption technology.

The techniques involving keys that are available in Microsoft Fax, Microsoft Exchange Server, and new Exchange add-ons make it possible for you to secure and sign messages intended for virtually any recipient.

Key Points

- Message security uses a system of keys to protect the privacy of a message and authenticate the identity of the sender.
- You can send secure messages directly to another person using Microsoft Fax and Binary File Transfer.
- Microsoft Exchange Server security uses a key management server to store keys for the entire organization.
- Messages sent via the Internet can be secured with Exchange add-ons such as PGP Extension for Exchange and Secure Messenger.
- S/MIME is a new specification for secure electronic mail that Secure Messenger, as well as several other e-mail programs, use.

For More Information

If the point-to-point message capability of Microsoft Fax interests you, check out the information on Binary File Transfer (BFT) in Chapter 14, "Sending Faxes." WinFax PRO 7.0 also supports BFT.

In Chapter 25, "Introducing Exchange Server 5.0," you'll learn how this newest version of Exchange allows you to exchange keys with Exchange Server users in other organizations.

Chapter 22

Working with Internet E-Mail

You may be able to reach a few dozen people or maybe even several thousand through your organization's e-mail system. But to extend your e-mail universe to tens of millions of people (a number growing every day), you need to be able to send messages on the Internet.

To reach the Internet via e-mail, yet stay within the Microsoft Exchange environment, you can choose a number of different approaches. What works best for you will depend on such things as your organization's e-mail scheme and the number and type of personal mail accounts you have.

In this chapter, we'll spotlight a variety of Internet mail approaches for Exchange and discuss some of the key issues you'll face once you are connected. These approaches will include both those for standalone Exchange users and for those of you who send mail via the Microsoft Exchange Server service.

Internet Mail Approaches

Internet
approaches for
Exchange
include
services for
large
organizations,
small
workgroups,
and
individuals.

Let's divide Internet mail approaches into three types, listed in Table 22.1:

Table 22.1 Internet Mail Approaches for Exchange		
Type	**Description**	**Examples**
Enterprise	Connects to the Internet through a mail server	Microsoft Exchange Server + Internet Mail Connector Microsoft Mail Server + an Internet mail gateway
Workgroup	Connects through a workgroup postoffice or workgroup mail server	netApps Internet Series (Office mode) Workgroup Internet Gateway (WIG)
Single-user	Connects directly to the Internet mailbox	Internet Mail service Netscape Internet Transport Single User Internet Gateway (SIG) netApps Internet Series (Personal mode)

The difference between enterprise and workgroup strategies is largely one of scale. Enterprise solutions use full-blown mail servers and often provide connections for multiple physical sites. Enterprise solutions are more likely to include a full-time (rather than dial-up) connection to the Internet. Workgroup approaches concentrate on a single group of users at one location; a chief advantage of workgroup solutions is the capability to offer dial-up access to Internet mail over a single phone line shared by all users.

Using Online Services for Internet E-Mail

Online services such as CompuServe, America Online (AOL), Prodigy, and The Microsoft Network (MSN) offer the capability to send and receive Internet mail, but sometimes with significant limitations. Some services do not allow file attachments or they can handle only MIME-encoded attachments but not UUENCODE, or vice versa (see the section "MIME vs. UUENCODE" later in this chapter).

Also, at this writing in the fall of 1996, the online services do not support the use of generic Exchange transports, such as the Internet Mail service; rather, they require their own separate Exchange information service. So far, these services are available only for CompuServe and The Microsoft Network with America Online planning to introduce its Exchange information service in early 1997.

However, this situation is likely to change. The online services are moving toward the POP3/SMTP mail standard. This means that in the future you may be able to set up the Internet Mail service to work with your online service mail account.

In the meantime, because of the potential problem with file attachments, if you frequently need to exchange files with people with Internet addresses, I recommend that you go ahead and get a standard Internet mail account from an Internet service provider. You can always use your online service's mail account as a backup or as a means of communicating with people who also use that service.

Online services offer the capability to send and receive Internet mail, but sometimes with limitations.

Delivery Issues

Two common concerns among Internet mail users are how to get mail from more than one mailbox and how to determine which of your Exchange services delivers your Exchange message.

Retrieving from Multiple Mailboxes

The multiple mailbox problem concerns users who have more than one mailbox with one Internet service provider (ISP) or mail accounts with multiple ISPs. The Internet Mail service available free from Microsoft (see Chapter 8, "Setting up Internet Mail") supports retrieval from only one POP3 account at a time.

There are three workarounds for this issue:

- Maintain a separate Exchange profile for each Internet mail account. Each such profile consists of Personal Folders, which always uses the same .pst file, and Internet Mail, which points to a different Internet mailbox in each profile. To get mail from a different mailbox, exit Exchange, then restart it with a different profile.

- Add a second single-user service to your Exchange profile. For example, you can use both Internet Mail and Netscape Internet Mail Transport in the same profile, connecting to two different mailboxes.

- Use netApps Internet Series in personal mode, configured to access multiple mail accounts.

Delivering Internet Messages

To send a message to the Internet, enter the recipient's address in the standard *name@domain* format; for example, joe@joesgrill.com. If your Exchange profile contains only one service that can handle such Internet addresses, that service will deliver the message.

But what if you have more than one Internet-capable service? You might have both Internet Mail and Netscape Internet Mail Transport installed, as noted in the previous section. As another example, you might have the Microsoft Exchange Server service with the Internet Mail Connector, plus MSN.

Where a profile contains more than one Internet-capable service, Internet messages — those addressed to *name@domain* addresses — are always delivered via only one service, which is the first one listed in the delivery order.

To check the delivery order of services, choose Tools, Options, then switch to the Delivery tab. Use the Move Up and Move Down buttons shown in Figure 22.1 to rearrange the delivery order. In general, you'll want the most reliable Internet mail service (or the one you access most frequently) to be first. You also can change the delivery order by accessing the properties for the profile through the Mail and Fax (or Mail) applet in the Control Panel.

Where a profile contains more than one Internet-capable service, Internet messages are always delivered via only one service, which is the first one listed in the delivery order.

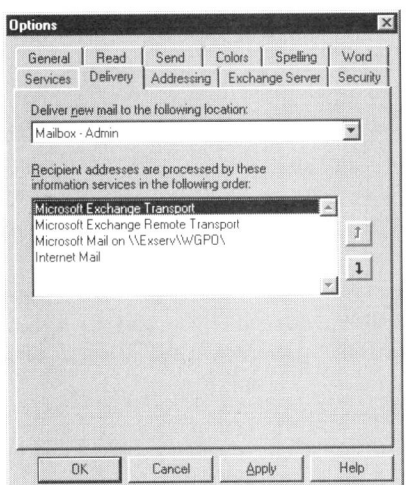

Figure 22.1

*The service you want
to use to deliver mail to
the Internet should be
at the top of the
delivery order list.*

Working with Mailto: Links

Internet Web pages typically include links to e-mail addresses. In the underlying HTML code for the page, these links say "mailto:*name@domain*," where *name@domain* is an actual address. You will also see blue mailto: links in incoming messages if you use an Exchange Server client or Deming Preview (see Appendix A, "CD Contents"), as seen in Figure 22.2.

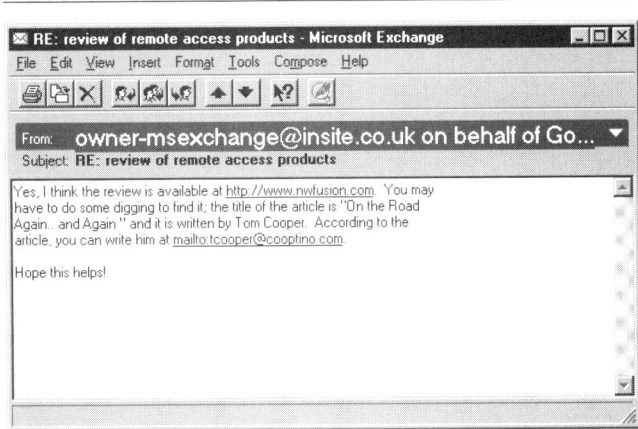

Figure 22.2

*A mailto: link is
underlined in blue.
Click the link to start
a new message
addressed to the
mailto: address.*

Internet mailto: messages are not delivered immediately; they go at the next scheduled delivery or when you use Tools, Deliver Now.

When you click a mailto: link, a new message window appears with the *name@domain* address already pasted in the To box. Add the subject and message text, then send the message. This places the message in your Outbox.

Note that the message is not delivered immediately, even if you are currently connected to the Internet. As with other Exchange messages, delivery depends on the service set up to deliver Internet mail (see the previous section) and the settings for that service. You may want to make a habit of using Tools, Deliver Now to deliver any Internet-bound messages from your Outbox before you quit your Internet browser.

For users of all versions of Exchange except the original Windows 95 operating system version, Exchange offers the capability for you to use a faster, simpler form to compose a message when you click a mailto: link. To enable this form, follow these steps:

1. Choose Tools, Options, then switch to the Send tab.
2. Check Use Simplified Note on Internet 'mailto:' and File, Send.
3. Click the OK button.

This form is available if you are using the Windows Messaging update to the Windows 95 operating system, the Windows Messaging program for Windows NT 4.0, or the Exchange Server client from Service Pack 2 or later.

Resetting the Mailto: Application

If you install another e-mail program, such as Eudora, the application used for mailto: links may change. To reset for use with Exchange, follow these steps:

1. In Windows Explorer, choose View, Options, then switch to the File Types tab.
2. Under Registered File Types, select URL:MailTo Protocol, then click the Edit button.
3. In the Edit File Type dialog box, under Actions, select Open, then click the Edit button.
4. In the Editing Action for Type: URL:MailTo Protocol dialog box (Figure 22.3), under Application Used to Perform Action, type the following:

        rundll32.exe url.dll,MailToProtocolHandler

5. Click the OK button, then click the Close button twice to save the change to the way mailto: links are handled.

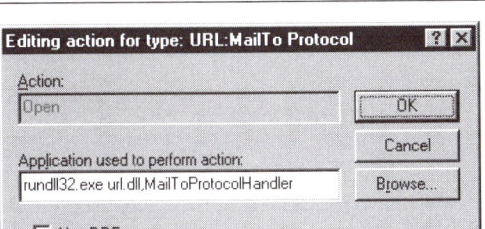

Figure 22.3
You can force mailto: links to use Exchange if you're switching from another e-mail program.

Mailing Lists

One of the great features about Internet mail is the capability for you to subscribe to mailing lists covering fields that interest you. Some mailing lists are heavily edited summaries of information and deliver only a couple of messages to you each week. Others function as lively discussion groups and can place dozens of messages in your Inbox each day. These are good places both to eavesdrop on other people's concerns and to post your own questions and comments.

Subscribing to a Mailing List

Where do you find out about mailing lists? You can ask in Internet newsgroups or look for links on World Wide Web sites. To subscribe, send a message to the specified address, using the format given. You should get a message back confirming that you have joined the list and giving instructions for sending messages to the list and canceling your subscription. Save this message. (I keep a Mailing List Subscriptions folder to keep track of the lists I've joined.) Many lists also append a signature to the end of each message telling you how to unsubscribe. Or they may send out a periodic message reminding you how to get off the list if it's no longer of interest to you.

Sending Messages to a List

When you join a list, you'll usually receive a welcome message containing instructions for how to use this list. It will tell you what address to use to send messages to the list. Go ahead and add that address to your Personal Address Book. You should clear the box for sending in rich-text format (RTF) for that recipient.

When you send to the list, the usual e-mail etiquette applies. Keep your message brief and well structured, and give it a distinct subject. If you reply to a list message, quote only as much of the original message as you need to. Notice that, even though the From box lists the person who sent the message, the reply is addressed to the list itself. You can, of course, change the address for the reply to send it not to the list but to the individual sender.

Choosing a Message Format

When you send anything other than plain text to an Internet address, the content must be converted to a format that can be sent over the Internet. This process is called *encoding* and is one of the main functions of any Internet e-mail utility. The two principle encoding methods for PCs are Multipurpose Internet Mail Extensions (MIME) and UNIX-to-UNIX Encode (UUENCODE) (BinHex is another, used mostly by Macintosh mail programs).

In this section, we'll consider when to use these two encoding formats and also when to use the RTF that Exchange supports. The encoding method can be set for each message; RTF can be enabled only on a per-recipient basis.

MIME vs. UUENCODE

Either MIME or UUENCODE is set as the default encoding format in the settings for the Internet service(s) in your Exchange profile. For the Microsoft Exchange Server service, the encoding format is set on the server, but you can override it; choose File, Properties from the new message window, then click the Send Options button and switch to the Internet tab.

If you use the Internet Mail service to send e-mail via the Internet, you can override the default setting for any particular message. Choose File, Properties, then switch to the Internet tab shown in Figure 22.4 and make your choice of format. (If you have both the Internet Mail and Microsoft Exchange Server services, you'll see an Internet tab in the Properties dialog box and a different one in the Send Options dialog box. Changing the encoding type in either place changes it on the message, and you see the change on the other tab.)

MIME provides the best handling for both RTF and file attachments, so it's the usual default choice. If you send to people who can't handle MIME — such as MSN members — you need to switch to UUENCODE. Also use UUENCODE if your recipients complain about what looks like garble at the bottom of messages, preceded by a line that reads

```
Content-Transfer-Encoding: base64
```

A default character set is also part of the message format set on the Internet tab (Figure 22.4). If recipients complain about stray odd characters appearing in otherwise clean text, that means their mail program can't handle certain extended characters. Try switching to the USASCII character set.

Figure 22.5 shows an example of a MIME-encoded message received by an Exchange service that handles only UUENCODE messages.

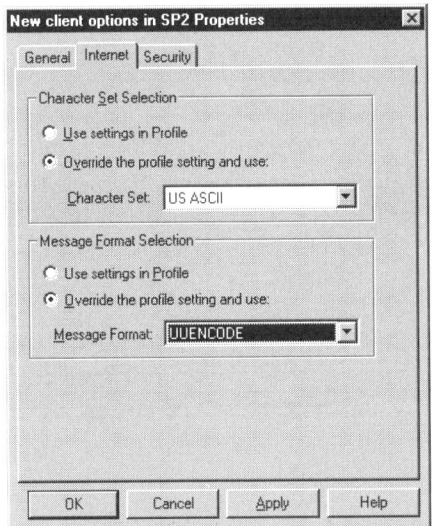

Figure 22.4
In the Internet Mail service, you can switch between UUENCODE and MIME and select a character set for any individual message.

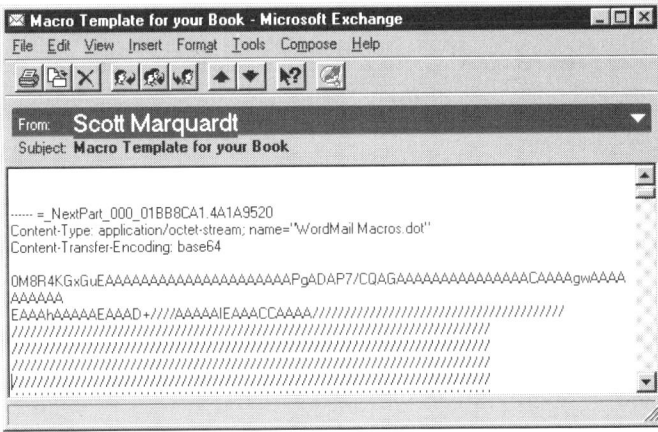

Figure 22.5
When a MIME-encoded message is received by a mail application that handles only UUENCODE formatting, the result is something like this. The message can be saved as a file and decoded with a utility such as CoderPad or Decode Shell Extension, which are included on the accompanying CD.

When to Use Rich-Text Format

Rich-text format (RTF) includes the fonts, bullets, colors, and other formatting available in the Exchange message editor. If you know that the recipient also uses Exchange, then use RTF and set the properties for that recipient to send in RTF. You do this on the Personal Address Book (PAB) entry for that person, as shown in Figure 22.6.

Figure 22.6
PAB showing SMTP tab.

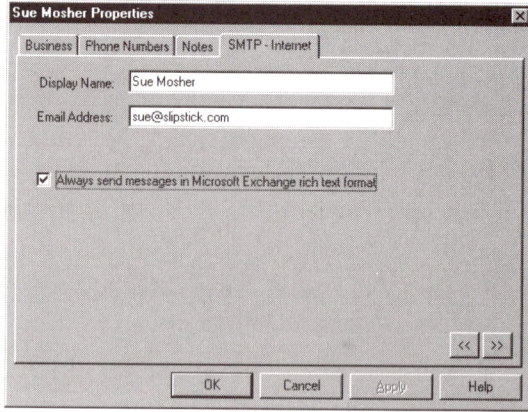

However, if a recipient complains of an indecipherable WINMAIL.DAT attachment (if you're using UUENCODE) or an odd section with the MIME content type of "application/ms-tnef," then you should turn off RTF to that recipient.

Special Note

The Internet Mail Connector for Exchange Server can be configured to turn off RTF for all recipients or for particular domains. This setting overrides any settings for individual recipients.

Tips and Tricks

To help you make the most of Internet mail, we'll show you how to determine whether a recipient can receive in rich-text format, what to do about recipients that don't wrap long lines, and how to work with mailto: links in CompuServe Mail.

Using Mailto: Links with CompuServe Mail

CompuServe Mail presents a problem to Internet browsers, because it cannot handle addresses in the standard *name@domain* format. This means that when you click on a mailto: link at a Web site, you must edit the address to convert to CompuServe's own format for Internet addresses.

If CompuServe is the only way you have to send Internet mail, follow these steps to change the address inserted by a mailto: link to a proper CompuServe Internet address:

1. Select the address in the To box, then press Ctrl+C to copy it to the clipboard.

2. Click the To button.

3. In the Address Book dialog box, click the New button.

4. In the New Entry dialog box, choose In This Message Only if you don't want to put the address in your Personal Address Book.

5. Select an entry type of CompuServe.

6. In the New CompuServe Properties dialog box, enter a Display Name.

7. In the E-mail Address field, type **INTERNET:**, then press Ctrl+V to paste the Internet address that you copied in step 1. Alternatively, you can choose an entry type of CompuServe/Internet and paste in the name and domain.

8. Click the Add To button to add the address and return to the new message window.

9. In the new message window, delete the address that was originally pasted into the new message window by the mailto: link.

10. Complete the message and send it.

Forcing Line Breaks

An Internet e-mail annoyance you're likely to run into is the fact that some e-mail programs (such as Digital's All-in-One or Netscape Navigator 2.0) do not automatically wrap lines to fit the display. Recipients may complain that they have to scroll far to the right to see all your paragraphs.

Microsoft Exchange Server can be set to force default line lengths to help overcome some of these problems. This adjustment must be made by the Exchange Server administrator and affects all messages and users.

However, the Internet Mail service does not offer any way to automatically break lines with a hard return at a certain length. Instead, you need to consider one of the following workarounds:

- Break lines yourself by pressing Enter where you want the break to occur.

- Use WordMail as your e-mail editor and a macro that inserts hard returns for you. An example of such a macro is included on the CD for this book.

- Use MIME with USASCII for your message format. However, the recipient may see an = character at the end of each line where a soft return is detected; and this method may not work for all recipients.

- Use UUENCODE with USASCII for the message format.

Finding RTF-Compatible Recipients

Earlier in the chapter, you were warned not to use RTF on messages to non-Exchange recipients. But how can you tell who's using Exchange and who's not? One indicator is whether you get a message with RTF. Does the incoming message have bullets, varying fonts, or colors? If so, then it's an RTF message, and you can confidently reply to the sender using RTF.

Another way to tell whether it's safe to send RTF is to look at the Internet headers for the incoming message, as described under "Viewing the Internet Headers," page 287 in Chapter 12. To see the header for a message, choose File, Properties and switch to the Internet tab. The presence of any of the following lines is a clue that it's OK to use RTF for that recipient:

X-MS-TNEF-Correlator

X-Mailer: Microsoft Exchange Server Internet Mail Connector Version 4.0.993.5

Content-Type: application/ms-tnef

X-MS-Attachment: WINMAIL.DAT 0 00-00-1980 00:00

Summary

Internet e-mail is the key to sending mail between individuals and organizations scattered across the globe. In this chapter, we've reviewed several methods for connecting you and your fellow workers to the Internet and for resolving some of the problems that can arise when sending Internet messages with Exchange.

Watch for the Microsoft Exchange Server service to continue to evolve to add features to make it easier to receive and send mail via the Internet. Exchange Server 5.0 (see Chapter 25) allows you to access your Exchange Server mailbox with any POP3 Internet mail program or even with your Web browser!

Key Points

- Internet approaches for Exchange include services for large organizations, small workgroups, and individuals.

- Online services offer the capability to send and receive Internet mail, but sometimes with limitations.

- Where a profile contains more than one Internet-capable service, Internet messages are always delivered via only one service, which is the first one listed in the delivery order.

- Internet mailto: messages are not delivered immediately; they go at the next scheduled delivery or when you use Tools, Deliver Now.

For More Information

One of the keys to successful Internet messaging is to get your Internet service set up correctly. Check back to the appropriate chapter(s) in Part II for the service(s) installed in your Exchange profile.

The Internet mail community has built up its own standard way of handling replies, quotations, signatures, and other e-mail elements. You'll find valuable information about these issues in the sections in Chapter 11 under "Understanding E-Mail Style." In that same chapter, look at "Adding Internet Links" for information about how to add Internet hot links to your messages.

Chapter 23

Managing a Workgroup Postoffice

Not every office needs the Microsoft Exchange Server service or even Microsoft Mail Server. In many cases, you can start connecting people with e-mail using the *workgroup postoffice* included with Windows 95, Windows NT, and Windows for Workgroups. Because you don't need to purchase any additional software — everything comes with the operating system — a workgroup postoffice is an excellent way to experiment with group e-mail.

A workgroup postoffice is so named because it is intended for use only in the somewhat limited setting where you have, at most, a few dozen users and no need for connections to other sites. In this chapter, you'll learn how to create and manage the postoffice and get some ideas for expanding its capabilities in the future. If you already have a workgroup postoffice, then skip ahead to the "Managing Users" section on page 516.

Special Note

The tools for creating and managing a workgroup postoffice are not included in the Exchange Server clients, only in the Windows 95 and Windows NT operating system clients. If you need to manage an existing workgroup postoffice at the same time you are upgrading to Exchange Server, first install the operating system Exchange client and the Microsoft Mail service, then run the setup program for the Exchange Server client.

Also, as noted in Chapter 6, "Setting Up Microsoft Mail," Windows 95 users may need to update their copy of the Microsoft Mail service to gain access to Microsoft Mail shared folders.

Planning for the Postoffice

The postoffice should be located on a computer that will be up all the time.

Two things you need to think about before you create the workgroup postoffice are

- Where the postoffice should be located, and
- Who will manage it

A workgroup postoffice is a hierarchy of files that contain information about users and store those users' messages until they can retrieve them. The workgroup postoffice is a passive structure; that is, there is no active application running to deliver the mail. Therefore, you can locate the postoffice on just about any system. However, to keep users from revolting when they can't get their mail, the postoffice should be located on a computer that will be up all the time, or at least during office hours. This computer could be a dedicated NetWare or Windows NT server, or even a Windows 95 system operating as a file server in a peer-to-peer network environment.

The postoffice doesn't need its own dedicated machine; it can easily share space with other files. Although you could put the postoffice on a machine that's used to run applications, I don't recommend it. If you don't have the resources to start with a dedicated mail server, then put the postoffice on the most lightly used system, the one least subject to crashes that require restarting Windows. The main reason for this approach is that if an application crashes in such a way that you need to restart Windows, then everyone will lose access to the mail server during that time, too.

Who will manage the postoffice is a completely separate issue, because the postoffice can be maintained from any workstation. You don't need to be at the server to add users and to compact shared folders. What is important is to assure continuity for the postoffice manager's account. The last thing you want to do is have the person who's been managing the postoffice leave the company without telling anyone the password. If that happens, you won't be able to create any additional users until you delete the old postoffice and create a new one. My recommendation is to have the postoffice manager use two separate accounts: one for managing the postoffice and one for getting personal e-mail messages. This approach makes it easier to hand off the postoffice functions to someone else during vacations or to switch postoffice responsibilities to another person if you need to do so.

Creating the Postoffice

Once you've decided where to install the postoffice and how to handle the postoffice manager's account, it's time to set up the postoffice. To install the postoffice, follow these easy steps:

1. Click Start on the task bar, then Settings, Control Panel.

2. In the Control Panel, double-click Microsoft Mail Postoffice. Note that this is a different applet from the Mail and Fax (or Mail) applet used to set up Exchange profiles.

3. In the first screen of the Microsoft Workgroup Postoffice Admin Wizard, choose "Create a new Workgroup Postoffice," then click Next to continue.

4. On the next screen, enter the location where you want the postoffice folder to be installed. This might be your local C: drive, or it could be a drive on the network. You can click the Browse button to locate the server where you want to install the postoffice, as shown in Figure 23.1.

Be sure to safeguard a copy of the postoffice manager's password; if you lose it, you will have no way to add or delete users.

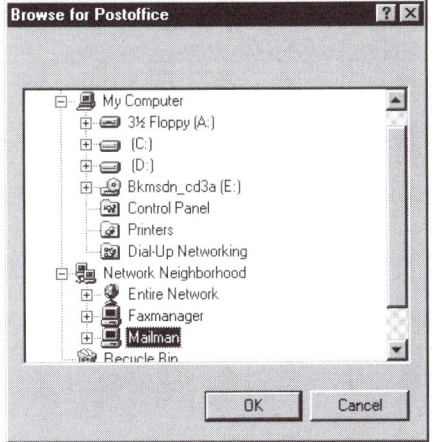

Figure 23.1
The workgroup postoffice can be located either on a local drive or on a network server.

Special Note

The postoffice setup program will automatically create a new folder on the drive or in the folder you specify. For example, if you enter C:\Windows as the postoffice location, Exchange will create a new C:\Windows\WGPO0000 folder and install the postoffice files there.

5. Once you've entered the location for the postoffice, click Next to continue.

6. The next step is to set up the account for the postoffice administrator. Exchange pops up the dialog box shown in Figure 23.2. Enter the Name, Mailbox, Password, and any other details you want to include. Be sure to safeguard a copy of the password; if you lose it, you will have no way to add or delete users and you'll be forced to re-create the entire postoffice.

Figure 23.2

As part of the process of creating a workgroup postoffice, you establish an e-mail account for the person who will add and delete new users.

Enter Your Administrator Account Details	
Name:	Postoffice Manager
Mailbox:	admin
Password:	aardvark
Phone #1:	
Phone #2:	
Office:	
Department:	
Notes:	

OK   Cancel

7. When you've set up the postoffice administrator's account, click OK, then click OK again when Exchange confirms the creation of the postoffice.

On a Windows 95 or NT system, share the postoffice folder with full access (see "Sharing Network Resources," page 57 in Chapter 3, for details about how to enable sharing and how to share a folder). If you created the postoffice on a NetWare server, assign access rights, including file scan.

Managing Users

Managing a workgroup postoffice is definitely a part-time job. Only a few tasks are involved:

- Adding users
- Deleting users

- Resetting passwords and changing other user details
- Compressing shared folders

We'll cover the user functions in this section, then turn to shared folders. As noted earlier in the introduction to this chapter, these functions are included only in the Microsoft Mail service installed as part of the operating system Exchange clients.

Here's how to launch the Postoffice Manager dialog box:

1. Click Start, then Settings, Control Panel.

2. In the Control Panel, double-click Microsoft Mail Postoffice.

3. Click on the "Administer an Existing Workgroup Postoffice" option, then click Next to continue.

4. Specify the Postoffice Location on this screen (the default is usually correct), then click Next to continue.

5. On the next screen, Exchange will fill in the mailbox name that you gave when you created the postoffice. You'll need to enter your password (you do remember the postoffice manager's password, don't you?). Click Next to open the Postoffice Manager dialog box, shown in Figure 23.3.

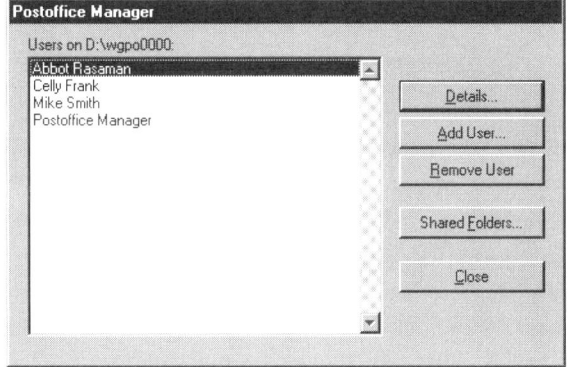

Figure 23.3
Administer user accounts and shared folders from the Postoffice Manager.

6. To close the Postoffice Manager dialog box, click the Close button.

Adding Users

Before anyone in the workgroup can use Exchange to access your postoffice, (s)he must have a user account. There is no option to create a user account on the fly, as there was with the version of Mail that came with Windows for Workgroups and Windows NT 3.x.

Think for a moment before you add that first user. How do you want names to appear in the postoffice address list? Should they be alphabetized by last name? If so, you'll want to enter the name that way; for example, "Jones, Sam." Or is your office run largely on a first-name basis? In that case, you should use "Sam Jones" as your name format.

To add a user, first launch the Postoffice Manager dialog box, as described above, then follow these steps:

1. From the Postoffice Manager dialog box (Figure 23.3), choose <u>A</u>dd User to display the dialog box shown in Figure 23.4.

Figure 23.4

Each user needs a Name, Mailbox, and Password. Whether to use the other fields is up to you.

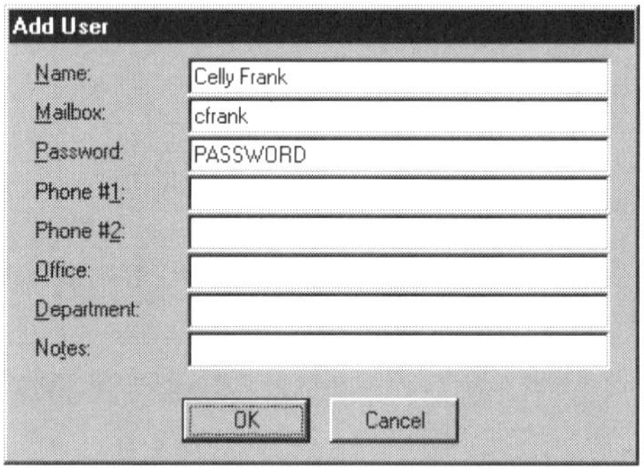

2. Enter the <u>N</u>ame as you want everyone else to see it on the Postoffice Address List.

3. Enter a <u>M</u>ailbox Name up to 10 characters long. You can use any combination of letters and numbers, but not spaces, hyphens, or other punctuation. Using the first initial plus the first nine characters of the last name is one good way to build mailbox names.

4. For <u>P</u>assword, you can keep the default, which is PASSWORD, or enter a different password to be used the first time the user connects to the postoffice. You can even delete PASSWORD and leave the Password box blank so no password is required, but that's not recommended.

5. Add other details at your discretion, as shown at the bottom of the Add User dialog box. These user details are not required, but they are displayed when users check the properties of recipients in the Postoffice Address List.

6. Click OK to add the new user.

Don't forget to create a personal mail account for yourself if you follow my advice and keep your postoffice administrator account separate. You'll also want to create two different Exchange profiles for yourself — one for each account. These profiles can share the same Personal Folders file if you prefer.

Deleting Users

Deleting users from your postoffice is easy. You just run the Microsoft Mail Postoffice applet in the Control Panel, log on as the postoffice administrator, highlight a user, and click the Remove User button. Note that once you delete a user, only the postoffice manager's mail account will be able to delete or rename any shared folders created by that user.

Changing Passwords and Other Details

Probably the most common task for the postoffice manager is resetting passwords for people who forget them. Here's how:

1. Open the Postoffice Manager as usual.
2. Select the user whose password needs to be changed, then choose Details.
3. In the dialog box for the user's account, the password will be masked with asterisks. Delete that password and enter a new one of your choice, which you can then give to the user.
4. Click the OK button to save the new password.

Use this same technique if a user changes his or her name. Just enter the new name in the Name box. Avoid changing the Mailbox, even in the event of a name change. If you change the Mailbox, the user also will have to update all profile(s) used to access that mail account.

Managing Shared Folders

As users create shared folders and add and delete items, the folders change in size (see "Creating New Folders," page 231 in Chapter 10). But unlike Personal Folders in Exchange, these shared folders never have the opportunity to be compressed automatically. Compressing the shared folders from time to time is your job as the postoffice administrator.

Don't forget that for Exchange under Windows 95, you must apply the Exchange update from Service Pack 1 or the Windows Messaging update on each workstation before users of that computer can access shared folders (see "Activating Shared Folders," page 128 in Chapter 6).

Special Note

To compress the shared folders, follow these steps:

1. Open the Postoffice Manager as usual. Click the Shared Folders button to display the Shared Folders dialog box, shown in Figure 23.5.

Figure 23.5
When a significant amount of free space can be recovered from shared folders, the Compress button will be enabled.

2. If the Compress button is enabled, click it to compress the shared folders. If it is not enabled, then there isn't enough free space worth recovering.

3. When compression is complete, click Close to return to the Postoffice Manager dialog box.

The other shared folder task that may need your attention is that of deleting obsolete shared folders if a user leaves your organization. You will need to run Exchange with a profile that uses the postoffice manager's account.

Tips and Tricks

If you have the job of workgroup postoffice administrator, you might like the tip below about creating a shortcut to the Postoffice Manager applet. You'll also learn how to move a workgroup postoffice.

Adding a Shortcut for the Postoffice Manager

If you anticipate adding or deleting users often, a shortcut to the Postoffice Manager on your desktop might be convenient. To create a shortcut, open the Control Panel, then drag the Microsoft Mail Postoffice icon to the desktop. Choose Yes when Windows offers to create a shortcut for you. Once you've created a shortcut, you also can copy or cut and paste it to any location on the Start menu. To change the Start menu, right-click the Start button, then choose Open or Explore.

Moving the Postoffice

Microsoft does not provide any special tools for moving a workgroup post-office from one machine to another. Because a postoffice is just a file structure, moving it is really pretty easy. There are three parts to the operation:

- Copying or moving all the files from the postoffice folder (usually WGPO0000) to the new machine
- Sharing the new postoffice folder
- Revising user profiles to enable access to the postoffice at its new location

The new postoffice folder does not need to use the same folder name or share name as the old one. Also, if you move the postoffice rather than copy it, users will get a message when they next run Exchange that the postoffice couldn't be found. They'll have the opportunity to enter the new path, which you will have given them by now (but not via e-mail!).

Keeping the Postoffice Path

If you must move the workgroup postoffice to a new machine, there is a way to avoid making changes to user profiles. The key is to maintain the same path to the postoffice — in other words, the same *computername**sharename*. For example, if your postoffice was located on a computer named Mailman in a folder named WGPO0000 and shared as WGPO0000, users' Exchange profiles would point the Microsoft Mail service to \\Mailman\WGPO0000.

To move this postoffice without making the users change their profiles, follow these steps:

1. Give the Mailman computer a new name using the Network applet in the Control Panel, then restart that system.
2. Give the new computer the name Mailman and restart it.
3. Copy or move the WGPO0000 folder from the old computer to its home on the new Mailman computer, keeping the same folder name.
4. Share the new WGPO0000 folder as WGPO0000.

To client workstations, it will appear as if the postoffice never moved because it's still located at \\Mailman\WGPO0000, the same path that it used on the old machine.

Summary

Creating and maintaining a workgroup postoffice is the first step toward providing people in your organization with a way to share ideas and information with Exchange. Once you set up the postoffice, your main job will be to add and delete users as people come and go and occasionally to reset passwords and compress shared folders.

Key Points

- The postoffice should be located on a computer that will be on and available all the time.
- Be sure to safeguard a copy of the postoffice manager's password. If you lose the password, you will have no way to add or delete users.

For More Information

You can find the basic steps for setting up the Microsoft Mail service for Exchange in Chapter 6, "Setting Up Microsoft Mail."

You'll also find information about working with Microsoft Mail shared folders in the "Working with Folders" section of Chapter 10.

Chapter 24

Troubleshooting

Throughout the book, we've tried to highlight the most common problems with Exchange and the available workarounds. This chapter reviews some general problems, provides more detailed procedures for trouble-shooting Microsoft Fax, and suggests some additional techniques for getting to the bottom of a glitch. We'll also use the Inbox Repair Tool to fix problems with Personal Folders files.

One technique that can be applied in all cases is to put the information service suspected of causing trouble in a new profile along with a fresh set of Personal Folders and a new Personal Address book. If you can get the service to work in isolation like this, then copy it to an existing profile (see the section "Working with Services" on page 78 in Chapter 4).

General Problems

Try to isolate a troublesome Exchange service in a profile by itself.

Two of the most perplexing Exchange service problems are messages that stay in the Outbox and are never sent (we'll look at this in an upcoming section) and messages that are returned as undeliverable. If a message can't be delivered for some reason, it is returned to your Inbox attached to a message from the System Administrator (see the section "When Messages Fail," page 269 in Chapter 11). The text of the message (Figure 24.1) should help you resolve whatever problem prevented the message from going through. If the trouble was with particular addresses, those recipients will be listed. Once you have fixed the problem, you can click the Se<u>n</u>d Again button to resend the message.

Figure 24.1
Sometimes messages can't be delivered for some reason. When this happens, Exchange notifies you with a message from the System Administrator.

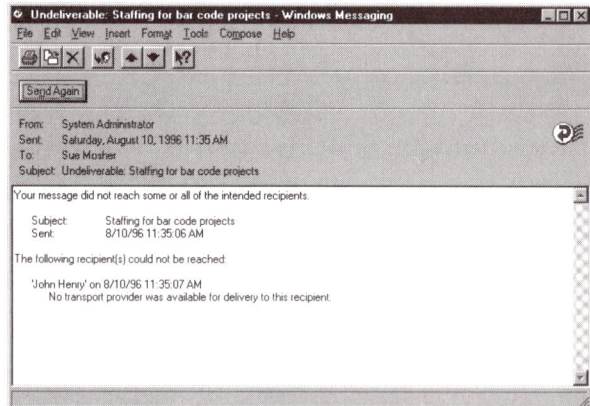

Special Note

The contents of the Sent Items folder can be somewhat misleading, because undeliverable messages are moved there, even though they were not successfully transmitted.

No Transport Provider

Perhaps the most mysterious undeliverable message is like the example shown in Figure 24.1, indicating that "No transport provider was available for delivery to this recipient." As you might recall from Chapter 2, the services that you install in your Exchange profile are mostly *transport providers*, services that handle the formatting and transmission of messages.

Receiving a "No transport provider..." message means there is a mis-match between the address(es) for the message and the transport services in the current Exchange profile. This can happen if you have multiple Exchange profiles on your computer, each with different services.

The easiest way to fix this problem is to first check the services installed in the profile, then check the addresses listed in the Undeliverable message notice as having had problems. To check the services, choose Tools, Services to display the Services dialog box shown in Figure 24.2.

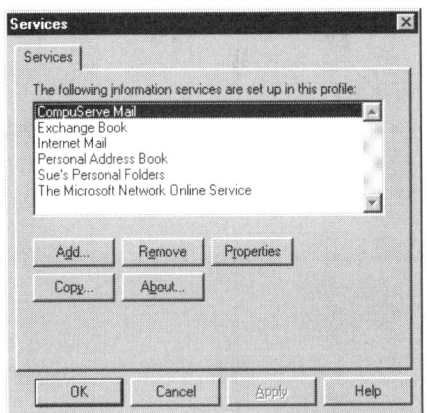

Figure 24.2

Transport services installed on this computer include CompuServe Mail, Internet Mail, and The Microsoft Network.

To check the addresses, click the Send Again button on the Undeliverable notice (Figure 24.1). Then right-click each name, choose Properties, and examine the Address tab shown in Figure 24.3 (additional tabs will be visible for addresses from the Address Book). In particular, you need to look at the "E-mail type" box. Table 24.1 lists some of the types you're likely to see.

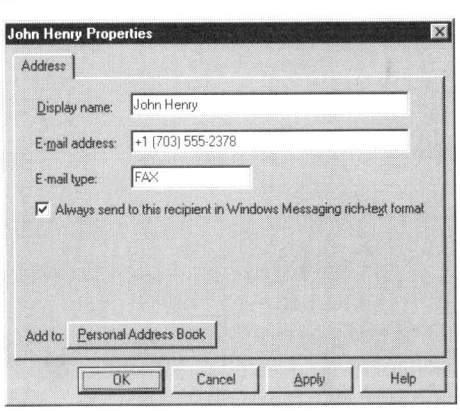

Figure 24.3

Look at the "E-mail type" to make sure it matches one of the transport providers in your Exchange profile.

Table 24.1 E-Mail Types	
Type	**Description**
COMPUSERVE	CompuServe address
EX	Microsoft Exchange Server address
FAX	Fax address
MS	Microsoft Mail address
MSN	The Microsoft Network address
MSNINET	Internet via The Microsoft Network
SMTP	Internet address

In Figure 24.3, the "E-mail type" is FAX. But there is no fax service listed in the Services dialog box shown in Figure 24.2. Because no fax transport is installed in the current profile, the message is undeliverable. Before resending the message, you would need to either

- Exit, then restart Exchange with a profile that includes a fax service, or
- Change the address for the message to an e-mail address that can be handled by one of the services in the current profile

When your Exchange profile contains more than one Internet-capable service, all Internet-bound messages are delivered via the first such service found in the delivery order.

Messages Stay in the Outbox

When messages stay in the Outbox folder without being sent, check for these possible situations:

- More than one service in the profile that can handle Internet mail
- Corruption in the Personal Folders file (on operating system Exchange clients)

We also discuss the Internet mail issue in Chapter 22, "Working with Internet E-Mail." What happens is that, if you have more than one service in your Exchange profile capable of delivering Internet mail (for example, both Microsoft Exchange Server and The Microsoft Network), all Internet-bound messages will go via just one of those services; *which* service is determined by the delivery order.

To set the delivery order, choose Tools, Options, then switch to the Delivery tab, shown in Figure 24.4. With the arrow buttons, rearrange the order of delivery so the service that you want to carry all messages to the Internet is listed above any other Internet-capable services.

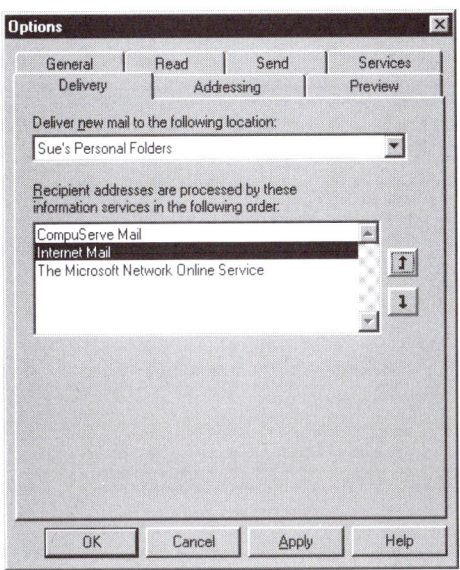

Figure 24.4
Use the up arrow to move your preferred Internet mail service to the top of the delivery order.

Using the Inbox Repair Tool

If the delivery order is not a problem, items sticking in the Outbox may be a symptom of Personal Folders corruption. This generally is an issue only with the Windows 95 and Windows NT operating system clients for Exchange (or for Windows Messaging).

Microsoft provides a utility to fix Personal Folders files. To use the Inbox Repair Tool, you will need to know the location of your Personal Folders file. To check the location of your Personal Folders file, choose Tools, Services. Then select the Personal Folders file from the Services dialog box (Figure 24.2) and click the Properties button. In the Properties dialog box for the Personal Folders service, look in the Path box for the location of the file.

To run the Inbox Repair Tool, follow these steps:

1. Click the Start button, then choose Programs, Accessories, System Tools, Inbox Repair Tool.

You will use the Inbox Repair Tool to fix Personal Folders files.

2. In the box provided in the Inbox Repair Tool dialog box, enter the name of the Personal Folders file you want to repair (you also can use the Browse button to locate the file). Then click the Start button.

3. The Inbox Repair Tool examines the file and reports on any errors, as shown in Figure 24.5. For more information, click the Details button (see Figure 24.6).

Figure 24.5

The Inbox Repair Tool analyzes a Personal Folders file, then lets you choose to repair any errors found.

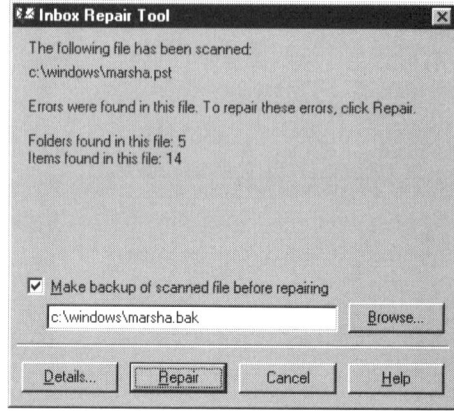

Figure 24.6

The Details dialog box provides more information about the errors in the file.

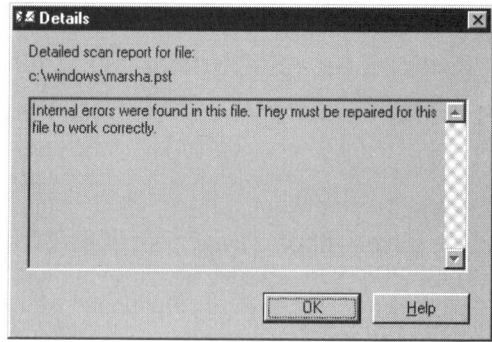

4. To perform the actual repair, click the Repair button.

If the Inbox Repair Tool does not repair apparent damage to the Personal Folders file, try running ScanDisk (also found on the Systems Tools menu), then run Inbox Repair Tool again. It's sometimes necessary to repeat this sequence — ScanDisk, then Inbox Repair Tool — several times.

Emptying the Outbox

Another way to deal with messages stuck in the Outbox on the Windows 95 and Windows NT operating system clients is to create a new profile that contains only the Personal Folders you used to create the messages. Do not include any transport services, such as Microsoft Fax or Internet Mail. Start Exchange with this profile. All the messages in the Outbox will automatically move to Sent Items, with Undeliverable notices sent to the Inbox, noting that no transport provider was available to send the message. You can then quit Exchange, restart it with your original profile, and try to resend the messages.

"Object Could Not Be Found"

On the Windows 95 operating system version of Exchange, you might get one of the following error messages when you try to read or compose a message:

```
- The item could not be displayed. The object could not be
  found.
Microsoft Windows Messaging System Forms Registry - 13085 -
  [8004010F]
```

or

```
- The command you specified could not be carried out. The
  object could not be found.
Microsoft Windows Messaging System Forms Registry - 13085 -
  [8004010F]
```

These messages indicate that either the Frmcache.dat file in the Windows\Forms folder is missing or corrupted, or the Program Files\Microsoft Exchange folder does not have a short folder name of Progra~1\Micros~1, possibly because of long-file-name damage. The Frmcache.dat file is used to store information about the forms used to display Exchange messages.

To fix this problem, it's best to quit Exchange and remove all existing Exchange profiles. Before quitting Exchange, you should write down all the key information (user IDs, mail server locations, and so on). Repeat for all profiles. The Personal Folders and Personal Address Book files should not be affected, but it's not a bad idea to back them up anyway by making a copy of those files. Once you've backed up this key information and quit Exchange, follow these steps:

1. Delete the Windows\Forms folder.

2. In the Control Panel, double-click the Mail and Fax icon, then click the Show Profiles button.

3. On the General tab, click the Remove button until all profiles have been removed.

4. Click the Close button.

5. Click Start, then Find, Files or Folders.

6. Under Named, enter **Mlset32.exe**, then click Find Now.

7. When the Mlset32.exe file has been located, double-click it to run it.

8. The wizard will ask whether you've used Microsoft Exchange before. Click No, then Next.

9. Set up services for an initial profile, using the Personal Folders and Personal Address Book already on your computer.

If the Mlset32.exe file does not turn up in step 6, you can extract the file from the Win95_07.cab file (floppy or CD). Here's an example of the syntax to extract it. It is essential that the case of the characters after the / switches be as noted.

extract /L C:\Windows D:\Win95\Win95_07.cab Mlset32.exe

You can modify this command to point to the particular drive and folder where Win95_07.cab is located on your system. This command will place Mlset32.exe in your Windows folder. You can then run it from there.

"MPREXE.EXE Caused a Page Fault"

When you start Exchange on a Windows 95 system, you may get the following error message:

```
MPREXE.EXE caused a page fault in KERNEL32.DLL
```

This error actually has nothing directly to do with Exchange. It's caused by a corrupt password list file. Your password list file is a .pwl file with your Windows user name. For example, if you log on to Windows as "LisaC," the password list file is LisaC.pwl, located in your Windows folder.

Another symptom of the same problem is that the option to remember passwords, "Save this password in your password list," may be grayed out or unavailable in various dialog boxes. An existing password list file has the potential to become corrupted if you have applied Service Pack 1 for Windows 95.

You can resolve the problem by either repairing or deleting the password list file. Try repair first, because if you delete the password list file, you will be forced to re-enter all the passwords you normally use. To repair the password list files on your computer, obtain the Windows 95 Password List Update from Microsoft (see Appendix B, "Exchange Resources") and run the Mspwlupd2.exe program.

If you continue to see this error, delete the password list file for your Windows user name, then restart Windows. A new password list file will be created automatically for you after you log on.

Restoring a Missing Service

After adding the Windows Messaging update to Windows 95 or installing the Exchange Server client, you may no longer see a particular service in the list available to add to a profile.

If the service is installed in any other profile, then you simply can copy it from that profile (see "Adding a Service," page 79 in Chapter 4). Otherwise, you will need to repair the Mapisvc.inf file, which apparently was damaged during the installation.

Mapisvc.inf is a text file that contains information about the Exchange services that have been installed on your system and are available to your profiles. In some cases, the details for Microsoft Fax or The Microsoft Network are removed during the client upgrade process. The files needed by those services are still on your system; you just don't have any way of telling Exchange how to use them!

The best way to prevent this problem is to make a copy of the Mapisvc.inf file before you install any new Exchange client. However, if you didn't take that precaution, you can get a fresh copy of the Mapisvc.inf file that contains the Microsoft Fax and The Microsoft Network entries by following these steps:

1. Insert the Windows 95 CD in your CD-ROM drive, or, if you are using Windows 95 disks, insert Disk 7.

2. Choose Start, Run.

3. In the Open box, type the following:

   extract /L C:\Windows\Temp D:\Win95\Win95_07.cab Mapisvc.inf

   You can modify this command to point to the actual drive where Win95_07.cab is located or to change C:\Windows\Temp to any other temporary location.

4. Click OK to extract a copy of Mapisvc.inf to the C:\Windows\Temp folder.

Next, make a backup copy of the old Mapisvc.inf file, found in your Windows\System folder, then open the Mapisvc.inf file in Notepad. Use a second copy of Notepad to open the copy of the Mapisvc.inf file that you just extracted. At the top of the Mapisvc.inf file, you'll see a [Services] section. Look in the extracted copy of the Mapisvc.inf file for the services you need that are missing in the old copy of the Mapisvc.inf file. These might include

AWFAX=Microsoft Fax

MSN=The Microsoft Network Online Service

Copy these lines from the [Services] section of the extracted Mapisvc.inf to the [Services] section of the Mapisvc.inf from Windows\System. The order doesn't matter, since Exchange displays available services in alphabetical order.

If you have added the line for AWFAX, now look in the extracted copy of the Mapisvc.inf file for sections whose names begin with AWFAX. You should find

[AWFAX]

[AWFAX_AB]

[AWFAX_XP]

For The Microsoft Network, you should see these sections:

[MSN]

[MSN_ABP]

[MSN_RXP]

For each service that you added to the [Services] section, copy the corresponding sections listed above to the end of the Mapisvc.inf file from Windows\System. Be sure to copy the entire section, including the heading and all the lines under it.

After you've edited the Mapisvc.inf file to copy the necessary sections, save it. You should now be able to add the restored services to any profile. Remember, though, that if you also are missing components for those services, they won't work. See "Reviewing Service Components" later in this chapter for information about how to tell whether you have all the necessary parts.

Microsoft Fax Troubleshooting

Troubleshooting Microsoft Fax errors can be tricky, because modems and phone lines are added to the possible causes. Problems can occur both in sending and in receiving faxes. Here is a general sequence of steps to follow to try to isolate the trouble:

1. Put Microsoft Fax in a profile by itself with a new Personal Folders file.
2. Check any faxes in the Outbox to make sure they have correct FAX-type addresses.
3. Check with your modem vendor to see if there is an updated .inf file with new setup strings for your modem.
4. Disable high-speed transmission and error correction, as described below.
5. Lower the modem transmit and receive buffers, as described below.
6. Experiment with a different phone line to try to eliminate line noise as a possible cause.
7. Manually remove faxes from the queue, as described below.

Adjusting the Modem Settings

To disable high-speed transmission and error correction, follow these steps:

1. Choose Tools, Microsoft Fax Tools, Options, then switch to the Modem tab in the Microsoft Fax Properties dialog box.
2. Select the active fax modem, then click the Properties button.
3. In the Fax Modem Properties dialog box, click the Advanced button.
4. In the Advanced dialog box (Figure 24.7), check "Disable high speed transmission" and "Disable error correction mode."

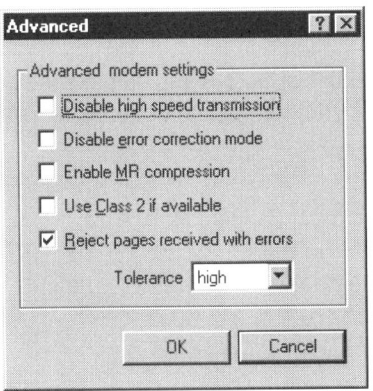

Figure 24.7
Advanced modem settings are usually changed only for troubleshooting Microsoft Fax problems.

5. Click OK three times to return to the Exchange Viewer.

Note that in the Advanced dialog box you also can adjust the threshold for rejecting faxes with errors.

To lower the modem transmit and receive buffers, follow these steps:

1. Click the Start button, then choose Settings, Control Panel.

2. Double-click the Modems applet.

3. In the Modems Properties dialog box (see Figure 24.9), select the modem being used for Microsoft Fax, then click the Properties button.

4. In the properties dialog box for the modem, switch to the Connection tab, then click the Port Settings button.

5. In the Advanced Port Settings dialog box (Figure 24.8), move the slider for the Receive Buffer down a notch. Repeat for the Transmit Buffer.

Figure 24.8
Reduce the Receive Buffer and Transmit Buffer settings to try to resolve Microsoft Fax connection problems.

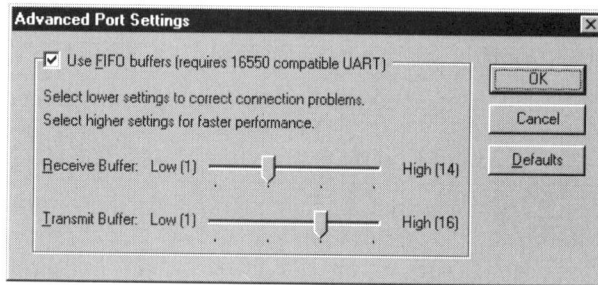

6. Click OK as needed to save the new settings and return to the Control Panel.

Manually Removing Faxes from the Queue

In the case where a fax is queued in the Outbox but isn't being sent, you can take the step of removing it from the queue by hand, then requeuing it. Follow these steps:

1. Choose File, Exit and Log Off to quit Exchange.

2. Choose Start, Programs, MS-DOS Prompt to open a DOS window.

3. At the DOS prompt, type **CD \Windows\Spool\Fax** to change to the Spool\Fax folder in your Windows folder.

4. Type these commands to remove the temporary fax files:

del *.mg3
del *.efx

5. Type **EXIT** and press Enter to close the DOS window.

When you restart Exchange, new files will be created in Windows\ Spool\Fax for any faxes that were in the Outbox. If you don't want the faxes to be requeued in this fashion, then start Exchange with a profile that contains the same Personal Folders file, but does not include the Microsoft Fax service (see "Emptying the Outbox" earlier in this chapter). The faxes should fail with an Undeliverable message sent to the Inbox indicating that no transport service was available. You can resend them later, if you wish, by starting Exchange with a profile that does include Microsoft Fax.

Information-Gathering Techniques

Sometimes the source of an Exchange problem is obscure. You may need to consult some of the resources listed in Appendix B. Before you do this, put together as much information about your configuration as you can. If you have a computer where Exchange is working fine, compare its settings and logs with the machine that's having problems.

Reviewing Service Components

Every information service is composed of one or more .dll (dynamic link library) files. If one or more of these files is missing, damaged, or the wrong version, you'll have problems with a service. Here's how to check these components:

1. In the Control Panel, double-click the Mail and Fax (or Mail) icon.

2. On the Services tab, select the service you suspect of problems, then click the About button.

3. In the About Information Service dialog box (see Figure 24.9), you will see the names of the .dll files that make up the service. You can select each file to review its version and date.

Use the About button in the Profile Properties dialog box to check the components for each service.

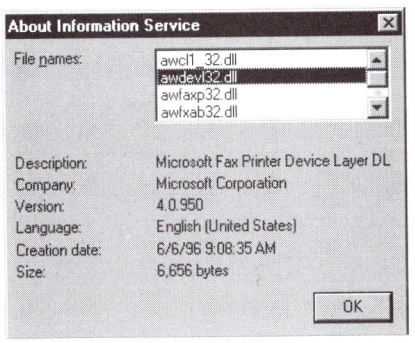

Figure 24.9

Each Exchange information service includes one or more .dll files, whose properties you can examine in this dialog box.

Table 24.2 lists the .dll files for Exchange services distributed by Microsoft.

Table 24.2 Information Service Components	
Service	**Components**
Microsoft Exchange Server	Emsabp32.dll
	Emsmdb32.dll
	Emsui32.dll
Microsoft Fax	Awcl1_32.dll
	Awdevl32.dll
	Awfaxp32.dll
	Awfxab32.dll
	Awfxcg32.dll
	Awrndr32.dll
Microsoft Mail	Msfs32.dll
The Microsoft Network	Mosabp32.dll
	Moscfg32.dll
	Mosrxp32.dll
Internet Mail	Minet32.dll
CompuServe Mail	Csmapa32.dll
	Csmapx32.dll
Personal Folders and Personal Address Book	Mspst32.dll

If any of these components is missing, the easiest thing to do is to re-install that service from your latest source — either the original system or application disk, or an update you may have downloaded. If the components are there, make a note of the date and version and include that information when you contact Microsoft technical support or post a message in a newsgroup.

Keeping Logs

Some Exchange services and Windows components include logging functions. We mentioned these in Part II, as we discussed the configuration of Exchange in general and the specific services. Table 24.3 summarizes these log files and others that may be useful.

Table 24.3 Log Files Useful for Exchange Troubleshooting	
Log File	**Description**
Modemdet.txt	Log file for modem detection during Windows setup
Modemlog.txt	Records modem session events and commands sent to the modem
Mailbox.log	Inbox Repair Tool log for Personal Folders file named Mailbox.pst (Logs for other Personal Folders files use the same name as the .pst file, but a .log extension.)
Msfslog.txt	Microsoft Mail connection and event log
Imail.log	Internet Mail connection and event log
Ppplog.txt	Log for dial-up networking connections
Synchronization Log	Log for offline folders synchronization (Exchange Server clients only), found in the Deleted Items folder in your Exchange mailbox

Not all log files will be present on every system. Most are located in the Windows folder. The easiest way to find a log file is to click the Start button, then Find, and search your computer for the file. Open the log file in either Notepad or WordPad.

Summary

In this chapter we have provided guidelines for solving common problems not associated with a particular Exchange service, and we have introduced the

Inbox Repair Tool for cleaning up damaged Personal Folders files. In addition, we have included details about Microsoft Fax troubleshooting to supplement the specific problem-solving tips we offered in the chapters on Microsoft Fax.

Key Points

- Try to isolate a troublesome Exchange service in a profile by itself.

- A mismatch between the address for a message and the services in your Exchange profile will cause a message to be returned as undeliverable because "No transport provider was available."

- When your Exchange profile contains more than one Internet-capable service, all Internet-bound messages are delivered via the first such service found in the delivery order.

- Use the Inbox Repair Tool to fix Personal Folders files.

- Use the About button in the profile properties dialog box to check the components for each service.

For More Information

Most of the common problems with Microsoft Fax are listed in Chapter 14, "Sending Faxes," and Chapter 15, "Receiving Faxes." You should try the troubleshooting suggestions in the current chapter after you've checked out the specific problems addressed in those chapters.

Similarly, particular problems known to affect different information services are covered in the chapters in Part II that discuss setting up those services.

Chapter 25

Introducing Microsoft Exchange Server 5.0

Throughout this book, you've learned about the features of Microsoft Exchange Server, whose initial release was version 4.0. The newest release, version 5.0, gives Exchange users several new and exciting ways to access their mailboxes on a Microsoft Exchange server and adds the capability to access Internet newsgroups via Exchange Server public folders. Also new are support for connecting to Lotus cc:Mail systems and a number of general enhancements to the Exchange Server client.

New Features in Exchange Server 5.0

Exchange Server 5.0 adds three new ways to access your Exchange mailbox.

For users, the biggest news in Exchange Server 5.0 may be the three new clients:

- Microsoft Outlook
- Internet (POP3) support
- Web browser support

Outlook is an entirely new client included with Exchange Server 5.0 that organizes mail and scheduling, plus all sorts of desktop information. It's also part of Microsoft Office 97. You'll get an in-depth look in the next chapter.

Exchange Server 5.0 turns the server into a POP3/SMTP mail server, which means you can access your Exchange mailbox from any mail software that can access a POP3 mailbox. That could be Exchange using the Internet Mail service, or it could be a completely different mail program such as Eudora. This change is important if you need quick, reliable access to your mail (but not to public folders) from a machine that might be underpowered for the standard Exchange Server client, or that is running an operating system for which there is no Exchange client.

The third new way to access your mail is via a Web browser that supports frames and Java, such as Microsoft Internet Explorer 3.0 or Netscape Navigator 3.0. You can not only see your mailbox, but also use public folders and search the address list.

Microsoft also has added Internet newsgroup support to Exchange Server, allowing you to read and post messages to newsgroups as you would with other public folders and to publish public folders so they can be accessed by newsgroup client programs.

Another new feature is a connector to Lotus cc:Mail systems, so you don't need to use a separate Exchange service such as MAPI ConnectorWare for cc:Mail or ccXchg (see "Enterprise Mail Services," page 194 in Chapter 9).

Let's start our survey of the new features by examining some general enhancements to messages, rules, and folders in the new Exchange Server 5.0 client. Then we'll look at the cc:Mail, POP3, Web, and newsgroup features.

Message Enhancements

Changes to the message window make it easier to browse items that you haven't read. Exchange has added a Reply To address for your messages. Also, you can specify either MIME or UUENCODE for any particular recipient in your address book. Finally, you also can now exchange security keys with Exchange Server users at other organizations.

Improved Browsing

When you have an item open, you can easily move to the first item in the next or previous group of items or view the next or previous unread item.

- To read the next unread item, choose View, Next Unread or click the Next Unread button.
- To read the previous unread item, choose View, Previous Unread or click the Previous Unread button.
- To see the first item in the next group of items, choose View, Next Group or click the Next Group button.
- To see the first item in the previous group of items, choose View, Previous Group or click the Previous Group button.

New buttons for Next Unread and Next Group are automatically added to the toolbar in the window used to read posts in folders. To add these buttons to the toolbar in the window used to read messages, open a message, then choose Tools, Customize Toolbar. You'll also need to customize the toolbar if you want to use the Previous Unread or Previous Group buttons for browsing either messages or folder posts.

Supporting "Reply To"

You can now specify that replies to your message be sent to a different address, rather than to your own e-mail address. This feature, called "Reply To," is often found in Internet mail programs.

To change the Reply To address for a message,

1. In the New Message window, choose View, Reply To Box.
2. The Reply To box appears at the top of the New Message form, as shown in Figure 25.1. Either type in the recipient's name or address, or click the Reply To button to use the Address Book to enter the address.

Like the Bcc box (see "Displaying the Bcc Box," page 273 in Chapter 11), the Reply To box will appear in every New Message window until you disable it by choosing View, Reply To Box again.

If you want both another person and yourself to get replies, enter both your own address and the other person's in the Reply To box.

You now have the option of specifying a Reply To address to redirect replies to a different address.

Figure 25.1

Use the Reply To box to specify that responses to your messages be sent to someone else.

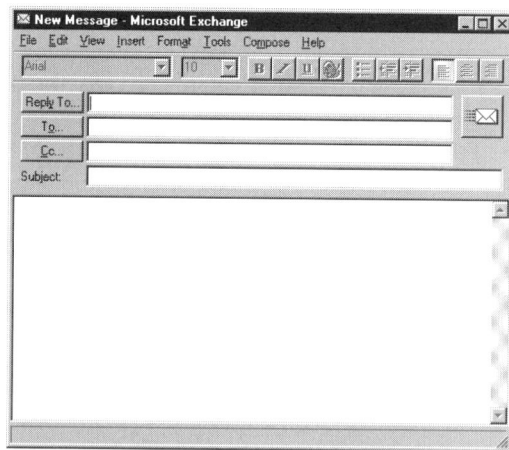

Specifying Per-Recipient Encoding

If you use MIME as the default for encoding Internet messages (see "Choosing a Message Format," page 506 in Chapter 22), but a particular recipient needs a different encoding method, you can now associate a specific format in that recipient's entry in your Personal Address Book. Here's how:

1. Choose Tools, Address Book.

2. Select an Internet recipient, then choose File, Properties.

3. On the SMTP - Address tab of the Properties dialog box, click the "Send Options…" button to display the "Send Options for this Recipient" dialog box shown in Figure 25.2.

4. Check the box labeled "I want to specify the format for messages to this recipient."

5. Select the format you want to use — MIME (plain text and/or HTML), UUENCODE, or UUENCODE with BINHEX for Macintosh attachments.

6. Click OK to save the format with the address book entry.

Note that this option works only when you have the Microsoft Exchange Server service in your profile, and does not affect messages sent through other Internet services.

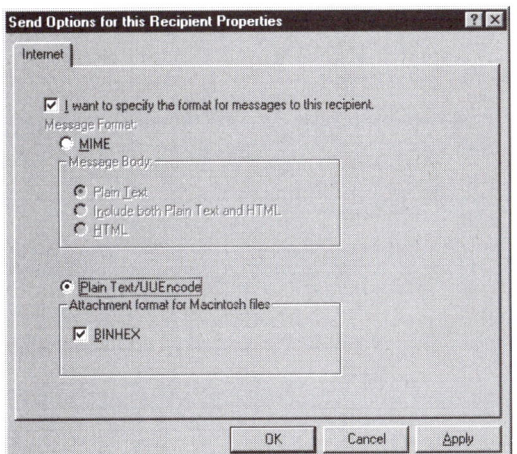

Figure 25.2

A separate message format can be specified for each Internet recipient in your Personal Address Book.

Sending Security Keys

If you use Exchange Server security (see "Working with Microsoft Exchange Server Security," page 491 in Chapter 21), your public security keys can be exchanged with users in other organizations that also use Exchange Server security. This will let you send and receive encrypted and digitally signed mail via the Internet.

Exchange Server 5.0 includes a special form for creating a message to exchange keys. When the recipient opens the message, it displays the option to add an entry to the Personal Address Book that includes the keys.

To send your keys to another user,

1. Choose Tools, Options, then switch to the Security tab.

2. Click the Send Security Keys button.

3. In the Microsoft Exchange Security Logon dialog box, enter your "Security password," the one you entered when you set up security for Exchange, then click OK.

4. In the Security Key Exchange Message window, shown in Figure 25.3, enter the addresses of the Exchange Server users to whom you want to send your keys. You can either type their addresses in the To box or click the To button and pick them from the address book.

5. Exchange automatically fills in Your E-mail Address with your Internet e-mail address. You should check both that and the Display Name, because these will be used to build a Personal Address Book (PAB) entry on the recipient's computer.

You can exchange security keys with Exchange Server 5.0 users in other organizations, letting you send and receive encrypted and digitally signed mail.

Figure 25.3

The Security Key Exchange Message form is used to send your public keys to Exchange Server users in other organizations so you can exchange encrypted and signed messages with them.

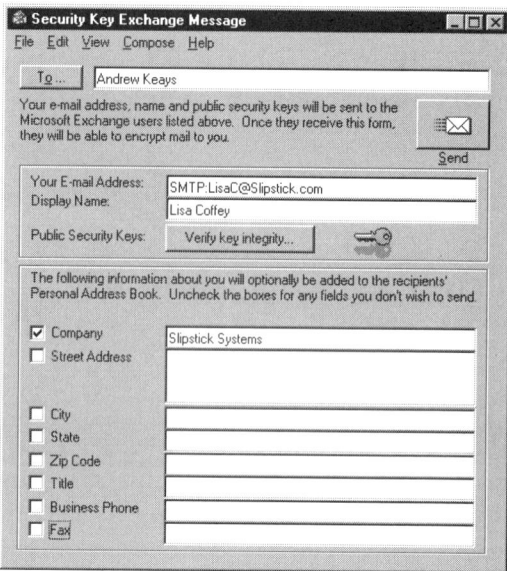

6. You can transmit additional information for the PAB entry that will be created. Enter your Company and other details in the boxes at the bottom of the Security Key Exchange Message window. If you leave any box blank, clear the corresponding checkbox.

7. Click the Send button when you've finishing filling out the form.

This message will appear in the recipient's Inbox with a green key icon and the subject, "Security Keys for" plus the name of the sender. To add the keys contained in the message to the PAB,

1. Open the message that displays the green key icon.

2. In the Security Key Exchange Message window, shown in Figure 25.4, use the fields at the bottom of the window to add any personal details that you want to store in the PAB.

3. Click the Add to Personal Address Book button to create a new PAB entry that includes this person's security keys. Enter your security password if you're prompted to do so.

4. Close the Security Key Exchange Message. You might want to retain a copy of the message in an archive folder in case you ever need to reconstruct that Personal Address Book entry.

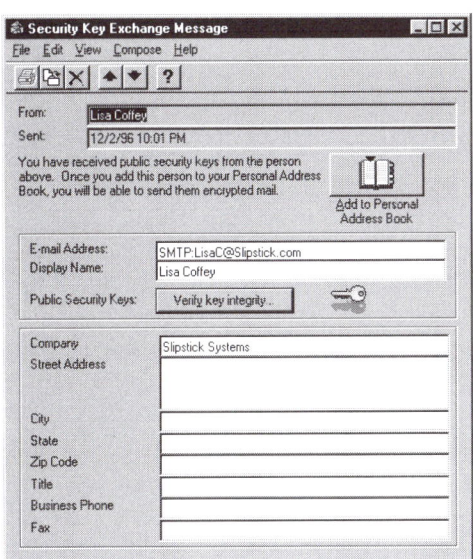

Figure 25.4

When you send your keys to another Exchange Server user, that recipient sees this message, including its distinct Add to Personal Address Book button.

Here are a few additional notes about exchanging security keys:

- You don't need to exchange keys with people in your own organization, because they can access your public keys through Exchange Server.

- The recipient must be using version 5.0 of the Exchange Server client and must be enabled for Exchange Server security.

- When you receive a key exchange message, both you and the sender can use the "Verify key integrity" button to display a series of codes that can be matched over the phone or by some other separate means to confirm the accuracy of the key exchange.

Assistant Rules Enhancements

The Exchange Server 5.0 client includes several enhancements to make working with Inbox Assistant rules easier:

- You can specify that a particular rule should be the last one applied to a message.

- You can forward a message so that the recipient sees the original sender and other header details.

- Rules can be associated with all your profiles, rather than being limited to the profile where you created the rule.

Enhancements to rules let you specify the last rule to be applied to a message, preserve a message when it's forwarded, and associate rules with multiple profiles.

These improvements, of course, also apply to Out of Office Assistant and Folder Assistant rules.

Specifying the Final Rule

When you create rules, it's often useful to build them as a series that gradually narrows to a final rule that's applied to everything that didn't fit the previous conditions. To accomplish this, you need to be able to stop the processing of an item once you've applied every rule designed for that type of item. Under Exchange Server 4.0, the only way to do that was to use a Delete rule, often after a Move rule, to remove the item from the Inbox.

You now can specify that processing of an item halt if a particular rule fires, without deleting the item from the Inbox. To do so, follow these steps:

1. Choose Tools, Inbox Assistant.

2. In the Inbox Assistant dialog box, click either Add Rule to start a new rule or Edit Rule to work with an existing rule.

3. Enter the conditions and action(s) in the Edit Rule dialog box (Figure 25.5).

Figure 25.5

To specify that a rule is the last one for a particular condition, check the "Do not process subsequent rules" box.

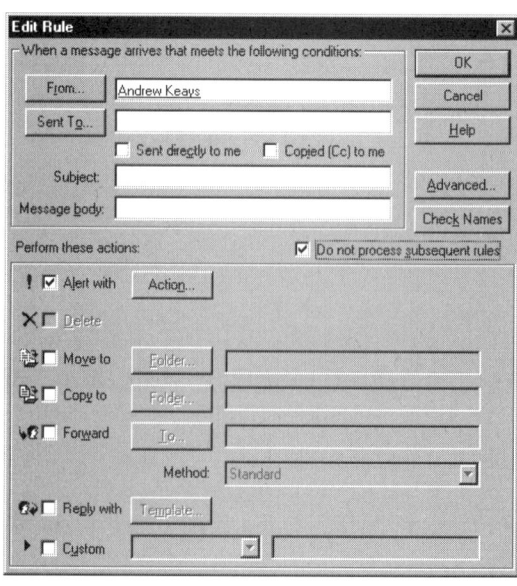

4. Check the "Do not process subsequent rules" box.

5. Click OK to save the rule, then OK again to close the Inbox Assistant dialog box.

Note that this technique also works with Outbox Assistant and Folder Assistant rules.

Associating Rules with Any Profile

In version 4.0 of the Exchange Server client, any Inbox Assistant or Out of Office Assistant rule was associated with a particular profile. A rule created in another profile appeared in the Inbox Assistant dialog box, but the rule was dimmed and unavailable. By copying folder properties, you could extend rules to other profiles, but not without a lot of work.

Exchange Server 5.0 takes care of this issue. Now you can extend a rule to apply to any profile. Here's how:

1. Choose Tools, Inbox Assistant.
2. In the Inbox Assistant dialog box (Figure 25.6), check the "Show rules for all profiles" box.

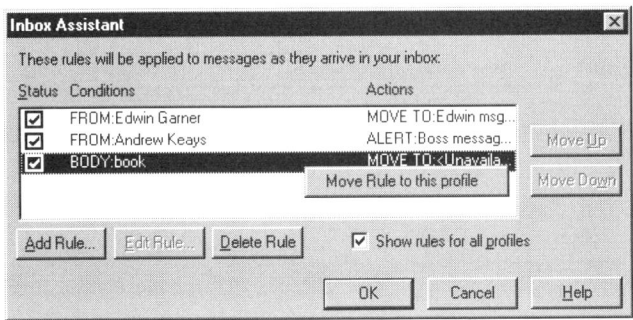

Figure 25.6

Right-click a dimmed (disabled) rule from another profile to have the option of using the disabled rule in the current profile.

3. Right-click a disabled (dimmed) rule that you want to make available to the current profile.
4. On the pop-up menu, choose "Move Rule to this profile."
5. Click OK to close the Inbox Assistant dialog box.

Note that this technique also works with Outbox Assistant rules.

New Forwarding Methods

When you use a rule to forward messages, you now can control how those messages look to the recipient — in particular, whether they carry the original sender's address or your address as the person who forwarded the message.

You'll find these new choices in the Edit Rule dialog box in a list under the T̲o box for the For̲ward rule, as shown in Figure 25.7. Standard is the original method of forwarding via a rule, while "Leave message intact" and "As an attachment" are the two new choices. Table 25.1 spells out what happens to the forwarded message when you use these different methods.

Figure 25.7
New forwarding methods let you send intact messages on to another user.

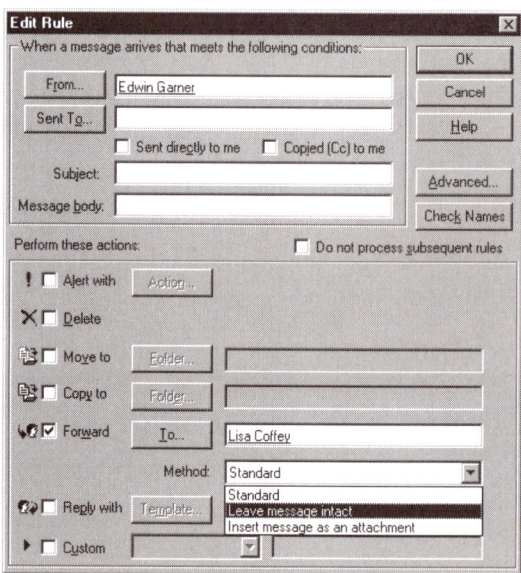

Table 25.1 Methods for Forwarding Rules			
Method	**To Field**	**Subject Field**	**Message Body**
Standard	Address of person who forwarded	FW: + original subject	From, Sent To, Subject from original message, plus "Auto forwarded by a Rule," followed by the text of the message
Leave message intact	Original sender	Original subject	Original message
As an attachment	Address of person who forwarded	FW: + original subject	Original message as an attachment

Here are a couple of additional notes on the new forwarding methods:

- "Leave message intact" is a good choice if you are forwarding messages to yourself at another address (see "Forwarding Messages to an Internet Mailbox," page 420 in Chapter 18).
- Use "As an attachment" only when you can be certain that the recipient is also using Exchange, because otherwise the attached message can't be opened.

Folder Enhancements

Another set of Exchange Server 5.0 enhancements makes it easier to work with folders, particularly public folders. For example, you now receive a warning whenever you delete a folder, asking if you're sure you want to permanently delete it. Other new features include a Follow-up To option and the ability to rename a folder in Favorites and store favorite folders as subfolders.

Supporting "Follow-up To"

Just as Reply To is now supported for messages, a Follow-up To option is available for posts in folders, to direct replies to a different folder rather than to the folder where the original message was posted.

To add a Follow-up To location for an item being posted in a folder,

1. In the New Post window, choose View, Follow-up To Box.
2. The Follow-up To box appears at the top of the post form, as shown in Figure 25.8. Click the Follow-up To button.
3. In the Follow-up To dialog box, select the folder where you want to direct replies, then click OK to return to the post form and complete the item.

Like the Reply To box, the Follow-up To box will appear on every New Post window until you disable it by choosing View, Follow-up To Box again.

When a user opens the item and chooses Compose, Post Reply to Folder or clicks the Post Reply in This Folder button, the reply will automatically be posted in the folder designated as the Follow-up To folder for that item.

This feature can be extremely useful where you allow read-only access to a folder but still want to encourage feedback by routing replies to a separate discussion folder. Examples include public folders containing company policies, technical support documents, or product descriptions.

Figure 25.8
*When you use a
different Follow-up To
destination folder, replies
are kept separate from
the original postings.*

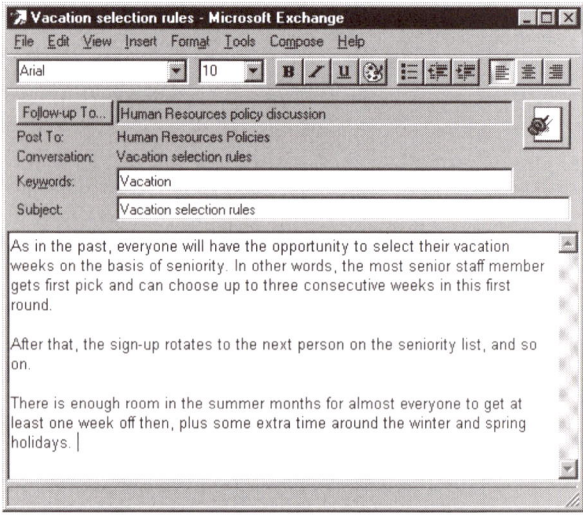

Working with Favorites Folders

You can rename folders in your Favorites list without affecting the original public folder names.

You'll recall that to add a public folder to your Favorites folders, you can select the folder, then choose File, Add to Favorites. In version 5.0, an Add to Favorites dialog box (Figure 25.9) appears, where you can specify the Favorite Folder Name that you want to use in your own Favorites folder.

In Figure 25.9, the Options button has been clicked to show another new Favorites folder feature. When you add a folder that has subfolders, you can choose whether those subfolders will also be added to Favorites.

You can rename a Favorites folder at any time by choosing File, Rename or by right-clicking on the folder, then choosing Rename. Renaming a folder in Favorites is strictly for your convenience and does not affect the name of the folder as it appears under All Public Folders.

Connecting to cc:Mail

Another new feature in version 5.0 is a connector to Lotus cc:Mail systems. What this means to you if you're a cc:Mail user is that you don't need to use a separate Exchange service such as MAPI ConnectorWare for cc:Mail or ccXchg.

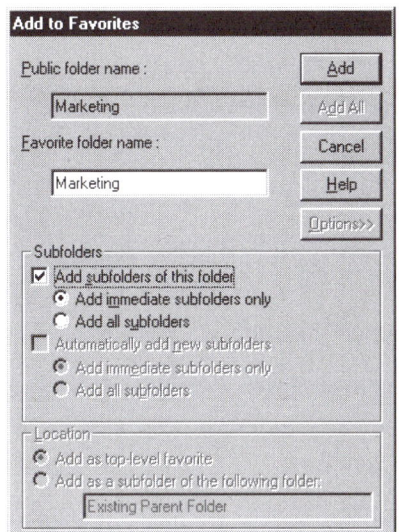

Figure 25.9
Folders added to your Favorites folder can use names that you choose. You also can choose to add subfolders to Favorites.

Setting Up cc:Mail

Actually, there's nothing for the user to set up. Your personal messages should be migrated by the Exchange Server administrator to your Exchange mailbox, while bulletin board information is copied to public folders.

How It Works

A connector works directly with Exchange Server to convert incoming and outgoing messages and provide access to address lists. Because all the work is done by the server on the "back" end, the user needs to do nothing special. Whenever you address a message to a cc:Mail user within your organization, Exchange takes care of delivery.

In fact, any cc:Mail addresses you may have entered in your PAB while using MAPI ConnectorWare or ccXchg should still work, because the addresses use the e-mail type of CCMAIL, the same type used by the new connector in version 5.0.

You also can add new cc:Mail addresses, of course. To do so, follow these steps:

1. Choose Tools, Address Book, or click the Address Book button.
2. Switch to the Personal Address Book if it's not already displayed.
3. Choose File, New Entry, or click the New Entry button.
4. On the New Entry dialog box, select "cc:Mail Address," then click OK.

The user needs to do nothing special to use the cc:Mail connector, because the Microsoft Exchange server does all the work.

5. In the New cc:Mail Address Properties dialog box (Figure 25.10), fill in the address details, then click OK to save the new address.

Figure 25.10

Addresses created for the cc:Mail connector use an e-mail type of CCMAIL.

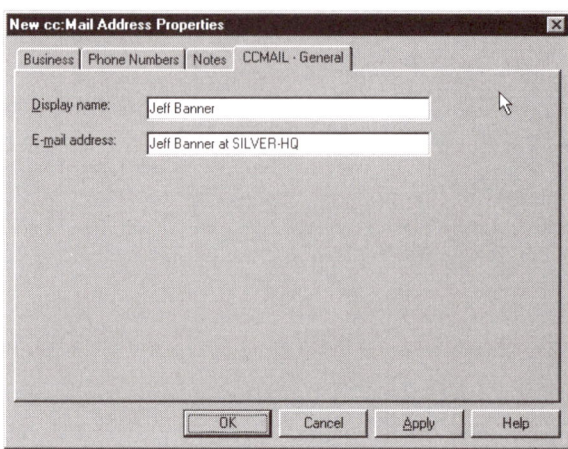

Connecting to Exchange Server with POP3/SMTP

Now let's turn to the new clients for Exchange Server 5.0, starting with the POP3/SMTP server capability.

How It Works

Under version 5.0, the Microsoft Exchange server can act as a POP3/SMTP mail server, so that it operates just like a mail server at an Internet service provider. The advantage to your whole organization is that this capability allows any computer to access an Exchange mailbox using whatever Internet mail software is appropriate for a particular computer, depending on its operating system and resources.

A computer running Microsoft Exchange Server 5.0 can act as a POP3/SMTP server, allowing you to use virtually any Internet mail program to get your messages.

Setting Up POP3/SMTP

Just as with any Internet mail service, you need to know your e-mail account, password, and mail server addresses (see "How to Get an Account," page 178 in Chapter 8). The syntax for the mailbox account can take three different formats, depending on how both the Windows NT user and Exchange user accounts are set up. Table 25.2 lists the variations you're likely to see. Your Exchange administrator can tell you which is appropriate for your use.

Table 25.2 POP/SMTP Account Name Formats

Syntax	Example	Usage
NT_Domain\NT_User\ Exchange_Mailbox	Verona\Rmontague\ Romeo	When the NT user account name and the Exchange mailbox name are different
NT_Domain\NT_User	Verona\Romeo	When the NT user account name and Exchange mailbox name are the same and you know the domain name
Exchange_Mailbox	Romeo	When the NT user account name and Exchange mailbox name are the same and you don't know the domain name

Using just the Exchange mailbox name as the POP3/SMTP account name isn't practical if your organization has a large number of domains and users, because the domains must be searched to locate the one that contains the indicated user account.

The POP3 server for incoming mail is the computer name of the Microsoft Exchange server where the mailbox account resides. The SMTP server for outgoing mail is the computer name of the system running the Internet Mail Connector that will deliver mail to the Internet. Often, it's the same as the POP3 server, but your Exchange administrator can tell you for sure. With POP3/SMTP, the password is always the Windows NT password for the primary NT account for the mailbox.

If you want to try connecting to Exchange Server as a POP3/SMTP mail client, you can create an Exchange profile using the Internet Mail service. Just follow the instructions in Chapter 8, "Setting Up Internet Mail," using the e-mail account, password, and mail server addresses described above.

Limitations

The POP3/SMTP capability of Exchange Server 5.0 isn't intended to be a full-time substitute for the more robust capabilities of the regular Exchange Server client. You can't synchronize your private folders with it, send or receive encrypted or digitally signed messages, or access public folders. You can send unencrypted messages and retrieve any new messages sent to you, but that's about it.

Connecting to Exchange Server from the Web

The Exchange Web Service provides access to your mailbox and turns Exchange into an Internet publication platform.

The other new Exchange client that we'll cover in this chapter is the Web browser client. As with the POP3/SMTP client, this expands the reach of Exchange Server to any computer with a compatible browser. But it goes way beyond the POP3/SMTP client to offer access not only to incoming e-mail messages, but also to any private folders you've created, to public folders, and to the list of other Exchange users in your organization. In addition, it provides anonymous access to public folders, turning Exchange into an Internet publication platform.

Setting Up Web Browser Access

The principle requirement for Web browser access is a browser that supports both frames and Java and has Java and JavaScript enabled. Microsoft has tested Microsoft Internet Explorer 3.0 and Netscape Navigator 3.0.

You'll also need the address for the Exchange Web Service and your mailbox, user ID, and password. No special setup is required. You'll simply enter the information when prompted to do so on the Web pages.

How It Works

To connect to Exchange Server with your Web browser, point your browser to the address that the Exchange administrator provides, such as http://exchserver. mycompany.com. You'll see a page like that in Figure 25.11. For access to your mailbox and folders, enter your mailbox alias in the box provided, then click on the text "Click Here." Your browser will pop up a dialog box where you'll enter your user ID and password, as you might at any other secure Web site.

Once you're logged in, you'll be able to access your mailbox and public folders and search the address list. The first thing you see is your Inbox (Figure 25.12). A frame on the left provides navigation links to switch you between your mailbox, public folders, a Find Names utility, and an Options page. Also use this area to leave the Exchange Web site by clicking Log Off.

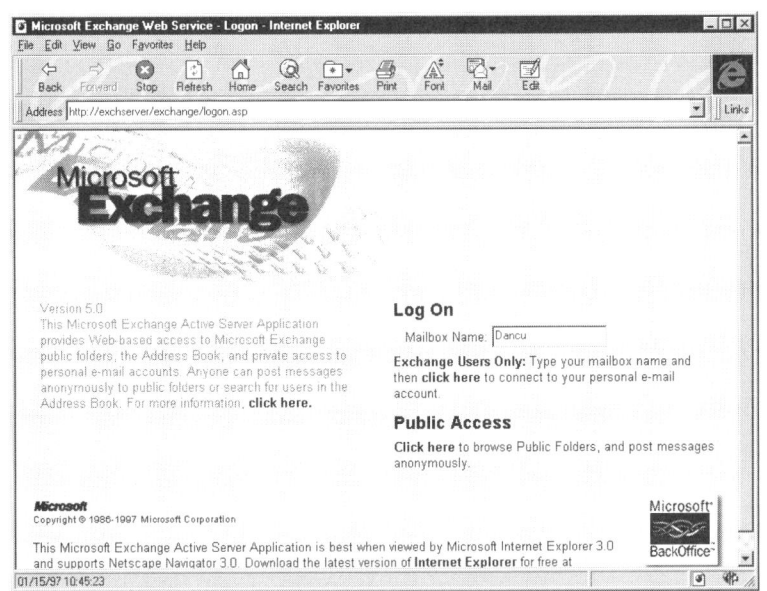

Figure 25.11

Exchange Server 5.0 offers the option of full access to your mailbox and folders or anonymous access to public folders.

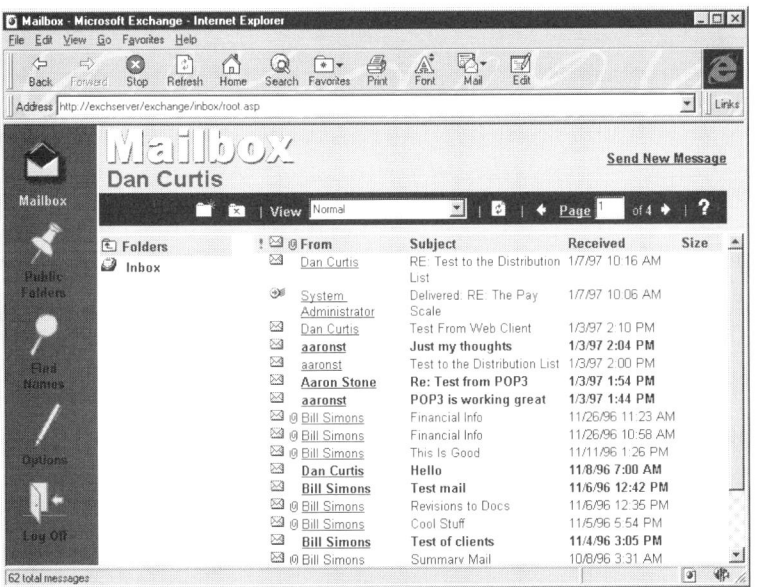

Figure 25.12

Click on any underlined hotlink in the From column to open the message. The graphics on the left of the screen provide the navigation tools for Exchange Web access.

Use the icons and underlined hotlinks just as you would on any other Web page; for example,

- To access the other folders in your mailbox, click on Folders near the top of the Mailbox page.
- To read a message (Figure 25.13), click on the underlined name of the sender in the From column.
- To send a new message, click on Send New Message. A page like that depicted in Figure 25.14 appears.

Figure 25.13

Rich-text formatting is preserved for Exchange Server messages read via the Web.

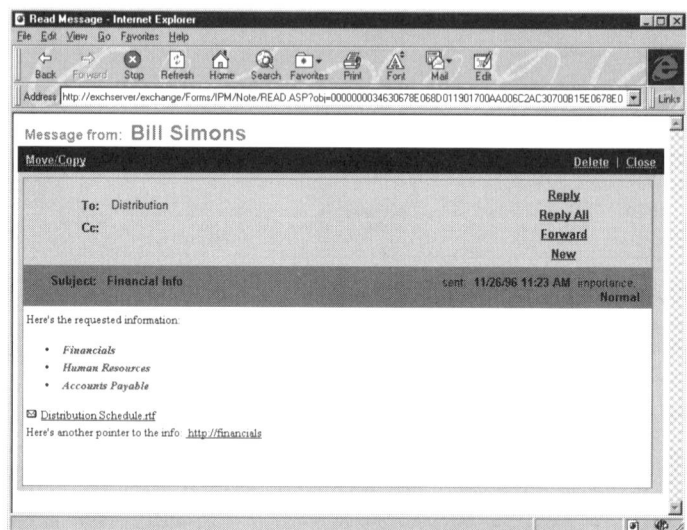

Don't forget that you can use your browser's Back and Forward buttons to move back and forth between the Web pages you've accessed.

To locate address details for another Exchange Server user, click the Find Names graphic in the frame shown on the left in Figure 25.12. Fill in one or more boxes on the Find Names page (Figure 25.15) with the information you want to search for, then click on Find. A list of matching names (Figure 25.16) will be displayed. You can then click any name to get details for that person, as shown in Figure 25.17.

If you used your Exchange Server mailbox to log on, you can get to public folders by clicking the Public Folders graphic on the left side of your browser window. To view only public folders without logging on, at the initial Microsoft Exchange Web Service page (Figure 25.11), under Public Access, click on Click Here.

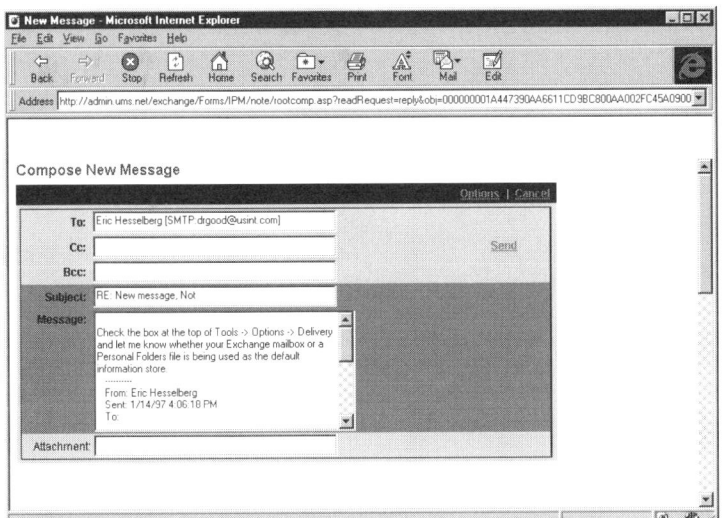

Figure 25.14
Creating a new message displays a page that closely resembles the New Message form.

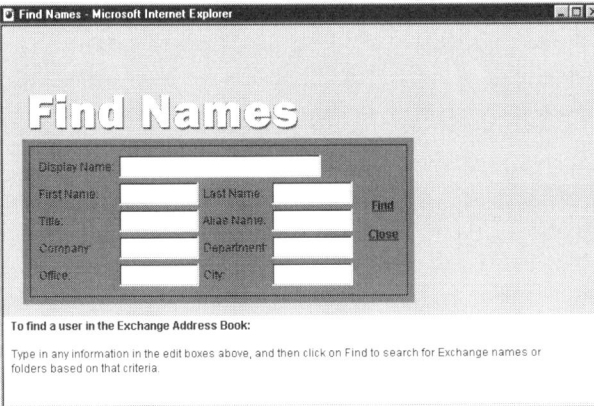

Figure 25.15
Search the user list by specifying a name, company, or other information.

Click any public folder to see its contents (Figure 25.18). To open an item, click the highlighted name of the person who posted it.

Figure 25.16

Click on any name listed for your search to display details for that user.

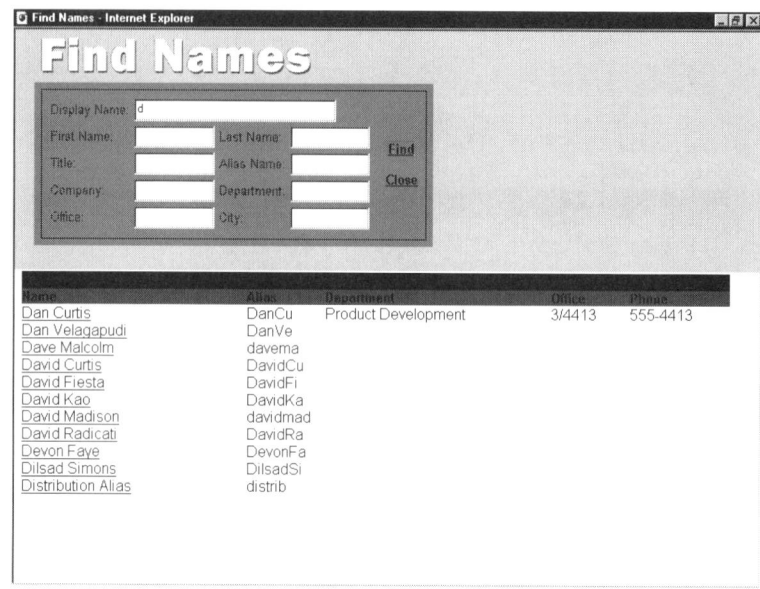

Figure 25.17

User details include location and phone number.

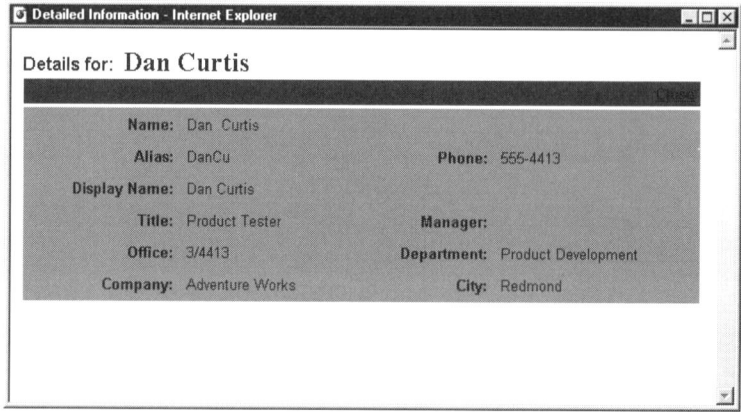

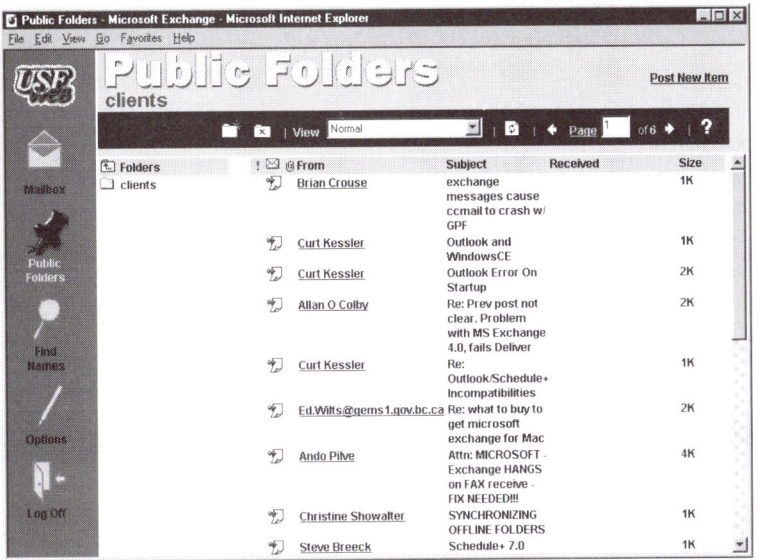

Figure 25.18

As with a message in your Inbox, open a public folder item by clicking on the underlined name of the sender.

Working with Newsgroups in Exchange

POP3/SMTP support and Web browser support are two of the ways in which Exchange Server 5.0 is bound closer to the Internet. Another is support for newsgroups. Exchange Server 5.0 can be set up to capture any of the thousands of newsgroups used as discussion forums on the Internet.

When this feature is added to the Microsoft Exchange server for your organization, a new folder named Internet News is created under All Public Folders. Under Internet News, you'll see a folder for each newsgroup to which the Microsoft Exchange server is subscribed. In many cases, the folders are nested in a hierarchy going several layers deep (see Figure 25.19).

Because newsgroup folders act just like any other public folders, no special techniques are needed. However, we do offer a few notes on newsgroups under Exchange:

- When you post an item to a newsgroup, users in your organization see the posting immediately because it's added to the public folder. However, it may take minutes, hours, or even days for the posting to reach all the other news servers around the world and generate responses from other people.

- Adding a newsgroup folder to Favorites is equivalent to subscribing to a newsgroup in a standard newsreader: Doing so allows Exchange to track read and unread messages for you.

Newsgroups in the Internet News folder under All Public Folders look and act just like any other public folders.

Figure 25.19

A Microsoft Exchange server displays Internet newsgroups in a hierarchy. See how newsgroups added to Favorites show the full name of each newsgroup and track the number of unread items.

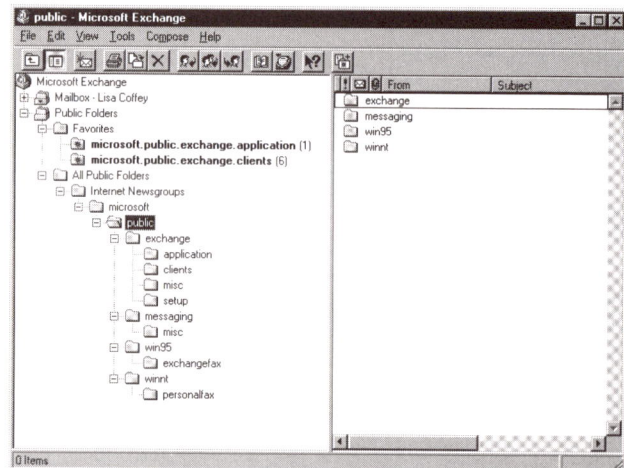

- The default view on newsgroup public folders is to show conversation threads. The threads with the most recent messages are at the top of the list, so you can easily find the newest messages and the hottest topics.

One more thought on newsgroups: Any public folder can be set up to be published as a newsgroup that can be accessed with an newsgroup reader application. This is just one more example of how Microsoft Exchange Server 5.0 can be used to present information on the Internet or on an intranet within your organization.

Summary

Microsoft Exchange Server 5.0 offers new ways to access your mailbox and public folders and ties Exchange closer to the Internet. You'll also find enhancements for working with messages, folders, rules, and security.

Key Points

- Exchange Server 5.0 adds three new ways to access your Exchange mailbox.
- You now have the option of specifying a Reply To address to redirect replies to a different address.
- You can exchange security keys with Exchange Server 5.0 users in other organizations, so you can send encrypted and digitally signed mail to each other.

- Enhancements to rules let you specify the last rule to be applied to a message, preserve a message when it's forwarded, and associate rules with multiple profiles.

- You can rename folders in your Favorites list without affecting the original public folder names.

- The user needs to do nothing special to use the cc:Mail connector, because the Microsoft Exchange server does all the work.

- A computer running Microsoft Exchange Server 5.0 can act as a POP3 server, allowing you to use virtually any Internet mail program to get your messages.

- The Exchange Web Service provides access to your mailbox and turns Exchange into an Internet publication platform.

- Newsgroups in the Internet News folder under All Public Folders look and act just like any other public folders.

For More Information

Your best bet for learning more about version 5.0 is to visit some of the resources on the Internet described in Appendix B, "Exchange Resources." Also, the final chapter in this book, coming up next, introduces you to Microsoft Outlook, a vastly enhanced Exchange client that's included with Exchange Server 5.0.

Chapter 26

Introducing Microsoft Outlook

As noted in the previous chapter on Microsoft Exchange Server 5.0, Microsoft Outlook is a totally new, enhanced Exchange client, included both with Exchange Server 5.0 and with Microsoft Office 97. Outlook works with your existing Exchange profiles and can replace either the operating system Exchange client or the Exchange Server client.

Outlook is an extremely ambitious program that ties together messaging, scheduling, and overall organization. In this chapter, we'll look just at the messaging aspects of Outlook, including the many address book enhancements, to try to give you a leg up if you're migrating to Outlook from one of the Exchange clients.

What Is Microsoft Outlook?

Microsoft Outlook is a desktop information manager combining messaging, scheduling, contact management, groupware, and task management.

Microsoft positions Outlook as a new type of application, a *desktop information manager* combining messaging, scheduling, groupware, task management, and contact management. Outlook certainly moves to the head of the class as Microsoft's premier messaging client, both for Exchange Server users and for people who connect to other types of mail systems.

Many of the features from the Exchange Server clients — such as AutoSignature, filters, views, and Internet hot links — are now available to everyone via Outlook. Even if you don't connect to Exchange Server, you can download a Rules Wizard from Microsoft to add automatic processing of incoming and outgoing messages.

Another aspect to examine as we explore Outlook is the way it is totally integrated with the Internet. Contact records can include Web and FTP addresses, while incoming messages format any valid Internet URL as a hot link.

Finally, as part of Microsoft Office 97, Outlook is tightly bound to the other Office applications and includes a new, streamlined version of WordMail.

Getting Started with Outlook

Before we get into the new features of Outlook, let's run through the steps you need to take to install it on your computer and set it up with the information you're going to want to work with.

Installing Outlook

If you want to import contacts from a database, make sure you install the database drivers during setup.

Before you install Outlook, make sure that your hard drive has 26–46 MB of free space for all the necessary files and that you disable any antivirus protection. If you have Windows NT Workstation 4.0, you must install Service Pack 2 or a later service pack. If you have Windows 95 and plan to send faxes with Outlook, make sure that Microsoft Fax (see Chapter 7, "Setting Up Microsoft Fax") is installed before you begin the Outlook setup procedure.

Also consider what kind of data you have that will need to be imported into Outlook; this will affect your setup choices. For example, if you have contacts in a Microsoft Access database, you'll want to install the database driver that lets you connect to an Access database. Drivers are also available for dBase, Microsoft Excel, and Microsoft FoxPro.

You don't need to remove Microsoft Exchange (or Windows Messaging) before installing Outlook. In fact, you can continue to use Exchange while you get acquainted with Outlook.

To install Outlook, run the Setup.exe program that you'll find on the CD for Microsoft Office 97, Microsoft Exchange Server 5.0 (clients), or Microsoft Outlook. You'll be asked to choose either a <u>T</u>ypical, <u>C</u>ustom, or <u>R</u>un from

CD-ROM installation. I'd recommend that you choose Custom, so you can select the exact components you need. Figure 26.1 shows the default components installed for Outlook.

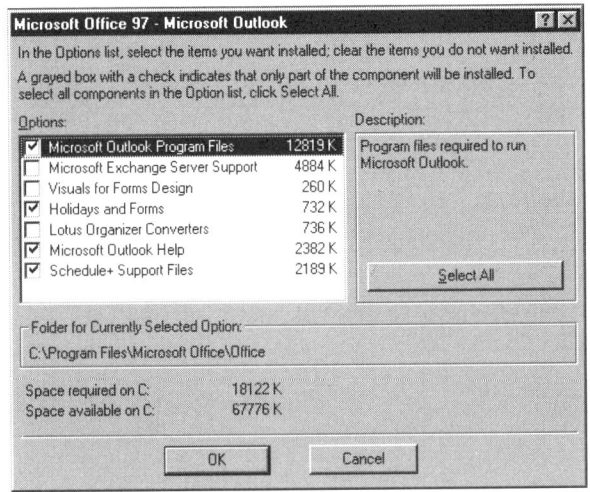

Figure 26.1

The default components for Outlook include the program files, holidays and forms, help files, and support files for Schedule+.

Here are some considerations to keep in mind as you select Outlook components:

- If you connect to Exchange Server, then you also must check Microsoft Exchange Server Support.
- If you have been using Lotus Organizer 1.1 or 2.1 and want to convert your data to Outlook, then check Lotus Organizer Converters (see the section "Importing Data" for details about how to convert Organizer data and data from other sources).
- If you don't need to import data from Schedule+ or view free/busy information for Schedule+ users, then you can clear the checkbox for Schedule+ Support Files.
- If you plan to design forms or continue to use Exchange along with Outlook, then check Visuals for Forms Design.
- Database drivers, such as those needed to import contacts from a Microsoft Access database, are found not under Outlook components, but under Data Access.

Note that, if you're installing Office 97, the Microsoft Office Upgrade Wizard will search your system for older versions of Office programs and offer to remove them.

Running Outlook for the First Time

The first time you run Outlook, you may be asked what profile to use. Outlook uses the same mail profiles as Exchange. The program will take quite a while to start because it makes a number of changes to your system. Here's what's going on:

- Five new folders are added to your Exchange Server mailbox or your Personal Folders file (whichever is the default information store) for Calendar, Contacts, Journal, Notes, and Tasks.
- The Outlook Bar is built with shortcuts to the new folders, as well as to your Inbox and other mail folders.
- Sample items are added to each of the new folders, welcoming you to each of these aspects of Outlook.

Once this process is complete, Outlook displays a Welcome to Microsoft Outlook! dialog box (Figure 26.2) to help you get started.

Figure 26.2

Outlook welcomes first-time users by suggesting some tasks to get you started.

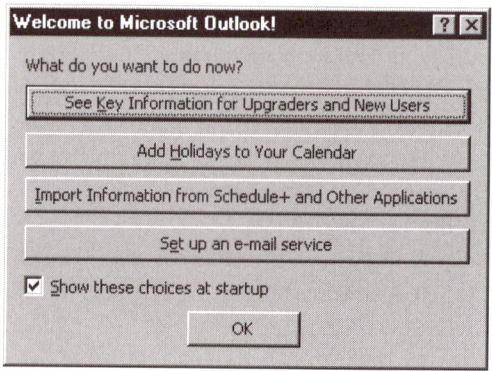

The two tasks you'll probably want to do right away are Add Holidays to Your Calendar (picking one or more countries — the United States is already checked by default) and Import Information from Schedule+ and Other Applications, which we'll examine in detail in the next section, "Importing Data." The following section, "Using the Add-In Manager," contains details about another task you may need to perform before you start using Outlook.

Importing Data

One of the first things you'll want to do with Outlook is import your contacts and other information from other sources, including an Exchange Personal Address Book, Microsoft Schedule+, databases, or personal information managers. If you want to do this right away, then click Import Information from Schedule+ and Other Applications when you see the Welcome to Microsoft Outlook! dialog box. You also can import these items at another other time by choosing File, Import and Export. Table 26.1 lists the different import sources you can use with Outlook and where to get the conversion components.

Table 26.1 Outlook Import Sources and Converters	
Import Source	**Required Converter**
Exchange Personal Folders file (.pst)	Included with Outlook
Exchange Personal Address Book (.pab)	Included with Outlook
Microsoft Mail file (.mmf)	Included with Outlook
Comma- or tab-separated values file	Included with Outlook
Lotus Organizer 1.0, 1.1, or 2.1	Install the Lotus Organizer files during Outlook setup
Microsoft Schedule+ 1.0 or 7.0	Install the Schedule+ support files during Outlook setup
Microsoft Access	Install the database driver during Outlook setup
Microsoft Excel	Install the database driver during Outlook setup
Microsoft FoxPro	Install the database driver during Outlook setup

continued

Table 26.1 Outlook Import Sources and Converters, continued	
Import Source	**Required Converter**
dBase	Install the database driver during Outlook setup
Symantec ACT! 2.0	Install the Outlook converter from the Office 97 Valupack
NetManage ECCO Pro 3.0, 3.01, or 3.02	Install the Outlook converter from the Office 97 Valupack
Starfish SideKick 1.0/2.0/95	Install the Outlook converter from the Office 97 Valupack

To install the additional Outlook converters from the Office 97 Valupack, look in the Valupack\Convert\Outlook folder on the Office 97 CD and run the Outcvt.exe file if you have either Windows 95 or Windows NT 4.0. You also can download the converter from the Microsoft Web site (see Appendix B, "Exchange Resources").

Because we're concerned in this chapter mainly with messaging and the Contacts folder that can become your new address book, we'll look at the specifics of importing from the Personal Address Book (PAB) and Schedule+, then we'll spend a little time with more general import techniques.

Importing a Personal Address Book

To import addresses from a PAB to the Contacts folder in Outlook,

1. Make sure that the PAB you want to import is in the current profile. To switch PABs, choose Tools, Services, then select the Personal Address Book service and click Properties. Enter the file name of another PAB, then click OK twice to complete the change.

2. Choose File, Import and Export.

3. In the Import and Export Wizard (Figure 26.3), select "Import from Schedule+ or another program or file," then click the Next button.

4. In the first Import a File dialog box (Figure 26.4), select Personal Address Book, then click the Next button.

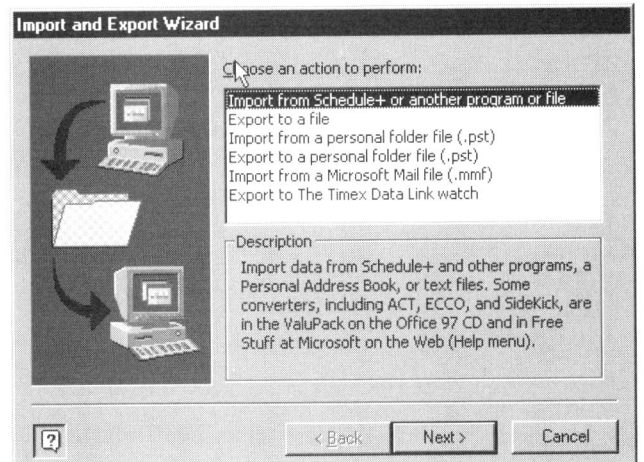

Figure 26.3
Outlook offers an extensive array of import and export choices.

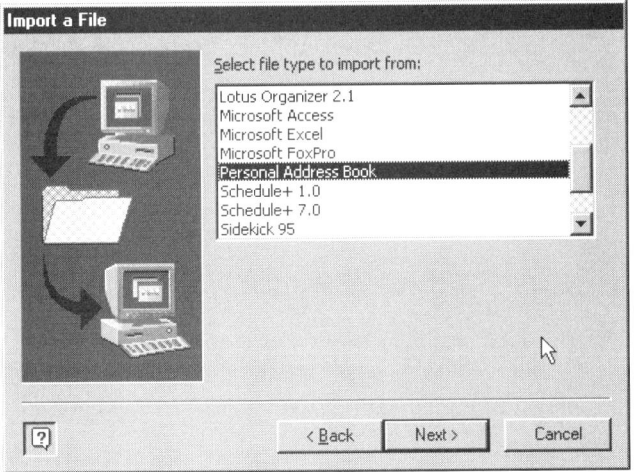

Figure 26.4
The files you can import from will depend on the converters you have installed.

5. In the next Import a File dialog box (Figure 26.5), choose the folder where you want to store the addresses, usually Contacts. Click the Next button to continue.

6. In the last Import a File dialog box (Figure 26.6), you have a final opportunity to Change Destination, and you can change the mapping of fields from the PAB to the Contacts folder (see the sidebar "Mapping Import Fields"). Click Finish to complete the import process.

Figure 26.5

Entries from the Personal Address Book are usually imported to the Outlook Contacts folder.

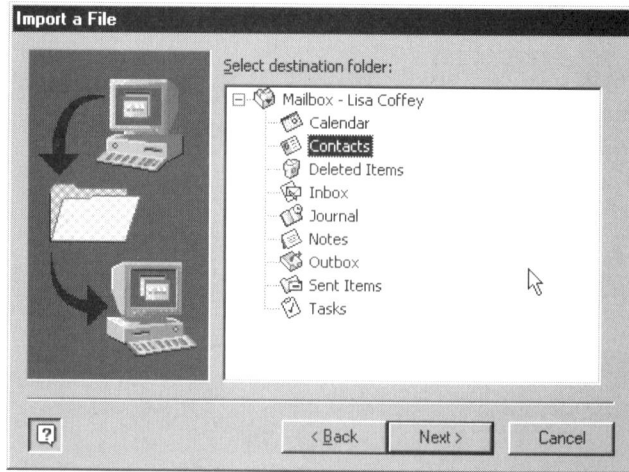

Figure 26.6

Importing from a Personal Address Book is a relatively simple process of copying data from one file to another.

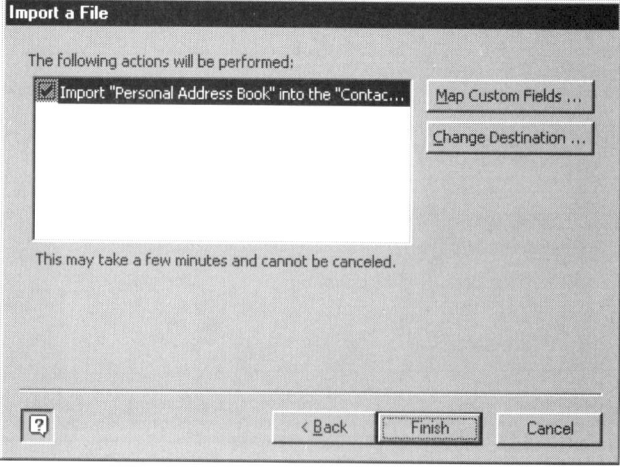

Mapping Import Fields

One of the features that makes the file-import function of Outlook so flexible is the capability to map fields from the source file to the destination folder. The mapping function is provided in the last Import a File dialog box (Figure 26.6). Click the Map Custom Fields button to display the Map Custom Fields dialog box shown in Figure 26.A.

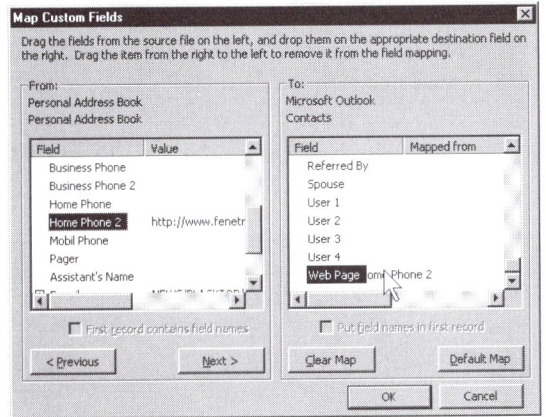

Figure 26.A
Mapping fields from the data source to the destination folder is a simple matter of dragging fields from the left side and dropping them in the target field on the right side.

The fields on the left side are from the source file, whether a PAB or a database, while the fields on the right represent the folder to which the data is being imported. Notice the Value column on the left side. Here you'll find sample values for the source data. Use the Previous and Next buttons to browse the source records and see more values. This should help you decide which field on the right is the best destination for you.

To change the mapping for a field, simply drag the field from the left side and drop it on the desired destination field on the right side. To remove a field from the mapping list, drag the field from the right back to the left.

Default mappings are created for any import, based on the similarity of field names. But you may have been using a field for a different purpose. For example, because you don't know anyone with two home phone numbers, you may have used the Home Phone 2 field in the PAB to keep a record of each person's Web site. To map the Home Phone 2 field to Outlook's Web Page field, drag Home Phone 2 from the left and drop it on Web Page on the right. This is the operation depicted in Figure 26.A.

Importing from Schedule+

If you've been using both Exchange and Schedule+, you may want to import the Schedule+ Contacts list instead of your PAB, then add e-mail addresses later. You must have Schedule+ on your computer to perform the import.

To import data from Schedule+,

1. Choose File, Import and Export.

2. In the Import and Export Wizard dialog box (Figure 26.3), select "Import from Schedule+ or another program or file," then click the Next button.

3. In the first Import a File dialog box, choose either Schedule+ 1.0 or Schedule+ 7.0, depending on which version you have, then click the Next button.

4. In the next Import a File dialog box (Figure 26.7), select the file to import and indicate how you want to handle duplicate items. Click the Next button to continue.

Figure 26.7

You can ignore Schedule+ items that duplicate existing entries, add them to your Outlook folders, or use them to replace existing items.

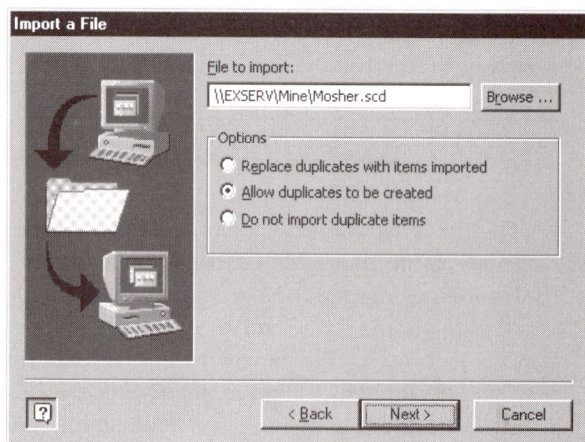

5. The final Import a File dialog box (Figure 26.8) lists the actions that will be performed. Schedule+ Contacts are imported by default into the Outlook Contacts folder, Appointments to the Calendar folder, and Tasks to the Tasks folder. Make any changes in the destination folder or field mappings (see the sidebar "Mapping Import Fields"), then click the Finish button.

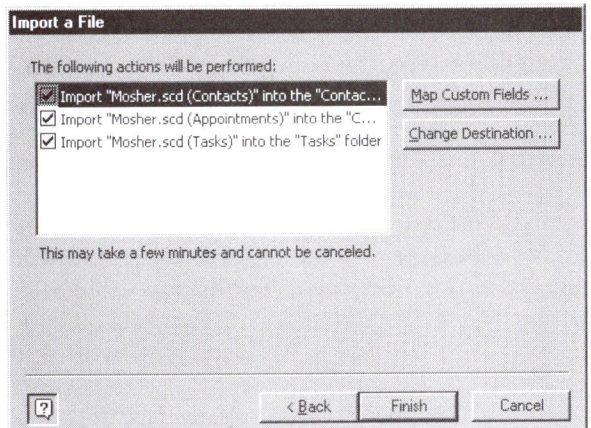

Figure 26.8
The tasks to be performed by the Import a File wizard are listed to give you a last chance to cancel them, change the destination folder, or alter the field mappings.

Importing from Other Sources

If you've followed the procedures described above for importing from a PAB or Schedule+, you should see a pattern that will be followed for every other type of import:

1. Select the type of data to be imported.
2. Select the source file containing the data.
3. Indicate how duplicates should be handled.
4. Select a destination folder for each type of data record.
5. Adjust the field mappings as needed.
6. Perform the import.

To import data from some applications, such as Lotus Organizer 2.1 or NetManage ECCO Pro, the program used to create the data file must still be installed on your computer.

Migrating Exchange Add-Ons

As an Exchange user migrating to Outlook, one question you might ask is whether all the services in your profile and any Exchange add-ons will continue to work with Outlook. Fortunately, most of them will. One known exception, though, is any service that uses its own information store, such as Lotus Notes.

To work with Outlook, an information store must completely implement the MAPI store specification, including support for named properties, hidden folders, and hidden messages. Because there haven't been applications to take advantage of the complete specification, not everyone has supported it. As this book was being written at the end of 1996, the only information stores certified by Microsoft as compatible with Outlook were Microsoft Exchange Server and Personal Folders.

Outlook users who need to connect to a cc:Mail postoffice will find what they need in the ValuPack included on the Microsoft Office 97 CD. Look in the Valupack\Ccmail folder, and run Ccmailsp.exe to install an Outlook-compatible version of the Transend MAPI ConnectorWare for cc:Mail discussed in Chapter 9, "Setting Up Other Information Services." You'll need to add this program to your profile using the Mail applet in the Control Panel and add the corresponding Outlook extension with the Add-In Manager, as described in the next section.

For other add-ons, you'll have to play it by ear. Many will no doubt become obsolete as Outlook fulfills their functions. Others will work fine, while still others will fail for no obvious reason. You'll want to check the online resources listed in Appendix B, "Exchange Resources," for the latest information on updates to your favorite add-ons to make them Outlook-compatible.

Using the Add-In Manager

When you use Outlook for the first time, check which add-ons are loaded and install any others you need.

To work, some information services need special Outlook components. These add-ons are copied to your system during Outlook setup, but not all of them are installed automatically. Other add-ons are used to provide additional functions to Outlook. The first time you start Outlook, it's a good idea to check which add-ons are loaded and install any others you need.

To work with add-ons, choose Tools, Options, switch to the General tab, and click the Add-In Manager button. The Add-Ins dialog box, shown in Figure 26.9, appears.

To install an add-on,

1. In the Add-Ins dialog box (Figure 26.9), click the Install button.
2. Select the add-on from the Addins folder. Add-ons have .ecf (extension configuration files) file names. Table 26.2 lists the add-ons included with Outlook.
3. Click the Open button to install the selected add-on.
4. Click OK to close the Add-In Manager.

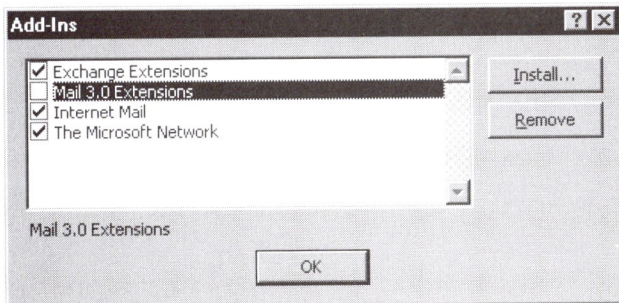

Figure 26.9
Install and Remove
Outlook add-ons through
the Add-In Manager.

Table 26.2 Outlook Add-Ons

Add-On	File Name	Description
cc:Mail	Ccmxp.ecf	Adds cc:Mail to the list of available mail delivery services
CompuServe	Cserve.ecf	Adds CompuServe Mail to the list of available mail delivery services
Delegate Access	Dlgsetp.ecf	Adds the Delegates tab to the Options dialog box (Exchange Server users only)
Digital Security	Etexch.ecf	Adds the Security tab to the Options dialog box for use of the digital signature and message seal features with Exchange Server
Exchange Extensions	Emsuix.ecf	Adds the Out of Office Assistant and Inbox Assistant commands to the Tools menu, for use with Exchange Server
Internet Mail	Minet.ecf	Adds Internet Mail to the list of available mail services
Mail 3.0 Extensions	Mail3.ecf	Lets Outlook use extensions created for Microsoft Mail 3.0

continued

Table 26.2 Outlook Add-Ons, continued		
Add-On	**File Name**	**Description**
Microsoft Fax	Awfext.ecf	Adds Microsoft Fax to the list of available information services
MSFS Menu Extensions	Msfsmenu.ecf	Lets Outlook use menu extensions created for Microsoft Mail 3.x
MSFS PropSheet Extensions	Msfsprop.ecf	Lets Outlook use dialog box extensions created for Microsoft Mail 3.x.
Schedule+	Msspc.ecf	Provides Schedule+ compatibility
The Microsoft Network	Msn.ecf	Adds The Microsoft Network to the list of available mail services

To remove an add-on,

1. Choose Tools, Options, switch to the General tab, then click the Add-In Manager button.

2. Select the add-on you want to remove, then click the Remove button.

3. Click OK to close the Add-In Manager.

Changing the Inbox Icon

The Microsoft Office 97 CD includes a small program to change the Inbox icon on your desktop to an Outlook icon and to open Outlook instead of Exchange or Windows Messaging. Look in ValuPack\Patch for Chnginbx.exe. You also can get this program from the Microsoft Web site (see Appendix B, "Exchange Resources").

Working with the Information Viewer

Now that you have Outlook installed, we can begin our whirlwind tour of the features you're most likely to notice if you're upgrading from Exchange. The obvious place to start is with the Information Viewer, the window where all your Outlook information appears.

Understanding the Information Viewer

Take a look at the Information Viewer, shown in Figure 26.10. Notice that there are two principle sections — the main window on the right displaying items in the current folder, and the Outlook Bar on the left. We'll get into more detail about the Outlook Bar later in this section.

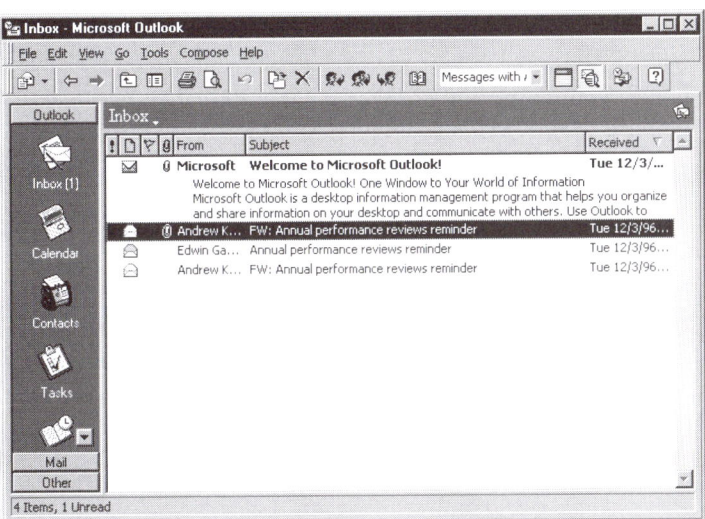

Figure 26.10
The Information Viewer in Outlook is a big change from the Exchange Viewer.

The toolbar at the top should have a lot of familiar buttons. Those for going up one level, displaying the folder list, printing, deleting, replying, forwarding, and using the Address Book are all the same as in Exchange. We'll highlight the important new buttons as we go along.

Previewing Messages

One of the first things you'll notice in the Information Viewer is that you can preview messages, with the first three lines shown in blue. To toggle previewing on and off, click the AutoPreview button shown in Figure 26.11, or choose View, AutoPreview.

Figure 26.11
The AutoPreview button turns previewing on and off.

The Outlook Information Viewer features AutoPreview, new message icons, and user-customizable views.

The default setting is to preview only unread messages, but it's easy to change that. You also can change the color. To make changes, follow these steps:

1. Choose View, Format View.

2. In the Format Table View dialog box (Figure 26.12), you'll find a section for AutoPreview. To change the font, or its color or style, click the Font button, make your change in the standard Font dialog box, then click OK.

3. To show preview lines for all items, choose "Preview all items." Notice that you can turn off AutoPreview by choosing No AutoPreview.

4. Click OK when you've finished changing the AutoPreview settings.

Figure 26.12

Control the appearance of the Inbox or any other folder laid out as a table.

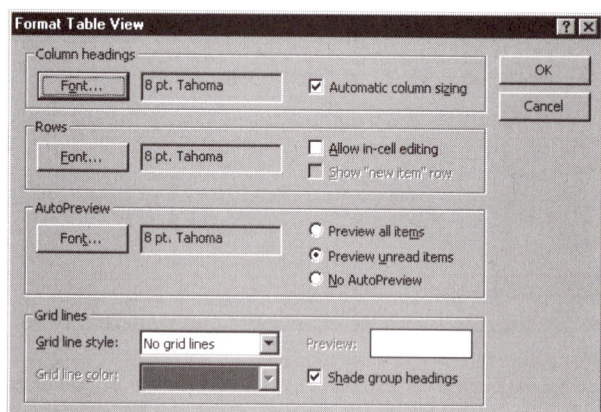

Switching Between Folders

When you first start Outlook, it displays the contents of your Inbox. But how do you get to your other folders? One way is to click the big Inbox button. This will display a complete view of your folder hierarchy, as shown in Figure 26.13, from which you can select any other folder to open.

Another method is to click the Folder List button (which looks the same as in the Exchange Viewer) or choose View, Folder List. This action divides the main Information Viewer window into two panes, one for folders, the other for messages or other items, just as you might have been using in Exchange. You can then easily click on any folder to open it.

To open a folder or folders from another Exchange Server mailbox or from a Personal Folders file (one that isn't in your profile), choose File, Open

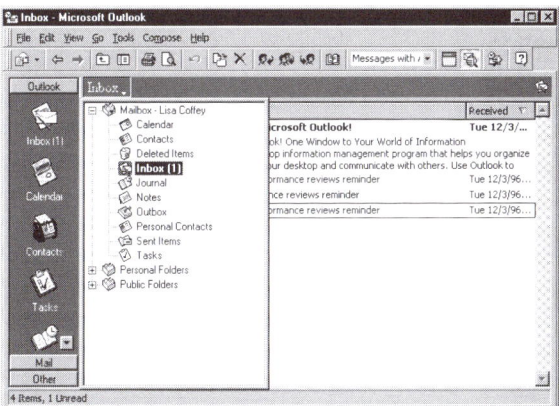

Figure 26.13
To switch from the Inbox to a different folder, click the Inbox button.

Special Folder. You then can choose either Exchange Server Folder or Personal Folder and select the one you want to open. The folder will appear in a new Outlook window, but it also will be accessible through any other Outlook window that's open.

Understanding the Icons

In addition to the variety of folder icons shown in Figure 26.13, Outlook also uses a much richer library of icons for messages and other items, distinguishing between read and unread messages with open and closed envelopes. It even has a special icon for drafts — in other words, for messages you haven't yet sent. Table 26.3 lists the icons you're most likely to encounter.

Table 26.3 Outlook Message Icons	
Icon	**Description**
	Read message
	Unread message
	Forwarded message
	Replied to message
	Draft (unsent) message
	continued

Table 26.3 Outlook Message Icons, continued	
Icon	**Description**
	Sealed message
	Digitally signed message
	Posted message
	Message recall attempt
	Notification of successful message recall
	Notification of unsuccessful message recall
	Notification that a message was delivered
	Notification that a message was read
	Notification that a message was not delivered
	Notification that a message was not read
	Remote Mail message header
	Header marked for download
	Header marked for download as a copy
	Message with an attachment
	Message flagged for follow-up
	Message flagged as complete

One thing Exchange Server users will find missing in Outlook is the special icons for folders that have been set up for synchronization.

Working with the Outlook Bar

The Outlook Bar on the left side of the Information Viewer is one of several nifty new navigation tools. This bar is a collection of shortcuts to folders. Each of the small horizontal buttons represents a group of shortcuts. For example, click the Mail button to see icons for your Inbox, Sent Items, Outbox, Deleted Items, and other private folders. Click the Outlook button to return to the icons for the Inbox, Calendar, Contacts, Tasks, Journal, and Notes.

Click Other, and you may be surprised. There you find icons not just for Public Folders and any folders in your Favorites folder (if you use Exchange Server) but also icons for My Computer and the Favorites file (not Exchange) folder (see Figure 26.14). This means you can use Outlook instead of Windows Explorer as a window into your entire system.

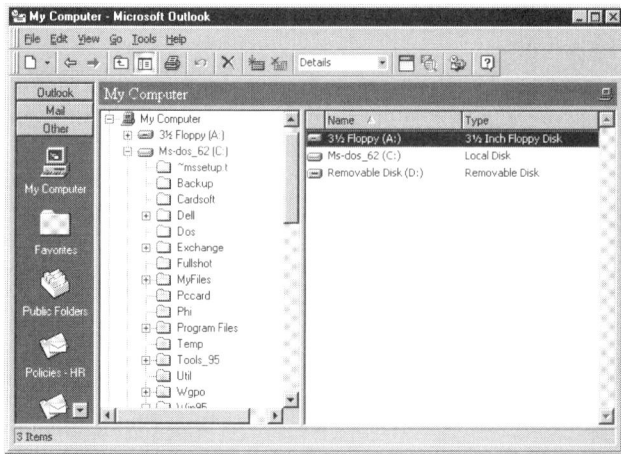

Figure 26.14
Use Outlook to explore not only messages and other personal information, but also public folders and even your entire computer.

Now let's look at the tools you need to manage the Outlook Bar:

- To add a folder to the Outlook Bar, just drag any folder either from Windows Explorer or from the Outlook Information Viewer to the group where you want to place the shortcut. If you're viewing folders in Outlook, you also can right-click the folder then choose Add to Outlook Bar to add the folder to the current group.

- A third way to add a folder to the current group is to choose File, Add to Outlook Bar. In the Add to Outlook Bar dialog box, you'll be able to choose between folders in Outlook and those in the File System — in other words, those that you would see in Windows Explorer.

- To add a new group, right-click on the button for any group or in any blank space on the Outlook Bar, then choose <u>A</u>dd New Group. You'll need to give the new group a name.
- To remove a folder from the Outlook Bar, right-click its icon, then choose Re<u>m</u>ove from Outlook Bar.
- To remove a group, right-click its button, then choose Re<u>m</u>ove Group.
- To rename a shortcut in the Outlook Bar, right-click its icon, then choose <u>R</u>ename Shortcut.
- To change the size of the shortcut icons, right-click on the button for any group or in any blank space on the Outlook Bar, then choose either Large Icons or S<u>m</u>all Icons.
- To hide the Outlook Bar, right-click on the button for any group or in any blank space on the Outlook Bar, then choose <u>H</u>ide Outlook Bar. You also can toggle it on and off by choosing <u>V</u>iew, <u>O</u>utlook Bar.

Note that you can include only shortcuts to folders on the Outlook Bar, not shortcuts to individual messages, contacts, files, or other items in your Outlook or system folders.

Using the Browse Buttons

Navigate through Outlook with the Outlook bar and the Back and Next browse buttons.

The Outlook Bar isn't the only new navigation aid in Outlook. On the toolbar, you'll also find browse buttons, shown in Figure 26.15, similar to those on a Web browser. These take you back and forth to the folders you've been working with during the current Exchange sessions.

Figure 26.15
The browse buttons on the Outlook toolbar work just like the Back and Forward buttons on a Web browser.

Working with Views

As we noted at the beginning of this chapter, Outlook supports grouping, filters, and views, as introduced with the Exchange Server client (see "Advanced Customizing with the Exchange Server Client," page 235 in Chapter 10).

Each type of folder — for messages, contacts, and so on — has its own default views. These views are already built for the folders you see initially in Outlook, and they can be added to any new folder you create.

To switch between views, click the drop-down list on the toolbar. As Figure 26.16 shows, you'll see a list of views from which you can choose. You also can choose View, Current View, then select from a menu of views for the current folder.

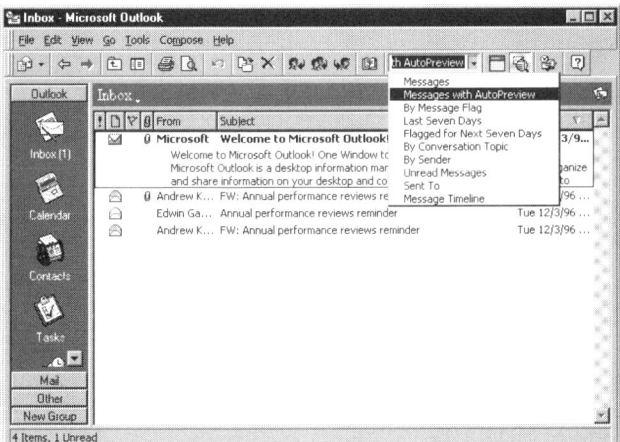

Figure 26.16
Each basic Outlook folder has a collection of ready-made views.

The View menu also contains a number of actions to help you change views and create new ones. Table 26.4 lists these actions, together with a comparison of similar functions in Exchange.

Table 26.4 Functions for Formatting Views (View Menu)

Function	Description
Show Fields	Select the fields to include in the view and the order in which to display them (similar to View, Columns in Exchange)
Format Columns	Change the display format, column heading, width, and alignment (not supported in Exchange)
Sort	Sort in ascending or descending order by up to four columns (whereas Exchange lets you sort on only a single column)
Filter	Display only selected items (similar to View, Filter in the Exchange Server client)
Group By	Group items in a hierarchy and sort them (similar to View, Group By in the Exchange Server client)
Expand/Collapse Groups	If grouping is in use, display all the items (expand) or hide the detailed items (collapse)
Format View	Control the fonts and other appearance settings (see Figure 26.12; not supported in Exchange)
Define Views	Modify, delete, and create views (similar to View, Define Views in the Exchange Server client)
Field Chooser	An interactive alternative to Show Fields (see Figure 26.17), allowing you to drag fields to the Information Viewer (not supported in Exchange)
Group By Box	Toggles on and off a bar at the top of the view showing which fields are being grouped on and how they're being sorted (not supported in Exchange)
AutoPreview	Toggles AutoPreview on and off (not supported in Exchange)

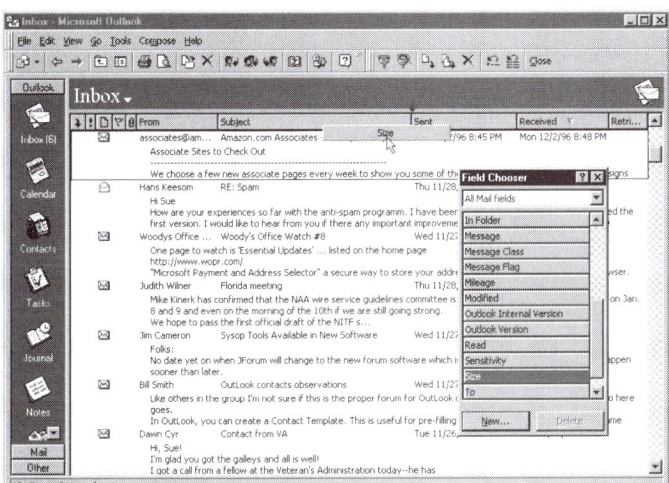

Figure 26.17
Drag a field from the Field Chooser to the Information Viewer to add it to the view.

Setting Categories

In addition to the types of fields you're accustomed to seeing for messages — for example, Received, Sent By, Subject, From — Outlook includes a new field called Categories that can be applied to any type of Outlook item. What makes Categories so exciting is that it is a multivalued field. You can mark an item for more than one category; in addition, you can select multiple Categories for use in a filter or in a Find operation.

To set the categories for an item,

1. Select one or more items, then right-click and choose Categories. You also can choose Edit, Categories.

2. In the Categories dialog box (Figure 26.18), select one or more "Available categories" to apply to the item(s), then click OK.

To add a new category,

1. Choose Edit, Categories.

2. In the Categories dialog box (Figure 26.18), click the Master Category List button.

3. In the Master Category List dialog box (Figure 26.19), enter the category under "New category," then click the Add button.

4. Repeat Step 3 if you want to add more categories, then click OK when you're finished.

Figure 26.18

Items can belong to as many categories as you choose.

Figure 26.19

Add items to the Master Category List to fit the way you work, and remove those categories that you're never going to use.

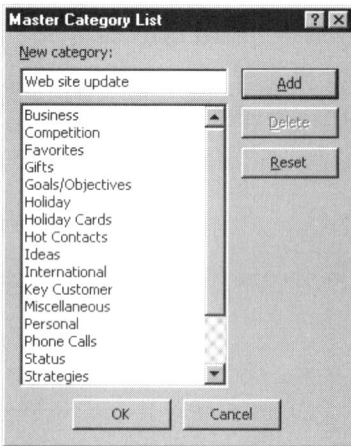

To delete categories,

1. Choose Edit, Categories.

2. In the Categories dialog box (Figure 26.18), click the Master Category List button.

3. In the Master Category List dialog box (Figure 26.19), select a category, then click the Delete button if you want to remove a single category.

4. To remove all categories that you have added, leaving only those that come with Outlook, click the Reset button.

5. Click OK when you've finished working with the Master Category List.

   Deleting a category from the master list does not affect any items that have been marked with that category. The items retain the category, even though it's no longer on the master list.

   To filter messages by category,

1. Choose View, Filter.

2. In the Filter dialog box, switch to the More Choices tab.

3. On the More Choices tab, shown in Figure 26.20, either type category names in the Categories box, or click the Categories button to select categories from the master list.

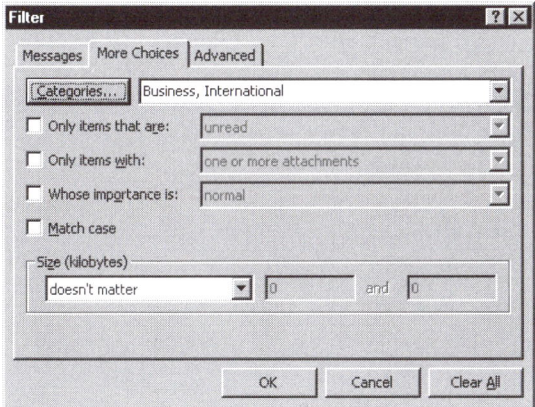

Figure 26.20
Messages can be filtered by category.

4. When you've finished selecting categories, click OK to display only those items that match the categories you chose.

Creating a View

There are two different ways to create a new view. One is to choose View, Define View and work through all the different field, group by, sort, filter, and format settings in a series of dialog boxes. Frankly, that's not much fun. The easier way, which I'll show you in a moment, is to use the different View menu functions (Table 26.4) to change the display in the Information Viewer then save that view as a new one.

One thing you need to know in advance is that there are five different types of views in Outlook:

Table Items arranged in rows and columns, with optional gridlines

Timeline Icons arranged in chronological order from left to right on a time scale

Card Items arranged as individal "cards" as in an address card file, with a letter index to the right for quick navigation

Day/Week/Month Items arranged on a calendar similar to a paper schedule planner

Icon Items arranged as large or small icons on an invisible grid or as a list of icons

Messages are most commonly arranged in a table view, addresses in a card view. To create a new view by modifying an existing one, you must start with a view of the particular type you want to use. In other words, you can't turn a table view into a card view.

If you need to create a view of a particular type as a starting point, follow these steps:

1. Choose View, Define Views.

2. In the Define Views dialog box, click the New button.

3. In the Create a New View dialog box (Figure 26.21), enter the "Name of the new view."

Figure 26.21

Five different types of views are available in Outlook.

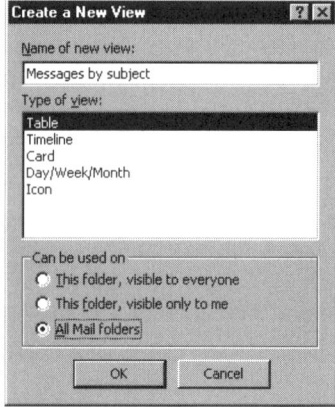

4. Select the "Type of view."

5. Indicate whether the view is specific to the particular folder or can be used on any folder for similar items. For Exchange Server users, if you make the view specific to the folder, you also can indicate whether others can use the view.

6. Click OK to create the new view.

Note that normally for new message views, you won't need to go through the above procedure. Just start with any of the table views already created for the Inbox or other message folders.

To create a new message view,

1. Use the drop-down list on the toolbar to switch to the existing view that most closely resembles the view you want to create.

2. Use the View menu functions (Table 26.4) to change the display.

3. Select a new view from the drop-down list. The Save View Settings dialog box shown in Figure 26.22 appears.

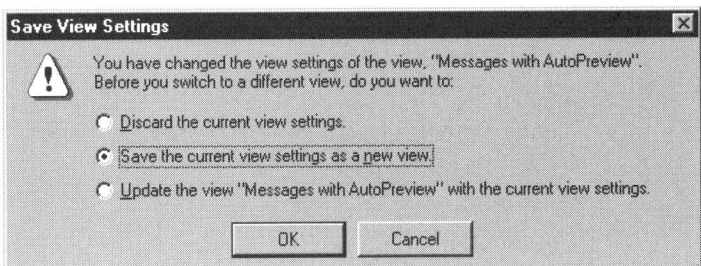

Figure 26.22
Any time you make changes to a view, you will have an opportunity to save those changes when you leave that view.

4. Choose "Save the current view settings as a new view."

5. Next, the Copy View dialog box (Figure 26.23) appears. Enter the "Name of the new view" and its usage, as described in Step 5 in the previous procedure.

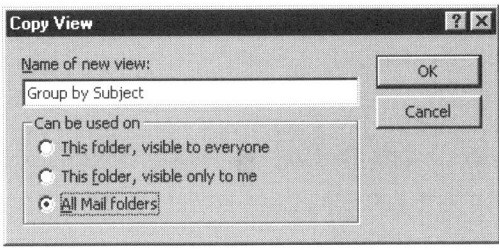

Figure 26.23
When you create a new view from an existing view, you need to give the new view a name and determine where and by whom it can be used.

6. Click OK to finish saving the new view, which will now appear on the drop-down list.

To delete a view,

1. Choose <u>V</u>iews, <u>D</u>efine Views.
2. In the Define Views dialog box, select the view, then click the <u>D</u>elete button.
3. Press Close.

Working with Contacts

Outlook solves many of the Address Book problems encountered by Exchange users.

The Contacts folders in Outlook solve many of the problems with addresses that have frustrated Exchange users. Table 26.5 lists some of the issues.

Table 26.5 Exchange Address Problems Solved by Outlook	
Exchange Problem	**Outlook Solution**
Need to make multiple entries for an individual with more than one e-mail address	You can keep up to three e-mail addresses, plus a fax number for each contact.
Need to create separate e-mail and fax entries	You can use numbers entered in the Business, Home, or Other Fax fields to send faxes.
Inability to access more than one Personal Address Book at a time	You add any number of Contacts folders to the address lists available in the Address Book.
Lack of shared contacts list	For Exchange Server users, you can maintain a Contacts folder in Public Folders. For other users, you can update a personal Contacts folder from a central list.

Throughout this section, we'll look at how to implement these solutions and other new Outlook features. For details about how to share contacts, turn to "Tips and Tricks" at the end of this chapter.

Viewing Contacts

When you switch to the Contacts folder (Figure 26.24), you'll see a view that's very different from the Inbox. This is a card-type view, showing contacts as individual cards, with alphabetical navigation buttons on the right.

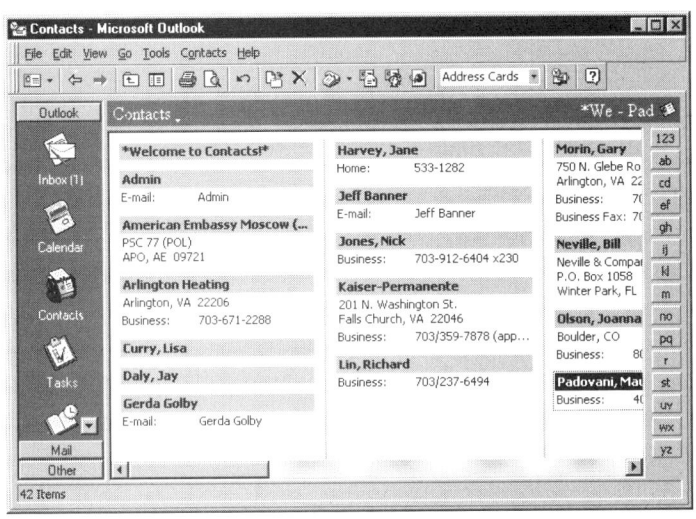

Figure 26.24
View names and addresses as cards in the Contacts folder.

To change the fields shown on the cards, choose View, Show Fields. Add the fields you want to see on the cards and remove those you don't want to see. For example, the default Address Cards view does not include the Company name. That's one field you might want to add right away.

Adding a Contact

Click the New Contact button (Figure 26.25) to open a new Contact record (Figure 26.26), which contains four tabs of information.

Figure 26.25
To create a new record in Contacts, click the New Contact button.

Figure 26.26
The contact information you use most frequently is contained on the General tab.

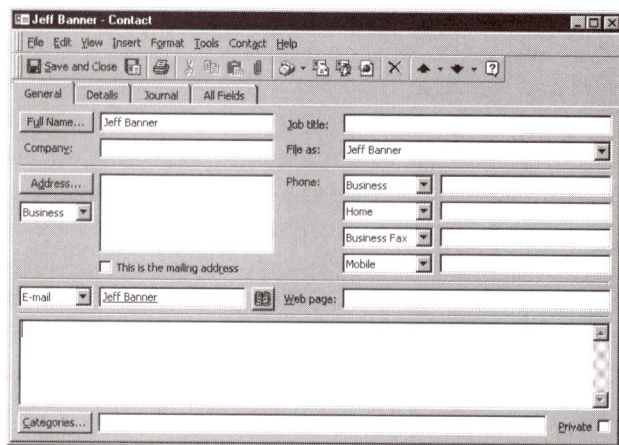

Type in the F_ull Name of a new contact you want to enter. After you enter the name and move to another field, a feature called AutoName goes to work, breaking the name into first and last names. You can see the result of this in the "Fi_le as" field, where you can choose to display the contact with last name first or by the first name.

Something similar happens when you type in an A_ddress. AutoAddress breaks the information into components, making it possible for you to sort later by city or state without having to tediously enter city and state in separate fields.

Entering Phone Numbers

If you plan to use automatic dialing with the phone numbers in Contacts and take advantage of Windows dialing properties (see "Configuring Dialing Locations," page 28 in Chapter 3), enter the numbers in international format; that is, as *+xx (yyy) zzz-zzzz*, where *xx* is the country code, *yyy* the area or city code, and *zzz-zzzz* the local number. The same goes for fax numbers that you want to use with Microsoft Fax or Personal Fax for Windows NT.

Notice that the General tab lets you display up to four phone numbers, with more than a dozen different types of numbers to choose from. For example, for some contacts, instead of Mobile, you might want to display Assistant for the number for the contact's assistant.

Entering E-Mail Addresses

If you imported entries from your PAB, then many of the entries in Contacts will already have an e-mail address. Each record has room for three addresses; so one of your cleanup tasks in migrating from Exchange will be to add addresses from old PAB records, because the PAB required a separate entry for each address.

To add an e-mail address,

1. Select E-mail, E-mail 2, or E-mail 3 from the drop-down list.

2. For an Internet address, enter the address in the box provided in the format *name@domain.*

3. For other addresses, refer to the table "One-Time Address Formats" on page 255 for the required syntax. For example, use **[COMPUSERVE:75140,543]** to add a CompuServe address.

4. To add an address from either your PAB or an organizational address list, click the address book button next to the box. Then in the Select Name dialog box, select the address you want to use and click OK.

You should use the method in step 4 to update the Contacts list with additional PAB addresses where you had several entries for one person.

Adding Your Own Fields

The Contacts record has many different fields, including one for "<u>W</u>eb page," which works with the Explore Web Page button (Figure 26.27) (and also with Contact, <u>E</u>xplore Web Page on the menu) to give you a way to track a person's main Web site and visit it with the click of a button. Be sure to check the Details and All Fields tabs to see what other fields are available.

Figure 26.27
Click the Explore Web Page button to view the Web page entered for a contact.

But maybe there aren't enough fields for you. No problem! You can add additional fields. Here's how to add a new field you can use in all Contacts records:

1. From the Information Viewer, choose <u>V</u>iew, Show <u>F</u>ields.

2. In the Show Fields dialog box, click the <u>N</u>ew Field button.

3. In the New Field dialog box (Figure 26.28), enter the <u>N</u>ame, <u>T</u>ype, and <u>F</u>ormat.

4. Click OK to save the new field.

Figure 26.28

In this example, we're adding a new Contacts field to track the Employee Start Date, the day each person started with the company.

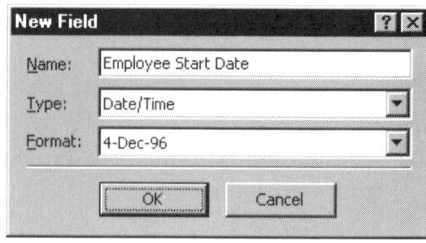

5. If you don't want to display the new field in the current view, click the Remove button.

6. Click OK to close the Show Fields dialog box.

Another way to add a field is from a Contacts record. Follow these steps:

1. Select or double-click on an existing contact to open the Contacts record.

2. Switch to the All Fields tab.

3. If you want to add a field available to all records, select "User-defined fields in folder" from the "Select from" drop-down list. To add a field for just this record, select "User-defined fields in this item."

4. Click the New button to open the New Field dialog box.

5. In the New Field dialog box (Figure 26.28), enter the Name, Type, and Format.

6. Click OK to save the new field.

To enter data in the new fields, type the information in the Value column for the field on the All Fields tab. If you don't see the new fields, then in the "Select from" list, choose "User-defined fields in folder."

Adding Multiple Contacts Lists

Another Exchange Address Book problem that Outlook solves is that of keeping multiple address lists, for example, to maintain personal and business lists. You can do this by using categories to filter the main Contacts list, or you can create additional folders for contacts and add them to your Address Book.

To create a new folder for storing contacts,

1. Choose File, New, Folder.

2. In the Create New Folder dialog box (Figure 26.29), give the folder a Name.

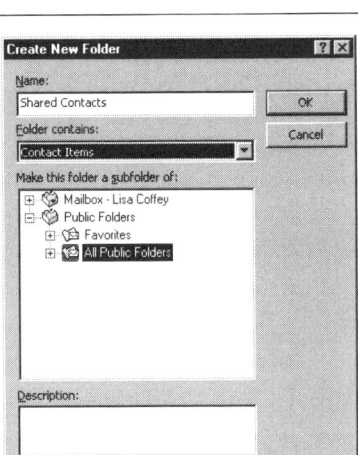

Figure 26.29
When you create a new Outlook folder, you specify what type of item it can contain.

3. Under "Folder contains," specify Contact Items.

4. Under "Make this folder a subfolder of," select the location where you want to create the new folder, either in your Exchange Server mailbox or in a Personal Folders file.

To make the new folder available to the Address Book,

1. Choose Tools, Services, then switch to the Addressing tab.

2. Click the Add button.

3. In the Add Address List dialog box, look under Outlook Address Book to find all the folders that have been set up for contacts. Select the folder you want to add to the Address Book, then click the Add button.

4. Click the Close button to close the Add Address List dialog box, then click OK to close the Services dialog box.

If in step 3 above you don't see the contacts folder you want to use, then close the Services dialog box. You will need to bring up the Properties dialog box for the folder (right-click, then choose Properties), switch to the Outlook Address Book and check the box labeled "Show this folder as an e-mail Address Book." Then you can complete the procedure above.

Special Note

If you don't see the Outlook Address Book in the Address Book (see Figure 26.30), then you need to add the address book to other profiles through the Control Panel with the Mail icon or through Tools, Services in Outlook. Each profile can have a different Outlook Address Book referencing a different set of contacts. Or you can use the same address book for every profile by copying it from your default profile to other profiles.

After you've added a new address list, you can take a look in the Address Book. Choose Tools, Address Book. Under "Show Names from the," look under Outlook Address Book for the new folder you just added. Figure 26.30 shows two new additional folders for contacts — Shared Contacts (see "Creating a Shared Contacts Folder (Method 2)" at the end of the chapter) and Personal Contacts.

Figure 26.30
New folders set up for contacts are listed under the Outlook Address Book once you add them to the Addressing settings for your profile.

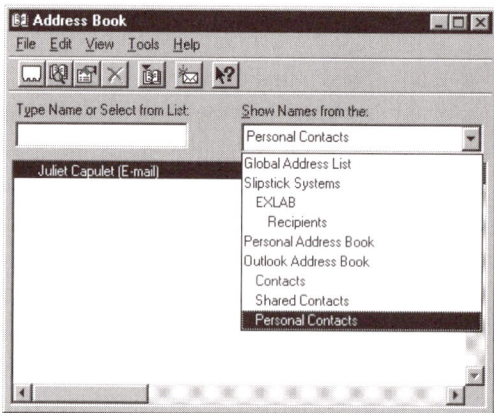

Making Contacts the Default Address List

If you have upgraded to Outlook from Exchange and are using the same profile, you probably still have Personal Address Book as one of your services, as well as the Outlook Address Book. Once you've had a chance to work with the Contacts folder, you may want to make it your default address list for checking names in outgoing e-mail messages (see "How Exchange Looks Up an Address," page 393 in Chapter 17).

To use the Contacts list first for checking names,

1. Choose Tools, Services, then switch to the Addressing tab.
2. Click the Add button.

3. In the Add Address List dialog box, select the Contacts folder you want to add, then click the A̲dd button. Click the C̲lose button to return to the Addressing tab.

4. On the Addressing tab, under "W̲hen sending mail, check names using these address lists in the following order," select Contacts, then use the up arrow button to move this particular group to the top of the list.

5. Click OK to save the change in the address list order, then quit Outlook and restart it.

When you check names against the Contacts list and there is more than one address for a contact, Outlook presents you with a list of all the available addresses. In the example in Figure 26.31, you can see both SMTP (in other words, Internet) and FAX addresses — drawn from a single Contacts entry.

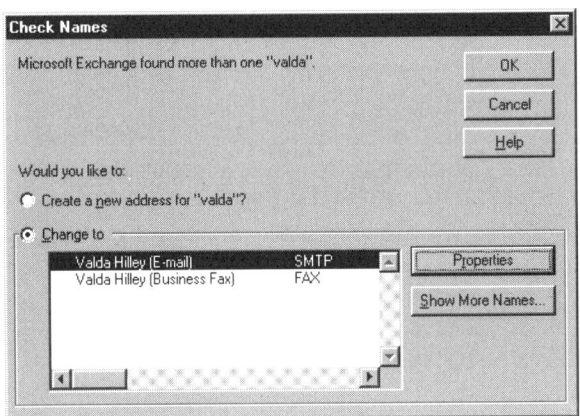

Figure 26.31
When checking names, Outlook displays all e-mail addresses available for a particular person.

Printing and Exporting Contacts

The formats available for printing contacts depend on the current view, particularly what fields are visible and whether it's a table or card view. Choose F̲ile, Print Prev̲iew to see how the printout will look and to make changes to the paper size, layout, and headers. You also can filter Contacts before printing to gather only the names and addresses you need.

If you don't find a print format that does exactly what you want, you can always use the Contacts in a Word 97 mail merge or export Contacts to another format for input into a different program. To export, choose F̲ile, Import̲ and Export, and select "Export to a file" on the Import and Export Wizard. Then continue with the wizard prompts to export in the format you prefer. You'll have the option to produce a tab- or comma-separated values file or, if you installed database drivers during setup, any of several database formats.

Other Contact Enhancements

We don't have space in this brief chapter to cover all the great features of Outlook Contacts, but Table 26.6 lists several you should explore.

Table 26.6 Additional Contact Enhancements

Feature	Description
Automatic Dialing	Choose Tools, Dial to dial any of the numbers associated with a contact and, optionally, to create a Journal entry.
New Contact from Same Company	Choose Contacts, New Contact from Same Company to copy Company and Business fields to a new record.
Templates	Create a Contacts entry containing details that you want to use in a number of other entries. Choose File, Save As, and save the file as an Outlook Template. To use a template to create a new entry, choose Contacts, Choose Template, then select the template you want to use and click OK.
Drag and Drop	Drag a contact and drop it on Inbox to create a new message, on Calendar to create a meeting with the contact, on Tasks to create a new task for the contact, or on Journal to start a new Journal entry for the contact.

Working with Messages

The processes of creating, delivering, retrieving, reading, and managing messages in Outlook are very similar to those in Exchange. This section highlights the many new options available and points out some major changes in Remote Mail.

Creating Messages

To create a new message, if you're in a mail folder, click the New Mail Message button (Figure 26.32) or press Ctrl+N. You also can choose File, New, Mail Message or press Ctrl+Shift+M, no matter where you are in Outlook. The Message tab of the new message window (Figure 26.33) that opens isn't that different from the message window in Exchange.

Figure 26.32
*Click the New Mail
Message button to create
a new message.*

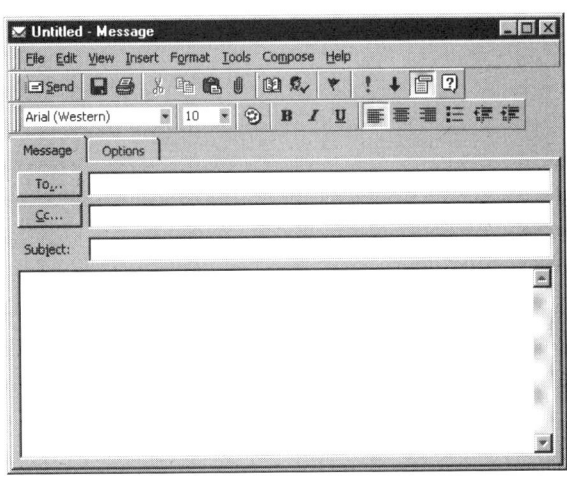

Figure 26.33
*A new message in Outlook
looks very much like a new
message in Exchange.*

However, much is new on the Options tab, shown in Figure 26.34. You see some of the same options you find when you use File, Properties to change the settings for a message. For example, the "Tracking options" section gives you a place to ask for delivery and read receipts. Importance and Sensitivity should also be familiar settings from Exchange.

Here's a quick rundown of the other options:

Use voting buttons   Add buttons to a message to other Outlook users
                                asking for their opinion

Figure 26.34
Most message properties
are gathered together
on the Options tab.

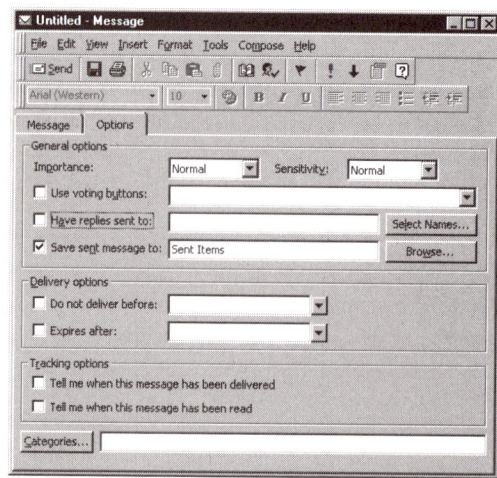

Have replies sent to	Add a Reply To setting to the message header so replies go to some other address(es) instead of your e-mail address
Save sent messages to	Keep this message in the specified folder after it's been delivered
Do not deliver before	Defer delivery until the specified date
Expires after	Force the message to become unavailable after the specified date
Categories	Mark the message with one or more categories (see "Setting Categories" earlier in the chapter)

Checking Names Automatically

When you start entering addresses, you'll begin to see some of the enhancements in Outlook. First of all, you can separate addresses with either a comma or a semicolon, whichever you prefer.

As you move from the To box to other fields in the message, Outlook begins to check the names you've entered. If it finds an exact, unique match, it underlines the name.

If there is more than one possible match, Outlook underlines the name with a red squiggle, just like Word uses for AutoSpell. Right-click on any name underlined with a red squiggle to select the address you want to use or to create a new one.

The real magic occurs the next time you enter that name. Outlook remembers which address you preferred earlier and uses that. But Outlook underlines the address with a green dashed line to indicate that this was an educated guess. As before, you can right-click on the name and select a different address if you need to.

Using AutoSignature

AutoSignature has been changed since it was introduced in the full Exchange Server client. You now have only one signature, but it's maintained as part of your profile, rather than kept in a text file that everyone else using your computer must share.

To set up your signature,

1. Choose Tools, AutoSignature from either a new mail message or from the Information Viewer if you're in a mail folder.
2. In the AutoSignature dialog box (Figure 26.35), enter the text, formatting it with the Font and Paragraph buttons as needed.

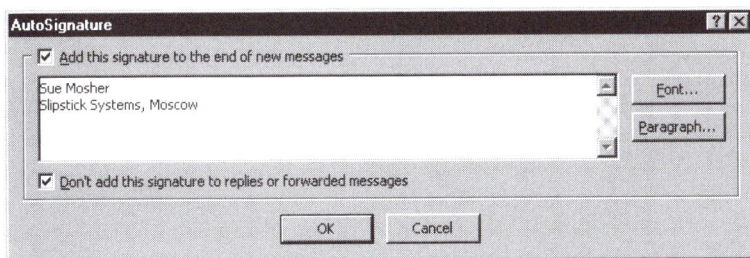

Figure 26.35
You can create one signature, which Outlook will use on all new messages, if you choose.

3. If you want the signature to be added automatically, check "Add this signature to the end of new messages." You may also want to check "Don't add this signature to replies or forwarded messages."
4. Click OK to save the signature.

If you didn't check "Add this signature to the end of new messages" in step 3 above, you still can add your signature to any message. Just choose Insert, AutoSignature.

If you use more than one signature, you can either use WordMail and enter the other signatures as AutoText or create an Outlook template (another new feature) for each additional signature. Creating a signature template is easy. Here's how:

1. Click the New Message button to create a new message.

2. In the body of the message, enter the text you want to use for your signature. Format the signature if you plan to use it in messages to recipients who can handle rich-text formatting.

3. Instead of sending the message, choose File, Save As.

4. In the Save As dialog box, under "Save as type," select "Outlook Template (*.oft)."

5. Give the template a "File name," then click the Save button to store it in the Outlook folder with other templates.

To use a template to create a message,

1. Choose File, New, Choose Template.

2. In the Choose Template dialog box, select the template you want to use, then click OK.

Delivering Messages

As with Exchange, Outlook offers two different ways to receive your messages. Check for New Mail works largely the same as Deliver Now in Exchange, but with the Check for New Mail option you have more flexibility in what mail services are accessed and which messages are delivered. However, substantial changes have been made to Remote Mail, and we'll look at them in detail.

Using Check for New Mail

On the Tools menu in Outlook, you'll see two Check for New Mail choices: Check for New Mail and Check for New Mail On. You can specify which services the first one, Check for New Mail, will use.

Choose Tools, Options. In the "Check for new mail on" list on the E-mail tab, check the services you want to access when you use Check for New Mail. In the example shown in Figure 26.36, I've cleared the box for Internet Mail, because I always access my mailbox with Remote Mail. Because I want to check all the other services with Check for New Mail, I leave them checked. This will let me choose Tools, Check for New Mail just once and get all the mail from each service.

The second function, Check for New Mail On, lets you decide what services to check at any time. When you choose Tools, Check for New Mail On, the dialog box shown in Figure 26.37 appears, with all services checked. Clear the checkboxes for any services you don't want to check at this time, then click OK to put Outlook into action downloading new mail and uploading anything pending in your Outbox.

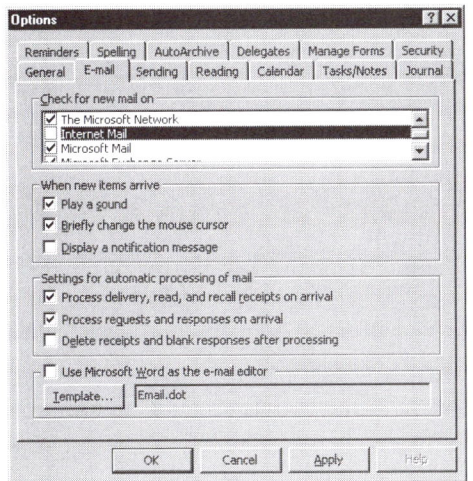

Figure 26.36

Select the services that you want to work with the Check for New Mail function.

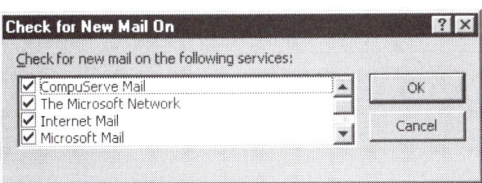

Figure 26.37

When you use Check for New Mail On, you have the opportunity to select which services to check.

Using Remote Mail

If you want more flexibility over what items are sent from your Outbox and which items are retrieved from your mail server, then use Remote Mail. Let's walk through a Remote Mail session to show you how the Outlook version works:

1. Choose Tools, Remote Mail, Connect to display the Remote Connection Wizard, shown in Figure 26.38.

2. Under "Connect to which information service(s)?" check the one(s) you want to access.

3. Check the "Confirm before connecting" box if you want the opportunity to change dialing locations (see "Configuring Dialing Locations," page 28 in Chapter 3).

4. If you want to send everything from the Outbox and retrieve message headers, and you want to use the current dialing location, then click the Finish button. Otherwise, click the Next button.

Figure 26.38
With Remote Mail, you can access mail services all at once or one by one.

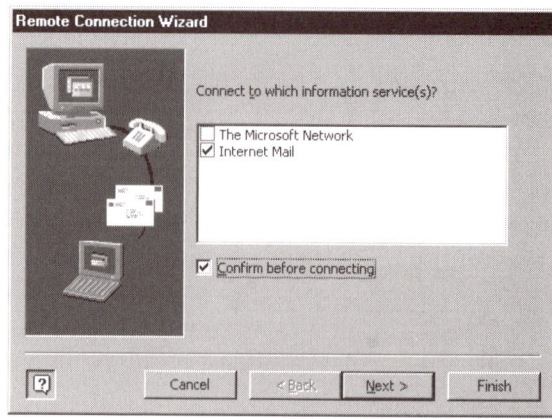

Outlook does not use a separate Remote Mail window; instead, it displays headers in the Inbox.

5. On the next Remote Connection Wizard screen (Figure 26.39), you'll see a check box for each item in your Outbox and for each header that you might have marked for retrieval from a previous Remote Mail session. If you don't want to send or retrieve a particular item, just clear its checkbox.

6. If you want to use the current dialing location, click Finish to start the process of uploading and retrieving mail. If you need to change locations, click the Next button and, on the next screen of the wizard, select the dialing location, then click Finish.

By now you should have noticed the first big difference between Remote Mail in Outlook and Exchange: Outlook does not use a separate Remote Mail window. Once the Remote Mail process is complete, headers are

Figure 26.39
Control the activities in the current Remote Mail session by clearing the checkbox for any action you want to skip at this time.

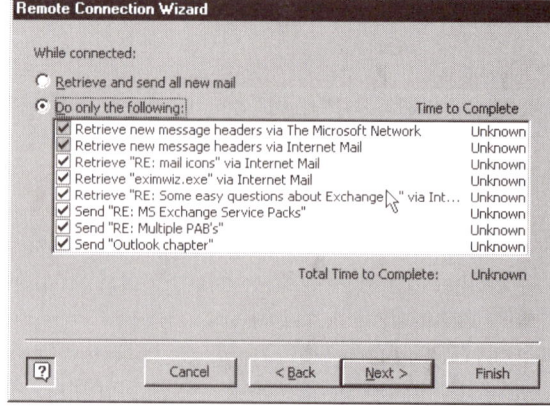

shown in your Inbox (Figure 26.40) and the Remote Tools toolbar is displayed. You can let the Remote Mail toolbar float or drag it up to the top of the Outlook window and dock it next to the regular toolbar.

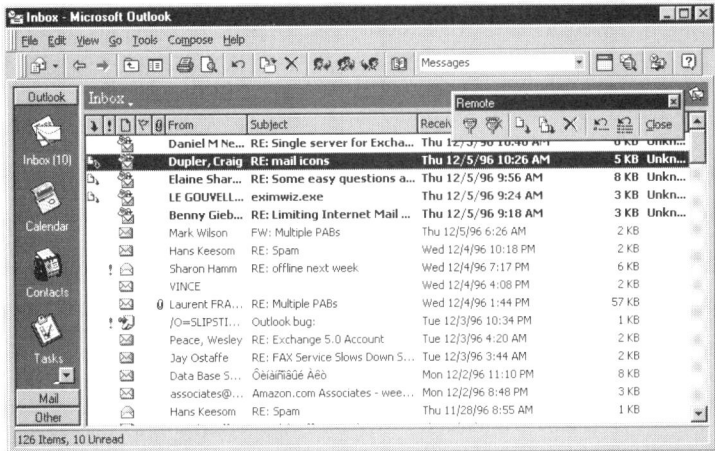

Figure 26.40
Headers downloaded via Remote Mail are mixed with regular messages in your Inbox.

To mark the downloaded headers, either use the buttons on the Remote Toolbar, right-click a header and pick from the pop-up menu, or use the choices on the Tools, Remote Mail menu. You have the same choices as in Exchange — Mark to Retrieve, Mark to Retrieve a Copy, and Delete. Headers marked for deletion go to your Deleted Items folder and will be deleted from the server the next time you connect.

Here are a couple of brief tips on working with headers:

- If you receive a lot of headers mixed in with other messages, it's easier to pick the headers out of the crowd if you turn off AutoPreview.

- You can create a filter to view only the message headers in your Inbox. On the Advanced tab in the Filter dialog box, add the field Message.Class (found under All Mail Fields) and specify IPM.Remote for its value.

Other Message Enhancements

As with Contacts, we can't fit all the new message features into this introduction to Outlook. See what happens when you drag a message to one of the other icons in the Outlook group on the Outlook Bar, such as Contacts or Tasks. Also, do some exploring on your own to check out the enhancements listed in Table 26.7.

Table 26.7 Additional Message Enhancements

Feature	Description
Improved WordMail	Choose Tools, Options, and on the E-mail tab check "Use Microsoft Word as the e-mail editor." This new version, which requires Word 97, adds enhanced formatting to the regular Outlook message window.
Insert Item	In a new message window, choose Insert, Item and choose an item from an Outlook folder — another message, a contact, a task, and so on.
Alternate location for sent messages	On the Options tab in a new message window, check "Save sent message to" and select the destination folder.
Message Recall	Open a sent message, then choose Tools, Recall This Message. You'll be given the option to have unread copies deleted or replaced.
Resend messages	Open a sent message, then choose Tools, Resend This Message.
Find similar messages	Right-click any message in a folder, choose Find All, then choose Related Messages or Messages from Sender.
Archive items	Choose Tools, Options, and switch to the AutoArchive tab to turn on automatic archiving. Then select each folder you want to archive and choose Tools, Properties; switch to the AutoArchive tab to set the schedule and destination. You also can choose File, Archive to archive manually at any time.
Journal	Logs are kept in the Journal folder of all Remote Mail sessions. Entries also can be made for e-mail sent to particular contacts. Open the contact record, switch to the Journal tab, and check "Automatically record journal entries for this contact."

continued

Table 26.7 Additional Message Enhancements, continued

Feature	Description
Undo	If you delete or move an item from a folder, then change your mind, choose Edit, Undo to reverse your action.
Synchronize All on exit	(For Exchange Server users only) Choose Tools, Options, then switch to the General tab. Check "When online, synchronize all folders upon exiting" if you want your folders to be synchronized automatically when you exit Outlook.
Link to the Internet	Incoming messages containing http://, mailto:, ftp://, and other valid Internet URLs show those resources as blue underlined hot links. Click on the link to access the resource. URLs in your outgoing messages are also formatted with blue underlining, but they won't be hot links unless the recipient's mail program supports that.
Move messages faster	Move to Folder is now on the right-click pop-up menu in the Information Viewer. Also, if you click the Move to Folder button on the toolbar, you'll see a list of the most recently used Move folders.
Flag messages for follow-up	Right-click a message in the viewer and choose Flag Message to mark it. Or open the message and choose Edit, Message Flag to set a specific follow-up action and/or due date.

Perhaps the biggest enhancement in Outlook is the multitude of methods it offers for tracking the information you receive via e-mail. For example, consider a message that arrives with a tip on a new utility for Exchange, and I decide I want to include the tip in the next update for my Web site. I can keep track of the message at least four different ways:

1. Choose Edit, Categories and mark the message with a category of My Web Site, which I add to the Master Category list.

2. From the main viewer window, choose Edit, Move to Folder to put the message in a folder I created, one named My Web Site. If you already have the message open, choose File, Move to Folder.

3. Open the message, then choose Edit, Message Flag. In the Flag box in the Flag Message dialog box, type in "Update web site" (flags aren't limited to just the actions on the drop-down list). In the By box, enter an optional due date. Click OK to save the flag.

4. Drag the message from the Information Viewer to the Tasks button to create a new task. If the message was already flagged with a due date, that date carries over to the task.

See if you can find more ways for Outlook to help you keep track of information!

Summary

Microsoft Outlook really is a complete desktop information manager, even giving you access to the system folders in My Computer. By dragging items among the different folders, you can use messages to create tasks, contacts, and other new items. The enriched Information Viewer and more complex Remote Mail options can take a little getting used to, but they pay off in flexibility.

Key Points

• Microsoft Outlook is a desktop information manager combining messaging, scheduling, contact management, groupware, and task management.

• If you want to import contacts from a database, make sure you install the Database Drivers during setup.

• Outlook uses the same mail profiles as Exchange.

• When you use Outlook for the first time, check which add-ons are loaded and install any others you need.

• The Outlook Information Viewer features AutoPreview, new message icons, and user-customizable views.

• Navigate through Outlook with the Outlook bar and the Back and Next browse buttons.

• Outlook solves many of the Address Book problems encountered by Exchange users.

• Outlook does not use a separate Remote Mail window, but instead displays headers in the Inbox.

For More Information

We've had space here to give only a brief introduction to Outlook, spotlighting only those features related to e-mail and the contacts you use to send messages. There's a lot more to it, of course — scheduling and task management, just for starters. Use the Help file to assist you in your explorations. Late-breaking information on Outlook is included in the OlReadme.txt file on the CD. Also take a look at the resource sites listed in Appendix B, "Exchange Resources," for the latest in how-tos and FAQs.

Appendix A

CD Contents

One of the features of Microsoft Exchange that quickly got me hooked is that it can be extended in so many ways. You can add service providers to access different types of e-mail systems. Utilities can be developed with MAPI to add new functions. You can design forms with the Microsoft Exchange Forms Designer to streamline information sharing. For Microsoft Word 7.0 users, macros can reformat mail and even update the Personal Address Book.

On the CD accompanying this book, you'll find a wide variety of Exchange add-ons that I hope will make Exchange work even better for you. The following table lists the location of each item on the CD. Notice that reference materials are also included to supplement what's in this book.

Exchange Add-Ons on the CD		
Type	**Name**	**Location**
Address Book Utilities	Import to Personal Address Book	Address Book\Import to PAB
	Schedule+ Address Book Assistant	Address Book\Schedule+ Assistant
Antivirus Utilities	ThunderBYTE Anti-Virus for MS Exchange	Anti-virus\ThunderBYTE
	VirusEx	Anti-virus\VirusEx
Dial-Up Networking Utilities	Dunce	DUN\Dunce
	Keep Going	DUN\Keep Going
Fax Utilities	Print Fax	Fax\PrintFax
	Scan and Fax Wizard	Fax\Scan and Fax Wizard
Forwarding Utilities	Forward as Attachment	Widgets
	Forward Mail	Forwarding\Forward Mail
	Robert's Auto Forwarding Extension	Forwarding\Robert's Auto Forward
Logon Utilities	Exchange Profile Selector	Logon\EPS
	MAPI Logon (Goetter)	Widgets

continued

Exchange Add-Ons on the CD, continued		
Type	**Name**	**Location**
	MAPI Logon (Mashlan)	Logon\MAPI Logon
Message Decoders	CoderPad	Decode\CoderPad
	Decode Shell Extension	Decode\Shell Extension
Message Utilities	Equipment Request Form	Equipment Request Form
	Exchange SMTP Migration Tool	Message\SMTP Migration Tool
	Internet Idioms	Widgets
	Janitor in a DLL	Widgets
	Resend Client Extension for Microsoft Exchange	Message\Resend
	Rich-Text Sentry	Widgets
	StikrZ Lite	Message\StikrZ
Notification Utilities	MailAlert	Notification\MailAlert
	MailFlag	Notification\MailFlag
Retrieval Utilities	E-mail Exchanger	Retrieval\Exchanger
	GetMail	Retrieval\GetMail
	MAPI Download	Widgets
	MSN Auto Dialer	Retrieval\MSN Auto Dialer

continued

Exchange Add-Ons on the CD, *continued*		
Type	**Name**	**Location**
Security Utilities	PGP Extension for Microsoft Exchange	Security\PGP Extension
	Secure Messenger	Security\Secure Messenger
Service Providers	ccXchg	Services\ccXchg
	Internet Series	Services\Internet Series
	Workgroup Internet Gateway	Services\WIG
Viewers	Deming Preview	Viewers\Deming Preview
	KEYview	Viewers\KEYview
WordMail Macros	WordMail Macros	WordMail Macros
References	Exchange FAQ	FAQ
	CD Software Hot List	CD.htm
	Exchange Resources	Resources.htm

The contents of the CD are included without warranty of any kind, either express or implied, including but not limited to the implied warranty of merchantability and fitness for a particular purpose. Neither Duke Press nor its dealers or distributors assumes any liability for any alleged or actual damages arising from the use of or the inability to use this software. (Some states do not allow the exclusion of implied warranties, so the exclusion may not apply to you.)

Note that some of the applications are freeware, while others are shareware (which require a payment if you decide to keep using the software) or demo versions (which may have certain features disabled or may expire after a certain period). Check for a Readme.txt or License.txt file with each application to see what restrictions the author has placed on its use and distribution.

Not all applications have been tested on Windows NT 4.0, so take care to read the description in this chapter and the documentation in each folder to find out whether the utility is suitable for your use. Ben Goetter's utilities in the Widgets folder include both Intel and Alpha versions for NT. Other utilities compatible with Windows NT will run on Intel systems only.

For more Exchange add-ons, you'll also want to browse through Appendix B, "Exchange Resources."

Before You Install

Before you install any of the CD software, read both the description in this chapter and any documents in the folder for the program. Also be sure to use File, Exit and Log Off to completely quit Exchange before you do the installation.

Address Book Utilities

To help you work with the Personal Address Book (PAB), the Import to Personal Address Book utility can add addresses from any data source. For export, the Schedule+ Address Book Assistant copies addresses from the PAB to the Schedule+ Contacts list. Another PAB utility is the address macro in the WordMail Macros collection, covered later in this appendix.

Import to Personal Address Book

Import to Personal Address Book consists of a Microsoft Word 7.0 template containing instructions and a macro that enables you to import contact data from an external data source into the Microsoft Exchange PAB. The data source can be any type of file that Microsoft Word 7.0 can use as a mail-merge source (e.g., Microsoft Access *.mdb files, Word documents, comma- or tab-delimited text files). You also can work with your Microsoft Schedule+ 7.0 Contacts data.

No setup is required. Simply open the ImpPAB1.dot document found in the Address Book\Import to PAB folder on the CD. To run the macro, click the "Run Import To PAB" button on the custom ImportToPAB toolbar. If you don't see the ImportToPAB toolbar, choose View, Toolbars from the View menu, then check the box next to ImportToPAB in the list of available toolbars, and click OK. Detailed instructions for mapping fields from the data source to the PAB are included in the ImpPAB1.dot file.

This program is freeware. For the latest version, visit http://www.slipstick. com/exchange. To contact the author, e-mail Graham Smith at Graham-Smith@ msn.com or 100125.1730@compuserve.com.

Schedule+ Address Book Assistant

The Microsoft Schedule+ Address Book Assistant is a Visual Basic 4.0 32-bit application (using Schedule+ OLE Automation) that allows you to grab address book entries and copy them into your Microsoft Schedule+ Contacts list. This gives you an easy way (through Schedule+) to print information about a contact or to add the contact to your Timex DataLink watch.

To install the Schedule+ Address Book Assistant, Windows 95 users should run the Schedaba.exe file found in the Address Book\Schedule+ Assistant\W95setup folder on the CD. For Windows NT, right-click on the Address Book\Schedule+ Assistant\Flatfiles\schedaba.inf file, then choose Install.

To use the Schedule+ Address Book Assistant to import addresses from the Personal Address Book,

1. Start Schedule+.
2. In Schedule+, choose File, Import, From Address Book.
3. In the "Select Entries to copy to Microsoft Schedule+" dialog box, select names from your address book (hold down the Ctrl key as you click to select more than one), then click the Schedule+ button to move those names to the right-hand list.
4. When you've selected all the names you want to import, click OK and the names will be added or updated in the Schedule+ Contacts list.

The Schedule+ Address Book Assistant is just one of the sample applications (including source code) available at the Microsoft Exchange Application Farm, http://www.microsoft.com/technet/appfarm/default.htm. To contact the author, e-mail appfarm@microsoft.com.

Antivirus Utilities

Two antivirus utilities, ThunderBYTE and VirusEx, are available for individual Exchange users. (Another interesting development is the creation of antivirus utilities for mail servers, but that's beyond our scope here.)

ThunderBYTE Anti-Virus for Microsoft Exchange

ThunderBYTE Anti-Virus for Microsoft Exchange scans file attachments in incoming and outgoing messages for viruses and notifies you when a virus is found.

To install ThunderBYTE for Microsoft Exchange, run the Tbavmb50.exe program found in the Anti-virus\ThunderBYTE folder on the CD. You will be asked whether you want to install ThunderBYTE in your default Exchange profile. If you choose No, you will need to add the service later. To change the settings for ThunderBYTE, from the Exchange Viewer choose <u>T</u>ools, Ser<u>v</u>ices, select ThunderBYTE Anti-Virus for MS Exchange, then click the P<u>r</u>operties button.

This product is a beta version. If you want to continue using it, you should obtain the released version from http://www.nemx.com. To contact Nemx, e-mail support@nemx.com.

VirusEx

VirusEx detects incoming message attachments that look like they might be viruses.

To install VirusEx, run the Virusex.exe program found in the Antivirus\VirusEx folder on the CD. Choose between German or English text for the setup wizard. You also can choose between using the THOR virus scanner engine included with VirusEx or relying on another virus scanner (such as McAffee or F-PROT) already working on your system. VirusEx will now be active whenever you start Exchange. To view and change its settings, choose <u>T</u>ools, <u>O</u>ptions, then switch to the VirusEx tab.

To see how VirusEx works, you can send yourself the Dummyvir.com file found in the VirusEx folder. I know this sounds alarming, but it's harmless and was created just to show you how a file with a pattern that resembles a virus can trigger VirusEx's detection program.

This product is an evaluation copy and includes only the German-language help file, not the English help. If you want to continue using VirusEx, you should obtain the released version. Visit Glück and Kanja GmbH at http://www.glueckkanja.de. To contact Glück and Kanja, e-mail info@ glueckkanja.de.

Dial-Up Networking Utilities

Two utilities can help you connect faster with dial-up networking. Both Dunce and Keep Going eliminate the need to click the Connect button every time you want to access mail on a remote server.

Dunce

Dunce (or Dial-Up Networking Connection Enhancement) version 2.4 allows for much easier dial-up networking than Windows 95 provides. The program will automatically press the Connect button in the Connect To dialog box, redial your Internet service provider if the line is busy, and reconnect if the connection is unexpectedly dropped. Dunce also supports scheduled connections (including connections to The Microsoft Network) and can run specified applications each time you connect.

To install Dunce, copy the files found in the DUN\Dunce folder on the CD to a new folder on your computer, probably C:\Program Files\Dunce. Then run the Dunce.exe file from this new folder to configure the program. By default, Dunce places an icon in the system tray on the task bar (the little guy with the red dunce cap). Click the icon with the left mouse button to turn Dunce on and off. Right-click the icon to change the Dunce settings.

This program is freeware. For more information, the latest version, or news about other Vector Development utilities, including an enhanced version called Dunce Gold, visit http://www.vecdev.com. To contact the author, e-mail vecdev@vecdev.com.

Keep Going

Keep Going eliminates the need to click the Connect button when you are using dial-up networking with a script (see "Scripting the Log-On Process," page 45 in Chapter 3).

To use Keep Going, copy the Keepgoin.exe and Keepgoin.hlp files from the DUN\Keep Going folder on the CD to your computer. Then put a shortcut to Keepgoin.exe in the Programs, StartUp folder, set to run minimized.

This product is shareware. If you want to continue using Keep Going, you must register it. Call 1-800-946-8769 with a credit card, or go to http://www.xmission.com/~wintrnx/regnet to register online. To contact the author, e-mail wintrnx@xmission.com.

Fax Utilities

For Microsoft Fax, you'll find Print Fax, which automatically prints and/or forwards incoming faxes, and Scan and Fax, for building multipage faxes with your scanner.

Another utility useful to Microsoft Fax users is MAPI Logon, discussed in the "Logon Utilities" section. Robert Mashlan created this so he could receive faxes without the need to start the full Exchange program.

Print Fax

Print Fax scans the Inbox folder for new incoming faxes and prints them or forwards those faxes to another e-mail user, or both.

To install Print Fax, run the Setup.exe program found in the Fax\PrintFax folder on the CD. A Print Fax item will be added to the Start, Programs menu. Use this item to start Print Fax, which is set by default to print all faxes to the computer's default printer.

To add forwarding of faxes, follow these steps:

1. Choose Options, Set Target.
2. Select one or more recipients to forward faxes to, then click OK.
3. Choose Options, Forward To (the names of your recipients) to check that menu option.

Print Fax must be running for faxes to be forwarded.

This program is freeware. For updates, visit http://www.slipstick.com/ exchange/gallery.htm. To contact the author, e-mail techsupport@axs.be.

Scan and Fax Wizard

If you worked through "Building a Multipage Fax with Imaging," page 331 in Chapter 14, then you no doubt think there must be a better way. This is it. The Scan and Fax Wizard automates the process of creating and sending a fax with your scanner and Imaging for Windows (see "Imaging for Windows," page 167 in Chapter 7).

To install the Scan and Fax Wizard, run the Setup.exe program found in the Fax\Scan and Fax Wizard folder on the CD. Run Scan and Fax from the icon on the Programs menu and follow the wizard steps.

This program is freeware. For updates, visit http://www.slipstick.com/ exchange/gallery.htm. To contact the author, e-mail John Sherda at JohnSherda@ msn.com.

Forwarding Utilities

You'll find two kinds of utilities in this section. Forward as Attachment lets you forward a single Exchange message as an attachment, in the same way multiple messages are forwarded. Then there are two automatic forwarding utilities, Forward Mail and Robert's Auto Forwarding Extension. We also mentioned another utility specifically for forwarding faxes (Print Fax) in the "Fax Utilities" section.

Forward as Attachment

If you first select more than one message in the Exchange Viewer, and you then choose Compose, Forward, Exchange includes each selected message as an attachment on the new message; but single messages are always forwarded as included text. Forward as Attachment provides the capability to forward a single message as an attachment, just as easily as you can forward multiple messages (note that the recipient needs to have Exchange to be able to read the attached message).

To install Forward as Attachment, follow these steps:

1. Copy the Fwdasatt.dll file from the Widgets\Intel or Widgets\Alpha folder on the CD to your system directory (usually Windows\System on Windows 95, Winnt\system32 on Windows NT).

2. Check your system directory for the file Msvcrt40.dll. If you don't see it, then copy it from the Widgets\Intel or Widgets\Alpha folder to your system directory.

3. Double-click the Fwdasatt.reg file to update the Windows registry with the necessary entries.

On the Compose menu of the Exchange Viewer and message windows, you now will see a new command, Forward as Attachment. Select the command to forward the current message as an attachment. You can place this command on the toolbar if you like, even replacing the standard toolbar Forward button with it.

This program is freeware. For more information, the latest version, or information about other Widgets for Microsoft Exchange, visit http://www.angrygraycat.com/goetter/widgets.htm. To contact the author, e-mail Ben Goetter at goetter@angrygraycat.com.

Forward Mail

Forward Mail is a small program that scans the Inbox folder for all incoming e-mail (including faxes) and forwards the e-mail to an address you choose. This address can be that of a user on your internal system, a fax recipient, or any other valid e-mail address. For example, you can use Forward Mail to forward all incoming faxes from an unattended computer to an administrator's account.

To install Forward Mail, run the Setup.exe program found in the Forwarding\Forward Mail folder on the CD. The first time you run Forward Mail, you'll be asked to specify a valid recipient to forward mail to and how often you want your mailbox checked for new mail.

This program is freeware. For updates, visit http://www.slipstick.com/exchange/gallery.htm. To contact the author, e-mail Franck Sidon at francks@msn.com.

Robert's Auto Forwarding Extension

Robert's Auto Forwarding Extension automatically forwards incoming Internet messages to one or more addresses, with the option of excluding mail from certain domains (so you don't forward mailing list messages, for instance).

One use of this utility might be to forward mail from your work account to your personal mail account.

To install Robert's Auto Forwarding Extension, right-click the Exch_fwd.inf file found in the Forwarding\Robert's Auto Forward folder on the CD, then choose Install.

To set the forwarding options, from the Exchange Viewer choose Tools, Options, then switch to the new Forwarding tab.

This program is freeware. For updates, visit http://www.slipstick.com/ exchange/gallery.htm. To contact the author, e-mail Robert Chou at rob_ chou@ix.netcom.com.

Log-On Utilities

In this section, Exchange Profile Selector and MAPI Logon by Ben Goetter both let you start Exchange with a particular profile, instead of requiring you to pick from the list of profiles on your computer.

A second MAPI Logon program, by Robert Mashlan, starts Exchange without loading the full client. This program was designed to receive faxes via Microsoft Fax.

Exchange Profile Selector

Exchange Profile Selector version 1.4.1 is a utility for starting Exchange with a specified profile, rather than selecting from the list of profiles.

To install Exchange Profile Selector, copy the Eps.exe file from the Logon\EPS folder on the CD to the Windows folder on your computer. Here is the command line syntax for using it:

eps <*"name of profile"*> [Exchange command line options]

Note that the profile name must be in quotes if it contains spaces. This will start Exchange using the specified profile, passing any optional command line options (see "Adding Command Line Settings to Exchange," page 245 in Chapter 10) directly to Exchange. For example,

> **eps "MS Exchange Settings"**
> **eps "MS Exchange Settings" /n**
> **eps "FAX Settings" /a**

You can use this syntax to create shortcuts either on the desktop or on the Start menu.

This program is freeware. For more information, the latest version, or information about other utilities, visit http://ourworld.compuserve.com/homepages/jsijm. To contact the author, e-mail Jan Sijm at 101451.1651@compuserve.com.

MAPI Logon (Goetter)

MAPI Logon by Ben Goetter is a utility for starting Exchange from a command line with a particular profile.

To install MAPI Logon, follow these steps:

1. Copy the Mlogon.exe file from the Widgets\Intel or Widgets\Alpha folder on the CD to your computer.
2. Check your system directory for the file Msvcrt40.dll. If you don't see it, then copy it from the Widgets\Intel or Widgets\Alpha folder to your system directory.

To use MAPI Logon, use Start, Run or create a shortcut using a command with this syntax:

Mlogon /p <*MS Exchange Settings*>

where "MS Exchange Settings" is an Exchange profile, surrounded by quotes if it contains spaces. You'll need to include the path to Mlogon.exe if you didn't put it in a folder in your path. Other switches are detailed in the Mlogon.htm file found in the Widgets folder on the CD.

This program is freeware. For more information, the latest version, or information about other Widgets for Microsoft Exchange, visit http://www.angrygraycat.com/goetter/widgets.htm. To contact the author, e-mail Ben Goetter at goetter@angrygraycat.com.

MAPI Logon (Mashlan)

MAPI Logon by Robert Mashlan is a simple utility that logs on to an Exchange profile, making it possible to receive faxes with Microsoft Fax without running the full Exchange program. MAPI Logon uses the default Exchange profile.

To install MAPI Logon, copy the Mapilogon.exe and Mapilogon.inf files from the Logon\MAPI Logon folder on the CD to a temporary folder on your hard drive. Right-click the local copy of Mapilogon.inf, then choose Install. Once MAPI Logon is installed, it will start automatically whenever Windows 95 starts. When the program is running, you will see a small M icon in the system tray on the taskbar. You can click once on the icon to display a small menu to log on and off or to start Exchange.

This program is freeware. For more information, the latest version, or information about other R2M Software utilities, visit http://www.r2m.com/. To contact the author, e-mail Robert Mashlan at rmashlan@r2m.com.

Message Decoders

Sometimes you may receive a message from the Internet in a format that Exchange can't decode. Instead, the message looks like gibberish. That's when you need a decoder utility such as CoderPad or the Decode Shell Extension included here.

CoderPad

To install CoderPad, copy the CoderPad.exe, CoderPad.hlp, and Uudeview.dll files from the Decode\CoderPad folder on the CD to a folder on your computer.

CoderPad (beta) was created in Microsoft Visual Basic 4.0 and requires the VB runtime support files. If you don't have VB installed (or any other utilities written with VB), run the Setup.exe file found in the CoderPad\VBRun folder on the CD. Doing this will install the necessary support files. Start Coder-Pad from the folder where you copied it. You'll be asked to specify where to store decoded files.

What makes CoderPad unique is that you do not need to save Exchange messages as separate files to decode them. Instead, you can copy message text to the clipboard, then pass that text directly to CoderPad to decode. Here's how:

1. Open a message containing an encoded file.
2. Choose Edit, Select All to select the text, then Edit, Copy to copy it to the clipboard.
3. Start CoderPad (or switch to it if it is already running), then click the Paste button.
4. In the Decode Files dialog box, CoderPad will indicate at the bottom box whether it found any files it can decode. If it did, then click the Decode button to decode them.

This software is shareware. If you plan to continue using CoderPad, you should register it. For details and the latest version, visit http://users.aol.com/lamprog/coderpad.html. To contact the author, e-mail Lou A. Moccia at lamprog@aol.com.

Decode Shell Extension

The Decode Shell Extension version 2.1 (from Funduc Software) adds a Decode menu item to your Windows 95 or Windows NT 4.0 Explorer context menu (the one you see when you right-click an item in Explorer). The Decode menu item appears only when exactly one file is selected.

When you right-click a file and choose Decode, the extension analyzes the file. If it detects a UUENCODE, BinHex, or MIME encoded file, it asks if you want to decode it. Multiple attachments are decoded as separate files.

To install the Decode Shell Extension, run the Setup.exe program from the Decode\Shell Extension folder on the CD. To use the program to decode Exchange messages, you must first save the message as a text file by choosing File, Save As. After you specify the name and location for the file, click the Save button. Then switch to Windows Explorer, right-click the file, and choose Decode.

This program is freeware. For more information, the latest version, or information about other Funduc Software utilities, visit http://home.sprynet. com/sprynet/funduc. To contact the author, e-mail Mike Funduc at 102372. 2530@compuserve.com.

Message Utilities

The collection of utilities in this section includes add-ons to make your messages look better, keep your private folders cleaned up, and move messages from your old Internet mail program. Another source for message utilities is the WordMail Macros template described later in this appendix.

Equipment Request Form

The project source for the Equipment Request form discussed in Chapter 20, "Collaborating with Exchange," is included along with the finished version. You must be using an Exchange Server client to work with this form. If you just want to install the form as-is, follow these steps:

1. In the Exchange Viewer, choose Tools, Options, then switch to the Exchange Server tab.
2. On the Exchange Server tab, click the Manage Forms button.
3. In the Forms Manager dialog box, click the Install button.
4. In the Open dialog, select the Equiprqt.cfg form found in the Equiprqt folder on the CD, then click the Open button.
5. Click OK when you see the Form Properties dialog box.

6. When you return to the Forms Manager dialog box, click the Close button, then OK in the Options dialog box to return to the Exchange Viewer.

You now can send equipment requests. Choose Compose, New Form, then choose Equipment Request from the New Form dialog box, and click OK. To modify the form with Microsoft Exchange Forms Designer,

1. Copy the Equiprqt.efp file from the equiprqt folder on the CD to a new empty folder on your computer.
2. In the Exchange Viewer, choose Tools, Application Design, Forms Designer.
3. Choose "Open an Existing Form Project," then click the Next button.
4. In the Open dialog box, select the Equiprpt.efp file in the folder where you placed it on your computer.

You now can see how the form was constructed and add your own embellishments.

Exchange SMTP Migration Tool

This is a tool for transferring the contents of SMTP mailboxes — such as those from Eudora, Pegasus, or Netscape — into an Exchange Server private mail store. It scans an SMTP mailbox and creates migration files suitable for transfer into Exchange using the Exchange Migration Wizard supplied with Exchange Server. This wizard is described in Chapter 2 of the Exchange Migration Guide (located in the directory Migrate\Docs on the Exchange Server CD). *Please note*: This is a tool for migrating messages to an Exchange Server mailbox, not to a Personal Folders file.

To install the Exchange SMTP Migration Tool, copy the files from the Message\SMTP Migration Tool folder on the CD to a new folder on your computer. Read the Readme.doc file for instructions on how to set up the required parameters in the Mailexp.ini file. The command line for the program is

Mailexp.exe <*C:\My Path*>\Mailexp.ini

where *C:\My Path*\Mailexp.ini is the full path to the .ini file. After running the Exchange SMTP Migration Tool, you then use the Exchange Migration Wizard included with Exchange Server to complete the migration process.

This product is shareware. If you want to use it beyond an evaluation period, you must register it. For updates, visit http://samantha.ccc.ox.ac.uk/

exchange. To contact the author, e-mail Matthew J. Dovey at matthew.dovey@ccc.ox.ac.uk.

Internet Idioms

Internet Idioms is an add-on that makes Exchange act more like some of the other Internet mail programs by adding a quote prefix and signatures. You also can use this software to control the font used to display incoming messages.

To install Internet Idioms, follow these steps:

1. Copy the Inetxidm.dll file from the Widgets\Intel or Widgets\Alpha folder on the CD to your system directory (usually Windows\System on Windows 95, Winnt\System32 on Windows NT).

2. Check your system directory for the file Msvcrt40.dll. If you don't see it, then copy it from the Widgets\Intel or Widgets\Alpha folder to your system directory.

3. Double-click the Inetxidm.reg file to update the Windows registry with the necessary entries.

When you choose Tools, Options, you'll now see a new tab, Idioms, where you can set the read font, signature, and prefix options.

This program is freeware. For more information, the latest version, or information about other Widgets for Microsoft Exchange, visit http://www.angrygraycat.com/goetter/widgets.htm. To contact the author, e-mail Ben Goetter at goetter@angrygraycat.com.

Janitor in a DLL

If you don't have Exchange set to empty the Delete Items folder when you exit (see "Deleting Messages," page 379 in Chapter 16), you'll appreciate this add-on, which adds a function to empty the Deleted Items folder on command.

To install Janitor in a DLL, follow these steps:

1. Copy the Mtwb.dll file from the Widgets\Intel or Widgets\Alpha folder on the CD to your system directory (usually Windows\System on Windows 95, Winnt\System32 on Windows NT).

2. Check your system directory for the file Msvcrt40.dll. If you don't see it, then copy it from the Widgets\Intel or Widgets\Alpha folder to your system directory.

3. Double-click the Mtwb.reg file to update the Windows registry with the necessary entries.

On the File menu of the Exchange Viewer you will see a new command, Expunge Deleted Items. Select it to empty your Deleted Items folder of all deleted messages.

This program is freeware. For more information, the latest version, or information about other Widgets for Microsoft Exchange, visit http://www.angrygraycat.com/goetter/widgets.htm. To contact the author, e-mail Ben Goetter at goetter@angrygraycat.com.

Resend Client Extension for Microsoft Exchange

The Resend Client Extension solves the dilemma of how to retransmit an item from the Sent Items folder, either to the original recipient or to a new recipient, without forwarding.

To install the Resent Client Extension, right-click on the Resend.inf file found in the Message\Resend folder on the CD. After you restart Exchange, you will see two new options on the Compose menu, Resend and Resend Now. Resend opens the message so you can change recipients. Resend Now resends the item with exactly the same recipients as the original.

This program is freeware. For more information, the latest version, or information about other Microsoft Exchange client extensions from the University of Wisconsin at Stevens Point, visit http://ems1.uwsp.edu/client_ext/. To contact the author, e-mail Stephen P. Johnson at sjohnson@uwsp.edu.

Rich Text Sentry

The Rich Text Sentry guards against the common mistake of sending Exchange rich-text format (RTF) messages to an Internet recipient not using Microsoft Exchange, which results in the recipient receiving either an odd and useless Winmail.dat attachment (if you sent with UUENCODE) or a lot of unusable binary data (if you sent with MIME).

Once installed, Rich Text Sentry watches every outgoing message for Internet recipients who were not selected from the Address Book and who have the "Send to this recipient in Microsoft rich text format" flag set. When Rich Text Sentry finds such a message, it warns the user, who may send the message as it is, stop sending the message, or have Rich Text Sentry eliminate the rich-text setting for that recipient.

To install Rich Text Sentry, follow these steps:

1. Copy the Rtfguard.dll file from the Widgets\Intel or Widgets\Alpha folder on the CD to your system directory (usually Windows\System on Windows 95, Winnt\System32 on Windows NT).

2. Check your system directory for the file Msvcrt40.dll. If you don't see it, then copy it from the Widgets\Intel or Widgets\Alpha folder to your system directory.

3. Double-click the Rtfguard.reg file to update the Windows registry with the necessary entries.

This program is freeware. For more information, the latest version, or information about other Widgets for Microsoft Exchange, visit http://www.angrygraycat.com/goetter/widgets.htm. To contact the author, e-mail Ben Goetter at goetter@angrygraycat.com.

StikrZ Lite

StikrZ Lite is a 16-bit program (it will even run on Windows 3.1) that lets you add emotions and tone to your messages by dragging pictures from a collection of "stickers" or by inserting them as objects in an Exchange message.

To install StikrZ Lite, run the Stk16b03.exe program found in the Message\StikrZ folder on the CD. To run StikrZ, click the Start button, then choose Programs, StikrZ, StikrZ. Keep StikrZ open if you want to be able drag a sticker into any Exchange message window. You also can insert a sticker into a new message by choosing Insert, Object, then choosing Sticker from the Object Type list.

This program is freeware. For more information, the latest version (StikrZ Pro, a 32-bit version, is in the works), or information about other Trax Softworks programs, visit http://www.traxsoft.com/~traxsoft. To contact Trax, e-mail info@traxsoft.com.

Notification Utilities

While Exchange gives you several options for being notified when new messages arrive, there's room for improvement in this area. Mail Alert and MailFlag both offer interesting enhancements.

Mail Alert

Mail Alert adds two features to Exchange — custom mail notifications (similar to those available with Inbox Assistant) and scheduled retrieval of messages via the Internet Mail service, without having to leave Exchange running.

To install MailAlert, follow these steps:

1. Copy the MailAlert.exe file from the Notification\MailAlert folder on the CD to your computer.

2. Copy the MailAlert.cnt and MailAlert.hlp files to the Help folder under your Windows folder, which usually is C:\Windows\Help.

3. Run the MailAlert.exe file. The properties dialog box will come up. Note that in the Default Settings property page you can check the "Load on Windows startup" box to create a shortcut to the MailAlert.exe file in your StartUp folder.

This product is shareware. If you want to continue using Mail Alert, you must register it. Follow the instructions in the help file. For more information or the latest version, visit http://www.diamondridge.com. To contact the author, e-mail MailAlert@DiamondRidge.com.

MailFlag

MailFlag enhances the message-notification options in Exchange by showing you whether an incoming message has an attachment or requests a receipt and by allowing you to set reminders for unread messages. You can combine MailFlag with a retrieval utility, such as Email Exchanger, to get notification of incoming messages without running the full Exchange program.

To install MailFlag, copy the Mflag32.exe file from the Notification\Mail-Flag folder on the CD to your computer. Copy the Mflag32.dll file to the system folder, usually Windows\System on Windows 95 or Winnt\system32 on Windows NT. MailFlag runs from a command line, using this syntax:

MailFlag.exe -u<"*MS Exchange Settings*">

where "*MS Exchange Settings*" is the name of a specific Exchange profile, enclosed in quotes if it contains spaces. Note that there is no space between the -u switch and the profile name.

This program is shareware. You may evaluate it for 30 days, after which you must register to continue using it. Registration is supported through the CompuServe shareware registration service (GO SWREG). See the Mfreg.txt file on the CD for details. To contact the author, e-mail Jeff Lundblad at 73537. 1203@compuserve.com.

Retrieval Utilities

Automatic retrieval of waiting messages isn't on option for every Exchange service, but a variety of utilities detailed in this section can help you set up scheduled retrieval sessions, even for Microsoft Network mail. Also check out the MailAlert utility in the previous section for its ability to perform automatic retrieval.

Email Exchanger

Email Exchanger version 2.0 is a utility for scheduling retrieval of messages for all the services in your Exchange profile. If you want Email Exchanger to work with The Microsoft Network, you need to use one of the programs listed under "Dial-up Networking Utilities" that can automatically click the Connect button for you.

To install Email Exchanger, run the Setup.exe program found in the Retrieval\Exchanger folder on the CD. During setup, a new Program Files\mapcall folder is created. When setup has finished, run the Emailex.exe file from this folder to place the yellow Email Exchanger icon in the system tray on the taskbar. Click the icon to set up the scheduled connections. You can find additional documentation in the Emailex.hlp file in the Retrieval\ Exchanger folder on the CD.

This product is shareware. If you want to continue using Email Exchanger, you should register it. Registration is supported through the CompuServe shareware registration service (GO SWREG, ID #7931). To contact the author, e-mail Jeffrey Levy at jeffrey@rhinestone.com.

GetMail

GetMail is a program designed to retrieve mail for a specified Exchange profile through an unattended dial-up connection without opening the full Exchange program.

To install GetMail, copy the Getmail.exe file from the Retrieval\Getmail folder on the CD to the Windows folder on your computer. To use GetMail, use Start, Run or create a shortcut using a command with this syntax:

GetMail <*"My Internet Service Provider"*> <*"MS Exchange Settings"*>

where "*My Internet Service Provider*" is the name of a dial-up networking connection and "*MS Exchange Settings*" is the name of an Exchange profile, each surrounded by quotes if it contains spaces.

GetMail will establish a dial-up session, instruct the service providers in the MAPI profile to transfer all mail, then hang up the phone. It should do this without any dialog boxes or prompting, as long as the services themselves do not require user interaction, or you have a program such as Dunce installed that can take care of pushing the Connect button on the Microsoft Network dialog for you. You can use the System Agent program included with Microsoft Plus! or another scheduling program to schedule GetMail to make mail runs every hour.

This program is freeware. For more information, the latest version, or information about other R2M Software utilities, visit http://www.r2m.com. To contact the author, e-mail Robert Mashlan at rmashlan@r2m.com.

MAPI Download

MAPI Download connects and downloads messages without ever starting the full Exchange program, making it suitable for running from scheduler programs. MAPI Download lets you specify the profile to use on the command line.

To install MAPI Download, follow these steps:

1. Copy the Mfetch.exe file from the Widgets\Intel or Widgets\Alpha folder on the CD to your system directory (usually Windows\System on Windows 95, Winnt\System32 on Windows NT).

2. Check your system directory for the file Msvcrt40.dll. If you don't see it, then copy it from the Widgets\Intel or Widgets\Alpha folder to your system directory.

To use MAPI Download, use Start, Run or create a shortcut using a command with this syntax:

Mfetch /p <*"MS Exchange Settings"*>

where "*MS Exchange Settings*" is an Exchange profile, surrounded by quotes if it contains spaces.

This program is freeware. For more information, the latest version, or information about other Widgets for Microsoft Exchange, visit http://www. angrygraycat.com/goetter/widgets.htm. To contact the author, e-mail Ben Goetter at goetter@ angrygraycat.com.

MSN Auto Dialer

The MSN Auto Dialer connects to The Microsoft Network and collects any waiting messages. You can use MSN Auto Dialer with any Windows 95 scheduling program to collect mail at specified times.

To install the MSN Auto Dialer, follow these steps:

1. Copy the Msndial.exe file from the Retrieval\MSN Auto Dialer folder on the CD to your computer.

2. In the Exchange Viewer, choose Tools, Services, then select The Microsoft Network, and click the Properties button.

3. Check the boxes for "Download mail when e-mail starts up from MSN" and "Disconnect after Transferring Mail from Remote Mail."

4. Click OK twice to save these settings.

You can now run Msndial.exe at any time to collect MSN mail.

To contact the author, e-mail Andy Fox at AndyFox@msn.com.

Security Utilities

The two security add-ons in this section, PGP Extension for Exchange and Secure Messenger, were introduced in the section "Using Other Security Methods," page 495 in Chapter 21.

PGP Extension for Exchange

The PGP Extension for Exchange adds PGP (Pretty Good Privacy) encryption and decryption functions. You must first obtain PGP (http://web.mit.edu/network/pgp) and configure it. You will find instructions in the Readme.doc found in the Security\PGP Extension folder on the CD.

To install the PGP Extension, follow these steps:

1. Copy the Pgpext32.dll file from the Security\PGP Extension folder on the CD to your system directory (usually Windows\System on Windows 95, Winnt\System32 on Windows NT).

2. Double-click the PgpExtRegistryValues.reg file to update the Windows registry with the necessary entries.

The Encrypt and Decrypt commands are added to the Tools menu.

This program is freeware. For the latest version, visit http://homepage.interaccess.com/~jon. To contact the author, e-mail Jon Whalen at jon@interaccess.com.

Secure Messenger

Secure Messenger uses S/MIME (Secure MIME) to digitally sign and encrypt messages either with a key pair you generate yourself or with keys registered with a trusted third-party.

To install Secure Messenger, run the Smb1_ww.exe file found in the Security\Secure Messenger folder on the CD. The Secure Messenger S/MIME service will be added to your default Exchange profile. If you want to use it with other profiles, you will need to add it yourself.

The first time you start Exchange after installing Secure Messenger, choose Sec<u>u</u>rity, <u>S</u>ecurity Settings. This dialog box consists of three tabs:

S/MIME Passphrase	Enter and change the passphrase used to access your security keys
S/MIME Keys	Generate and manage your private keys
S/MIME Options	Set digital signature and encyption options for outgoing messages

Consult the Readme.wri file found in the Security\Secure Messenger folder for details about how to generate and use your encryption keys. To set S/MIME options for individual messages, from the Compose New Message window, choose <u>F</u>ile, P<u>r</u>operties, then switch to the S/MIME tab.

This is a beta version of Secure Messenger, provided for your evaluation. For information about the released version and other Deming Internet Security products, visit http://www.deming.com. To contact Deming Internet Security, e-mail beta@deming.com.

Service Providers

Here are trial versions of three complete information services that you can add to Exchange — ccXchg to access an account on a cc:Mail server, and Internet Series and Workgroup Internet Gateway for receiving and sending Internet mail.

ccXchg

ccXchg is a cc:Mail transport service that lets you read and send messages from your cc:Mail account through Exchange.

To install ccXchg, run the Install.exe program found in the Services\ccXchg folder on the CD. Once the installation program has completed, you must add the newly installed service to your Exchange profile (see "ccXchg," page 198 in Chapter 9).

This product is shareware. If you want to continue using ccXchg, you must register it. Registered users also will be informed of the release of a planned version that supports the cc:Mail Mobile product and an update tested on Windows NT 4.0. Registration is supported through the CompuServe shareware registration service (GO SWREG, ID #10784). To contact the author, e-mail Irving Caplan at 100270.2671@compuserve.com.

Internet Series

As introduced in Chapter 9, "Setting Up Other Information Services," the Internet Series software (Personal or Office mode) from Nemx (formerly netApps) is a service for retrieving and sending Internet mail. Internet Personal operates as a single-user service with the capability for you to access more than one mail account. Internet Office operates as a gateway connected to a Microsoft Mail postoffice, either a full Microsoft Mail Server or a workgroup postoffice (see Chapter 23, "Managing a Workgroup Postoffice").

This software lets multiple users work through a single Internet mailbox. Two components are involved:

* The Internet Series service for Exchange
* Internet Server — a separate program run on the local machine in Personal mode or on a server for Office mode

The Internet Server used in Office mode must be able to connect to the Internet, either with a modem or via a direct network connection. It does not need to be the same machine as the Microsoft Mail postoffice.

Detailed installation instructions for both modes are found in the Netapps1.doc file in the Services\Internet Series folder on the CD. This document supplements the documentation provided by netApps and deals with the specific issues of installing the software with Exchange.

A trial version of Internet Series is included on the CD. If you want to continue using this service, you must license it. See Order.wri in the Services\Internet Series folder on the CD. For more information, the latest version, or details about other Nemx products, visit http://www.nemx.com. To contact Nemx, e-mail info@nemx.com.

Workgroup Internet Gateway

Like Internet Series, Workgroup Internet Gateway (see "Workgroup Internet Gateway," page 203 in Chapter 9) lets you use a single modem to receive and send Internet mail for a group of people. An extensive manual, with screen shots, is included in the Services\WIG folder on the CD. Follow the setup instructions you find there.

This copy of Workgroup Internet Gateway is a 10-day trial version. To use it beyond that time, you must register the software. Follow the instructions in the Register.txt in the Services\WIG folder on the CD. For more information, the latest version, or details about other Sareen Software products, visit http://www.sareen.com.

Viewers

The two viewers in this section enhance Exchange in very different ways. Deming Preview adds a viewer pane to the Exchange Viewer window, while KEYview lets you look at files attached to messages without launching the applications for those files.

Deming Preview

Deming Preview adds a third pane to the Exchange Viewer window, allowing you to read messages without opening them. Internet http://, mailto:, and other URLs become hot links. Click on a highlighted link in the preview pane to access that Internet resource. See "Adding a Preview Pane," page 243 in Chapter 10.

To install Deming Preview, run the Preview.exe program found in the Viewers\Deming Preview folder on the CD.

This program is freeware. For more information, the latest version, or information about other Deming Internet Security utilities, visit http://www.deming.com.

KEYview

KEYview enhances Exchange by adding the capability for you to view and print a variety of documents that appear in messages as attached files, without opening them in their native applications. Nearly 200 different file formats are supported.

To install KEYview, copy the Keyview.exe file to a temporary, empty folder on your hard drive. Run Keyview.exe to extract the setup files. Then run the Setup.exe file. After the installation is complete, you will be able to open a message with an attachment, then right-click the attachment and choose View with KEYview.

The version on the CD is a 30-day limited evaluation copy. If you want to continue using KEYview, you must purchase the full product. Visit http://www.ftp.com. To contact the author, e-mail keyview@ftp.com.

WordMail Macros

The WordMail Macros template contains macros to automate many Exchange functions if you use WordMail as your e-mail editor (see "Using WordMail," page 270 in Chapter 11). Here's a list of the macros and what they do:

Macro	Lets you
address	Copy the highlighted address to the Personal Address Book
explorer	Access the highlighted URL (http://, etc.) with Microsoft Internet Explorer
netscape	Access the highlighted URL (http://, etc.) with Netscape Navigator
open	Access the highlighted URL (http://, etc.) with your default browser
HardWrapGlobal	Insert hard line breaks in the entire message, wherever lines appear to end in the current message window
HardWrapLocal	Insert hard line breaks at 75 characters (or fewer) in the current paragraph only
quotes	Add a quote character, >, to the beginning of each line in a message or to just selected lines
signature	Insert text chosen from a list of text files
CleanUp	Remove extraneous quoting characters and =20 line-break characters from selected text

To install the WordMail macros, follow these steps:

1. Copy the "Wmailmac.dot" template from the WordMail Macros folder on the CD to your Wordmail folder, usually Office95\Winword\Wordmail.

2. In the Exchange Viewer, choose Compose, WordMail Options.

3. In the WordMail Options dialog box, select the Wmailmac template, then click the Edit button.

4. When the WordMail Macros template opens, delete all the text in it, then close it.

The WordMail Macros template is now ready for use. From the Word-Mail Options dialog, you can select the WordMail Macros template, then choose <u>C</u>ompose. You also can make this template the default template. An alternative is to copy the macros from the WordMail Macros.dot template to your present WordMail template using Word's Macro Organizer.

This program is freeware. For the latest version and more WordMail macros, visit http://www.wwa.com/~sam. To contact the author, e-mail Scott Marquardt at sam@wwa.com.

References

Several reference tools are included to help you find quick answers to your Exchange questions and stay up-to-date on the latest developments.

Exchange Client FAQ

The Exchange Client FAQ contains answers to the most frequently asked questions about Microsoft Exchange and Windows Messaging and was the inspiration for this book. This FAQ is a fully searchable Windows Help file.

To use the Exchange Client FAQ, start the Exchfaq.hlp found in the FAQ folder on the CD. To have this FAQ handy all the time, copy the Exchfaq.hlp and Exchfaq.cnt files to the Windows\Help folder or WinNT\Help folder. Then right-drag (with the right mouse button) the Exchfaq.hlp file to the Windows desktop to create a shortcut. You also can drag this shortcut into an Exchange folder so you can get to the FAQ any time you're using Exchange.

CD Software Hot List

You can find updated links to the developers of all the software on the CD on the CD.htm file in the root directory of the CD. Just open this file in your Internet browser.

Exchange Resources

Additional Internet resources for Exchange users are summarized in the Resources.htm file in the root directory of the CD. Open this file in your Internet browser, and you'll be able to jump to the latest FAQs, software updates, utilities, mailing lists, and other information, including the Slipstick Systems Exchange Center, home of *The Microsoft Exchange User's Handbook*.

Appendix B

Exchange Resources

Keeping up with Microsoft Exchange means occasionally checking various resources on the Internet to learn about new updates and enhancements. To accompany this appendix, the CD includes a Resources.htm page, which you can open in your Internet browser to reach all the links described here.

Slipstick Systems Exchange Center

The Exchange Center (http://www.slipstick.com/exchange) is the official home of *The Microsoft Exchange User's Handbook*. Here you'll find updated versions of both Resources.htm and the CD.htm page that links to all the developers of the add-ons on the accompanying CD. Other features are extensive FAQs, tips, and links to just about every Internet site that deals with Exchange.

Microsoft Resources

Microsoft is now supporting its products exclusively on the Internet. Updates to Windows 95, Windows NT, and Exchange Server (including new client versions) are posted on Microsoft's World Wide Web (http://www.microsoft.com) and FTP (ftp://ftp.microsoft.com) sites. The main support page for all Microsoft products is found at http://www.microsoft.com/support.

If you want to browse the FTP site, start with the index to many updates for Windows 95 and Windows applications, found in the Softlib folder as Index.txt. The updates themselves are in the Softlib/Mslfiles folder. For Windows NT, look in the Bussys/Winnt/Winnt-public folder. For Exchange Server updates (including new versions of the Exchange Server client), look in the Exchange/Exchange-public folder.

An essential resource is the Microsoft Knowledgebase. Located at http://www.microsoft.com/kb, the MSKB is a searchable archive of thousands of known bugs, fixes, and how-to tips. It's the first place to look if you have a problem that isn't documented in the help file or any FAQ.

You can ask questions about Exchange in the Microsoft newsgroups. The microsoft.public.exchange.* groups are for Exchange Server issues. For the Windows 95 and NT operating system versions, you can post questions in microsoft.public.win95.exchangefax, microsoft.public.messaging.misc, microsoft.public.windowsnt.apps, and microsoft.public.windowsnt.mail.

Another general resource is the Get ISDN for Microsoft Windows kit, available at http://www.microsoft.com/windows/getisdn. This free kit lets you request an ISDN line electronically by forwarding your request to the appropriate telephone company.

Windows 95

Here are some specific sites of interest for Windows 95 users, including Exchange updates:

Windows 95 Home Page	http://www.microsoft.com/windows95	
Windows 95 Software Library	http://www.microsoft.com/windows/software.htm	Service packs, other updates, Power Toys, Kernel Toys
Microsoft Fax Cover Page Fix	http://www.microsoft.com/windows/coverpg.htm	Replaces Awfxcg32.dll to solve the problem with cover pages being unavailable
Internet Mail Service	http://www.microsoft.com/windows/inetmail.htm	Separate download for the Internet Mail service
Exchange Update	http://www.microsoft.com/windows/software/exupd.htm	Windows Messaging update, including the Internet Mail service and an update for the Microsoft Mail service to allow access to shared folders
Password List Update	http://www.microsoft.com/windows/passwd.htm	Fixes a problem with Service Pack 1 that causes passwords not to be saved and/or Mprexe.exe crashes

Kernel Update for Windows 95	http://www.microsoft.com/windows/krnlupd.htm	Replaces Kernel32.dll to solve a problem with gradual memory loss when connecting to the Internet
TapiTNA Telephony Location Selector Power Toy	http://www.microsoft.com/windows/download/tlocmgrc.exe	Places an icon in the taskbar system tray for switching dialing locations

Windows NT 4.0

The home page for Windows NT Workstation is located at http://www.microsoft.com/ntworkstation. For updates on Windows NT Server, see http://www.microsoft.com/ntserver.

Microsoft Office 7.0b

To post Microsoft Office documents to Exchange Server public folders, Microsoft Office version 7.0a or later is required. At this writing, 7.0b was the latest version. This update cannot be downloaded. In the U.S., you can obtain it from the Microsoft Order Desk at (800) 360-7561. Outside the U.S., contact the Microsoft subsidiary for your area. If you need help locating the subsidiary, call the Microsoft International Sales Information Center at (206) 936-8661.

Microsoft Outlook

For more information about Microsoft Outlook, visit http://www.microsoft.com/outlook. You'll be able to read the Resource Kit and download add-ons such as the Rules Wizard.

Microsoft Exchange Server

The place to start learning about Microsoft Exchange Server is on the product home page at http://www.microsoft.com/exchange. Service packs are listed on the What's New page at http://www.microsoft.com/exchange/nwseven.htm.

A fascinating group of applications created for Exchange Server is located at the Microsoft Exchange Applications Farm at http://www.microsoft.com/technet/appfarm/default.htm. Source code is included, to help you learn more about creating applications with Microsoft Exchange Forms

Designer and other tools. Some applications, including the Schedule+ Address Book Assistant, also can be used with the operating system versions of Exchange.

Other utilities, such as a command-line mail sender, preview pane extension, and Crystal Reports for Microsoft Exchange, are included on the Microsoft Exchange Technical Resource CD. You can download this CD or order it for delivery. See http://www.microsoft.com/Exchange/freesoft/techcd.htm for details.

Still more applications are included in a Sampapps.pst file that ships with Exchange Server. Your system administrator already may have installed these applications in public folders. If not, you can obtain the Sampapps.pst file from the administrator and add it to your Exchange profile as another copy of Personal Folders.

Exchange Trial Server

A trial server running Microsoft Exchange Server and offering free downloads of the Exchange Server client software is a remarkable opportunity to give the full product a whirl and, in particular, to see what it's like to connect to Exchange Server over the Internet.

The trial server is located at http://www.ms-exchange.com. After filling out a registration form, you will be able to download the software and actually use an Exchange account on the server, testing Inbox Assistant, public folders, and other unique Exchange Server features.

For those interested in technical details, the Exchange trial server runs on Digital Prioris HX MP dual Pentium 100 and Digital AlphaServer 2000 5/250 dual DECchip 21064 Alpha servers supplied by Digital Equipment Corporation. Software provided by Microsoft Corporation includes the following products: Exchange Server Enterprise Edition, SMS Server, SQL Server, and Internet Information Server. The Internet gateway is an ISDN 128K link using an Ascend Pipeline 50 router provided by USConnect Vancouver.

Fax Resources

If you have an Intel SatisFAXtion 400I CAS modem, you can visit Pure Data at http://www.puredata.com/satwin95.html to obtain a firmware revision to make the modem Class 1 compatible for use with Microsoft Fax.

The latest version of the Imaging for Windows 95 program is available at Wang's Web site at http://www.wang.com.

Several products are available to apply optical character recognition (OCR) to incoming faxes using the Microsoft Fax .awd file format. Here's where to get more information via the Internet:

Cfax Pro-for-a-Change	http://www.cfax.com/change.htm
Imaging for Windows Professional Edition	http://www.imaging.wang.com
OmniPage Pro 7.0	http://www.caere.com

If you don't have a fax modem, you still can send faxes through a variety of e-mail services on the Internet. A detailed list of such services is maintained at http://www.northcoast.com/savetz/fax-faq.html.

Other Exchange Resources

Mailing lists and a number of other Web sites make it easy to stay up-to-date on Microsoft Exchange. There are at least three Exchange mailing lists. My Exchange Center Update newletter comes out irregularly to highlight client issues. Drop me a line at sue@slipstick.com with the subject line "subscribe." I'll assume you can handle RTF messages unless you tell me otherwise in the body of the message.

For a discussion of Exchange Server issues, send a message to msexchange-request@mail.insite.co.uk (keep hyphen) with a message saying "SUBSCRIBE" (without quotes or other punctuation). The MSEXCHANGE list is archived by Anjura Technology Corporation at http://www.anjura.com/notes.html. The list also has been boiled down into an excellent Exchange Server FAQ by Stephen A. Gutknecht at http://www.computek.net/public/SGutknec/exchfaq.

For an information-only mailing list (no discussion, but lots of good news articles), send a message to lists@lists.useast.net. Put "Join Exchange" in the body of the message.

Here is a selection of Exchange resource sites on the Web:

The Exchange Page	http://www.donadams.com/exchange.htm
Cool Add-ins for Exchange	http://home.istar.ca/~anthony/add-ins.html
Exchange Suggestion Database	http://www.useast.net/EXSuggest.htm
Gordon Fecyk's Windows 95 FAQ: Section 10, Windows Messaging	http://www.orca.bc.ca/win95/faq10.htm
Get Help with Microsoft Windows Featuring Microsoft Exchange	http://ourworld.compuserve.com/homepages/G_Carter/default.htm

General Internet Resources

To learn more about Microsoft Exchange on the Internet, you might start by using one of several search sites, such as Yahoo at http://www.yahoo.com or my favorite, Alta Vista, at http://www.altavista.digital.com/.

If you're looking for a mailing list on a particular subject, check Catalist at http://www.lsoft.com/lists/listref.html, a catalog of LISTSERV mailing lists you can join to participate in discussions of just about any subject you can imagine.

The detailed workings of the Internet are spelled out in RFC (Request for Comments) documents. There are many sites where you can read them. I like http://www.pmg.lcs.mit.edu/, because you can see the links between different RFCs. Several RFC documents of interest to Exchange users include

RFC 1521: MIME, Part I

RFC 1522: MIME, Part II

RFC 1855: Netiquette

Exchange-Compatible Products

Many Exchange-compatible products are included on the CD accompanying this book. More are emerging or being updated every week. In this section, you'll find Web site information for many transport providers that plug into any Exchange client and for special applications designed for Exchange Server.

Transport Providers

Quite a few additional information services that plug into Exchange are available, especially to link to proprietary mail services and to support wireless communications. Here is a selection of such transport providers:

AT&T Mail	http://www.att.com/easycommerce/ easylink/winmail.html
MCI Mail	http://www.slipstick.com/exchange/ mcimail.htm
Mobileware Personal	http://www.mobileware.com/
Transend MAPI ConnectorWare for cc:Mail	http://www.transendcorp.com/cware.html
PilotMail	http://www.algonet.se/~fth/Pilot/index.html

Exchange Server Add-Ons

To search for connectors and other add-ons for Microsoft Exchange Server, visit http://www.microsoft.com/Exchange/ExISV/. Here is a partial list of providers and products:

Company	Product	Web Site
Active Voice	ViewMail	http://www.activevoice.com/
Ardis	Mobile Office	http://www.ardis.com/ardis_hp/amoexch.htm
Crystal	Crystal Reports for Exchange	http://www.seagate.com/software/crystal/
Desktop Data	NewsEdge for Exchange	http://www.desktopdata.com/neexchng.htm
Fenestrae	Faxination	http://www.fenestrae.com/
Fulcrum	Fulcrum Find	http://www.fulcrum.com/
Individual	First! for Exchange	http://www.individual.com/
Integra	Wireless Messaging Server	http://www.integra.net/
JetForm	Jetform	http://www.jetform.com/
Keyfile	Keyflow	http://www.keyfile.com/
Mesa	Conference+	http://www.mesa.com/
Mustang	Wildcat! 5	http://www.mustang.com/
Octel	Unified Messaging	http://www.octel.com/
Omnitrend	PageMaster/ex	http://www.omnitrend.com/
Omtool	Fax Sr.	http://www.omtool.com/
Optus Software	FACSys	http://www.optus.com/
PC DOCS	Interchange for Exchange	http://www.pcdocs.com/
Trax	TeamTalk	http://www.traxsoft.com/~traxsoft
Verity	Search 97, Team 97	http://www.verity.com/

Appendix C

Windows Messaging Update for Windows 95

The Windows Messaging Update for Windows 95 (http://www.microsoft.com/windows/software/exupd.htm) is required for users of the operating system version of Exchange who have not installed Service Pack 1 and want access to Microsoft Mail shared folders. This update also offers speed improvements, especially for computers with 8 MB of RAM. Some add-ons to Exchange require Windows Messaging, rather than the operating system version of Exchange.

Users have experienced a variety of problems with the Windows Messaging update, though, including the following:

- Inability to add previously available services to profiles
- Splash screen not disappearing until quitting Windows Messaging
- Problems with shortcuts to Exchng32.exe and with opening messages saved as .msg files
- Inability to uninstall Windows Messaging

Fortunately, you can avoid these problems with a little preparation and follow-up.

Special Note

As this was written in the fall of 1996, international versions of the Windows Messaging update were not available. Users of versions of Windows 95 other than the U.S. English version can install Windows 95 Service Pack 1 to get the Microsoft Mail shared-folders functionality.

Preparing to Install Windows Messaging

Before installing Windows Messaging, make a backup copy of the Mapisvc.inf file in your Windows folder. This file contains certain settings used when you add services to a profile. If, after installing Windows Messaging, you can't add a particular service — one that you previously were able to use — to a profile, rename Mapisvc.inf, then copy the backup you made earlier, using that as the new Mapisvc.inf.

Do not uninstall Microsoft Exchange through the Control Panel, Add/Remove Programs before installing Windows Messaging. If you do so, you will not be able to use Microsoft Fax or The Microsoft Network without uninstalling Windows Messaging, then re-installing Exchange, then installing Windows Messaging again.

Note that, if you have the Exchange Server client, the Windows Messaging setup program prompts you to uninstall Exchange before proceeding. If you are connecting to Exchange Server, you must keep the Exchange Server client and not install Windows Messaging.

Cleaning Up After the Installation

Windows Messaging usually installs in the Program Files\Windows Messaging folder. If the older version of Exchange remains on your system, any shortcuts to the older version will start Windows Messaging but leave the splash screen up until you exit Windows Messaging.

To fix this problem, after installing Windows Messaging, you should check the Program Files\Microsoft Exchange folder for any .pab (Personal Address Book) or .pst (Personal Folders) files and copy them to another location. Then delete the Microsoft Exchange folder and its contents.

After deleting the old Microsoft Exchange folder, you should remake any shortcuts to Program Files\Microsoft Exchange\Exchng32.exe, instead pointing them to Program Files\Windows Messaging\Exchng32.exe. In general, you can simply start the shortcut, then indicate the new location when Windows tells you it can't find the old file.

If you save messages outside Exchange as .msg files, then you also need to point the actions for that file type to the new Exchng32.exe. To do so, follow these steps:

1. In Windows Explorer, choose <u>V</u>iew, <u>O</u>ptions, then switch to the File Types tab.

2. Under "Registered file types," select Mail Message, then click the Edit button.

3. On the Edit File Type dialog box, under <u>A</u>ctions, select "open," then click the <u>E</u>dit button.

4. On the Editing Action for Type: Mail Message dialog box, under "Application used to perform action," enter **"C:\Program Files\Windows Messaging\Exchng32.exe" /f**, including the quotation marks (or use the exact path to the new Exchng32.exe on your computer), as shown in Figure C.1.

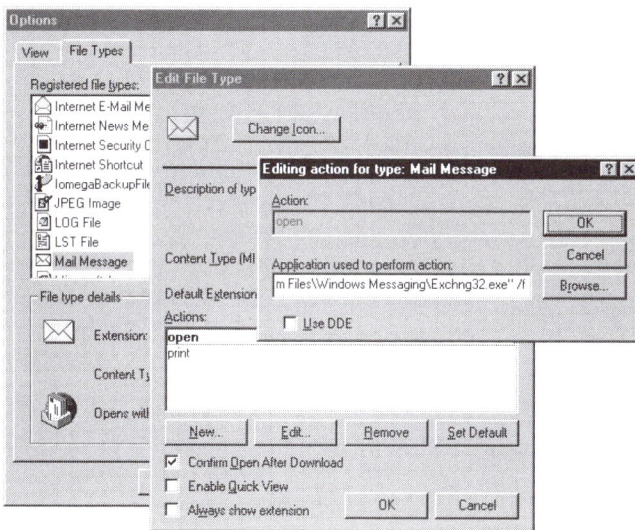

Figure C.1
The actions for the Mail Message file type need to be edited after you install Windows Messaging.

5. Click OK to return to the Edit File Type dialog box.

6. Repeat steps 3 and 4 for the "print" action, using "C:\Program Files\Windows Messaging\Exchng32.exe" /p as the application.

7. Click OK twice to save the new file type association and return to Windows Explorer.

Uninstalling Windows Messaging

Do not attempt to uninstall Windows Messaging through the Control Panel, Add/Remove programs. The only way to remove Windows Messaging is by using the original setup program.

To retain the capability to uninstall Windows Messaging, you should keep the Exupdusa.exe file that you downloaded from the Microsoft site. If you need to uninstall, then follow these steps:

1. Start Exupdusa.exe (the update file you downloaded from Microsoft).
2. After this action extracts components into your Temp folder, you will see the options shown in Figure C.2.

Figure C.2

To remove the Windows Messaging update, you must run the update file downloaded from Microsoft, then choose Remove All.

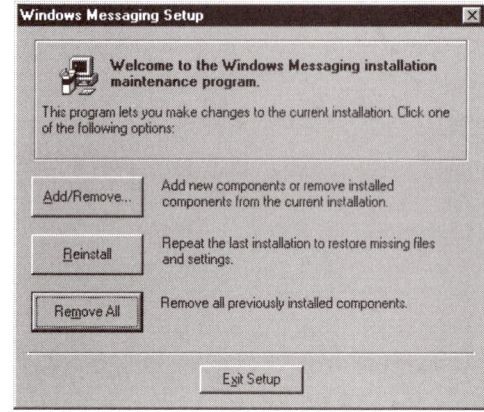

3. Click the Remove All button.
4. When the Remove Shared Component dialog box appears, click the Remove button to completely remove Windows Messaging.

Removing Windows Messaging does not remove any Personal Folders (.pst) or Personal Address Book (.pab) files on your system.

For More Information

For updated information on Windows Messaging, I maintain an FAQ at http://www.slipstick.com/exchange/msgfaq.htm.

Appendix D

Personal Fax for Windows NT

Just a few weeks before this book went to press, Microsoft released its first add-on for Windows Messaging for NT 4.0, a beta version of Personal Fax for Windows NT. Personal Fax performs both as an information service within Windows Messaging (or Exchange) and as a standalone desktop fax program. The fax receiver operates as an NT service and logs fax events so they can be examined with Event Viewer. A cover page editor is included, along with several ready-to-use cover pages.

In many ways, Personal Fax is a big improvement over the Microsoft Fax service that ships with Windows 95, though this beta release has some significant limitations. Perhaps by the time you read this, those will have been resolved.

Installation

You can download the self-extracting file for Personal Fax from Microsoft at http://www.microsoft.com/ntworkstation/fax.htm. Versions are available for all Windows NT processors. To install the software, run the file that you download, then answer the questions in the Setup Wizard. If you plan to use Personal Fax with Windows Messaging or Exchange, be sure to check the appropriate box in the wizard.

The setup procedure adds a Fax menu to the Programs menu, a Fax applet to the Control Panel, and a Fax printer to the Printers folder.

Here's a list of some of the important features in Personal Fax:

Send Features   You have the option of including a banner at the top of each page with the date, time, page number, and telephone number for the sending fax machine.

Cover pages created with the Windows 95 Cover Page Editor can be used in Personal Fax, but are first converted to a new .cov format.

Outgoing faxes can be archived in a file folder as .tif images, showing exactly what was sent.

Receive Features   With a modem that supports adaptive answer, you can receive faxes via Personal Fax and take incoming RAS calls on the same modem.

You can automatically print incoming faxes, route them to a file folder on your computer or on the network, and/or route them to your Exchange Inbox.

General Features   Because Personal Fax is an NT service, Exchange does not need to be running for you to send or receive faxes.

Incoming and outgoing faxes are stored as .tif images and can be viewed and annotated with Imaging for Windows.

Fax events are recorded in the Windows NT event log; you can control the extent of logging.

Limitations

The following limitations existed in the initial beta version of Personal Fax, but may be eliminated in later versions:

- The fax modem cannot be shared with other workstations on the network.
- Binary file transfer — sending editable documents to a modem using compatible software — is not supported.
- There is no Compose, New Fax command in the Exchange Viewer menu; to send a fax with a note on the cover page, you must use the Fax Send Utility on the Programs, Fax menu or print to the Fax printer.

Index

New Books in the Duke Press Library

MIGRATING TO WINDOWS NT 4.0

By Sean Daily

A comprehensive yet concise guide to the significant changes users will encounter as they make the move to Windows NT 4.0. Includes a wealth of tips and techniques. 9 chapters, 450 pages.

POWERING YOUR WEB SITE WITH WINDOWS NT SERVER

By Nik Simpson

Explores the tools necessary to establish a presence on the Internet or on an internal corporate intranet using WWW technology and Windows NT Server. 500 pages. CD included.

MICROSOFT EXCHANGE — UP & RUNNING

By Bill Kilcullen

A practical guide to incorporating the Exchange model. This book is the link between technical manuals and everyday concerns faced by professionals charged with the task of implementing and managing a complex messaging system. 300 pages. CD included.

THE ADMINISTRATOR'S GUIDE TO MICROSOFT SQL SERVER 6.5

By Kevin Cox and William Jones

Delivers expert technical advice, practical management guidelines, and an in-depth look at the database administration aspects of the Microsoft SQL Server 6.5 product. 450 pages.

THE MICROSOFT EXCHANGE SERVER INTERNET MAIL CONNECTOR

By Spyros Sakellariadis

Presents everything you need to know about how to plan, install, and configure the servers in your Exchange environment to achieve the Internet connectivity users demand. 200 pages.

DEVELOPING YOUR AS/400 INTERNET STRATEGY

By Alan Arnold

Addresses the issues unique to deploying your AS/400 on the Internet. Includes procedures for configuring AS/400 TCP/IP and information about which client and server technologies the AS/400 supports natively. Don't put precious corporate data and systems in harm's way. Arnold shows you how to reconcile the AS/400 security-conscious mindset with the less secure philosophy of the Internet community. This enterprise-class tutorial evaluates the AS/400 as an Internet server and teaches you how to design, program, and manage your Web home page. 225 pages.

THE TECHNOLOGY GUIDE TO ACCOUNTING SOFTWARE
A Handbook for Evaluating Vendor Applications

By Stewart McKie

Are you involved in recommending or selecting financial software for your department or company? Whether you are a CFO, an IS professional, or a practicing accountant, if the answer is Yes, then this book is must reading! It is designed to help managers evaluate accounting software, with an emphasis on the issues in a client/server environment. McKie cuts the marketing hype and provides a range of useful checklists for short-listing products to evaluate in more detail. More than 50 vendors are profiled, and a resource guide and a glossary are included. 225 pages.

Also Published by *NEWS/400* and Duke Press

THE A TO Z OF EDI

By Nahid M. Jilovec

Electronic Data Interchange (EDI) can help reduce administrative costs, accelerate information processing, ensure data accuracy, and streamline business procedures. Here's a comprehensive guide to EDI to help in planning, startup, and implementation. The author reveals all the benefits, challenges, standards, and implementation secrets gained through extensive experience. She shows how to evaluate your business procedures, select special hardware and software, establish communications requirements and standards, address audit issues, and employ the legal support necessary for EDI activities. 263 pages.

APPLICATION DEVELOPER'S HANDBOOK FOR THE AS/400

Edited by Mike Otey, a **NEWS/400** *technical editor*

Explains how to effectively use the AS/400 to build reliable, flexible, and efficient business applications. Contains RPG/400 and CL coding examples and tips, and provides both step-by-step instructions and handy reference material. Includes diskette. 768 pages, 48 chapters.

AS/400 DISK SAVING TIPS & TECHNIQUES

By James R. Plunkett

Want specific help for cleaning up and maintaining your disks? Here are more than 50 tips, plus design techniques for minimizing your disk usage. Each tip is completely explained with the "symptom," the problem, and the technique or code you need to correct it. 72 pages.

AS/400 SUBFILES IN RPG

On the AS/400, subfiles are powerful and easy to use, and with this book you can start working with subfiles in just a few hours — no need to wade through page after page of technical jargon. You'll start with the concept behind subfiles, then discover how easy they are to program. The book contains all of the DDS subfile keywords announced in V2R3 of OS/400. Five complete RPG subfile programs are included, and the book comes complete with a 3.5" PC diskette containing all those programs plus DDS. The book is an updated version of the popular *Programming Subfiles in RPG/400*. 200 pages, 4 chapters.

C FOR RPG PROGRAMMERS

By Jennifer Hamilton, a **NEWS/400** *author*

Written from the perspective of an RPG programmer, this book includes side-by-side coding examples written in both C and RPG clear identification of unique C constructs, and a comparison of RPG op-codes to equivalent C concepts. Includes many tips and examples covering the use of C/400. 292 pages, 23 chapters.

CL BY EXAMPLE

By Virgil Green

CL by Example gives programmers and operators more than 850 pages of practical information you can use in your day-to-day job. It's full of application examples, tips, and techniques, along with a sprinkling of humor. The examples will speed you through the learning curve to help you become a more proficient, more productive CL programmer. 864 pages, 12 chapters.

CLIENT ACCESS TOKEN-RING CONNECTIVITY

By Chris Patterson

Attaching PCs to AS/400s via a Token-Ring can become a complicated subject — when things go wrong, an understanding of PCs, the Token-Ring, and OS/400 is often required. *Client Access Token-Ring Connectivity* details all that is required in these areas to successfully maintain and troubleshoot a Token-Ring network. The first half of the book introduces the Token-Ring and describes the Client Access communications architecture, the Token-Ring connection from both the PC side and the AS/400 side, and the Client Access applications. The second half provides a useful guide to Token-Ring management, strategies for Token-Ring error identification and recovery, and tactics for resolving Client Access error messages. 125 pages, 10 chapters.

COMMON-SENSE C
Advice and warnings for C and C++ programmers

By Paul Conte, a **NEWS/400** *technical editor*

C programming language has its risks; this book shows how C programmers get themselves into trouble, includes tips to help you avoid C's pitfalls, and suggests how to manage C and C++ application development. 100 pages, 9 chapters.

CONTROL LANGUAGE PROGRAMMING FOR THE AS/400

By Bryan Meyers and Dan Riehl, **NEWS/400** *technical editors*

This comprehensive CL programming textbook offers students up-to-the-minute knowledge of the skills they will need in today's MIS environment. Progresses methodically from CL basics to more complex processes and concepts, guiding readers toward a professional grasp of CL programming techniques and style. 512 pages, 25 chapters.

DDS BY EXAMPLE

By R S Tipton

DDS by Example provides detailed coverage of the creation of physical files, field reference files, logical files, display files, and printer files. It includes more than 300 real-life examples, including examples of physical files, simple logical files, multi-format logical files, dynamic selection options, coding subfiles, handling overrides, creating online help, creating reports, and coding windows. 360 pages, 4 chapters.

DDS PROGRAMMING FOR DISPLAY & PRINTER FILES

By James Coolbaugh

Offers a thorough, straightforward explanation of how to use Data Description Specifications (DDS) to program display files and printer files. Covers basic to complex tasks using DDS functions. The author uses DDS programming examples for CL and RPG extensively throughout the book, and you can put these examples to use immediately. Focuses on topics such as general screen presentations, the A specification, defining data on the screen, record-format and field definitions, defining data fields, using indicators, data and text attributes, cursor and keyboard control, editing data, validity checking, response keywords, and function keys. A complimentary diskette includes all the source code presented in the book. 446 pages, 13 chapters.

DATABASE DESIGN AND PROGRAMMING FOR DB2/400

By Paul Conte

This textbook is the comprehensive guide for creating flexible and efficient application databases in DB2/400. The author shows you everything you need to know about physical and logical file DDS, SQL/400, and RPG IV and COBOL/400 database programming. Clear explanations illustrated by a wealth of examples, including complete RPG IV and COBOL/400 programs, demonstrate efficient database programming and error handling with both DDS and SQL/400. Each programming chapter includes a specific list of "Coding Suggestions" that will help you write faster and more maintainable code. In addition, the author provides an extensive section on practical database design for DB2/400. This is the most complete guide to DB2/400 design and programming available anywhere. Approx. 772 pages, 19 chapters.

DESKTOP GUIDE TO THE S/36

By Mel Beckman, Gary Kratzer, and Roger Pence, **NEWS/400** *technical editors*

This definitive S/36 survival manual includes practical techniques to supercharge your S/36, including ready-to-use information for maximum system performance tuning, effective application development, and smart Disk Data Management. Includes a review of two popular Unix-based S/36 work-alike migration alternatives. Diskette contains ready-to-run utilities to help you save machine time and implement power programming techniques such as External Program Calls. 387 pages, 21 chapters.

THE ESSENTIAL GUIDE TO CLIENT ACCESS FOR DOS EXTENDED

By John Enck, Robert E. Anderson, and Michael Otey

The Essential Guide to Client Access for DOS Extended contains key insights and need-to-know technical information about Client Access for DOS Extended, IBM's strategic AS/400 product for DOS and Windows client/server connectivity. This book provides background information about the history and architecture of Client Access for DOS Extended; fundamental information about how to install and configure Client Access; and advanced information about integrating Client Access with other types of networks, managing how Client Access for DOS Extended operates under Windows, and developing client/server applications with Client Access. Written by industry experts based on their personal and professional experiences with Client Access, this book can help you avoid time-consuming pitfalls that litter the path of AS/400 client/server computing. 430 pages, 12 chapters.

ILE: A FIRST LOOK

By George Farr and Shailan Topiwala

This book begins by showing the differences between ILE and its predecessors, then goes on to explain the essentials of an ILE program — using concepts such as modules, binding, service programs, and binding directories. You'll discover how ILE program activation works and how ILE works with its predecessor environments. The book covers the new APIs and new debugging facilities and explains the benefits of ILE's new exception-handling model. You also get answers to the most commonly asked questions about ILE. 183 pages, 9 chapters.

IMPLEMENTING AS/400 SECURITY, SECOND EDITION

A practical guide to implementing, evaluating, and auditing your AS/400 security strategy

By Wayne Madden, a **NEWS/400** *technical editor*

Concise and practical, this second edition brings together in one place the fundamental AS/400 security tools and experience-based recommendations that you need and also includes specifics on the latest security enhancements available in OS/400 Version 3 Release 1. Completely updated from the first edition, this is the only source for the latest information about how to protect your system against attack from its increasing exposure to hackers. 389 pages, 16 chapters.

INSIDE THE AS/400
An in-depth look at the AS/400's design, architecture, and history
By Frank G. Soltis

The inside story every AS/400 developer has been waiting for, told by Dr. Frank G. Soltis, IBM's AS/400 chief architect. Never before has IBM provided an in-depth look at the AS/400's design, architecture, and history. This authoritative book does just that — and also looks at some of the people behind the scenes who created this revolutionary system for you. Whether you are an executive looking for a high-level overview or a "bit-twiddling techie" who wants all the details, *Inside the AS/400* demystifies this system, shedding light on how it came to be, how it can do the things it does, and what its future may hold — especially in light of its new PowerPC RISC processors. 475 pages, 12 chapters.

INTRODUCTION TO AS/400 SYSTEM OPERATIONS
by Patrice Gapen and Heidi Rothenbuehler

Here's the textbook that covers what you need to know to become a successful AS/400 system operator. System operators typically help users resolve problems, manage printed reports, and perform regularly scheduled procedures. *Introduction to AS/400 System Operations* introduces a broad range of topics, including system architecture; DB2/400 and Query; user interface and Operational Assistant; managing jobs and printed reports; backup and restore; system configuration and networks; performance; security; and Client Access (PC Support).

     The information presented here covers typical daily, weekly, and monthly AS/400 operations using V3R1M0 of the OS/400 operating system. You can benefit from this book even if you have only a very basic knowledge of the AS/400. If you know how to sign on to the AS/400, and how to use the function keys, you're ready for the material in this book. 234 pages, 10 chapters.

AN INTRODUCTION TO COMMUNICATIONS
FOR THE AS/400, SECOND EDITION
By John Enck and Ruggero Adinolfi

This second edition has been revised to address the sweeping communications changes introduced with V3R1 of OS/400. As a result, this book now covers the broad range of AS/400 communications technology topics, ranging from Ethernet to X.25, and from APPN to AnyNet. The book presents an introduction to data communications and then covers communications fundamentals, types of networks, OSI, SNA, APPN, networking roles, the AS/400 as host and server, TCP/IP, and the AS/400-DEC connection. 210 pages, 13 chapters.

JIM SLOAN'S CL TIPS & TECHNIQUES
By Jim Sloan, developer of QUSRTOOL's TAA Tools

Written for those who understand CL, this book draws from Jim Sloan's knowledge and experience as a developer for the S/38 and the AS/400, and his creation of QUSRTOOL's TAA tools, to give you tips that can help you write better CL programs and become more productive. Includes more than 200 field-tested techniques, plus exercises to help you understand and apply many of the techniques presented. 564 pages, 30 chapters.

MASTERING AS/400 PERFORMANCE
by Alan Arnold, Charly Jones, Jim Stewart, and Rick Turner

If you want more from your AS/400 — faster interactive response time, more batch jobs completed on time, and maximum use of your expensive resources — this book is for you. In *Mastering AS/400 Performance*, the experts tell you how to measure, evaluate, and tune your AS/400's performance. From the authors' experience in the field, they give you techniques for improving performance beyond simply buying additional hardware. Learn the techniques, gain the insight, and help your company profit from the experience of the top AS/400 performance professionals in the country. 259 pages, 14 chapters.

MASTERING THE AS/400
A practical, hands-on guide

By Jerry Fottral

This introductory textbook to AS/400 concepts and facilities has a utilitarian approach that stresses student participation. A natural prerequisite to programming and database management courses, it emphasizes mastery of system/user interface, member-object-library relationship, utilization of CL commands, and basic database and program development utilities. Also includes labs focusing on essential topics such as printer spooling; library lists; creating and maintaining physical files; using logical files; using CL and DDS; working in the PDM environment; and using SEU, DFU, Query, and SDA. 484 pages, 12 chapters.

OBJECT-ORIENTED PROGRAMMING FOR AS/400 PROGRAMMERS
By Jennifer Hamilton, a **NEWS/400** *author*

Explains basic OOP concepts such as classes and inheritance in simple, easy-to-understand terminology. The OS/400 object-oriented architecture serves as the basis for the discussion throughout, and concepts presented are reinforced through an introduction to the C++ object-oriented programming language, using examples based on the OS/400 object model. 114 pages, 14 chapters.

PERFORMANCE PROGRAMMING — MAKING RPG SIZZLE
By Mike Dawson, CDP

Mike Dawson spent more than two years preparing this book — evaluating programming options, comparing techniques, and establishing benchmarks on thousands of programs. "Using the techniques in this book," he says, "I have made program after program run 30%, 40%, even 50% faster." To help you do the same, Mike gives you code and benchmark results for initializing and clearing arrays, performing string manipulation, using validation arrays with look-up techniques, using arrays in arithmetic routines, and a lot more. 257 pages, 8 chapters.

POWER TOOLS FOR THE AS/400, VOLUMES I AND II
Edited by Frederick L. Dick and Dan Riehl

NEWS 3X/400's Power Tools for the AS/400 is a two-volume reference series for people who work with the AS/400. *Volume I* (originally titled *AS/400 Power Tools*) is a collection of the best tools, tips, and techniques published in *NEWS/34-38* (pre-August 1988) and *NEWS 3X/400* (August 1988 through October 1991) that are applicable to the AS/400. *Volume II* extends this original collection by including material that appeared through 1994. Each book includes a diskette that provides load-and-go code for easy-to-use solutions to many everyday problems. *Volume I:* 709 pages, 24 chapters; V*olume II:* 702 pages, 14 chapters.

PROGRAMMING IN RPG IV
By Judy Yaeger, Ph.D., a **NEWS/400** *technical editor*

This textbook provides a strong foundation in the essentials of business programming, featuring the newest version of the RPG language: RPG IV. Focusing on real-world problems and down-to-earth solutions using the latest techniques and features of RPG, this book provides everything you need to know to write a well-designed RPG IV program. Each chapter includes informative, easy-to-read explanations and examples as well as a section of thought-provoking questions, exercises, and programming assignments. Four appendices and a handy, comprehensive glossary support the topics presented throughout the book. An instructor's kit is available. 450 pages, 13 chapters.

PROGRAMMING IN RPG/400, SECOND EDITION
By Judy Yaeger, Ph.D., a **NEWS/400** *technical editor*

This second edition refines and extends the comprehensive instructional material contained in the original textbook and features a new section that introduces externally described printer files, a new chapter that highlights the fundamentals of RPG IV, and a new appendix that correlates the key concepts from each chapter with their RPG IV counterparts. Includes everything you need to learn how to write a well-designed RPG program, from the most basic to the more complex, and each chapter includes a section of questions, exercises, and programming assignments that reinforce the knowledge you have gained from the chapter and strengthen the groundwork for succeeding chapters. An instructor's kit is available. 464 pages, 14 chapters.

PROGRAMMING SUBFILES IN COBOL/400

By Jerry Goldson

Learn how to program subfiles in COBOL/400 in a matter of hours! This powerful and flexible programming technique no longer needs to elude you. You can begin programming with subfiles the same day you get the book. You don't have to wade through page after page, chapter after chapter of rules and parameters and keywords. Instead, you get solid, helpful information and working examples that you can apply to your application programs right away. 204 pages, 5 chapters.

THE QUINTESSENTIAL GUIDE TO PC SUPPORT

By John Enck, Robert E. Anderson, Michael Otey, and Michael Ryan

This comprehensive book about IBM's AS/400 PC Support connectivity product defines the architecture of PC Support and its role in midrange networks, describes PC Support's installation and configuration procedures, and shows you how you can configure and use PC Support to solve real-life problems. 345 pages, 11 chapters.

RPG ERROR HANDLING TECHNIQUE
Bulletproofing Your Applications

By Russell Popeil

RPG Error Handling Technique teaches you the skills you need to use the powerful tools provided by OS/400 and RPG to handle almost any error from within your programs. The book explains the INFSR, INFDS, PSSR, and SDS in programming terms, with examples that show you how all these tools work together and which tools are most appropriate for which kind of error or exception situation. It continues by presenting a robust suite of error/exception handling techniques within RPG programs. Each technique is explained in an application setting, using both RPG III and RPG IV code. 164 pages, 5 chapters.

RPG IV BY EXAMPLE

By George Farr and Shailan Topiwala

RPG IV by Example addresses the needs and concerns of RPG programmers at any level of experience. The focus is on RPG IV in a practical context that lets AS/400 professionals quickly grasp what's new without dwelling on the old. Beginning with an overview of RPG IV specifications, the authors prepare the way for examining all the features of the new version of the language. The chapters that follow explore RPG IV further with practical, easy-to-use applications. 500 pages, 15 chapters.

RPG IV JUMP START, SECOND EDITION
Moving ahead with the new RPG

*By Bryan Meyers, a **NEWS/400** technical editor*

In this second edition of *RPG IV Jump Start*, Bryan Meyers has added coverage for new releases of the RPG IV compiler (V3R2, V3R6, and V3R7) and amplified the coverage of RPG IV's participation in the integrated language environment (ILE). As in the first edition, he covers RPG IV's changed and new specifications and data types. He presents the new RPG from the perspective of a programmer who already knows the old RPG, pointing out the differences between the two and demonstrating how to take advantage of the new syntax and function. 204 pages, 16 chapters.

RPG/400 INTERACTIVE TEMPLATE TECHNIQUE

By Carson Soule, CDP, CCP, CSP

Here's an updated version of Carson Soule's *Interactive RPG/400 Programming*. The book shows you time-saving, program-sharpening concepts behind the template approach, and includes all the code you need to build one perfect program after another. These templates include code for cursor-sensitive prompting in DDS, for handling messages in resident RPG programs, for using the CLEAR opcode to eliminate hard-coded field initialization, and much more. There's even a new select template with a pop-up window. 258 pages, 10 chapters.

S/36 POWER TOOLS

Edited by Chuck Lundgren, a **NEWS/400** *technical editor*

Winner of an STC Award of Achievement in 1992, this book contains five years' worth of articles, tips, and programs published in *NEWS 3X/400* from 1986 to October 1990, including more than 280 programs and procedures. Extensively cross-referenced for fast and easy problem solving, and complete with diskette containing all the programming code. 738 pages, 20 chapters.

STARTER KIT FOR THE AS/400, SECOND EDITION

An indispensable guide for novice to intermediate AS/400 programmers and system operators

By Wayne Madden, a **NEWS/400** *technical editor*
with contributions by Bryan Meyers, Andrew Smith, and Peter Rowley

This second edition contains updates of the material in the first edition and incorporates new material to enhance its value as a resource to help you learn important basic concepts and nuances of the AS/400 system. New material focuses on installing a new release, working with PTFs, AS/400 message handling, working with and securing printed output, using operational assistant to manage disk space, job scheduling, save and restore basics, and more basic CL programming concepts. Optional diskette available. 429 pages, 33 chapters.

SUBFILE TECHNIQUE FOR RPG/400 PROGRAMMERS

By Jonathan Yergin, CDP, and Wayne Madden

Here's the code you need for a complete library of shell subfile programs: RPG/400 code, DDS, CL, and sample data files. There's even an example for programming windows. You even get some "whiz bang" techniques that add punch to your applications. This book explains the code in simple, straightforward style and tells you when each technique should be used for best results. 326 pages, 11 chapters, 3.5" PC diskette included.

TECHNICAL REFERENCE SERIES

Edited by Bryan Meyers, a **NEWS/400** *technical editor*

Written by experts — such as John Enck, Bryan Meyers, Julian Monypenny, Roger Pence, Dan Riehl — these unique desktop guides put the latest AS/400 applications and techniques at your fingertips. These "just-do-it" books (featuring wire-o binding to open flat at every page) are priced so you can keep your personal set handy. Optional online Windows help diskette available for each book.

Desktop Guide to CL Programming

By Bryan Meyers, a **NEWS/400** *technical editor*

This first book of the **NEWS/400** *Technical Reference Series* is packed with easy-to-find notes, short explanations, practical tips, answers to most of your everyday questions about CL, and CL code segments you can use in your own CL programming. Complete "short reference" lists every command and explains the most-often-used ones, along with names of the files they use and the MONMSG messages to use with them. 205 pages, 36 chapters.

Desktop Guide to AS/400 Programmers' Tools

By Dan Riehl, a **NEWS/400** *technical editor*

This second book of the **NEWS/400** *Technical Reference Series* gives you the "how-to" behind all the tools included in *Application Development ToolSet/400* (ADTS/400), IBM's Licensed Program Product for Version 3 of OS/400; includes Source Entry Utility (SEU), Programming Development Manager (PDM), Screen Design Aid (SDA), Report Layout Utility (RLU), File Compare/Merge Utility (FCMU), and Interactive Source Debugger. Highlights topics and functions specific to Version 3 of OS/400. 266 pages, 30 chapters.

Desktop Guide to DDS

By James Coolbaugh

This third book of the **NEWS/400** *Technical Reference Series* provides a complete reference to all DDS keywords for physical, logical, display, printer, and ICF files. Each keyword is briefly explained, with syntax rules and examples showing how to code the keyword. All basic and pertinent information is provided for quick and easy access. While this guide explains every parameter for a keyword, it doesn't explain every possible exception that might exist. Rather, the guide includes the basics about what each keyword is designed to accomplish. The *Desktop Guide to DDS* is designed to give quick, "at your fingertips" information about every keyword — with this in hand, you won't need to refer to IBM's bulky *DDS Reference* manual. 132 pages, 5 major sections.

Desktop Guide to RPG/400

By Roger Pence and Julian Monypenny, **NEWS/400** *technical editors*

This fourth book in the *Technical Reference Series* provides a variety of RPG templates, subroutines, and copy modules, sprinkled with evangelical advice that will help you write robust and effective RPG/400 programs. Highlights of the information provided include string-handling routines, numeric editing routines, date routines, error-handling modules, tips for using OS/400 APIs with RPG/400, and interactive programming techniques. For all types of RPG projects, this book's tested and ready-to-run building blocks will easily snap into your RPG. The programming solutions provided here would otherwise take you days or even weeks to write and test. 211 pages, 28 chapters.

Desktop Guide to Creating CL Commands

By Lynn Nelson

In this most recent book in the *Technical Reference Series*, author Lynn Nelson shows you how to create your own CL commands with the same functionality and power as the IBM commands you use every day, including automatic parameter editing, all the function keys, F4 prompt for values, expanding lists of values, and conditional prompting. After you have read this book, you can write macros for the operations you do over and over every day or write application commands that prompt users for essential information. Whether you're in operations or programming, don't miss this opportunity to enhance your career-building skills. 164 pages, 14 chapters.

UNDERSTANDING BAR CODES

By James R. Plunkett

One of the most important waves of technology sweeping American industry is the use of bar coding to capture and track data. The wave is powered by two needs: the need to gather information in a more accurate and timely manner and the need to track that information once it is gathered. Bar coding meets these needs and provides creative and cost-effective solutions for many applications. With so many leading-edge technologies, it can be difficult for IS professionals to keep up with the concepts and applications they need to make solid decisions. This book gives you an overview of bar code technology including a discussion of the bar codes themselves, the hardware that supports bar coding, how and when to justify and then implement a bar code application, plus examples of many different applications and how bar coding can be used to solve problems. 70 pages.

USING QUERY/400

By Patrice Gapen and Catherine Stoughton

This textbook, designed for any AS/400 user from student to professional with or without prior programming knowledge, presents Query as an easy and fast tool for creating reports and files from AS/400 databases. Topics are ordered from simple to complex and emphasize hands-on AS/400 use; they include defining database files to Query, selecting and sequencing fields, generating new numeric and character fields, sorting within Query, joining database files, defining custom headings, creating new database files, and more. Instructor's kit available. 92 pages, 10 chapters.

USING VISUAL BASIC WITH CLIENT ACCESS APIs

By Ron Jones

This book is for programmers who want to develop client/server solutions on the AS/400 and the personal computer. Whether you are a VB novice or a VB expert, you will gain by reading this book because it provides a thorough overview of the principles and requirements for programming in Windows using VB. Companion diskettes contain source code for all the programming projects referenced in the book, as well as for numerous other utilities and programs. All the projects are compatible with Windows 95 and VB 4.0. 680 pages, 13 chapters.

FOR A COMPLETE CATALOG OR TO PLACE AN ORDER, CONTACT

NEWS/400 and Duke Press

Duke Communications International
221 E. 29th Street • Loveland, CO 80538-2727
(800) 621-1544 • (970) 663-4700 • Fax: (970) 669-3016
or shop our Web site: **www.dukepress.com**

Subscribe Now No Risk!

Subscribe now to *Windows NT Magazine* and save over 32% off the newsstand price for a year!

Windows NT Magazine is the leading publication for IS professionals and other technical decision makers using the Windows NT operating system. *Windows NT Magazine* delivers helpful strategies for migration, enterprise networking, interoperability, and software development on Windows NT.

Try it at no risk – Satisfaction guaranteed!

❏ **Yes,** rush me my first issue of ***Windows NT Magazine*** and bill me for 1 year (12 issues) at $39.95*. If I decide not to subscribe, I'll return your invoice marked "cancel" and keep my first issue **FREE.**

Name

Title   Phone

Company

Address

City, State, Zip

E-mail
       * Canada CDN$69+7% GST, Mexico US $49, elsewhere US $89.

❏ Please send me information about new Duke Press books on the subject of